CHICAGO SOUL

Music in American Life

A list of the volumes in the series
Music in American Life
appears at the end of this book.

CHICAGO SOUL

ROBERT PRUTER

UNIVERSITY OF ILLINOIS PRESS

Urbana and Chicago

Publication of this book was made possible in part
by grants from Robert E. Stallworth
and from the National Academy
of Recording Arts and Sciences, Inc.

First paperback edition, 1992

This book is printed on acid-free paper.

Library of Congress Cataloging-in-Publication Data

Pruter, Robert, 1944–
    Chicago Soul / Robert Pruter.
       p.   cm. — (Music in American life)
    Includes bibliographical references.
    ISBN 10: 0-252-06259-0 (alk. paper). / ISBN 13: 978-0-252-06259-9
    1. Soul music—Illinois—Chicago—History and criticism.
    I. Title. II. Series.
    ML3537.P78   1991
    781.644'09773'11—dc20   89-78326
                                                  CIP
                                                MN

To Margaret and Robin

Contents

Preface

In Gary, the old rust-belt city in northeast Indiana, the sky is often overcast and dreary from industrial pollution, but one rainy day in July 1986 was particularly cheerless for fifty friends and relatives of an old man who before his death a few days earlier, on July 9, had seemed to age well beyond his sixty-one years. They gathered in one of the city's funeral homes to pay their respects, and while the minister intoned his reverential words over the sound of the drizzle outside, among the listeners was a lone celebrity, Jerry Butler, one of soul music's all-time great singers.

Butler was there as a personal friend of the deceased, but there was a business tie as well. The man being buried was Calvin Carter, another celebrity of the record industry. As A&R director of Vee Jay Records during the 1950s and 1960s he was responsible for the launching and developing of the careers of Jimmy Reed, the Spaniels, the Dells, the Impressions, Curtis Mayfield, Dee Clark, Betty Everett, as well as Jerry Butler. Carter's creative energy helped build Vee Jay into the biggest black-owned record label of its day. He should be considered one of the founding fathers of Chicago soul music, because it was he who took a chance in 1958 to record a new group, the Impressions, who composed a gospelized r&b song called "For Your Precious Love." It represented a new sound, the sound later identified as "soul," and many observers regard the song as Chicago's first soul record. Out of the Impressions came Curtis Mayfield and Jerry Butler, two titans of the soul music industry in Chicago during the 1960s.

Despite his eventful career and long list of magnificent achievements, Calvin Carter died in obscurity. Only the Gary newspapers mentioned his death.[1] It went unnoticed in the Chicago dailies, the *Chicago Defender*, and all the industry's trade journals. When Carter died there was no longer a soul music industry in Chicago. The last substantial label, Chi-Sound, had closed its doors two years earlier. Ashes to ashes, dust to dust, Carter and Chicago soul music had come full circle. Like the life of Calvin Carter, the story of Chicago soul has been overlooked and ignored. I have written *Chicago Soul* to rectify the neglect that it has suffered over the years from commentators on popular music.

Chicago Soul tells the story of the soul entertainers who lived, worked, and recorded in Chicago and put the city on the map as an internationally famed recording center during the 1960s and 1970s. Profiled in these pages are some of the biggest names in black popular music, notably Curtis Mayfield and the Impressions, Jerry Butler, Gene Chandler, Tyrone Davis, the Dells, the Chi-lites, and the Five Stairsteps. I have not neglected the writers, arrangers, producers, A&R directors, record company owners, and other "record men" who helped create, shape, and market Chicago soul music, notably Carter of Vee Jay, Carl Davis of OKeh and Brunswick, Bunky Sheppard of Constellation, Billy Davis at Chess, and George Leaner at One-derful.

These artists and record men, as important as they were to the development of Chicago soul, are only a part of the story; perhaps, if you will, they should be likened to no more than a few tiles in a vast mosaic that made up this richly variegated regional music scene. This history then necessarily must include many of the "small-time" artists and record men. Thus it is the story of Tony Gideon, who saw a high-school youth do a funny dance and created the first "Watusi" record. It is about the Radiants, a vocal group who auditioned at all the companies up and down South Michigan Avenue's Record Row, trying to get signed. It is about classically trained Holly Maxwell, who practiced to Aretha Franklin records to learn how to sing "soul," and about the Starlets, a girl group who breached their contract on tour to record as the "Blue-Belles" and thereby launched the career of Patti LaBelle. Then there were the nameless black school-kids who created the dances that shaped the rhythms on records that sold across America, as well as the neophyte, obscure young writers and singers inspired to create one great record only to fade out of the picture when inspiration failed.

Chicago Soul is the story of Bill Erman, an owner of a coal company whose love for music drove him to start up a record label, and it is the story of former Ikette Joshie Jo Armstead who with her husband, Melvin Collins, started a mom-and-pop firm with the improbable name Giant. In short, this story is about the people of Chicago, mostly black, who created a vibrant, thriving recording industry.

Were I to focus on just the limited number of major figures in telling this story, the reader would gather the same impression of Chicago soul as would a person who is transported back to the city in 1964, listens to the local radio station, hears the hits of Jerry Butler, the Dells, the Impressions, and the major Chicago stars of the day, but fails to hear the hits by the lesser lights, such as the Daylighters, the Radiants, the Drew-vels, Otis Leavill, Johnny Sayles, Mitty Collier, all of whom made a contribution that year to the city's music scene. To omit the latter group would result in bad history. In a sense this is history from the bottom up, which concentrates on the experiences and events of the artists and small record men as much as the careers of the major movers and shakers of the industry.

For the stories of most of the well-known artists and record men, I drew my profiles from published sources written by various researchers and from interviews I conducted; for the less well known and the obscure I invariably worked from my interviews. A list of the people interviewed and the places and dates of the interviews appears as an appendix at the end of this book. Most of the artists discussed in *Chicago Soul* have had longer and more richly detailed histories published about their careers, written either by me or by one of the many British writers on the subject. These have appeared in various magazines over the last fifteen years. Notes in each chapter of this book not only indicate where the reader can find additional information on each artist discussed, but also provide a source list of published items I used in putting together my profiles.[2]

I have chosen not to discuss such artists as Sam Cooke, who was born and raised in the city but recorded elsewhere, and I have devoted only cursory examinations to such artists as the Emotions, who recorded in other cities for most of their careers. In selecting artists for inclusion in *Chicago Soul*, I decided to choose all artists, Chicago-based or not, who recorded hits in the city for Chicago-based producers and companies. By "hits" I mean local successes as well as records that made national charts. I gleaned local hit information from the hit-sheet playlists of local radio stations from the period and from the *Chicago Defender*'s weekly hit list. For information on national hits I consulted charts printed in the trade publications *Billboard* and *Cash Box* as well as in books compiled from those charts.[3]

I am not especially keen on discussing the artists' successes on the pop charts, largely because this is irrelevant. The artists had already achieved substantial success by making the black charts, and calling attention to pop-chart hits has the unfortunate and insidious effect of seeming to downgrade the black-chart hits. Also, the buyers of records from the pop charts were mostly white rock 'n' roll fans, who tended to buy black records with obvious hooks and strong beats and who often ignored the more nuanced black records that emphasized vocal skills and interpretation. So too the best examples of soul music often were not crossover hits, which is why a better measurement of quality in black records—if we are to assume that the better records tend to make the charts—would be the black-chart hits.

At this writing, in the late 1980s, the United States record industry is centered in three national recording centers—New York, Los Angeles, and Nashville. But this situation only developed in the last ten years, because during most of its history the recording industry was spread out among various regional recording centers that not only produced hits in the field of pop, rhythm and blues, country and western, and jazz for the national market, but also produced loads of regionally successful hits. One writer on the music business, David Dachs, wrote in the early 1960s that the popular music industry had seven "Tin Pan Alleys"—New York, Los Angeles, Nashville, Philadelphia, Detroit, Chicago, and "the rest of the world."[4] I would single out two other cities, namely New Orleans and Memphis, both of which had thriving rhythm-and-blues recording scenes during that decade.

The kind of popular music that fueled the success of the recording industries in Chicago, Detroit, Memphis, Philadelphia, and New Orleans was soul music. This music may be subsumed under a broader category of black music called rhythm and blues, or r&b. Whereas rhythm and blues of the 1950s had something of a straight-ahead rock 'n' roll beat with a blues feel, soul music as a new form of the music had a gospel feel and approach. Melisma, call and response, and screaming of vocals, long common approaches in black gospel music, crossed over in the 1960s to flavor much of the new rhythm and blues. Soul obviously then cannot be distinguished by musical notation from earlier rhythm and blues, but rather, as music historian Michael Haralambos notes, by the "overall sound, quality and feeling" of the music.[5]

Chicago during the soul era easily ranked as one of the major centers for the production of soul and equalled or surpassed other regional centers in putting records on the charts. Yet the city's self-evident role has not only *not* received the proper amount of recognition by writers on popular music; too often it has been completely ignored. I will not cite chapter and verse, but the reader should consider some of the following examples: Los Angeles, New York, and Nashville by virtue of their being the loci of the recording industry get the ink in any book that discusses popular music. From the standpoint of New York's regional soul music scene, there have also been books written on Brill Building pop-soul (named after one of the two buildings on Broadway that served as the center of the New York recording industry) and on Atlantic Records.[6] No books, however, have covered as a collective whole such New York operations as Bell-Amy-Mala, Sue, Scepter-Wand, Laurie, and Red Bird, as well as Atlantic.

Detroit has had five substantial books written about its largest record company, Motown, but as yet none about the city's entire industry.[7] Philadelphia has had one book published about its recording scene, but as a British publication it was generally unavailable in the United States.[8] Memphis was well covered in two books on the southern soul centers, one from the United States and the other from Great Britain.[9] New Orleans, remarkably, has benefitted from three marvelous surveys of its r&b industry.[10] But surprisingly no book has ever been written covering even a part of the Chicago soul music industry.[11]

The general histories of popular and soul music have also slighted Chicago. Gerri Hirshey's *Nowhere to Run* (1984) was ostensibly about the history of soul music, but the author devoted as an afterthought only nine inaccurate pages to Chicago soul.[12] A British book, *The Soul Book*, covered the South, Philadelphia, Detroit, and other regional scenes, but omitted any mention of Chicago.[13] Turning to the *New Grove Dictionary of American Music* (1986), one finds that its articles on Chicago, soul music, and the soul music section in the article about popular music all omitted any mention of a Chicago soul music scene.[14]

Lack of recognition of Chicago's soul heritage, alas, extends to my hometown as well—to Chicago itself. In 1985 the Chicago Historical Society mounted a special exhibit on music in Chicago, and it very generously treated the city's classical, Tin Pan Alley, jazz, blues, gospel, and folk traditions, but it ignored Chicago's largest contribution in rhythm and blues.[15] The *Illinois Entertainer*, which covers the popular-music scene in the Chicago area, ran separate series about the history of rock, the history of blues, and the history of jazz in the city, but never a series on rhythm and blues. For several years in the late 1970s and early 1980s Chicago featured a lakefront music festival that had stages for rock, jazz, folk, and blues, but none for the city's soul performers. I could go on with many more examples, but are more needed?

It should be evident by now that *Chicago Soul* is not a musicological examination of Chicago-based soul music, but rather a history of the soul music industry in the city, from its rise in the early 1960s out of an already thriving rhythm-and-blues industry, to its decline and virtual disappearance in the early 1980s. The end of the soul music industry also put an end to the city as one of the major regional recording centers, a fate shared by Detroit, Memphis, New Orleans, and Philadelphia as well. I hope my examination of the years of the record industry's decline in Chicago will help the reader gain insight and understanding as to why the industry evolved from a collection of regional scenes to a trio of national centers.

NOTES

1. Tollie Carter interview.

2. The best writing and research on soul music has been done by the British, who, as in the field of blues, were the first to appreciate and study the music with the seriousness it merited. Much of the research has been done by buffs, autodidacts whose enthusiasm for the music led them to trace down and interview many popular and semipopular artists that the mainstream press such as *Rolling Stone* and *Creem* ignored. Their articles would appear in "fanzines" (fan magazines), often mimeographed publications of their own effort. Pioneers in this area were Tony Cummings and Clive Richardson with *Shout* magazine, John Abbey with *Blues and Soul*, Chris Savory with *Hot Buttered Soul*, and Mick Vernon with *R&B Monthly*. There were many others as well. The best historical writing on soul appeared in the British monthly *Black Music*, a thick glossy magazine that published regularly during the 1970s. Many of the sources I have used were by writers appearing in these magazines, namely John Abbey, Tony Cummings, David Nathan, Clive Richardson, and Cliff White.

In North America, coverage of soul music, especially the Chicago variety, has been abysmal. As in the UK, the best writing and research has been done by buffs for fanzines, and I am virtually alone in doing any research on Chicago artists. The leading North American fanzines that cover soul music are *Soul Survivor* (put out in Canada by transplanted Britons), *It Will Stand* (put out by beach music enthusiasts in the Carolinas), and *Goldmine* (a magazine for record collectors published in Wisconsin). The best magazines put out by blacks were *Soul* (published in Los Angeles from 1966 to 1982) and *Black Stars* (published in Chicago from 1971 to 1981), in which I have found many useful articles on the lesser-known artists ignored by the rock press. Another useful source was the *Chicago Defender*, which in the 1960s was especially vigilant in covering local entertainment developments. For record company information, the trade publications *Billboard* and *Cash Box* were invaluable resources. Most of these publications can be found in major cities' public libraries, which have special collections of popular music magazines and fanzines.

3. George Albert and Frank Hoffman, comp., *The Cashbox Black Contemporary Singles Chart, 1960–1984* (Metuchen, N.J.: Scarecrow Press, 1986); Joel Whitburn, comp., *Joel Whitburn's Top Rhythm and Blues Records 1949–1971* (Menomonee Falls, Wis.: Record Research, 1973).

4. David Dachs, *Anything Goes: The World of Popular Music* (Indianapolis: Bobbs-Merrill, 1964), p. 16.

5. Michael Haralambos, *Right On: From Blues to Soul in Black America* (London: Eddison Press, 1974), p. 96.

6. The best book that covers Brill Building pop-soul is Alan Betrock, *Girl Groups: The Story of a Sound* (New York: Delilah Books, 1982). The most comprehensive coverage of Atlantic is found in Charlie Gillett, *Making Tracks* (New York: E. P. Dutton, 1974).

7. The books on Motown are: Peter Benjaminson, *The Story of Motown* (New York: Grove Press, 1979); Sharon Davis, *Motown: The History* (Enfield, Eng.:

Guinness Books, 1988); Nelson George, *Where Did Our Love Go?: The Rise and Fall of the Motown Sound* (New York: St. Martin's 1985); J. Randy Taraborrelli, *Motown* (Garden City, N.Y.: 1986); Don Waller, *The Motown Story* (Charles Scribner's Sons, 1985).

8. Tony Cummings, *The Sound of Philadelphia* (London: Eyre Menthuen, 1975). This is a superb history of the Philadelphia r&b and rock 'n' roll recording industry from the late 1940s to the mid-1970s, with special emphasis on the soul era.

9. The regional histories on the South are both excellent: Peter Guralnick, *Sweet Soul Music* (New York: Harper and Row, 1986); Barney Hoskyns, *Say It One Time for the Broken Hearted* (Glasgow: Fontana/Collins, 1987). Guralnick covers the entire South as a regional recording scene with special attention to Memphis and Muscle Shoals. Hoskyns's book is not as detailed as Guralnick's but he covers soul music activity in Nashville and Louisiana, two scenes neglected by Guralnick.

10. New Orleans, despite its small recording industry, holds a special fascination for rhythm-and-blues researchers. Notable works include John Broven, *Walking to New Orleans: The Story of New Orleans Rhythm and Blues* (Bexhill-on-Sea, Sussex, Eng.: Blues Unlimited, 1974). Broven also wrote a fascinating survey of the southern Louisiana recording scene, a separate regional industry of its own: *South to Louisiana* (Gretna, La.: Pelican, 1983). Also noteworthy is Jeff Hannusch, *I Hear You Knocking: The Sound of New Orleans Rhythm and Blues* (Ville Platte, La.: Swallow, 1985). Hannusch's book has a heavier concentration on the 1960s soul artists than does Broven's book. A superb work is Jason Berry, Jonathan Foose, and Tad Jones, *Up from the Cradle of Jazz: New Orleans Music since World War II* (Athens, Ga.: University of Georgia Press, 1986). This book includes extensive original research on the "Indian tribes" of Mardi Gras and other aspects of New Orleans black music not covered in the other sources.

11. Jim Miller, ed., *The Rolling Stone Illustrated History of Rock & Roll* (New York: Random House/Rolling Stone Press, 1980 [revised and updated from 1976]). This resource does an excellent job in surveying each of the country's regional recording scenes, but Joe McEwen's essay on Chicago, "The Sound of Chicago," as excellent as it is, is disgracefully short; perhaps space considerations prevented McEwen from discussing major developments in Chicago soul music history.

12. Gerri Hirshey, *Nowhere to Run: The Story of Soul Music* (New York: Times Books, 1984), pp. 250–58.

13. Ian Hoare, Clive Anderson, Tony Cummings, Simon Frith, *The Soul Book* (New York: Delta Books, 1976).

14. Wiley Hitchcock and Stanley Sadie, eds., *New Grove Dictionary of American Music* (London: Macmillan, 1986), vol. 1, pp. 418–25; vol. 3, pp. 606–9; vol. 4, pp. 263–64.

15. Robert L. Brubaker, *Making Music Chicago Style* (Chicago: Chicago Historical Society, 1985). To be fair to Brubaker, who programmed the exhibit, we should note that he was well aware of the role of rhythm and blues in the city's history but was working under severe space constraints.

Acknowledgments

This history was made possible by the many participants who gave me their time and their stories, and who loaned me photos and other items relating to their entertainment and business careers. I am, of course, indebted to everyone I talked to, but the following individuals were especially helpful and always eager to take my calls and provide assistance: Joshie Jo Armstead, Jerry Butler, Gene Chandler, Otis Clay, Carl Davis, Tony Gideon (of the Daylighters), Clarence Johnson, Otis Leavill, Mickey McGill (of the Dells), Curtis Mayfield, O. C. Perkins (of the Sheppards), Eugene Record (of the Chi-lites), and Eddie Sullivan (of the Classic Sullivans). I should not leave out Barbara Acklin, Jan Bradley, Alvin Cash, Dee Clark, Jack Daniels, Charles Davis, Syl Johnson, Major Lance, Maurice McAlister (of the Radiants), Melvin Mason (of the Marvelows), Holly Maxwell, Jackie Ross, and Marvin Smith (of the Artistics), all of whom gave me marvelous interviews.

This project was made much easier by the band of indefatigable r&b researchers who at every request were generous with their help. Special thanks are extended to Peter Grendysa, who supplied me with hundreds of *Billboard* chart items previously unavailable to me; Dave Hoekstra, entertainment reporter at the *Chicago Sun-Times,* who supplied me with tapes of interviews and file copies of his many fine profiles on Chicago r&b artists; and Richard Pack, editor of *Soul Survivor,* who supplied me with copies of numerous articles that had appeared in British publications. Also, without the outlets for my articles afforded me by Pack and other magazine editors— Chris Beachley of *It Will Stand,* Cilla Huggins of *Juke Blues,* and Rick Whitesell and Jeff Tamarkin of *Goldmine*—my research would have come to a standstill. I must not forget the record collectors—John Cordell, Wayne

Jancik, Edward Keyes, Richard Murray, Doug Seroff, Bob Sladek, Steve Towne, and Steve Wisner—who supplied discographical information, many leads and contacts, and copies of recordings from their collections. Special appreciation goes to collector Bob Stallworth for his generous contribution.

To my editor at the University of Illinois Press, Judith McCulloh, whose guidance and astute suggestions at the various stages of the manuscript encouraged me to reshape my work into a much deeper and richer study than one I had originally envisioned, lasting thanks. I'm also gratefully indebted to copy editor Carol Bolton Betts for her fine touch with the blue pencil.

Finally, loving thanks go to my wife, Margaret, and my daughter, Robin, who gave me much-needed encouragement to persevere with the project when my enthusiasm flagged and my energy was down. There is nothing like family support to help a researcher to recharge his batteries.

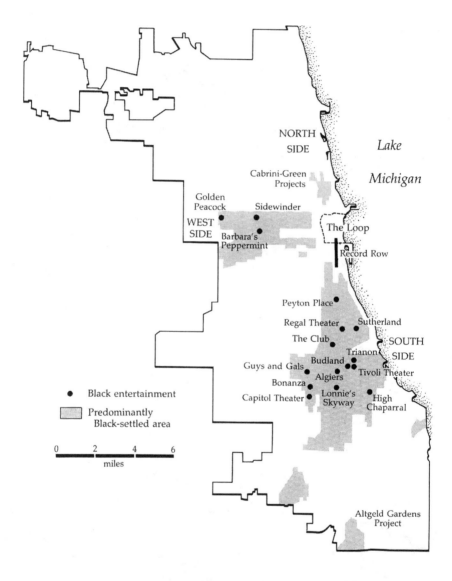

NORTH
SIDE

Lake

Michigan

Cabrini-Green
Projects

Golden
Peacock   Sidewinder

WEST
SIDE   Barbara's
Peppermint

The Loop

Record Row

Peyton Place

Regal Theater   Sutherland

The Club   SOUTH
                                  SIDE
                    Trianon
          Budland
Guys and Gals   Tivoli Theater
          Algiers
    Bonanza
Capitol Theater   Lonnie's   High
                   Skyway   Chaparral

● Black entertainment

Predominantly
Black-settled area

0   2   4   6
        miles

Altgeld Gardens
Project

Chicago in the 1960s: The Black Entertainment World.

CHAPTER

1

Chicago at the Dawn
of the Soul Era

The Lay of the Land

The central downtown section of Chicago, popularly called the Loop for the elevated-train structure that circles through it, abuts Lake Michigan on the east. Fanning out from the Loop to the north, west, and south are the residential, business, and industrial districts of the city. In the 1870s Chicago adopted the nickname "The Garden City," and a visitor might well believe the appellation still applies were he to enter the city from Lake Michigan, because all along the length of the city's lakefront are parks, beaches, and museums. This beautiful veneer is barely a few blocks deep in most places. Beyond it lies some of the most impoverished and downtrodden areas of the city, along with areas of great wealth and commercial growth.

Chicago streets are in a grid pattern and the city uses a house-numbering system that begins at "1" at Madison and State streets in the center of the downtown. As one travels north, west, and south the address numbers go higher. The crosswise streets to the west and north are given names, the streets to the south are given numbers. For example, Forty-seventh Street, the black community's central business district from the 1930s to the early 1960s, is forty-seven blocks south of Madison Street in the Loop. Roughly eight blocks is a mile, so the street is about six miles south of the Loop.

The sections of Chicago in the three directions from the Loop are informally called the North Side, West Side, and South Side. Close to the Loop the areas are called the near North Side, near West Side, and near South Side. During the early 1960s, the bulk of the black population lived on the South Side, from approximately Twenty-second Street to approximately Ninety-fifth Street. As a rule, as one traveled south the black areas would be progressively newer and better off economically. The West Side was largely black and had fewer middle-class areas than the South Side. On the near North Side there was a pocket of blacks located in the Cabrini-Green housing project. Most of the North Side, the Northwest Side, Southwest Side, and far South Side were white-populated areas.

In 1960 Chicago had a population of some 3,550,000 residents, and 22.9 percent of them, or 812,000, were black.[1] These census figures show a startling increase in the black population from 1940, when the total population was 3,397,000, and only 8.2 percent, or 278,000 of the residents, were black.[2] Much of the increase in the black population was due to migration from the South, principally from the states of Tennessee, Arkansas, Alabama, and especially Mississippi.[3] These figures will be underscored as the reader will discover time and time again that most of Chicago's soul entertainers were born in those southern states. The streams of blacks flocking to the city served to develop a huge constituency that could give rise to and sustain a great regional recording scene largely developed by and for blacks.

Chicago before the soul era had a long history of deep involvement in the recording industry, especially with regard to black music. In the early days of the industry Chicago and New York were the two main centers for all kinds of recorded music.[4] In the 1920s, however, the city developed a special reputation as a blues recording center, when such companies as Paramount, Brunswick-Balke-Collender, Victor, and OKeh recorded many blues artists there. Some maintained studios there as well.[5] With its large South Side black entertainment district from Thirty-first to Thirty-fifth streets along State Street, the city was a particularly rich fount of recording talent.[6] It was not surprising then that during the 1930s and 1940s Chicago-based artists dominated the blues recording field. A&R man Lester Melrose claimed he recorded 90 percent of all blues talent for RCA Victor and Columbia while working out of the city from 1934 to 1951.[7]

During the late 1940s and 1950s, after the independent record companies seized control of the black market from the majors, Chicago was one of the prime centers for rhythm-and-blues music.[8] This music, along with country and western, fed the rock 'n' roll revolution of the late 1950s. In other areas of popular music, RCA Victor, Columbia, Decca, and other major labels from the 1930s through the 1950s maintained studios and offices in the city, and recorded big band, jazz, Tin Pan Alley, country and western, and gospel music there.[9] By the late 1960s, the predominant recording activities in the city were in the soul field, with a small amount of recording in the rock 'n' roll area.

The city was also the center for the manufacture of juke boxes. Wurlitzer, Rock-Ola, and Seeburg, three companies that monopolized the juke box industry, all had their headquarters and plants in the city.[10] In the early 1960s, juke boxes accounted for about half of all single records sold in the United States.[11]

Record Row

Michigan Avenue, or South Michigan Avenue, several blocks south of the Loop, was the center of the city's flourishing popular music industry. There along a twelve-block stretch, from Twelfth to Twenty-fourth streets, were located most of Chicago's record companies and record distributors, and therefore the avenue popularly became known as Record Row. South Michigan was not always a record industry strip. The thoroughfare was originally one of the more western streets of the "Prairie Avenue Section," the most exclusive and prestigious residential area in Chicago from the 1870s through the 1890s.[12] During the early 1900s, South Michigan was invaded by automobile repair shops, car dealerships, parts stores, and other establishments serving the needs of the burgeoning automobile manufacturing industry. By the 1920s Michigan Avenue had become Automobile Row.[13]

Twenty years later South Michigan's Automobile Row was being superseded by other "automobile rows" throughout the city, such as Cicero Avenue on Chicago's Northwest Side. As the street became more of a backwater it became more valuable to such enterprises as the recording industry. The street was located close to the Loop, yet it had low rents because it was off the beaten path. At first in the 1940s only Decca, Capitol, and Mercury, with distribution branches, were located on the avenue.[14]

In the early 1950s as far as rhythm-and-blues recording was concerned, "record row" was located much further south, on Cottage Grove from Forty-seventh Street to Fiftieth Street. There record companies King, Vee Jay, Chess, Chance, and Parrot, a well as United, Bronzeville, and other distributors made their headquarters.[15] But during the middle to late 1950s most record companies and distributors gravitated toward South Michigan Avenue, and by the early 1960s it had fully blossomed as Record Row.

By 1963 the soul music industry had been launched. An observer looking down South Michigan Avenue in the latter part of that year would not be impressed or even notice particularly that the street was filled with record industry–related enterprises.[16] Because the business was not directed toward the public at large, no prominent signs were necessary, and often just lettering on the door was all that identified the business inside. The street looked like the backwater it had become.

Starting at the 1200 block of the street one would find the headquarters of Cosnat Distributors (1239 South Michigan), a branch office of a New York-based firm. In 1963 the company was distributing thirty-five labels, most all from the East Coast. The 1300 block had a number of distributors, notably Capitol Distributors (1326) and Liberty Record Distributors of Illinois (1329), both firms owned by large West Coast labels. On the west side of the street was Pan American Records Distribution (1344), which was distributing seventy-four tiny labels specializing in Latin American music, and on the east side was Music Distributors (1343), with eighteen labels, including that of a major, MGM. The company was owned by Jimmy Martin, who had been distributing since the 1940s, and it was headed by Jack Solinger.

The 1400 block was likewise filled with firms. On the west side of the street was Potter Record Distributing Corporation (1410), owned by Kirk Potter and headed by Joseph Cerami, and the famed All State Distributing Company (1450), owned by Paul Glass, who founded the firm in 1955. Among its thirty-one labels were Checker and Chess from Chicago, and Motown, Stax, and Mercury's Smash subsidiary. The address also housed the headquarters of Glass's USA Records, which put out notable rock 'n' roll hits during the 1960s. An associate said of Glass upon his death in 1986, "He really made a lot of records. He could smell a hit. He could pick the winner and consequently became one of the biggest independent record distributorships in the country. . . . He was known then as the 'boy wonder of the record industry.' "[17] Perhaps the key man at All State was promotion man Howard Bedno. "He had a reputation for having a particularly good ear," said one distributor, Jack White, "and I know he had a lot to do with the success of that outfit."[18]

Across the street were headquarters of Constellation Records (1421) and Vee Jay Records (1449). Also on the east side was Big Town Distributors (1455), headed by Kent Beauchamp. Among its fifteen labels were Vee Jay and United Artists. At the same address was Garmisa Distributing Company, owned by Leonard Garmisa and headed by his nephew, Edward Yalowitz. Also there was the Garmisa-owned Midwest Mercury Distributors, which distributed Mercury labels exclusively. (Beauchamp and Yalowitz would later team up to form Royal Disc Distributors at 1239 South Michigan.)

Skipping down to the 1700 block was one of Record Row's biggest distributors, M.S. Distributing Company, at 1700 South Michigan. It was owned and headed by Milt Salstone, who founded the firm in 1946. Leonard Garmisa began at M.S. before he founded his own firm. In 1963 M.S. was distributing some forty-eight labels, including Chess's Argo subsidiary.

Several more blocks south on the east side of the 2000 block were two distribution firms. Kent Distributors was at 2011 and it handled some twenty-five lines, including the local Firma and Foxy labels. The firm was owned by Bill Berman and Bert Loob. At 2029 was United Record Distributors, headed and owned by brothers Ernest and George Leaner, two of the few black men in a business dominated by persons of Italian and Jewish heritage. The company distributed some thirty-six labels, including Tamla, Duke, Wand, and Scepter, as well as labels of the One-derful Records group owned by George Leaner. In late 1963 One-derful was operating at 2642 South Michigan, but within a few months would be at 1827 South Michigan along with United Distributors.

On the 2100 block were two famed record companies, Chess (2120) and the Chicago headquarters of Cincinnati-based King Records (2131). On blocks further south were Advance Distributing (2335), managed by Art Velen; James H. Martin Distributors (2419), with Dot, London, Monument, and other substantial lines; and the distributorship of Decca Records (2441) with its r&b subsidiary, Brunswick.

About a quarter of a block east of Michigan Avenue on Twenty-second Street was Batts Restaurant, a delicatessen and hub of Record Row. Related Jack White, "Along with the London House, at Wacker and Michigan, up north, Batts was the place where everybody in the record business went and hung out—promotion people, people from Chess, All State, M.S., everybody. They would go there for lunch and for dinner, and the record business just throbbed in that place."[19]

Elsewhere around Chicago were the worldwide headquarters of Mercury Records, at 35 East Wacker Drive (in the downtown area), RCA Victor Distributors, at 5050 South Kedzie (on the Southwest Side), and Columbia Records' Chicago headquarters, at 630 North McClurg Court, and distribution branch, at 2240 North Milwaukee (both on the North Side).

At 1345 Diversey Parkway (on the North Side) was one of the largest independent distributors, Summit Distributors, owned by Seymour Greenspan and Jack White. It distributed some nineteen labels including Columbia's Epic and OKeh subsidiaries, A & M, and Warner Brothers. The firm was founded in 1960 following the failure of Warner Brothers' branch distributorship. Greenspan, its Midwest operations manager, and White, its Midwest sales manager, built an "indie," as independents came to be called, from its ashes and Summit quickly became a major competitor to the chief independents—M.S., All State, and Garmisa. Charles "Deke" Atkins, who handled r&b promotions for the firm, gave Summit strength in the r&b area. (For a short time, 1968–71, Summit had an r&b label of its own, Duo.)[20]

Throughout the South and West sides were many mom-and-pop record companies in which the owners operated out of their own homes or from retail record shops. Such was Charles Colbert Sr.'s Nike Records at 7601 South Stewart and Richard Stamz's Paso Records at 3346 West Roosevelt.

To make sense of this almost bewildering list of distributors, a few amplifications are in order, starting with what a distributor did. Record distributors were middlemen; they bought records from the record companies and distributed them at wholesale to retail outlets. They also did much more by trying to promote the sales of the record labels they carried, primarily by having promotion men call on the radio stations and talk up the latest releases to provide the push to get the records exposed and played. Also, it was standard practice to lavish promotion copies on the deejays so they could build their personal collections or have something to sell for cash. Promotion men also provided discount deals to retail outlets to carry a larger number of releases.[21] By the 1980s, however, much of the promotional work had been taken over by the record labels.

A distributor would also represent local labels nationally. For example, Summit represented the Zodiac label owned by Ric Williams and would act as its agent in placing the label with distributors in other parts of the country. This service helped immeasurably in getting mom-and-pop labels distributed nationwide in a matter of days.

The essence of a distribution operation in 1963 was captured by an industry observer, David Dachs:

> Somewhere in your city or near where you live, there is an un-impressive one-story red-brick building, in the center of town or perhaps on the low-rent outskirts. In Chicago, the building may be a store with big-glass windows on "Record Row," South Michigan Avenue. . . . Inside there are few glamorous offices—just girls working on bills at files and desks. In the back or front of the building, there is generally parking space. Throughout the day, Railway Express or private trucks park, bringing records to this structure or store. From it shoots out little trucks, Railway Express ones, or snub-nosed Volkswagons, carrying cartons of Ray Charles, Chubby Checker, Connie Francis, Bent Fabric—"singles," LP's, good music, bad music, jazz, children's recordings, and no-music (spoken-word recordings).[22]

Record Row had two kinds of distributors, company-owned branches and independent operators. The former were owned by the major recording companies and handled just their own records. One of the characteristics of major record companies—RCA, Columbia, Decca, Mercury, Capitol, and MGM—is that they owned their own distribution branches and record-pressing plants. Chicago, for example, had company distribution arms of RCA, Columbia, Capitol, and Decca. Independent record distributors handled many record lines. Usually the average was about fifteen labels, and most majors in the early 1960s also gave certain of their subsidiary labels to independent distributors.[23] With their own sales representatives and promotion men, the indies were often more adept at reaching certain markets, such as the rhythm-and-blues market. For this reason, Columbia, for example, had Summit handle its r&b label, OKeh, in the Midwest.

Because of the vast array of distributors, most record companies would release their records on two or more labels and market each label with different distributors, to benefit from the multiple promotion and push of their records. This is why Chess Records placed its Chess label with All State and its Argo label with M.S., and why Motown placed its Motown label with All State and its Tamla label with United. Also, radio stations at that time would not play more than a certain number of records from any one label. Most of the Chicago distributors would cover a three- or four-state area—usually Illinois, Indiana, and Wisconsin.

There were two other, new kinds of distributors in 1963: the rack jobbers, a fast-growing business that distributed and stocked the entire record departments of drug stores, department stores, and chain stores; and one-stops, which carried all record-company lines—hence the name "one-stop." The one-stops were originally established to provide records to juke box operators, but by the early 1960s they were supplying mom-and-pop record stores, especially in the black community.[24] One-stops in black Chicago in the early 1960s were Barney's (1144 South Kedzie) on the West Side, and Joe's Records (550 East Forty-third), Gardner's (748 East Seventy-fifth) and Singer's (6920½ South Halsted) on the South Side.[25]

The distribution business was both an exhilarating one and a tough, aggravating one filled with conflict, where overstuffed inventories, slow collections from retail dealers, and excessive returns were basic facts of the business. Recalled Jack White of Summit,

> We had a hell of a lot of inventory...the companies wanted us to take three or four times as many records than we needed. They didn't do this on the rhythm-and-blues singles, which you could order as you needed. They did this mostly on rock and pop LPs. They were constantly after us to take more inventory on a new record....So we would fight and fight and fight and fight. We'd end up taking 75 percent when we wanted to take 25 or 35 or 40 percent. And then we had to take back returns from dealers. The general procedure was that you sent the records out to the dealers, and if they didn't sell the dealers would send them back to you.
>
> Then we had a lot of trouble collecting from our dealers, and we had a problem of paying the companies we owed money to. Seymour [Greenspan] and I both had headaches. Seymour had headaches you wouldn't believe. You want to know headaches— he was the guy who paid the bills.

But like a combat veteran who recalls his war years as a time when he never lived his life more intensely, White concluded, "I had a great time.

It was a wonderful experience."[26] Mind you, Summit was one of the more successful indies. No wonder that David Dachs in *Anything Goes* called his chapter on distribution "The Distribution Jungle" and referred to the business as a "record war."[27]

Chess, One-derful, and Brunswick usually relied on their in-house recording studios, but much of the recording by other companies was done at outside studios. The preeminent studio in the 1950s and 1960s (and into the 1980s) was Universal Recording, founded in 1946 by Bill Putnam, Bernie Clapper, and Bob Weber. It was located on the near North Side at 46 East Walton. Other top independent studios of the soul era were RCA (445 North Lake Shore Drive), Sound Studios (230 North Michigan), Stereo-Sonic (526 North Michigan), and Paragon (9 East Huron), all on the near North Side; and P.S. Recording (323 East Twenty-third) on the near South Side.[28]

The soul era in Chicago was the heyday of the in-house studios, and George Leaner contended that "the hottest studios in the era were in-house."[29] An owner of Universal seemed to offer confirmation when he was interviewed in 1980: "There was an eight-year period, 1967–75, when our previous owners lost touch with the record industry, that's when you saw Brunswick building their own [studio]."[30] Truth to tell, however, the situation was hardly bleak for Universal, because throughout the soul era the studio always did good business even in the face of increased in-house competition. Paul Serrano remembered that when he opened P.S. in 1966 he considered the only major competition to be Chess, RCA, and Universal.[31]

This portrait of the firms on Record Row and elsewhere in the city should be considered no more than a snapshot, especially with regard to the distributors. The distribution scene was one of constant upheaval and change.[32] *Billboard* during the 1960s was filled with announcements of distributors in Chicago opening and closing their doors, and losing and gaining lines.[33]

The many distributors in Chicago, especially the independents, were a crucial part of the foundation that supported the city as a recording center. There was the advantage of proximity, by which the record companies could establish valuable ties with the distributors' promotion men. Also, many distributors and one-stops would form labels of their own: United formed One-derful Records, All State formed USA Records, Summit formed Duo Records, and Barney's One-Stop formed Four Brothers Records. Most important, there were countless intertwining relationships that served in a symbiotic fashion to feed both the success of the record firms and the success of the distributors. Chicago was typical of other regional scenes in which the promotion activities of indie distributors helped create a recording industry of independent record companies.[34]

The Entertainment Venues

On the South and West sides were the theaters, nightclubs, social clubs, and high schools that were the venues where the record companies discovered and drew talent. In a matter of weeks a local high-school talent-show winner could be transformed by a local company into an internationally known recording star.

The biggest and brightest venue was the Regal Theater, at Forty-seventh and South Parkway (later King Drive), which was equivalent to New York's Apollo Theatre. The Regal was part of what was popularly called the chitlin' circuit, a string of theaters in the northeast section of the country at which all the major soul revues would play. The theaters included the Howard in Washington, D.C., the Uptown in Philadelphia, the Royal in Baltimore, the Fox in Detroit, as well as the Regal and the Apollo. Every Chicago soul act during the 1960s that achieved a modicum of national success played at one or more of these theaters.[35]

The chitlin' circuit was the last remnant of the vaudeville tradition. Each show at the Regal and its sister theaters took the form of a revue. The core of each show was, of course, soul music, but on the bill were usually a dance act, sometimes a gospel act, and always a comedian (often doubling as MC). Each theater had a house band that would provide accompaniment to the acts, who usually did not bring any musicians except perhaps a guitarist. The Regal house band in the 1960s was the Red Saunders Orchestra.

The Regal was built and opened in 1928 as the showcase theater of the black community. Next door to the Regal was the Savoy Ballroom, opened in 1926. The opening of the two entertainment palaces was the catalyst that moved the heart of the black entertainment district from Thirty-first to Thirty-fifth and State to Forty-seventh Street in the late 1920s.[36] During the 1930s and 1940s the Regal served as the home to the big bands, but by the mid-1950s it was presenting revue shows of rhythm-and-blues artists. The theater, with a seating capacity of thirty-five hundred, was of middling size. The interior and exterior design was "Spanish baroque with heavy Moorish influence," according to local jazz historian Demsey Travis.[37] As such, the theater exuded a classy, dignified air.

The Regal presented about twelve to fifteen shows a year, each of which usually lasted seven days, Friday through Thursday. An inveterate attendee at those shows, rhythm-and-blues authority John Cordell, recalled how a typical revue show at the Regal was presented:

> There were four shows a day. The doors opened at 1:30, and
> there would be a movie first. The first show was about 3:00. There

would be about six to nine acts, and many of the acts would only do two or three songs. Headliners wouldn't be on for more than fifteen minutes, and the whole show would be about an hour long. The Red Saunders Orchestra would open with a theme, which I always liked but I never knew what it was. Then the MC would come out. He was usually a comedian, like Flip Wilson. I saw him on several shows before he got famous. The MC would tell a few jokes for about five minutes to warm up the audience. Some of the comedy was pretty racist, but not real bad, talking about some southern racist going to heaven and meeting St. Peter at the Gate, and St. Peter is black. . . .

Most of the shows I saw would have as an opening act someone who had only one record out. Bobby Miller with "Uncle Willie Time," somebody like that. If they had any gospel group at all, it was towards the beginning, and I didn't pay attention to the gospel groups; they could have just as well stayed home.

If they had a big-name comedian like Moms Mabley or Pigmeat Markham, he would come in the middle of the show. The headliner would close, and the movie would come on to empty the theater. You could stay for a second show if you wanted to, but you had to sit through the movie. The movies were only about seventy-five minutes; they weren't real long films.[38]

A ticket for the matinee shows was $1.25; for the evening show it was $1.50, and in later years, $2.00.[39] Imagine in April 1966 paying $1.25 to see in one show Smokey Robinson and the Miracles, Bobby Bland, Maxine Brown, the Mad Lads, Ronnie Milsap, Sam and Bill—four Chicago acts— the Five Stairsteps, the Radiants, Jackie Ross, and Billy Stewart.[40] It is mind-boggling.

"The Regal shows," said r&b collector Dr. Robert Stallworth, "never had a poor draw. They had so many singers, somebody for everybody. A lot of local singers, too. You get somebody like Darrow Fletcher, he was at the Regal once. Well, a lot of local people went to see him even though he was no big star. He may have had fifty to seventy-five people of his out in the audience."[41] During the height of the soul era and Chicago glory years in the business, from 1962 through 1968, some 40 percent of the Regal acts were locally recorded soul stars.[42]

Even though the Regal featured many acts who during the 1960s had records played on the top-forty lists of pop radio stations and who had wide appeal with white audiences as well, the theater was so far in the black ghetto that it attracted few white customers. The audience overwhelmingly consisted of black kids and adults, with a larger percentage of kids at the shows during the summer. Cordell, who is white, recalled, "If a show had Ray Charles or Sam Cooke, maybe 10 percent of the audience was white, but I've gone there when there was no whites at all. None at all. I was the only one there, and nobody ever bothered me."[43]

Besides the Regal, Chicago could boast of three other large venues that occasionally featured large revue-type shows: the Capitol (Seventy-ninth and Halsted), the Trianon Ballroom (Sixty-second and Cottage Grove), and the Tivoli Theater (Sixty-third and Cottage Grove). Said Cordell, "It seemed like the Tivoli was a classier theater, but it didn't have as good as acts as the Regal. That was one of the biggest theaters in Chicago."[44]

Chicago had a rich club tradition before most of the city's nightclubs offering live entertainment bit the dust in the 1970s from the impact of disco, urban decay, and the spiraling costs of name entertainment. During the 1930s two black nightclubs achieved particular national renown, the Club DeLisa (Fifty-fifth and State) and the Rhumboogie Club (Fifty-fifth and South Parkway). These clubs were especially noted for their fabulous reviews featuring floor shows with loads of gorgeous chorines, comedians, tap dancers, exotic dancers, and nationally known singers and bands.[45]

Chicago in the 1960s was well served by nightclubs, which generally would feature a revue format but on a lesser scale. Gone were the chorines, but a club show invariably had an MC doubling as a comedian, and would have two or three acts—some first-time amateur acts—preceding the star of the show. Sometimes a show would include a shake dancer, which was the black community's equivalent of a belly dancer.

One of the more famous 1960s spots was the Club, a successor to the Club DeLisa owned by two deejays, Purvis Spann and E. Rodney Jones. Another notable South Side spot was the High Chaparral (Seventy-seventh and Stoney Island Avenue). It was perhaps the city's most successful black club, and featured more big names than any other club. Other South Side clubs included the Algiers Lounge (359 East Sixty-ninth), the Bonanza (7641 South Halsted), Guys and Gals (846 Sixty-ninth), Lonnie's Skyway Lounge (131–35 West Seventy-fifth), Budland in the Pershing Hotel (Sixty-fourth and Cottage Grove), and the Sutherland Lounge in the Sutherland Hotel (Forty-seventh and Drexel). On the West Side were Barbara's Peppermint Lounge (3219 West Harrison), the Golden Peacock (4654 West Madison), and the Sidewinder Club (3147 West Madison).[46]

The adult fan of soul music was not only served by theaters and nightclubs, but by social clubs. Many club meetings would feature entertainment by local singers, and members were occasionally treated to a performance by a shake dancer.[47]

For the city's teenagers, local recording stars would make appearances at high-school record hops and dances around the city sponsored by local deejays. A "performance" at those kinds of gigs was usually "lip synced" to the artist's record. "Lip sync" is short for lip synchronization, wherein the performer would pantomine the song by moving his lips to the recording. Some of the principal black high schools were Phillips, DuSable, Dunbar, and Hyde Park on the South Side, and Marshall, Crane, Farragut, and St. Philip on the West Side.

The Emergence of Soul Radio

The existence of at least one and usually several twenty-four-hour radio stations specializing in playing black music is taken for granted in the 1980s. But such stations did not exist for the most part before the soul era. In Chicago radio, the soul era did not begin until 1963, when Leonard and Phil Chess founded WVON. Black radio in the city, however, had existed for many decades, as an aspect of ethnic radio.[48]

The stations that Chicago blacks listened to in the forties and fifties were WHFC, WGES, and WOPA, all of which interspersed black deejays playing rhythm and blues with Greek, German, Lithuanian, Polish, Czech, and other ethnic shows. Such stations worked on a brokered system: deejays would buy the time from the station and then solicit advertising to support the shows. There was intense competition among the black deejays to obtain accounts, especially the national-brand soft drinks that could bring in the bucks. The soda pop accounts were important even before black radio. Richard Stamz, who started at WGES in 1951, began his career driving an advertising truck, selling Seven-Up. Such a truck would be covered with billboards—the largest promoting a national soft drink—and Stamz would drive his around the black community to advertise products.[49]

The station with the largest amount of black programming was WGES, where such deejays as Al Benson, Richard Stamz, and Sam Evans held sway. The famed Benson, whose real name was Arthur Leaner, was an uncle of Ernie and George Leaner. He worked at several stations, up to ten hours a day, but his base was WGES, where he had a variation on the brokerage concept. He was not charged for his time, but instead acted as a salesman for WGES, receiving a commission for the accounts.[50] A top Chicago soul producer, Carl Davis, got his start in the music business with the legendary deejay, and he related the following:

> Al Benson believed in advertising the product. He really gave
> you a good shot for your money. The other thing, he didn't try
> to be an A&R man with your record. If you brought him a record,
> and he put your record on, he didn't sit up there and tell you to
> bring the drums up or bring the vocals up. He just played your

record, and if he put your record on, you were going to sell some records.

He used to have two boxes that you could put records in. The same records were in each stack. He would play down one stack and when he got through he would play down the other stack. He had brokered his show down to three hours then, so in three hours you were guaranteed that your record was going to be played twice. And what he was doing—I don't know how many distributors there were in town—if there were eight distributors he would actually allot each certain slots. If you were Paul Glass of All State you had maybe eight slots. Leonard Chess might have had three slots. Milt Salstone of M.S. might have had eight, and on down to Leonard Garmisa and other distributors. They each had a certain amount of records in that stack. If you wanted to change your eight, all you do was call up. You come in, take out the eight you had in, and put in a new eight. Benson didn't care what you put in. He was something else.[51]

The distributors and the labels "earned" Benson's confidence. In January 1960, the *Chicago American* revealed the deejay was getting payola from local firms totaling $855 a month—$200 from All State; $100 each from Vee Jay, Chess, Garmisa, M.S., and Apex; $80 from Midwest Distributors; $50 from Peacock Records; and $25 from lowly King.[52] Milt Salstone downplayed the revelations: "I didn't see anything wrong with it. Businesswise, it was a good deal. His programs sold a lot of records for me. If I didn't pay him and he stopped playing my records I'd have lost a lot of money."[53]

Benson in the late 1950s was clearly resting on the laurels of his earlier years as Chicago's most popular deejay. There were others coming up who would replace the likes of Benson, Stamz, and Evans, and who would make a name for themselves in the next decade as purveyors of soul. One man was Herb Kent, who started out at WBEE, a small station in the south suburbs, and then went to WHFC. "I went there," said Kent, "and became an immediate success. I've always been the biggest jock in any station I've worked at."[54] He soon was on twice a day, from 2:00 to 6:00 in the afternoon and from 8:00 to midnight.

The black radio station as represented by Benson was fading across the country by 1960. In the late forties and early fifties the first stations offering all-black programming came on the air, but these were concentrated in small communities and the South.[55] Around 1957 the first stations emerged in the major cities in the North providing teen-oriented black programming twenty-four hours a day. Some of these early all-black music stations were WUFO in Buffalo, WILD in Boston, and WAMO in Pittsburgh.[56]

Chicago in the 1940s and 1950s was acknowledged as the capital of black radio and as the pioneering city in black programming. It had always had more hours of black programming than any other city.[57] Surprisingly, however, its first twenty-four-hour black-oriented station did not arrive until 1963, after one of the most bizarre situations in the history of black radio. In the summer of 1962, Gordon McLendon, who owned a chain of stations, purchased WGES, which was broadcasting a five-thousand-watt signal at 1390 on the dial. McLendon got rid of the brokered programs, including all the programs of the black deejays, and provided around-the-clock programming ostensibly directed at the black community. All the new deejays were unknowns brought in from other cities, and except for the evening deejay, Dick Kemp, the radio personalities, notably Lucky Cordell and Yvonne Daniels, were black.

The station was renamed with the acronym WYN-R, and all through the day and evening the deejays would scream over the airwaves "WIN-NERRR!!" The deejays seemed at that time to be incredible screamers, incoherent half the time. The evening deejay, Dick Kemp, would have a phony Negroid-sounding patter in which he would stutter, laugh, cackle, and come up with various noises without ever completing a thought. No cool at all; it was dreadful.

What was mystifying about the station was the music it played—the same top-forty pop music as rival rock 'n' roll station WLS, the powerhouse fifty-thousand-watt station that dominated the Midwest. The rhythm and blues and the emerging soul music that was the staple of the WGES deejays were no longer heard. Instead WYN-R played surf tunes, such as Jan and Dean's "Surf City," folk tunes, such as the new Christy Minstrels' "Green Green," country sounds, such as Bill Anderson's "Still," as well as pop-ish sort of r&b, such as Brook Benton's "True Confession." The music was virtually indistinguishable from that of WLS, except for an occasional solidly r&b-styled record on the playlist.[58]

Presumably the station was going after Chicago's black audience and a white rock 'n' roll audience at the same time.[59] Many white kids did listen to the station, and for a while WYN-R actually contended with WLS for this audience. At times the station made it to number three in the general audience ratings and to number one among blacks.[60] The station's hold on the blacks was tenuous, and it lost them as soon as competition developed.

That competition arrived in March 1963, when Leonard and Phil Chess purchased WHFC for one million dollars, and turned it into a twenty-four-hour station with an overwhelming diet of uncompromising soul-style rhythm and blues. The new station had the call letters WVON, "Voice of the Negro." Its signal at 1450 on the dial was unbelievably weak; during the day it was only a thousand watts, which went down to two-fifty after 7:30

PM. The station did manage to reach the West- and South-Side black areas. It's original line-up of deejays included Ric Riccardo and Herb Kent (who were both with WHFC), Franklin McCarthy and Al Benson (who had both been with WGES), Purvis Spann (who came from WOPA), and E. Rodney Jones (who came from St. Louis).[61] Benson only lasted a few months at WVON.

The top deejay was Herb Kent, who was on from 7:30 to 11:00 each evening. Unlike many other deejays of the day, black or white, he never shouted or screamed or used an artificial patter. He always talked in a conversational, ultra-cool style. One of the most popular shows was his Saturday night "dusty oldies" show, when he played r&b classics of the fifties. Kent would always close his daily show with a marvelous gospel tune called "Open Our Eyes," by the Gospel Clefs.

Purvis Spann, who came on at midnight, was the "all-night blues man." Actually, his "all-blues" format did not begin until 3:00 AM, when B. B. King hit it off with "3 O'Clock Blues." WVON began the day at 5:00 AM with a gospel show hosted by Bill "Doc" Lee. The most popular daytime deejay was E. Rodney Jones, who curiously had worked at WYN-R, where he lasted only three weeks before being canned.[62]

From a South Side newspaper, *The Courier*, WVON hired Wesley South to conduct a nightly interview–talk show from 11:00 PM to midnight on issues and subjects relating to the black community. Isabel Johnson (from WHFC) joined the station to handle public affairs and gospel shows. Later, Bernadine Washington was brought in to do short segments during the day on fashion, etiquette, household tips, and other topics that would presumably interest women. Sundays were given over to gospel shows and to remote-broadcast church services (by local churches who brokered the time). From its beginnings, WVON was highly community-centered, which contrasted sharply with WYN-R, which brought in outside deejays and offered little to the black community.[63]

With Kent at the helm in the crucial evening spot and other veteran Chicago deejays in the other times, and with a steady diet of soul music, WVON exploded on the metropolitan radio market. By September 1963, WVON had overtaken rival WYN-R, according to the C. E. Hooper Ratings service. The *Defender* writer, Bob Hunter, attributed the WVON victory to the better WVON personalities, and he made a snide comment concerning WYN-R's musical format, calling it "rock-a-billy."[64] A week later a WYN-R deejay dropped into the *Defender* offices to explain his station's music policy, contending, as the newspaper reported, that WYN-R was attempting to "elevate the listening habits of Negro radio listeners." A *Defender* columnist sarcastically replied, ". . . if such rock-a-billy songs as 'Abilene,' 'Six Days on the Road,' 'Ring of Fire,' and 'Detroit City' are elevating the habits of Negro radio listeners, then what about Muddy Waters, Memphis Slim, Ray Charles, and the rest?"[65]

In early 1964 Chicago radio people were stunned by the release of the Pulse general audience ratings of AM radio listenership for November-December 1963. The ratings covered an eight-county area, and as expected, top-forty rocker WLS took the number-one evening spot. In number two was tiny WVON, ahead of three large MOR (middle-of-the-road pop music) stations. WYN-R did not make the top five. WVON had so completely gobbled up the black market that despite its extension into a small area of Cook County, it beat out stations that reached into the entire eight-county survey area.[66]

WYN-R's problems were not limited to its lack of soul music programming and its frantic deejay approach. The station's owner, McLendon, was a right-wing ideologue, and during the 1964 presidential campaign he broadcasted specifically to the black community frequent editorial endorsements of the Goldwater candidacy. That was the end. Within a few months WYN-R threw in the towel, changed its call letters to WNUS, and became an all-news station.

During the WVON vs. WYN-R radio war, there was a tremendous outcry from the Chicago ethnic communities.[67] Within a few months foreign-language programming had been eliminated from two stations. The anger of the ethnics was justified. Congressman Roman Pucinski, a Polish-American, led the futile protest, as many of his constituents were served by WGES and WHFC. The loss of the two stations was inevitable. Chicago was becoming less European ethnic and more an Americanized city in which blacks were a growing element.[68]

WVON's black competitors during the remainder of the 1960s were varied, but collectively they were landing only powder-puff blows when the fight really called for one mighty knock-out puncher. During the sixties a demographic change from white to black, similar to that which took place in many areas of Chicago, was occuring in many of the south suburbs. To serve this new market new stations arose. In 1955, WBEE in Harvey, Illinois, was launched with a fulltime r&b music format. It was located at 1570 on the dial and broadcast a thousand watts of power during daylight hours. Its most famous deejay was Mary Dee, "The Honey Bee." The station was less rigidly formatted than WVON. One Saturday afternoon, for example, a kid walked into the studio with a handful of oldies. The deejay enthusiastically responded, "Hey, let's see what you've got," and proceeded to play them.

But WBEE's daylight hours–only schedule was a handicap. However, its signal was able to reach listeners in suburbs, both south and west, that

WVON could not. Nonetheless, WBEE gave up the challenge in 1968, and went to an all-jazz format.

WVON's other south suburban contender was WMPP, the first black-owned station in the Chicago area. The company that owned it, Seaway Broadcasting Company, was headed by William Marden and Charlie Pincherd. WMPP was located at 1470 on the dial, and also was a thousand-watter daytime operation. Its signal was blocked out in Chicago by WVON's 1450 signal, but the station could be picked up throughout the south suburbs and the largely black communities in northwest Indiana. WMPP came on the air in August 1963, but was never much of a competitor to WVON.[69]

Another thousand-watt daytime operation in Chicago began in 1967, when the longtime jazz station WAAF (950 on the dial) became WGRT ("W-Great!" as the deejays exclaimed). The station had a high-quality soul music format, but was not able to compete against WVON even though it did seem to have certain advantages, such as a policy not to talk over the records and to broadcast soul music on Sundays. Located in Oak Park was WOPA, which was started by Egmont Sonderling in 1950.[70] It was a foreign-language station throughout its history, but at various times of the week it presented Big Bill Hill, who on his brokered-time program played blues and southern-style soul. He developed a considerable following among the working-class middle-aged blacks on the West Side.

Within three incredible years black radio was completely transformed in Chicago. Whereas in 1962, the black community was just another ethnic-audience segment in the splintered brokered-time system of ethnic programming, by 1964 that audience was being served by several fulltime radio stations with programming entirely devoted to black interests. And the central appeal of the stations was the new style of rhythm and blues called soul music.

Michael Haralambos, a British sociologist who surveyed black radio during 1967–68 in his fine study *Right On: From Blues to Soul in Black America,* found that statistically, soul music was the primary music of black radio. "The sound is the same in black ghettos across America," he wrote. "The broadcasting format of black radio varies little from station to station. Chicago's WVON broadcasts rather more gospel music than most, but in other respects is typical." Examining the percentage of soul music played on three of Chicago's stations, Haralambos found that WVON's percentage was 91.8, WBEE's was 97.4, and WMPP's was 92.5. WVON was named "favorite station" by 64 percent of all black families, a percentage "more than double of the next four stations combined."[71]

Haralambos in his explanation of soul music did not choose to delineate the differences in styles of the music, but even from its very beginnings a casual listener could detect some broad distinguishing marks by the way the music was programmed on radio. The stations, reflecting demographic considerations, played a "hard" kind of soul music and a smattering of blues during the daytime (to reach the housewives) and late at night (to reach the nightshift workers). The late afternoons and early evening hours were given over to "soft soul," a more pop style of music that had teen appeal, to reach the teenagers.

By "hard soul" I mean a vocal music that relied on a raw delivery and made heavy use of melisma (bending of notes) and screaming. Vocals were often shouted rather than smoothly delivered. Hard soul drew more heavily on blues and gospel than did its soft-soul counterpart, and as with blues, hard soul tended to appeal to a largely adult audience and black working-class constituency. Hard-soul singers tended to have deep, adult-sounding voices. The music has also been called "deep soul," "downhome soul," and "southern soul" (the latter designation because so much of the music was developed in the South).

By "soft soul" I refer to a style that owed perhaps as much to aesthetic considerations of mainstream popular music as to r&b traditions. The music tended to emphasize a strong melody and obvious hooks, vocals were more "correctly" sung, and the instrumentation was more formally arranged and fuller (often with strings for "sweetening"). Some types of artists endemic to the soft-soul style were balladeers, girl groups, young female sopranos, and male vocal groups who used barbershop harmonies in their delivery. Soft soul has also been called "uptown soul," "pop soul," and most inaccurately, "Motown," after the most successful purveyor of the music, Motown Records out of Detroit. Much of soft soul came out of the northern cities of Philadelphia, New York, Chicago, as well as Detroit.

In Chicago, radio played a consistent role during the 1960s in promoting the soul-music industry. Deejays such as Herb Kent were instrumental in promoting and getting certain acts recorded by local companies, and then playing their records upon release. During the middle to late 1960s, WVON and other local stations regularly devoted a third of their playlists to locally produced records, and frequently gave an extra push to records released by local talent.[72] WVON deejays, notably Kent, E. Rodney Jones, and Purvis Spann, were heavily involved in the ownership of clubs, and in promoting concerts, which provided venues for local acts to play. Chicago black radio was thus intimately and intricately intertwined with the local recording industry and helped immensely in fueling its success.

The local companies were not unaware of radio programming differences but perhaps were not as conscious of the distinctions in soul styles as drawn by later observers. They did tend to specialize in either hard- or soft-soul styles, but some, such as Chess, recorded with equal facility in both styles. Records in the hard-soul style were mostly small but steady sellers and rarely big hits. R&b during much of the soul era was a singles market (as opposed to albums), and most singles recorded were then directed at the teenage market.[73] Thus, most Chicago r&b companies directed their energies at creating and selling soft soul, which had the better potential for getting big sales. Major labels, such as the OKeh subsidiary of Columbia, and companies that aspired to be major labels, such as Vee Jay, usually ignored hard soul because the returns were either not cost effective or not worth the bother.

The key men who determined the record companies' approaches to recording soul were the A&R men. A&R, short for artists and repertoire, is the crucial area of responsibility at a record company. The A&R man signs the singers and other talent to the label, chooses the songs for the recording artist, often suggests the tone of the arrangement, and, in the r&b field especially, acts as producer. In short, the A&R man is the tastemaster for the label.[74] The leading A&R men in Chicago were Carl Davis of OKeh and Brunswick, Billy Davis of Chess, and Calvin Carter of Vee Jay.

The strategies used by Chicago record companies to sell records and gain a niche in the marketplace were ultimately determined by the owners, who then hired not only the A&R men but also administrators and promotion men to put those strategies into effect. In the following pages we will see how each Chicago company succeeded in the record business, how they created and marketed soul music, and how they chose the artists they recorded.

NOTES

1. United States Department of Commerce, Bureau of the Census, *Sixteenth Census of the United States: Population, Vol. 2, Characteristics of the Population: Part 2, Florida-Iowa* (Washington, D.C.: Government Printing Office, 1943), p. 640.

2. United States Department of Commerce, Bureau of the Census, *Census of Population, 1960; Vol. 1, Characteristics of the Population: Part 15, Illinois* (Washington, D.C.: Government Printing Office, 1963), p. 15-107.

3. United States Department of Commerce, Bureau of the Census, *1950 United States Census of Population: State of Birth* (Washington, D.C.: Government Printing Office, 1953), pp. 4A-37; United States Department of Commerce, Bureau of the Census, *Mobility for Metropolitan Areas* (Government Printing Office, Washington, D.C.), p. 44.

4. Dave Dexter, Jr., "Music Cities, U.S.A.," *Billboard*, December 27, 1969, p. 45.

5. Robert M. W. Dixon and John Godrich, *Blues and Gospel Records 1902-1943*, 3rd ed., rev. (Chigwell, Eng.: Storyville, 1982), pp. 16-27.

6. Robert Pruter, "The Emergence of the Black Music Recording Industry, 1920–1923," *Classic Wax* 3 (May 1981): 4–6. This essay describes the birth of the black music-recording industry in the context of Chicago's black entertainment world.

7. Mike Rowe, *Chicago Breakdown* (London: Eddison Press, 1973), p. 17.

8. Arnold Shaw, *Honkers and Shouters: The Golden Years of Rhythm and Blues* (New York: Macmillan, 1978), p. xxi.

9. Perry Duis, *Chicago: Creating New Traditions* (Chicago: Chicago Historical Society, 1976), p. 99. Dexter, "Music Cities, U.S.A.," p. 45.

10. Wayne Jancik, "After Ninety Years: A New Generation of Juke Boxes," *Illinois Entertainer*, May 1979, pp. 1, 22–23; "Chicago: Jukebox World Capital," *Billboard*, April 19, 1975, p. C-23.

11. David Dachs, *Anything Goes: The World of Popular Music* (Indianapolis: Bobbs-Merrill, 1964), p. 209.

12. Robert Pruter, "The Prairie Avenue Section of Chicago" (Master's thesis, Roosevelt University, Chicago, 1976), p. 11.

13. Paul Gilbert, "Prairie Avenue, Chicago's Ghost Street," *Townsfolk*, June 1947, p. 23; Pruter, "Prairie Avenue Section," p. 36.

14. *Red Book* (Chicago: Reuben H. Donnelley Corp., 1945, 1948, 1949, 1950, 1951).

15. *Red Book* (Chicago: Reuben H. Donnelley Corp., 1954).

16. *Billboard 1963–1964 International Music-Record Directory and Buyer's Guide* (Cincinnati: Billboard Publishing Company, 1963), pp. 59–60; Nick Biro, "Lots of Smoke, No Fire in Chicago Distrib Picture," October 26, 1963, pp. 6, 8; [Chicago] *Yellow Pages* (Chicago: Reuben H. Donnelley Telephone Directory Co.), 1964.

17. Kenan Heise, "Paul Glass 60, Once Top Record Distributor," *Chicago Tribune*, April 1, 1986.

18. Jack White interview, July 6, 1988.

19. Ibid.

20. Greenspan interview; White interviews. Throughout this book, dates and places of interviews not given in notes may be found in the appendix to this book.

21. Dachs, *Anything Goes*, pp. 176–77; Peter Grendysa, letter to author, April 16, 1986. In Dach's *Anything Goes*, the chapter on distribution provides a particularly vivid portrait of record distribution in the 1960s.

22. Dachs, *Anything Goes*, p. 176.

23. Ibid., pp. 176, 181.

24. R. Serge Denisoff, *Solid Gold: The Popular Record Industry* (New Brunswick, N.J.: Transaction Books, 1975), p. 190.

25. [Chicago] *Yellow Pages*, 1964.

26. White interviews.

27. Dachs, *Anything Goes*, p. 171.

28. Cary Baker, "Recording Activity in Chicago: From 4-Track to State-of-the-Art," *Illinois Entertainer*, May 1980, pp. 4–5; idem, "The Chicago Recording Co.," *Triad*, August 1976, pp. 25–28; Neil Tesser, The Men in the Glass Booth,"

Chicago *Reader*, December 5, 1975, pp. 1, 32–35; Joan Tortorici, "The Chicago Recording Scene—Past, Present and Future through the Eyes of a Man Who's Seen It All," *Illinois Entertainer*, July 1976, pp. 1, 21; Bill Williams, "Chicago Gains as a Studio Center," *Billboard*, April 19, 1975, pp. C-3, C-20; [Chicago] *Yellow Pages*, 1964–75.

29. Baker, "Recording Activity in Chicago," p. 4.

30. Ibid., p. 5.

31. Tesser, "Men in the Glass Booth," p. 35.

32. Dachs, *Anything Goes*, p. 177.

33. The titles of the following news items in *Billboard* suggest these changes: "Chicago—Changing Distrib Scene" (August 21, 1965, p. 1) and "Lots of Smoke, No Fire, in Chicago Distrib Picture" (October 26, 1963, p. 6).

34. Steve Chapple and Reebee Garofalo, *Rock 'n' Roll Is Here to Pay* (Chicago: Nelson-Hall, 1977), p. 24.

35. Most of the sources relating to the chitlin' circuit have concerned the Apollo Theatre, which has been the topic of three books: Ted Fox, *Showtime at the Apollo* (New York: Holt, Rinehart, and Winston, 1983); Jack Schiffman, *Uptown: The Story of Harlem's Apollo Theatre* (New York: Cowles, 1971); Jack Schiffman, *Harlem Heyday* (Buffalo: Prometheus Books, 1984). The Fox Theater in Detroit was subject of a profile: Paul Eisenstein, "Motor City's Rebirth in High Gear," *Christian Science Monitor*, July 14, 1987. The many sources about the Regal include: Steve Tomashefsky, "Farewell to the Regal," *Living Blues* 15 (Winter 1973–74): 20–21; and Dempsey J. Travis, *The Autobiography of Black Jazz* (Chicago: Urban Research Institute, 1983). The latter contains two extensive chapters on the Regal covering its history during the 1930s and 1940s. Also revealing is a rock 'n' roll fan's look at the package black reviews that toured the southern theater circuit in the early 1960s: Bob Kinder, *The Best of the First: The Early Days of Rock and Roll* (Chicago: Adams Press, 1986).

36. Travis, *Autobiography*, p. 145.

37. Ibid., pp. 146–47.

38. John Cordell interview.

39. Dr. Robert Stallworth interview.

40. Regal advertisement, *Chicago Defender*, April 23, 1966.

41. Stallworth interview.

42. Survey by author of Regal show advertisements in *Chicago Defender* from January 1962 to December 1968.

43. Cordell interview.

44. Ibid.

45. Travis, *Autobiography*, pp. 110–23. Travis paints a splendid portrait of Chicago night life in the 1930s and 1940s, especially of clubs on Fifty-fifth Street (Garfield Blvd.). For a full picture of a typical review as presented by the Rhumboogie Club, see Helen Oakley Dance, *Stormy Monday: The T-Bone Walker Story* (Baton Rouge: Louisiana State University Press, 1987), pp. 62–67.

46. Survey by author of nightclub advertisements in the *Chicago Defender*, 1964–68, as well as firsthand experience.

47. Carl Merritt interview.

48. The story of black radio in Chicago can best be gleaned by examining *Billboard* and other trade magazines, which regularly featured items and stories on the city's radio wars. The *Chicago Defender* during much of the 1960s also kept up with the story. A remarkable history of black radio in Chicago from the 1920s to 1954 is provided in Mark Newman, *Entrepreneurs of Profit and Pride: From Black-Appeal to Radio Soul* (New York: Praeger, 1988). Michael Haralambos, *Right On: From Blues to Soul in Black America* (London: Eddison Press, 1974), takes the story into the 1960s. See also Edward Eckstine, "Natra: Black Music in the '70s," *Soul and Jazz Records,* August 1974, pp. 6–7; Chris Heim, "Radio Roots," *Chicago Tribune Magazine,* February 12, 1989, pp. 10–14, 23–28; Robert Pruter, "How Herb Kent, the Kool Gent, Got Burned," Chicago *Reader,* April 15, 1977, pp. 11, 17; David Smallwood, "Radio's Great Black Sound," *Chicago Sun-Times Midwest,* January 8, 1977, pp. 6–9.

49. Richard Stamz interview.

50. Newman, *Entrepreneurs,* pp. 83–84.

51. Carl Davis interview, March 9, 1986.

52. Norman Glubok, "D.J. Al Benson Tells of $855 Monthly Take," *Chicago American,* January 7, 1960.

53. Norman Glubok, "Howard Miller in Payola Quiz," *Chicago American,* January 4, 1960.

54. Herb Kent interview, April 8, 1977.

55. Newman, *Entrepreneurs,* pp. 86, 90.

56. Eckstine, "Natra," p. 6.

57. Newman, *Entrepreneurs,* p. 82; Heim, "Radio Roots," p. 13.

58. "WYN-R Top 40 Disks" hit sheet (Summer 1963).

59. Sandra J. Logan, "Randolph of New Radio Station Makes WYNR a Winner with Teens," *Chicago Defender,* October 20, 1962.

60. "McLendon's Hardest Sound in Town Makes Rating Noise," *Billboard,* March 16, 1963, p. 70.

61. "New Chess R.&B. 'Baby' Shows Face in Chicago," *Billboard,* April 13, 1963, p. 24.

62. Bob Hunter, "WVON New King of Chicago Radio," *Chicago Defender,* September 21, 1963.

63. "New Chess R.&.B. 'Baby,'" *Billboard.*

64. Hunter, "WVON."

65. Ole Nosey, "Everybody Goes when the Wagon Comes," *Chicago Defender,* October 19, 1963.

66. Nick Biro, "Chicago Radio: Kings Remain Assumptive; Heirs Presumptive," *Billboard,* March 28, 1964, p. 12

67. "WYNR Case Goes to D.C. as Probe Here Closes," *Chicago Defender,* April 20, 1963.

68. The following figures for the censuses of 1930 to 1960 give percentages of black and foreign-born white populations in Chicago:

	1930	1940	1950	1960
Black	6.9	8.2	13.6	22.9
White Foreign-born	25.5	19.9	14.5	12.3

Sources: 1940 census, p. 640; 1950 census, p. 13–92; 1960 census, pp. 15–107, 15–235.

69. "New Radio Station Opens," *Chicago Defender,* August 31, 1963; Nick Biro, "R&B Roundup," *Billboard,* May 11, 1963, p. 22.

70. "WBMX Sold Kernie Anderson to Remain," *Chicago Defender,* January 26, 1987.

71. Haralambos, *Right On,* p. 94.

72. Survey by author of local playlists. WBEE and WVON both put out lists in the 1960s of the top-selling records, which like most radio surveys were partially determined by record sales and partially by the stations' choices of what to play. The "Soul 45" WVON list from July 17, 1964, listed sixteen Chicago-produced records, only four of which were from Chess Records. The latter fact is important because it shows that the determination of the playlist was not unduly influenced by the station's ties to Chess Records. The recording company as well as all local firms had to put out records that deserved their place on the charts. The WBEE list from February 18, 1966, which featured thirty records, listed ten Chicago-produced records. Also each week the station listed and played a "Chicago Talent Spotlight" record.

73. Dachs, *Anything Goes,* pp. 30–31.

74. Ibid., p. 72.

2

Vee Jay Records

Vee Jay was one of Chicago's most successful labels, and until the advent of Motown during the early 1960s it was the largest black-owned record label. The company was founded in mid-1953 by the husband-and-wife team of Jimmy Bracken and Vivian Carter. In 1948 Vivian won a talent contest for new deejays conducted by Al Benson of WGES. She worked three months at WGES and then moved to WWCA and later to WGRY, both in her hometown of Gary, Indiana. Bracken in about 1952 opened a record store, Vivian's Record Shop, in the city, and after several months of scrimping and saving the couple decided to start a record label. About the same time, two acts, a vocal group called the Spaniels and a blues singer by the name of Jimmy Reed, had come into the store inquiring about recording opportunities. These acts would become two of Vee Jay's biggest recording stars during the fifties. The Brackens set up the company's headquarters in Chicago on Forty-seventh Street.[1]

During the winter of 1953/54, the first Vee Jay records by Jimmy Reed and by the Spaniels were released and became strong local hits. The company was firmly established following the appearance in 1954 of the Spaniels' third release, "Goodnight Sweetheart, Goodnight," which became a top r&b hit and, as covered by the McGuire Sisters, a million seller.

In 1955, Ewart Abner, Jr., a black record executive at the failing Chance label in Chicago, joined Vee Jay. One of the musicians at Vee Jay, Red Holloway, said, "Abner's role in Chance had been as administrator. In fact, he learned his tools of trade at Chance Record Company, he learned the business there, but Chance just couldn't stay in business. Vivian and Jimmy didn't really know all that much about business things when it got into the real paperwork, so since Abner had been doing that at Chance, they just made a deal with him and he went over there. Abner became pretty much the boss. Jimmy and Vivian still called the shots, because they owned the label, but when it came to the final details of making deals and stuff, that's where Abner was the boss, because he knew more about it and had more insight into what was happening."[2] Abner's first title at Vee Jay was general manager, then it was vice president, and in 1961, president. Calvin Carter, Vivian's brother, became the label's A&R man and principal producer.

By 1955, the Vee Jay house band had been established. It usually included Lefty Bates (guitar), Quinn B. Wilson (bass), Paul Gusman and Al Duncan (drums), and Horace Palm (piano). The brass section usually included Red Holloway and Lucius Washington (tenor saxes), Vernel Fournier and McKinley Easton (baritone saxes), and Harlan "Booby" Floyd (trombone). Von Freeman and Riley Hampton were the principal arrangers. Al Smith was the band leader and in charge of rehearsing and preparing Vee Jay acts for recording sessions.

While Carter was the producer in name, there was often a collective approach in producing the sessions, most of which at first were recorded at Universal Studios. Said Holloway,

> Calvin Carter was in charge of the recording sessions. Calvin was a singer, and when we recorded singers he would be saying things like, "Hey, you all didn't sing the do-do-wop right," or "you're out of tune with this one." When it came to the musicians' parts, certain fellows in the band, usually Lefty and I, would listen to the playback and take it upon ourselves to say, "let's take that over," or "you're not doing this or that," or "hey, that's not right, let's straighten that up." We in the band basically directed our part of it. When it came to the vocals, though, Calvin Carter would do that. He had a good idea of what harmonies were supposed to sound like. Abner would come around to the sessions every once in a while, but he didn't usually have much to say. Musically, Abner wasn't that sharp, but he was good at making deals and doing things administratively.[3]

Jerry Butler fondly recalled, "Carter was basically not a musician; he just had a great ear and a great feel for songs, and a great feel for artists, and a great feel for the people. And that was how he made his records. He's got a track record that Phil Spector would be envious of, and Phil Spector is the 'sound cat'! Carter's record stands for itself, but his recognition is non-existent."[4]

Many persons decades later listening to Jerry Butler's or Dee Clark's output on Vee Jay look askance—perhaps justifiably—at the type of standard tunes given the performers and the sometimes overly pop-like arrangements and chirpy chorusing on some of the r&b material. Both Clark and Butler had remarkable crossover success for black artists in the late 1950s and early 1960s, however, and these commercial considerations should not be easily dismissed. Regarding the "whitening" of artists, Butler said,

> History will say it was a good philosophy, because if he [Carter] had not taken that approach to it, perhaps a Dee Clark would not have been as big a star as he was. And also you have to understand that Calvin had to deal with the time frame that he was living in, and he had been to the water a couple of times with acts he had produced and had good commercial product, such as the Spaniels, only to see the McGuire Sisters and acts like that cover his product and sell more records than he. "And why did that happen," he said, "because mine sounded black and theirs didn't. So now I've got to try to figure how to make mine sound not so black!"[5]

By 1963, with the emergence of the soul era, Vee Jay could feel more comfortable about doing unabashedly black-sounding records on their top artists. Carter proceeded to do it with great success, and what is interesting is that he did not think of Vee Jay as a regional r&b company but as a company competitive in the same popular-music market as the majors. This approach is what distinguished Vee Jay from its Chicago counterparts, who never aspired to be anything more than purveyors of r&b music. Carter, alone of all the Chicago A&R men, made frequent trips to New York, still the songwriting capital of the world, to obtain top-notch songs for his soul artists. And many of Vee Jay's top hits by Butler, Betty Everett, and Dee Clark came from New York.

Abner formed Vee Jay's first subsidiary label, Falcon (which later changed its name to Abner), in 1957. Two years later he established the company's jazz line with such artists as Wynton Kelly, Wayne Shorter, Eddie Harris, and Lee Morgan. A separate jazz LP series was launched in 1960 and before the company went under it came out with some forty albums.[6] Put in as A&R head of the jazz department was Sid McCoy, who by the mid-1950s had become one of the city's premier jazz deejays.

Early on, Vee Jay became involved in gospel music and recorded many of the top acts in the field, notably the Staple Singers, Swan Silvertones, Harmonizing Four, and Highway QCs. In 1959 Vee Jay started its LP line on gospel artists, and within four years the company had seventy-seven releases.[7]

With hits in the 1950s by such artists as the Dells, the El Dorados, the Impressions, Wade Flemons, Dee Clark, John Lee Hooker, as well as the Spaniels and Jimmy Reed, and with steady sales in jazz and gospel, Vee Jay was growing by leaps and bounds. In August 1959, after a short stay at 2129 South Michigan, the company moved into larger headquarters at 1449 South Michigan. It was a two-story building and the company occupied both floors. Abner was fast expanding the administrative staff. In 1960 he hired veteran record man Randall Wood (a light-skinned black) as the company's West Coast regional representative in Los Angeles. Other hirings included Red Schwartz for Philadelphia and Steve Clark for Atlanta. Vee Jay was ready for significant expansion in the sixties as it was in a strong position to make its presence felt in the emerging soul field, and, as events would transpire, in the rock 'n' roll field as well.

Vee Jay got its first million-selling record in early 1962 with Gene Chandler's "Duke of Earl," fueling the company's expansion. During the summer the company took over the distribution of Johnny Vincent's Ace Records out of Jackson, Mississippi. Abner set up Dart Record Sales with himself as head to handle distribution. Also in 1962 Randall Wood discovered the rock 'n' roll act the Four Seasons and brought the group to the company. As true of most rock 'n' roll acts of the 1960s, the Four Seasons presented the company with a completed product, writing their owns songs and playing on and producing their own records. The Four Seasons, working in New York, immediately produced a spate of million sellers, "Sherry," "Big Girls Don't Cry," and "Walk Like a Man." Another important signing in 1962 was the British singer Frank Ifield, who Vee Jay signed for his European hit "I Remember You." The Ifield signing would scarcely be considered important if EMI in England had not asked Vee Jay to sign another act as a "throw-in." Vee Jay assented to that and readily signed the then unknown Beatles. When the United States finally discovered the Beatles in early 1964, Vee Jay was able to parlay millions of sales from the group's records before the company's sixteen Beatle recordings reverted to EMI's United States label, Capitol Records.

The late 1950s and early 1960s were thus good years for Vee Jay. With the goundwork laid by Abner and Carter, the management team of the mid-sixties did not approach the market as an r&b company but as a versatile company that recorded rock 'n' roll, folk, middle-of-the-road (MOR) pop, comedy, and jazz. No other Chicago independent label achieved the success Vee Jay did as an all-around company, but then no other Chicago independent made the attempt. Vee Jay also had notable success in the development of soul. For the most part the company's soul performers grew out of their rhythm-and-blues acts of the 1950s. Dee Clark and Jerry Butler were spin-offs from vocal harmony groups, the Kool Gents and the Impressions respectively, who were recording for the company.

Dee Clark

Dee Clark is one of the truly legendary names in rock 'n' roll/rhythm-and-blues history. Just about anybody, even the most casual follower of popular music, if he or she had attended high school during the late 1950s and early 1960s and had listened to radio, can still recognize his name. His skilled, highly expressive and warm high-tenor voice gave us "(Hey) Little Girl," "Nobody But You," "Raindrops," "Just Keep It Up," and "How About That," just to name a few of his Vee Jay hits. Unfortunately, since he hadn't had any big hits after his Vee Jay years, the rock histories and the rock 'n' roll magazines never properly did their jobs in bringing this terrific entertainer's achievements to the attention of the public.[8]

Dee Clark was born Delecta Clark on November 7, 1938, in Blytheville, Arkansas, but at the age of three his family moved to Chicago's West Side. When he was thirteen he joined with his schoolmate Sammy McGrier from Calhoun School and Ronnie Strong from Douglas Elementary School on the South Side to form a Hambone group. Hambone was a routine involving the slapping of the thighs, chest, and other body parts to create a dancing rhythm (essentially a Bo Diddley beat). "In 1952 we recorded a song called 'Hambone' for OKeh," said Clark. "Red Saunders backed us up with his big orchestra. Hambone was a big fad then."[9] The novelty record rode the Hambone fad pretty well, breaking into a number of pop markets as well as the r&b markets.[10]

After the Hambone had run its course, Clark got involved in the vocal-group scene, joining an ensemble called the Goldentones at Marshall High. The group was formed about 1951 and Clark joined as lead singer in 1953. The Goldentones came under the mentorship of deejay Herb "The Kool Gent" Kent, who not only gave them a new name, the Kool Gents, but got them entree to Vee Jay Records. From 1955 to 1957, with Clark's seductive leads, the Kool Gents became one of the top vocal groups in the city, even though they had negligible national impact.

In 1957 Clark was ready to leave the Kool Gents. The group had recorded "Mother's Son," "Gloria," and "Kangaroo Hop" in 1956, but the latter two were released the following year under the name of Dee Clark rather than the Kool Gents. "The group and I," said Clark, "we weren't getting along too well, different things came about and I came around to the company and asked Calvin Carter and Ewart Abner if they would record me as a single. Calvin said, 'I'm glad you asked because we've been wanting to do that anyway.' So it wasn't much longer after that that I told the fellows I was leaving to go it alone."[11]

Clark's debut as a solo artist was not the most auspicious. The haunting but pedestrian "Gloria," which utilized the "chalypso" beat (combining the calypso with the cha-cha) popular in that era, and "Kangaroo Hop," a mediocre dance number at best, were simply not strong songs. There then came a bunch of strange follow-ups in which Clark mimicked the styles of two great rhythm-and-blues performers, Clyde McPhatter and Little Richard, with "Seven Nights" and "Wondering" (McPhatter) and "Twenty-four Boy Friends" and "Oh, Little Girl" (Little Richard). Vee Jay seemingly was trying to break its new solo artist by having him ape the vocals of two big contemporary stars. The records fared well locally but nowhere else.

"Twenty-four Boy Friends" produced an interesting development. "I liked Little Richard's style 'cause he was like number one back then and I could imitate fairly well for having a tenor voice," said Clark. "About the same time I cut 'Twenty-four Boyfriends,' Little Richard had thrown his rings in the water, quit that scene. The guy who was booking Little Richard on the coast heard my record and had me come in [November 1957] and do the remaining dates that was on Little Richard's itinerary. I more or less did the same routine, not so much the dancing but the same tunes in order, much like he would do his show."[12] Clark would tour for five months with Richard's former band, the Upsetters, and also record with them.

The stylistic breakthrough in which Clark became an original came with a song he wrote and released in December 1958, "Nobody But You," an excellent up-tempo love song that sounded only like the man singing it. An interesting coloration of a prominent flute and other approaches that gave the record a pop flavor set a pattern for later releases. In the spring of 1959 Clark reverted to a McPhatter sound-alike, "Just Keep It Up," but the quality of the song obscured any comparisons.

Clark made his first solid break into the rock 'n' roll market in August 1959 with "(Hey) Little Girl," an Otis Blackwell composition propelled by a Bo Diddley beat. "When Blackwell gave me the demo on it," said Clark, "it was like [sings softly] 'Hey little girl in the high school sweater, whoosh. Gee I like to know you better, whoosh.' What the whoosh was for I don't know. But anyway, we had been doing on my show 'Hey Bo Diddley,' and my guitarist, Phil Upchurch, was just kind of thumbing around with the guitar and started doing the Bo Diddley rhythm and I said, 'Hey, whoa, let's see if we can't make that fit with '(Hey) Little Girl.' It did and that was the birth of '(Hey) Little Girl.'"[13] The song lasted fifteen weeks and rose as high as twenty on the pop charts.

Other hits followed in the next two years—"How About That" (1959), "At My Front Door" (1960), "You're Looking Good" (1960), and "Your Friends" (a big hit in Chicago in 1961)—but none was as distinguished as his first three hits. It seemed as though whatever Clark touched turned into a chart record.

In May 1961 Clark came out with not only the best song of his career but also his biggest, "Raindrops." On the pop chart the song went as high as number two in the nation. "I felt very good about that tune," said Clark. "I had a lot of help musically from Phil Upchurch. The way the tune was kind of put together, we were coming from New York heading back to Chicago on the turnpike. It was coming down like all cats and dogs, just raining. I was sitting back and Phil was driving. And I was keeping time to the windshield wipers—'oh rain, oh rain'—you know, and I went to the first line and then I got my tablet out of the glove compartment, and just started writing. Inspiration struck! When I got to Chicago, I said, 'Ooh man, I may have something here.'"[14]

Have something he did. From the record's dramatic cloudburst opening followed by a rolling beat, to Clark's finely wrought lyrics, to his finishing high-piercing wail, the song was a triumph. "Raindrops," a harbinger of the coming soul era, was Clark's first break from 1950s-styled songs.

Clark's remaining few records on Vee Jay were considerably more modest. The best of them were "I'm Going Back to School," which despite its noble sentiments was a corny rock 'n' roll tune that made some noise in October 1962, and "I'm a Soldier Boy," which was released in early 1963. "Soldier Boy" was a pretty good march-step type of song that had the added distinction of breaking its young composer, Otis Leavill, into the business. In late 1963 Clark left Vee Jay and never again attained recognition in the pop market, and precious little in the soul market.

Impressions

The Impressions while they were at Vee Jay were famous for only one song, "For Your Precious Love," in 1958, and for serving as the genesis of two of the most famous talents to grace the Chicago soul scene—Jerry Butler and Curtis Mayfield. Much of the group's work on the label did not have the ingredients to become pop hits, and many persons listening to their songs decades later might find that the songs lack engaging hooks. But to me and to many fans of the early soul sound, the Impressions on Vee Jay made highly appealing music.[15]

The Impressions traced their origin to Chattanooga, Tennessee. About 1956 Fred Cash, Sam Gooden, Emanuel Thomas, and the brothers Richard and Arthur Brooks formed a vocal ensemble called the Roosters. Opportunities for advancement in rhythm and blues were nonexistent in eastern Tennessee, and the Roosters did what many a group did during that era—they moved to a city with a recording industry, in this case Chicago. Three of the Roosters, the Brooks brothers and Gooden, made the move in 1957 with the intention of adding the rest of the group later on. The three moved up to the near North Side, in the Cabrini-Green project.

Regarding his involvement in the group, Butler said, "When they came here I was in my last year, my senior year, of high school. They were trying to find a person to take the place of two of the guys in their group who had not come from Chattanooga with them, and I was called to act as a replacement until they could find somebody on a permanent basis."[16]

"I listened to the group," noted Butler, "and I decided that what we needed was someone who could play an instrument and who could help us get our harmony together. I had known Curtis Mayfield from church and we sang in various choirs together and so I persuaded him to join us. He was only sixteen years old then and already very talented. So he joined the group and we really started to get an identity, so to speak, of our own—a sound of our own. About six months after that, we made our first record for Vee Jay, 'For Your Precious Love.'"[17]

The Roosters were discovered by record man Eddie Thomas, who became their first manager and changed the group's name to the far more appealing "Impressions." The group practiced in the field house at Seward Park in the Cabrini-Green area. (Seward Park in later years would serve as the home of many other up-and-coming groups during the soul era.) Soon the Impressions were appearing at social-club affairs, fraternity parties, house parties, and other modest events of that type.

The Impressions were soon brimming with songs and eager to record. They went to South Michigan and started traipsing from door to door looking for an on-the-spot audition. Related Calvin Carter,

> They came to us on a Saturday. We were distributing our own label in Chicago, so we were open a half day on Saturday. Jerry had been all up and down Michigan Boulevard trying to record a record. So [the Impressions] finally came to us, these five guys walked in the door. They sang about five or six numbers and sounded pretty good, but I was not hearing that thing that sounds like money in the bank. On a hunch, I told them, "Sing something you're ashamed to sing! Sing something you don't usually feel like singing in public." So one of them told the rest, "Hey, how about that spiritual thing we worked out?" The rest of them argues about it, but they finally sang it. It was a beautiful ballad. It was called "For Your Precious Love." It sold over nine hundred thousand copies on its first issue.[18]

What Carter was doing here was based on the idea that the next hit record is not the sound-alike of current records but often a different-sounding tune that captures the public imagination because it is fresh and new. In auditions, acts will invariably present sound-alikes of hits they have heard.

Carter signed the Impressions on the spot and recorded them the very next Wednesday. What excited him so was the spiritual feel of the song. Most vocal groups of that day were doing doowop harmonies, in which they harmonized barbershop-based nonsense syllables behind their lead vocalists. "For Your Precious Love" was a genuine departure. Butler's baritone lead had a nice churchy feel that suggested a deep emotion, and the group chanted and moaned in the background but did not sing nonsense syllables. The Impressions, unlike any of the other groups of that era, brought a significant influence of black gospel singing into their music.

The company followed with two more ballads that evoked much of the sound and spirit of "For Your Precious Love," but not quite the quality. "Come Back My Love" hit in October 1958, making the lower reaches of both the r&b and pop charts of *Billboard*, but "The Gift of Love" failed to make any chart impact upon its release in early 1959.

After "The Gift of Love," Butler split off from the Impressions and became a solo artist at Vee Jay. Mayfield explained what happened.

> It wasn't so much Jerry, because we were all quite close, having worked together. And of course I've known Jerry for years. What began to create the tension was that Vee Jay chose to put on the record "Jerry Butler and the Impressions." And of course you can understand all these fellows having worked and sacrificed evenly in trying to become somebody, for anyone's name to be put out front was sort of a blow to the rest of the gents. Of course, in doing so and having such a big record, its happening just immediately, all the attention began to go to Jerry Butler. The disc jockeys when they played the record, it was "Now here's Jerry Butler and 'For Your Precious Love.'" And of course the fan mail would come, which we got gobs of, to Jerry Butler. This kind of crushed the fellows. Because of that the label change did create somewhat of a tension with the fellows and it probably did promote Jerry to have to decide to move on.[19]

What Vee Jay did with the Impressions was not unusual, according to Mayfield. "Back during those times most record companies if they had a five-man group that was beginning to do well, they immediately wanted to pull the lead artist away, sensing they could sell more records and get into the crossover market, over into the white market. They did it with Dee Clark and the Kool Gents, they did it with Frankie Lymon and the Teenagers, Clyde McPhatter and the Drifters—I mean you name it, they did it with all of them."[20]

The Impressions were bereft of their most recognizable asset, Butler's baritone lead, but Mayfield asserted that losing Butler was "probably a blessing in disguise." The reason? "Simply because," he said, "when Jerry left it allowed us to regroup and start getting into our own selves, and it allowed me to generate and pull out my own talents as a writer and a vocalist."[21]

The Impressions regrouped by bringing up Fred Cash from Chattanooga to join them. Mayfield took over the lead, which at first did not work out too well for the group. Mayfield sang in an exceedingly light falsetto tenor, and if the background harmonies or support instrumentation for such a voice is not done in the appropriate manner one can get a thin-sounding record. The records that the Mayfield-led Impressions did for Vee Jay in 1959—"Senorita I Love You" and "That You Love Me"—were lovely songs, but the thinness of the leads undoubtedly contributed to their lack of success. Vee Jay released the group before the year was out. Of course, within two years the Impressions would begin an immensely successful association with a major label, ABC-Paramount.

One can bet Vee Jay later rued their decision to let the Impressions go. "To be honest, it was my fault that they went away," Carter confessed. "I was not excited about Curtis' falsetto voice. A falsetto voice has never gotten over to me. At that time we also had the Dells, the Magnificents, the Spaniels, the Orioles—we had acts coming out of our ears. We just couldn't launch the Impressions."[22]

Jerry Butler

Jerry Butler's rich warm baritone voice was put to great use on a spate of Vee Jay ballad hits which epitomized the Chicago style of light and subtle soul during the early 1960s. Unlike most of Vee Jay's artists, he was not solely dependent on Carter for his supply of hit tunes. Butler got some from his good friend Mayfield ("Need to Belong" for example) and others were collaborations with Mayfield ("He Will Break Your Heart" and "Find Another Girl") or with his brother Billy ("I Stand Accused"). Of course, Carter got him some terrific songs from New York, notably "Make It Easy on Yourself," "Moon River," and "Giving Up on Love." Butler contributed significantly to making Vee Jay the powerhouse company it was in the 1960s which in turn helped bring the Chicago recording industry into the soul era. Butler during his Vee Jay years became a nationally renowned recording star.[23]

Butler was born in Sunflower, Mississippi, on December 8, 1939, but when he was three years of age he went with his parents to Chicago, which has been his home ever since. His earliest experience with music was singing in various church choirs. While he was attending Washburne Trade (which, after he graduated, became Cooley High of the movie fame) on the near North Side, he and three other classmates formed a group called the Quails. The other members were Willie Wright, "Doolaby" Wright, and Ronald Sherman. But Butler's father died when he was fourteen and he had to drop out so he could go to work and support the family.

The Quails replaced Butler with another fellow and went on to record a song called "If Love Is Wrong." Butler had written the tune but the group did not credit him on the label. Said Butler, "I remember Sam Evans playing it one night on the radio. And I said, 'That's my song!' I called the guys up but they were all covering their eyes and feeling ashamed."[24] The Quails broke up soon afterward, but Willie Wright went on to become a fairly successful folk singer in Chicago during the early 1960s. Butler's other significant early musical experience was with a gospel group, the Northern Jubilee Gospel Singers, which besides Butler consisted of Curtis Mayfield and his three cousins.

Butler, as mentioned earlier, had his solo career launched from his membership in the Impressions. His first solo release, "Lost," on Vee Jay's Abner subsidiary, was unimpressive but because his name was still potent the song got on the charts. "Rainbow Valley" and "Couldn't Go to Sleep" didn't make the charts during 1959, but "A Lonely Soldier" briefly entered the r&b chart in June of 1960. These songs were somewhat in the pop mode and had the same kind of fluffy arrangements as those of Dee Clark's records then. A flute, tinkling piano, chirpy girl chorus and syrupy strings, and bouncy rhythm worked better with Clark's tenor than Butler's forceful baritone. The songs were good, but Carter was saddling them with ill-advised production.

Butler switched to the Vee Jay label in 1960 and began working with Curtis Mayfield, who replaced Phil Upchurch as his guitarist on the road. The Impressions were somewhat moribund at this time, and Mayfield started touring, writing, and recording with Butler. Their first collaboration, "He Will Break Your Heart," was Butler's first number-one r&b hit as a solo artist and first national top-twenty pop record. The pop success was ironic because the record eschewed the pop arrangements of Butler's earlier discs and had a blacker, tauter sound. It was set to a Brazilian baião rhythm, which had great popularity in the early 1960s, especially on New York–produced r&b records.

During 1961 Butler sustained his recording career with two other fine collaborations with Mayfield, "Find Another Girl" and "I'm a Telling You." Mayfield then left Butler to take leadership of a newly revived Impressions group. Butler recorded a thoroughly pop song, Henry Mancini and Johnny Mercer's "Moon River," which was both an r&b and crossover hit in late 1961 and early 1962. Said Butler, "During that period it was just very difficult for folks to deal with waltzes and that whole thing. So we changed the tempo and made a kind of cha cha or bossa nova, something like that out of it, and recorded the song and it was a big smash."[25]

The year 1962, recording-wise, was weak for Butler. The one bright spot resulted from a trip to New York he made to record under the writing/producing team of Burt Bacharach and Hal David, who were having great success with Dionne Warwick and Lou Johnson at the time. The team gave Butler a great ballad, "Make It Easy on Yourself," which hit the charts in September 1962. Inexplicably, the equally good "Message to Martha" was kept in the can until released on an album two years later.

Butler came out with a number of fine records in 1963, but did not hit again until he put out the ballad "Need to Belong" in November (a case of Mayfield's writing to the rescue again). The song was his most soulful up to that time and served to bring the artist solidly into the soul era.

Butler's best year with Vee Jay was 1964. The hauntingly soulful "Giving Up on Love" was a sizable hit for him in the spring, and the summer produced the best double-sided record of his career with two ballads—"I Stand Accused," written with his brother Billy, and "I Don't Want to Hear Anymore," one of Randy Newman's earliest and best songs. Butler was also compatibly teamed up with Betty Everett, which resulted in chart success with "Let It Be Me" and "Smile." Despite the quality of the 1964 records, Butler got only limited recognition in the pop market. The British invasion was going full force and soul was still largely unknown. Paradoxically, Butler probably had greater pop recognition in 1961.

The years 1965 and 1966 at Vee Jay were wasted years for Butler. The company was in financial trouble and the in-house creative staff was breaking down. Vee Jay seemed unable to match Butler with good songs. He told Cliff White in *Black Music*, "We knew that Vee Jay was in trouble, so at the end of 1965 I negotiated to get out of my contract. But because they were the first black company to reach that size, and because they were owned by friends, I then re-signed for another six months, after they filed for bankruptcy, to see if they could save the company. After the fact, when it had gone down that they were definitely going under and couldn't be saved, that's when I got into the Mercury situation."[26]

During his Vee Jay years, however, Butler had a white constituency prior to rock criticism. In the Carolinas, among middle-class white youth, especially those of college age, rhythm and blues was the music of choice. They called it "beach music" because it first became popular on the juke boxes in the many beach clubs found in the Carolinas.

Butler first realized he had a special popularity on the southeast seaboard fairly early in his career:

> I was involved in the whole beach-club circuit in the early days of r&b, or what have you. We used to do extensive traveling on the southeastern seaboard, from Virginia to Miami, and we played all those clubs—which were basically clubs where kids came for summer vacation. They were usually located on the beach, for instance Myrtle Beach, South Carolina, and places like that. Because of the great influx of colleges in the area, we used to play a lot of college gigs during that period when college gigs was the thing to do. Now I've played almost every school from VPI to the University of Miami, and that's a lot of schools I'm talking about—Clemson, Furman, Western Carolina College, North Carolina State, and Duke, to name a few.
>
> The movie *Animal House* was a perfect example of the kind of stuff that was going down through Florida, Georgia, and the Carolinas: Fraternities bringing in black bands while they partied and drank. And they got so into the music that pretty soon when they had the proms, when they had the homecomings, it just wasn't hip unless they had some black performer on the set. So you built a whole audience out of those kinds of venues.[27]

Butler's reminiscence is supported by an exceedingly interesting statistic from a 1974 publicity release on him which listed all the institutions of higher learning where he had played. The list contained names of thirty-nine institutions, and twenty were located in just four states—Virginia, North Carolina, South Carolina, and Georgia.[28] Little did Vee Jay realize when it was shaping Butler's career that they were creating a beach-music artist.

Betty Everett

Betty Everett for a time in the 1960s was one of the hottest female vocalists in the soul field. Her bittersweet voice was equally at home with blues, soul, MOR pop, and teenage rock 'n' roll, and the result was a number of memorable songs for several Chicago companies, most notably Vee Jay from 1963 to 1966. Everett was born in Greenwood, Mississippi, November 23, 1939, and attended Broad Street High in the city. With her two sisters and two brothers she received a deeply religious upbringing, and as was true of a good many soul singers she got her start in the church. Beginning at age fourteen, she sang and played piano for choirs in her home church, Jones Chapel Baptist Church, and two other congregations in the area.[29]

In early 1957 Everett moved with her sister to Chicago, settling on the West Side. Not long after arriving she was discovered by the famed bluesman Magic Sam. Said she, "My sister and I went to Mel's Hideaway one night and Magic Sam was there. He knew I sang, and asked me to get up and sing, and so I sang. And the club owner, Mel, heard me and hired me, and from that I got with Cobra Records."[30] The label was owned by Eli Toscano and Howard Bedno and at the time they were putting out some of the greatest blues recordings by such artists as Otis Rush, Magic Sam, and Walter "Shakey" Horton.

Cobra teamed up their new signing with some of the city's top blues musicians and the results were sides that strongly evoked the jump blues and blues ballad sound of the 1940s and early 1950s. Dated though the sound may have been, Everett's voice is thrilling to hear. Her young girl soprano had a touch of edgy soulfulness and succeeded admirably in getting across a genuine blues feeling. The first sides, "My Life Depends on You" and "My Love," were not her best for Cobra, however. "Ain't Gonna Cry" and "Killer Diller," featured in a later session, were more solid achievements and a tad blusier as well. Upon their release in 1958, however, they hardly sounded suitable for the emerging rock 'n' roll market.

Everett returned to the studio in 1959 with members of the Ike Turner Band as her sidemen. The two numbers from the session, "I'll Weep No More" and "Tell Me Darling," were both top-notch Everett. "Weep" was a bluesy gospel moan with an excellent chorus from the sidemen, and "Tell Me" was a fine jump blues, far more aggressive than her previous jump numbers.

Cobra went out of business before 1959 was up. Everett continued to sing in clubs around the city under the management of a disc jockey, George "G. G." Graves. In 1959, Graves, who thought the trend in the business was toward male groups headed by female leads, teamed Everett with a young group, the Daylighters. The ensemble with Everett then gigged around the city, and recorded a single for Carl Jones's small outfit, C.J. Records, "Why Did You Have to Go"/"Please Come Back," released in 1960. The top side, although billed as a group, featured Everett alone and was a superlative jump number with classic blues drive courtesy of the Ike Perkins Band. The flip was a quality deep r&b ballad in which Everett's declarative vocals were nicely answered by the Daylighters' first-rate chanting.

In 1961, Everett followed with a solo release recorded with the Perkins Band, "Happy I Long to Be"/"Your Lovin' Arms," both quality ballads. Notwithstanding my appreciation for Everett's C.J. sides, they are obscurities today and were obscurities when they were released. The public was not interested.

While with C.J., Everett was having second thoughts about continuing her career in rhythm and blues. She said, "In 1961, I found God and got saved. I decided I wanted to do gospel for Carl Jones, but he wouldn't do it. So I eventually just went back and did blues again."[31] This would not be the only time in her career that Everett would feel the pull of her religious beliefs and express a desire to do gospel and get out of secular music.

Everett's next association was with independent record producer Leo Austell. He recalled getting Everett:

> I happened to hear a record by Betty Everett that was cut on C.J. Records, "Happy I Long to Be." I heard the girl sing and said the girl is a tremendous singer. Whoever the guy is, he really isn't recording her like he should. I happened to know a guy by the name of Big Jock. He told me he knew her and took me over to her home over on the West Side by Kennedy Expressway. I met and talked with her, and she was interested in singing. She didn't have a contract with C.J.; it was a kind of an understood thing. So she agreed to record with me. That's how I met Betty Everett and became her producer as well as her manager.[32]

In November 1961, Austell recorded four sides by Everett—"Your Love Is Important to Me," "I'll Be There," "Please Love Me," and "I've Got a Claim on You." The production and arrangement were handled by Milton Bland (Monk Higgins), one of his first efforts. The result was a departure from Everett's usual 1950s stylings and a more modern soul sound. "Your Love Is Important to Me," a ballad and the strongest of the four, was released first on Austell's Renee label, but then when George Leaner launched One-derful in March 1962, he leased from Austell all four sides for five hundred dollars.

"Your Love Is Important to Me" made a little local noise in March 1962, but it never caught on. The next One-derful release, "Please Love Me," in 1963, had lots of verve but the song was really only a harbinger of Everett's great future.

During 1963 Austell was busy working to get his new find on a top record label. Said Austell, "One-derful had the first right of refusal on the next thing we did. Then from there King offered me a deal, and I turned them down. Then I met Calvin Carter, whom I knew his sister [Vivian Carter] quite well. He liked Betty, and Vee Jay signed her, and the very first thing we cut was 'Prince of Players.' I think it was a little bit too early."[33] The last comment was Austell's way of saying the record failed to sell, but quite frankly it was a weak disc. It had a pop sound, however, the type of sound with which Vee Jay wanted to establish Everett's career.

Carter had obtained the song in New York, the same city from which he would get Everett's first big hit, "You're No Good."

As Carter told interviewer Mike Callahan in 1981:

> I first selected the tune for Dee Clark. Then when I went to rehearsal with the tune, it was so negative. I said, "Hey, guys, don't talk negative about girls, because girls are the record buyers." [They were then.] So I gave the song to Betty Everett. Then we got into the studio and we're recording it, and the Dells were just sitting in on the recording date. They were sitting on the wooden platform where the string players would sit. Well, they were sitting there on the playback and just stomping their feet on this wooden platform to the beat of the song as it was playing back. So the mikes were open and I heard it. I told the engineer, "Let's do it again, and let's mike those foot pounds, 'cause it really gave it a hell of a beat." So we did that, and boom, a hit. Betty Everett with the Dells on feet. That's how things would happen in those days, you know, by accident. You kept the mikes open and your ears all over the place, and when anything unusual happened you'd just tape it.[34]

Carter was not the only record executive to pick up the song. Jubilee Records in New York first recorded "You're No Good" for a new singer of theirs, Dee Dee Warwick, the younger sister of Dionne. Everett's record killed Warwick's and proved to be a pop hit as well. On *Cash Box*'s r&b chart, "You're No Good" went to the five position and lasted sixteen weeks in late 1963 and early 1964.

Before "You're No Good" slipped off the charts, Carter went fishing in New York again and snagged another fine catch, Rudy Clark's "It's in His Kiss (The Shoop Shoop Song)." Vee Jay gave the upbeat song a great punchy arrangement with flashy horn flourishes, and Everett's vocals simply soared on that kind of material. The number proved to be the only million seller of Everett's career, peaking on *Cash Box*'s r&b chart at number one and lasting sixteen weeks.

Vee Jay followed with "I Can't Hear You," an up-tempo number written by the famous Brill Building composing team of Gerry Goffin and Carole King. It was given an aggressive Motown-style incessant beat, but the song, surprisingly weak for Goffin-King, did not give the Vee Jay staff much to work with. The record went to number thirty-nine on *Cash Box*'s r&b chart, essentially a non-hit.

In December 1964, Everett was again into the hit-making groove, at least in the soul market, with the rousing "Getting Mighty Crowded." The hit came from yet another eastern songwriter, Van McCoy, who provided just the sort of defiant lyrics that Everett could sink her teeth into with her saucy vocals. The record did not break pop, but it did well enough in the black community to keep her r&b career on track.

Everett was also scoring hits during 1964 with Vee Jay stable-mate Jerry Butler. Their duets tended to sound a bit stiff and a mite incompatible, but on the hits the arrangements suited the pair and they came up with some winners. Their best and biggest duet was "Let It Be Me," a remake of the Everly Brothers' hit of four years earlier. The Everlys in their turn had taken this classic French pop tune by Gilbert Becaud and remade it with English lyrics. The song is essentially an Everett vehicle as it is her voice that dominated the harmony parts and it was her lead that Butler had to answer.

The Everett/Butler version is easily better than the Everlys', which seemed to lack the proper romantic ambience that singers of opposite sexes could give it. The strings on the Everlys' arrangement were also too sticky-sweet; the Vee Jay string arrangements were much more suited to the song. Both versions sold a million copies, but the Vee Jay version did marginally better on the charts, number five to the Everlys' number seven on *Billboard*'s pop chart.

"Let It be Me" gave rise to an album by Everett and Butler called *Delicious Together*, which was not exactly the case. On most of the cuts the vocal arrangements tended to be unimaginative and routine. There were only two outstanding cuts, "Let It Be Me," of course, and a zesty cover of the Jimmy Reed hit, "Ain't that Loving You Baby," which was the flip to "Let It Be Me."

At the end of the year, Vee Jay released a follow-up to "Let It Be Me," and as an indication of how weak the *Delicious Together* LP was, Vee Jay didn't opt for a cut from the album. They went with Charlie Chaplin's "Smile," which, depending on one's tolerance toward soul singers doing old standards, is a mighty appealing version. The song went to a respectable sixteen on *Cash Box*'s r&b chart and lasted nine weeks.

During 1965, as Vee Jay seemed to lose its touch, Everett had an exceedingly poor year and was again losing her enthusiasm for secular music. She asked Carter to let her do a gospel album but he refused. When I asked her what she did then, she replied fatalistically, "I didn't do nothing but accept it. That's all, that's my way of living."[35]

Everett's first release in 1965 was a duet with Butler, "Since I Don't Have You," which was one of the weak cuts from the *Delicious Together* LP. Then Everett came out with a solo release, "The Real Thing," a Valerie Simpson/Nick Ashford/Joshie Jo Armstead song that Carter picked up in New York. But unlike previous efforts in which Vee Jay smashed its East Coast competitors, Everett's version did not overpower the original version by Philadelphia singer Tina Britt. The song was a moderate-size r&b hit, but only Britt's version charted. Vee Jay tried again in 1965 with another Simpson/Ashford/Armstead song, "Too Hot to Hold." It was an appealing song, sharply aggressive in the Detroit manner, but it did not chart and got little airplay.

While Vee Jay was fast closing in on bankruptcy in early 1966, it put out a last-gasp release on Everett, "The Shoe Won't Fit." The song was another Simpson/Ashford/Armstead composition, but the borrowing from Diana Ross and the Supremes was too obvious for radio programs to give it a shot. The record was a sad finale for the very good association Everett had with Vee Jay. With the collapse of the company, Everett moved in June 1966 to a major, ABC Records, which was already the home of such Chicago acts as the Impressions and the Marvelows.

Fred Hughes

Fred Hughes was one of the happy products of Vee Jay's move to the West Coast in early 1964. During the company's dying days he was one of the few artists to score top hits for it, specifically "Oo Wee Baby I Love You" and "You Can't Take It Away." His dry tenor vocal was put to superb use on those numbers, conveying a soulful, haunting sound.

Hughes was born in Arkansas, and later ended up in California. There he formed his own band, the Creators, and worked the clubs for two years before being discovered by Vee Jay's West Coast A&R director Richard Parker (who once recorded in a duo called the Dutones).[36] Parker wrote and produced Hughes's two Vee Jay hits. "Oo Wee Baby I Love You" in the spring of 1965 went to the three position on *Billboard*'s r&b chart and lasted fifteen weeks. "You Can't Take It Away" in the fall of the year lasted twelve weeks and went to the twelve position. The records certainly should have launched Hughes on a thriving career but his label collapsed. Vee Jay had planned to release an album on Hughes in the fall, but it and a bunch of others were cancelled at the last minute as the company retrenched.

Vee Jay failed Hughes on the creative end as well. Parker could not seem to come up with solid songs for the singer during his last months with the company. After Vee Jay suspended operations in May 1966 and the Brackens began selling records under the Exodus label, Hughes came out with two Parker-produced singles that did little.

Hughes did not have much of a career after his Vee Jay years. During 1968–69 he had two singles out on Chess that did not do anything. In 1969 he went to Brunswick where Parker was working as a producer. He got two singles, "Baby Boy" (1969) and "I Understand" (1970), on the lower reaches of *Billboard*'s r&b chart.

The Fall of Vee Jay

The Vee Jay bankruptcy in 1966 and the shutting of its doors on South Michigan Avenue came as no surprise to anybody in the record industry. For the previous three years the company was the talk of people in the business. During that time Vee Jay was selling millions of records and ranking as one of the top-ten companies in sales, yet it was in a constant state of turmoil from repeated management turnovers, relocations of head-quarters, and being subject to an endless welter of lawsuits.[37]

The genesis of Vee Jay's decline can probably be dated as early as August 1963, when Vivian and James Bracken expelled Ewart Abner from the presidency and the firm. With him went public-relations chief Barbara Gardner and promotion and A&R man Bill Sheppard. The news of the managerial shake-up, reported *Billboard*, "hit the industry with the force of an explosion."[38]

Billboard did not address the reason for Abner's departure at the time, but Gene Chandler got to the nub of the situation when he said, "Abner liked to spend, and that was the problem. He'd go to a hotel and buy the whole floor, top floor, penthouse, and the disc jockeys would come up and party. He knew how to be a fantastic host. That's how Vee Jay got into trouble. He overspent, accounts receivable all the time. He blew some money in Vegas, maybe two hundred and some thousand dollars. That was enough to get the company in some kind of trouble. He would have brought Vee Jay out of it, but Jimmy got upset. But Abner knew what he was doing."[39]

In 1967 *Billboard* revealed that a July 1963 audit turned up that Abner took $178,482.59 from the company as a "loan." Abner admitted to gambling in Las Vegas with company funds, but claimed he lost only $6,000.[40]

To be an executive in an independent record company, which depends on a continued production of hit records for its month-by-month existence, is to be a naturally gambling type. A number of executives at Vee Jay seemed to be "gambling types" and seemed especially attracted to high-stakes gambling. Said one Chicago songwriter, "Ewart Abner and Bill Sheppard used to gamble at Leo Austell's house every week. One day I recall Bill Sheppard came over to Leo's house with a small suitcase. He had $55,000 in it. They used to gamble for days—E. Rodney Jones, Bill Sheppard, and Abner. They were all making money at the time. Everybody use to come to his place, and on weekends nobody but the big record guys like Calvin Carter would go over there and gamble."[41] And as it turned out with Vee Jay the gambling habits of the executives may have contributed something to the company's instability. And then again it may have not.

The loss of two of the company's biggest soul artists, Gene Chandler and Dee Clark, was damaging to Vee Jay's future. They went with Abner when he established his own label, Constellation Records.

Randall Wood, who described himself as "neither white enough nor black enough," was named president.[42] He brought in an old New York associate, Jay Lasker, as vice president. Wood told r&b researcher Arnold Shaw:

> We were trying to reconstruct the company from every standpoint—the location of the masters to what our real obligations were to creditors, suppliers, artists, etc. When I took over as president, they came out of the woodwork. We found one pressing plant to whom we owed a quarter of a million dollars. At one point we had no fewer than sixty-four legal actions going.
>
> All this had accumulated over a period of four years. . . . Ewart Abner had the whole thing in his head. And how you can run a company that's doing two to three million dollars a year—keeping the facts and figures in your head—is an enigma. I guess he had the sixth sense of knowing what to put where, which is, perhaps, the qualities that make a president. But they also serve to fuck up that company, pretty badly.[43]

Most of the new management team under Wood lived in Los Angeles, and in February 1964 they moved the company's headquarters to plush and spacious offices on Santa Monica Boulevard. Carter stayed in Chicago and kept operational the building at 1449 South Michigan. When Wood talked to Shaw he put the best possible light on his tenure as president, as one would assume, but according to many observers the new management team brought a load of new troubles to the company despite their valiant efforts to clear up the old difficulties. The company was split into two factions—the largely white management team in California and the Brackens and Carter in Chicago. Said Carter, "We were making money, and all they were doing out there was blowing it." In 1964 Vee Jay did fifteen million dollars' worth of business, but the management team was signing such money-losing artists as Arthur Godfrey, Gary LeMel, and Buddy DeFranco, and operating out of expensive headquarters whose existence was wholly unnecessary. Concluded Carter, "It was just a bad job of managing."[44]

But how did Vee Jay manage to do fifteen million dollars worth of business, bad management or not? One answer was the company's bizarre situation regarding their Beatles album. Carter related to Mike Callahan, "We put the album out, and EMI, through Capitol, sued us to cease and desist. They got an injunction against us seemingly every week. They would get an injunction against us on Monday, and we would get it off on Friday, then we'd press over the weekend and ship on Monday; we were smooth, we had everybody alerted, and we were pressing records all the time on weekends."[45] Before 1964 was over Vee Jay had to give up the Beatles to Capitol. Vee Jay was a much smaller company and could not afford to fight a lawsuit even though it felt its contractual right to the Beatles was unassailable.[46] In the record business in the 1960s, might made right, which is one reason why the majors were able to seize control of the rock 'n' roll and rhythm-and-blues market from the independents.

In February 1965 the Brackens fired the California management team, excepting Randall Wood who remained as the "titular president."[47] Bracken assumed the presidency in June and hired Ewart Abner as general manager.[48] Vee Jay then returned to its Chicago headquarters in October. Having lost both the Beatles and the Four Seasons in 1964, by late 1965 Vee Jay had once again become a small family-owned business specializing in rhythm-and-blues music.

However the r&b end had not held up well during 1965. Perhaps because of the turmoil, the creative end was collapsing. The only top-twenty r&b chart hits that Vee Jay could come up with were a Joe Simon hit, a Little Richard hit, and two solid hits by Fred Hughes.

Vee Jay went under Chapter 11 of the bankruptcy law in May 1966, and abruptly suspended all operations. How abruptly? Related Chuck Barksdale of the Dells: "I came down to Vee Jay one day, because I was working as part of the A&R staff. I met a couple of guys who were also on the staff, Richard Parker and Barrett Strong, and they told me the company's closed. I said, 'Closed, what do you mean closed?' They said, 'Hey, they got this big padlock on the door upstairs and nobody puts a padlock on the door like the government.' "[49] The reference to the government was an allusion to the fact that besides having a $1.8 million debt to creditors, Vee Jay owed $1.5 million to the government in taxes.[50]

With Vee Jay in Chapter 11, Jimmy and Vivian continued to put Vee Jay product out during the summer on their newly formed Exodus label. Some of the albums in the back catalogue were put out under the Exodus imprint, and a few artists who weren't grabbed by other companies came out with new singles. The Brackens' principal Exodus artists were Fred Hughes and bluesman Jimmy Reed, the latter of whom made the charts with "Knockin' at Your Door" in June. In August, Vee Jay formally went bankrupt, and that put an end to Vee Jay as well as Exodus. In February 1967, the company's furniture, masters, and other assets were auctioned off.[51]

Of the principals in Vee Jay, the executive who fared the best was Ewart Abner, Jr. He eventually served as president of the giant independent,

Motown Records. James and Vivian Bracken were divorced sometime after the end of Vee Jay. James Bracken made several feeble attempts at resurrecting a label, and died in 1972 owning a hole-in-the-wall record shop. Vivian Carter returned successfully to radio in her hometown of Gary. She died in 1989, three years after her brother, Calvin, passed away.[52]

NOTES

1. Vee Jay has been the most extensively documented of all the Chicago record companies, probably because its spectacular rise and equally spectacular fall has captured the imagination of researchers. Also, Vee Jay was making such controversial news during its last three years of existence that *Billboard* and other trade magazines provided a complete corporate history in their pages. The best research on Vee Jay has been done by Mike Callahan, who in *Goldmine,* May 1981, wrote "The Vee Jay Story" in three parts: part 1, "Scenes from a Family Owned Company," pp. 6–18; part 2, "Vee Jay Is Alive and Living in Burbank," pp. 161–63; part 3, "Both Sides Now, the Story of Stereo Rock and Roll, Vee Jay Records," pp. 170–72.

2. Callahan, "Vee Jay Story," p. 7.

3. Ibid., p. 8.

4. Jerry Butler interview.

5. Ibid.

6. Callahan, "Vee Jay Story," p. 18.

7. Ibid., pp. 16–18.

8. Robert Pruter, "The Dee Clark Story," *Goldmine,* May 1981, pp. 19–21; Cliff White, "Dee Clark: In from the Cold," *Black Music* (December 1975): 23 and 61; Dee Clark interview; H. Sam McGrier interview.

9. Clark interview.

10. Robert Pruter, "The Hambone Kids," *Goldmine,* September 1980, pp. 180–81; "Hambone Kids," *Ebony,* June 1952, pp. 71–76.

11. Clark interview.

12. Ibid.

13. Ibid.

14. Ibid.

15. Serious articles on the Impressions per se, and not specifically on Curtis Mayfield, have been surprisingly few: Bob Fisher, "The Impressions," *The Marshall Cavendish Illustrated History of Popular Music,* vol. 7, 1967–68 (New York: Marshall Cavendish, 1989), pp. 793–95; Joe McEwen, liner notes, *The Vintage Years: Featuring Jerry Butler and Curtis Mayfield,* Sire 3717-2, 1976; Cliff White "Jerry Butler, Curtis Mayfield and the Impressions," *Time Barrier Express* 23 (July–August 1977): 28–32; Cliff White, "Keep on Pushing," *Black Music,* September 1974, pp. 16–19; Curtis Mayfield interview.

16. Lawrence N. Redd, *Rock Is Rhythm and Blues: The Impact of Mass Media* (Grand Rapids, Mich.: Michigan State University Press 1974), p. 137.

17. John Abbey, "The Ice Man," *Blues and Soul,* April 10-23, 1970, p. 21.

18. Callahan, "Vee Jay Story," p. 9; Clarence Page, "Does Curtis Mayfield Sincerely Want to Be Rich?" *Chicago Tribune Magazine,* February 10, 1974, p. 35.

19. Mayfield interview.

20. Ibid.

21. Ibid.

22. Page, "Does Curtis Mayfield Want to be Rich?" p. 35.

23. Jerry Butler, as one of the most visible of the Chicago soul stars, has had a great many superb articles documenting his career: John Abbey, "The Ice Man," *Blues and Soul,* April 10–23, 1970, pp. 20–23; Vince Aletti, "Jerry Butler," *The Rolling Stone Rock 'n' Roll Reader,* ed. Ben Fong-Torres (New York: Bantam, 1974), pp. 123–32 (article originally published in *Rolling Stone,* April 30, 1970, pp. 34–36); Lacy J. Banks, "Jerry Butler: The Anti-Perspirant Iceman," *Black Stars,* August 1972, pp. 19–27; Marcia L. Brown, "Jerry Butler: The Ice Man Keeps on Rolling Along," *Black Stars,* September 1974, pp. 11–16; Robert Pruter, "The Jerry Butler Story," *It Will Stand* 27/28 [1982]: 6–10; Redd, *Rock Is Rhythm and Blues,* pp. 135–46; Cliff White, "History of an Ice Man," *Black Music,* February 1977, pp. 44–53; Butler interview.

24. Butler interview.

25. White, "History of an Ice Man," p. 45.

26. Ibid., 46.

27. Butler interview.

28. Undated publicity release, "Jerry Butler Revue: College Engagements to Date."

29. Robert Pruter, "Betty Everett: Thirty Years of Bitter-Sweet Recordings," *Goldmine,* April 10, 1987, pp. 97–99; liner notes, *Betty Everett/Lillian Offitt,* Flyright 589, 1985; Leo Austell interview; Betty Everett interview.

30. Everett interview.

31. Ibid.

32. Austell interview.

33. Ibid.

34. Callahan, "Vee Jay Story," p. 11.

35. Everett interview.

36. Liner notes, Fred Hughes, "Oo Wee Baby, I Love You," DJM Records, DJS 10717, undated.

37. Vee Jay advertisement, *Billboard,* March 7, 1964, p. 37.

38. "Ewart Abner Exits Vee Jay; Big Shake-Up," *Billboard,* August 3, 1963 (n.p.)

39. Chandler interview, February 6, 1979.

40. "Bribe Case Turns Touchy and Go," *Billboard,* March 4, 1967, p. 4.

41. My source prefers anonymity. The interview was conducted by telephone, Chicago, January 16, 1979.

42. Arnold Shaw, *Honkers and Shouters* (New York: Macmillan, 1978), p. 337.

43. Ibid., p. 338.

44. Callahan, "Vee Jay Story," p. 12.

45. Ibid., p. 11.

46. Ibid., p. 12.

47. "Top Level Changes Made at VJ," *Billboard,* February 27, 1965, p. 3.

48. "Randall Woods Exits," *Billboard,* June 19, 1965, p. 10.

49. Chuck Barksdale interview.

50. "Combine Bids for VJ—With Condition," *Billboard,* May 14, 1966, p. 4.

51. "Five Thousand Vee Jay Masters on Auction Block on February 24," *Billboard,* February 11, 1967, p. 10.

52. Eileen Southern, "James Bracken," in *Biographical Dictionary of Afro-American and African Musicians* (Westport, Conn.: Greenwood Press, 1982), p. 43; "Vivian Bracken, Sixty-nine; Brought Records of the Beatles to U.S.," *Chicago Sun-Times,* June 15, 1989.

Pam Productions / Constellation Records

Pam Productions was formed by two small record entrepreneurs, Carl Davis and Bill "Bunky" Sheppard, in early 1961. They set up their operation on the near West Side at 2400 West Madison. The company started putting out records in the soft-soul vein on three labels—Nat, named after an accountant for the firm; Pam, named after one of Davis's daughters; and Wes, short for William E. Sheppard. Pam Productions almost immediately began getting hits with such acts as the Starlets, Sheppards, and Dukays. It was a Dukays record, "Duke of Earl," that launched Carl Davis, Bunky Sheppard, and Gene Chandler as major figures in the Chicago soul music scene. Davis became the preeminent record producer and executive in Chicago with posts first at Columbia Records and later at Brunswick Records. Sheppard became an executive first at Vee Jay and later at Constellation. Chandler left the Dukays to become one of the biggest soul stars of the 1960s.

Pam Productions lasted only a few short years, but it cemented the creative and business alliances that kept Davis, Sheppard, and Chandler working together while each was with separate companies, especially when Chandler was with Vee Jay (1961–63) and Constellation (1963–66). Constellation was formed in August 1963 by Ewart Abner following his dismissal from the presidency of Vee Jay. The formal name of the company was Dart Record Sales, which Abner had started in July 1962 under the Vee Jay banner to distribute Ace records. Constellation was the name of the label. The company had three owners—Ewart Abner, president; Bunky Sheppard, vice president; and Art Sheridan, secretary. Sheridan had owned Chance Records in the early 1950s and had started Abner in the record business. Constellation was headquartered at 1421 South Michigan Ave.[1]

Constellation can be viewed as basically a continuation of Pam Productions. When Sheppard joined Vee Jay in 1961 he formed a close friendship with Abner, and when Abner left the company, Sheppard followed. Most important, Sheppard brought Chandler, who while at Vee Jay was under contract to Pam Productions, which although not a separate label was still a legal entity. Dee Clark had a similar kind of business arrangement with Abner and also joined Constellation. Sheppard was in charge of A&R and had his friend Carl Davis produce most of the Chandler sides. On most of the Chandler Constellation releases that say "A Bill Sheppard Production," the actual production was by Carl Davis.[2] With Ace distribution, Chandler and Clark in the stable, and Davis helping in the producing, Constellation had an auspicious start.

Behind the saga of Pam Productions were two remarkable men, Carl Davis and Bill Sheppard. Davis was born on the South Side of Chicago, April 4, 1934, the last of eleven children. He was born Carl Adams, his father later adopting his mother's maiden name of Davis. His parents were blue-collar workers, his father working as a custodian and his mother as a housekeeper, and with eleven children to raise there were not many resources to go around. Still, at age seven Carl moved with his family from the more impoverished area around Forty-eighth and Champaign to the middle-class Englewood area at Sixty-ninth and Langley.

Davis attended Englewood High, where he played football and was pretty good at it. He had the potential to become a star college athlete, but threw away his budding football career by quitting high school and joining the Air Force in 1951. There he went to clerical school and learned how to operate a DSJ composomatic machine, which was used in typesetting and printing. When Davis got out of the Air Force in April 1954, he did not know what he was going to do, and drifted from job to job. His first job was at a composomatic machine in an office with forty other machines. But he tired of the routine and quit after six months. He then worked at Argo Starch, then the post office, then a filling station, and then attended Cortez Business College.

While attending school, Davis, still rudderless, went to the manufacturer of the composomatic machine to find out the names of the customers to whom they sold the machines, figuring one of them might need an operator. He spied the name of Al Benson, the legendary black deejay who at that time was the most powerful in the city. Benson used the composomatic machine to make up his own top-twenty r&b hit sheet that he distributed to the record shops. Davis applied for and got the job as operator, his modest entrance into the music business.

Davis prior to this time was mainly interested in jazz and had only a fleeting acquaintance with rhythm and blues. He also had no familiarity

with musical instruments, although three of his older brothers were musicians—Herman, a bass player; Arlington, a tenor saxophone player; and
Clifford, the most accomplished musician in the family, a tenor saxophone
player.

Davis's job with Benson was not only to put the top twenty and the
second tier of twenty "up-and-coming records" on the hit sheet. He also
had to conduct a survey of the stores and gather the sales figures to determine
the order of the top twenty and the up-and-coming records. The up-and-
coming listing was based less on sales figures and more on seat-of-the-pants
guesswork. Davis soon found himself developing a good knack at gauging
what records would become hits.

Davis's job also brought him in contact with all the distributors on
Record Row, who, cognizant of his influential position, didn't hesitate to
load him up with his favorite jazz records. In 1959 Morry Price, a one-
time vice president at Mercury Records, opened his own distributorship,
Arnold Distributing, at 1329 South Michigan Avenue. He hired Davis as
one of his promotion men. One of the labels Arnold was handling was
Amy. Davis made his reputation at the firm in 1960, when two records were
out that exploited the popularity of the Madison dance craze. Ray Bryant's
"The Madison Time," on Columbia, was the top national seller and easily
bested Al Brown and the Tunetoppers' "The Madison," on Amy. In Chicago,
it was a different story. With Davis's promotion efforts the Amy record was
the top seller.[3]

After a brief stay at Summit Distributors, 1345 West Diversey Parkway,
Davis went to Columbia's distribution branch at 2240 North Milwaukee in
1960. Davis got the job as local promotion manager, replacing Granville
White, who became regional promotion manager for the firm.

Meanwhile, Davis and Bunky Sheppard together were independently
working in various recording endeavors. Davis originally met Sheppard in
1958 when he was working at Favor Ruhl, an art supply store in the Chicago
Loop. Sheppard was trying to get a hit in the record business, recording
an occasional record on one of Chicago's many street-corner groups. Said
Davis:

> He had a group called the Bel Aires, and he was trying to do
> something with their record, "Rockin' and Strollin." I remember
> he brought the record over to Al Benson. He came upstairs and
> he had a fifth of gin. His intent was to give Al this fifth of gin
> to play his record. I don't know why, I just took a liking to him.
> I said, "Don't go offer that man no gin 'cause I know Al. He
> don't want no gin." I said, "Let me hear your record." I listened
> to it. I didn't think it was a hit, but I thought it was good enough

to be played on radio. So I told him, "Let me take it in and see if I can get it played for you." Al played it and the record did all right. The important thing, it brought Bunky and I together."[4]

While at Columbia Record Distributors, Davis began to get the itch to make records on his own. Sheppard was getting some success on the successor group of the Bel Aires called the Sheppards, so Davis teamed up with him to form Pam Productions in 1961.

The Sheppards

The Sheppards are highly regarded today by those familiar with the group's music, but by and large they remain unknown to the vast majority of rhythm-and-blues fans. Their relative obscurity perhaps can be attributed to the fact that they were popular during the long-denigrated early-1960s era of rock 'n' roll, when doowop was largely a memory and soul had a few years to go before it would make its impact. But the Sheppards, as well as certain other rhythm-and-blues stars from this period, deserve wider recognition, because they are the artists who redeemed the early 1960s by creating a marvelous transitional style of r&b unique to the period. It was a music drawing much of its character from the earlier doowop, yet it incorporated instrumentation and vocal stylings that in later years would inform soul music.

The Sheppards were formed in 1959 out of two earlier groups managed by Bill Sheppard, the Ballads and the Bel Aires. Members were Millard Edwards (lead and bass), Jimmy Allen (baritone), and James Dennis Isaac (bass and fifth tenor) from the Bel Aires; and Murrie Eskridge (lead and top tenor), O. C. Perkins (second tenor), and Kermit Chandler (guitar) from the Ballads.[5] Isaac and Perkins were the oldest veterans of the Chicago vocal group scene, having recorded with various groups since the mid-1950s.

The group featured two first-rate leads—the smooth ballad voice of Edwards and the sharper-edged, gospelly vocals of Eskridge. The Sheppards were also blessed with excellent songwriters as virtually all their material was written by group members. Perkins and Chandler teamed up on nearly a third of the songs and created most of the hits, and Edwards proved prolific with the pen as well. The Sheppards, in short, combined the strengths of two groups. Sheppard signed the group to Apex, which, with subsidiary labels Mad and Dempsey, he co-owned with Tommy "Madman" Jones and Dempsey Nelson. The operation was located at 951 East Forty-seventh Street.

The Sheppards' first Apex release paired "Island of Love," which came from the Bel Aires, and "Never Felt Like This Before," which came from the Ballads. The latter song, with the strong, soulful lead by Eskridge, got a lot of play on the East Coast, but it was the enchanting and romantic Edwards-led "Island of Love" that became a national hit. The song was not a chart success, however, but after its release in the spring of 1959, it sold strongly and steadily for almost a full year and as a result became the group's trademark tune. While "Never Felt Like This Before" seemed to be a harbinger of the coming soul era, "Island of Love" seemed to hark back to the past glories of doowop.

Because of their initial recording success, the Sheppards were given the opportunity to tour the chitlin' theater circuit in the summer and fall of 1959. In their first show, at the Tivoli Theater in Chicago, the group was billed behind LaVern Baker, Roy Hamilton, and Huey Smith and the Clowns. In their second show, at an auditorium in Calumet City (a suburb south of Chicago), the Sheppards and the Skyliners were first-billed and it was that show that proved most memorable to the group. Perkins remembered: "That was the first time I really saw our name up in lights. They had it in some kind of sequins or something. It was just dynamite for me to see this, and after we got in, we worked the auditorium. Like four or five thousand kids were in there. The crowd was excited, and it was really exciting to see them excited, because I've never seen this in nowhere but the movies and I thought it was bullshit. Then you get to see it with your own eyes, and then you realize this is for real and its happening to you. . . . And all those kids—I actually saw this one girl just faint when we hit 'Island of Love.'"[6]

Nothing much happened for the Sheppards on the next few releases, but their fifth release, "Come Home, Come Home," had some pop success in the fall of 1960. The group's next release, "Tragic," proved even more successful. It got quite a bit of play on the r&b outlets in early 1961 and was the song that the group sang on the Dick Clark show.

The Sheppards left Apex after "Tragic," and joined Pam for their next release, a fine double-sided effort, "Never Let Me Go"/"Give a Hug to Me." The latter side made some noise in the Midwest, but turned out to be only a "radio hit" with few record sales. Two other fine songs from the Pam session, "Queen of Hearts" and "Forgotten," later came out on the Sheppards' first album released on Constellation in 1964 as part of an oldies series.

With the release of "The Glitter in Your Eyes," in December 1961 (first on Wes, but then on Vee Jay when Sheppard moved to that label), the Sheppards were rewarded with their first national hit since "Island of Love." The song featured exotic but splendid warbling that sounded fiftyish, but it had a certain degree of soul styling to place it between eras. The Sheppards, still on Vee Jay, then re-recorded "Tragic" with an echo effect. It came out in the spring of 1962 and proved to be another national hit for the group. Later releases on Vee Jay bombed.

After Vee Jay, the Sheppards never had a subsequent hit, and their career went into a decline. In 1963, Sheppard got Davis to release on OKeh "Pretend You're Still Mine," a fine doowopy ballad. The song never caught on, however, perhaps because it sounded somewhat dated. Following that release, Edwards left the goup to go it alone as a single under the name Mill Evans. The Sheppards continued as best they could without Edwards on a number of records, but they hadn't any success. They finally called it quits in 1969.

The Sheppards were a much better group than the modest success of their records indicated. The group had such talent that it could have eventually made it to the big-time as did the Dells and the Temptations, but they did not. Perkins explained why: "The most unfortunate thing that ever happened to the Sheppards was that they didn't ever get someone to take the act and really polish it and produce it to what it could have been. No one took us and said, 'I'm going to make you an act instead of a record.'"[7] Notwithstanding Perkins's remarks, the Sheppards have made an indelible mark on the history of rhythm-and-blues and soul. This was evidenced by a *Time* magazine profile of the group in January 1981, some nineteen years after the group's last hit record. The profile was prompted by *Time*'s selection of *The Sheppards,* a Solid Smoke reissue LP, as one of the top ten pop records of 1980.[8] The Sheppards made music that had staying power.

The Starlets

The early 1960s were the heyday of the strident girl-group sound and in all the major recording centers across the nation record entrepreneurs were searching out ensembles who had a forceful and unmistakable teenagy-girl sound. New York and Los Angeles seemed to produce most of the groups of that genre, but other cities made their contributions, albeit minor, to the sound. Chicago gave us the Starlets, who had "Better Tell Him No" in 1961, and, in one of the peculiar twists of the record industry of that time, also had a much bigger hit, "I Sold My Heart to the Junkman," as the Blue-Belles in 1962.

The Starlets began in early 1961, when a young lady a few years out of high school, Jane Hall, began gathering a group together on the city's South Side. She found Maxine Edwards at a pecan-processing plant where they both worked. Edwards, later called Maxine Lightner, was the sister of Earl Edwards, one of the members of the Dukays. Other members Hall added to the Starlets were Mickey McKinney and Jeannette Miles. When the girls felt they were ready, Hall took them to Bernice Williams, a local songwriter in her Englewood neighborhood. At that time Williams was writing songs for the Dukays and helping them get material together for recording on Pam Productions. Williams felt the Starlets needed another voice and brought into the group a girl called Liz Walker (she also called herself Dynetta Boone, and the girls never knew which was her true name).[9]

Williams gave the Starlets a strident-sounding song, "Better Tell Him No," and after a week's rehearsal the girls went down to Pam Productions to audition it. It was partly done as a dialogue with Edwards and Williams respectively singing first lead and second lead as daughter and mother. Davis and Sheppard were impressed with the song and with Edwards's forceful lead, but sent the group back home to give the song more polish and to come up with more material for a recording session.

Preparing for a session would not be a problem because as Lightner told it, Williams vigorously worked the girls: "Sometimes we would start rehearsing at 4:00 in the afternoon while she was cooking dinner. She had a family then. By the time she gets through cooking for and feeding her family, we're sung out. And then she would come in there and we had to do what she said and had to go over the songs again. We were sort of tired, and would often say, 'Hey, aren't we finished yet!'"[10]

Prepared, the Starlets returned to Pam and recorded "Better Tell Him No," and for a flip, "You Are the One," which Liz Walker led. "Better Tell Him No" entered the *Billboard* pop chart in April 1961 and went to position thirty-eight, lasting sixteen weeks. On the magazine's r&b chart it lasted two weeks and went to the twenty-four position in June. The record was obviously a bigger rock 'n' roll hit than an r&b one. Despite its undeniable success and notwithstanding its rock 'n' roll spiritedness, the song lacked a memorable melody and hooks. The flip, "You Are the One," was more engagingly melodic and soulful.

With a top-forty hit, the Starlets were in demand for live appearances and were soon touring the entire northeast section of the country. Lightner recalled going to Cleveland; Washington, D.C.; Philadelphia; New York; and Newark. "Our first show," she said, "we did away from home in Newark, New Jersey. We did a show with Gladys Knight and the Pips, Mary Wells, the Spinners, Van McCoy, and Jackie Wilson. We were the second ones on the show. It was very exciting. By us being so young, we were so eager to sing we weren't even nervous."[11]

While on tour in Philadelphia the Starlets recorded "I Sold My Heart to the Junkman." Said Lightner:

> By us being eager to sing, we got caught up in a situation where we breached our contract. We went into the recording studio for another company and did "I Sold My Heart to the Junkman."

We really were thinking that we were gonna change over and make big money. This man, Harold Robinson, who got us to do this, he owned a car place in Philadelphia. He had us record—the recording studio was inside his car place—and he was telling us he had seen us and heard us perform. And he said he could do a lot with us. Now we knew we weren't making a whole lot of money with Bernice Williams, so we just figured, "Hey, this is a way we could make money," not thinking we were breaching a contract. We just thought Pam would be happy and sell us out and make money too. So we recorded the song. And when we came back to Chicago, we heard our song in about two or three weeks.[12]

"I Sold My Heart to the Junkman" became a huge pop and r&b hit in the spring of 1962. On *Billboard*'s r&b chart it lasted seven weeks and went to position thirteen, and on the pop chart it lasted eleven weeks and went to position fifteen. The record is a classic girl group and thoroughly typified the mainstream rock 'n' roll approach to the genre. The record had loads of drive, Edwards's lead voice had great soulful urgency, and the rest of the girls chorused sharply. The song, curiously, was originally recorded by Etta Jones in 1947 as a lazy jazz ballad.

When a record is made under cloudy circumstances as "Junkman" certainly was, and the record dies, everybody forgives and forgets. But "Junkman" was a big hit, lots of money was involved, so the lawsuits were flying. Phil Terry, the record's producer, took Robinson into court. Said Lightner, "He pursued the court action because Mr. Robinson didn't want to give us money from the record and he didn't want to give Phil any money. So we went into court on that."[13]

"In court," continued Lightner, "they did state I was on lead, but in the background Mr. Robinson said he had faded out the background and put all his girls, the Blue-Belles, in the background. But what he did, he dubbed over again the same girls background to make it sound real full, and he claimed that he dubbed in his girls. But that wasn't so. Phil Terry was through it all and he was with us, 'cause he didn't like what was happening. We didn't get any more than $4,000 to $5,000 apiece on the record."[14]

Although "$4,000 to $5,000 apiece" sounds like a hefty chunk of money for 1962, Lightner contends, "I feel we should have gotten so much money for plays on the record. The money we got wasn't for the plays, it was just a settlement to just quiet down on who sang on the record. We couldn't tour off the record; Mr. Robinson's girls did that."[15]

By mid-1962, Carl Davis was with OKeh records and he released one more record by the Starlets, "You Belong to Me"/"Impression." Dynetta

Boone soulfully led on both sides and both were fiftyish in sound, with high sweet harmonies. The songs were old stuff that were in the can and merely put out routinely without any push from the company. By the time of the record's release the Starlets were no longer associated with Davis. Said Lightner, "When they dropped us they also told us that we would never be able to sing anywhere, because they got us tied up. They told us that we were still under contract to them and they weren't going to do anything with us. They would just sit us on the shelf."[16]

The Starlets were not all that pleased with Pam Productions either. "We got disgusted," said Lightner, "because a lot of times when we made money we did not receive it because they would always tell us that it was eaten up by the recording costs. They would also tell us that the money went on our uniforms. We would say, 'What uniforms?' We remember putting money in towards uniforms, our own personal money. Then they got angry with us too, saying we were dumb and stupid because we went out and recorded under contract. We just got tired of being called dumb."[17]

The story of the Starlets might well leave the impression that it was one filled with conflict, bitterness, and heartbreak. But there were many happy and positive times as well, as Lightner easily recalled with fondness: "...Remembering back when we first started, and just merely walking down the street getting our harmony together before we got to Bernice Williams's house, standing on Bernice Williams's porch at all times of night and just singing. I mean it was really fun, and just concerning ourselves with getting ready to do TV hops, you know. It was really something!"[18]

The Dukays

The Dukays were known for a few moderate soul hits, but few followers of popular music realized in the early 1960s that they also recorded one of the most famous early rock 'n' roll records of all time, "Duke of Earl." The song was made famous by Gene Chandler. Eugene Dixon, to use Chandler's birth name, was the Dukay's first lead singer and as lead he recorded the song with the group, but a marketing decision on top of record company politics resulted in the turn of events that had him alone credited on the record. Chandler became the "Duke of Earl" and went on to national fame, while the rest of the group continued on a few more years with only intermittent, modest success. The Dukays as an act are worthy of interest, however, because artistically, as with the Sheppards, they helped bridge the earlier doowop era and the emerging soul era by creating a music that partook of both styles. The Dukays helped pioneer soul.[19]

The Dukays came out of the Englewood neighborhood of Chicago and got together when they were high schoolers, about 1957. Earl Edwards—

the Dukays' spokesman, leader, founder, and self-confessed "daddy" of the group—formed the group with Ben Broyles, James Lowe, and Eugene Dixon as lead. He got Dixon from another group.

"A man had a barbershop in the neighborhood and his name was Cooper," related Edwards. "He picked the name for us, and said he was going to call us the 'Dukays.' We would go into his shop and rehearse and have little contests. That's the way Gene Chandler joined my group. He liked the way we did things so he decided to leave his group, the Gaytones, and sing with us."[20]

Dixon soon left the Dukays to join the Army. While he was stationed with the 101st Airborne Division in Germany, he did some performing with the Special Services. The Dukays continued to stay together in his absence, and when Dixon got out in 1960 he reclaimed his place as lead. He also brought along his cousin, Shirley Jones, who the group felt would be a novel attraction because it was not all that common for females to be in male groups. At this time, the group consisted of lead vocalist Eugene Dixon, baritone Earl Edwards, second tenor James Lowe, bass Ben Broyles, and Shirley Jones, who did the customary male part of first tenor. The Dukays were now ready to go beyond street-corner harmonizing to making records, but they were weak on original material and sought the help of Bernice Williams.

Williams worked with the Dukays, polished their act, and developed some songs for them, and after some months the group was ready for the recording studio, and to record with Carl Davis and Bunky Sheppard. The sessions resulted in the following songs: "The Big Lie," "Festival of Love," "Kissin' in the Kitchen," "Girl Is a Devil," "Nite Owl," and "Duke of Earl." These songs were typical of the period—partly in the group-harmony tradition and partly in the soul style. The vocal parts were allowed to assert themselves well in front of the few instruments employed in the mix, but despite this 1950s complexion, there is a subtle soul element in the hard-edge vocals.

"Girl Is a Devil," the first release, came out on the Nat label in the spring of 1961. After the record entered *Billboard*'s pop top-hundred on May 15, it lasted a relatively long thirteen weeks on the chart, going as high as sixty-four. The song, written by Williams, had a terrific urban flavor well conveyed by Dixon's soulful and perfectly enunciated delivery. The follow-up to "Girl Is a Devil" was the equally masterful "Nite Owl," another Williams composition thoroughly evocative of the ghetto streets of Chicago. "Nite Owl" broke into the top-hundred chart on January 20, 1962, slipped off the chart on February 24, but returned for one week on March 31.

The Dukays' next record, "Duke of Earl," was released in November 1961, only weeks after "Nite Owl." The story of how the song came to be recorded and how the name "Gene Chandler" came to appear on the record is related by Chandler:

> We used to rehearse at my house every day, and when we rehearsed in order to open our cords we would sing "ah, ah, ah, ahh" on the scale, something like that, OK? Or "du, du, duu." This particular day, everybody was hitting their notes, "du, du, du, duu." You see what I'm gonna get to? All of a sudden I told them to hold those notes. We started getting them in place. I said, "Hold those notes and keep doing that." So I thought about "Duke!" We couldn't go round singing "Du du," so I said "Duke!" So I say, "Duke, Duke, Duke of Earl!" If you think about it, it's only going up the scale and going back down...Duke, Duke, Duke of Earl, Duke, Duke, Duke of Earl, Duke, Duke, Duke of Earl... right? We were rehearsing. Earl Edwards made me think of Earl. It wasn't originally intended to be a song. It was only intended to just hold our notes and open up.
>
> Now I said, "Take it up to [the chorus]." They took it up to [the chorus] and I just started throwing any kind of lyric to it ... "As I walk through this world, nothing can stop the Duke of Earl," whatever came out of me. So the song sounded good, so we ran out the house and went up the street to where Bernice lived. She was our manager then. We say to Bernice, "We got a million seller, a million seller!" At that time we didn't know we had a million seller, but it sounded so great, it was the greatest thing we had done, out of the songs she was writing and whatever we received from people.
>
> Anyway, Bernice changed some lyrics from the lyrics I had given her. So Bernice Williams is named as co-writer. And since we were using Earl Edwards's name in the song, we gave him a piece of it. At that time I wasn't up on writing and all that. That was the first song I had ever written.[21]

Chandler's version of the song's creation pretty much left out Earl Edwards. Edwards has contended and Carl Davis has agreed, however, that he had an important role in genuine authorship of the song. Edwards told me a story about the genesis of the song along the same lines that Chandler did, but with him directing and shaping the creation instead of Chandler.[22]

Davis related how the "Duke of Earl" got to be recorded. It was a typical seven-hundred-dollar, four-songs-per-session deal as was customary of the period:

> We listened to the Dukays and they had a song called "Nite Owl." I said that "Nite Owl" sounds like it would be a smash. So Bunky

and I, we were trying to find the money to cut it. I remember I went to this girl I was dating. I went to her and told her I needed seven hundred dollars. Between her and her mother, they came up with the seven hundred dollars. I got my brother Clifford to write out the chord changes. We got the musicians in there. In those days I think it was only two-track; the music's on one, the singing is on the other.

The night before the session the Dukays were in our office, and they were rehearsing the songs they were going to record the next day. When they got through rehearsing, I was in my office, and they were in this outer office, and through the door I kept hearing—I thought they were singing "do cover"—the "Duke of Earl." I thought it was something else, man. I said, "What is that!" They said, "We're just rehearsing our next session. We haven't even written the lyrics to this song yet." And I said, "Run it down, let's hear it." They started and the song just knocked me. I said, "Let me tell you something, if you don't cut this song tomorrow, there ain't no session."[23]

Following the session, Davis sent both "Nite Owl" and "Duke of Earl" to their New York-based distributor, Lesgal Productions, to pick which one it wanted. Lesgal preferred "Nite Owl" over "Duke of Earl" and released the record on Nat. Davis then had something of an option of taking "Duke of Earl" to someone else. Said Chandler, "Calvin Carter of Vee Jay Records, which had just bought the publishing [rights] for 'Nite Owl,' wanted to hear the other Dukays' songs from the session. He heard the 'Duke of Earl' master and went ecstatic, and wanted to buy it right away. Davis, however, pointed out that the group doing the record was the Dukays and they were already assigned to the other distributor. So Calvin said, 'We don't care. We want that song. We'll put anybody's name with the song, the group, or whoever.'"[24]

After Vee Jay purchased "Duke of Earl," Davis and Sheppard began trying to determine what artist would be on the record. At the same time, O. C. Perkins—a member of the Sheppards—was attending a show in Gary, Indiana, where a young singer by the name of Charles Davis was performing. Charles Davis recalled, "Perkins heard me sing and said, 'Sheppard needs a singer; you're a single artist and I like the show so come on down.' So I met with Bill Sheppard and Carl Davis and auditioned. It was just about all set and I was going to be "Gene Chandler...."[25]

Carl Davis, however, then presented the situation to Dixon. "I could either stay with the group," said Chandler, "and they would let Charles Davis become whoever they were gonna have for the 'Duke of Earl' record.

Or vice-versa, they would take Davis and put him with the group to replace me and I would go out as a single with Vee Jay. But I had to change my name, because it was signed to the group under the contracts that were there. So alright, Carl Davis was a fan of Jeff Chandler, and I liked Jeff Chandler, and we thought that was a long sort of *white* name," he said with a semi-conspiratorial air. "And my name was Eugene, so we just changed it to Gene...Gene Chandler."[26]

Chandler continued, "I decided to split from the group because I was really tired of groups—the rehearsals, the hassles—and I always wanted to be alone. But we had 'Nite Owl' happening, so it was a real choice for me. 'Duke of Earl' was not even released yet. I just took a chance and I went with 'The Duke' record."[27]

"I told him that the song wasn't going to make it," Edwards confessed, "This is what I thought, you know. I told him, 'You make your couple of bucks and come right on back to the Dukays.' It didn't work out that way."[28]

The "Duke of Earl," beginning on January 13, went on to stay fifteen weeks on *Billboard*'s pop chart, including three weeks in the number one position. The record was a million seller. Chandler recalled:

> No time at all I was a household word. Everything happened so fast I didn't have a chance to think about it. They were taking me here, taking me there, and I didn't have time to get my head together about what I was going to be. I was more or less saying "How do I do this?" or "How do you do that?" You know, "What's happenin' next?"
>
> I didn't know.
>
> For a time I wore a "Duke of Earl" costume—tux, cape, top hat, monocle, the whole bit. At the time I was totally brainwashed into what was happening. I wore it for a time, naturally. Then after a while I discarded it, especially because of the different types of songs I was doing. They moved me around so fast that when finally the "Duke of Earl" record was finished I didn't realize what I had until it was really over with. And then I realized how much more I could have capitalized off it.[29]

Asked what it was that so struck him about "Duke of Earl," Davis replied, "It was really that haunting chant, 'Duke, Duke, Duke of Earl.' They didn't have a song written at the time. But they had the vamp, that haunting thing, and this is what sold me. I didn't care what the lyrics were. It was just a giant record, and Gene Chandler immediately was a pop act. It had to be one of the first black records to be a million seller. A million seller was hard to come by in those days, especially on black product."[30]

Meanwhile, the Dukays were left with no credit and no glory from the song, although they collected royalties on the record. But with Davis as their new lead, they did obtain a contract with Vee Jay through Bunky Sheppard and were able to continue to reap rewards on their past hits as well as on their later, more modest successes. Before the first Vee Jay session dates, however, Shirley Jones left the group and was replaced with Margaret "Cookie" Stone.

The first record for the Davis-led Dukays was "Please Help," a novelty number, backed with "I'm Gonna Love You So," a ballad. Both songs in the spring of 1962 got a lot of play on a regional basis in Chicago, Philadelphia, and Indianapolis, but did virtually nothing nationally. "Please Help" even went pop in Chicago on the powerful WLS station. The next records on Vee Jay did nothing, and in 1963 Davis, Broyles, and Stone left the group. Charles Davis explained what happened:

> We fell into a lull. I always relate it back to the money the group got from "Duke of Earl." It seemed as if the group kind of lost its enthusiasm at that time. The record was a top record and the Dukays never got that much credit for it. Locally, everybody knew the group did the record, but from a national standpoint, nothing. They received substantial royalties from the record, and when that happened, I think Ben Broyles was the first to kind of drift away. They received close to seven grand apiece all at one time. Earl was always the stabilizing force—he really kind of kept it together—but then after he bought a building, the group started drifting away and stopped rehearsing. They just sort of lost motivation.[31]

The Dukays continued with some new members—Claude McCrae and Richard Dixon—and lasted a few more years. They recorded a local hit in 1964 called "The Jerk" for Jerry T. Murray's Jerry-O label, but the following year when a follow-up failed they disbanded.

Gene Chandler

The association of Gene Chandler with the "Duke of Earl" hit is so well known that it has tended to obscure his greater achievement as a leading purveyor of Chicago-style soul. Chandler was one of soul music's best balladeers, and few soul artists could express achingly lovelorn feelings as well as he. These emotions were superbly interpreted in his biggest ballads, notably "Just Be True," "What Now," "Bless Our Love," "Here Comes the Tears," and "The Girl Don't Care." But he was also a master of the mid-tempo song, such as "Think Nothing About It," "Nothing Can Stop Me," and "There Goes the Lover." In commercial terms he had twenty-one national chart records from 1961 to 1969, and in Chicago he had at least thirty hits during that period.[32]

Chandler was great not only because he sold a lot of appealing records, but because he brought to his songs a high degree of artistry, in the highest sense of the word. His artistry rested in his voice. Though in a technical sense somewhat limited in range and lacking resonance and tone quality, it had a personality and a clarity of expression that were magnificent. This timbre, as musicologists would call his vocal coloration and intonation, is often hard for the uninitiated to grasp; they do not hear all the nuances and subtleties that separate soul music from pop, but Chandler sang lyrically uncomplicated songs that were highly sophisticated in their manner of expression. To know Chandler and understand his music is to appreciate truly the "soul" in soul music.

Chandler said of his younger years:

> I was born Eugene Dixon on July 7, 1937, and raised in Chicago. I lived at 429 East Forty-sixth Place, which is between Vincennes and South Park, a half block from Forty-seventh Street, which is where the Regal Theater was at. I lived there from a baby till I was around eleven years old. Then I moved to Englewood. When I first moved there I would have to say the neighborhood was upper working [class]. It was black and white. As a matter of fact it was more white than it was black. Blacks were moving in and they started having a lot of racial conflict and then finally the neighborhood changed over. And only a few whites stayed and just became a part of the neighborhood. It wasn't a poor neighborhood, no. The building that I stayed in, the fellow that owned it, he lived on the first floor and had a grocery store also on the first floor. My mother owned a beauty shop across the street, right across Racine on Fifty-ninth Street. There was a young lady I used to date; her mother owned the bar that was on the corner. It was sort of like that; those kinds of people and then there were those who worked regular jobs. My father worked in a steel mill.[33]

The mid-1950s was the heyday of the vocal group, when the cities were alive with the sounds of harmonizing street-corner ensembles each in vigorous competition with the other. At Englewood High, when he was fifteen, young Dixon got caught up in emulating the great doowop groups of the day and formed his own aggregation, the Gaytones, with some schoolmates. "I never went to voice school," noted Chandler. "I used to just copy the groups like the El Dorados, the Danderliers, and what have you. Listen to their sounds and just sing their songs on the street corner."[34]

With years of vocal-group experience under his belt, first with the Gaytones and then with the Dukays, Chandler in 1962 was more than ready to make it on his own. He first went on a frenetic schedule of touring to reap the benefits of the "Duke of Earl" hit. "I played before black audiences, before white audiences, and then there were places I played that were mixed," said Chandler. "Then there were situations, places that you went to in the South. If you took a big show in—with me and a bunch of people—then they had what they called a segregated audience. The whites would sit in front, then the blacks would sit in the back or up in the balcony. And they had a rope dividing them in two. That sounds ancient and old...but that's not true, it wasn't that long ago."[35]

After "Duke of Earl," Chandler had some trouble coming up with another hit for awhile. His first follow-up, "Walk on with the Duke," was a contrived sound-alike. With six songwriters listed under the title, the song was obviously a product of a brainstorming session, as were many follow-ups to hits during that era. (Among the songwriters listed was Irv Nahan, a Philadelphia manager and song-publishing executive who undoubtedly had nothing to do with the composition.) The song proved a well-deserved failure. Following two more dismal releases, the spirited and sophisticated "Tear for Tear" broke the impasse in September 1962. The record did not make the national r&b chart, but the song did well enough in some markets to return Chandler to recognition, if not on the pop stations, then on the r&b outlets.

Late in 1962, "You Threw a Lucky Punch," an answer song to Mary Wells's Motown hit "You Beat Me to the Punch," again got Chandler pop play on the lower reaches of the top-forty charts. It was the flip, "Rainbow," a deep soul ballad somewhat out of character for Chandler, which firmly reestablished him with the r&b audience. "I had to beg them to record 'Rainbow,'" said Chandler, "And they wound up putting it on the flip. I was so crazy about 'Rainbow' that I refused to sing 'Lucky Punch.' Even Curtis Mayfield, whom I got the tune from, said 'You can't sing this.' I said, 'Hey, man, you'd better give me that song, ballads are my meat.' Then they didn't want to release it because they said that it went on too long before it went on to the break. But when I got them to put it on the back side, I ran with it everywhere I went, to try to get the record turned over. Finally, a couple of stations turned it over, I think one was in New Jersey and the other in D.C., and it took off."[36] "Rainbow," which finally broke in January 1963, proved a bigger hit than the A side.

"Man's Temptation," a hit in the summer of 1963, was the first Mayfield ballad that got the classic Chandler treatment, mellow, soulful, and intense, but not gut-wrenching as in his "Rainbow" performance. The imprint of Carl Davis was clear on this record, which Davis later claimed to have produced. Chandler was also fast demonstrating himself as one of the best interpreters of Mayfield songs, and the legendary songwriter agreed: "Gene seemed to sing my songs in his own way, and he had such an enthusiasm for them. He was a seller of them. Whatever it was, even if the song wasn't the best, Gene just had a way of putting himself totally into a tune. He proved that with 'Rainbow,' which was different than 'Duke of Earl.' Those 'Duke of Earls' are the kind of tunes that you find yourself being competitive with to prove that you really are a singer. So Gene came back with 'Rainbow.' He always was capable of putting his own influences, his own feeling, into a tune, but also being true to the original intention of the writer."[37] Just as Chandler was getting back into a hit-making groove, however, he left Vee Jay with Abner and Sheppard when they set up Constellation.

Chandler's first two releases with Constellation were deserving flops. Sheppard then brought in Davis to save the situation, and the third release in early 1964, the Mayfield-composed "Think Nothing About It," was a gem. It was a big hit only in Chicago; nationally it lasted only seven weeks and went to position twenty-eight on *Cash Box*'s r&b survey. "'Think Nothing About It' was a great record," said Chandler, "but it didn't happen that big. And I was crazy about it. I said, 'How could this record miss?' These are the things that'll turn your head around sometimes about re-cording."[38] Despite the record's relative lack of success, the team of producer Davis and composer Mayfield was so potent that Sheppard prevailed upon Davis to produce all of Chandler's Constellation records.

The remainder of 1964 proved far more fruitful for Chandler, when he came out with a succession of stunning Davis-produced ballads. The first of these, in June, was "Just Be True," a Mayfield tune that went to position four and lasted sixteen weeks on the *Cash Box* survey. It was Chandler's biggest hit since "Duke of Earl." A Billy Butler composition, "Bless Our Love," followed in September and went to the four position. The intense emotion that Chandler projected in this long underrated song makes it one of his best. "What Now," in November, was somewhat derived from the previous two songs, but it was still an excellent Mayfield ballad and proved to be a top-ten r&b hit.

Chandler's Constellation years were truly his golden years, as it seemed every release proved to be either a blockbuster commercial hit or an artistic triumph. The year 1965 was no less successful than 1964, with "You Can't Hurt Me No More" in February, "Nothing Can Stop Me" in March, "(Gonna Be) Good Times" in July, "Rainbow 65" and "Here Comes the Tears" in September. "You Can't Hurt Me No More," a cover of the Opals' local hit from a year earlier, featured a magnificent wall-of-sound orchestral backing. Gerald Sims, who worked on the record, was reluctant to claim it a success: "Gene, his head was blown up," he said sadly. "It wasn't that he initiated the idea so much; we worked it out together. But he'll go to New York and see the Temptations get this big orchestra and things. So he'll come back and say, 'I want an oboe, I want a French horn, I hear a piccolo, I want a harp.' A harp, of all things! Next thing you know we got an orchestra. It didn't have to be that way."[39] "Nothing Can Stop Me" was a delightful up-tempo anthem of positive thinking and was a top-twenty pop hit for Chandler. "(Gonna Be) Good Times," a fabulous sound of summer, captured the atmosphere of the streets in Chicago in the mid-1960s.

For most of 1966, Chandler suffered a lean time on the national charts, but that didn't mean he wasn't coming out with good records. Early in the year, he had two marvelous mid-tempo gems, "Bet You Never Thought" (a Bobby Miller composition) and "(I'm Just a) Fool for You" (a Gerald Sims/Carl Davis composition). Incidentally, the latter, because Davis had left OKeh Records at the end of 1965, was the first Chandler release in which Davis's production was actually credited. Both records got good play in Chicago, but nowhere else. One more Chandler record in 1966 made the local charts, "I Can Take Care of Myself" (a Van McCoy composition), but it was not an inspiring disc. Constellation was rapidly running down both creatively and in terms of marketing.

Dee Clark–Nolan Chance–Holly Maxwell

Constellation, during its three years of existence, was virtually kept afloat by Gene Chandler. The Ace distribution pact produced no hits and Dee Clark got no sizable national hits either. However, the label did produce a number of interesting records and garnered some solid regional hits with Clark as well as with some of their little-known artists, specifically Nolan Chance and Holly Maxwell.

Clark was not the pop star of his Vee Jay years, but during his alliance with Constellation he came out with enough hits in the r&b market to sustain himself as a successful soul artist. His first release on Constellation, "Crossfire Time," sold enough to return the artist to the national charts—albeit for only five weeks—in October 1963. The record was supposed to promote a new dance but the dance never caught on with the kids. Then in April 1964, he broke into Chicago and a few other locales with the Bob Gaudio–penned "Come Closer." The song was one of the best of his career, but despite its pop origins (Gaudio was a member of the Four Seasons), its soulful delivery limited crossover success. In 1964, most white kids were not ready for soul music.

Two months later, Clark came out with a fine double-sided hit: "Warm Summer Breezes," a song thoroughly in the Chicago soul tradition, and

"Heartbreak," a reprise of the old Jon Thomas song from 1959. Both songs rose high on regional r&b charts and ranked among Clark's better efforts.

Clark's last hit on Constellation, "TCB" came out in January 1965. (The initials stood for "Taking Care of Business," and it is amusing to think about all the kids who thought the rock group Bachman Turner Overdrive invented this ancient expression with their hit "Taking Care of Business" in 1974.) "That was a Sam Cooke idea," Clark said in explaining the genesis of the song. "We were on tour together and were just sitting in the back, and I was singing to myself almost, 'TCB, TCB, everybody TCB . . .' Sam said, 'Hey, Dee, that'd be a good tune,' and added the line, '. . . don't mean nothing but taking care of business.' So I continued working on it until I came up with the song."[40] "TCB" was a pleasant up-tempo tune, but it does not have the staying power of Clark's other hits.

The most mysterious aspect of Clark's career began after Constellation folded in 1966. This singer who possessed fine writing talents, an excellent voice, and an enviable track record for success in the music business began an odyssey, moving from one company to another with never more than one release for each, and with no notable recording success. He continued to play all over the country, and after 1966 lived a nomadic existence. "I stayed in L.A. for a year and some, you know, off and on, in and out. Atlanta, Georgia—worked out of that area for about four years. Orlando, Florida—two years there. I spent quite a bit of my time in the South. Chuck Jackson and I bumped heads a lot, playing the same lounges and shit, playing the same caliber of clubs."[41] In the 1980s he was still in the South, living from motel room to motel room, playing small bars where he could get a few dollars to entertain small audiences who still remembered his hits.

Nolan Chance, whose real name is Charles Davis, had a rich and varied career, made some very good records, yet never had a giant hit, and as a result his recording opportunities were limited. Davis was born on November 11, 1939, in Vidalia, Louisiana, but while he was still a toddler his family moved to LaGrange, Illinois, a suburb west of Chicago. There he attended Lyons Township High School, where he began singing as a member of a doowop group.[42]

After the breakup of the group, Davis continued to sing, and was soon making the rounds of local nightclubs in the western suburbs. Around 1959 Davis was asked to join another doowop aggregation, the Trinidads. Its members, besides Davis, who sang lead and tenor, were Claude Forch (bass), Norman Price (baritone), Hosea Brown (lead and tenor), and Charles Colbert, Jr. (lead and first tenor). (Colbert would later become a member of the influential Chicago group the Daylighters.) The Trinidads recorded two obscure records for Don Talty's Formal label.

Singer Otis Clay performs at the High Chaparral, Seventy-seventh and Stoney Island, the premier nightclub of black Chicago during the soul era. Courtesy Otis Clay.

An advertising sign for WVON, the dominant black radio station in Chicago in the 1960s, adorns the side of the Chess Records building at 2120 South Michigan Avenue, along Record Row. Photo by Cary Baker.

Record distributor Ernie Leaner (right) and deejay Richard Stamz. In the early 1960s, record distributors aggressively pushed their records on black radio. Courtesy Richard Stamz.

Unless noted otherwise, all photographs are from the Robert Pruter Collection.

The Vee Jay brain trust, left to right: James Bracken; Ewert Abner, Jr.; Vivian Carter; and Calvin Carter. Vee Jay was the largest black-owned record label before Motown. Courtesy Tollie Carter.

Vee Jay artist Dee Clark was one of Chicago's first big rhythm-and-blues stars.

The Impressions, 1958. Clockwise from top left: Jerry Butler, Fred Cash, Richard Brooks, Curtis Mayfield, and Arthur Brooks. This group recorded Chicago's first soul-style hit, "For Your Precious Love."

Jerry Butler. With Curtis Mayfield writing the songs, Butler brought Vee Jay into the soul era with hit after hit.

Betty Everett. Everett was Vee Jay's top female artist in the 1960s.

The Sheppards, 1961. Left to right: Murrie Eskridge, O. C. Perkins, Millard Edwards, James Dennis Isaac, Jimmy Allen, and Kermit Chandler.

The Starlets, 1961. One of the first acts produced and recorded by Carl Davis and Bunky Sheppard, this group also recorded as the Blue-Belles on "I Sold My Heart to the Junkman." Left to right: Mickey McKinney, Maxine Edwards, Jane Hall, and Jeanette Miles. Courtesy Maxine Edwards Lightner.

The Dukays, 1961. This group recorded "Duke of Earl," the million-selling record in which the artist was billed as "Gene Chandler." Top: Eugene Dixon (Gene Chandler); center: Ben Broyles; bottom, left to right: James Lowe, Shirley Jones, and Earl Edwards.

Gene Chandler in his "Duke of Earl" regalia. After "Duke of Earl" launched Chandler's career, he became one of the most consistent hitmakers in soul music and helped put Chicago on the map as a soul-music recording center.

Holly Maxwell, 1964.

Walter Jackson, 1965. Jackson became OKeh Records' premier balladeer after being discovered by Carl Davis in a Detroit nightclub.

Seward Park Recreation Center. In the shadow of the Cabrini-Green Housing Project, many an OKeh act practiced the essentials of their art in this building.

Major Lance pushing "Monkey Time" records, 1963. One of the earliest and biggest stars of Chicago soul, Lance built his career recording dance records for Carl Davis's OKeh Records operation. Courtesy Michael Ochs Archives, Venice, California.

Billy Butler and the Chanters, 1964. The group's mid-tempo, cheerful songs virtually defined Chicago-style soul. Left to right: Jesse Tillman, Billy Butler, and Errol Batts.

The Artistics, 1964. While at OKeh, Carl Davis recorded this group with Motown-style songs. Clockwise from top left: Marvin Smith, Larry Johnson, Aaron Floyd, and Jesse Bolian.

The Opals, 1964. This group under the mentorship of the Dells came out with some of the most delightful OKeh records. Courtesy Melvin Mason.

Gerald Sims. Sims, who began his behind-the-scenes career at OKeh, became a producer, music director, arranger, and writer who was a mainstay of the Chicago soul scene. Courtesy Gerald Sims.

For the next two years Davis fronted the Lorenzo Smith and Turbo Jets band, doing local cabaret dates. Then in late 1961, O. C. Perkins came across Davis's act in Gary, Indiana, and as related in the Dukays story, he got a lead position in the Dukays. Davis acquitted himself with the group before leaving in early 1963. Then for a number of months, in 1963–64, he served as lead for the Artistics, but the arrangements never worked out and no records resulted from the union.

Davis decided to try performing as a single artist again and hooked up with Bunky Sheppard at Constellation Records in 1964. It was decided that the name "Charles Davis" was insufficiently show business, so Davis took the name "Nolan Chance" as a stage name. Soon he was recording, and the first result was "She's Gone," a wonderful ballad about a country boy who lost his girl to the big city. It was a perfect vehicle for Davis's plaintive, vulnerable-sounding vocals and seemed to offer a promising future for the young singer. "She's Gone" did not make the national charts, but in the first months of 1965 it was number one in Los Angeles, number one in Atlanta, and a large hit in Chicago and certain other cities.[43]

Later in the year, Davis had considerably less success with "Just Like the Weather," which was unfortunately a much weaker effort than "She's Gone." Not long afterward Constellation went out of business, and as Davis put it, "After Constellation went down the tube, so did Nolan Chance."[44]

Davis built a career as an accountant, so for several years he stayed away from the entertainment business. He recorded again for Eddie Thomas, first on the Thomas subsidiary label of Curtom Records in 1969 and then for the New York–based Scepter label in 1972, but without garnering more than a bit of regional success.

Holly Maxwell typified the light, airy soprano voice that was very popular in Chicago, perhaps to excess, because on her records she sounded almost too young at times. But she had a pretty voice and it was put to good use on a number of fine records, particularly for Constellation Records. She was born October 17, 1945, in Chicago. She came out of Parker High on the city's South Side, where for a brief time she was a part of girl group called the Tourjourettes.[45] But most of her early experience in music consisted of the classical-music training she got as a student of voice and piano at the Chicago Musical College from age nine to seventeen. "I was raised in a European background," related Maxwell, "because of the classical music. My mother was not like the average black mother. I went to modeling school. I went to finishing school, and I had classical musical training. Okay, therefore when you're black and you're raised in that environment, it's kind of hard to know who you are. So for a long time I was trying to figure who Holly was. I could sing in German, French, and Italian. Well, who was I gonna curse out in Italian going to black school. It took me a long time to figure who I was, where my niche was."[46]

Maxwell only discovered soul music late in high school. "Around the age of seventeen," she said, "I started sneaking off to the nightclubs and looking at Harold Burrage, Otis Clay, and Little Johnny Williams. I used to watch these artists because they seemed to have so much soul, so much whatever."[47]

In early 1965, Maxwell was discovered by Bunky Sheppard and he signed her up. The first release was the delightfully melodic "One Thin Dime," which succeeded despite the thin arrangement (an organ rather than horns was used to fill the holes). Not long after the record was released and garnered good play in Chicago in the summer of 1965, a *Chicago Defender* columnist, Beatrice Watson, featured Maxwell in her column. In it, Holly's mother, Eula Maxwell, took pains to assure the *Defender* reporter that her daughter was still progressing toward becoming an opera singer. Holly herself pointed out that she had been singing jazz for two and a half years and was singing r&b as a step up. (Poor lowly rhythm and blues!)[48]

Protests aside, Maxwell continued in the soul music field, and a few months later hit with the lovely "Only when You're Lonely," which featured a marvelous interaction between her soprano and the chorus. It was a strong local record but inexplicably never broke as a national hit. Both of her Constellation records were produced by Bill Sheppard. By the end of 1965 Maxwell was on another label, Star, and under the direction of Monk Higgins. Her next record was a dance number called the "Philly Barracuda," which got good local play in Chicago.

Maxwell appeared in many local clubs: the London House and the Happy Medium, where she sang jazz; and the Algiers Lounge (359 East Sixty-ninth Street), The Club (Fifty-fifth and State), Lonnie's Skyway Lounge (131–35 West Seventy-fifth Street), and Peyton Place (Thirty-ninth and Indiana), where she sang rhythm and blues—or, as she told me, attempted to. Despite having come out with a number of recordings, Maxwell does not believe she learned how to sing soul music until around 1967, when she was twenty-two years old.

"You know I could sing pretty," said Maxwell, "I could hit all the notes in the world, but it was like something inside of me that said you got more to give." The watershed in her career came at an engagement at Peyton Place, where gay singer Hi Fi White and his Jaguars Band were then creating a sensation. "I got up and sang 'Misty' with my hands folded operatic style—'loook at meeeh'...they started to laugh and throw oranges and stuff at me, and beer bottles. And I ran in the dressing room and I went to cry. And Hi Fi White, who had called me up on the stage, he said 'Honey, you ain't got no soul.' From that point on I was determined to get this 'soul.' I listened to Gladys Knight. I listened to Aretha Franklin. I listened to everyone who hollered and screamed."[49]

Maxwell went back to Peyton Place four months later, persuaded a reluctant Hi Fi White to give her another chance, and knocked the audience dead with a dynamite version of Aretha Franklin's "Respect." She had become a soul singer.

Maxwell came out with a few more modestly received records in the following years. She surfaced on Curtis Mayfield's Curtom Records in 1969 with a lovely ballad, "Suffer," written by Mayfield and Donny Hathaway. But it never hit, probably because the song did not have a strong hook. The following year she had an East Coast hit with a Philadelphia-produced record called "Never Love Again."

During most of the 1970s and early 1980s, Maxwell lived in California. She owned a nightclub for a while, sang jazz with organist Jimmy Smith for three years, sang Tina Turner songs in the Ike Turner Review for two years, and toured many foreign countries. In 1985 she returned to Chicago to be with her ailing mother. Holly Maxwell had a modest but eventful career, and during her teenage years in Chicago she made a positive contribution to the Chicago soul scene and gave Constellation two local hits besides.

Constellation's Demise

With the small number of artists in its stable, Constellation was extremely vulnerable to collapsing if the company ever hit a cold spell. That is exactly what happened in 1966. Chandler was only getting local hits, which was poor for him. Dee Clark just went stone cold, and nothing at all was coming out of the minor artists. Abner, who returned as the head of Vee Jay in the summer of 1965, was preoccupied with a fruitless attempt to save Vee Jay. During the months after Vee Jay went under in May 1966, Abner began closing up shop at Constellation, selling off as many assets he could. The chief asset was Gene Chandler, whose contract was sold to Chess Records. Constellation went out of business at the end of the summer. Chandler succinctly summed up why Constellation failed: "I wasn't enough to sustain the company."[50]

NOTES

1. There have been no articles per se on Pam Productions or on Constellation Records, but some on Carl Davis, notably: John Abbey, "Behind the Scenes with Carl Davis," *Blues and Soul,* August 3–16, 1973, pp. 22–24; Dave Hoekstra, "The

Chicago Sound," *Suburban Sun-Times,* June 11, 1982, p. 12; see also Carl Davis interviews, 1982, and April 27, 1986.

2. Davis interview, April 27, 1986.

3. Davis interview, 1982.

4. Ibid.

5. Robert Pruter, "Island of Soul: The Sheppards," *Time Barrier Express* 27 (April–May 1980): 69–73. "Collectible Bel Aires Disc Precursor of R&B/Soul Hits by Chicago's Sheppards," *Record Collector's Monthly* 34 (February–March 1986): 4; James Dennis Isaac interview: O. C. Perkins interviews.

6. Perkins interview, October 24, 1977.

7. Ibid.

8. Jay Cocks, "Sounds Like Old Times," *Time,* January 5, 1981, p. 75.

9. Robert Pruter, "Chicago's Starlets Created 'Junkman' Sound that Launched Blue-Belles' Career," *Record Collector's Monthly* 36 (December–January 1986–87): 1, 10–11; Maxine Edwards Lightner interview.

10. Lightner interview.

11. Ibid.

12. Ibid.

13. Ibid.

14. Ibid.

15. Ibid.

16. Ibid.

17. Ibid.

18. Ibid.

19. Robert Pruter, "The Dukays," *Record Exchanger* 27 (1978): 4–7; idem, "Gene Chandler," *Goldmine,* January 1980, pp. 13–17; Gene Chandler interview, February 6, 1979; Charles Davis interview; Earl Edwards interview.

20. Edwards interview.

21. Chandler interview.

22. Edwards interview.

23. Davis interview.

24. Chandler interview.

25. Charles Davis interview.

26. Chandler interview.

27. Ibid.

28. Edwards interview.

29. Chandler interview.

30. Davis interview.

31. Charles Davis interview.

32. For an artist of Gene Chandler's fame and stature there have been surprisingly few serious articles published on his career: Roland Bynum, "I'm Ready if I Don't Get to Go," *Soul,* February 28, 1972, p. 14; Aaron Fuchs, "The Duke of Earl Gets into Studio 54," *Village Voice,* April 16, 1979, pp. 69–71; Robert Pruter, "Gene Chandler"; idem, "The Gene Chandler Story," *It Will Stand* 35 [1987]: 6–11. A fascinating look at the world of teenagers in Chicago in 1962 and

how that world related to "The Duke of Earl" is found in Jack Clark, "Mercury Vapor Nights," Chicago *Reader,* January 21, 1977, pp. 9–10; Gene Chandler interviews 1979 and February 6, 1979.

33. Chandler interview, February 6, 1979.
34. Ibid.
35. Ibid.
36. Chandler interview, 1979.
37. Curtis Mayfield interview.
38. Chandler interview, February 6, 1979.
39. Gerald Sims interview.
40. Dee Clark interview.
41. Clark interview.
42. Robert Pruter, "Nolan Chance," *Goldmine,* July–August 1978, p. 23; Charles Davis interview.
43. Charles Davis interview.
44. Ibid.
45. Robert Pruter, "Holly Maxwell: From Opera to Soul," *Goldmine,* January 1, 1988, pp. 100, 106–7; Beatrice Watson, "From Bea...to You," *Chicago Defender,* June 19, 1965; Holly Maxwell interview.
46. Maxwell interview.
47. Ibid.
48. Watson, "From Bea...to You."
49. Maxwell interview.
50. Chandler interview, February 6, 1979.

4

OKeh Records

OKeh was Columbia's r&b independently distributed subsidiary label. The major record companies during the 1950s and 1960s generally used independent distributors for their country and rhythm-and-blues lines because at that time the indies were in closer touch with the record shops, clubs, disc jockeys, and radio stations involved with those forms of popular music.

OKeh had a long and rich history before the arrival of Carl Davis. The label began in 1918 as a New York company that recorded all kinds of music, but in 1920 it launched the black-music recording industry with the release of Mamie Smith's "Crazy Blues." In the following decade OKeh made a name for itself recording blues and jazz discs, most notably the seminal sides of Louis Armstrong's Hot Five and Hot Seven combos. During the 1950s, as a subsidiary label of Columbia, OKeh had such hits as "Hambone" (1953) by the Hambone Kids, and "I Put a Spell on You" (1956) by Screamin' Jay Hawkins, but very little else. By the early 1960s OKeh was producing so few hits that the label was practically moribund.[1]

In June 1962, Columbia brought in Carl Davis as A&R producer for Columbia and in April 1963, he was made A&R director specifically for the OKeh label. (In July 1965 he would be promoted to executive producer.) Davis almost immediately rejuvenated OKeh and within a year it had become one of the major soul labels in the country. Nearly all the OKeh hits were written by Curtis Mayfield and produced by Davis; it was truly a magical team. The OKeh brand of soul that Davis developed and dubbed the "Chicago sound," not without good reason, was somewhat light and subtle music that had highly melodic vocals with just a touch of gospel. Brass instruments, especially trombones, were prominently featured. OKeh recordings did not have the simplistic appeal of Motown and Stax recordings, which had more of a rock 'n' roll beat to them, but they did have more of that almost indefinable quality called soul: soul that did not have to hit you on the head to convey deep feeling—quintessential soft soul. Hard soul was a rare commodity at OKeh, both because Carl Davis was not generally interested in that kind of music and because the label, as a subsidiary of a major, did not make a practice of signing hard-soul and blues artists. There was one exception at OKeh, Ted Taylor, who was produced by Davis and who sang both ballads and blues in a hard-soul manner.

Davis related:

> How I came to be associated with Columbia was a result of the "Duke of Earl." I was working for the local distribution branch at Columbia Records as a salesman/promotion man. In those days it was a combination of the two jobs. Dave Kapralik at that time was head of the A&R department at Columbia Records, and when he found out that "Duke of Earl" was my production, he offered me a position at Columbia as an A&R guy to head up the OKeh label.
>
> They made me A&R producer and they also allowed me to promote my own product. In other words, I used to travel with Granville White, who at that time was regional promotion executive. Granville taught me a whole lot on how to promote product. That's how I really got started with OKeh.[2]

To discuss the Chicago sound, one has to start with Curtis Mayfield. To quote Gerald Sims, a member of Davis's team at OKeh, "the Chicago sound came from basically one source—Curtis Mayfield."[3] Davis recalled in 1986:

> Curtis and I, we knew each other for a long time. I knew all the Impressions, Sam and Fred, and all. I used to go out to Curtis's house a lot of times and sit down, and Curtis would have a shopping bag full of tapes, and a lot of them were songs that he would only have six or eight bars to. Because when Curtis used to get an idea he would go to a tape recorder and put the idea down. Then he would go off into something else, and he would come back to it later on. A lot of times you'd pick up a tape and play it, and you'd get off into it, and then it would stop! You'd have to go back and ask him to finish this tune or finish that tune or finish this one. So he would do it; he was very obliging about it and would go write you a complete tune.[4]

Davis chuckled as he made the next comment: "You would have to be careful with Curtis. Because if Curtis came up with six tunes and he'd play them, you'd say, 'That's the one I want!' He'll say, 'Oh, that's the one I'm cutting on the Impressions.' So what I would do is let him play all the tunes he had available, and then I'd ask him which songs were available for me. Because I learned that if I just walked in there and say 'Oh, I really like that one,' he'll say, 'Oh yeah, I'm cutting that one on the group.' You had to learn to work around Curtis."[5]

Davis in 1963 hired Mayfield as associate producer. "I had offered him a job 'cause quite frankly I just wanted to have talented people around me," said Davis. "So he accepted it, and we worked out differences. He was mostly on the road weekends, and there were times where he would have to leave Wednesday in order to get a gig to wherever they were going. I had no problem. CBS gave me a free rein, not so much CBS but Dave Kapralik."[6]

One of the keys to the OKeh sound was that in contrast to much of 1950s rhythm and blues, it was a highly arranged music—as was much of soul music in the northern cities then. In the South, "head arrangements" were the norm, in which the musicians worked out the arrangements at the recording session. Davis made use of two of the city's best free-lance arrangers, Riley Hampton, who was good with strings and who worked on a lot of ballady songs, and Johnny Pate, who was especially good on the medium tempo and fast songs.

As Davis recalled the situation:

> Johnny Pate had been an accomplished musician, a bass player for quite a while, and he always had visions of being an arranger, but not having the opportunity. Because in this town during the time we were coming up, Riley Hampton pretty much had it sewed up, and rightfully so because he was successful with most of his endeavors—"Moon River" with Jerry Butler and on and on and on. He did quite a bit of the Vee Jay stuff and the early Etta James stuff on Chess. He was about the hottest arranger in town. Johnny wanted to get into it, and so because I wanted to create a different kind of sound I chose to use Johnny in particular with the OKeh records. Because at that point I was trying to get away from strings, except on Walter's stuff. I wanted to develop what I thought was indicative of the Chicago kind of things. I always felt we were a bit of the South and a bit of the North combined. So I liked the syncopated rhythm, and I liked the fact that he did the things with horns.
>
> I think the whole idea of the heavy horns approach was a combination of my idea and Johnny's only because I did not know what I wanted the horns to do. I just knew that I wanted to do

something that was not being done at the time. The records that had been successful had a lot of strings, lot of sultry things. I wanted to attack. I wanted someone to say, "Hey, wait a minute, what was that!"

What we were doing...Johnny Pate used to come out to my house. In those days the term "putter-downer" was invented. In other words, you brought in an arranger and rather than let him arrange willy-nilly, you wanted him to "put-down" what it was you wanted, then allow his own talent to take over from that point. I would sit there and would say I wanted such and such beat. Basically I was following Curtis's lead on his guitar—"ta-dum dum, ta-dum, dum, dum dum" [opening riff of "Monkey Time"]. And then I wanted a "da dahh!"—the horns to accent the beat. I wouldn't write it; I would play back the song as written by the writer and then we would take parts the way he played the guitar and turn it into various instruments—this might be horns, that might be something else. You gave Pate the basics and let him do it.[7]

The musicians who played for OKeh began with Curtis Mayfield, as it was the arrangers who had to orchestrate the songs he wrote. But Mayfield also had a unique guitar sound. Billy Butler said, "The Curtis Mayfield type of guitar—it was a very fluid type of sound. Not rigid, very liquidy. Soft sound, almost fluid. Curtis was an innovator."[8] Said Gerald Sims, "His style of playing was unique, the way he tuned to a natural chord. Also, Curtis played slightly different. He might play a certain song in D chord, where someone else might use a C. Everyone in Chicago would imitate his guitar style."[9] Said Otis Leavill, one of Davis's administrative assistants and a recording artist in his own right, "Most of the guitar players either tried or did play similar to Curtis. You notice Billy Butler. He played on my 'Let Her Love Me' and 'To Be or Not to Be,' but a lot of people confused Billy with Curtis because of the way he played. You got a guy named Danny Reed, who was in my band. He idolized Curtis, so he basically played like Curtis would."[10] Besides Curtis, Davis would also use Phil Upchurch, Gerald Sims, Billy Butler, and Kermit Chandler on OKeh sessions.

"As we went along," said Davis, "we used Kermit Chandler on guitar and Bernard Reed on bass. They were half brothers and we used them on most of things we did with the Artistics."[11] For most of the other OKeh artists Davis usually used Louis Sattersfield on bass, who along with Maurice White, whom Davis often used on drums, was a founding member of the famous 1970s group Earth, Wind, and Fire. Al Duncan, a veteran of the 1950s rhythm-and-blues scene who appeared on most of the Vee Jay recordings during that decade, was used on most of the OKeh records as the session drummer. Said Billy Butler, "Duncan played with a lighter touch. It was not that incessant Motown beat or the funky beat of Memphis. He would have a nice clean sound."[12]

Regarding OKeh piano players, Davis said, "We used different piano players—Ken Boyd, Floyd Morris, John Young. Floyd was probably the main one we used in the beginning. John Young was a jazz piano player."[13]

The famous OKeh brass section, as one might expect of a brass section, was often changing, but there were certain players who seemed to appear on most of the sessions. On trumpet were Maury Watson and Paul Serrano; Serrano later founded a successful recording studio in Chicago called P.S. Recording Studio. On trombone were Morris Ellis and John Avant (who played both bass and valve trombone). Most often on saxophone was Carl Davis's brother Cliff. Major Lance characterized the Chicago sound in terms of the brass section: "It was the sound of the horns, their depthness. We were using a lot of lows. Like we were the first to use those two trombones and the baritone sax. We had the bass trombone and the regular trombone, like if you take a bass trombone and a baritone sax and sustain that note you got the blahh, like on 'Monkey Time.' We were the ones who started that."[14]

These session musicians did more than merely follow the charts as written down by the arrangers. They contributed ideas to the records as well. Said Davis, "In those days we allowed the musicians some latitude. You would pass out the charts and more or less let them know what you wanted them to do, but then you gave them some room to do what they wanted to do." Added Butler, "The distinctiveness of the Chicago sound had a lot to do with the musicians at that time—they were very creative."[15]

One curious element in the development of the Chicago sound was Cabrini-Green. Most of the OKeh acts came out of a small area on Chicago's near North Side called Cabrini-Green after the two housing projects located there. The area, well known from its portrayal in the movie *Cooley High* and the television show "Good Times," was one of the worse crime-infested pockets in Chicago. Although it had few redeeming qualities, the area can be credited as a fertile field for r&b talent. Aside from Jerry Butler, Cabrini-Green gave rise to Curtis Mayfield, Major Lance, Otis Leavill, Billy Butler and the Chanters, and through the Lance connection the West Side group, the Artistics. Said Davis, "They were all raised up together in Cabrini-Green, Curtis and Billy and Jerry, and Major Lance and Otis Leavill."[16] Added Butler, "We were all into trying to sing. That was about the only thing to do really. . . . the area didn't have street gangs at the time. Everyone would form a group and go into Seward Park, which had a recreation building and club rooms, in which everyone would practice."[17] The kids attended one of three high schools—Wells, Waller, and Cooley Vocational. Only Cooley was all black, the other two were each 50 percent white. Most of the acts that gravitated to OKeh Records attended Wells.

Incidentally, those who recall the movie *Cooley High*, which was about ghetto high-school kids of the 1960s, may also recall that the soundtrack included nothing but Motown hits. No Jerry Butler, no Curtis Mayfield and the Impressions, no Billy Butler, no Major Lance, no Otis Leavill.

The Cabrini-Green connection with OKeh was due perhaps to chance. All it took was the signing of Major Lance to the label in the summer of 1962, and all his friends from the area who had any musical ability made their way to Davis's office.

With regard to Davis's approach to recording his artists, it would be hard to escape comparisons with Berry Gordy's Motown organization, which was the most successful soul label in the 1960s. Said Davis,

> This is not directly a criticism of Motown's methods, because they've been tremendously successful at what they've done. But they would take an artist, to use an example of a painting... Motown used to put a picture frame together, paint in all the background, and then they would take the artist and put him in the picture. They would make a complete record, record it in a certain key that they thought would fit the song. Then the singer had to come in and sing the song in the key they had already determined, whether or not it was appropriate for the artist or not. I didn't go that far. Sometimes I would have a singer sing in one key higher than he normally would to get that urgency in the vocals. But the OKeh approach was to take each artist, paint the background in, and then put the frame around to fit the subject. I've never thought an artist should be confined to what an arrangement and music is. They should surround the artist. I didn't do the same thing with Major Lance as I did with Walter Jackson, they were different artists who needed different approaches.[18]

Ted Taylor

Ted Taylor was not a Cabrini-Green artist. He was not even a Chicago artist; he came from Los Angeles. But Columbia A&R director Dave Kapralik signed Taylor in 1962 and gave him to Davis to produce as one of his first projects. Davis's early work with Taylor showed that the "Duke of Earl" was not a one-shot happenstance. Taylor was no newcomer, having been recording and writing since 1955. One can understand why Kapralik wanted to sign this talented artist, even though his track record was limited to only a few regional hits.[19]

Taylor's soaring bittersweet tenor was, if anything, soulful, and one of the most captivating in black music. The bread and butter for Taylor was normally his excellent soul ballads and southern-style hard-soul numbers, but every now and then he chose to work in the blues idiom.

Ted Taylor was born in Okmulgee, Oklahoma, near Tulsa, on February 16, 1934. As early as fourteen years of age he was singing in gospel quartets, and while still in his teens he gravitated to Los Angeles. After spending some time in gospel he moved into r&b, becoming a member of the Cadets/ Jacks vocal group that recorded for Modern Records in Los Angeles during 1955-56. In 1957 Taylor began recording as a solo artist, and during the next four years he put out blues and bluesy r&b for such labels as Ebb (1957–58), Duke (1959), Top Rank (1960), Laurie (1961), and Golden Eagle (1961). His most successful record during this time was his own composition "Be Ever Wonderful" for Duke.

During the first two years of Taylor's contract with OKeh, Davis did the producing, and what a marvelous job he did. Most of the best material of Taylor's career was done with Davis, notably "Can't Take No More" (1963), a remake of "Be Ever Wonderful" (1963), "You Give Me Nothing to Go On" (1963), and "So Hard" (1964). Davis also produced the excellent *Be Ever Wonderful* album (1963), Taylor's first.

Taylor's recordings were made in Chicago with Riley Hampton or Johnny Pate arranging and in Nashville with Bill Justis as arranger. Taylor wrote most of his songs, and what is most interesting was the range of material he wrote and sang, from romantic ballads, to hard soul, to downhome blues. This varied diet caused Taylor no distress, but many a critic hearing the smorgasbord years later usually gets indigestion. Taylor did not confine himself, and more power to him.

In 1964 OKeh took Taylor out of Davis's hands and sent him down to Nashville to record with country-and-western producer Billy Sherrill. With Sherrill, Taylor had the biggest hit of his career, "Stay Away from My Baby," in November 1965. The song went to position fourteen and stayed twelve weeks on *Billboard*'s national soul chart. Other outstanding releases under Sherrill included "Don't Deceive Me" (1964), the Chuck Willis standard; and "Love Is Like a Ramblin' Rose" (1965), a cover of a Jerry Lee Lewis tune. Taylor continued as a hitmaker for many more years with Stan Lewis's Ronn Records, out of Shreveport, Louisiana. Taylor was reviving his career as a blues artist in 1987 when he died in a car accident in Louisiana.

The Dutones

Taylor would not be the only non-Chicagoan Davis would work with. In 1962 Davis went to Nashville and recorded the Buttons on a strident girl-group song, "Shimmy Shimmy Watusi." The song got a lot of airplay in Chicago, in November 1962, and was something of a local hit on the top-forty stations, but not the r&b stations, which found the record devoid of r&b content. For the most part, however, Davis worked with the talent he found in the city. When Davis assumed his A&R duties at Columbia, most of the top talent in the city seemingly was already associated with the established companies, notably Vee Jay and Chess. The earliest artists that Davis picked up were Walter Jackson (out of Detroit), Joyce Davis, and a duo singing group called the Dutones, all of whom appeared on the Columbia label in 1962.

The Dutones, Richard Parker and Jerry Brown, had Davis's most successful Columbia label release, "The Bird," which was a solid top-forty and r&b hit in the Midwest in January 1963. It lasted four weeks on *Cash Box*'s r&b survey after entering the chart in February. Davis gave the record an exuberant-sounding ambience, but despite its undeniable energy, the record sounded somewhat comical. Records promoting dance fads were supposed to sound like fun, but "The Bird" seemed a tad too minstrel in tone. Parker would become a principal songwriter for Davis in the early 1970s, when he was at Brunswick.

So where did Davis get the artists to launch OKeh, when all the other companies in the cities seemed to have all the top artists locked up? Said Davis, "When I first got the job, everybody was saying, like Vee Jay when an act came to them and they didn't want to be bothered with it, they sent the act over to me, that kind of thing. As a matter of fact that's how I got Major Lance. He went into Vee Jay and Calvin Carter didn't see nothing, no potential in him, so he said, 'I got the greatest idea in the world. We'll send you to another guy.' And they sent him over to me. A lot of the people in Chicago, those who were in the production area, would do that. So it was important to me to take what they thought were losers and turn them into winners."[20]

Major Lance

The most successful OKeh artist was Major Lance. Aside from the Curtis Mayfield–led Impressions, he was the largest-selling artist from Chicago in the years 1963-66. It seems hard to believe today, but Lance for a few years achieved greater crossover success than his Chicago counterparts, Gene

Chandler and Jerry Butler. His thin but interestingly forceful vocals were perfectly showcased by Davis, and the result was a series of sparkling dance records that virtually defined the more energetic side of the Chicago sound. For Lance, he employed a deep rich brass sound, perhaps the brassiest in the business. Especially prominent was the use of the bass trombone with its characteristic "blaht blaht" riffing.[21]

Lance was born in Chicago on April 4, 1941, and grew up in a family that ultimately included eleven children. He spent most of his childhood years on Chicago's rugged West Side. One of his earliest friends was Otis Leavill. The two youngsters early on took up boxing in order to get along in their neighborhood, and eventually both became quite proficient at the sport. Lance first attended the West Side's Crane High School, but after his family moved to the Cabrini-Green projects he went to Wells High.

As was true of many Chicago-sound artists, Lance during his Wells days hung out at Seward Park, along with Leavill, Butler, and Mayfield. He emphasized that he was not all that interested in music at first; rather his principal enthusiasm was sports, particularly boxing, which he and Leavill continued to pursue into the amateur ranks. But Lance was also participating as a regular dancer on the "Jim Lounsbury Record Hop," a local television show in Chicago. Through Lounsbury, he was able to get a one-shot deal to do a record for Mercury, "I've Got a Girl," written and produced by Mayfield and backed by the Impressions. It ranks as one of the earliest songs in the Chicago-sound genre, and though an exceedingly weak effort, it got a little play in Chicago in 1959.

Lance did not enter a recording studio again until 1962, when he was signed by Carl Davis to OKeh Records. But of all the talent in the city, why did the young A&R chief sign Lance, who was not the greatest talent in the world? "Persistency, persistency," Davis repeated for emphasis.

> Major came to me through the Curtis Mayfield situation. I recall I was just given this office at the CBS building on McClurg Court. He used to be there every morning when I got to work. He would go out and get me coffee. I must have had ten cups of coffee a day and Major would go out and he would just sit there and expound on the fact if I gave him the chance he would make us both some money. He and Curtis—Curtis wasn't working for me then—were very close, and Curtis was going to write a tune for him. That in itself, and plus the fact that I happened to take a liking for him as a person, 'cause he's really a nice person.[22]

We have in Davis's remarks three reasons for signing Lance—Lance's persistency, Lance's likability, and Curtis Mayfield's tunes. It's likely that the first two reasons would not have amounted to much had not Lance been able to bring in some great tunes from the fast-emerging talent of Curtis Mayfield.

Regarding his approach to recording Lance, Davis said, "Major, you see, he was not a god-given talent singing-wise, so you had to put something around him. You had to put background vocals where he was weak, and music had to be a real important part of his product. You just couldn't give him a song and he would learn it and take him into the studio and just cut it. You had to do a lot more."[23]

The first Mayfield tune Lance recorded for Davis was "Delilah," which was no bigger than a minor hit. Nonetheless, it was a marvelous tune with the patented Chicago mid-tempo lope and Johnny Pate's piano-led arrangement that perfectly showcased Lance's reedy but engaging vocals. Pate had not yet developed the bass trombone–dominated brass arrangements that would later characterize Lance records.

On May 8, 1963, Lance went into the studio again and made what has to be considered recording history. He did three songs—"Monkey Time," "Please Don't Say No More," and "Mama Didn't Know," the latter an answer to Jan Bradley's splendid hit from early in the year, "Mama Didn't Lie." "Monkey Time" was paired with "Mama Didn't Know" for Lance's second release on OKeh, and the record became a monster hit during the summer and early fall, eventually selling more than a million copies. On *Billboard*'s pop chart "Monkey Time" lasted fifteen weeks and reached as high as number eight in the country, and on its r&b chart the song lasted an equal number of weeks and as high as the second spot on the chart. The flip also got substantial play. "Monkey Time," featuring the classic brassy sound that distinguished later OKeh hits, launched the OKeh label and popularized a dance of the same name.

The success of "Monkey Time" caught everyone by surprise. Lance related, "I was still working in a drugstore on the North Side by Perry Street called Cabrini Drugs. The record hit so fast, I had to have clothes made. I was so small I couldn't buy anything off the rack. Everything was like panic because people were calling me for personal appearances. I wasn't ready really—but I got ready though."[24] Lance began touring right away and made the whole chitlin' circuit.

While "Monkey Time" was still hot, Lance went into the studio in August to record "Hey Little Girl" and "Um Um Um Um Um Um" (two magnificent compositions of Mayfield), and "Sweet Music" and "Crying in the Rain" (two fine examples of Leavill-Lance collaborations). "Hey Little Girl" was released in the early fall, and lasted ten weeks on the top-hundred but only three weeks on the r&b survey. The record was bigger than this chart action indicated (*Billboard*'s r&b chart at this time was not the most reliable).

"Um Um Um Um Um Um"/"Sweet Music" was released in December. "Sweet Music" got the more favorable *Billboard* review, but it was "Um Um Um Um Um Um" that entered the charts in January 1964. The song lasted thirteen weeks and reached the top position on *Cash Box*'s r&b survey. "Sweet Music" received a lot of play in Washington, D.C., but the side never broke.

Throughout 1964 Lance's chart action did not let up. Just as "Um x 6" was slipping off the surveys, "The Matador" slipped on. The song was written by Lance and Billy Butler. According to Lance, on all his Davis-produced OKeh sides Mayfield played guitar, and where the records had male background vocals the Impressions were used—all except "Matador," which featured Billy Butler on guitar and his group the Chanters on the background vocals.[25] Although the record was supposed to promote a dance, no one ever did a Matador dance to it. It lasted twelve weeks and went to the four position on *Cash Box*'s r&b chart in the early spring of 1964.

Lance's next record, "It Ain't No Use"/"Girls," was a double-sided hit during the summer. Neither side made it higher than position twenty-five on the *Cash Box* chart. Although both were fine Mayfield tunes and rank among Lance's strongest efforts, their lesser success may have reflected on the relative sameness of sound the public was perhaps perceiving in Lance's records. In late summer and early fall, Lance bounced back with another big record, "Rhythm." Although it echoed his previous efforts, the Mayfield-quality writing and Davis/Mayfield production were so perfectly realized for Lance's vocals, the record just had to be a hit. On the *Cash Box* chart it lasted sixteen weeks and went to position three.

Heretofore all of Lance's hits had been in the bright, bouncy danceable mode. On his next release he tried something different with "Sometimes I Wonder, " in which Mayfield introduced a more somber, melancholy mood and theme. A change was probably necessary, but this deviation from the formula was less successful artistically than Lance's earlier efforts. "Sometimes I Wonder" charted during the winter of 1964/65.

"Come See" in March and April of 1965 continued Lance's virtually uninterrupted string of successes written by Mayfield, but there was nothing really to distinguish this song, and it is the least remembered of his hits. The last of the Mayfield songs was "Ain't It a Shame," popular during the summer of 1965. It was a quality song, but as compared to his earlier records there was almost no crossover success with it.

By late 1965, Mayfield had removed himself from writing songs for Lance and other OKeh artists to concentrate on his career with the Impressions. Not long afterward Davis departed from the company. These developments effectively closed the book on Lance's most magnificent recording era, a period that assured him his reputation in soul music history. During that time, Lance not only toured on the chitlin' circuit but also on Dick Clark's Caravan of Stars. On the tour he played to appreciative, largely white audiences across the nation. He was not considered only an r&b star but a popular rock 'n' roll artist as well, and this observation is borne out in his sales. From the summer of 1963 and continuing for two years, Lance was almost continuously on the charts and sold more than five and a half million records.[26]

The next few years on OKeh proved to be frustrating for Lance and those concerned with his career. There were few subsequent hit records after "Ain't It a Shame," and no one could come up with the special combination to produce anything comparable to a "Monkey Time" or an "Um Um Um Um Um Um." Lance did have a minor success with "Too Hot to Hold" in the fall of 1965. Gerald Sims wrote the song and produced the record with Davis.

Columbia then decided to send Lance to Nashville to have him produced by Billy Sherrill, one of their top country-and-western producers. The first record produced by Sherrill, "Investigate," bombed, but the second, "The Beat," became a minor hit in the fall of 1966. The record, however, had to rank as one of Lance's weakest efforts up to that time. OKeh put out three more releases on Lance up through early 1968, two productions by Ted Cooper in New York and one by Gerald Sims in Chicago. The shift from one producer to another reflected the desperate search for a hit combination that could sustain Lance's career. OKeh was going downhill rapidly in 1968 and Lance left to join up with Dakar Records, an operation that Davis and Leavill had started. He also moved to Atlanta, Georgia, to live.

Walter Jackson

Walter Jackson was the master of the love ballad. His husky baritone was in the mode of such sophisticated pop entertainers as Arthur Prysock and Billy Eckstine, but it was put to excellent use by Davis at OKeh. The end result was obviously a brand of pop soul, but unlike the pop-soul Motown artist, Jackson was far more adult and subtle. Jackson was born on March 19, 1938, in Pensacola, Florida, but while still a baby he moved with his parents to Detroit.[27] In his formative years, young Walter contracted polio, which left him on crutches, crippled but not handicapped, as he was fond of telling interviewers.

Jackson attended Northwestern High and while there he did what many teenagers did in the late 1950s, he joined a vocal group. The ensemble was called the Velvetones, and its members besides Jackson were Ronald Head,

Neil Magby, Bobby Jones, and a young lady Jackson only remembered as "Marion."[28] The Velvetones did get an opportunity to record in 1959, releasing "Stars of Wonder" on Deb Records. It was an amateurish effort and the inexperience of the group was telling.

The group soon broke up and its members—except for Jackson—drifted into other areas of endeavor. He continued in the field more energetically and soon became a regular cabaret performer in the Detroit area, singing largely pop material. Among the clubs he worked were the Phelps Lounge and the famed Twenty Grand. Then in 1962, Carl Davis ran across one of Jackson's performances while visiting Detroit and invited Jackson to Chicago to record.

Davis had made his reputation as a producer of rhythm and blues, but the acquisition of Jackson necessitated a slightly different approach. Jackson considered himself a pop performer, not an r&b or rock 'n' roll singer. As a consequence, Davis took a two-fold approach to recording his new talent. First, Davis favored r&b songs—or ballads with at least an r&b flavor—in Jackson's single releases; here Jackson could demonstrate his ability to do material that required a moderate display of roughness and funkiness in the vocals. Secondly, Davis also pushed Jackson as an album artist, which was unusual for an r&b performer at that time. Jackson was perhaps the only Chicago-sound act promoted in this manner. His second album, *Welcome Home*, reflected Davis's dual treatment as it contained both some of his r&b hits and old evergreens such as "My Funny Valentine" and "Moonlight in Vermont," with suitably lush arrangements by Riley Hampton.

Jackson's first 45 release, "I Don't Want to Suffer," was frankly a mediocre song, but it made a little noise in August 1962, and got the singer his first notices. Nothing much happened for the next two years, however, but Jackson and Davis kept plugging away, hoping to come up with that magic formula that results in hits. They found it when Curtis Mayfield, Chicago songwriter-guitarist extraordinary, entered the scene.

Mayfield first wrote for Jackson "That's What Mama Said," an answer song to Jan Bradley's "Mama Didn't Lie." It was backed with an excellent ballad, "What Would You Do?" Unfortunately for Jackson, both sides died. His next release, however, hit paydirt. It was another Mayfield composition, "It's All Over," which became a national hit, lasting thirteen weeks and going to position ten on *Cash Box*'s r&b chart in late 1964. The record's flip, "Lee Cross," in which Jackson sings of the lover-boy qualities of Lee Cross ("they say that Madame Nhu wants to be his wife"), had sparkling airplay as well.

More national hits followed in quick succession: the wistful "Suddenly I'm All Alone" in January 1965; the magnificent "Welcome Home" in May; and the sophisticated "Funny (Not Much)," which capped off the trio of ballad hits in February 1966. "Funny (Not Much)," with its supper club ambience, should not even be considered r&b, but it is Jackson's all-time favorite, revealing something of his pop sensibilities.

"The song is complete within itself," said Jackson. "I think 'Funny (Not Much)' afforded me a lot more of those 'Ummmm' [raised his eyebrows] kind of attitudes—'Because he sings *that* kind of song, he must be a hell of a guy.' I think that has enhanced my career more than any other particular piece of music I could name."[29]

Luckily for Jackson's fans much more "enhancement" would follow. With Davis's departure at the end of 1965 he got a new producer in Ted Cooper, who although working out of New York, hewed perfectly to the Chicago-style soul sound Davis had established by using the same Chicago musicians and arrangers. The first Cooper-produced release was "Uphill Climb to the Bottom," backed with an old Gene Chandler hit, "Tear for Tear," and it came out in May 1966. These songs were a little more upbeat, calling for a bit more aggression in the vocalizing than that of the ballad material Jackson had been doing, but in no way was there any loss of the Jackson touch. "Uphill" was the side that made the national charts, but in Chicago both sides got equal play. Other strong Cooper-produced songs quickly followed: "After You There Can Be Nothing" in August; "A Corner in the Sun" in October; and one of his biggest, the hauntingly beautiful "Speak Her Name," in March 1967.

There was one other number, released in late 1967, which, however, never made the national charts, a superb rendition of Jimmy Radcliffe's hit from 1965, "My Ship Is Coming In." The song ended a remarkable three-year period for Jackson in which he, with his producers, created a formidable and enduring body of music that easily ranked with the best soul music of the day. Looking back on them, Jackson was not totally happy with some of the songs, however: "You see, I was introduced to rock 'n' roll. That kind of rubbed me the wrong way when I first heard it, because I didn't think I had displayed that much definite direction. I think I was a bit related to rhythm and blues though. So in trying to climb a little higher, give myself a wider field, these songs just happened, I think."[30]

After "My Ship Is Coming In" the good songs as well as the hits stopped coming. Even his label faded, and Jackson was switched to the larger Epic label, but with no better results. Other records on other labels followed, but Jackson just could not connect. His return to the charts would not occur until he hooked up with Carl Davis again in 1976.

Billy Butler and the Chanters

One of the most compelling acts to come out of Chicago in the mid-1960s was Billy Butler and the Chanters. The lead vocalist and songwriter of the group was the younger brother of Jerry Butler, and although Billy's substantive body of Curtis Mayfield–styled work is not as well known as that of his brother and other Chicago acts, it ranked right up there with the best.[31] Butler was born in Chicago on June 7, 1945, the youngest child of Jerry and Arvella Butler. Besides his older brother, Jerry, he had two sisters, Dorothy and Mattie. The family was raised in the Cabrini-Green area. Speaking about when his interest in music was first sparked, Butler said, "I guess it was when Jerry and Curtis came to the house and rehearsed. I used to sit up and watch them. That really turned me on. I liked that. I kept bugging my family to get me a guitar. So when I was twelve they gave me one. I never did learn how to play it, you know, the technical aspect of it. But I did learn how to play it well enough to write my songs."[32]

While attending Wells High, Billy got together with a group of classmates and formed the group Billy Butler and the Four Enchanters. Members of the group besides Butler were Errol Batts (tenor), John Jordan (second tenor), Alton Howell (bass), and Jesse Tillman (baritone). During early 1963, the group went from record company to record company on Michigan Avenue, attempting to get themselves heard but without success. "We also went to Jerry," Butler added, "the closest thing to us. Jerry said, 'Okay, I like the sound of the group, I think it's cool. But, I don't know, maybe you need some more material.' "[33] When Jerry returned from a tour and saw them again, they were apparently ready, because he sent them to Curtis Mayfield, who was then working with Carl Davis. Mayfield and Davis had Butler and his group do a demo session of several songs, including Butler's superb "Found True Love." That turned out fine and they followed with a regular session, in May 1963.

Said Davis, "When Billy came to me, I bought him a guitar and amp, because I really believed, based on some of the things I heard, that he was a fantastic songwriter. We always had the problem of him being in his brother's footsteps. What I tried to do was get him out of Jerry Butler's areas, and that is why I'd preferred to sign him up as a group rather than as a solo artist."[34]

"Found True Love" was released in late summer, and sold well enough in Chicago to establish the name of the group. The song never made it nationally, but on November 2 on the strength of Midwest sales, it reached "Bubbling Under" status on *Billboard*'s top-hundred chart for a week. "Found True Love," of all the group's songs, best reflected the close-harmony fifties doowop tradition, probably because it had more voices in a fuller range than most of the later records. This range decreased because after one more session in October 1963 the group's second tenor and bass, Jordan and Howell, departed. "They were under the impression that we were getting cheated with the 'Found True Love' record," Butler explained. "But I don't think we could have been because it was only played in this area. It sold just enough records for us to break even on the account. But because of the phenomenal success that we were witnessing here in the area, they seemed to think it was that way across the country. They figured that we were getting cheated and because I didn't squawk about it I had to be in on it."[35]

To reflect the new makeup of the group, the name was changed to Billy Butler and the Enchanters on the next record, "Gotta Get Away," recorded in February 1964. The song was written by Mayfield and came out in the early spring of that year. Although Butler doubted that it was any bigger than a regional hit, the up-tempo "Gotta Get Away" did last three consecutive weeks on *Cash Box*'s national r&b chart.

About the same time "Found True Love" hit, a Philadelphia group, Garnett Mimms and the Enchanters, had "Cry Baby" and several other records on the charts. So to get away from the confusion of names, Butler's group shortened its name to Billy Butler and the Chanters. During the summer and early fall, the group had a truly splendid record called "Can't Live without Her," which was written by Butler and recorded at the "Gotta Get Away" session. With its relaxed medium tempo, its bright bubbly sound, it ranks as one of the most outstanding OKeh records. The group continued its string of regional hits in the fall with the faster and more frenetic "Nevertheless," another Mayfield composition.

Billy Butler and the Chanters played the whole theater circuit. Butler mentioned the Howard, the Royal, the Apollo, the Uptown, the Fox and the Freeport (in Brooklyn), as well as the Regal. They also appeared on national television, playing on "Shindig" and Dick Clark's "Where the Action Is."[36] Unlike most soul groups, Billy Butler and the Chanters did not do choreography. "We never did have a dance routine," said Butler, "because I was always holding the guitar—I wouldn't be able to do all the splits and everything that everyone was doing, not that I couldn't. It was very awkward looking with the guitar. We were singing a subtle type of r&b that really didn't call for a lot of movement. We tried, however, to accent little beats with our hands and bodies."[37] And try they did; the group was exciting to watch as Tillman and Batts on both sides of Butler bobbed back and forth to songs such as "Nevertheless." Their performance was quite intense, and their appearance on the "Shindig" show was one of the highlights of that series.

The group's biggest and last hit was another Mayfield composition, "I Can't Work No Longer," a rousing song in the "Chain Gang" tradition. It came out in the spring of 1965, and lasted six weeks on the top-hundred ·chart and eleven weeks on *Billboard*'s r&b chart. After "I Can't Work No Longer," the group broke up. The split was caused when one of the members, Batts, decided at the last minute not to play an engagement because he was getting married. "That created a hassle," Butler explained, "that probably would have been avoided at a later date if we all had been a little older and more mature about it."

In August 1965, OKeh released "You're Gonna Be Sorry," which achieved regional breakouts in Miami and Milwaukee, according to *Billboard*, but ultimately went nowhere. The Mayfield composition had something of the punch of a Major Lance record that was very appealing. It was recorded before the breakup of the group but only Butler's name appeared on the label.

In the summer of 1966, Butler got a national hit with the energetic "Right Track," lasting twelve weeks on *Billboard*'s r&b chart. By this time Pate had left for ABC and Davis had Gerald Sims arrange the number. Sims adhered to the typical OKeh formula by giving the song punchy, brassy flourishes and a clean bright sound. About the same time "Right Track" was breaking, Davis took Butler and another OKeh act, the Artistics, with him to Brunswick. At Brunswick, the Artistics went on to greater success, but Butler's career foundered. In the shadow of his more famous brother, Billy's achievements were largely overlooked. For true aficionados of soul music, however, Billy Butler holds a revered place in the history of Chicago popular music.

The Artistics

The Artistics were not a major act while at OKeh. They had only a couple of minor national hits, but all their records on the label were appealing. Unlike other OKeh acts, in which Davis forged a distinctive "Chicago Sound," the Artistics were recorded with the idea of imitating the sound of Detroit. Only after the Group left OKeh and joined Davis at Brunswick Records did they get any top hits.[38]

The Artistics' story was typical of most vocal groups of their era: they traced their origin to the street-corner scene of the 1950s when *a cappella* harmonizing held sway. The group got together in 1958 when its members were freshmen at Marshall High on the West Side. The Artistics at this time consisted of Curt Thomas on lead, Larry Johnson as first tenor, Jesse Bolian as second tenor, and Aaron Floyd as baritone-bass. "We started singing in social affairs, high school functions, things like that," remembered

Johnson. "There were a lot of groups at Marshall, but we were the most popular, probably because we had more gall than anybody. We would do more things you know. We were competitive. If there was another group, we would always want to outshine them, so we would go to more extremes than the other groups would."[39]

Within two years the Artistics had jelled to the point where they were invited to sing at the Democratic National Convention when it was held in Chicago in 1960. The group continued to kick around with no further advance until a break came in 1963: "We formed the group with another lead singer, Robert Dobyne," related Johnson. "We were rehearsing up north in that area where Major Lance lived, Cabrini-Green. Major asked us to back him up on a record. So he came over to our rehearsals and we would rehearse his tunes. [They ended up backing Lance on a tune on his first album, *The Monkey Time*.] His manager, Carl Davis, heard our backing and liked the way we sounded, and he signed us up to a contract on OKeh. Needless to say, all the records we put out on OKeh didn't really go off."[40]

The Artistics' first record, "I Need Your Love," was released in October 1963, and as Johnson contended it did not do much. But it was a fine song and was expertly done, and although not perhaps hit material, it hinted of better things to come. But the group was experiencing some difficulties. "Dobyne felt like he wanted to control the group, I guess," said Johnson. "There were conflicts. We felt that the group should remain as it was, a democratic organization."[41] So Dobyne was out.

The Artistics picked as their new lead Charles Davis, a singer of some experience who had been with the Dukays. However, the association did not work out and after some months the Artistics got another new lead, Marvin Smith. Smith likewise was a singer with earlier professional experience, having sung for two years with the famed Chicago 1950s group the El Dorados.

With Smith, the Artistics had an immediate local hit with a cover of Marvin Gaye's "Get My Hands on Some Lovin'." The record was a top-five hit in Chicago in July 1964, but it did little elsewhere, going to the forty-five position on *Cash Box*'s r&b chart. The song was indicative of the type of tunes the group was doing at OKeh. A good many of the songs were from Detroit songwriters, and many, from a production standpoint, had that Detroit sound even though all of their material was recorded in Chicago. "We were doing Detroit material," said Smith, "because Motown was what was happening then. Carl just had that thing about singers and productions up there."[42]

The most successful of the OKeh songs was a tune composed by Barrett Strong, "This Heart of Mine," which made it on the national soul survey for five weeks beginning in December 1965. Although the group's other material from this period did not hit the charts, "This Heart of Mine" was more than equalled by two more strong songs, "I'll Come Running" and "So Much Love in My Heart." Compared to what some other groups were doing at the time perhaps the material was modest, but it was good enough and successful enough to get the Artistics playing live dates and touring.

In November 1965, the group played at a homecoming dance at Crane High School in the West Side, sharing the bill with another West Side aggregation, the Vontastics. In January of the next year the Artistics played the prestigious Regal Theater with such acts as the Impressions and Otis Redding. That engagement initiated their first tour of the black theater circuit. Despite their considerable success at this point in their career, the Artistics would achieve much greater success on another label, Brunswick, when they followed Carl Davis over to the label in 1966.

The Opals

The Opals were a girl group from East Chicago, Indiana, and were still in high school when they were discovered by the Dells. The members of the group were Rose Addison, who sang lead, Myra Tillison, "Tootsie," and "Betty." The Opals sang in the teen-soprano manner that was so typical of girl groups of the era, which is why they were called "girl groups." Davis put out only three records on the group, but all three were wonderful.[43]

Mickey McGill of the Dells explained how the Opals ended up with OKeh: "They were singing in East Chicago and we had a manager named Charles Bucko, and I think he knew somebody that knew the Opals, and that's how we got to hear them. They sounded pretty good so we started teaching them. We didn't manage the group, but we took them as little kids and showed them how to sing and everything. We took them to Vee Jay and they did a lot of background work. They did some things with Otis Leavill, and they did a lot of sessions with Betty Everett. Then we took them to Carl Davis, and when he heard them he wanted to record them."[44] By this time, "Betty" had already left the Opals, leaving the three-member group shown in the publicity photos.

Near the end of January 1964, the Opals came out with their first release, a Billy Butler song called "Does It Matter." It had an appealing, forceful drive and was more of a rock 'n' roll sound than a soul sound. The second release, "You Can't Hurt Me No More," was a typical OKeh record from 1964—Curtis Mayfield songs, Johnny Pate arrangements, and Carl Davis productions—which is why it was so good. The song had a pretentious quality and fittingly got a full orchestrated production, but lead singer Addison emoted so soulfully in the best tradition of teen anguish, the song could not miss. It became a solid local hit in the summer of 1964.

The Opals' "Restless Days"/"I'm So Afraid," from the summer of 1965, was a double-sided treat. "Restless Days" was written by Mickey McGill and Verne Allison and was recorded by the Dells in the 1950s. The Dells' rendition, however, remained unissued until it appeared on a European reissue in 1983. Meanwhile, Davis had the Opals record their simply excellent version. "I'm So Afraid" was a Mayfield song with something of a Motown beat that had equally as strong appeal. It managed to chart locally for a month, but not long afterwards the Opals broke up.

The Opals records were not the only OKeh recordings Davis made that had the teen-soprano sound. He had some truly standout releases with the Kavettes' "You Broke Your Promise" (1964) and Marlina Mars's "Just Another Dance" (1965), a Mayfield song that came out shortly before Mayfield released it with himself and the Impressions. Neither of these two records did anything, and these commercial failures prompted Davis to question his ability to record women: "I don't know whether or not I was as successful with female acts as I was with male acts. Barbara Acklin we did well with at Brunswick, but very few other females."[45]

Gerald Sims

One of the most active members of the Chicago soul scene was the ubiquitous Gerald Sims. As songwriter, producer, and, with Carl Davis, in his position as "vocal and orchestra director," Sims worked with such artists as Gene Chandler, Major Lance, Otis Leavill, the Artistics, the Radiants, and the Daylighters. He also had an artistically modest career as a performer in his own right recording on the OKeh label.[46]

Gerald Sims was born January 5, 1940, in Chicago, but spent his early life in Kalamazoo, Michigan. As was true of most persons who got involved in popular music, he never received formal musical training, but was self-taught on guitar and in other aspects of music.

In 1959, Sims moved to Chicago and there hooked up as guitarist with a struggling group recently arrived from Alabama, the Daylighters. The group had already recorded a few mediocre songs in a basically 1950s doowop style. The Daylighters' next two releases, however, moved the group toward what later would be called a soul style. Instrumental to this change was the emergence of Sims as producer, writer, and lead vocalist. The first, "Oh What a Way to Be Loved," released in the winter of 1961–62, was a haunting ballad that was strikingly sophisticated and urbane. Dot picked up its distribution but the record's national sales were never more than spotty. The other Sims vehicle followed in September 1962, "Cool Breeze," which became the Daylighters' biggest hit, crossing over on some top-forty stations.

With these records, Sims came to the notice of Carl Davis. While the Daylighters went on to record a number of excellent records with distinction, Sims left the group and signed a contract with Columbia to record as an artist. Two releases soon followed. "Cool Breeze," re-released under Sims's name alone and backed with the equally superb "There Must Be an Answer Somewhere" (also previously released), became a mild hit in some parts of the country in late 1963. However, Sims became more interested in the production side of the entertainment business and aborted his career as an artist after the second release in 1964.

At first Sims worked with Davis on OKeh releases by such artists as Major Lance, Billy Butler and the Chanters, and Walter Jackson, learning the ropes. Eventually he was given projects of his own, sometimes receiving credit and sometimes not. The artists he worked closest with were Gene Chandler, the Artistics, and Otis Leavill. Some of his best work in association with Davis was with Chandler on such numbers as "Here Comes the Tears" (written by Sims), "Nothing Can Stop Me," and "You Can't Hurt Me No More."

Sims's work with the Artistics was listed on the records as that of "director of vocals and orchestra," and thus he shared in the credit for their two biggest hits, "I'm Gonna Miss You" (1966) and "Girl I Need You" (1967). In the same capacity he assisted in the success of Marvin Smith's "Time Stopped" (1966). Sims also wrote for other artists not associated with Davis. He scored major successes with the Radiants, writing their great mid-1960s hits, "Voice Your Choice" and "It Ain't No Big Thing."

By the end of the 1960s, Sims had broken with Davis. "I became disillusioned with Carl," said Sims. "He taught me everything, but then he didn't want to pay me. Our relationship was getting strained, and I was tired of being a 'student.' But he didn't pay me and I left."[47] For several years in the early 1970s Sims worked with Jerry and Billy Butler for their Fountain Productions.

OKeh Downfall

The downfall of OKeh began with a corporate shuffle at CBS that resulted in Davis's no longer reporting to Dave Kapralik, but to Len Levy. "That was a sad moment for us," declared Davis. "For some reason Columbia decided to separate the Epic and Columbia labels. Columbia became one entity, Epic the other. OKeh fell under the Epic label and Len Levy headed Epic. Len Levy and I never got along, and I never could figure out why, because I had proven I could produce hits."[48]

In 1965 Davis and Levy had an acrimonious clash that eventually spelled Davis's doom at the label. Said Davis:

What happened, there was an item in one of the New York papers. A columnist had put in that "OKeh prez Carl Davis was seen courting Motown superstar Mary Wells. Is there something going on there?" Somehow or another someone gave that article to Len Levy, and he called me in Chicago and wanted to know why I was representing myself as the president of OKeh Records. I said, "What are you talking about?" He said, "I've been hearing you're going around telling people you're the head of OKeh." I said, "Len, let me tell you this. Whenever a disc jockey would call to talk to you relative to the OKeh label, you would always refer them to Carl. You didn't want nothing to do with those guys. So maybe as a result of that people took the position that I was running the label."

They actually called me into New York. He waited until he got in front of the whole A&R staff and began to lambaste me about this newspaper report. I just got up and walked out of the room, and left with the impression that they were either gonna fire me or ask me to resign. Bob Morgan, who at the time was head of the A&R department, patched things up, but it was going downhill after that. Because then Levy wanted me...whatever was current he wanted me to record. If Chuck Jackson was the hottest thing out there, he would want me to go back and cut a Chuck Jackson. I used to try to tell him I was trying to develop the Chicago sound. I was trying to develop something that was uniquely ours.[49]

There was more than just personality and philosophical differences involved in Davis's departure. There was the question of his outside producing activities. Davis had long been discreetly producing Gene Chandler on Vee Jay and Constellation, a situation that Kapralik while he was in command pretended not to notice. Said Gerald Sims, "Those were the days of staff A&R. There wasn't all these independent production deals then. Carl had a contract with OKeh. I wasn't on contract with them, but we were hustling. We were cutting Mary Wells on Atlantic, cutting things on Constellation. The new guy in New York, Len Levy, did not get along with Carl. New York then looked at Carl's moonlighting and the whole thing blew up."[50]

In November 1965, Davis recorded a session on Mary Wells in Chicago, which produced a big hit for her in early 1966 called "Dear Lover." Said Davis,

That was discovered by CBS and they started pressuring me with that. I remember Bob Morgan and Len Levy flying into Chicago one day. I got a call at home from my engineer, Jim Felix, who said, "Hey, I just thought I'd let you know that Bob Morgan and Len Levy are in your office looking around, and asking if you were doing sessions for anybody other than CBS, stuff like that." I jumped in my car and went down to the office. So when I got there they were just nodding and grinning and saying they were in Chicago for some other reason and thought they'd stop by. At that point I knew they would either find a way to fire me or make things miserable, so I just put in my resignation.[51]

By the time "Dear Lover" was released in February 1966, Davis was gone from OKeh, so he could be fully credited as producer. He did a great job, too, giving Wells her biggest hit since leaving Motown in early 1964. The song was written and produced by Davis and Gerald Sims, and arranged by Sonny Sanders, who had been recently brought to Chicago from Detroit. "Dear Lover" featured that great bubbly pop-soul sound that Wells sang at a Chicago-style medium tempo.

OKeh was able to have a fairly successful year in 1966 with the remainder of Davis-produced recordings that had yet to be released when Davis left and with a spate of Walter Jackson hits produced in New York by Ted Cooper with Chicago musicians and arrangers. But the company was in a double bind, since it had lost not only Davis but arranger Pate and writer Curtis Mayfield, who were concentrating their work elsewhere.

During 1967–68, OKeh had, besides some more Jackson hits, minor hits with Larry Williams and Johnny Watson's "Mercy Mercy Mercy," Ray Thompson's "Sookie Sookie," and the Vibrations' "Pick Me" and "Love in Them There Hills," none of which was recorded in Chicago. In February 1969, Dave Kapralik brought in Richard Parker as A&R director and executive producer for OKeh to try to revive the label's work in Chicago.[52] Parker failed to get much going, and after only three releases in 1970, OKeh was quietly closed down at the end of the year, a sad end to one of the most famous labels in recording history.

NOTES

1. Martin Koppel, "The Chicago Sound of OKeh," *Soul Survivor* 5 (Summer 1986): 24–25; Joe McEwen, liner notes, *Okeh Soul*, Epic 37321, 1982; Billy Butler interview; Carl Davis interview, March 9, 1986; Otis Leavill interview, April 19, 1976; Gerald Sims interview.

2. Davis interview.

3. Sims interview.

4. Davis interview.

5. Ibid.

6. Ibid.

7. Davis interview.

8. Butler interview.

9. Sims interview.

10. Leavill interview.

11. Davis interview.

12. Butler interview.

13. Davis interview.

14. Major Lance interview.

15. Butler interview.

16. Davis interview.

17. Butler interview.

18. Davis interview.

19. Jim O'Neal and Dick Shurman, "Living Blues Interview: Ted Taylor," *Living Blues* 25 (January–February 1976): 10–18; Clive Richardson, "Ted Taylor" (obituary), *Juke Blues* 11 (Winter 1987/88): 18–19.

20. Davis interview.

21. Dave Hoekstra, "Major Lance," *Goldmine*, October 1983, pp. 114–26; Robert Pruter, "The Chicago Soul of Major Lance," *Time Barrier Express* 25 (July–August 1979): 31–34; idem, "The Major Lance Story," *It Will Stand* 34 [1986]: 6–10; Davis interview; Lance interview.

22. Davis interview.

23. Ibid.

24. Lance interview.

25. Ibid.

26. Leavill interview.

27. Robert Pruter, "The Uphill Climb of...Walter Jackson," *Goldmine*, August 1979, pp. 20–22; Walter Jackson interview.

28. Jackson interview.

29. Ibid.

30. Ibid.

31. Clive Anderson, liner notes, Billy Butler and the Enchanters, *The Right Track*, Edsel 147, August 1985; Peter Burns, "Billy Butler: Nearly a Decade of Writing and Recording," *Blues and Soul*, June 8–21, 1973, pp. 24–25; Robert Pruter, "The (Other) Butler Did It...(Too)!!: The Billy Butler Story," *It Will Stand* 19 (1981): 16–18; Butler interview.

32. Butler interview.

33. Ibid.

34. Davis interview.

35. Butler interview.

36. Ibid.

37. Ibid.

38. Robert Pruter, "Beach Music from the Windy City: The Story of the Artistics," *It Will Stand* 12/13 (1980): 14–16; Larry Johnson interview; Marvin Smith interview.

39. Johnson interview.

40. Ibid.

41. Ibid.

42. Smith interview.

43. Mickey McGill interview, April 28, 1986.

44. McGill interview.

45. Davis interview.

46. [Cary Baker], "Gerald Sims' Homecoming," *Illinois Entertainer,* February 1981, p. 4; Robert Pruter, "Gerald Sims," *Goldmine*, December 1978, p. 26; Sims interview.

47. Sims interview.

48. Davis interview.

49. Ibid.

50. Sims interview.

51. Davis interview, April 27, 1986.

52. "Richard Parker to OKeh A&R Post," *Cash Box*, February 22, 1969, p. 30.

5

Chess Records

Chess Records was founded by Leonard and Philip Chess, two Jewish immigrants from Poland who came to Chicago in 1928. They got involved in the liquor business and by the 1940s owned a string of South Side bars, including a large nightclub, the Macomba, at Thirty-ninth and Cottage Grove. Feeling that the black talent they had seen at the club was not being adequately recorded, the Chess brothers in 1947 entered into partnership with Evelyn Aron, who had just started Aristocrat Records with her husband to record jazz, blues, and r&b. In late 1949 the Chess brothers bought out their partner and in early 1950 reorganized the company as Chess Records. As the company grew, it added the Checker label in 1952 and the Argo label in 1956. Checker tended to concentrate on blues singers and Argo emphasized jazz.[1]

During the 1950s, Chess flourished in the burgeoning rhythm-and-blues field, recording blues artists such as Muddy Waters, Howlin' Wolf, and Sonny Boy Williamson, and vocal groups such as the Moonglows and Flamingos. The company's biggest successes were with Chuck Berry and Bo Diddley. These artists, who were steeped in the blues, emphasized the beat in the form and helped forge a new kind of music for teenagers called rock 'n' roll.

During Chess's early years, Leonard and Phil Chess were "record men" in every sense of the word. They were not only businessmen who owned a record company, they lived, breathed, and loved the music they were recording. Because the brothers were intimately involved in the creative end, the company felt little need to bring in A&R men and producers. As the company grew, however, the brothers gradually delegated more and more of the creative work to their employees. The nucleus of the 1960s creative staff was established in 1959, when the white veteran producer Ralph Bass came over from King/Federal records to serve as Chess's new A&R director.[2]

When the 1960s began, Chess had a stable of artists that included Muddy Waters, Howlin' Wolf, Chuck Berry, Bo Diddley, and other veteran 1950s artists. The company was hardly ready for the coming soul era, but the Chess brothers were able to adapt by bringing in from Detroit in 1961 Roquel "Billy" Davis as the company's new A&R director and staff producer. This move was the most significant development for Chess Records in that decade and paved the way for the company to become an important force in soul music and to grow as a major independent.

Billy Davis, who was born on July 11, 1937, brought to Chess a strong creative hand and, by being young and black, a sensibility attuned to the new sounds and developments in black music. Davis was born and raised in Detroit and attended Northern High School (a source of a lot of black musical talent in the 1960s), Wayne State University, and the Maurice King School of Music. His first musical association was as a member of the Four Tops vocal group. He wrote the group's songs and acted as its spokesman and manager. In 1956 he took the group to Chess, which agreed to record the act in exchange for two of Davis's songs, "See Saw" and "A Kiss from Your Lips," which the company gave to the Moonglows and the Flamingos respectively. Although the Four Tops' release bombed, both "See Saw" and "A Kiss from Your Lips" became big hits, and thereafter Davis's association with Chess grew. Said Davis, "So I had a relationship going with them over the years, working with their artists, Bo, Chuck Berry, and Muddy. Quite often, whenever I was in town, they would request for me to come over."[3]

Davis was also building a successful career in Detroit. With Berry Gordy he wrote most of Jackie Wilson's early hits, and the two songwriters then went into independent production work, recording talent around the Detroit area. The arrangement eventually evolved into Motown Records. In 1958 Davis founded Anna Records with Berry Gordy's sister, Gwen Gordy, and had the label distributed first by New York-based End and then by Chess. All these successful activities by Davis prompted Chess to hire this talented young man. Davis terminated his Anna association in 1961 and turned over to Berry Gordy the interests they had held jointly, namely contracts with certain artists such as the Miracles and Marv Johnson.

For the first year with Davis at the helm, Chess tried to operate a newly formed Detroit-based label, Check-mate, with Davis in charge. (Davis also shared with Chess equal ownership in the Chevis publishing company.) But the label never got off the ground and expired in early 1962. Davis then became a full-time Chicago employee. In Chicago, Chess assented to Davis's program to beef up substantially their in-house production, arranging, and writing staff. Valuing his predecessor's experience, Davis also asked and got permission to keep on board Ralph Bass, who then handled A&R for the gospel and blues performers.

Davis, as both a producer and an excellent songwriter, was the key creative person. Almost equally important as far as the soul acts were concerned was the staff arranger, Phil Wright, who Davis discovered working in Chicago nightclubs as a band arranger. Said Davis, "He understood r&b and what we were trying to achieve. He had ability to orchestrate r&b and add the pop flavor to it."[4] Indeed, if anything typifies the Chess sound of the 1960s it is Wright's full-bodied arrangements that superbly enhanced the soulful vocals of the performers.

Many of Davis's songwriting staff people came out of acts that came to the company. Maurice McAlister and Leonard Caston, Jr., came out of the Radiants, and Raynard Miner came out of the Gems. Miner in turn brought to the firm a talented partner, Carl Smith. Miner and Caston also served as producers. In 1964 Phil Chess brought in veteran saxophonist Gene "Daddy G" Barge as staff producer and director of the rhythm section.

The rhythm section on most of the records included Maurice White on drums, Louis Sattersfield on bass, and on guitar Gerald Sims, Bryce Robertson, and Pete Cosey. Robertson was one of the few white persons at Chess, and according to Barge, he "played very funky and bluesy."[5] (Years later White and Sattersfield would form the immensely successful aggregation Earth, Wind and Fire.) On organ Chess would use Sonny Thompson and on piano Leonard Caston, Jr., and Raynard Miner. Chess never had a regular horn section, and would gather them ad hoc for each session.

With the new staff gathered by Davis, Chess was soon producing soul records in its own unmistakable style—fully orchestrated and arranged, often horn driven and deeply touched with gospel and blues fervor. Chess had entered the soul era. Perhaps because of the company's rich tradition in recording blues, Chess was the one major independent in the city that was as strong in recording hard soul as it was in soft soul. Davis tended to concentrate his production work on the soft-soul acts and let Bass and Barge work with the hard-soul and bluesy acts. The one artist who best exemplified both the soft-soul and hard-soul aspects of the Chess sound was Etta James. She was their preeminent hard-soul sister who could belt like a blues shouter, yet she was also a great singer of ballads and pop standards.

The Hard-Soul Sisters

Etta James was Chess's first soul star. The singer had initially made a name for herself at the age of seventeen with the early rock 'n' roll hit "Roll with Me Henry" in 1955, but when she joined Chess in 1959 she had been cold for several years. Her career at Chess was one of ups and downs, but she was prolifically recorded by the company and she had innumerable hits showcasing her biting, intense vocals.[6]

James was born Jamesetta Hawkins in Los Angeles on January 25, 1938, of a teenage black mother and an Italian father. She was raised by her grandparents, but after her grandmother died in 1950 she relocated in San Francisco to live with her mother, Dorothy Hawkins. Around 1954 she and two high-school friends, sisters Abbysina and Jean Mitchell, formed a vocal trio called the Peaches. The group made up an answer song to the Midnighters' "Work with Me Annie" called "Roll with Me Henry," and auditioned the song to bandleader Johnny Otis. Impressed, Otis took them into the studio in November 1954, had them record the song, and a rock 'n' roll classic was born.

The success of "Roll with Me Henry" on the Bihari brothers' Modern label prompted James to split from the Peaches and pursue a solo career. She had a few more but minor hits, notably "Good Rockin' Daddy" (1955) and "Tough Lover" (1956). She also did some appealing duets with Harvey Fuqua of the Moonglows as "Betty and Dupree," but by the late 1950s James had fallen into obscurity.

James and Fuqua were also romantically involved, and Fuqua, who was becoming more immersed in A&R work for Chess, was thus the reason that James left Modern and joined Chess in 1959. James and Fuqua were quickly recorded together under the name of "Etta and Harvey," and came up with a fine double-sided hit, "My Heart Cries"/"If I Can't Have You" (1960). But the songs harked back to the 1950s and did not represent James's subsequent work at Chess.

With James, Chess launched its new era of recording soul with a beefed-up production, arranging, and writing staff. James's output during her first several years at the company was primarily string-laden ballads, many of them old standards. The healthy tension generated between the pop-like arrangements of Riley Hampton and the gospel/blues vocals of James produced an early type of soul heavy on melodrama. From 1960 through 1962 most of her songs were of this type and most were top-ten hits in the r&b market, thus launching James as a major soul artist.

James's first solo hit, "All I Could Do Was Cry" (1960), was brought from Detroit by Billy Davis, and it helped facilitate his entry into the Chess organization the following year. James quickly followed up with "My Dearest Darling" (1960), "At Last" (1961), "Trust in Me" (1961), "Fool that I Am" (1961), "Sunday Kind of Love" (1961), and "Seven Day Fool" (1961). Interrupting the string of ballads was the hard-driving "Something's Got a Hold on Me" (1962), in which James's soulful vocals were unleashed to exhibit a raw, shouting style. (The record was a double-sided hit, with the flip featuring a magnificent ballad, "Waiting for Charlie to Come Home".) For the remainder of the year, James returned to her melodramatic ballad style with "Stop the Wedding" and "Would It Make Any Difference to You?"

During this time Chess came out with a slew of albums on James, but years later she dismissed most of them, except for an album of standards she recorded in 1962: "Those early albums are so embarrassing," she told journalist Bob Fukuyama in 1976. "We'd just throw stuff together to fill an album. My favorite album might be *Etta James Sings for Lovers,* because it was a collection that held together. We found oldies I had always liked, and we did them right. Instead of cutting each track as a separate thing, we used strings, cellos, harps, like a symphony, for the whole album to make it unified. It was beautiful."[7] When few r&b artists of the day had albums out, and when their LPs were nothing more than collections of singles, the approach Chess used for James was exceedingly novel and generous. The heavily orchestrated approach forced a little mental adjustment on Leonard Chess's part: "That was really amazing to Leonard Chess," related James. "He said, 'Oh my God, is this going to be a symphony or something?' 'Cause really, his true thinking wasn't beyond Muddy Waters and Howlin' Wolf and them, that was the bag he loved."[8]

By 1963, with the emergence of soul as the predominant r&b style, James's records became harder and more aggressive as blaring horns replaced strings and the beat became heavier and more insistent. Launching her in this phase of her career were "Two Sides (To Every Story)" (1963), "Pushover" (1963), and "Baby What You Want Me to Do" (1963).

After 1963, James's hits became more sporadic. She was fighting a drug habit, and for that reason the company's commitment to her career was perhaps not all it could have been. She did come up with two hard-soul hits in 1964, "Loving You More Every Day" and "Mellow Fellow." But in 1965 Chess did not release anything on her. The company, especially Leonard Chess, did not allow James to drift during her difficulties. Said James of Leonard, "He always looked after me, even though I was the company's black sheep, always getting into trouble. When I was a junkie he set me up with the rehabilitation center and made sure I was staying straight. I mean, there are a lot of companies who couldn't care less."[9]

In 1966, James returned from her layoff with a dynamic duet with Chess stablemate Sugar Pie DeSanto, called "In the Basement," one of the most uncompromising hard-soul songs Chess ever recorded.

Sugar Pie DeSanto was a little four-foot eleven-inch bundle with a big contralto voice. She had only a few hits with Chess, but they were powerfully sung and gripping songs and should not be overlooked. DeSanto, the progeny of a Filipino father and a black mother, was born Umpeylia Marsema Balinton, in New York City, October 16, 1935. In 1951, at the Ellis Theater in San Francisco, she won a talent contest seen by Johnny Otis. He liked what he saw and brought her to Federal Records, who signed her up. Her Filipino name would not do for show business, so Otis dubbed her "Little Miss Sugar Pie."[10]

DeSanto got no hits in her association with Federal and later with Aladdin, but things turned around for the singer in 1959 when she signed with Bay Area record man Bob Geddins. Her first release for Geddins, "I Want to Know," became a national chart hit that lasted nine weeks and went to position four on *Billboard*'s r&b survey. The song was rather laid back compared to the later songs she recorded for Chess, but it effectively showcased DeSanto's bluesy voice and established her career.

Chess was sufficiently enamored with her recordings to pick up her contract from Geddins in 1961. DeSanto moved to Chicago and Chess immediately released an album, *Sugar Pie*, which consisted primarily of sides cut with Geddins. Her best work lay ahead. The year 1964 saw a series of singles that presented DeSanto the way she was meant to be recorded—as a bluesy hard-soul singer. Her first success was "Slip-In Mules," an answer record to Tommy Tucker's monster blues hit of the same year, "Hi-Heel Sneakers." ("Sneakers" was also a Chess release, but it was produced in New York and leased to the company.) DeSanto's record lasted fourteen weeks and went to position ten on *Cash Box*'s r&b survey in the early spring. The company followed up with another superb chart hit in the late summer, "Soulful Dress," a fine McAlister composition. The flip, "Use What You Got," written by Davis, was equally fine. Both sides exemplified DeSanto at her aggressive best, shouting out her sexual prowess over a stinging blues guitar.

After two undistinguished releases in 1965, DeSanto returned to form with "Go Go Power," a solid local hit in December 1966. The forceful song was her last release put out by Chess Records, but her excellent duet with Etta James, "In the Basement," should not go unmentioned.

DeSanto went to Chicago rival Brunswick Records, but her two releases with that company were uninspiring. In 1969, she was back in San Francisco, where for the next two decades she came out with lackluster releases on a variety of labels.

Mitty Collier, with her rich deep contralto, must be counted among the best soul singers of all time, even though she had only a few hits with Chess. She was born June 21, 1941, in Birmingham, Alabama. There she attended Western Olin High School and went to college at both Alabama A&M and Miles College. While in high school, she sang in church and even toured the state and neighboring Georgia as a member of a traveling gospel group, the Hayes Ensemble. By the time she was attending college she had branched out into rhythm and blues, and was working the local clubs.[11]

Said Collier:

> I came to Chicago in the summer of 1959 to visit my brother who was living here, and while I was here I met my French teacher from college, who had helped me a lot in Birmingham. He came here the same year also visiting, and he found different talent shows for me to be on while I was here. One of the talent shows was Al Benson's Talent Show at the Regal Theater. I won that for six weeks straight, first place. I did a song called "Someday You'll Want Me to Want You." Della Reese recorded it at that particular time. Ralph Bass, who was with Chess Records, was out there in the audience and he heard me and offered me a contract to sing for Chess. That's how I got a contract with them in 1960.[12]

Chess knew they had something with Mitty Collier, but the company at first had some difficulty providing her with suitable material. After several failed releases, her break came when Little Johnny Taylor's "Part Time Love" became a huge blues hit in the summer of 1963. Chess's response was to have Collier record an answer song, "I'm Your Part Time Love." The song was a natural for her and she got great support from Gerald Sims's fine stinging guitar work. In October the record made the national r&b charts.

Collier came out with the remarkable "I Had a Talk with My Man" in August 1964. It was a wonderfully crafted production, opening with rhythmic strings, breaking off into one soaring note by a French horn, which leads into some gospel piano notes, which leads into Mitty's vocals, virtually solo except for muted strings in the background. The juxtaposition of Collier's deep contralto with the sweetening strings produced a profoundly moving and soulful sound.

"I Had a Talk with My Man" was a secular gospel number. Said Collier, "We got it from a gospel song that James Cleveland had done, 'I Had a Talk with God Last Night.' We had a musician at the studio who played for church. His name was Leonard Caston. So he had this album and he came down to the studio and played it, because he was going to teach some songs from it to his church. Billy Davis, who was my manager and producer, heard the song and kept telling Leonard to play it over and over. And so they took it and changed the words, and we cut it in the next couple of weeks or so."[13] The record lasted thirteen weeks and went to number three position on *Cash Box*'s r&b chart.

In December 1964 Collier successfully followed up with "No Faith, No Love," which was another secular gospel tune. It too came from the Cleveland songbook, his wonderful "No Cross, No Crown." In early 1965 it lasted eleven weeks and went to position four on the *Cash Box* survey, keeping Collier's name before the public. Following a local Chicago hit with "For My Man" in September 1965, Collier scored the third-biggest hit of her career, "Sharing You," a cover of a southern hit by Carl Henderson. Her reading of the southern-style song effectively and dramatically conveyed the impression that she felt the lyrics down to her bone. Maybe she did. The song was soul music in every sense of the word and the public bought it. It lasted nine weeks and went to position ten on *Billboard*'s r&b chart.

The next five releases on Chess by Collier, from 1966 to 1968, were not hits, but included some interesting songs nonetheless. Some were produced by Leonard Caston, Jr., and Monk Higgins in Chicago and some were produced by Rick Hall in Muscle Shoals, Alabama. Collier left Chess in 1969 and joined Peachtree Records out of Atlanta, Georgia. After several unsuccessful releases, in 1972 she gave up secular music for gospel music, and the world of soul lost one of its finest practitioners.

Teen Sopranos

Chicago record men in the 1960s were especially adept at recording teenage girls with high pretty voices. Chess Records, in particular, seems to have had this ability, coming out with many of the best teen-soprano records by such artists as Jan Bradley, Jackie Ross, the Gems, and JoAnn Garrett. Chess songwriters Raynard Miner, Carl Smith, and Billy Davis had the talent to write songs that captured the innocence of these marvelous voices.

Jackie Ross was born in St. Louis, Missouri, on January 30, 1946. She was the daughter of a husband-and-wife team of preachers, and by the age of three little Jackie was beginning her career singing gospel tunes on her parents' radio program. At the age of eight, after her father passed away, she and her mother moved to Chicago.[14] Her mother was a good friend of Sam Cooke, who on one of his trips to Chicago discovered Ross's singing abilities. In 1962 he recorded her "Hard Times" for his Sar label, a modest effort in which Ross's youth was truly telling.

Jackie Ross continued to sing gospel in the Chicago area, but she was also working to establish herself in the rhythm-and-blues market. Her break came at a talent contest at the Trianon Ballroom. Related Ross:

> Syl Johnson's band was playing there, and I went there and won
> a singing contest. The award was a weekend of singing and being
> paid. And that started me singing in Syl Johnson's band. We

worked a lot of places, and I was working with Syl Johnson when Bill Doc Lee discovered me.

Well, at the time, Leonard Chess owned the radio station on which Bill Lee played gospel records. He took me down to Chess Records and told me that he thought I had something. They listened to me just singing and after they heard me they had the writers there, Carl Smith and [William] Flash McKinley. They said they had the perfect song for me, which was "Selfish One."[15]

The song was Ross's biggest hit and epitomized the Chess approach to recording young female singers, pop-like yet soulful. (The instrumental fanfare was so exciting that a Detroit company copied it two years later for the intro of Edwin Starr's "Stop Her on Sight.") The song lasted thirteen weeks and went to position four on *Cash Box*'s r&b chart in the late summer of 1964.

After several mediocre records, some of them undeservedly modest hits, Ross came out with the excellent "Take Me for a Little While," in July 1965. With its rolling, catchy beat and plaintive plea, the song was a perfect vehicle for the young singer. It was, however, a cover of a just-released record by Evie Sands, a young white singer in New York. The Sands record was just beginning to break in most of the black markets when the Ross record hit the street. Because Ross's version was on the veteran Chess label and sung by an established black star, it knocked off Evie Sands's song in most cities.

Recalled Ross:

What happened is that someone in the Chess organization had gotten the tune from someone in New York. And I didn't know anything about it. Evie Sands's manager approached me when I was in New York. I even often think about it now. He came to me and said, "How could you?" I looked at him, I had no idea who he was. I said, "How could I what?" He said, "You made it, you got a name for yourself, how could you deliberately take this tune and take it away from someone who is trying to make it now?" I feel even to this day that he really didn't believe me when I told him that I did not know what he was talking about. And it just really hurt me.[16]

Jackie Ross also did a lot of touring at this time. "We did all kinds of tours," said Ross "We toured the South, Canada, everywhere. With Chess, we had an all-Chess show, and went across the country, hitting all the theaters in the different spots. We called ourselves the Chess family, 'cause at each theater everybody would pitch in and make it very enjoyable.

We would just get gobs of food and stuff and stay backstage and eat. The acts on the tour were Fontella Bass, Little Milton, Tony Clarke, Mitty Collier, Sugar Pie DeSanto, and the Radiants."[17]

Because of disappointment with Chess over the meager royalties she earned on "Selfish One," Ross left the company not long after "Take Me for a Little While." Her later recording associations, with Brunswick (1967–68), Jerry Butler's Fountain Productions (1969–71), and her manager, Jimmy Vanleer (1971–82), were all unproductive as far as hits were concerned. She recorded some excellent tunes, but she never got more than local play in Chicago with them. Her Chess years were her glory years.

The Gems never established a national reputation in the few years during the 1960s that they were around, but they did firmly establish themselves as local stars in Chicago. They were originally formed in 1961 as the Lovettes by Vandine Harris from among her classmates at Marshall High on the West Side. Joining Harris as members of the group were Jessica Collins, Theresa Washum, Dorothy Hucklebee, and Raynard Miner (who played piano and was their musical director). They were all about fourteen or fifteen years old at the time. In late 1962 the Lovettes signed with Chess as a backup and recording group. They also added another girl, Bertha Watts.[18]

The Lovettes became the Gems in 1963 and under their new name recorded one of their finest songs, "A Girl's Impression." The song was led by Collins and featured pretty r&b-type harmonizing. Miner wrote the song and seemed to capture perfectly the innocence of teen romance. "A Girl's Impression" garnered some local play.

Harris left the group following "A Girl's Impression," and recruited in her place was Minnie Riperton, who Miner and the group's manager, Rose Miller, plucked out of Hyde Park High School A Cappella Choir. The group's next release was more in the rock 'n' roll vein, "That's What They Put Erasers on Pencils For," and it featured Collins again on lead. The song had been recorded earlier for Chess by the Four Jewels, a Washington, D.C., girl group, but the staff at the company did not consider it successful. As recorded by the Gems, the song got strong play in Chicago in early 1964.

The Gems' next release, "I Can't Help Myself," had a classic Chess mid-1960's soul sound in the manner of Jackie Ross records. Theresa Washum acquitted herself well on the lead, and the result was the biggest record of the girls' career. Though the song never made the national charts, it did well enough to become a hit in several regional markets. The group's last release, "Happy New Love," featured Minnie Riperton in the lead. As was true of some of their earlier releases, its lack of success was not a reflection on its quality.

The Gems may rate no more than a minor footnoote in the history of soul, but they came out with some nice records and served as a training ground for two artists who made a much bigger mark, namely Minnie Riperton and Raynard Miner.

Miner was born in Chicago, March 18, 1946. Although born with vision, at an early age he went totally blind. He was largely reared by his grandparents, because his mother died when he was four and his father died when he was eight. Early on, he developed an interest in music and by his early teens he was playing piano and composing with the Gems. With the Gems he made his entry into the Chess organization, where he prospered into one of their finest songwriters.[19]

Aside from his work with the Gems, Miner's composing credits include "Rescue Me" for Fontella Bass; "We're Gonna Make It" for Little Milton; "Higher and Higher" for the Dells, Jackie Wilson, and Rita Coolidge; "There Is," "Show Me," and "Run for Cover" for the Dells; as well as numerous other top-flight songs.

Minnie Riperton, the brave coloratura soprano of popular music, died of cancer in July 1979 after several years of acclaim as a California-based solo artist. But as evident from the Gems story, her roots were in Chicago, where she had an extensive recording career besides her association with the Gems.[20] Riperton was born on the South Side on November 8, 1947, and was the youngest of eight children. When she was ten years of age her mother enrolled her in the cultural programs at the Lincoln Center in the Oakwood community (one of the poorest and roughest in Chicago). "Lincoln Center was a great center for a lot of black people," recalled Riperton, "I studied toe and ballet for years, long before I was singing, and arts and crafts. There were some really great people helping out in the community. Because after all, it was right around Thirty-ninth Street, and it was 'Dopeville' and 'Junkyville' and that trip. But it was really nice. I studied music until I was about sixteen, but I got swayed off my path once I got a little rock 'n' roll dangling in front of my eyes."[21]

By 1966, the Gems were dissolved, and Riperton was recording as a solo act under the name Andrea Davis, a name she detested that was picked for her by the company. Her one release as Andrea Davis, "Lonely Girl," was a magnificent performance in which she showcased her lovely three-octave range. It was a local hit in Chicago in 1966. In the black community, in the clubs, Riperton proved less than stunning. Johnny Sayles, one of Chicago's best hard-soul singers, used to feature her as his opening act. He remembered: "I liked Minnie's singing, but the black folks didn't like her singing, then. I'd have her working for me, and shit, hell, you couldn't even tell she was singing, there be so much loud talking. They gave her no kind of respect."[22]

From her less than rewarding career as Andrea Davis, Riperton would go on to great fame first as a member of Chess's one progressive rock group, the Rotary Connection (1967–70), then as a highly successful solo artist in California (1971–79).

Jo Ann Garrett had one of the prettiest teenage soprano voices at Chess. Although she achieved little national success, Garrett was a local phenomenon in Chicago, and deservedly so. On her best songs—notably "Stay by My Side," "Thousand Miles Away," and "One Woman"—she offered a well defined and artistically successful teenage soul sound to the young people of the city.[23]

Garrett was born in Chicago, on March 3, 1949, and grew up in the rough West Side Maxwell Street area with seven brothers. She first attended Harrison High, but then her family moved to Robert Taylor Homes projects on the South Side, and she attended DuSable High. She built a reputation as a talented singer at school, and in 1966 fellow student Cormie Vance (who sang in the Para-Monts) encouraged Garrett to audition for deejay and promoter Purvis Spann, who owned The Club. She passed, which led to a talent show at the Regal Theater. She took second to the Five Stairsteps, and both acts walked away with contracts. Jo Ann was the tender age of fifteen.

Garrett came under the management wing of Spann and Bob Lee and was soon making regular appearances at The Club and other local spots. Garrett's first release was a marvelous song written by Lee and Sherman Nesbary called "Stay by My Side." The song was recorded at Universal Studio, and when Chess heard the final product the company picked it up. It proved to be a well-played local hit in May 1966. Subsequent Garrett releases were recorded at Chess.

In March 1967 "You Can't Come In" teamed Garrett up with the Dells. It was a bouncy number that was a partial take-off of "The Three Little Pigs," but the record did not have a corny juvenile sound. It made a lot of noise in Chicago but had little national impact. Teamed up with the Dells again, Garrett came out with a remake of the old Heatbeats standard, "Thousand Miles Away," in December 1967. It was produced to perfection by Andre Williams, but the song got no more than local sales. Despite the lack of national chart action, Garrett's records gave her some recognition in selected markets across the country and she managed to tour based on her recordings.

In 1968 Garrett and Williams joined a new company, Duo, owned by distributors Jack White and Seymour Greenspan. Garrett immediately achieved success with the Williams-composed "One Woman." The song with its relaxed vocals over a gentle lope was her most subtle and sophisticated effort, but for whatever reason it did not break big. During the 1970s,

Williams recorded Garrett on various labels, including Chess again, without any real success. By the mid-1970s Jo Ann Garrett was out of the music business.

The Dells

"I don't know whether or not we came to our singing natural, or what it was, but maybe because we were so together we never really had to do hard, drawn-out practices on songs. It just always seemed to fall into place for us. We never had to plan that much for a recording session. What we would do was learn the melody to get the right background, then we would go into the studio and that was the magic."[24] So the great baritone lead Marvin Junior of the Dells explained what most observers had always assumed about this exceptionally talented group, which was formed in Harvey, Illinois, in 1953. The original members were Johnny Funches (tenor lead), Verne Allison (second tenor), Mickey McGill (baritone), Chuck Barksdale (bass), and Marvin Junior (baritone lead). Throughout the 1950s they achieved moderate fame with such vocal harmony classics as "Dreams of Contentment" (1955) and "Oh What a Nite" (1956) on the Vee Jay label.[25]

In late 1958 the Dells' career was temporarily halted when the group fell apart following a serious automobile accident. It took a while before the singers could be reunited, which happened in 1960. Funches, however, could not be persuaded to come back. Marvin Junior, who had been singing most of the leads on the road, became the sole lead, and the group obtained first tenor Johnny Carter, who had been a member of the Flamingos earlier. The new Dells ensemble soon developed the patented Dells style of the soul era, using the trade-off leads of Junior's gruff baritone and Carter's mewling falsetto tenor. Reflecting the greater forcefulness of soul music, Junior usually sang the principal lead, but more often than not Carter would come in with a sweet-sounding answering lead.

The Dells' return to recording was a bit inauspicious. They came out with four releases on the Argo label, but only one, "The (Bossa Nova) Bird," sold anything. The song was punchy and forceful and was a perfect vehicle to introduce the Dells to the era of soul. The record was a big hit in Chicago and several other locales but unfortunately went to only the thirty-eight position and lasted only five weeks on *Cash Box*'s r&b chart.

While at Argo, the Dells were also doing extensive work in Chicago at cocktail lounges and jazz clubs. "We were singing predominately jazz," said Barksdale. "One of the clubs we worked at was the Pro-Bowl in Buffalo Grove [a Chicago suburb], which was owned by a football player, Rick Casares. We worked up there for about six to eight weeks, five, six nights a week, driving from Harvey with the Sonny Cox Trio. We were a lounge-type act then."[26] Much of what the Dells were doing then was a style of singing called modern harmony, which used big-band arrangements for singing by vocal ensembles.

The Dells returned to Vee Jay in 1964, and the four singles the company put out on the group were an uneven lot. Only "Stay in My Corner," which made it on the lower reaches of the charts in June 1965, was worthwhile. Vee Jay, however, was in economic difficulty and was rapidly going downhill and could not give the record the push it deserved.

In 1966 the Dells moved back to Chess, and there they immediately came out with two fine records, "Thinking about You," a kicking number with a steady lope that sold briskly in Chicago in the summer, and "Run for Cover," a great rousing up-tempo song that hit locally in December. Referring to the two songs, Barksdale cracked, "After you got outside of Gary, Indiana, they were out of earshot. No airplay. We thought they were big until we saw the so-called royalty statements."[27]

In the summer of 1967, Chess took the Dells out of the hands of their usual producer and arranger, Billy Davis and Phil Wright, and gave them to producer Bobby Miller and arranger Charles Stepney. Said McGill:

> Bobby Miller doesn't get a lot of credit. Before Bobby Miller, we were cutting tunes, some were good and some weren't so good. He came along and Leonard Chess and all the producers and writers had a meeting and Chess said, "We got to get some hit records on the street." So Chess told these producers to take whatever artist they wanted, and you either got to get a hit on these artists or else your job is on the line. So Bobby Miller said, "Well, give me the Dells." So Billy Davis and all those guys, they all started laughing, and said "You got them, because you can't get a hit on them no way!"
>
> So Bobby Miller called me on the phone. He said, "Listen, we're going to start rehearsing tomorrow and we're going to cut a bunch of hit records. I got a lot of songs, a lot of ideas." So we got together. Bobby brought us these songs, "Ooo I Love You" and "There Is." The guy was a fantastic songwriter. Most of the songs he wrote were good clear songs with good lyrics.
>
> Bobby Miller was our producer but he received a lot of help from our arranger, Charles Stepney. He would go to Stepney and they would collaborate. Stepney was a talented musician and would put in all the right chords and the whole bit. We would rehearse with Bobby, and when we would get to a session, Stepney would show us a chord he had changed and whatnot. We can sing any chord and would sing what we were suppose to sing. We had more

hits with Bobby and Charles together than with anybody else. We had the perfect combination, good arranger and a great songwriter, and that combination is hard to find.[28]

And that combination resulted in a tremendous payoff for the group, the *There Is* album, from 1968. The album contained six hit songs. Besides the earlier mentioned "Run for Cover," three other up-tempo songs—"There Is" and "Show Me" (released back-to-back in January 1968), and "Wear It on Your Face" (March 1968)—were likewise outstanding cuts. The cream of the up-tempo cuts was "There Is," but the Dells were not much impressed with it at first. As Barksdale related to interviewer Wayne Jones, "'There Is' was written by Bobby Miller. Now Bobby was one of those songwriters who did not have the greatest musical timing in the world. He had such bad timing that the rhythm for 'There Is' was what we called 'cut time.' So, when we first heard the song our reaction was, what the hell is this? But the lyric content was great. When we finally took it into the studio to record it, Stepney put the song in its proper perspective with the right meter, et cetera, and it came out fantastic."[29]

The *There Is* LP was also packed with ballads with great lush, mellifluous harmonies, including two that charted, "Ooo, I Love You" (August 1967) and a remake of their Vee Jay song, "Stay in My Corner" (number one on the r&b charts in June 1968). Barksdale explained how the "Stay in My Corner" remake came about:

> We brought up redoing the song to Stepney. The song was quite long so Charles suggested we cut it down. We said no, stating that we preferred to stay with the long version, which was the exact same way we were singing it in concerts. We ended up recording 'Stay in My Corner' in its entirety, six minutes and ten seconds long. The deejays picked up on playing that one from the album and it started getting more and more requests. I remember we had just come back from overseas and we were in South Carolina where Leonard Chess called us to tell us how well the record was received and that it just jumped into the top-hundred pop chart at the number forty-two position with a bullet. I was so surprised, I asked to make sure he was talking about the right record. He said the pressing plants were having difficulty keeping up with the demand.[30]

"Stay in My Corner," surprisingly, became a big pop hit and was the Dells' first big-seller to the white audience.

There Is ranked as one of the finest examples that worked 1950s harmonies into 1960s soul production. The Chess in-house production system was peaking at the time and was able to supply the best collection of songs the Dells ever put out. Said McGill, "*There Is* is fabulous. That album was so great that when it came out, it took us completely by surprise, because at that time we were working in Chicago a little bit. We immediately began a tour, we went to the Apollo. We left the Apollo and went to the Howard in Washington, D.C. By the time we got through working in D.C., which was about two weeks later, we had the biggest album on the East Coast. And it scared us, because it got so big so fast, and we had been out of the mainstream of having hit records. When we looked around, we were getting work and a lot of gigs."[31]

When Chess released the second Dells album in late 1968, few expected another *There Is*. Such albums as that are rarities. However, no one expected the drop in quality would be so precipitous as with the *Always Together* LP. The title single was a fine ballad, but much of its great chart success in the fall of 1968 was due to the spillover from the "Stay in My Corner" hit earlier in the summer. "Does Anybody Know I'm Here," "Hallways of My Mind," and "I Can't Do Enough" were other cuts from the LP that charted in 1969, so the album was a solid commercial success.

Miller and Stepney continued their commercially winning ways with the *Love Is Blue* album from 1969. The album contained only one original song, but it produced three strong chart entries during the year. The first, an "I Can Sing a Rainbow/Love Is Blue" medley, raced up the r&b and pop charts in the spring. Next was "Oh, What a Nite," a remake of their classic doowop, and it topped the r&b chart in the summer. "Sitting on the Dock of the Bay" followed in the fall, and it was the Otis Redding hit dreadfully speeded up in Dells style. Another cut from the LP, "Glory of Love," got a belated release and entered the lower reaches of the r&b chart in January 1971. Despite the album's considerable success, it was a most distasteful effort. Every song was given the most overblown and inflated arrangement to milk the most drama possible from each song. Each cut featured pretentious breaks to allow Junior to shout declaratively his lyrics over the thunderous background.

At the end of 1969, the Dells came out with perhaps their second-best Miller/Stepney collaboration, *Like It Is, Like It Was*. As with the *There Is* LP, it was a marvelous blend of doowop harmonies with the feeling of soul. One side featured oldie tunes, and the other, new tunes. The new side produced the most successful single, "Oh What a Day," a superb McGill neo-doowop that utilized the background riffing of "Time Makes You Change," the Dells' up-tempo classic from 1957.

The Dells' next single was a double-sided hit, featuring the Miller tune, "Open Up Your Heart," a peppy number from the new side, and "Nadine," a fantastic rendition of the Coronets' tune from the oldie side. In Chicago, "Nadine" got the most play, but in the rest of the country "Open Up My

Heart" got the stronger play. "Long Lonely Nights" (oldie side), the old Lee Andrews hit, did mildly well upon its release in the spring of 1970. This was the last record the Dells did with their producer, Bobby Miller, and ranks as the last recording on the Dells before the company moved to New York.

The Radiants

The Radiants fittingly represented the early 1960s, when the shuffle beats and the doowops were giving way to the new sound of soul. The group was an important pacesetter in this transition, along with such outstanding groups as the Sheppards and the Impressions. The group created a spirited and highly melodic yet sophisticated form of rhythm and blues. The story of the Radiants began in 1960, when Maurice McAlister distilled a vocal group from the members of the Greater Harvest Baptist Church youth choir. He sang the lead and first tenor, and rounded out the group with Wallace Sampson (baritone), Jerome Brooks (second tenor), Elzie Butler (bass), and Charles Washington (first tenor). The group sang gospel and toured the local churches, but the singers were also working on secular material. After a few months, Green McLauren, also a member of the youth choir, replaced Washington.[32]

By 1961, the Radiants had given up gospel completely and had recorded a demo of McAlister-written songs. They sent it to a number of recording companies, including Chess and Motown, but none expressed interest. Said McAlister, "We had been trying, walking up and down Michigan Avenue, which was Record Row then, going to companies. We went to Chess four or five times, but they never did have the time for us. They said, 'Leave your tape,' this, that, and the other, you know."[33] Added Brooks, "Fortunately, Lee Jackson, our manager, knew Leonard Chess. Lee was a supervisor for a meat-packing company, and he used to go to Chess Records and talk to Leonard. A lot of time he would bring him a thing of bologna or salami, so they got pretty tight. Then he introduced us to Leonard by the way of the demo."[34] Said Sampson, "They signed us up, and we recorded our first session in May of 1962. We had a release out in August of the same year, 'One Day I'll Show You' and 'Father Knows Best.' "[35]

The Radiants' first release, though no blockbuster, was a solid double-sided hit. "Father Knows Best," which the company deemed the A side, was essentially a Miracles-styled variation of the group's big hit, "Shop Around," but several steps down from the original. It did well in Chicago and a few other locales. "One Day I'll Show You" was a medium-tempo cross between doowop and soul, with McAlister's forceful lead strongly supported by full-bodied chorusing. The song ranks with the Radiants' best and is McAlister's all-time favorite.

In February 1963 the Radiants followed up with "Heartbreak Society." The song was first-rank Radiants' material, but the record failed to make an impact in the market. McAlister's arresting timbre, plus a great hook of a refrain, in which the rest of the guys riffed behind his chanting of "hearrt...breeaaak," combined to make the record a richly rewarding listening experience. "Shy Guy," a fast rocking tune, was the group's next release, in October 1963. In Chicago, it made the top-forty radio stations and became a hit in the city's dance halls. "Shy Guy" introduced a new member of the group, Frank McCollum, a replacement for McLauren, who entered the Army in the latter part of 1963.

In 1964 the Radiants began experiencing internal difficulties, fell into disarray, and broke up. Only McAlister and Sampson were left to continue the group. At that time, however, a fellow choir member and organist at the Greater Harvest Church, Leonard Caston, Jr., had just gotten out of the Army. The three got together and formed a new Radiants ensemble.

The three-man lineup inaugurated its career with a bang when "Voice Your Choice" was released in November 1964. Using three-part harmony and the switch-off lead made famous by the Impressions, the Radiants created an instant classsic in Chicago-style soul music. The song, written by McAlister and Gerald Sims, became number one in Chicago and the group's most successful nationwide hit.

The Radiants strongly followed early in 1965 with "It Ain't No Big Thing," a masterpiece composed by McAlister. Here the switch-off lead was exceedingly pronounced and immensely effective, and even though the song was based on the Impressions' format, the Radiants' manner of doing it was distinctive enough to give them a unique sound. The marvelous vocal interplay of the song worked like a constant flux of voices slipping in and out of the musical mix, a technique later copied by the progressive r&b groups of the 1970s, Sly and the Family Stone, and Earth, Wind and Fire. Not coincidentally, Maurice White, the drummer behind EW&F, played on all the Radiants' sessions.

In 1965 Caston decided to leave the group to work in-house as a songwriter and producer. Replacing Caston was James Jameson, who appeared with McAlister and Sampson on the next release, "Baby You've Got It," in March 1966. The Motownish record was a departure from the Radiants' sound and, frankly, was overproduced and not very good.

McAlister left after "Baby You've Got It," and the group was without its lead and principal songwriter. This loss theoretically should have ended the group, but it did not, and why it did not is a little complicated to tell. Chess had recorded a group called the Confessions in 1965. The group had a terrific gospelly lead in Mitchell Bullock, whose voice was somewhat similar in timbre to McAlister's. They recorded a great single, "(Don't It Make You) Feel Kind of Bad," but before Chess could release the song, the group broke up, and the record ended up on the shelf. Chess had one singer, a terrific record, and no group.

Meanwhile, Sampson and Jameson were left adrift after McAlister left the group. Chess still had a valuable asset in the Radiants' name, but it lacked the Radiants group. Billy Davis then suggested the obvious—that Sampson and Jameson team up with Bullock; to round out the group, he added Victor Caston, the younger brother of Leonard.

The first release of the new Radiants, in early 1967, was "(Don't It Make You) Feel Kinda Bad," which was the original Confessions' record. The record lasted only two weeks on *Billboard*'s national r&b chart, but it was a much bigger hit than that in Chicago and a number of other cities.

Leonard Caston wrote for and produced the new material for the Radiants, but his only success was "Hold On," a true piece of inspiration that lasted seven weeks on the national r&b chart in the spring of 1968. When follow-up productions by Caston and then Bobby Miller all bombed, the Radiants left Chess in 1969. The group broke up in 1972.

The Washington, D.C., Connection

One would think that Washington, D.C., with its large black population, would have developed a significant rhythm-and-blues recording industry, or that at least, nearby Baltimore would have. But neither city did; they formed the largest urban complex in the North without a substantial regional recording industry. Most of the talent that developed in D.C. gravitated to New York City or Philadelphia in search of recording opportunities. Chess, surprisingly, was able to draw a number of D.C. artists within its orbit almost from its inception. During the late 1950s, after Bo Diddley moved to the city, the company's contacts with its artists intensified. Diddley brought, most significantly, Billy Stewart to the company. Besides Stewart, Chess got a later Moonglows ensemble, the Knight Brothers, and the Four Jewels.

Billy Stewart had an unforgettable, unique style of vocalizing, which involved a stuttering, rapid-fire explosion of words. Nicknamed "Motor-mouth," he called his style "doubling of words," which he said came from his early interest in calypso. Despite having achieved substantial r&b fame and recognition, Stewart remains virtually unknown among rock critics, let alone among rock fans. And this is inexplicable, because Stewart was the kind of r&b performer who rock critics went out of their way to praise. He stood apart because he was more than an entertainer, he was an artist who created a thoroughly original and intensely personal style of singing. His vocalizing was exceedingly effective in conveying the bittersweet emotions of his lyrics. Many of those lyrics involved what is reportedly the classic paradox of the obese person (as Stewart was), who is outwardly jolly but who is crying inside. He made a listener feel in his wistful, yearning songs that he wanted to love someone and ached to have someone love him. Clearly, Stewart was a first-rank r&b artist, despite the small number of hits to his credit.[36]

Born William Larry Stewart on March 24, 1937, in Washington, D.C., he grew up in the capital and spent all his adult life there. Stewart's first involvement with music was through his mother's church, and during his early teen years he was a member of his mother's gospel group, the Stewart Gospel Singers. His mother also encouraged Stewart to develop an interest in the piano, the first instrument on which he became proficient. He attended Armstrong High in D.C.

Stewart was discovered by fellow D.C. resident Bo Diddley. While the rock 'n' roll legend was appearing at the Capital Arena Theater, he noticed Stewart amusing himself on the piano backstage. Much impressed with what he heard, Diddley asked the young man to join his band. While he was with Diddley, for a period of several years, Stewart developed his talents beyond piano playing and singing, becoming competent on the organ, bass, and drums as well. His tenure as a journeyman talent obviously did much to nurture his later, far more successful career.

Through Diddley, Stewart got an opportunity to record only a few months after joining the band. His record, called "Billy's Blues," which came out in July 1956, was a pretty raw effort, but one could see the seed of what would become a much better talent. For OKeh Records in 1957 he recorded two numbers, "Billy's Heartache" and "Baby, You Are My Only Love," backed by a D.C. group, the Marquis. Both songs were nice efforts— the Marquis backed him splendidly—and because of Stewart's wistful vocals one could already appreciate his personal approach to a song.

Stewart did not record for another five years. In 1962 he contracted with Chess Records again. The first release for the company, in May 1962, was "Reap What You Sow," a fine debut, which he had recorded with his road band. Not only did the song exhibit his classic doubling of words, it also revealed his songwriting skills, a talent evident on virtually all his subsequent hits. The song made both the pop and r&b charts.

Stewart's next success came in September 1963 with the gently rolling, atmospheric ballad "Strange Feeling," in which he employed to perfection his doubling of words. He confessed he has "lived his life in a sad world," but finding the right girl has changed his life around. The song was easily one of the outstanding releases of 1963.

In March 1964 Stewart followed up with a superb up-tempo tune, "Count Me Out," written and recorded by Chess studio talent. Notwithstanding, "Count Me Out" was typical Stewart, a song in which he expressed all his insecurities as a lover. The song proved to be a big seller in Chicago, but elsewhere it failed to make an impact.

Stewart released his best and most famous song, the lovely "I Do Love You," in February 1965. It was a terrifically etched ballad in which all the ingredients, lead vocals, choruses, and instrumental support, coalesced into a perfect record. Stewart expressed his insecure feelings that the girl he loved will not stay true. He prayed, he got on his knees to plead. He had no self-assurance at all, but nevertheless he always expressed a joyous feeling of hope.

Stewart's genius was recognized by the public, who made "I Do Love You" his most successful record ever in the r&b market. It lasted twenty-one weeks and went as high as number six on the *Billboard* survey. Although the record was also listed on the magazine's pop chart, it made the listing solely on the strength of r&b sales. The record was too subtle to reach a crossover audience.

Before "I Do Love You" left the charts, another Stewart masterpiece, "Sitting in the Park," entered. In this song he wallowed in self-pity again while sitting in the park anxiously awaiting for his girl to show up for their date. Musically, the ballad was much in the same vein as "I Do Love You," down to the familiar-sounding guitar intro, but "Park" employed less of the word-doubling than usual. It was Stewart's second-most successful single on the r&b charts, lasting thirteen weeks and going as high as position four.

Despite the success Chess was having with Stewart, it was a struggle to get him into the studio, partly because the singer found touring more lucrative than record royalties. And when Billy Davis got him into the studio, he never came in with a finished song, preferring to work it to completion with the studio musicians.[37] Sometimes the product of this method was inspired, and sometimes dismal.

In the summer of 1966, in what perhaps might be seen as a desperate but inspired move following three failed original compositions, Stewart came out with a speeded-up remake of his favorite old standard, "Summertime." Never was the doubling of the words more pronounced, never was the name "motormouth" more applicable; this recording was both exaggerated and quintessential Billy Stewart.

"Summertime" was Stewart's third-most successful single on the r&b chart, lasting eleven weeks and going as high as the seven position. Strangely, though the record was not his best, it garnered the singer his first real pop recognition. On the *Billboard* pop chart, "Summertime" reached as high as position ten. His success with the crossover audience with "Summertime" but not with "I Do Love You" was telling evidence that the music on r&b radio in the mid-1960s was far more nuanced and subtle than the standard fare on top-forty radio. In the years hence, rock critics would primarily identify Stewart with "Summertime," and as all Stewart fans know, they missed the mark.

In October 1966 Stewart came out with the old Doris Day standard, "Secret Love," which followed the same formula as "Summertime." Though not as good and a little too calculated in its intentions, "Secret Love" was still able to get Stewart considerable pop play and recognition.

Stewart refused to do any more standards after "Secret Love." Explained Davis to writer Adam White, "He wanted to go back to his own material. In fact, he insisted. It's like a lot of artists who become successful and realize there's more money to be made from their own songs; economics become part of the struggle."[38] But Stewart was never again able to come up with hit songs of his own.

"Cross My Heart" returned Stewart to the charts in October 1967 with a backward glance at the singer's ballad style. The Chess composing team marvelously evoked Stewart's writing style of the "I Do Love You" era. "Cross My Heart" lasted eight weeks on *Billboard*'s r&b chart but went only as high as the thirty-four position. It was the last hit the singer ever had. Stewart died in an automobile accident while on tour in the Carolinas in 1970.

The early 1960s saw the emergence of a new entity in r&b music, the impassioned gospelly duos, the most significant being the Righteous Brothers and Sam and Dave. Among these groups that brought black music into the soul era were the Knight Brothers, Richard (Dunbar) and Jimmy (Diggs). Dunbar (born May 31, 1939) and Diggs (born ca. 1937) were natives of Washington, D.C. Their one significant hit was "Temptation 'Bout to Get Me," from 1965, but both singers over the years were associated with a sizable body of music. Both were veterans of the D.C. vocal-group scene and recorded a few records during the 1950s, but without much success.[39]

In 1963 the Knight Brothers were signed to Chess. Their first three releases were recorded in D.C. and New York City, and all bombed despite the excellence of some of the sides. The company brought the duo to Chicago to record in 1964. The payoff was one of the most magnificent records ever to come out of Chess, "Temptation 'Bout to Get Me," produced by Billy Davis. The song combined a superb arrangement highlighted by a French horn intro, with one of the greatest singing jobs by a duo ever to appear on wax. The soulful lead by Dunbar, the answering of Diggs, and the harmonizing of the two voices resulted in a simply perfect record. It lasted eight weeks on *Billboard*'s r&b chart and went as high as position twelve in the spring of 1965. Although it was the Knight Brothers' only chart record, it gave them lots of work and they toured extensively.

During 1964–65, Diggs was also working with another D.C. group, the Carltons. They recorded three records, mostly in the style of the Impressions, for Chess's Argo subsidiary. The members of the group on record were lead singer Larry Bell, Jerry Norris, and Jimmy Diggs. When the group made live appearances, however, a fellow whom Dunbar recalled only as "Bo" took Diggs's place.[40]

The first two releases—"Can't You Hear My Heart Beat" and "Hey Mr. Lonesome"—were simply Impressions sound-alikes in which the Mayfield-type high-tenor harmonies were answered by a Gooden-type bass. The Carltons last release, in 1965, "I'm a Man," featured a good soulful lead that was more natural-sounding than the high tenor used on the previous records. The Carltons had found a sound, their sound, but unfortunately, as with the other releases, the record did not hit.

Meanwhile, the Knight Brothers continued to record for Chess and later for Jerry Butler's Fountain Productions with releases on Mercury. They got no other hits, however, and broke up in 1969. Richard Dunbar established a career for himself in the 1970s and 1980s as a member of a revived Orioles vocal group.

The Four Jewels were a group of girls who came to Chess as a result of the company's D.C. pipeline via Bo Diddley and Billy Stewart. The girls—Carrie Mingo, Sandra Bears, Grace Ruffin, and Margie Clark—first sang together in the school choir at Roosevelt High before deciding to form a group called the Impalas.[41] The girls knew a lot about harmony—they came up with one of the most angelic blends of voices I have ever heard. Clark and Mingo did most of the leads and both were in the teen soprano mode, with voices that sounded clear, sweet, and innocent.

The group's first release, recorded in Bo Diddley's basement studio, was not successful upon its release on Checker in 1961. The following year the girls came under the wing of D.C. manager and producer Bob E. Lee, who composed most of the group's subsequent recordings. He persuaded them to change their name to the Four Jewels, and in early 1962 the group entered the studio and sang the Lee-composed "Loaded with Goodies," a wonderfully harmonized ballad led by Mingo. It was put out on the local Start label, and before the year was out two more records by the group came out on the label.

The Start records were not heard outside the Washington D.C./Baltimore area, but also in 1962 Lee got Chess interested in the group. The company brought the Four Jewels to Chicago to record a session on three Lee songs— "Dapper Dan," a harsh shouter with Ruffin as lead; "Time for Love," a lovely ballad with Mingo as lead; and "That's What They Put Erasers on

Pencils For," a bouncy and pleasingly strident number with Mingo as lead. But Chess was slow in putting out the records, releasing them during 1963–64 with no commercial success.

Then, as the Jewels, the group signed with the New York-based Dimension label in 1964 and recorded "Opportunity." It was a fine song that most decidedly had that Brill Building pop rock 'n' roll sound, in which the girls, especially Sandra Bears, effectively switched off the lead work. "Opportunity" was the group's only hit, going to position eighteen on *Cash Box*'s r&b chart in November 1964.

The St. Louis Connection

St. Louis was a valuable talent conduit for Chess during the soul years. The city was practically devoid of recording companies and to get on record the singers and musicians had to look elsewhere. From 1961 to 1964 Chess picked up three artists who would produce big hits for the company in the following years, Little Milton, Fontella Bass, and Bobby McClure. Although Milton and Bass had both recorded in St. Louis, teaming them up with Chess writers, arrangers, and producers made a world of difference for the artists. All three were associated with veteran sax player Oliver Sain, who directed Little Milton's band and then formed his own band employing Bass and McClure as vocalists.

Little Milton came to Chess as a respected blues artist and left the company as an average soul performer. But Chess was extremely beneficial for the bluesman's career, turning him into one of the country's biggest blues artists, almost equal in stature to such greats as B. B. King, Lowell Fulsom, and Bobby Bland. The company originally respected Milton's blues roots and built his reputation as a blues stylist along the lines of Bobby Bland's gospel-blues vocal stylings and B. B. King's guitar approach. The result was a whole spate of hits that captured the essence of 1960s urban blues. His last few years with the company, however, were more successful commercially than they were artistically as Milton was given soul-style songs and covers of soul hits to record.[42]

Little Milton was born Milton Campbell, Jr., on September 7, 1934, and like many blues greats he came out of the Mississippi Delta region in western Mississippi. He was born in Inverness but was raised on a farm between Greenville and Leland. At adolescence he learned to play the guitar, and a few years later, around 1950, he took up electric guitar. In 1953, Milton, under the aegis of Ike Turner, recorded his first sides for Sam Phillip's fledgling Sun label in Memphis. During 1956–57 he recorded a few more sides in Memphis for Les Bihari's Meteor label.

Billy Davis. As A&R man at Chess Records, Davis was the architect of the company's success in the soul market in the 1960s. His departure in 1968 left a void that was never adequately filled. Courtesy Billy Davis.

Etta James, early 1960s. James was Chess Records' first soul star. She began her career in Los Angeles in 1955. Courtesy MCA-Chess Records.

Jackie Ross, 1964. Ross's big hit was "Selfish One." Courtesy Maurice McAlister.

The Lovettes, 1962. This early version of the Gems included Raynard Miner, who became a standout writer during the 1960s. Left to right around Miner: Vandine Harris, Theresa Washum, Dorothy Hucklebee, Jessica Collins, and Bertha Watts.

The Gems, 1964. This grouping of the Gems included, left to right, Jessica Collins, Minnie Riperton, Dorothy Hucklebee, and Theresa Washum.

Jo Ann Garrett, 1966. "One Woman," recorded in 1968, was Garrett's most outstanding achievement.

The Dells. These singers were veterans of the 1950s when they went to Chess Records in the 1960s, but with a contemporary soul sound they became the company's biggest hitmakers.

The Radiants, 1964. This vastly underrated group made some of the best soul music to come out of Chess studios and Chicago. Clockwise from top left: Wallace Sampson, Maurice McAlister, and Leonard Caston, Jr.

Billy Stewart, late 1960s. Stewart was perhaps Chess Records' most original soul stylist. Courtesy MCA-Chess Records.

Fontella Bass, 1962. The young Fontella Bass started out in St. Louis before joining Chicago-based Chess Records. Courtesy Bill Greensmith/Fontella Bass.

Laura Lee, 1967. This Detroit-based singer was taken by Chess to Muscle Shoals, Alabama, to record, resulting in some great southern-style hits, notably "Dirty Man."

The Impressions, 1964. This is the classic lineup that recorded on ABC-Paramount some of the greatest Chicago-style soul songs of the 1960s. Left to right: Fred Cash, Curtis Mayfield, Sam Gooden.

The Fascinations, 1963. This Detroit-based group was recorded in Chicago by Curtis Mayfield, first for ABC-Paramount and then on Mayfield's own Mayfield label.

The Five Stairsteps, 1967.
Courtesy Richard Pack.

The Marvelows, 1965. Discovered
by ABC-Paramount arranger and
producer Johnny Pate, the
Marvelows went on to record "I
Do," which was later covered by
the J. Geils Band. Top, from left:
Melvin Mason and Frank Paden:
bottom, Sonny Stevenson, Jesse
Smith, and Johnny Paden.
Courtesy Herb Turner.

Not long after recording for Meteor, Milton moved to East St. Louis, Illinois. While in the St. Louis area he formed a band and had Oliver Sain, a long-time friend from Mississippi, direct the organization. In 1958 Bob Lyons, a station manager at local station KATZ, heard Milton doing a live broadcast on the remote from an East St. Louis nightclub. Impressed, he formed the Bobbin label in partnership with Milton to record the singer. From 1958 to 1961 Lyons released fourteen sides on the artist, but the first release, "I'm a Lonely Man," was the most sizable hit. The late-1950s sides of Milton show a talented blues musician whose clean, elegant guitar picking owed a debt to T-Bone Walker and B. B. King.

In 1961 Milton signed with Chess, and the company started putting him out on its Checker subsidiary. The first few releases were basically leased masters from Lyons, one of which, "So Mean to Me," a terrific number in the Bobby Bland mode, made it on the national charts in 1962.

Milton and Sain and the band split in 1963, and the bluesman began recording in Chicago. The release that made him a star was a cover of Bland's "Blind Man," a national hit for Milton in 1964. The following year he came out with the biggest hit of his career, "We're Gonna Make It," which shot to the number one position and lasted fifteen weeks on *Billboard*'s r&b chart in the spring.

During the mid-sixties Milton recorded many successful sides in the urban blues mode, and these were captured on two excellent albums, *We're Gonna Make It* (1965), produced by Billy Davis, and *Little Milton Sings Big Blues* (1966), produced by Gene Barge. By the late 1960s and early 1970s, however, the company felt that black people were moving away from blues and so it had Milton record soul songs, such as "Baby I Love You" (a cover of a Jimmy Holiday hit) and "Somebody's Changin' My Sweet Baby's Mind" (a Tyrone Davis–styled number). Chess succeeded in keeping Milton on the charts at great sacrifice. His lovely blues guitar was rarely heard and he often seemed out of his element. Most of the soul records were produced by Barge or Stepney.

In 1971 Milton could not see eye to eye with Chess at contract renewal time and he left for Stax, the company based in Memphis. It was obvious that when Chess lost an artist of Milton's stature—in all probability because they could not match the offer that Stax was able to provide—the company was faltering. At Stax, Milton returned to making blues records for a while, and throughout the remainder of his career this artist would shift back and forth between recording blues and recording soul. His most memorable records remain those he recorded for Chess in the mid-1960s.

Fontella Bass was the daughter of gospel singer Martha Bass, a member of the famed Clara Ward Singers and then a soloist of some note. Fontella was born July 3, 1940, in St. Louis, and at the age of four she was already being coached by her mother. The next year she was playing piano at funerals, and by adolescence she was playing churches throughout the St. Louis area.[43]

During Bass's teen years, secular music began to beckon her. With the connivance of some sympathetic uncles, she got around her mother's ban on secular music by sneaking out of her house to play nightclubs. After graduating from Golden High in 1958 she began performing more openly. In 1961 while working for the Leon Claxton Show, Oliver Sain discovered her and brought her into the Little Milton Band as a pianist and chorus singer only. Milton did not want another feature vocalist competing with him. Bass played piano behind Little Milton recordings in the early 1960s on Bobbin and Checker. Lyons heard her sing at a show when she was temporarily standing in for Milton and was persuaded by the talent he saw to record her on four sides in 1962, but the recordings didn't do anything.

In 1963 Oliver Sain and Little Milton got into their spat and Sain took the band, reorganizing it as the Oliver Sain Review with Bass and Bernard Mosley as featured vocalists. Soon Mosley was replaced by Bobby McClure. In January 1964 Sain fired Bass for not making a gig. Not unhappy about being fired, Bass took the opportunity to move up to Chicago and there she contacted Chess Records, who immediately signed her up as an artist.

Bass's first recordings at Chess were with Bobby McClure, who Chess had signed a few months after her. Ironically, Sain was hired by Chess to produce Bass and McClure, both as solo artists and as a duo. The teaming of Bass and McClure was proposed by Leonard Chess. The first record, "Don't Mess Up a Good Thing," written by Sain, was recorded in June 1964, and released in January 1965. The song married a fast beat devised from a popular dance of the day, the Uncle Willie, with switch-off leads by Fontella and Bobby and a swinging sax break courtesy of Gene Barge. The song was released on the Checker label and lasted fifteen weeks and went as high as position five on *Billboard*'s r&b chart, an impressive debut. The duo followed with "You'll Miss Me (When I'm Gone)," which reprised the switch-off-lead approach with great effect. The Davis and Barge composition lasted six weeks and went to position twenty-seven on the r&b chart in the summer of 1965. The pairing of Bass and McClure, however, did not last beyond the duo's first tour together.

Bass's solo career at Chess was launched with the biggest hit of her career and one of the best records to come out of Chess during those years, "Rescue Me." The record was a solid crossover hit, lasting thirteen weeks on *Billboard*'s pop chart and going to position four. On the r&b chart, the record lasted an outstanding nineteen weeks and went to the number one position. With its riveting bass-line intro that magnificently layers on instruments, to Bass's great soprano lead, to the electrifying call-and-response chorusing, "Rescue Me" was a terrific example of the Chess studio system at its finest. Typically, the song came out of a woodshedding situation. ("Woodshedding," as rhythm-and-blues musicians use the term, refers to practicing, but always with the hope that something creative would be the end product.) One Saturday in August 1965, Bass was sitting in a rehearsal studio with producers-writers Carl Smith and Raynard Miner. They were fooling around with the song when arranger Phil Wright walked in, and the ensuing four-way jam session brought forth "Rescue Me." Davis produced the side, and on the flip the company put "The Soul of a Man," a song written and produced by Sain and done earlier. It was a great gospelized blues that did not deserve to be buried on a B side, and was so good that the *Billboard* reviewer singled it out as the hit side.

Following "Rescue Me," the Smith-Miner-Davis team came up with several undistinguished follow-ups—"Recovery" (January 1966), "I Surrender" (May 1966), and "Safe and Sound" (August 1966). The titles alone tell the lack of imagination that went into those songs. They all reprised the bubbly sound of "Rescue Me," and the first sold very well, making both the r&b and the pop charts and sustaining Bass's career through 1966.

While at Chess, Bass got the company to record her mother for their gospel line. Martha Bass recorded four albums for the company. Fontella had only one album on Chess, the quickly recorded *The New Look* LP from November 1965. It contained "Rescue Me," "Soul of a Man," and filler in the form of covers of contemporary soul hits.

Bass left Chess in 1967 and signed a deal with Jerry Butler's Fountain Productions, and later she moved to Paula and then Epic. Despite recording regularly, she never had another hit. Occasionally she appeared as a vocalist on jazz albums recorded by her husband, Lester Bowie, trumpeter in the famed Art Ensemble of Chicago.

Bobby McClure did not have much of a career after he and Fontella Bass split. In 1966, he scored a national hit, "Peak of Love," which lasted an impressive ten weeks and went to position sixteen on *Billboard*'s r&b chart. He never had another chart record, but his expressive tenor voice was put to good use on a number of hard-soul records over the years.[44]

McClure was born April 21, 1942, in Chicago, but at the age of two moved with his parents to East St. Louis. McClure began singing gospel at the age of nine, fronting a group of ladies called the Spirit of Illinois. He sang gospel until his early teens, sharing the stage with some of the greatest names in gospel music. In 1963 McClure began fronting a local r&b band, the Big Daddy Jenkins Band, which played the entire St. Louis-area circuit of clubs, such as the Red Top, Manhattan, and Paramount.

After about a month with the Jenkins organization, McClure was hired by Oliver Sain for his review. In mid-1964, Sain began working with Chess

Records, and McClure signed a recording contract with the company and moved to Chicago. The first fruits of the association were the two duets he recorded with Bass. In 1966 he came out with his first solo release, on Checker, "I'm Not Ashamed," a solid southern-style soul ballad written by Sain. The record failed and Davis took over producing McClure and came up with "Peak of Love." With McClure shouting declaratively over an aggressive blues-style riff, the DeSanto-and-Davis–composed song probably appealed to the same adult working-class constituency that was buying blues records.

The following year, McClure came out with a song Caston wrote and produced, "Baby You Don't Love Me," a mid-tempo, southern-style ballad. The song had lots of appeal but it bombed, and McClure not long after left Chess Records. None of his later recording associations panned out for McClure, who continued to make records into the 1980s.

Jazz and other Connections

For many years Chess had a jazz catalogue that helped sustain the company with steady album sales. Its jazz stable included such notable artists as Ahmad Jamal, James Moody, Sonny Stitt, Yusef Lateef, and the Ramsey Lewis Trio. Vocalists close to the jazz tradition included Lorez Alexandria, Jean Dushon, and Marlena Shaw. When these artists recorded a jazz cut that the company felt might have appeal in the r&b market, the company would release it as a single on its Argo (later Cadet) label. During the 1960s Chess got hits on the r&b charts from the Ramsey Lewis Trio and Marlena Shaw. For its jazz artists Chess employed different producers and arrangers; for example, Richard Evans arranged and produced Shaw, and Esmond Edwards produced and Evans arranged Ramsey Lewis records.

The Ramsey Lewis Trio for most of its history consisted of pianist Ramsey Lewis (born May 27, 1935, in Chicago), bassist Eldee Young (born January 7, 1936, in Chicago), and drummer Isaac "Red" Holt (born May 16, 1932, in Rosedale, Mississippi). The group came together as teenagers on the South Side in 1956. Through the urging of local jazz deejay Daddy-O Daylie, Chess signed the group and recorded them in December of 1956.[45]

The trio's eighteenth album, *The In Crowd*, a live recording of a May 1965 engagement at the Bohemian Caverns, Washington, D.C., yielded their first r&b hit, the title cut, in the summer of 1965. The instrumental was a stylish piano-driven, cocktail-lounge jazz cover of the Dobie Grey soul hit from earlier in the year, and not a great departure from the group's usual oeuvre. "The In Crowd" was such a hit, however—top-ten on both the r&b and pop charts—that the trio essentially reshaped itself as an r&b group specializing in instrumental renditions of pop hits. In quick succession came "Hang on Sloopy" (1965), "Hard Day's Night" (1966), and "Hi-Heel Sneakers" (1966), all chart hits.

Ironically, the success of the act served to break up the ensemble in the summer of 1966. Eldee Young and Red Holt departed to form the Young-Holt Trio with a new piano player, and Ramsey Lewis with the support of bassist Cleveland Eaton and session drummer Maurice White continued to put out highly successful records, notably "Wade in the Water" (1966), "Uptight" (1966), "Daytripper" (1966), and "One Two Three" (1967). The last record Chess released on Ramsey Lewis was in 1972, and thereafter he recorded for Columbia for many years.

Marlena Shaw produced the solo-vocalist version of the kind of music that Ramsey Lewis was doing, cocktail-lounge jazz. Shaw did the vocal counterparts of such jazz hits as Cannonball Adderley's "Mercy Mercy Mercy" and the Ramsey Lewis Trio's "Wade in the Water." She was born in 1944 and raised in New Rochelle, New York, and got her singing start in the church choir. In 1963 she began a professional career singing sophisticated pop in East Coast night spots, and in 1965 got on the Playboy Club circuit, which favored her cocktail-lounge jazz approach. While working at the Chicago Playboy Club in June 1966 she was discovered by Chess, and she signed to the Cadet label in September.[46]

Shaw's first single, "Wade in the Water," released near the end of 1966, got good play in Chicago but seemingly nowhere else. Her second single, "Mercy Mercy Mercy," became a national hit on *Billboard's* r&b chart in March 1967. Chess released six more singles and two albums on Shaw, but never got any more r&b success out of her. She left Chess in 1969 and built a moderately successful career during the 1970s, recording jazz and sophisticated pop albums, first on Blue Note and then on Columbia.

Chess had an extensive gospel catalogue, but very few of its r&b artists came from its gospel acts. One such singer who came through its gospel line was James Phelps, who sounded like a gospel-voiced Sam Cooke. Phelps was born and raised in Shreveport, Louisiana, and at a young age was singing gospel. In the early 1960s he was a member of the Chicago-based Clefs of Calvary, who came out with several albums while Phelps was their lead. From the Clefs of Calvary he graduated to the Soul Stirrers around 1963 to serve as their lead.[47]

The Soul Stirrers had spawned a number of great soul singers. Sam Cooke and later Johnnie Taylor both used the Soul Stirrers as a launching pad for a career in secular music. In 1965, Phelps with perhaps a bit of inspiration from the careers of Cooke and Taylor took the advice of a disc jockey to try his hand at soul music. On his very first release, "Love Is a Five-Letter Word," he got a hit, in May 1965. The song was written by Gene Barge, who gave it a heavy-on-the-horns production in the same manner that Little Milton was being recorded for the company. It was a terrific urban blues and has become a staple often heard in blues clubs.

Phelps followed up with the rousing "La De Da, I'm a Fool in Love," another Barge composition that was a strong local hit in July of 1965. When "Oh What a Feeling" did nothing upon its release in 1966, Phelps joined Fontana, a subsidiary of Mercury. He was not able to get another hit, however, and soon disappeared from the entertainment world.

Tony Clarke was one of the Chess songwriters who because of his success at writing hits for the company was given an opportunity to record. He was a protégé of Billy Davis, whom he had known in Detroit before the A&R chief moved to Chicago. Clarke was born in New York City, but not long after his birth his family moved to Detroit, where he grew up. He had been dabbling in the music business for several years when his break came in 1961 with the ascension of Davis to A&R director at Çhess. Davis began making use of Clarke's songwriting talents, and after two of his compositions, "Pushover" and "Two Sides (To Every Story)," became big hits for Etta James in 1963, Davis in effect rewarded Clarke by signing him to Chess as a recording artist.[48]

During his brief career, Clarke had twelve sides on Chess, from 1964 to 1966. His one smash, "The Entertainer," became a top-ten soul hit, lasting eleven weeks on *Billboard's* r&b chart in the spring of 1965. The record had all the ingredients of a quality hit—Clarke's superb lyrics that managed in a few words to convey strong images of the entertainer, an engaging melody, Wright's tasteful arrangements that made use of an organ to provide an appropriate calliope sound, and a nice lyrical guitar lead at the bridge. The flip, "This Heart of Mine," was another masterful song, but was unfortunately obscured by the success of "The Entertainer."

No hits followed, and Clarke left Chess in 1966 and moved to Hollywood, California. He formed his own production company, Earthquake Productions, and recorded "Ghetto Man," a minor West Coast hit. Clarke also tried to start a career in acting, and appeared in a bit part in a Sidney Poitier vehicle, *They Call Me MISTER Tibbs!* (1970). Not long afterwards, Clarke died in his Detroit home, killed by his wife while she defended herself from one of his frequent beatings.[49]

The Muscle Shoals Connection

The Muscle Shoals connection was a reversal of Chess's usual alliances. Instead of drawing upon talent from an area and bringing it to Chicago as the company did with D.C., Detroit, and St. Louis performers early in the 1960s, Chess in the late 1960s was taking its talent to Muscle Shoals, Alabama. The company's in-house production staff was not coming up with the hits as in previous years, and the people at Chess felt the Muscle Shoals studio was an ideal environment in which to record some of its acts—notably Bobby Moore and the Rhythm Aces, Laura Lee, Maurice and Mac, Mitty Collier, and Etta James. Chess also sent the famed New Orleans singer Irma Thomas to Muscle Shoals, and among her three releases the company got a minor hit with "Good to Me" in 1968.[50]

Muscle Shoals, as it was known in the record industry, is a shorthand term for an area in northwestern Alabama around Wilson Dam on the Tennessee River that has four close-by towns—Florence, Sheffield, Tuscumbia, and Muscle Shoals (the smallest of the four). The Fame Recording Studio, where Chess sent its acts, was actually located in Florence. Fame was founded in 1962 by Rick Hall, who developed a flourishing enterprise producing and recording black acts with white session musicians. Vee Jay and later New York-based Atlantic Records had developed fruitful alliances with Hall's operation. Atlantic especially benefitted during the years 1966–67 when it took Wilson Pickett and Aretha Franklin down to the studio and got million sellers with Muscle Shoals songs and productions. These developments did not go unnoticed at Chess. To get Hall interested in recording his acts, Leonard Chess provided Fame with a larger royalty rate for the producer (Hall) and more money up front than Atlantic ever did.[51]

Bobby Moore and the Rhythm Aces was the first Chess act to record at Muscle Shoals. The group was formed in Montgomery, Alabama, in 1961, and was essentially a cocktail-lounge band. On record, they performed a brand of light mid-tempo soul with lead vocals that had a nice soulful edge. The ensemble's members were Bobby Moore (tenor sax and leader), his son Larry Moore (alto sax), Chico Jenkins (guitar and lead vocals), John Baldwin, Jr. (drums), Joe Frank (bass guitar), and Clifford Laws (organ). In 1966 Moore and his group were signed to the Checker label.[52]

The group's first record was "Searching for My Love," which became a top-ten r&b hit for the company in early 1966. Chess followed with an album in June, which consisted of all Moore originals, and a sound-alike hit, "Try My Love Again," in December, all recorded at the Fame studio. A poor "Chained to Your Heart" briefly entered the charts in August 1967, but thereafter the company was not able to get hits on the group. Chess released its last Bobby Moore record in 1970.

Laura Lee was an ideal signing for Chess in 1967. She had a deep, mean-sounding gospelized vocal approach that matched perfectly the kind of songs and productions for which the company was noted. But ironically Chess felt compelled to send her to Muscle Shoals to get her hit recordings.[53]

Laura Lee was born on March 9, 1945, in Chicago, but was raised in Detroit. Her birth name was Laura Newton. At the age of nine, when her mother was going through a serious illness, she was adopted by her church's pastor and his wife, the Rev. E. A. Rundless and Ernestine Rundless. She then took the last name of Rundless. Steeped in gospel music early on, Lee by the time she was in her middle teens was, along with her adoptive mother, a member of the famed Meditation Singers (of which Della Reese was a member at one time).

In 1965, as Laura Lee, she made her first secular disc, on the Detroit-based Ric Tic label, after which she signed with Chess Records. Her first hit was "Dirty Man," but the genesis of the song reveals some of the trouble the company was having in the late 1960s. Said Lee, "I went into the studio in Chicago with Leonard Caston and Billy Davis, but we just couldn't get it together. There was something that I wasn't giving of myself. So they sent me down to Rick Hall in Muscle Shoals."[54] That Chess seemed unable to produce directly a hard-soul singer such as Lee was indicative that the company's in-house system was faltering.

"Dirty Man," a smoldering, down-home bluesy ballad written by Bobby Miller, lasted eleven weeks and went to postition thirteen on *Billboard's* r&b chart in the fall of 1967. Four other chart hits on Chess followed, all in the hard-soul style; the most notable were "Up Tight Good Man" in December 1967, and an intense remake of the Jerry Butler hit from 1963, "Need to Belong." In 1969 Lee had her last hit on Chess, and during the early 1970s she had a spate of hit records for Holland-Dozier-Holland's Hot Wax label, singing with the same deep intensity but featuring long recitations called "raps." By late 1970s Laura Lee had returned to the gospel field.

Maurice and Mac were a Chicago act made up of two former members of the Radiants, Maurice McAlister and Green McLauren. The duo demonstrated a superb mastery of the deep-southern soul style in McAlister's soulful high-pitched wailing counterpointed by McLauren's deeper gospel shouting. The duo was formed in late 1966 after McAlister had left the Radiants and McLauren had returned from the Army.[55]

The duo's first release, a soulful remake of the Ben E. King hit "So Much Love," failed to generate any excitement in 1967. However, they got a big southern hit in March 1968 with "You Left the Water Running," a cover of Barbara Lynn's hit from a year and a half earlier. Although the song only scraped the bottom of the *Cash Box* r&b chart for three weeks in the spring of 1968, McAlister said he made more money from it, touring the South, than he ever did performing with the Radiants. There were six more releases in the next two years, but Maurice and Mac were not able to repeat their initial success. The duo broke up in 1972, a year after leaving Chess.

After Chess saw the success it achieved by sending its lesser acts to Rick Hall, it made the logical decision to send its original soul artist, Etta James, down to the operation. James had not had a top-ten r&b hit since

1963 and many of her records during the 1964–66 period were poor efforts. As one of the company's principal artists, she needed some hits to sustain her career and, just as important, to uphold Chess as a viable hit-making organization. Muscle Shoals seemed to be the solution.

The result was the best album of James's career, *Tell Mama*, and a number of outstanding southern-soul style hits—"Tell Mama" (1967), "I'd Rather Go Blind" (1967), and "Security" (1968), the latter a cover of the Otis Redding hit that put the original to shame. The Muscle Shoals records were the last big hits in James's career. She stayed with Chess until the company's collapse in the mid-1970s, but the company had to rely increasingly on outside producers during its waning years and few of her records could properly be called Chicago records.

The End of Chess

The decline and fall of Chess seemed surprising at the time. During the late 1960s, the fortunes of the company was clearly on the upswing. In September 1966 Chess moved around the corner from its Michigan Avenue headquarters to 320 East Twenty-first Street.[56] The new location elated Davis: "It had a couple of studios, and I had offices there for all the writers and producers, *finally*, with a smaller demo rehearsal studio."[57] But within three years the whole operation would come unhinged.

Leonard Chess was becoming more involved with WVON, but Phil stayed more in contact with the company. Said Davis, "He dealt with a lot of the artists, and was involved in a lot of the signing of artists—artist relationships you might say."[58] Max Cooperstein was given more day-to-day control of the company, and Davis was becoming more dissatisfied with what was happening. Said he, "With Leonard Chess I was pretty close as friends. I sort of looked on him as a godfather the whole time I was there. He sort of treated me more as a son than as an employee. I was unhappy with a few things that were going on in management there at the time. Leonard was getting more into the business end of it, more into the radio station. And Max Cooperstein was going to run the company. I saw a lot of changes that were going to happen. I wasn't too sure I wanted to remain there."[59] He did not. Near the end of 1968 he left to join the McCann Erickson Advertising Agency as music director. The offer of an appealing job was sufficient encouragement for Davis to decide to leave.

The year 1969 proved to be immensely unsettling to the company. In January, the Chess brothers sold Chess (which included nineteen corporations) to General Recorded Tape (GRT) for $6.5 million plus twenty thousand shares of GRT common stock.[60] GRT probably should have demanded that the company knock some three million off the price tag to compensate for the departure of Billy Davis. A lot of the cohesion in the creative staff was undoubtedly lost when Davis left. In 1968 arranger Phil Wright left for Capitol Records, and in 1969 two of the better songwriters, Leonard Caston, Jr., and Raynard Miner, departed to go to Motown. The following year Bobby Miller also left for Motown. Earlier, in 1967, Carl Smith left and joined Carl Davis; add the loss of the songwriting and producing skills of Billy Davis and a hefty chunk of the creative staff was gone. Ralph Bass and Gene Barge jointly inherited the A&R job but they had to work with a greatly depleted font of talent.

Another huge blow to the company came with Leonard Chess's death in October 1969. The company was then put through a succession of executive changes, moves that undoubtedly did not help to provide stability. Leonard's son, Marshall, was named president, but he showed little interest in the job and was replaced early in 1970 with the record industry veteran Len Levy. Levy moved the executive offices to New York and reduced the Chicago headquarters to a branch office.

The Chicago staff members had lost their morale at this point. The creative people under Bass and Barge were no longer coming up with hits. Conceded Barge, "We went cold for a while, after the big surge of hits. We found ourselves in the hands of people who did not know how to run Chess Records. GRT gave you a good example of how to dismantle an excellent record company, because they had no idea what to do with it. They were in the tape business. They bought the company and they put insensitive people in control. We were just browbeaten to a point where we just didn't feel we were going to make it. We just had that feeling, and the promotion got bad, and the rapport on the street got bad with the jocks and the marketing people."[61]

There was a precipitous loss of artists. Billy Stewart died in 1970, but others were simply let go or decided to leave. Said Barge, "We could just stand there and look at [GRT] let the artists get away, one by one. Ramsey Lewis went to Columbia, Little Milton went to Stax, and the rest of the people flew the coop because they had the feeling that nothing was going to happen. They also lost a lot of jazz artists. They didn't try to keep the people they had. Eventually what happened was a great company was disintegrated."[62]

By the summer of 1972 Chicago music journalist Cary Baker was reporting that the Chess offices were "virtually empty." The Chess distribution company, National Record Distributors, and their pressing company, Midwest Pressing, had both shut down, and only the company's studio, Ter Mar, was operating with about a half dozen employees.[63] And the studio operation was not going great guns either, according to an *Illinois Entertainer* reporter: "Little by little it could be seen that the new Chess organization had few sentimental feelings for Chicago, the only home that the company had really known. The Chess studio in Chicago never received any new equipment and soon garnered a reputation as a second-rate studio. Cheap commercials and low budget bands became denizens of South Michigan."[64]

In March 1971 Marvin Schlacter, who was president-founder of Janus, was named president of Chess, and he brought the company a little stability.[65] He had a difficult task, as he explained to Michael Gray in 1973: "You have to understand what was happening in the company. GRT owned Chess, they also had their own label, the GRT label, and then they had this joint venture called Janus Records. So they experienced a great deal of difficulty because Leonard Chess died. They brought in Len Levy, who moved Chess Records from Chicago to New York and integrated it with GRT Records. So there was a great deal of turmoil and on top of it all, there was so much indecision as to what to do. The whole situation just deteriorated. Chess started losing money."[66] Schlacter consolidated all three companies into one corporation, but continued the separate label identities. With the reorganization he returned the company to profitability, at least for a time.

The one act that sustained Chess in the 1970s was the Dells. The year 1971 saw the Dells enter a new phase of their career with the first Chess album without the service of Bobby Miller, *Freedom Means*, produced and arranged by Charles Stepney. The album produced one outstanding single, "The Love We Had (Stays on My Mind)," an engaging ballad that proved to be the Dells' biggest hit since 1969. The direction Stepney was taking the Dells became more dubious in 1972, with the release of two poor albums, *The Dells Sing Dionne Warwicke's Greatest Hits* and *Sweet as Funk Can Be*, neither of which produced any hits. The problem was that Stepney was not a songwriter and the Chess stable at this point was devoid of top-notch songwriters. The Dells needed to be put into new hands.

Schlacter sent the group to Detroit producer Don Davis, who had already developed a good track record with Johnnie Taylor and with such Detroit-based acts as J. J. Barnes, Steve Mancha, and the Dramatics. Davis found the magic groove and the result was a creative and commercial rejuvenation for the Dells during their final years at Chess. Hits with Davis included the million-selling "Give Your Baby a Standing Ovation" (March 1972), "My Pretending Days Are Over" (September 1973), "I Miss You" (November 1973), and "Bring Back the Love of Yesterday" (1974). But the Dells, as was true of Chess at this time, were no longer strictly a Chicago phenomenon. In subsequent years they would record in Detroit, Los Angeles, and Chicago, and mostly for major labels.

Stripped of artists as Chess was, the Dells were insufficient to sustain the company. By the summer of 1975 GRT began dismantling Chess. Related Bass, "GRT laid everybody off, and I stayed on for about another month getting all the tapes down to Nashville where GRT had a warehouse. I went down there and had a vault built just like at Chess. I had all the master tapes boxed, crated, put on a truck and sent down there and then had two guys help me. And I set up the tape storage just like at the Chess vault."[67]

In August 1975, with all of GRT record operations closed down, what remained of Chess was sold to an Englewood, New Jersey, firm called All Platinum, a small independent owned by Sylvia and Joe Robinson.[68] With overseas financial help from Polydor, All Platinum paid $950,000 for Chess. The Robinsons had intended to operate Chess as an active label, but they had run short of capital and were forced to reduce Chess to nothing more than a reissues label. For example, they could not afford the Dells' pricey contract and the group went to a major, Mercury Records. The sale of Chess to All Platinum effectively put an end to a great Chicago company.

The Chess building at 320 East Twenty-first Street was sold. The building's new owner brought in several dumpsters and a crew of day laborers with chain saws. They proceeded to destroy a quarter of a million records—Etta James, the Dells, Billy Stewart, Muddy Waters—that had been abandoned in the storerooms. The records and all other remaining accumulations were pitched in the dumpsters and carted away.[69]

NOTES

1. The story of Chess Records has been extensively documented over the years. The following sources provide the most useful information: Cary Baker, "Marshall Chess Comes Full Circle," *Goldmine*, November 1982, pp. 14–16; John Fleming, "A Life Recording," Chicago *Reader*, March 7, 1980, p. 1, 29–32; Peter Galkin, "Black White and Blues: The Story of Chess Records, Part One," *Living Blues* 88 (September/October 1989): 22–32; idem, "Part Two," *Living Blues* 89 (December 1989): 25–29; Michael Gray, "Chess at the Top," *Let It Rock*, September 1973, pp. 30–33; Robert Pruter, "A Talk with Daddy G," *Goldmine*, March 1982, pp. 24–25; Mike Rowe, *Chicago Breakdown* (London: Eddison Press, 1973); Gene Barge interview, September 8, 1981; Ralph Bass interview; Billy Davis interview.

2. In interviews with the author and others Bass has claimed with equal certainty both 1958 and 1960 as the year of his move. I believe he came to Chess in 1959, because he was still at Federal when Syl Johnson signed with the company in 1959 and may have discovered Mitty Collier for Chess the same year.

3. Davis interview.

4. Ibid.

5. Barge interview.

6. The career of Etta James has been the most extensively documented of all the Chess soul artists. The following features are the best: David Booth, "Etta James," *Soul Survivor* 3 (Autumn 1985): 4–8; Bob Fukuyama, "Etta James: Twenty

Years On," *Soul and Jazz*, April 1976, pp. 46–48; Norbert Hess, "Living Blues Interview: Etta James," *Living Blues* 54 (Autumn/Winter 1982): 12–20; Cliff White, "James the First," *Black Music and Jazz*, October 1978, pp. 22–23.

7. Fukuyama, "Etta James," p. 48.

8. White, "James the First," p. 23.

9. Fukuyama, "Etta James," p. 46.

10. David Nathan, liner notes, Sugar Pie DeSanto, *Down in the Basement*, MCA-Chess 9275, 1988; Robert Pruter, "Sugar Pie DeSanto: Go Go Power," *Goldmine*, July 31, 1987, pp. 20, 26; Cliff White, "Sugar Pie DeSanto: Use What You Got," *Black Music*, July 1974, p. 10.

11. Robert Pruter, "The Mitty Collier Story," *Goldmine*, November 1981, pp. 25–26; Mitty Collier interview.

12. Collier interview.

13. Ibid.

14. Robert Pruter, "Jackie Ross," *It Will Stand* 20 (1983): 6–8; Jackie Ross interview.

15. Ross interview.

16. Ibid.

17. Ibid.

18. Robert Pruter, "The Gems," *Goldmine*, December 1979, pp. 25–26; Jessica Edmund interview; Raynard Miner interview.

19. Earl Calloway, "Raynard Miner Gets BMI Award," *Chicago Defender*, July 8, 1978; Arnold Rozenzweig, "Blind Collegian-to-be Likes It That Way, Making It as R&R Composer," *Chicago Defender*, February 29, 1964.

20. Shirley Hawkins, "Queen of Soul?...Who Cares?," *Soul*, December 19, 1977, p. 19; Robert Pruter, "Minnie Riperton 1947–1979, *Goldmine*, October 1979, pp. 10–11; Al Rudis, "...and a Singer with Sounds that Are Beyond Belief," *Chicago Sun-Times*, July 14, 1974.

21. Rudis, "A Singer with Sounds."

22. Johnny Sayles interview.

23. Robert Pruter, "Jo Ann Garrett," *Goldmine*, January 1981, p. 173; Jo Ann Garrett interview.

24. Marvin Junior interview.

25. The Dells have been the beneficiary of voluminous documentation, but much of it is of the "fan profile" variety. Serious students of soul music should consult the following: Michael Lenehan, "Conversations with the Dells: Twenty-eight Years of Rhythm and Blues, From Doowop to Disco," Chicago *Reader*, November 14, 1980, pp. 1, 20–40; Robert Pruter and Wayne Jones, "The Dells, Part 2: The Soul Years in Chicago, 1960–1972," *Goldmine*, July 20, 1984, pp. 15–26; Clive Richardson, "The Dells," *Shout* 61 (December 1970), unpaged; Jack Sbarbori, "The Dells...Twenty-three Years Later," *Record Exchanger* 22 (1976): 4–11; Chuck Barksdale interviews; Marvin Junior interview; Mickey McGill interviews.

26. Barksdale interview, January 15, 1981.

27. Ibid.

28. McGill interview, February 21, 1981.

29. Pruter and Jones, "The Dells, Part 2," p. 22.

30. Ibid.

31. McGill interview, February 21, 1981.

32. Robert Pruter, "The Radiants Story," *It Will Stand* 22/23 (1981): 4–7; idem, "The Radiants," *Soul Survivor* 1 (1985): 9–13; Jerome Brooks interview; Leonard Caston, Jr., interview; Maurice McAlister interview; Wallace Sampson interview.

33. McAlister interview.

34. Brooks interview.

35. Sampson interview.

36. Robert Pruter, "Billy Stewart: The Fat Boy Lives On...," *It Will Stand* 17/18, (1981): 18–20; idem, "Billy Stewart," *Soul Survivor* 9 (Summer 1988): 18–20; Adam White, liner notes, Billy Stewart, *One More Time—The Chess Years*, MCA-Chess 6027, 1988.

37. White, liner notes.

38. Ibid.

39. Robert Pruter, "Knight Brothers," *Goldmine*, December 1983, pp. 137–39; Richard Dunbar interview.

40. Dunbar interview.

41. Max Oates, liner notes, The Four Jewels, *Loaded with Goodies*, DJM 001, 1985; Robert Pruter, "The Jewels: The Most Angelic Voices Ever Waxed," *Goldmine*, January 2, 1987, pp. 14, 20.

42. Cary Baker, "Little Milton Still Singin' Big Blues," *Goldmine*, May 1981, pp. 164–65; Cilla Huggins, "A Little More on Milton," *Blues Unlimited* 144 (Spring 1983): 30–34; Lynn S. Summers and Bob Scheir, "Living Blues Interview: Little Milton," *Living Blues* 18 (August 1974): 17–24.

43. Bill Dahl, "Oliver Sain: Soul Sax Serenader," *Goldmine*, October 21, 1988, pp. 34, 103; Bill Greensmith, "The Fontella Bass Interview," *Blues Unlimited* 147 (Spring 1986): 18–22.

44. Bill Greensmith, "The Bobby McClure Interview," *Blues Unlimited* 147 (Spring 1986): 23–25.

45. Cary Baker, "Ramsey Lewis: Anatomy of a Reunion," *Goldmine*, November 23, 1984, pp. 46, 48; Tom Nuccio, "History of Chicago Jazz, Part 16: Ivory Trios," *Illinois Entertainer*, April 1986, pp. 62–69.

46. Geoff Brown, "Just a Matter of Time," *Black Music*, January 1978, pp. 18–20; David Nathan and John Abbey, "Marlena Shaw: Sweet Beginnings...," *Blues and Soul*, August 2–15, 1977, pp. 5–6.

47. Undated program notes from an unidentified concert are the basis for this sketchy profile.

48. Michael Haralambos, "Tony Clarke—A Summary of the Official Biography," *Hot Buttered Soul* 20 (July 1973): 9; Robert Pruter, "Tony Clarke: The Entertainer," *Goldmine*, January 30, 1987, p. 22.

49. Chris Beachley interview, June 7, 1986.

50. Muscle Shoals sources are voluminous. The best information is found in the following: Peter Guralnick, *Sweet Soul Music* (New York: Harper and Row,

1986); Barney Hoskyns, *Say It One More Time for the Brokenhearted* (Glasgow: Fontana/Collins, 1987).

51. Guralnick, *Sweet Soul Music*, p. 375.

52. "Bobby Moore Tells How It Happened," *Soul*, July 21, 1966, p. 6.

53. Doug Wright and Richard Pack, "Laura Lee," *Soul Survivor* 5 (Summer 1986): 4–7.

54. Wright and Pack, "Laura Lee," p. 5.

55. Robert Pruter, "The Radiants Story"; idem, "The Radiants"; Maurice McAlister interview.

56. "Chess Moves into Its Own Building," *Billboard*, September 3, 1966, p. 4.

57. Davis interview.

58. Ibid.

59. Ibid.

60. "GRT Wrap-Up Near of Chess Purchase," *Billboard*, January 4, 1969, p. 1.

61. Barge interview, September 8, 1981.

62. Ibid.

63. Cary S. Baker, "Chicago Blues News," *Blues World* 43 (Summer 1972): 16.

64. "Chicago Loses Chess Records," *Illinois Entertainer*, December 1975, p. 25.

65. "Schlachter Will Head GRT Records Group," *Billboard*, March 13, 1971, p. 3.

66. Gray, "Chess at the Top," p. 31.

67. Bass interview.

68. "All Platinum Purchases Three GRT Labels," *Billboard*, August 30, 1975, p. 8.

69. Bob Sladek interview.

6

The ABC-Paramount
Chicago Connection

Curtis Mayfield and Johnny Pate

Curtis Mayfield with his group the Impressions recorded for the New York-based ABC-Paramount label during the 1960s. The group made some of the best records of the soul era, the most outstanding of more than two dozen hits being "Gypsy Woman" (1961), "It's All Right" (1963), "Keep on Pushing" (1964), and "People Get Ready" (1965). With producer and arranger Johnny Pate's horn-punctuated charts and the Impressions' lightly gospelized three-part harmonies, the group of Mayfield, Fred Cash, and Sam Gooden became one of the standard-bearers of the Chicago style of subtle soft soul.

The success of the Impressions served to inspire both ABC and Mayfield to record other acts in Chicago in the soft-soul idiom, and the Marvelows, Fascinations, the Five Stairsteps emerged as notable hitmakers. Like most large companies ABC-Paramount avoided hard soul as something not commercially viable and not something their creative people, meaning Pate and Mayfield, were attuned to. The stable of artists developed by Pate and Mayfield constituted a major creative force in Chicago in the same manner as such companies as Vee Jay, Chess, and OKeh.

ABC-Paramount was founded in August 1955 as a record division of the ABC broadcast network, formally called American Broadcasting–Paramount Theatres, Inc. The company concentrated on all forms of popular music, but was weak in country and western. Much of the company's growth was fueled by the success it had with young rock 'n' rollers, notably Paul Anka, Danny and the Juniors, the Elegants, and Lloyd Price (a veteran r&b artist who became a rock 'n' roller).

In 1960 ABC signed Ray Charles, which was considered a major coup, and the following year signed the Impressions, which went unnoticed. Charles, with his remakes of country-and-western tunes, within two years became one of the nation's top recording artists. The Impressions' road to success took more time to build, but by the mid-sixties they were a top group and Pate was made A&R director in the Midwest. An office was established at 1413 South Michigan. By 1965, on its tenth anniversary, ABC–Paramount was described by *Billboard* as "a major label, in every sense of the word."[1]

Mayfield Productions

The signing of the Impressions in 1961 signaled the emergence of Curtis Mayfield as a creative force in Chicago. Mayfield had struggled to make his mark for several years, yet was still a surprisingly young man, eighteen years old. He was born in Chicago on June 3, 1942, to an impoverished family. His family was always moving from neighborhood to neighborhood and by Mayfield's high-school years had settled on the near North Side in the Cabrini-Green projects. As true of many youngsters of the day, Mayfield formed a short-lived vocal group while attending a West Side grammar school. The group was called the Alphatones and besides Mayfield consisted of Al Boyce, James Weems, and Dallas Dixon.

Mayfield's strongest musical influence came out of his membership in a local gospel group called the Northern Jubilee Gospel Singers, which included his three cousins—Sam, Tommy, and Charles Hawkins—and Jerry Butler. The ensemble, which mainly sang in the Traveling Souls Church, was where Mayfield first took up the guitar. Said he, "One of the fellows from the group had gone into the Army. When he came back he brought this guitar, but nobody could play it and it sat in the corner for a long time. Finally I picked it up and started working it, tuning it in F# like all the black keys on a piano."[2]

At Cabrini-Green, Mayfield attended Wells High along with another future soul star, Major Lance, but he did not stay past his sophomore year. Butler had lured him into the Impressions, and high school just did not have the appeal of a vocal group. The Impressions signed with Vee Jay and after their first success with "For Your Precious Love" in 1958, Butler split from the group. The remaining Impressions made a few more releases for Vee Jay but the group was dropped by the label in 1959.

Related Mayfield,

> We scuffled some. For a time we would do gigs as the Impressions,
> but nobody was really aware of the Impressions. So it was quite

hard for us to get gigs. When we did gig, I can recall even having done some gigs as Jerry Butler and the Impressions when Jerry wasn't with us, and Sam would do "For Your Precious Love." This was in some of the lowlands, like down in Mississippi, just in little night spots like that. We ended up splitting up. Some moved to Detroit to live with their relatives. Of course, I still lived in Cabrini-Green. That's when I got my first job, with Alfred Dunhill, a cigar store. So I delivered cigars up and down the Gold Coast [the wealthy lakefront area on the North Side] for Alfred Dunhill."[3]

Mayfield did not drop his music endeavors, and in 1960 he began a successful career as songwriter and guitarist for Jerry Butler, helping to build Butler's career at Vee Jay. Butler's call came at the right time in his life. "I had nothing to do," said Mayfield, "as a matter of fact the Internal Revenue Service was looking for me for four-hundred bucks. They found me in Cabrini-Green and wanted payment. I had a Webcor tape recorder and they wanted me to sell it to get them the money. Anyway I got away from them by playing with Jerry. That's how I did nothing but play for Jerry and sleep with my guitar and write songs."[4]

By the following year Mayfield had earned enough money to get the Impressions off the ground again. "I had saved a thousand dollars," said Mayfield, "and we went to New York to record. All the fellows came together again, and we checked into this hotel in Manhattan, and I guess we were there about a week when we recorded 'Gypsy Woman.' "[5]

That was in July 1961, and "Gypsy Woman" proved to be one of the most important records of the Impressions' career. It reestablished them as an act. The group at this time consisted of Curtis Mayfield, Sam Gooden, Fred Cash, Arthur Brooks, and Richard Brooks. Mayfield wrote a light, delicate song to match his high-tenor lead and the subdued chorusing by the rest of the group. The use of castanets and muted instrumental support gave the record a dreamlike fantasy flavor. The record made it high on *Billboard*'s r&b and pop charts; on the r&b chart it went to the two position and lasted eleven weeks in the fall of 1961.

The *Billboard* r&b chart was only limited to the top thirty during the early 1960s and failed to reflect the Impressions' first several hit records after "Gypsy Woman." *Cash Box*, which had a top-fifty r&b chart, gave evidence of considerable chart activity by the Impressions.

In February 1962 the Impressions came out with the light, airy "Grow Closer Together," which briefly entered *Cash Box*'s chart at position forty-six for a week. In the summer of 1962 the jaunty "Little Young Lover" lasted eight weeks and went to position thirty. The flip was especially good, in which the Impressions using neo-doowop harmonies created a flavorful version of the old Johnny Ace hit "Never Let Me Go."

"Minstrel and Queen," a feathery light fantasy in the same vein as "Gypsy Woman," was a sizable hit for the group in the fall of 1962. The record lasted seven weeks and went to position twenty-seven on the *Cash Box* survey and should have made it on the *Billboard* survey. "I'm the One Who Loves You," released in early 1963, was another solid effort by the group, but it failed to chart anywhere. The song was recorded in March 1962, and that session, which included "Minstrel and Queen," was the last in which the Brooks brothers were a part of the Impressions. They left before the year was out.

It would seem strange for the Brooks brothers to leave just as the Impressions' career was gathering steam. But Mayfield attributed it to "frustration, their admiration of other acts that were making it then." Mayfield explained, "Our style was so different than what was really going on. My music and my own personal creations were so dominant. They being from the South, Chattanooga, the people they loved were the Five Royales, the Midnighters, James Brown. Between 'Minstrel and Queen' and 'I'm the One Who Loves You,' it just wasn't their music. They were trying to write their own tunes and put it into the group, but they just weren't good songs."[6]

The new three-man Impressions returned to Chicago and in January 1963 recorded their first session there with arranger and producer Johnny Pate. The best product of the session was the moody ballad "Sad Sad Girl and Boy." Although recorded much in the same light, airy style as their earlier hits, the song showed something a bit different in the vocal approach. No longer were the rest of the Impressions quietly echoing in a subdued chorus Mayfield's lead; they now showed a stronger presence with interjections and call-and-response patterns. The song was not much of a commercial success, however, lasting four weeks and going no higher than position forty-five on the *Cash Box* chart in the spring of 1963.

An August 1963 session yielded the first single to define the classic style of the 1960s Impressions. That single was "It's All Right," on which Pate lifted the energy level considerably, adding blaring horns and a more forceful, percussive bottom. The vocal style of the three was now fully developed, the lead switching off from among the three and the two others singing in harmony with the lead on the end phrases. The record was a successful crossover hit and went to number one on *Billboard*'s r&b chart in the fall of 1963.

The three-part switch-off lead of the Impresssions was a fresh new sound in rhythm and blues, but it was not new to black music. Related Mayfield,

I think it was probably original for the Impressions in r&b and contempoary music, but there was nothing original about it if you ever sang gospel. In gospel, you knew how to be a good singer, not only to sing lead but to be able to incorporate oneself into the blending of the group, too. And sometimes everyone comes out and sings in harmony a portion of the lead part. It was something totally different during those times. It made us a three-man group stronger than we were as a five-man group. It locks everybody in; you really know where the voices are. You know how to blend in. When you have four or five men, if one moves up, the other doesn't know where to go. Of course, other groups imitated us.[7]

With the success of "It's All Right," ABC-Paramount released in 1963 the Impressions' first album, *The Impressions*. A collection of the groups best songs from the previous three years, the album was a stunning debut on long play for the group.

The Impressions became a major act with a series of marvelous singles during 1964. On *Cash Box*'s r&b chart the group during the year had two singles that reached number one, two that reached number two, and one that reached number three. The group opened the year with a nice loping, medium-tempo song called "Talking about My Baby." It lasted thirteen weeks and went to the two position. They followed in the spring with one of their all-time best ballads, "I'm So Proud," which lasted fifteen weeks and went to the two position. The group also came out with their second album, *The Never Ending Impressions*. It was dreadfully thin on good songs, the only outstanding one being "I'm So Proud."

On their third album, *Keep On Pushing*, the Impressions redeemed themselves. The album included "Talking about My Baby," and two other top chart records—the rousing number that intimated new black pride, "Keep On Pushing," which went to number one and lasted fifteen weeks, and "Amen," which lasted twelve weeks and went to the top as well. "Amen" seems to me the most tiresome hit the Impressions ever recorded. Another top song from the album was the excellent ballad "I've Been Trying," which was also recorded by Jerry Butler with great success.

Continuing their splendid hit streak, the Impressions opened 1965 with their best album, *People Get Ready*. Just about every cut on the album was a musical treat, and it included several hits. The most outstanding was the title cut, with its heavy gospel-style imagery and feel. "People Get Ready" lasted ten weeks and went to the three position on *Billboard*'s r&b chart. Other hits from the album were "You Must Believe Me," a forceful mid-tempo song that lasted sixteen weeks and went to the number three position on the *Cash Box* survey in the fall of 1964, and "Woman's Got

Soul," which lasted seven weeks and went to the nine position on *Billboard*'s chart in the spring of 1965.

The year produced two more outstanding singles: "Meeting over Yonder," which lasted nine weeks and went to twelve position in the summer, was a churchy number that was a splendid example of the way Pate used horns for percussion. "You've Been Cheating," released in December, lasted eleven weeks and went to the twelve position. It had a propulsive drive made famous by Motown but the production was thoroughly Chicagoan in sound. The ballad flip, "Man Oh Man," ranks as a great undiscovered Impressions masterpiece.

The years 1966–67 were somewhat down years for the group. *Ridin' High* was the group's one album from 1966 and it was less than a stellar achievement. It consisted of mostly Mayfield songs that had earlier been done by other artists. Mayfield appeared to be running out of inspiration. The group's one big hit during the year was the rousing "Can't Satisfy." It had the same impelling drive as a Motown record, and no wonder: it borrowed heavily from the Isley Brothers' Motown hit "This Old Heart of Mine." Mayfield eventually had to settle with Motown and give the publishing of "Can't Satisfy" to the Detroit company. Mayfield was heavily involved in starting up two labels in 1966, Mayfield and Windy C, and perhaps was not giving enough attention to the group.

The Fabulous Impressions, from early 1967, continued the Impressions' artistic slide, yielding only mediocre singles. The year was partly salvaged by the single "We're a Winner," which entered the *Billboard* chart in December, lasted seventeen weeks, and went to the number one position. The driving song with the funky beat evoked the spirit of the times as blacks inspired by the civil rights movement were asserting themselves as equal human beings in American society. The album, *We're a Winner*, did not contain much, however, producing one other hit, the fine ballad "I Loved and I Lost," which lasted nine weeks and went to the nine position in the summer of 1968.

The Impressions had one other hit single on ABC in 1968, "We're Rollin' On," which directly aped "We're a Winner" but with less inspiration. The record lasted seven weeks on the chart and went to position seventeen. Surprisingly at that time, black radio had not kept pace with its black constituency and there was a lot of resistance by programmers over playing such "overtly" political songs. The popularity of those songs had the effect of pushing black radio in the direction its listeners were going. And many white programmers were not playing those songs either, feeling the message of black pride might alienate their white listeners. WLS, which controlled 14 percent of the national market then, refused to play "We're a Winner."[8]

Mayfield commented, "When you're talking about songs such as 'We're a Winner,' that's locked in with Martin Luther King. It could have been the very controversy of it even existing. But it was a song with a message; it had an inspiring message. And this wasn't really what radio was all about in those times."[9] After the summer of 1968 the Impressions were recording on Mayfield's newly formed Curtom Records.

The Fascinations featured one of the great teen-soprano soul sounds of the 1960s. Lead singer Bernadine Boswell Smith possessed a piercingly high soprano voice with a marvelous soulful edge that had a youthful teenage appeal. In addition she and the rest of the group were exceptionally talented singers who could make a song really swing. Throughout their career they were under contract to Curtis Mayfield, who was their manager, wrote many of their songs, and produced all their records, first for ABC-Paramount and later for his own Mayfield label.[10]

The Fascinations came from Detroit, but as they entered Mayfield's orbit they were part of the Chicago recording scene. Fred Cash and Sam Gooden discovered the group and brought them to the attention of Mayfield in 1961. The group had been formed a year earlier by Shirley Walker, and when the Fascinations met Mayfield, members were Bernadine Boswell Smith, her sister Joanne Boswell Levell, Fern Bledsoe, as well as Walker.

The first record Mayfield cut on the Fascinations was curiously "Mama Didn't Lie," the same song he had produced on Jan Bradley. Whereas Bradley's version had a straight-ahead drive, Mayfield gave the Fascinations' version a more syncopated, funkier sound and had the girls sing with more forcefulness. The girls' version in many respects had more appeal, but it was the Bradley version that became the big hit.

The following year, Mayfield recorded a fine Bernadine Smith–composed ballad, "Tears in My Eyes," in which Bernadine emoted with great relish in one of her strongest vocal performances. The record, alas, did not do anything, and ABC-Paramount gave up on the group and dropped them.

Mayfield did not give up. He knew he had come out with two excellent records on the Fascinations that did not happen for whatever reason, but the reason was not in the grooves. In 1966 he formed Mayfield Records and arranged for Calla Records in New York to handle distribution. The focal point of the company's efforts would be the Fascinations, and during the next three years the label came out with five releases on the group.

The first release, "Say It Isn't So," was a rousing upbeat number written and produced by Mayfield. The record only went to position forty-seven and lasted two weeks on *Billboard*'s r&b chart in the fall of 1966. In Chicago, however, the record got the recognition it deserved and was a big hit. The girls' next record and only truly national hit, "Girls Are Out to Get You," lasted ten weeks and rose to position thirteen on the r&b

chart in early 1967. The song was not much different from "Say It Isn't So" in having the same cheerful bounciness, but why one should become far more successful is one of the mysteries of the record business.

Mayfield was never able to duplicate the success of "Girls Are Out to Get You" in three more releases. In 1968 the Fascinations' contract was up and Mayfield decided not to renew it. He had found it difficult for his small company to properly push the girls as a recording act, conceding, "It became quite rough trying to promote the girls and get them off the way we wanted to. I guess for every hit I've had, I've probably had two misses."[11] The Fascinations, deciding their career was over, broke up.

There is a postscript to this story. Great Britain, which has had a habit of resurrecting old stateside records and turning them into hits, made "Girls Are Out to Get You" a pop hit in July 1971, when it reached position thirty-two on the English chart. The Fascinations regrouped briefly and made a tour of England on the basis of the record in August 1971.

The Five Stairsteps were solid r&b stars as chart regulars from 1966 to 1971, and before Motown's Jackson Five came to prominence, they were known in the black press as the "First Family of Soul."[12] The group released some twenty-five singles and seven albums, but its first album, *The Five Stairsteps*, which yielded five chart singles, was one of the most impressive debuts of the soul era.[13] The same year that Mayfield formed Mayfield Records he also formed the Windy C label and arranged for it to be distributed by Cameo-Parkway Records, a company with offices in New York but with studios in Philadelphia. Windy C was essentially a vehicle for Mayfield's work with the Five Stairsteps. As with the Fascinations, it was Fred Cash who brought the group to the attention of Mayfield.

The Five Stairsteps at the time they were signed were a five-member brothers and sister act ranging in age from thirteen to seventeen. The children of Clarence and Betty Burke, they were lead tenor Clarence Jr. (sixteen years old), contralto Alohe (seventeen), first tenor James (fifteen), baritone Dennis (fourteen), and second tenor Kenneth (thirteen). Four of the children attended Harlan High, which among all the South Side high schools in the 1960s was the premier public school for blacks. The parents who sent their children to Harlan owned their own homes, instilled in their offspring middle-class values, and provided an upbringing free from poverty, drugs, crime, and street gangs. Clarence Burke, Sr., was a detective in the Chicago police force and he firmly kept his kids on the straight and narrow. The group's second album, *Our Family Portrait*, included fifteen family snapshots that captured the very essence of the Five Stairsteps' upbringing.[14]

Clarence Sr.'s great passion was music and he raised his children as a singing and dancing group. Eventually they were performing in school functions and church gatherings. In 1965 the Five Stairsteps entered a talent contest at the Regal Theater and walked off with first prize. However, their father, known as "Papa Burke," turned down several record-company offers. He played bass guitar for the Five Stairsteps, wrote their songs (with Clarence Jr. and Gregory Fowler), and managed them. And as manager he was taking care that the group got the kind of contract it deserved. A chance meeting between Papa Burke and Fred Cash got the group on Mayfield's label.[15]

The Five Stairsteps' debut single was "You Waited Too Long"/"Don't Waste Your Time," in March 1966. The A side was a slow ballad written by the Burkes and the flip was a gently up-tempo number written by Mayfield. With Mayfield's sympathetic production, Clarence Jr.'s dry lead, and the group's harmonies providing an understated eloquence and soulfulness without sounding mannered and overly pretty, the result was like much of Chicago soft soul—engagingly subtle rather than obvious in appeal. Both sides of the single were big hits in Chicago, but only the ballad side made the national charts, lasting ten weeks and going as high as position sixteen on *Billboard*'s r&b chart.

The *Five Stairsteps* album soon followed and hits came in quick succession, all performed with the same understated eloquence. In June 1966, "World of Fantasy," a ballad written by Burke, was released, and it lasted ten weeks and went to position twelve on the r&b chart. Another Burke ballad, "Come Back," lasted nine weeks and went to position fifteen in late 1966. In January 1967, "Danger! She's a Stranger," co-written by the Burkes and Mayfield, entered the *Billboard* chart and lasted eight weeks and went to position sixteen. Its flip, "Behind Curtains," written by Mayfield, got good play as well.

In the spring of 1967, the Five Stairsteps came out with their first single not taken from their first album, "Ain't Gonna Rest (Till I Get You)," a routine hard-driving song that had nothing going for it. Apparently the deejays were willing to play anything by the group, because the record managed to last five weeks and go to position thirty-seven on the *Billboard* r&b chart. For the next release, Mayfield went back to the album again and put out a cover of the Miracles' hit from 1965, "Ooh, Baby Baby." The record lasted seven weeks and went to position thirty-four on the chart in the summer of 1967.

In late 1967 Cameo-Parkway was collapsing, and that put an end to the Windy C label. Neil Bogart, an executive at Cameo-Parkway, then joined Art Kass's newly formed Buddah Records as co-president with Kass. In short order he brought the Five Stairsteps to the company. The group's second album, *Our Family Portrait*, was produced by the fast-developing Clarence Jr. in Chicago. As a gimmick they added three-year-old Cubie Burke to their lineup and renamed themselves the Five Stairsteps and Cubie.

The album yielded two chart singles, the fine Burke composition "Something's Missing," which lasted eight weeks and went to position seventeen on the chart at the end of 1967, and a cover of the 1960 Jimmy Charles ballad, "A Million to One," which lasted seven weeks and went to position twenty-eight in early June. The album, however, was mighty thin and except for about three cuts was virtually unlistenable. Before the year was out, Mayfield had set up Curtom Records with distribution by Buddah, and the Five Stairsteps rejoined him.

Pate Productions

Johnny Pate, as a result of his success in arranging and producing the Impressions, was given the job as Midwest A&R man for ABC in about 1964.[16] Pate was born in 1923 in Chicago Heights, a suburb south of Chicago. While a youngster he played piano and tuba. During 1944–46, as a member of the 218th AGF Band while in the Army, he studied bass and arranging. Upon his discharge, he joined the Coleridge Davis Band in Atlantic City and later joined a trio in Chicago. In the 1950s he worked as a staff arranger for the Club Delisa house band and as a bassist at the famed Blue Note nightclub. Pate scored with a hit record in 1959, when recording as the Johnny Pate Quintet he came out with a jazz-flavored instrumental called "Swingin' Shepherd Blues," which was released on the Federal label.[17]

It was obvious why ABC was interested in establishing an A&R man in Chicago, as Carl Davis pointed out: "ABC Records at that time knew what was happening in Chicago. They knew that the Chicago sound was a definite happening."[18]

Apart from his work with the Impressions, Pate's A&R work at ABC was not a great success. He signed a few acts, but had commercial success only with the male vocal group the Marvelows. Three other signings were the girl group the Kittens; a male vocal group, the Trends; and Betty Everett. The Kittens did not sell any records, but Pate knew what he was doing, because these girls were talented. The group was from Chicago's West Side and consisted of eighteen-year-old Bernice Willis, out of Farragut High, and nineteen-year-old cousins Laurel Ross and Thelma Mack, both out of Marshall High. The lead singer of the group had a splendid gospelized mezzo-soprano voice that was perfect for soul music. The girls got together in May 1963, while still attending high school. They were coached and managed by Chicago veteran manager Ruth Moore, who had worked with dozens of Chicago acts for many years. In 1964 Pate discovered the group and signed the girls to ABC.[19]

Pate put out three records on the Kittens during 1965–66. He obtained songs, such as "I Got to Know Him" and "Lookie Lookie," from the hot New York team of Ashford-Simpson-Armstead. But despite Pate's arranging talents, the excellent singing abilities of the girls, and songs from presumably a top source, all three records failed. The inability of Pate to get the girls a hit stemmed from the poor songs they recorded. Even Cole Porter and Irving Berlin put out a few clunkers, and Ashford-Simpson-Armstead are entitled to their share as well. The Kittens in 1967–68 recorded three more records, two for Chess Records, with the same lack of commercial success and for the same reason. The Kittens probably closed their career bitterly disappointed with the popular music industry. They were far more talented than many groups who sold millions of records, and they hardly sold a handful.

The Trends were a young West Side group, one of many groups from the area who were trying to make it in the exploding soul music scene. Three of the members—Emmett Garner, Jr., Ralph O'Neal, and Jerome Johnson—were out of Marshall High, and the fourth member, lead singer Eddie Dunn, was from DuSable High. They were formed around 1964 and recorded two records that year for Mercury's Smash subsidiary without any success. Pate signed the group in 1966, and put out seven singles on them before letting the group go in late 1968. The Trends never had any hits, although some of their records, "Not Too Young to Cry" (1966) and "Check My Tears" (1967), got a bit of play in Chicago. The group broke up after being dropped by ABC, and Emmett Garner, Jr., continued in the music business for more years as a producer and promotion man in Chicago.

Pate also had a poor track record with Betty Everett, who left the collapsed Vee Jay organization in May 1966 to sign with ABC. With her move, she shed her longtime manager Leo Austell and went with another veteran record man, Al Smith. The first ABC release on Everett was "Nothing I Wouldn't Do," written by our old friends Simpson and Armstead. The rousing number arranged by Pate and produced by Pate and Smith was a local hit in Chicago but failed to do much anywhere else. Everett's three subsequent ABC releases also failed to do anything chartwise, and for good reason. Few of the original songs she sang had anything going for them, and the remakes of oldies such as Mary Wells's "Bye Bye Baby" (a lousy song the first time around) and Everett's "Your Love Is Important to Me" (wasn't a hit the first time around) were inexplicable.

Late in 1968 Everett left ABC and hooked up with Leo Austell again. He got her a contract with MCA's Uni Records in California. Austell joined with Archie Russell and Hillery Johnson to produce Everett's records. For her first single they chose a real zinger from the pens of Eugene Record and Floyd Smith (Record at this time was just emerging as the top songwriting member of the Chi-lites). "There'll Come a Time" was classic Everett, a wistful, sad song that was just right for her bittersweet vocals. The song went to number two on *Billboard*'s soul chart. Everett had three more chart records on Uni, but by 1970 was recording for Fantasy Records with ex-Vee Jay A&R producer Calvin Carter. In 1980, after years of mediocre records, she quit the music business.

The Marvelows, like such 1960s vocal groups as the Temptations, Whispers, and Manhattans, added a fine 1950s-style harmony to their brand of soul music. Pate built arrangements so sympathetically around the group's own vocal arrangements that listening to the Marvelows, one feels he is standing on the street corner doowopping with the neighborhood gang. But the Marvelows, who recorded for ABC from 1964 to 1969, were not anachronistic—they sang contemporary soul music.[20]

The group came out of the south suburb of Chicago Heights and was organized by Melvin Mason, the group's songwriter and frequent lead. In 1959 he was attending Bloom High when the Paden family, which included a pair of brothers who could sing, moved into town. Mason, who had been singing in groups since the age of eleven, got together with Johnny Paden, who sang bass, and Frank Paden, who sang lead and tenor, to form a group. When tenor Willie (Sonny) Stevenson, joined the group, the Marvelows were born. After some years doowopping on the corner the group broke up.

In the summer of 1964 the Marvelows came together again, but now as a five-man ensemble with the addition of first tenor Jesse Smith. They also obtained a manager, Herb Turner, a record-store owner and self-confessed vocal-group fan. By this time, the group was working with original material and developing a formidable local reputation. Mason explained how the group got a recording contract:

> Well, to be frank, that wasn't even what I was after. I was singing because I loved to sing. I saw so many groups under the streetlights, so that's where I wanted to be, under the streetlights. What happened was, my wife's cousin, Jesse Smith, turned out to be the stimulus in getting the contract. Smith's mother told him about a guy that she went to school with who used to live in Chicago Heights. His name was Johnny Pate. She said, "Why don't you check with him and see if he could do something for you, because you guys sound pretty good?" So Jesse unbeknownst to us went to the guy's house, [and after introducing himself] he told Pate, "Hey man, I got a group and we're tough!" Pate said, "If you're that tough, let's hear some tapes or something."[21]

Pate came and listened to the Marvelows, taped them, and got them a contract with ABC-Paramount in October 1964. From the original *a cappella* tapes he made, Pate wrote the arrangements for the first session. They recorded "A Friend," "Hey Hey Baby," "My Heart," and "I Do." The session featured Mason on lead for everything but "Hey Hey Baby," for which Frank Paden sang lead. Shortly after the session, the Marvelows added guitarist Henry Bardwell to the group.

"A Friend," which showcased the marvelous bass of Johnny Paden, was released in late 1964, but unfortunately attracted no interest. However, the group's next single, "I Do," turned out to be a hit in the spring of 1965.

"I Do" had an interesting origin: "We used to sing in the park because all the girls would be there," Mason recalled, "and we needed some type of song to warm our voices up on. At that time a lot of the groups were doing a thing like a baritone starting with 'woo,' and the others coming in with 'wo, woo, woooh.' So we said let's do something different. So we came up with this thing—'do doo, do doo, do doo.' I said I'm going to write some words for that, and that's what we came up with."[22] "I Do" went as high as number seven and lasted ten weeks on *Billboard*'s r&b chart. "'I Do' surprised everybody," Mason exclaimed. "It went pop, which was very surprising."[23]

The Marvelows got a lot of work from "I Do," playing such chitlin' circuit theaters as the Nixon in Philadelphia, the Howard in Washington, and the Apollo in New York. Mason remembered not so fondly that at the Apollo the Manhattans "burned" them with a super-choreographed act that made the Marvelows' efforts look amateurish. After the show, Honi Coles, longtime choreographer and manager at the Apollo, took the time to give the singers a few pointers and they somehow survived the week. When the Marvelows returned to the Apollo in 1968 they had a quality stage act that prevented any upstaging by rival groups.[24]

During 1966–67, the Marvelows failed to dent the charts with any of their records. In 1966, Smith was dropped for not following the group's discipline. "It was a thing about a reefer," related Mason. "We were really afraid because we've been hearing about so many people who were getting messed up on drugs and what not. We felt that a reefer might be the first step."[25]

After about a year with the four-man group, Mason brought in Andrew Thomas, who had sung a few years earlier with the Naturals (of "Let Love Be True" fame). The Marvelows also changed their name to the Mighty Marvelows to better distinguish themselves from a West Coast group called the Marvellos, who recorded for Loma. Mason pointed out that "everybody called us the Marvellos, and we kept explaining that it was a different spelling. A soul music magazine had a big write-up on both us groups in which the group from the West Coast was saying we stole their name. The Marvellos worked our tunes and got a lot of gigs off our records. Oh man, they burned California up. Groups were touring Europe under our name, and would call themselves names like the Fabulous Marvelows."[26]

The Mighty Marvelows with their new lineup came out with their first record, "In the Morning," in early 1968. The song had been in the group's repertoire for years, but Mason saw too many faults in it to record it. Just prior to a recording date, however, Pate rejected one of the group's proposed songs and asked that they come up with another tune for the session. "I was furious," said Mason, "so we left Chicago and came back to Chicago Heights and stopped in a tavern. We got a drink and we sat in the car and got our old song, 'In the Morning,' together."[27] The song was a beautifully mellow ballad, but because it was a slow side, the record did not have the crossover success of "I Do." On the *Billboard* r&b chart, "In the Morning" lasted ten weeks and went to the twenty-four position.

A follow-up, "I'm without a Girlfriend," was as superb as its predecessor but inexplicably failed to win a national chart position. The song did have fair success on a regional basis. The last two releases by the group made no impression at all, and the Marvelows, discouraged at the continual expense and trouble of staying together, broke up in 1969 before their contract had expired.

Despite the successes of the Marvelows, they never made it big. They were highly polished in their singing, which might well be expected of a group who had been singing together nearly five years before cutting their first record. But for all their talent, the Marvelows had it rough. "It wasn't fun," said Mason, "now that I look back on it, a lot of things happened that I can laugh and say, yeah, we had a good time, but at the time it was happening it was chaos, man. We were hungry a lot of times out there."[28] Not many persons realize just how financially unprofitable the chitlin' circuit was. The first time the Marvelows played the Apollo a full week in 1965, the entire group got only a thousand bucks for their efforts. Three years later, they got $2,800, not much better. Regarding song royalties, Mason said, "We never expected to cut a record, just the thrill of doing it was enough. A lot of things happened to us. We got beat out of a lot of money because we didn't know anything about publishing."[29]

The Marvelows made music that lasted. In 1977, "I Do" was recorded by the rock group J. Geils Band, and its version received much praise by rock critics, who typically had not the foggiest notion where it came from, invariably describing it as a Motown cover. The song also appeared in an episode of the television dramatic series "The White Shadow," which had a brief run in the late 1970s. In the episode, a group of black students decides to form a vocal harmony group, but the kids were a little weak on the technical aspects of music. They enlist the aid of a white teacher (played by Ken Howard), who teaches the finer points of vocal harmony on the song "I Do." By the time the group got it right for the finale of the show, the song sounded great.

The Marvelows' departure from ABC in 1969 put an end to the company's activities in Chicago. ABC apparently was not interested in maintaining a presence in the city, a reflection perhaps of the declining importance of Chicago as a recording center.

NOTES

1. Eliot Tiegel, "New Home, Face, Philosophy—ABC/Dunhill on 15th Anniversary," *Billboard*, September 12, 1970, pp. ABC-4 and ABC-8; "ABC-Paramount through the Years," and "Executive Line-Up," *Billboard*, September 18, 1965, p. 32.

2. Curtis Mayfield interview.

3. Ibid.

4. Ibid.

5. Ibid.

6. Ibid.

7. Ibid.

8. Michael Alexander, "The Impressions," *Rolling Stone*, December 27, 1969, p. 29.

9. Mayfield interview.

10. Sammy Chapman, "The Fascinations," *Soul Survivor* 1 (1985): 30–31; Robert Pruter, "Fascinations: Girls Are Out to Get You," *Goldmine*, March 27, 1987, pp. 20, 94.

11. Mayfield interview.

12. G. Fitz Bartley, "Stairsteps Unimpressive at Apollo," *Soul*, December 4, 1972, p. 12.

13. G. Fitz Bartley, "The Stairsteps Take a Step Back," *Soul*, December 6, 1971, p. 12; Judy Spiegelman, "Five Little Stairsteps and How They Grew," *Soul*, August 24, 1970, pp. 1–6; idem, "Why Are The Stairsteps Hiding?," *Soul*, August 30, 1971, p. 1.

14. The 5 Stairsteps and Cubie, *Our Family Portrait*, Buddah 5008, 1967.

15. Spiegelman, "Five Little Stairsteps," p. 2.

16. "ABC Paramount," *Billboard*, September 18, 1965, p. 32.

17. Leonard Feather, "Johnny Pate," *The New Edition of the Encyclopedia of Jazz* (New York: Horizon Press, 1960), p. 377; Jeff Lind, "1950's–60's Chicago Scene: Predecessor of Jazz-Rock Style," *Illinois Entertainer*, January 1978, p. 6.

18. Carl Davis interview, March 9, 1986.

19. "Cunningham and 'Kittens' Headline at Blue Angel," *Chicago Defender*, November 27, 1965; Bob Lee interview.

20. Robert Pruter, "The Marvelows," *The Time Barrier Express* 24 (April-May 1979): 19–22; Melvin Mason interview.

21. Mason interview.

22. Ibid.

23. Ibid.

24. Ibid.

25. Ibid.

26. Ibid.

27. Ibid.

28. Ibid.

29. Ibid.

7

The Small Entrepreneurs of the 1960s: Soft Soul

Undoubtedly because of the resurgent activities of Chicago's larger labels in exploiting the fast-growing soul market, the city was filled in the 1960s with hustling, ambitious men and women willing to make a go at it in the record business. Some of these small-time owners included Dick Simon, Bill Erman, Maurice Alpert, and Chuck Colbert, Sr., and usually they got into the business as a sideline to their main enterprises—insurance, coal, construction, whatever. Notable A&R men/producers included Richard Pegue, Bob Catron, Joshie Jo Armstead, and Bob Lee. These people, however, often wore several hats—owner, A&R director, producer, songwriter, arranger. For example, Bill Erman, owner of the Witch/Cortland/Ermine combine of labels, also wrote songs, produced records, and did A&R work.

Following the lead of Vee Jay, Chess, OKeh, and Constellation, the small entrepreneurs tended to work mainly with soft-soul acts, especially with vocal groups and teen sopranos. Over the years critics outside of the rhythm-and-blues field have generally given little consideration to vocal groups, who during the soul era usually made choreographed routines an aspect of their performances. *New York Times* critic John Rockwell most typically reflected the bias against vocal groups when he commented in a letter to me: "Yes, I am lukewarm about soft, harmonized soul groups. . . . It's a matter of taste, I guess. I get a lot of pleasure from a good ballad; it's just the mooning barbershop-quartet derivations that get to me."[1]

Not surprisingly there has been precious little criticism of substance on vocal/dance groups. Rather than contend with nuances of the falsetto tenor, the deep bass, and the textures of harmony, most critics just cover their ears; and when it comes to the subtleties of choreography, they close their eyes as well.

Despite the massive critical indifference to the vocal/dance-group genre, it has always been one of black music's richest traditions, as deeply embedded an art form as jazz, blues, or gospel. Few persons realize that on record, black vocal harmony predates all other forms of black music. Evidence unearthed in the 1970s indicates that Columbia put black vocal groups on wax as early as 1894, and since 1921, when the Norfolk Jazz Quartet came out with their seminal sides, there have been vocal groups regularly recorded on record.[2] They were on the cutting edge in the creation of rock 'n' roll and contributed significantly throughout the 1960s to the sound of soul. If anything, the male vocal/dance groups constituted the most popular form of soul music.

It should be obvious why Chicago record men concentrated so much of their energy and resources on recording vocal groups. Time and time again I've heard the refrain "vocal groups were the thing then." Yet the ensembles the record men worked with should not be considered mere transitory entertainers, but should be appreciated as valued disseminators of a long-honored form of popular music.

Also, during the 1960s one could frequently hear over the Chicago air waves records by young teenage girls with high pretty voices singing pop-soul confections. A few songs became national hits, notably Jan Bradley's "Mama Didn't Lie," but most had no more than local popularity, largely because these records were put out by small entrepreneurs—Chess Records being the exception—who had little ability to push the records beyond the city's environs.

Many critics, especially those of the rock persuasion, have over the years tended to dismiss female singers with light, airy soprano voices as something less artistically valid than mezzo-sopranos and contraltos. They would heap praises on such deep-thoated singers as Aretha Franklin and Laura Lee, but such nationally prominent sopranos as Barbara Lewis and Carla Thomas would get barely a nod. Incidentally, Detroit singer Lewis, who is best known for "Hello Stranger" (1963) and "Baby I'm Yours" (1965), recorded many of her "teen soprano" records in Chicago—the natural home of the sound. It seemed as though many critics felt the lower the voice, the closer the singer was to authentic soul. Of course, soul fans knew the aridity of that argument, which was simply personal bias disguised as considered criticism.

The earliest of the Chicago teenage sopranos was Joyce Davis, who hit with "Stop Giving Your Man Away" (1961), "Mean to Me" (1962), and "Moments to Remember" (1962), all produced in Chicago but leased to New York-based United Artists. Following her lead, teen sopranos such as Jan Bradley and others who recorded for Chess, Barbara Green who hit with "Young Boy" (1964 and 1968), and Tammy Levon who hit with "A

School Girl's Dream" (1967) helped to firmly establish Chicago as a center for the teen-soprano soul sound.[3] Small record men such as Clarence Johnson, Don Talty, and Peter Wright understood this sound and worked to produce such records for the soul market.

Formal Records

Don Talty, a construction engineer by trade, started in the record business in the spring of 1959 when he took over the operation but not ownership of Angelo Giardini's Formal Records. The label was founded in February 1956 by Giardini, who owned a formal-wear shop on Chicago Avenue on the West Side. Giardini was an aspiring songwriter and basically began the label to get his songs recorded. After nothing happened with his first three releases, Talty stepped in. Talty was born August 16, 1911, in downstate Illinois, and by the late 1940s was the owner of his own excavating business in the Chicago area.[4]

Talty was not young and was not black, but he had a lifelong love for black music, especially jazz and blues, and thought he could achieve something. He gradually withdrew from the construction business so that by 1962 he was a full-time record entrepreneur. He operated the business out of his home at 8501 South Harlem Avenue in the southwestern suburb of Oak Lawn with the help of his wife, Zelda, and his two teenage daughters, Janice and Joanne. His recording acts would all fondly relate how Talty always brought his daughters around to the recording sessions and the shows he promoted. For a time Talty operated his publishing company, JanJo, in the Woods Theater building at 54 West Randolph in the heart of Chicago's old Tin Pan Alley district. Several of Talty's acts, such as Jan Bradley from Robbins and the Trinidads from Argo and LaGrange, were also from the southwest suburbs.

Talty was not that interested in the Formal label per se, preferring to lease records to other companies over putting them out himself. He had his most successful artist, Jan Bradley, record mainly for Chess from 1963 on.

Before Talty had his big success with Bradley in 1963, he released records on the Trinidads (who included future soul stars Chuck Colbert, Jr., and Nolan Chance), the Masquerades (the Scott brothers), soul singer Ace St. Clair (brother of Johnny Ace), jazz pianist Earl Washington, and solo blues artists Guitar Red (Paul Johnson) and Willie Mabon. He got local hits out of Guitar Red's "Red Hot Red" in 1960 and Willie Mabon's "Got to Have Some" in 1962.

One of Talty's biggest hits was the instrumental "You Can't Sit Down" by the Philip Upchurch Combo. It became a top-ten r&b hit and top-thirty pop chart hit in 1961 after it was leased to Oklahoma-based Boyd Records and distributed by United Artist Records. Talty, curiously, never seemed to own a label, yet for various labels that his productions appeared on—such as Formal, Boyd, and Night Owl—he had logos designed, labels printed up, and records pressed.

Philip Upchurch was born in Chicago, July 19, 1941. His father, a pianist, introduced him to the ukulele, and he soon graduated to electric guitar and bass. He began his professional career playing in backing bands for r&b acts, working successively for the Kool Gents, the Spaniels, the Dells, and Dee Clark. It was when he was a member of Clark's band that "You Can't Sit Down" was recorded. The band's organist, Cornell Muldrow, had written the song and earlier recorded it for the Dasher label in Baltimore.[5]

On a tour in the southern states in 1960, the band found that the instrumental proved very effective as a warm-up number with audiences. In New Orleans Clark financed a studio recording of "You Can't Sit Down" by his group consisting of Upchurch on guitar, Muldrow on organ, David Brooks on saxophone, Mac Johnson on trumpet, and Joe Haddrick on drums. Vee Jay was given the recording, but sat on it. Rumor of this great instrumental filtered around town and Talty approached Upchurch, who had access to the recording. Talty had Upchurch put a bass overdub on the organ part and added vocal shouts to the mix, and the rest is history. Upchurch during the sixties became one of the most in-demand session musicians on the bass and guitar and helped significantly to shape the Chicago sound of soul.

Jan Bradley was born Addie Bradley, July 6, 1943, in Byhalia, Mississippi, and at around four years of age moved with her family to Robbins, Illinois.[6] Early on, she exhibited a talent for singing, which her family nourished by providing her with formal voice lessons. Her vocal abilities eventually led to a professional career, as she explained: "All through grammar school I was singing in the church choir, was lead soloist, and I was singing at different affairs, weddings and so forth. I was like a sophomore in high school, Blue Island Eisenhower, and I met this group of guys, the Passions. They asked me to sing with them and I did. We had a talent show in Robbins, and I guess that's when someone called Don Talty. He was looking for talent. He heard our group, liked me, liked my voice, and thought he could do more with me as a solo act."[7]

That was in 1959, and Bradley's parents decided that their daughter would finish high school before committing herself to a career in popular music. Upon completion of high school in 1961 she joined Talty.

Talty made a most wise decision in launching his singer: he obtained the services of Curtis Mayfield, who was just beginning to write for other artists besides his own Impressions. Talty was managing Phil Upchurch and knew he was friends with Mayfield. One thing led to another, and, said Mayfield, "He brought Jan Bradley and asked me to write and produce her. She was a very cute young lady and she had—sometimes as a singer it's not how well you sing, it's just that innocence or that certain something about the artist that makes a song appealing. Jan had that innocence in her voice."[8] Mayfield then wrote and produced "We Girls" on Bradley.

Talty's original intention was not to release "We Girls" on Formal. Said Bradley, "He put it out on that label because he couldn't get a big company to pick it up. He tried in New York with Columbia and with United Artists. I remember hearing a conversation he had with Art Talmadge, who was in charge of United Artists. He didn't think it was very commercial, because I was a black singer singing about something called 'We Girls.' Don Talty came back and put it out on his own label to try to get it off the ground and get me recognized and heard. And that happened. It sold pretty good and a lot of people bought it."[9]

Bradley was simply delightful on the song, exhibiting perfectly that innocence that Mayfield heard. When she sang in her clear youthful soprano, "Girls, we can't help it, we were born to hypnotize," one became a transfixed believer. "We Girls" became a top r&b hit in Chicago in the spring of 1962, and got play on WLS and some crossover sales as well. When Talmadge saw the record was selling, he finally expressed interest in it, but Talty rebuffed him. Although one can understand Talty's feelings, it was probably an unfortunate decision, because without the distribution muscle that UA could provide, "We Girls" remained a local phenomenon.

Following a few commercial failures in late 1962 Bradley came out with her biggest hit, "Mama Didn't Lie," a Mayfield composition almost perfectly realized in the studio. The recording had a highly compelling arrangement worked out by Eddie Silvers, Bradley, and her guitarist, Freddy Young. Using a prominent electric bass guitar, Young gave the record a medium-tempo drive to carry Bradley's pop-soul vocals. "That was the whole idea," said Bradley, "to get a real good flowing bass sound going and kind of not overpower my voice, and it worked really well. We knew we had a hit right after we did a few takes of it and got it down."[10] The record was released on Formal in November, and after Chess picked it up the following month, it zoomed up the charts in early 1963 to become a pop as well as a soul hit. It did best on the *Cash Box* r&b chart, lasting fifteen weeks and going to four position.

If Bradley could have followed "Mama Didn't Lie" with an equally strong Mayfield song, her career might have gone upward and onward. Instead, record company machinations interfered. "After 'Mama Didn't Lie,'" said Bradley, "I didn't get another song from Curtis, because he and Chess had some kind of disagreement. I think Chess wanted a part of the publishing, and Curtis was not willing to give up any. They said, okay, if he's not willing to give up anything we just won't use any of his material. That hurt me because I needed his material. They really did harm to me."[11]

Bradley had to fall back on her songwriting talent and on Talty's producing skills, the former a bit stronger than the latter. The next two Bradley releases on Chess were weak songs and did not do much, but in December 1964 she came out with a terrific record, "I'm Over You," written by Bradley. This was the first Chess record of Bradley's produced in-house by Billy Davis. "When Phil Chess heard that song," said Bradley, "he felt it had a lot of possibilities and he wanted his people to work with it."[12] The mid-tempo song with Riley Hampton's imaginative arrangements and a great guitar riff by Upchurch provided a superb showcase for Bradley's vocal. The song lasted ten weeks and went to position fifteen on *Cash Box*'s r&b survey in early 1965.

Bradley's next success was "Just a Summer Memory," written by Bradley and Talty and produced by Leonard Caston, Jr., and Billy Davis. The fully orchestrated Phil Wright arrangements gave the record a typical Chess-studio sound, which was to Bradley's benefit. The song was a minor hit on Chicago r&b radio in September 1966. Her last local chart record was "It's Just Your Way," a pleasant-sounding Kermit Chandler composition. It got good play in the city in December 1967. It was obvious that neither the Chess songwriters nor Bradley was able to come up with songs strong enough to sustain her career, and Bradley called it quits in 1969. She got married and returned to school, and when I interviewed her in 1987 she had earned an M.A. degree and was employed in social work.

Meanwhile Talty had closed down Formal in 1963. He continued his work with Bradley on Chess as well as on various other labels he was associated with through the 1960s, such as Adanti and Night Owl. By the early 1970s he was out of the record business, and in 1979 he passed away.

Nike Records

Nike Records was formed in 1961 by Charles Colbert, Sr., a musician and restaurant owner. His son, Charles Colbert, Jr., had just joined a vocal group, the Daylighters, who had recorded some sides for Talty at the RCA studios. Talty had lost interest in the Daylighters, and the members of the group did not have the money to pay for the studio costs to retrieve the masters. They went to the senior Colbert, who not only gave them the money but set up a company to put out the record on the Nike label.[13]

The principal partners in CaCoOl Productions, as the operation was first called, were both Colberts, Bob Catron (a musician married to Colbert's daughter, Claudette), and Doc Oliver (a songwriter). Colbert Jr. (born

August 30, 1939, in Argo) was the principal producer and songwriter, and Catron and Tony Gideon (founding member of the Daylighters) were the initial promotion men. Bandleader Burgess Gardner and Johnny Pate did the arranging. The company's offices were at the Colbert home at 8956 South Wallace. Recording was carried out at various studios, but a lot of woodshedding was done at a place at 800 East Sixty-third Street where many South Side r&b acts would write songs, rehearse, and work up material.

The company reorganized in 1962. Oliver and Catron left, the latter to work A&R and produce for the Witch/Cortland label group. The reorganized Nike company introduced new subsidiary labels, Tip Top and Jive. Catron, who was still part of the family, retained a little bit of stake in the company and as a result there was a bit of cross-fertilization between Witch/Cortland and Nike/Tip Top/Jive. For example, the Nike vocal group, the Candles, recorded as the Blenders on Witch. In 1966, Colbert Jr. added the Mellow label to the operation.

The Colbert labels specialized in vocal groups—specifically the Daylighters, of course, but also the Dolphins, the Salvadores, and Guys and Dolls. The only group that achieved any measure of success was the Daylighters, however. After Mellow was established the company got good sales with a fine solo artist, Marvin L. Sims.

The Daylighters were not originally from Chicago, but from Birmingham, Alabama. The group was formed by Hooper City High School student Tony Gideon in 1956. After scuffling for nearly two years, the Daylighters determined that Birmingham was no place to establish a recording career, and when some members made plans to move to Chicago at the end of the school year, the rest of the group followed. The group that came to Chicago consisted of Gideon, Levi Moreland, Eddie Thomas, and brothers Dorsey and George Wood. (Thomas died in 1986.)[14]

The Daylighters searched around the city for a record company, but met with no success after trying at Chess, Federal, and other labels. After two months Moreland, a bit homesick, returned home to Alabama. Things began looking up after the Daylighters obtained the managerial services of a local deejay, George "G.G." Graves, then the morning man at WGES. He brought the group to Cadillac Baby (Narvel Eatmon), the owner of the Cadillac Baby Club at Forty-eighth and Dearborn, a record shop, and Bea and Baby record company. The Daylighters did backup work as well as coming out with "Mad House Jump," their first record, in September 1959.

Shortly after "Mad House Jump," the group found itself in need of a guitarist. Graves worked his magic again and brought in a highly talented musician and creative songwriter from Kalamazoo, Michigan—Gerald Sims. About the same time, the group started an association with Betty Everett.

Graves thought the trend was toward male groups headed by female leads, so Everett was teamed up with the Daylighters for gigs around the city. They recorded together on one record, "Please Come Back," on Carl Jones's CJ label.

Up until 1961 nothing was happening with the Daylighters. The association with Everett did not work out and she departed. Lesser groups struggling in the business with as many years as the Daylighters under their belts probably would have packed it in, but the group was made of sterner stuff and was unusually persistent and enterprising. The turnabout came when the group joined Nike. Gideon at this point was forced out of the group over creative differences and was replaced with Colbert Jr. Gideon worked briefly as promotion man before being drafted into the service in September 1961.

The Daylighters' first Nike release was "This Heart of Mine," a dated doowop led by Dorsey Wood that did not do much. More promising records soon followed, however. Two releases reflected the ascendency of Gerald Sims, who contributed significantly to a modern soul style in the group. The first was the beautiful "Oh What a Way to be Loved," which combined a supper-club soul feel with haunting vocal-group harmonies. Sims, who wrote the song and sang lead, had created a magnificent transitional tune bridging the doowop and soul eras.

The second Sims-led record, "Cool Breeze," was a sensational local hit in September 1962. It even got a little bit of pop play on the top-forty stations, reaching as high as seventeen on WLS. "Cool Breeze" was a genuine soul record, the first real break from the group's 1950s stylings. As with most records of the soul era, it owed as much to the arrangement and production as to the vocal artistry. Pate did the imaginative string arrangements that conveyed a blowing wind affect.

After achieving two successive hits with the Daylighters, Sims's talents did not go unnoticed. In 1962 Sims left to join Carl Davis at OKeh records. The Daylighters' next record was slow in coming out; in fact, the group was drifting apart. The Wood brothers, Thomas, and Colbert were together again on only one more session, in the summer of 1963. They recorded four songs—four Colbert compositions—"Bottomless Pit" and "I Can't Stop Crying," in which Colbert took the leads, and two others in which Dorsey took the leads. But before these records came out, some records from Catron were released using the Daylighters' name.

With the Daylighters assumed to be inactive, Catron decided to push a new record in the summer of 1963, "Elephant Walk," by Donald Jenkins and a group consisting of Ronald Strong, Walter Granger, and some members of the Daylighters. The record was billed as being by "Donald Jenkins and the Daylighters." "Elephant Walk" became a national hit and Colbert Sr.

protested the use of the Daylighters' name. When the record was peaking, Catron changed the name on the label to the "Delighters."

In October, Gideon had finished his Army commitment and returned to Chicago at the tail end of the "Elephant Walk" brouhaha. The Wood brothers had left the group, and the decision was made to re-form the Daylighters with Gideon, Thomas, Colbert, and two new members, baritone Curtis Burrell and tenor Ulysses McDonald (both of whom had been in the Dolphins).

"Bottomless Pit" and the flip, "I Can't Stop Crying," meanwhile broke in November. Throughout the winter both sides got substantial airplay. Both were solid songs in the soul idiom and rank among the group's best. The group's other success during the winter was "Oh Mom (Teach Me How to Uncle Willie)," probably the most successful of the Uncle Willie dance records whose popularity swept the city in early 1964. Colbert wrote and sang lead on the song. Backing the Daylighters on some of their releases was a local rock group, Gary and the Knight Lites. Colbert, who played bass, had teamed up with the band in 1963, and during the next three years Gary and the Knight Lites emerged as one of the leading dance-hall bands in the city.

The Daylighters' next successul release was "Whisper of the Wind," in December 1964. Gideon sang lead on this delightful tune with a light wispy beat that presaged the similar reggae beat of the 1970s. The record was leased to Vee Jay, which put it out on its Tollie subsidiary. The group had another local success in June 1965 with the incredibly intense "For My Baby," again with lead work by Gideon.

Based on their rather modest recording successes, the Daylighters were able to get a few gigs, mostly locally. During the Christmas season of 1964 the group made a tour of Alabama and Mississippi, but the Daylighters essentially broke up after "For My Baby." Colbert was more interested in the Knight Lites, who were metamorphosing into the American Breed (in 1967 the group had a million-selling hit, "Bend Me, Shape Me").

While Colbert was pursuing his career in the American Breed, he and his father continued the record company activities with the Tip Top label and with its new label, Mellow. The most successful artist on Mellow was Marvin L. Sims, who had a number of records that were regional successes and one national hit, "Talkin' 'Bout Soul," in 1968. Sims was born on December 11, 1944, in Sedalia, Missouri. He graduated from high school in 1961 and joined the Air Force, and soon found himself stationed at Chanute Air Force Base, in Rantoul, Illinois.[15]

Sims finished his Air Force obligation in 1965, but before his discharge he had already gravitated to a civilian band in nearby Champaign called the Gaypoppers. The band was very much a family affair, featuring among its four or five pieces brothers Edward Lane (drums) and Bobby Lane (guitar), and their father John Green (saxophone). Sims with Bobby Lane started writing some songs and in late 1965 made the acquaintance of Marshall Neil of USA Records. Neil in turn brought the pair to Mellow Records.

During 1966-67, Colbert Jr. released six sides on Sims, mostly of Lane/Sims compositions, and sold most of them in the South. Explained Sims, "Our drawing market was Chicago and in major black areas in the South. We sold there a lot, partly because Colbert's sister and brother-in-law, Bob Catron, owned a record distributorship in Memphis. So every time we got a record out, it shot through the South really big. I went through Memphis, Arkansas, and those places all the time, every record I had."[16] The best of his Mellow records was an achingly beautiful rendition of the Donnie Elbert classic, "What Can I Do?" (1966).

In 1968, after some three years in the music business, Sims was still treading water: no forward movement. But fortune smiled on him with the next release, "Talkin' 'Bout Soul," an up-tempo song by Lane and Sims. The brighter-sounding arrangements by Lane perhaps spelled the difference as much as the distribution that Colbert obtained on MCA's Revue label. Sims said, "One report I read in either *Record World* or *Billboard* at the time stated that 'Talkin' 'Bout Soul' sold close to eight hundred thousand copies. However, Colbert Productions and I never saw that kind of a return. I do know that Uni/Revue promoted and pushed it nationwide."[17] Sims never was able to repeat his success. Several fine releases came out on Revue and later on Mercury, but when nothing happened with them Sims basically left the business in 1972. He went back to school and obtained an advanced degree in psychology.

By the last half of the 1960s the Nike Company was essentially Colbert Jr.'s operation. The Nike and Tip Top labels were ended by 1967 and Mellow by 1969. The younger Colbert continued into the mid-1970s occasionally releasing records through major labels. His father continued his restaurant business with two barbeque outlets on the South Side. When I first interviewed Colbert Jr. in 1974 he was writing jingles and commercials in the advertising field. Colbert Sr. passed away around 1985.

Erman Record Company

The success of Erman Record Company was fueled by equal amounts of enthusiasm for soft soul and for hard black coal. Bill Erman was the owner of Diamond Coal Company, at 1501 West Cortland on the North Side. He made his money from coal and oil, but his real love was music. Erman was born in Chicago on December 26, 1930, and inherited the coal business from his family. While in college he started his own band in which he played saxophone and clarinet, and the group played in Ivy League schools. Erman eventually graduated to songwriting, composing a couple of songs for Johnny Desmond along the way. He soon established his own publishing firm, Venetia Music, and from there it was no great leap to his own record firm.

Erman founded the company in 1961 and operated it from the offices of his coal company. His labels were Witch and Cortland for r&b music and Ermine for rock 'n' roll and country music.[18] He produced most of the rock 'n' roll records and wrote many of the songs for the acts, including the black ones. He handled A&R for Ermine, but had a black musician, Bob Catron, do the A&R and producing work for Witch/Cortland. Catron usually did the arranging, but sometimes brought in Johnny Pate.

Catron had a long career in music before his association with Nike and Witch/Cortland. He was born August 28, 1934, in Memphis, where he was raised. He was a music major in college, but while still in school he began gigging in r&b bands in the city's flourishing music scene. During the early 1950s he played in the Beale Streeters Band—which included Johnny Ace, Roscoe Gordon, Earl Forest, and Bobby Bland—both on tour and on record. Catron played saxophone and other brass instruments in the band. For the next decade, he worked in bands, and around 1960 ended up in Chicago where he was drawn into the recording scene.

The third key man in the Erman Record Company was Earl Glicken, the operation's aggressive promotion man. The efforts of Glicken were instrumental to the substantial local success the company enjoyed with many of its records.

The company had some success with rock 'n' roll, getting local hits with Johnny Cooper's "Bonnie Do" (January 1963) and Angelo's Angels' "Spring Cleaning" (April 1964) and "I Don't Believe It" (July 1964). The biggest hits were on the r&b end and were usually produced by Catron. The company's first release was an r&b record produced by Erman called "Son-in-Law," an answer song to Ernie K-Doe's "Mother-in-Law." It was performed by a Chicago lounge pianist/singer, Louise Brown, and made it on *Billboard's* pop chart for five weeks in the spring of 1961. After that, Catron took over r&b A&R and concentrated his efforts on soft-soul vocal groups. "Groups were the thing then" was his explanation. The basic sound Catron established was a kind of transitional music, half evoking the 1950s era of doowop and half presaging the emerging era of soul. Most of the artists he worked with began their careers in the 1950s, notably Donald Jenkins.

Donald Jenkins with his group the Delighters were a veteran outfit that had been intermittently together for some eight years before recording their big hit on Cortland, "(Native Girl) Elephant Walk" (1963). The original group went back to 1955 when each of the members was about twelve or thirteen years old and attending grade school on the South Side. Jenkins as lead singer got together with Ronald Strong (tenor), Walter Granger (baritone), and William Taylor (bass). (Strong had in 1952 sung with Dee Clark and Sammy McGrier in the Hambone Kids.)[19]

The group was originally called the Fortunes, and their break in the business came when they won a singing contest at the Pershing Hotel, the prize being a chance to audition for a recording contract. The upshot was that the group recorded one record for Chess in 1955, called "Believe in Me."

The Fortunes broke up before the members had finished Dunbar High. Jenkins went into the Navy for a hitch of three years, and after he was discharged in the early 1960s he got together with Strong and recorded a few records. As Rico and Ronnie, Jenkins and Strong recorded "It Takes a Long Time" (1962) for Chess; as the Starr Brothers, they recorded several records for Cortland, notably "Don Juan," which got some play in Pittsburgh and Chicago in early 1963, and "Mr. Auctioneer," which made a little noise in Chicago in April of that year.

Granger rejoined Jenkins and Strong in mid-1963, and the new group came out with "Elephant Walk," first as the Daylighters and then as the Delighters. Jenkins's haunting lead vocals, the fine use of background vocals, the clashing cymbals, plus the addition of jungle sound effects, all added up to a song atmospherically evocative of the subject. The song entered *Billboard's* pop chart on September 14 and left the chart after November 2 at position sixty-four. With more aggressive distribution the record could have done much better. In some markets, the song was not played at all, while in others it was a top-five record.

The later releases, "Adios (My Secret Love)" and "I've Settled Down," were superb sounds that never became hits. Jenkins went on the "Dick Clark Show" and sang "Adios" to a national audience, but then Cortland backed off the record. The problem was that the song was a rewrite of a Nolan Strong and Diablos record from nine years earlier called "Adios My Desert Love." It was written by Devora Brown, who headed Fortune Records, the label that released the song. The Jenkins version was credited to Jenkins and Catron. Said Brown, "When we found out about it, our attorney wrote them a strong letter. They apologized and they said that we could even use their master. I thought it was a good master, better than Nolan Strong's version. But Cortland apparently quit plugging it, because I guess they couldn't keep their name on it. It seemed to be going real good, too."[20] "Adios" made its noise in November 1963.

The "Adios" fiasco could have been avoided, according to Catron, had he listened to advice proffered by Billy Davis at Chess: "Billy Davis heard it and said 'Man, I've heard that song somewhere before.' I said, 'Oh no, Donald wrote this. In fact, he hummed this to me, and I wrote the music down for it.' He said, 'No, Bob, I've heard that. If I were you I'd find out where the guy got that song. He's changed it around a little, but I have heard that song.' I went ahead and put it out and it got a beautiful reception. It seemed about every time we got something started we ran into legal problems."[21]

During his stay at Cortland, Jenkins with the help of Catron penned a number of songs for a girl group he brought to the company from Marshall High, the Versalettes/Trinkets. "Shining Armor" was a local hit for the Versalettes in the fall of 1963. The song had an appealing young soprano lead that made it especially attractive to high schoolers. As the Trinkets the group recorded a Jenkins tune called "The Fisherman," and the girls sang on the record with such passion it was almost camp.

The Delighters did few live gigs—mainly high-school lip-sync engagements. They did, however, play some Chicago nightclubs and tour on Dick Clark's Caravan of Stars. After the Catron association ended, the group made records only sporadically. By the early 1970s they were no longer together. Ronnie Strong died in about 1983.

The Ideals made their name with an aggressive dance tune called "The Gorilla" in 1963 and were commonly thought of as a soul-era group. But long before the Ideals had ever made their name on wax, they had established a reputation during the 1950s as one of the best West Side r&b ensembles.[22] The group was formed about 1952 when the singers were freshmen in high school. The original members were Frank Cowan (lead), Leonard Mitchell (first tenor), Wes Spraggins (second tenor), Robert Tharp (baritone), and Clifford Clayborn (bass). Most of the members attended Crane High.

The Ideals knocked around the city for years before getting their first opportunity to record in 1961. The group at this time consisted of Reggie Jackson (lead), Leonard Mitchell (lead tenor), Robert Tharp (baritone), and Sam Steward (bass). Deejay Richard Stamz had a record label called Paso on which he put out four heavily doowop sides on the group, but nothing came of them.

The Ideals cooled their heels for a while before their next opportunity to record presented itself, in 1963. By that time they had added a new lead, Eddie Williams. A former member of the Five Chances, Howard Pitman, had started a record company, Concord, and chose the Ideals to record a song he composed called "The Gorilla." With this record, the Ideals broke with their doowop past. Williams's rough-hewn aggressive lead gave the record a decidedly soul sound.

"The Gorilla," in September 1963, near the end of the Monkey dance craze, proved to be the Ideals' biggest hit. Jackson related that Herb Kent would take the group around to all the high schools along with a guy in a gorilla suit to promote the record. With the powerful influence of Kent the record sold some ninety thousand copies in Chicago.[23] Very early it proved beyond the capabilities of Pitman and Concord sold it to Cortland along with the Ideals' contract. Cortland made the record a national hit, and the Ideals toured the entire chitlin' circuit. Unfortunately for the Ideals they could not sustain their success with decent follow-up hits.

Pitman with a fellow ex-member of the Five Chances, Hilliard Jones, brought to Witch/Cortland the Blenders, who during 1962-63 came out with a half dozen excellent releases. The group consisted of Jones and Albert Hunter, the latter also a veteran of the 1950s, and three young ladies—Goldie Coates, Delores Johnson, and Gail Mapp (lead).[24] The group scored with a national hit with the Jones-penned "Daughter" in the summer of 1963, and recorded other terrific songs such as Jones's "Boys Think" and Erman's "Love Is a Treasure." The Blenders last recording was "Junior," an answer song to "Daughter" that they recorded as the Candles on the Nike label.

Before the end of 1964, Erman closed down his record operation. Catron returned to Memphis and opened a distributorship as well as a chain of record stores. He continued to dabble in recording, most notably coming out with Calvin Leavy's "Cummins Prison Farm" in 1970. Earl Glicken helped establish Dick Simon's Satellite/St. Lawrence operation in 1965, taking the Ideals with him to the label.

Satellite Record Company

Satellite Record Company was founded by Dick Simon in 1965. Simon was the owner of an insurance agency, S. M. Simon and Company, at 4849 North Western on the North Side, and the record company operated out of the insurance offices.[25] The Impressions' old manager, Eddie Thomas, was brought in to run a subsidiary label, Thomas, and Earl Glicken came in to do promotion. The principal labels were Satellite and St. Lawrence, both distributed by Chess.

Simon hired Don Clay as general manager and made Monk Higgins his principal producer and A&R director. St. Louis hard-soul singer Chuck Bernard was signed not only to record records but also to produce and perform some A&R work. Higgins and Burgess Gardner did the arranging. The company had its biggest hits with soft-soul records, but because of the backgrounds of Higgins and Bernard there was a strong line of hard-soul records that came out of the operation. Two of them were solid local hits sung by Bernard, "Indian Giver" (1965) and "Funny Changes" (1966). Higgins, as a producer, arranger, composer, and saxophone player, was one of the principal architects of the hard-soul sound in the city. He was born Milton Bland in Menifee, Arkansas, October 17, 1936. He graduated from Arkansas State University with a music degree, and did advanced studies at the Chicago School of Music. After some years first as a school teacher and then as a social worker in Chicago, he joined One-derful Records shortly after the label's founding in 1962. After joining Satellite, Higgins with his tenor saxophone produced some nice instrumental hits, a national r&b chart hit with "Who-Dun-It?" (1966) and a double-sided local hit with "Ceatrix Did It"/"What Fah" (1966).[26]

The veteran Ideals were one of the company's first acts. The group by 1965 was reduced to three members—Reggie Jackson, Leonard Mitchell, and Sam Steward. Eddie Williams had been drafted into the armed services and Robert Tharp had dropped out to join Jerry Murray in a dance duo called Tom and Jerrio, specializing in Boogaloo dance records. The group's biggest record with the company was the Higgins-produced "Kissin'," which managed to make *Billboard's* national r&b chart in February 1966. Their best number was perhaps "You Lost and I Won," produced by Chuck Bernard and Bruce Scott. Sadly, the Ideals were attracting little interest among record buyers during 1965-67 and they were forced to call it quits, an uneventful end for a group that had been together fifteen years.

Satellite had much better success with the Vontastics, whose recording career began through a talent contest sponsored by radio station WVON. As the winning act, their group's prize was a recording contract with Satellite/St. Lawrence and a name derived from the station's call letters.[27] E. Rodney Jones from the station became the group's mentor. The Vontastics in 1965 consisted of Bobby Newsome, Kenneth Gholar, Jose Holmes, and Raymond Penn. Newsome wrote most of the group's material.

The Vontastics' first record was the up-tempo "I'll Never Say Goodbye," a substantial hit in Chicago in the summer of 1965. They followed with "Peace of Mind," a remarkable mid-tempo ballad that virtually defined the Chicago brand of soft soul, but as with the earlier record it remained a local phenomenon. By the second record the Vontastics had garnered considerable local celebrity, and in August they appeared on local television.

The Vontastics' next record, "I Need You," was one of the group's lesser sides, but it still got good airplay and sales in Chicago. In the fall of 1966, the group had its biggest hit with a cover of the Beatles' "Day-tripper," and was rewarded with an engagement at the Regal in September. "Daytripper" made the national pop and r&b charts. That was the last real success for the group. Its final record came out on Chess in 1967.

The most typical work of Higgins at the company was the records he made with Mamie Galore. The singer was born Mamie Davis in Erwin, Mississippi, on September 24, 1940. She began singing in church and school, graduating from O'Bannon High in Greenville, Mississippi, in 1958. She joined a local band, Herman Scott and the Swinging Kings, and worked with them until 1961. Then for a year Davis worked with the Ike and Tina Turner Review. From 1962 to 1965 she toured with the Little Milton Band and ended up in Chicago where Little Milton was making his home and recording.[28]

The singer's first record for the company, "Special Agent 34-24-38," gave Mamie her new name—" 'cause I'm special agent, double-o, 34-24-38, and I answer to the name of Mamie Galore." The record came out at the height of the spy-story craze in 1965, when James Bond movies, television shows "I Spy" and "Get Smart," and so on were capturing the imagination of the public—and apparently record producers as well. There were many soul records out at the time in the same vein, notably Detroit artist Edwin Starr's "Agent Double-0 Soul" (1965). Hard-soul singer Jamo Thomas, who was based in Chicago at the time, got a national hit out of "I Spy (for the F.B.I.)," which was produced by Higgins and was a national hit on the Thomas label in 1966.

In March 1966, Galore got her only hit, albeit local, with "It Ain't Necessary," which was somewhat in the Motown style with strong chick chorusing and a driving beat. But Galore brought to the record a somewhat funky flavor that could only come from her Mississippi roots. In 1968 she followed Higgins to California and in 1972 returned to Mississippi, where she continued to perform.

Cash McCall had perhaps the company's biggest selling hit with "When You Wake Up" in 1966. He was born Maurice Dollison in New Madrid, Missouri, January 28, 1941. Essentially a hard-soul singer, he began his career in gospel. He made his first public appearance at the age of twelve, singing with the Belmont Singers, a group from the area. By the time he graduated from high school, he had developed his musical skills on guitar, bass, and tenor saxophone. The early 1960s saw him in Chicago taking part in the gospel scene, playing guitar for various quartets, including the Five Blind Boys of Mississippi, the Pilgrim Jubilee Singers, and the Gospel Songbirds.[29]

Dollison began his secular-music career in 1963 when he signed with One-derful Records. In 1966 he was signed to the Thomas label and hit with his very first release, "When You Wake Up," which went to position nine and lasted thirteen weeks on the *Cash Box* r&b chart. Dollison was billed as "Cash McCall," because of the custom of the time of giving singers "marketable" names. "When You Wake Up," written by Dollison and Higgins and produced by Higgins, was a bright, up beat song with the typical Chicago medium-tempo lope. Befitting the song, McCall sang with a light, uptown approach.

In 1967 McCall and Higgins moved to Chess Records and put out two records on the Checker label in McCall's more customary hard-soul style. But the songs were not good. In 1976 McCall left Chicago and moved to Los Angeles to work as a studio musician.

Dick Simon folded his record company in early 1967. Chess picked up most of the company's assets, both tangible (recording equipment and so forth) and intangible (creative talent). Don Clay and Higgins joined Chess, as did many of the artists, such as the Vontastics, Cash McCall, and Johnny Sayles. Higgins stayed at Chess no longer than a year before moving to Los Angeles, where he worked for United Artists, ABC, and other large labels as a producer. His best success was producing the blues singer Bobby Bland during the late 1970s and early 1980s. In 1986 Higgins died at the age of fifty. Meanwhile, Thomas joined Curtis Mayfield and reestablished his Thomas label as a subsidiary of Curtom Records.

Don Caron Productions

Don Caron Productions was owned by Peter Wright and Don Caron, and the company recorded both rock 'n' roll acts and r&b acts. Offices were at 185 North Wabash on the near North Side. Recordings were usually done at Chess studios. The company had its most notable r&b success with a girl group called the Drew-vels and with Patti Drew, who was pulled out of the group. Both acts had records released through Los Angeles-based Capitol Records. Another r&b act of the production company was the Naturals, a male vocal group whose records were released on the Mercury subsidiary, Smash.[30]

Don Caron was a schoolteacher who also headed an orchestra that was popular in the area throughout the 1960s. The orchestra was the house band at Adventureland amusement park in the western suburbs, and also the studio band for a local rock label, I.R.C., owned by Jerry Mann and Leonard March. In 1962 the Caron Orchestra got an instrumental hit on a reworking of an old traditional number, "The Work Song." Released on I.R.C., the record lasted two months on the WLS survey chart.

Peter Wright (born in Chicago in 1935) began in the music business playing trumpet in area bands, but it was the behind-the-scenes record business that intrigued him. After successfully promoting a record as a free-lancer, he got a job in 1955 with United Distributors, opening and running the company's new branch office in Indianapolis. In the late 1950s, he was working as United's North Side sales manager, and Maury Lathowers, a friend he brought into the business, was working the South Side.

By 1963 Wright was teamed with Don Caron and producing and managing rock 'n' roll acts such as the New Colony Six. Lathowers was working as regional promotion man for Capitol Records. The entry of these record men into r&b was with a group of talented singers from Evanston, a suburb north of Chicago.

The Drew-vels had their origin in the Drew family, whose brood consisted of six daughters—Patti, Lorraine, Erma, Cynthia, Tina, and Rosalind. Patti, the eldest, was born in Charleston, South Carolina, on December 29, 1944. In the early years the girls were raised in Nashville, Tennessee, but in 1956 the family moved to Evanston, Illinois. By the time the three oldest girls—Patti, Lorraine (born 1946), and Erma (1948)—were in their teen years and attending Evanston High, they were strongly involved in singing in their mother's church.[31]

The girls' break into the record business came through their mother, who at that time was working as a domestic for Maury Lathowers. Mrs. Drew asked him to come listen to her daughters at church. Instead, he invited the entire family to his place for an audition. Lathowers liked what he heard and took an audition tape to Peter Wright. Impressed, Wright signed the girls to his production firm and Lathowers facilitated a contract with Capitol.

The group's first record, "Tell Him," featured the three elder Drew sisters plus the writer of the song, Carlton Black. The group was a total family affair, as Black was married to Erma. "Tell Him" was a huge success in Chicago during December 1963, both on the pop and the r&b charts, but it had only spotty sales nationwide. The beautiful follow-up, "It's My Time," was also a moderate hit, in April 1964, but with lesser sales. "I've Known" had good radio play in August, but did not have the ingredients to sell in any appreciable numbers. The Drew-vels got some work as a result of the records. Their most prestigious date was at the Regal Theater in March 1964, playing on a bill that featured Gene Chandler and Major Lance. Things had gone fast for the Drew-vels in only a few months, perhaps too fast, because the group was finding it difficult to get along, and broke up.

Before the breakup of the Drew-vels, Carlton Black achieved some success as a lead singer of a vocal group called the Naturals, consisting of fellow Evanstonians Charles Perry (tenor), Charles Woolridge (second tenor), Arthur Cox (baritone), and Andrew Thomas (bass).[32] The group came out with a beautiful mellow ballad, written by Black in the Impressions switch-off lead style, called "Let Love Be True." The record was big in Chicago, reaching as high as number three on WVON's survey in early spring, 1964.

The record did not make the national charts, however. Several follow-ups did nothing and by early 1965 the group had disbanded. The only member of the Naturals to continue in the recording field was Andrew Thomas, who in 1967 joined the Mighty Marvelows of "In the Morning" fame.

Meanwhile, more than a year after the Drew-vels broke up, Wright called Patti Drew and said he wanted her, but not the rest of the group. She first recorded without success for Wright's label, Quill—as did her sisters without Patti—but then in 1967 signed again with Capitol. She immediately hit with a re-recording of "Tell Him," with Black again doing the bass part. "Tell Him" was a minor national hit in October 1967, reaching as high as twenty-two on *Billboard*'s r&b chart.

Drew's next notable success, in July 1968, was a song Neil Sedaka wrote, "Working on a Groovy Thing." It was a bigger hit for the Fifth Dimension, but many soul fans considered Drew's version the superior rendition. Drew's career at Capitol was successful—she came out with five albums over a half decade—and she built a substantial career touring. Drew mentioned that she appeared in every state except Alaska and Hawaii, and even toured South America.

The touring, however, took a toll. Drew, perhaps somewhat jaded by playing before too many unappreciative audiences, cracked, "I worked the Playboy circuit so long I thought I was a bunny." She admitted that in 1971 she "freaked out," taking acid and getting involved in a heavy drug scene in Southern California. She recalled, "I completely lost contact around me. I became very militant, and finally my manager suggested that I take some time off."[33] To her disappointment, however, she was never asked to come back into the business on a serious basis.

By the time Patti Drew left the business, Wright was heavily involved in the operation of an r&b label he owned with Howard Bedno called Twinight. Maury Lathowers had gone to the West Coast and had risen to vice president of A&R at Capitol. In the 1980s he was the A&R man for jazz at Columbia. Don Caron had continued his principal career as a teacher.

Roulette Records

Roulette was a New York independent owned by Morris Levy, one-time owner of the Birdland Club, famed in the 1950s for featuring jazz greats. In November 1963 Levy announced that the company had set up an office in Chicago and that Chess A&R man Ralph Bass would run the operation.[34] Bass established the office at 2642 South Michigan in the Sammy Dyer School of Theatre, where his wife, Shirley Hall, was a dance instructor.[35] Helping Bass out at Roulette were arranger Johnny Pate and Chess writer Raynard Miner. Roulette was active in Chicago only a half year.

There is a mystery to all this, however. When I asked Billy Davis, the A&R chief at Chess, about the departure of Bass and Miner he asserted that they were never gone while he was there. Moreover, he expressed astonishment at learning from me the existence of two Henry Ford records put out by Bass and Miner on Roulette.[36] Most surprisingly the records were recorded in Chess studios.[37] When I asked Bass about this he denied ever working for Roulette, but could not clearly explain the existence of the Ford records.[38]

The records were actually put out by a group called the Gifts, in which Ford sang lead. The lead was born Henry Yarbrough in Chicago on September 30, 1948. When he made the records he was about fifteen years old and was attending Hirsch High on the South Side. Yarbrough began his professional career as a member of a family group. One of the members took an audition tape to Bass while he was at Chess, but there was a hitch, as Yarbrough related: "Bass liked it, but at the time my cousins were under contract to someone else. We had to break up. Bass was inspired to form a group around me, because he liked that young girlish type of voice I had. Now my uncle, Ronald Mays, he stayed with the group. And then Bass got two females and a guy—Natalie Smith, Gwendoline Little, and a guy I only recall as 'Frank.'"[39]

Bass teamed the new group, dubbed the Gifts, with songwriter Miner, who served as the group's coach.[40] Shirley Hall taught the group choreography and stage presentation. The Gifts ended up on Roulette where their first record was "It's Uncle Willie"/"Teardrops Are Falling," a splendid double-sided hit upon its release in January 1964. Both sides were written by Miner, produced by Bass, and arranged by Pate. The songs were bright and peppy and the leads by Smith and Ford perfectly evoked the great young-teen sound that Frankie Lymon and the Teenagers established in the 1950s.

The good sounds continued in April with the release of "Treat Her Right," written, produced, and arranged by the same team. There was a personnel change, however, when "Frank" was replaced by a cousin of Miner, Thomas Blunt. Ford was again super as lead on this typical Chicago-style medium-tempo workout. The Gifts, who shared the same manager with the Gems, Rose Miller, played gigs throughout the Chicago area with the Chess girl group.

By the summer of 1964, the Gifts had disintegrated in a breakup caused by an unsavory situation that neither Miner nor Yarbrough would discuss for the record.[41] Miner washed his hands of the group. The Gifts were one for the history books, and like a world-class female gymnast, Henry Yarbrough was a has-been at the age of sixteen. Roulette ended its foray into Chicago, and Bass and Miner returned to Chess, although in reality they had never left.

Kellmac Records

Kellmac Records got its start in late 1965 when Ace Leon Singleton and Harry Mitchell were driving past a park and spied a trio of fellows harmonizing under the street lamp. They stopped to listen, were bowled over by their talent, and decided on the spot to start up a company for the express purpose of recording the group, who came to be known as the C.O.D.s. The neophyte entrepreneurs brought in several other partners, including choreographer Bill Cody; Harry's wife, Edith; Eugene Mason, a South Side dentist; and Nelson Brown, a lawyer related to Oscar Brown, Jr.[42]

Mitchell was the president/treasurer of the company and basically handled all administrative chores. His home at 8337 South Indiana could be considered the company's offices. Ace Leon Singleton was the A&R man, producing the records and tutoring the acts in the finer points of singing. He was a graduate of the Chicago Conservatory of Music and had many years of gospel experience as a pastor of a church and as a member of the Original Singing Crusaders gospel quartet in the 1940s and 1950s. Bill Cody worked with the company's acts in their stage presentations and choreography and served as road manager.

Kellmac put out records by Ruby Stackhouse (Andrews), hornman Paul Bascomb, bluesman Guitar Red, as well as the C.O.D.s—about a dozen releases in all—but only scored with one hit. That was "Michael (The Lover)" by the C.O.D.s, which entered *Billboard*'s r&b chart December 18 and hit number five position before leaving the chart after ten weeks. The record was a solid national crossover hit as well. Kellmac arranged distribution through George Leaner's One-derful label.

The C.O.D.s consisted of Larry Brownlee, Robert Lewis, and Carl Washington.[43] In the *Chicago Defender,* the boys told of how their career developed: "We met in our neighborhood and decided to do something for kicks. That something was to form our group and sing. Then we contacted several companies and were turned down as having no talent." Then the group signed with Kellmac and they began working with Bill Cody (who also gave the group its name). A group member recalled, "He demanded we bring him a good tune. We brought him 'Michael (The Lover).' You see, there's this guy in our neighborhood who tells everybody that he is Michael the lover. We wrote it, practiced it, and got it up tight, and then recorded it."[44]

Brownlee wrote "Michael" and all the group's subsequent efforts, numbering eight more sides. The other songs lacked that melodic quality that made "Michael" so fine and they died without getting airplay and buyer response. Failing to keep themselves on the charts, the C.O.D.s disbanded at the end of 1967. Brownlee later achieved much success as a member of the Lost Generation (on Brunswick) and as a member of Mystique (on Curtom), but in 1978 he was murdered on the streets of Chicago.

Kellmac's last release was in October 1967, and by that time all the principals in the company had lost their shirts. Singleton attributes many of the problems to the fact that they were all "green as grass" and knew little about the business. The contract deals they made, such as the distribution arrangement made with George Leaner, proved to be highly disadvantageous to them. They paid for huge pressing bills for "Michael (the Lover)," but did not see nearly a proportionate amount in return.[45] The company was reorganized as Emase but the few releases on the label did nothing, and by the early 1970s Singleton, Mitchell, and the other partners had had their fill of the record business.

Crash Records

Crash was owned by the legendary deejay Al Benson and operated on Record Row at 1823 South Michigan. Subsidiary labels were Mica and Glow Star. The company was founded in 1965 and lasted until early 1967, and during that short time managed to get a number of local hits. In the summer of 1966 the company achieved good sales with a blues record, Magic Sam's "Out of Bad Luck," and in the fall got terrific local sales on "Wrong Wrong Wrong" by a South Side duo called Ray and Dave, and "What Is Love?" by Jimmy Dobbins. The latter two were produced by the label's A&R man, Bob Lee, a ubiquitous figure in the Chicago r&b industry at the time.

There were few records from the soul era that could match "What Is Love?" in vocal emoting, a perfect example of the black approach to balladry, achieving high emotional intensity in a controlled manner. It was the type of record that black buyers loved but few rock fans would find appealing—nor would rock critics. "Wrong Wrong Wrong" was a marvelous record that in its mid-tempo lope could only come out of Chicago. Lee sarcastically commented, "It got good play, but you know Al Benson. He was a crook. I really didn't get anything out of that."[46]

The company's most impressive act was the Steelers. This vocal group never made a truly bad record; they were too good a group. Their upbeat pop-like harmonies put a smile on your face and got your toes a-tapping, and the harmonies were simply ethereal. The ensemble was largely a brothers act, consisting of lead singer Wes Wells, Alonzo Wells, George Wells, Leonard Truss, and F. Allen.[47] The group was formed on the West Side in 1965, and not long afterward made its first record with veteran producer

Al Smith on the Glow Star label, "Crying Bitter Tears." The song featured excellent soul harmonies and used highly effective switch-off leads with falsetto the primary lead. "The Flame Remains," from 1966, was almost an equally appealing record, but neither record sold much.

The Steelers only scored a national hit after they left Crash. The 1969 song "Get It from the Bottom," written by Wes Wells and Al Smith and produced by Smith and Calvin Carter, was apparently impressive enough for Columbia to pick it up and release it on its Date subsidiary. The zesty up-tempo number, reminiscent of the Esquires sound, made it on *Cash Box*'s r&b chart for three weeks. The Steelers never had another national hit, but they never called it quits. In the late 1980s they were still performing on the West Side and still coming out with records.

The career of Crash was far more short-lived. In early 1967, Bob Koester, owner of the blues label Delmark, was sitting in the office of All State Distributors talking with owner Paul Glass. The phone rang, Glass excused himself and picked it up, made the usual telephone talk—"ah-hum," "yep," "Okay"—then hung up and turned to Koester and said, "Crash just went crash."[48]

Penny Records

Penny Records was part of the Met Music Record Shop operation owned by Maurice Alpert. Met Music, located at 328 East Fifty-eighth Street, under the elevated stop, was practically an institution on the South Side. When South Siders needed the latest "jams," they made it a habit to head to the Met. The Penny label was active twice—first in 1962 when two releases were put out, and then during 1966–70 when ten releases were put on the Penny label and about the same number on the sister Nickel label.[49]

The two 1962 releases, produced and arranged by Johnny Pate, were an instrumental by the Joy Rockers called "The Gouster Bop" and a vocal-group doowop by the Creations called "We're in Love." Both got some play on local radio, but sales were not substantial enough to sustain Alpert's interest in the label.

Four years later, an enthusiastic young man named Richard Pegue was working at the Met. He was born in Chicago, July 29, 1943, and as a student at Hirsch High in 1962 he made a record while a member of a vocal group called the Norvells (other members were Richard Steele, William Smith, Claude Wyatt, and Victor Trice). Pegue was a kind of guy who lived and breathed the record business, and he was still dabbling in music when he came across a box of old Penny records in the Met basement.

Related Pegue, "I went upstairs and asked Maury, 'Hey, what's this?' He said 'Oh that was something we did but nothing happened.' I said, 'I got some groups and I've worked up some songs and stuff.' He then gave me the funding to go into the studio and do it."[50] One group Pegue was working with was the Cheers, and one song he had written was "(I'm Not Ready to) Settle Down."

The Cheers were a family affair, consisting of Ben (Little Ben) Norfleet as lead, John Norfleet as second tenor, Merlon Norfleet as bass, and Frank Norfleet as first tenor. Although they weren't all brothers, the singers were related in various ways to the famous gospel-jubilee group the Norfleet Brothers.[51] Naturally the young Norfleets got their start in gospel, but within a year or two they gravitated toward popular music. Their first record was "Settle Down," and it was a monster in Chicago, selling in excess of forty thousand copies there but virtually nothing elsewhere. Pegue gave the record a seductive, subtle sound in the Billy Stewart ballad vein. The record returned to the local charts in November 1969, and sold for two solid months.

The Cheers had one more local success before they disappeared from the scene. It was "Since You Came into My Life," released in late 1974 on Ray Haley's and Don Goodman's Mocha Records. The song had an appealing Motown slickly produced sound, circa 1966. The record sold ten thousand copies in the Midwest and then died from what appeared to be a combination of dated sound and anemic distribution and promotion. The Cheers are perhaps totally unknown outside of the environs of Chicago, but their existence and local hits provide evidence enough that during the 1960s success in soul music was as much a regional phenomenon as it was national.

Pegue, meanwhile, recorded other groups on Penny and Nickel, mainly in various permutations of the original Norvells, but never achieved success equal to his "Settle Down" hit. After leaving Penny in 1969 he became a successful deejay on Chicago radio and a promoter of oldies shows.

Bunky Records

Bunky Records was formed by Bill "Bunky" Sheppard in late 1966 following the collapse of Constellation. He worked out of the old Constellation offices at 1421 South Michigan.[52] Sister labels of Bunky were B&G and BBS, but the company only had hits on Bunky and only with one act, a vocal group from Milwaukee called the Esquires. Other artists of Sheppard's were his namesake group, the Sheppards; another vocal group called the Impalas; and pianist Floyd Morris. Distribution was handled by Scepter-Wand out of New York.

Sheppard did the A&R and producing work, and used one of the best arrangers in Chicago, Tom Washington. The arrangements on Bunky records were always bright, bouncy, and eminently pop-like soul. Sheppard used the preeminent studio in the city, Universal Recording, and it showed in the quality of the records, which were always top-notch no matter how poor the material. As a long-time producer of vocal groups, Sheppard felt most comfortable working with them and therefore specialized in recording them. With the Esquires he was fortunate to have one of the best.

The Esquires hit during the late 1960s and early 1970s with a number of terrific soul numbers, notably "Get On Up," "And Get Away," and "Girls in the City." The group, with their falsetto-led, mid-tempo hits, sang harmonies that were strong and distinctive. They evoked the doowop sound of the 1950s, and if they sounded as though they came off a street corner circa 1957, it is only because they did.[53]

The Esquires began with the Moorer family, when Gilbert, Alvis, and Betty Moorer formed a vocal group about 1957. The Moorers attended North Division High on Milwaukee's North Side, and over the years other neighborhood teenagers passed in and out of the group. By 1965 the group consisted of the Moorer brothers plus Shawn Taylor and Sam Pace, and the singers were working on original tunes. Gilbert, the group's lead, came up with two notable ones, "Get On Up," and "Listen to Me." They made a dub and in 1966 decided to try their fortunes in Chicago, which had the recording companies that Milwaukee lacked.

The Esquires contacted Bill Sheppard. He listened to the group's rendition of "Get On Up," but was not quite satisfied, so one Sunday afternoon he called his friend Mill Edwards to give a listen. Edwards, a veteran of the Sheppards, related, "Bill said he felt something was missing from the song and asked what it needed. I told him there's a hole there. They're singing 'Get on up' and then there's a big hole there! Well, he said, you know it's not there so do something, give me something. I worked on it and came up with the bass parts for the song. It was to fill in the hole."[54]

When "Get On Up" became a monster hit upon its release in the summer of 1967, Edwards found himself a part of the group. The song became a million seller and was a hit on both the pop and r&b charts. In the fall, the Esquires came out with "And Get Away," and it immediately zoomed up the charts. The Gilbert-penned song followed the same formula as "Get On Up," with brassy flourishes, falsetto-led harmonies, and Edwards's bass counterpointing, but unlike many pale-imitation follow-ups, "And Get Away" was an original enough and solid enough accomplishment to work.

In March 1968 the Esquires hit the national charts again with "You Say," and in June with "Why Can't I Stop," but both were weak numbers. Switching from Bunky to the Wand label, they scored big with "You've Got the Power," a well-sung song with an appealing hook. It stayed eleven weeks on *Billboard*'s soul survey in the fall of 1968. "I Don't Know" followed in March 1969, and it too made the charts, but only for five weeks. It was the first Esquires record not to have been recorded at Universal. Wand took the group to New York to record.

In 1971 the Esquires were no longer recording for Wand but for Walter and Burgess Gardner's Lamarr label on the South Side. Sheppard was still producing the group. The group had Shawn Taylor sing lead on "Girls in the City," which despite its release on a small label became a solid national hit, lasting eleven weeks and reaching as high as position eighteen. In 1976 the Esquires returned one last time to the national charts with "Get On Up 76," recorded in Detroit under Richard Parker.

Sheppard closed down his Bunky label in 1969, and concentrated his efforts with the Esquires on Wand. Sometime in the early 1970s he moved to the West Coast to work as an executive in several record companies, notably Motown, where his old partner Ewart Abner was ensconced as president for several years.

Olé Records

Olé Records made a little blip of an impression in late 1966 and early 1967 with two releases, Otis Brown's "Southside Chicago" and the Para-Monts' "Come Go with Me." The label was owned by King Bevill and was operated out of his home at 9734 Princeton on the South Side.

The first release on the label was the Brown record. Nothing is known of Brown other than the existence of a half dozen of his records. His first was "Southside Chicago," which with its mid-tempo Chicago lope captured the flavor of the milieu from which the city's r&b singers came. The song got good play on local radio in late 1966, but Brown never made a subsequent impact.

The Para-Monts' "Come Go with Me," which came out in January 1967, was a simple, unsophisticated song, but its fetching soprano lead vocal and its insistent but sparse rhythm track made the record irresistible. The group, a neighborhood ensemble out of DuSable High, consisted of lead singer Cormie Vance; her sister, Earlene Vance Coleman; Rose Rice; and McKinley Norris.[55] After getting together in late 1966, and after some months of working out on the popular songs of the day, Norris suggested that the group try out at a talent show sponsored by the Regal Theater. The singers showed up but were not given the opportunity to perform. All was not lost, however, because King Bevill saw them rehearsing and was impressed enough to ask the group to try out on his label.

Bevill demanded some original material, so the group went to Earlene's husband, Walter Coleman, who played guitar, in hopes that he could come up with something. He wrote a number of songs, and from the batch Bevill took two for the group's first session. It was Coleman's guitar that was heard on both sides of the record: "Come Go with Me" (led by Vance) and "I Don't Wanna Lose You" (led by Earlene). The record did well in Chicago, Memphis, St. Louis, and a few other places.

The Para-Monts continued to sing together for a few more years, but recording opportunities eluded them. Before they broke up, however, they performed for a spell in Oscar Brown, Jr.'s, review, "Opportunity Please Knock." The review was devised by Brown to give members of the notorious Blackstone Rangers street gang a worthy outlet that presumably would lure them away from their hoodlum ways. Although it was advertised as being a review consisting of gang members, Brown apparently drew from all the youth in the area, which explains the participation of the Para-Monts.

Giant Productions

Giant Productions was founded in 1967 by Mel Collins and Joshie Jo Armstead. Collins was a Chicago native and Armstead was a New York songwriter who had just moved into the city. They formed both a personal and professional relationship and soon got married. Original offices were at 5622 South Maryland, later at 8144 South Cottage Grove. The team both leased records to larger firms and put out records on their own Giant, Gamma, and Globe labels. Their best successes were productions leased to other labels, notably on Ruby Andrews, Shirley Wahls, and Garland Green. Artists released on their own labels included Little Jimmy Scott, Smokey Smothers, Fenton Robinson, and Joshie Jo Armstead.[56]

Giant was a somewhat schizophrenic company. Collins had a preference for recording blues artists, such as Robinson and Smothers, which could be a steady but small market. Armstead preferred the softer, more pop variety of soul music, as in recordings by herself, Garland Green, and Ruby Andrews. The conflict between the two started with the company's first hit record, Andrews's "Casanova (Your Playing Days Are Over)." The medium-tempo, highly melodic song was recorded in Detroit with a superb arrangement by Mike Terry. But it was not easy getting the record done there, as Armstead explained: "Melvin at that time had artists like Fenton Robinson. I wasn't too much on the blues. That was the first thing that we fought over. Something happened and I just went to Detroit anyway. Broke, no money. If I had two dollars, I'd kiss you all over. I met Mike Terry there, and I said this is really the type of music that I hear. This is what I want to do."[57]

The Andrews recording established the Terry connection for Giant Productions, and with the songs of Armstead and the arrangements of

Terry, the company was able to come up with some notable hits during the late 1960s, especially on Armstead herself.

Armstead (born in Yazoo City, Mississippi, October 8, 1944) brought a wealth of experiences with her as a composer, producer, background singer, recording artist, and actress. In the early 1960s she was a member of the Ike and Tina Turner Review as one of the original Ikettes, the female backup group to Tina. The group recorded "I'm Blue," a big hit in 1962. From 1964 to 1967, she was part of the songwriting team of Nick Ashford and Valerie Simpson, writing such songs as "Let's Go Get Stoned" for Ray Charles, "Never Had It So Good" for Ronnie Milsap, "Real Thing" for Tina Britt, and "Nothing I Wouldn't Do" for Betty Everett.

In 1967 Armstead moved to Chicago, where she not only started Giant but also resumed her recording career. Her second release on Giant, "A Stone Good Lover," made it on *Billboard*'s r&b chart in the spring of 1968. The Terry-arranged, Armstead-composed-and-produced song was typical Armstead with its strong lilting melody and solid story line in the lyrics. It was one of her all-time best. Two other fine releases by Armstead— "There's Not Too Many More" (1969) and "I'm Gonna Show You" (1970)— did not get off the ground. By 1970 Giant was faltering.

Garland Green was the one artist on whom Giant was able to get a million-selling record, "Jealous Kind of Fellow," in 1969. Green was born on June 24, 1942, in the Mississippi Delta region in a little town called Dunleath, just outside Leland. Mississippi offered few opportunities for a poor black kid in the 1950s, so at the age of sixteen Green went up to Chicago to further himself and finish his education. He attended Englewood High, and afterward went to work at the Argo Corn Starch plant in suburban Argo.[58]

While in Mississippi, Green sang in spiritual groups, but in Chicago he developed a passion for secular music as well and proceeded to demonstrate his talent wherever and whenever he could. One day in 1965 while singing in a community recreation center, he was discovered by Chicago's barbeque king, Argia B. Collins, who owned a string of barbeque houses and marketed Mumbo Bar-b-que Sauce, a local favorite. Collins was not related to Mel Collins.

Argia B. Collins began sponsoring Green at the Chicago Conservatory of Music, where he trained in piano and voice. While attending school Green worked in the local clubs on amateur nights. While singing in a club Green was seen by Mel Collins and Armstead. Said Armstead, "Well, I saw Garland one night. I really liked his voice. There was that pleading quality that I knew that women would just love. I was with Melvin, and I told Melvin I believe I can get a hit on him. And he approached Garland. He was more than happy to work with me."[59]

The first song Collins and Armstead had Green record was "Girl I Need You," which although not an Armstead composition still possessed her mid-tempo melodic soul approach. It was recorded in Detroit with Terry. The record was released first on the Gamma label, and when it showed promise, MCA leased the record, in October 1967, and put it out on its newly formed r&b subsidiary label, Revue. The label marked MCA's direct entry into the soul music field, with much of its product being leased masters from independent Chicago producers. MCA at the time also owned half of Brunswick.[60] "Girl I Need You" never became more than a regional hit, but it did succeed in establishing Green as a staple in the then thriving club scene in the city.

In July 1969 Green followed with not only his biggest record of his career but his best, "Jealous Kind of Fellow." It had all the ingredients—chorus, instrumental track, lyrics, vocals—that seemed to jell into a satisfying whole. "Jealous" spent sixteen weeks on *Billboard*'s soul chart and went as high as the five position. The song was credited to four writers, two of whom were Armstead and Green, but Armstead said: "A lot of mean things happened. Garland brought me a piece of a song that he loved, and I really didn't want to work with it. But he kept insisting. So I sat down and gave it its title, its punch line, and cut him on it, and it was 'Jealous Kind of Fellow.' The thing is, after we recorded the song, the fellows who did the skeleton were assigned to some other company, and the company snatched the song. So consequently, I made no money."[61]

Green's second-biggest hit was "Plain and Simple Girl," in March 1971. It was produced by Syl Johnson and arranged by Donny Hathaway and marked a break with Giant Productions. The song with its melodic light-soul approach was very much in the same vein as Green's Armstead songs.

During the next several years Green had trouble scoring hits, and with good reason. On record after record his material proved sadly lacking the vitality and imagination that informed his best work, despite spirited interpretations. Finally, in December 1974, he blew Chicago wide open with his Spring Records release of the engaging "Let the Good Times Roll" (not the Shirley and Lee song). However, the record did not happen anywhere but in Chicago. It turned out to be Green's last Chicago hit; a few years later he moved to California.

Shirley Wahls was born in Marvel, Arkansas, on December 28, 1941. When she was nine she moved with her parents to Chicago's South Side. There she attended Phillips High, and while still going to school she began developing a considerable local reputation singing in church choirs. In 1963 she was invited to join the Argo Singers, an association followed by stints with the Gertrude Ward Singers and the Dorothy Norwood Singers. She recorded with all three groups, taking occasional leads.[62]

By late 1966 Wahls had become increasingly involved in secular music. One of the things she was doing was making demos for a friend, songwriter Karl Tarlton (who died sometime in the 1970s). One demo was "Why Am I Crying." Bill Sheppard heard the record and was so bowled over by Wahls's interpretation that he had her record the song for release. Sheppard leased the record to King, which according to Wahls sold some sixty-five thousand copies in Chicago.[63]

Wahls joined Mercury Records in 1968 under the Giant producing team of Armstead and Collins. The material, some of it written by Wahls and her husband and some by Armstead, was heavily gospel in feeling and manner of expression. The best songs from the association were "Prove It Everyday" (1968), "Half a Man" (1969), and "Cry Myself to Sleep" (1969). In 1970 Wahls appeared on the Giant label with "Tell the Truth." This hard-soul number made the local charts but had no impact anywhere else. It was Wahls's last record as a solo artist. Following a brief foray as a lead singer in the New Rotary Connection, a rock group produced by Charles Stepney for Chess, Wahls left the world of secular music in 1972.

Ruby Andrews was born Ruby Stackhouse in the Delta town of Hollandale, Mississippi, on March 12, 1947. She went to Chicago about 1953 and attended Hyde Park High.[64] Around late 1964, Ruby began working with the Vondells, who earlier in the year had hit with "Lenore." Their mentor was Bill Cody who owned a club on Eighty-seventh Street where they used to rehearse. In 1965 Cody recorded them on the Kellmac label. The record, Kellmac's first release, was "Please Tell Me" and it was credited on the label as by Ruby Stackhouse.

Nothing happened for Ruby Andrews for a while and she kept herself in show business as a dancer at a nightclub. It was as a dancer that she was discovered again. Disc jockey Lucky Cordell introduced her to local record entrepreneur Ric Williams, who was starting up Zodiac Records. Andrews's third release for the label was "Casanova (Your Playing Days Are Over)," which made her a nationally famous recording star.

In early 1968, Andrews launched her most artistically and commercially successful period with "You Can Run (But You Can't Hide)." The song introduced a new Ruby Andrews. Whereas "Casanova" was a melodic delight, "You Can Run" featured hot, forceful, arrangements that created an ideal support for Andrews's biting and shouting-style vocals. This was r&b music at its most rocking and rolling; it had loads of energy and excitement while still retaining enough control and professionalism so that the swing and listenability remains. "You Can Run'" was written by the Brothers of Soul vocal group (Richard Knight, Fred Bridges, and Robert Eaton). In April 1968, incidentally, the Brothers of Soul got on the national charts with an excellent single of their own, "I Guess that Don't Make Me a Loser."

The Bridges-Knight-Eaton team in the years that followed kept Andrews on the charts and contributed immensely to her success, notably with "The Love I Need" (1968), "You Made a Believer (Out of Me)" (1969), "Everybody Saw You" (1970), and "You Ole Boo Boo You" (1971). Most of her records were recorded in Detroit and Memphis. She recorded for ABC in the late 1970s but never returned to the charts after her Zodiac years.

Meanwhile, things were far from smooth at Giant Productions. Armstead said, "I dislike to talk about it because it was very rough in those days. The money was just squandered away. There was really no business sense."[65] The company in its collection of releases did have some big-selling records, but with all small companies there comes a time when there are more bills coming in than money, and that time was in 1970 for Giant. Also, things had gotten to a point between Armstead and Collins that their marriage was on the rocks as well.

So Armstead decided to pitch it all in Chicago and go to New York. Said she, "There were personal problems I was having, everybody fighting, and pulling this way and that. I called it like killing the goose that was laying the golden egg. It made everything to me distasteful, and so I just got away from it. I fled."[66] Mel Collins continued for several years more putting out an occasional blues record on the Gamma label, but by the late 1970s he had given up the secular market for the gospel field. Armstead recorded again, for Stax Records in Memphis, and got a national r&b hit with "Stumblin' Blocks, Steppin' Stones," in May 1975. In the late 1980s, back in Chicago, she managed a boxer, Alonzo Ratliff, a WBC cruiserweight champion.

Lock Records

Lock Records, founded in 1968, was a partnership of producer Clarence Johnson, arranger Johnny Cameron, songwriter Eddie Sullivan, and businessman Eddie O'Kelly. Offices were at 6724 South Stoney Island Avenue, on the far South Side.[67] The company specialized in recording young teen sopranos, notably Denise Chandler and Debbie Cameron, because all the officers in the company seemed most adept and experienced in that style of music.

Johnson and Sullivan had earlier experience with a young singer called Diane Cunningham, who came out with "Someday Baby" in late 1967. Cunningham was born in Detroit in 1949, but while still a youngster went to Chicago with her family, settling on the South Side. There she got her start in music in church choirs. Local producer Kenneth Wells discovered her while searching for a girl group to record.[68]

"Someday Baby" was written by Sullivan and co-produced by Sullivan, Johnson, and Wells. They got a nice understated approach out of the accompanying musicians that allowed Cunningham's vocals to shine. The record was released on the local New Breed label in August 1967, and on the strength of making the WVON top-ten list and selling five thousand copies locally it was picked up by Fontana, a Mercury subsidiary label. Despite the muscle of Mercury, the engaging song never caught on nationally.

Moving to Lock, Sullivan and Johnson put their biggest hopes on Denise Chandler. The company produced twelve single sides and an album on her, but all were mediocre. In later years, however, she would reprise her Chicago teen-soprano style as Deniece Williams with such hits as "Let's Hear It for the Boy" and "It's Gonna Take a Miracle." Chandler/Williams was born on June 3, 1951, in Gary, Indiana.[69]

Chandler's first record, "Love Is Tears," was produced by Wells and Johnson and released on the Lock label. The song got her a fair amount of play in Chicago in the spring of 1968, but subsequent releases on Lock and later on Ernie and Tony Leaner's Toddlin' Town label failed to capture a response. Mused Johnson, "I did an album on Niecy, and if you can hear it, she was good. Of course you're talking about a seventeen-year-old Niecy compared to a thirty-seven-year-old Niecy, so quite naturally she's gonna grow. At that time the only persons who liked her were myself and Ernie Leaner. We really believed in her."[70]

Lock collapsed in 1970, but not before the company got a national hit with the Lovelites' "How Can I Tell My Mom and Dad" (1969), a song featuring the teen-soprano sound. Sullivan during this time also earned outstanding writing credits when Candace Love on Ric Williams's Aquarius label got a national hit with "Uh Uh Boy, That's a No No" (1969), and Sunday Williams came out with "That's What You Want" (ca. 1970), the latter arranged by Cameron and produced by Johnson. (Williams earlier had a big local success with "Ain't Got No Problems" in 1969 on Nat Meadows's Al-teen label).

During the early 1970s Sullivan would join his two sisters, Barbara and Lorraine, in a vocal group called the Classic Sullivans, and they hit with "Paint Yourself in a Corner" on Marshall Thompson's Kwanza label in 1973. Johnson would go on to become one of the city's leading independent producers of the decade.

NOTES

1. John Rockwell, letter to the author, April 16, 1973.

2. Doug Seroff, "Polk Miller and the Old South Quartette," *78 Quarterly* 1, no. 3 (1988): 27–41. Seroff discusses a variety of turn-of-the-century vocal groups in the context of black vocal harmony traditions. Also of interest: Doug Seroff, "Pre-History of Black Vocal Harmony Groups," *Goldmine*, March-April 1977, p. 17; and idem, "Pre-History of Black Vocal Harmony Groups, Part 2," *Goldmine*, October 1977, p. 10.

3. No researcher has been able to locate Joyce Davis, Barbara Green, and Tammy Levon, and there have been no published profiles about their careers.

4. Robert Pruter, "Don Talty and Formal Records," *Juke Blues* 19 (Spring 1990): 6–11; Private papers of Don Talty, held by Janice McVickers, Sandwich, Illinois; Jan Bradley interviews; Angelo Giardini interview; Janice McVickers interview.

5. Howard Mandel, "Phil Upchurch Greases the Groove with His Intellectual Guitar Creativity," *Illinois Entertainer*, May 1981, pp. 34–35; Robert Pruter, "The Philip Upchurch Combo," *Goldmine*, December 30, 1988, pp. 24–25; Joan Tortorici, "Phil Upchurch a Natural Resource as a Studio Guitarist," *Illinois Entertainer*, December 1976, p. 16; "Upchurch and Fennyson [sic], Explosive New Duo," *Soul*, July 5, 1976, p. 10; Philip Upchurch interview.

6. Robert Pruter, "Jan Bradley," *Soul Survivor* 8 (Winter 1987/88): 18–20; Bradley interviews.

7. Bradley interview, June 9, 1987.

8. Curtis Mayfield interview.

9. Bradley interview, June 9, 1987.

10. Bradley interview, June 14, 1987.

11. Bradley interview, June 9, 1987.

12. Bradley interview, June 14, 1987.

13. Bob Catron interview; Chuck Colbert, Jr., interviews; Tony Gideon interviews.

14. Robert Pruter, "The Daylighters," *Goldmine*, February 1981, pp. 12–14; Colbert interview, August 20, 1974; Gideon interviews.

15. Robert Pruter, "The Marvin L. Sims Story," *Soul Survivor* 4 (Winter 1985/86): 14–15; Marvin L. Sims interview; Marvin L. Sims, letter to the author, November 30, 1985.

16. Sims interview.

17. Sims letter.

18. Bob Catron interview; Bill Erman interview; Tony Gideon interview, January 20, 1988.

19. Robert Pruter, "Donald Jenkins' Story," *Record Exchanger* 28 (1979): 14–15; Donald Jenkins interview.

20. Devora Brown interview.

21. Catron interview.

22. Robert Pruter, "Windy City Soul," *Goldmine*, February 1979, pp. 11–13; Reggie Jackson interview; Wes Spraggins interview; Robert Tharp interview.

23. Jackson interview.

24. Robert Pruter, "The Five Chances and Their World of Chicago R&B," *Goldmine*, April 6, 1990, pp. 18–19, 33; Hilliard Jones interview.

25. Don Clay interview; Tony Gideon interview, January 20, 1988; Jackson interview; Earl Glicken, telephone conversation with the author, February 6, 1988.

26. Kenan Heise, "Musician, Composer, Monk Higgins, Fifty" [obituary], *Chicago Tribune*, July 16, 1986; [Robert Pruter], "Monk Higgins 1936-1986," [obituary], *Living Blues* 72 (1986): 41.

27. Penni, Terry, Joe, Pip, Brandi, and Tee, "The Low Down," *Chicago Defender*, September 4, 1965; Robert Pruter, "The Vontastics," *Goldmine*, January 1978, p. 20.

28. Malcolm Walls and Robert Pruter, "Mamie Davis," *Living Blues* 57 (Autumn 1983): 31.

29. Robert Pruter, "Cash McCall: When You Wake Up," *Goldmine*, August 14, 1987, p. 107; Clive Richardson, "Cash McCall—A Biography," *Soul Music* 2 (January 1968); liner notes, Cash McCall, *No More Doggin'*, L&R Records 42.058, 1983.

30. Jeff Lind, "1950's-60's Chicago Scene: Predecessor of Jazz-rock Style," *Illinois Entertainer*, January 1978, p. 7; Peter Wright interview.

31. Robert Pruter, "Evanston Soul: Patti Drew and the Drew-vels," *Record Exchanger* 26 (1978): 22-24; idem, "The Patti Drew Story," *It Will Stand* 20 (1981): 14–15; Patti Drew interviews.

32. Pruter, "Evanston Soul"; Carlton Black interview.

33. Drew interview, July 15, 1977.

34. "Roulette Opens Chicago Office," *Billboard*, November 30, 1963, p. 33; Ralph Bass interview; Raynard Miner interview; Henry Yarbrough interviews.

35. Yarbrough interviews.

36. Billy Davis interview, August 28, 1986.

37. Yarbrough interview, April 29, 1988.

38. Bass interview.

39. Yarbrough interview, August 17, 1986.

40. Robert Pruter, "Henry Ford and Gifts Keep Kid-Lead Vocal Group Sound Alive in Chicago," *Record Collector's Monthly* 37 (May/June 1987): 1, 5; Miner interview; Yarbrough interviews.

41. Miner interview; Yarbrough interview, August 17, 1986.

42. Ace Leon Singleton interview.

43. Negro Press International, "Teen Musical Notes," *Chicago Defender*, January 15, 1966; Robert Pruter, "The C.O.D.s," *Goldmine*, December 1977, p. 12.

44. *Defender*, January 15, 1966.

45. Singleton interview.

46. Bob Lee interview.

47. Dee Duncan, "The Steelers (Re-emerge)," *After Five*, July/August 1982, p. 33.

48. Bob Koester interview.

49. Richard Pegue interview.

50. Ibid.

51. Jim Fishel, "Specialty Labels Abound," *Billboard*, April 19, 1975, p. C-20; Robert Pruter, "The Cheers," *Goldmine*, March 1979, p. 29; Ray Haley interview; Pegue interview.

52. Millard Edwards interview, February 16, 1988.

53. Robert Pruter, "Get On Up...And Get Away: The Esquires," *It Will Stand* 26 (1982): 6–9; Millard Edwards interview, September 8, 1981; Alvis Moorer interview; Gilbert Moorer interview.

54. Edwards interview, September 8, 1981.

55. Robert Pruter, "Windy City Soul," *Goldmine*, November 1978, p. 25; Cormie Vance interview.

56. Robert Pruter, "The Multifaceted Career of Joshie Jo Armstead," *Soul Survivor* 5 (Summmber 1986): 20–23; Joshie Jo Armstead interview; Mel Collins interview.

57. Armstead interview.

58. John Abbey, "Garland Green: The Story," *Blues and Soul*, June 20-July 3, 1975, p. 8; Robert Pruter, "Garland Green," *Soul Survivor* 7 (Summer 1987): 12–14; Armstead interview; Garland Green interview.

59. Armstead interview.

60. *Billboard*, October 7, 1967, p. 3.

61. Armstead interview.

62. Robert Pruter, "The Shirley Wahls Story," *Goldmine*, December 1981, p. 172; Shirley Wahls interview.

63. Wahls interview.

64. Steve Bryant, "Ruby Andrews," *Souled Out* 2 (May 1978): 2–5; Frederick Douglas Murphy, "Ruby Andrews Explores Her Bittersweet Career," *Black Stars*, February 1978, pp. 26–29; Robert Pruter, "Ruby Andrews," *Goldmine*, July 1982, pp. 26–27; Ruby Andrews interview.

65. Armstead interview.

66. Ibid.

67. Clarence Johnson interview; Eddie Sullivan interview.

68. "Will It Be Any Day for Young Diane?" *Soul*, December 11, 1967, p. 15.

69. Lacy J. Banks, "Deniece Williams: Niecy's Musical Medicine," *Black Stars*, June 1976, pp. 7–9; Geoff Brown, "Free!," *Black Music*, June 1977, pp. 24–26; Denise Hall, "LA Lowdown," *Black Music*, November 1976, p. 10; Johnson interview.

70. Johnson interview.

8

Chicago Black Dance

Chicago was the most significant center of black popular dance during the 1960s. The city can boast of giving rise to more dances and records promoting specific dances than any other city during the period. A host of choreographic fads—the Bird, the Barracuda, the Monkey, the Watusi, and many, many more—and loads of best-selling dance records by such artists as Major Lance, Alvin Cash, the Five Du-Tones, and Tom and Jerrio served to put the city on the map. Chicago producers made it a habit to scan the dance floors at the city's high schools and teen spots for the latest creations and then race to get the dance rhythms on record. But Chicago's achievement in the area of black popular dance has never been recognized.

There has been a myopia on the part of music writers regarding popular dance as a whole. The reasons for this are many but mostly it is because the subject of black dance and dance records has been generally misunderstood, and because few writers have exerted any effort or shown any interest in getting an understanding. Perhaps the following comments will help to illuminate the subject. Dance fads have been usually associated with "dance records," records released either to create and promote a specific dance or to exploit the popularity of a dance that had emerged spontaneously from the youth audience. A dance record may also be a record that was selected by an audience to do a certain dance to even though it made no reference to that dance.

What should not be forgotten is that any record is a "dance record" if one wants to dance to it. Up to the mid-1960s most rock 'n' roll records and virtually all r&b records were made for dancing. This was evident when kids on "American Bandstand" or on a local bandstand show would review records in terms of their danceability. "It's got a good beat, you can dance to it. I'll give it an 89," was the classic line that many writers would make much condescending fun of years later. However, these unsophisticated one-line reviews often showed a greater appreciation and awareness of what characterized the essence of rock 'n' roll than many later (should I say folk-music influenced) rock critics. Although classic rock 'n' roll was virtually synonymous with dance, for clarity I will use the term "dance record" to refer to those records that have a direct relationship to dance fads.

The evident lack of enthusiasm of chroniclers of popular music to survey dance records is somewhat understandable when one considers that this special genre of r&b/rock 'n' roll was often characterized by atrocious singing, dumb lyrics, and vapid, unimaginative music. Many dance records were unfortunately the product of the commercial practice of rushing out a record—any record, as long as it had the name of the necessary dance on it—to cash in on a dance fad before it went out of favor. This is how popular-music historian Charlie Gillett saw dance fads in his groundbreaking work *The Sound of the City*:

> With [the success of the Twist] dance music was thoroughly es-
> tablished, and a marvelous range of new dance names, though not
> new rhythms, was concocted to give people something "new" to
> do. Cameo-Parkway was behind many of the names, including
> "Mashed Potato Time" and "Ride" (Dee Dee Sharp). "Bristol
> Stomp" (the Dovells), and "Wah-Watusi" (the Orlons)—all hits;
> Chubby Checker went on to "The Fly," "Slow Twisting," and
> "Limbo Rock." Occasionally, a relatively authentic dance was
> introduced, such as the "Pop Eye."...the isolation of rhythm (for
> dancing) as the dominant part of popular music distorted the
> music's character, and none of the successful records had much to
> recommend them beyond their insistent beat.[1]

Gillett's sentiments—one could hardly call them research findings—were echoed repeatedly by popular-music writers. Langdon Winner in his essay "The Strange Death of Rock and Roll" characterized the early 1960s as an era of "manufactured dance fads."[2] Nik Cohn in *Awopbopaloobop Alopbamboom* expressed a similar sentiment: "The Twist itself didn't last long. Well, it wasn't really meant to. In any case, it was replaced by other dances, other campaigns, and the same people went on making the money."[3] Mike Jahn in *Rock* took the view that "dance-craze records," as he called them, were examples of the dark ages of commercial, insincere rock. He could only perceive the existence of four "dances"—the Twist, the Mashed Potato, the Wah-Watusi, and the Locomotion—a view which demonstrated the shallowness of the book. He did not mention dancing after the early-1960s and I doubt very much that he was aware of its existence.[4] This lack of perspicacity extends even to writers on r&b. Lynn McCutcheon wrote a book called *Rhythm and Blues*, in which one of his defining characteristics of soul music was that the music has "a very distinct danceable beat."[5] What is inexplicable is that he never elaborated beyond that statement.

True, there is some validity to what these critics wrote, especially with regard to the dances and records they mention. But there were also many less-popular records in the early 1960s that were individualistic, of high musical merit, and based on authentic dances. The real failure of most researchers is their lack of interest in dancing itself and the various dance fads that emerged. The giant role of dance in rock 'n' roll and r&b demands a thorough investigation and by necessity a survey of dance records as well. The errors of these writers arose because they apparently reported on the dance phenomenom as it existed with the white audience, neglecting the vast number of dances and dance records that existed in the lives of black kids. They seemed to be unfamiliar with most black dance fads.

Marshall and Jean Stearns in their remarkable book *Jazz Dance* carefully delineated the folk and popular black dances as well as professional black rhythm acts from slavery up through the 1940s. Although they called such dancing "jazz dance," their survey covered more than just dance performed to jazz. The authors explored virtually all dancing that "swung." But they neglected the popular dance fads of the 1950s and 1960s, their one failure in what otherwise is the definitive work on the topic.

The Stearnses did venture some brief comments on popular dancing of the rock 'n' roll era. They postulated two waves of dances—the first "before and during Presley's initial success" and the second during and after the Twist rage of the early 1960s (the book was written before the disco rage of the late 1970s). However, they mistakenly listed such dances as the Fly, Mashed Potato, Madison, and Roach as being in the first wave when in fact they were all part of the second wave, which reveals their lack of research of the period.[6]

The Stearnses' attitude toward dance fads of the 1950s and 1960s was generally belittling, as the following passage from their book makes clear:

> A second wave of dances crashed over American dance floors during and after the Twist; the Monkey, Bug, Pony, Frug, Hitch-hike, Watusi, Hully Gully, Jerk, Boogaloo, and so on. Several of them showed traces of ancient lineage: the Frug harked back to the Shimmy, the Bug and the Monkey borrowed from the old Heebie-Jeebies, and the Pony employed bits of the Slow Drag. In fact, their debt to earlier dances was the chief thing that made them distinguishable. But something was missing. As the dances multiplied, the quality deteriorated. Many such new dances as the

Swim, the Woodpecker, the Hitchhike, and the Monkey were simply charades, pantomimes with hand-and-arm gestures and little body and footwork.[7]

The Stearnses at least perceived the existence of a great number of dances. Their highly perceptive assertion that quality declined with the multiplicity of dances would have assuredly been valid had they sufficiently qualified it. The deterioration was certainly evident, exactly along the lines they described, but it was largely confined to the white rock audience not found among the r&b audience, who continued to develop creative and authentic dances. The high quality of black dance throughout the 1960s was evident in the professional choreography of the r&b vocal groups who often incorporated popular dances into their routines.

Indeed, it seems strange that the Stearnses, who concentrated on dance as it was performed by blacks, suddenly switched in their brief 1960s survey to concentrate mainly on rock 'n' roll dancing performed by white kids, without drawing any of the distinctions that did exist between the two audiences. This caused their assessment of the 1960s popular dancing to be confused, inaccurate, and incomplete.

The rock chronicler Carl Belz in his fine book *The Story of Rock* understood the differences between the black and the white dance audiences, and as a result provided the best written account, brief as it was, of the role of dancing in popular music. Belz emphasized that dancing was a spontaneous folk-creation. By this he meant that dances were devised by persons unaware that they were creating art. Belz noted that status among a young person's peers was often determined on how up-to-date one was with dance fads. Most important, dancing was a way that young persons expressed their appreciation of popular music.

Belz was satisfied simply to list the names of the dances, making little attempt to delineate the various styles. He did determine that the vast majority of the dance fads emerged from the black audience; and it was this audience, he believed, that continued to make dance an expressive part of their appreciation of their music long after the white community largely ceased to find dancing an important physical response to rock.[8]

By far the most knowledgeable and perceptive of the popular dance authorities was motion picture director John Waters. In his brilliant film *Hairspray* (1988), he recreated with remarkable accuracy many of the most popular black dances of the early sixties, notably the Madison, Dog, Roach, and Bird. The film, as no written account can, takes one into the world of early 1960s teenage dance.[9] A careful viewing of *Hairspray* will give one an appreciation of the dances that are discussed in this chapter.

My esthetic examination of Chicago dances and dance records reflects both the Belz understanding of popular dance and the images presented in

Hairspray. As dance developments in Chicago clearly demonstrated, most popular rhythm-and-blues dances were rich and varied in style, and for the most part did not originate from records. Rather, before any records were made, they were the spontaneous outcome of the dance experiences of black high-school youth from the urban ghettos.

Fad Dances, 1960–62

The first new dance of the 1960s was an r&b dance called the Madison, popular in Chicago and nationwide. Perhaps the most electrifying scene in *Hairspray* was the Madison dance number. The story of the movie centers around a teen dance television show loosely patterned after the Buddy Deane dance show in Baltimore. The Madison in fact originated on that show.[10] It was a line dance with regular steps, and was made popular by Al Brown's Tunetoppers' "The Madison" and Ray Bryant's "The Madison Time" in the spring of 1960. Bryant's version, with dance instructions recited by Baltimore deejay Eddie Morrison, was the bigger nationwide hit. Brown's version, however, because of the promotional efforts of Carl Davis, succeeded in becoming the hit version in Chicago.

Of all the dance records of the 1960s the lyrics of the Madison records were the most specific as to how to do the dance. Most dance records, especially after about 1962, gave little or no information as to the nature of the dance. It was presumed that the dance was learned from one's peers, and it was. Remarkably, in this way dances could spread across the country within a matter of weeks, and as would be expected, regional differences would crop up.

Any discussion of dance fads must obviously include the Twist, the biggest dance rage of the decade.[11] Among Chicago blacks, however, the dance did not reach great levels of popularity and it prevailed for only a short time during 1959–60. The black style of the Twist was not all that bad to look at, and although the same in form as the dance done elsewhere, it bore only a faint resemblence to the hokey, cornball style most persons associate with the dance. One large Chicago suburban high school, which had a student body that was about 90 percent white (the remainder black), would provide dancing in the school's recreation room during lunch hour. The small handful of blacks who went always had difficulty in getting permission to do their dances. The Twist, for example, was banned for being too suggestive. Actually the dance was quite tame, and the racist nature of the ban was evident a year later when every kid in the school was doing the dance months after it had died out in the black community.

The record that brought popularity to the dance was naturally Chubby Checker's "The Twist" (1960), a cover of a Hank Ballard record from two years earlier. The revival of the dance had its genesis among Baltimore teenagers, according to Ballard: "We were doing the Twist for approximately two years before it caught on. We were in Baltimore on a ten-day engagement at the Royal Theater. And the kids saw us doing the Twist there. There was a show in Baltimore, the Buddy Deane Show, which was similar to American Bandstand. Deane saw those kids out there doing the Twist, because they had seen us doing it at the Royal. So he called Dick Clark and said the kids over here are going crazy over a record by Hank Ballard and the Midnighters called 'The Twist,' and they're not even touching!"[12] The upshot was that Clark got Cameo-Parkway to record a slightly more pop-ish version for his bandstand audience, the Checker record.

Ideal for twisting were numerous Ballard numbers popular in 1960-61 and similar to "The Twist." These included "Finger Poppin' Time," "Let's Go, Let's Go, Let's Go," and "Nothing But Good." There were of course hundreds of other Twist records, but the vast majority did not relate to the black community.

From approximately 1959 to 1961 there was a moderately popular r&b dance called the Slop. While the dancers moved rhythmically back and forth, their hands were held palms down, wavering up and down at hip level as though they were in the act of slopping mud or something. No particular record became successful in promoting the dance, but perhaps the impetus for its spread across the country came from the Olympics' "Slop," which was the flip to their wildly popular "Big Boy Pete" of 1959. The dance dates back to 1956 in Philadelphia, when Little Joe and the Thrillers got a successful East Coast regional hit with "Let's Do the Slop." The group's lead, Joe Cook, was earlier one of Philadelphia's premier teen dancers and claimed to have created the Slop dance.[13]

The r&b dance the Horse had limited popularity in Chicago in the early 1960s. The dance required circular swaying of the hips and kind of resembled a stripteaser's grind. One of the routines had one partner bend far backward, allowing the other to follow snugly on top. Then the partners repeated the same in reversed positions. As one early participant put it, the Horse was a "real low-down dirty dance." One may legitimately question whether or not these movements constituted a dance or not, but the Horse demonstrably became one when it was performed by groups of dancers in unison, in parallel lines. Wilburt Harrison had a unique-sounding record in 1960 called "The Horse," which helped to promote the dance, but Ike and Tina Turner's "It's Gonna Work Out Fine" (1961) was the most popular number for dancing the Horse.

One of the biggest r&b dances of the early 1960s was the Watusi. The hit record of the dance, "The Watusi," was recorded by a veteran vocal group from Los Angeles, the Vibrations, and came out in 1961. The record lasted fourteen weeks and went to position six on *Cash Box*'s r&b chart. The Vibrations' recording as the Jayhawks had a novelty rock 'n' roll hit in 1956 with "Stranded in the Jungle," but had not done much until Ralph Bass brought them to Chicago and signed them to Chess's subsidiary label, Checker, in 1960. On Checker the group consisted of Richard Owens (lead), James Johnson (first tenor), Carlton Fisher (second tenor and lead), David Govan (baritone), and Don Bradley (bass). In the next several years Chess would record the Vibrations on two kinds of songs, frantic dance numbers and dreamy ballads. The group in live performance was one of the most spectacular in their dance movements and became one of the most popular acts at the Regal Theater.[14]

The early dance called the Watusi bore no similarity to the better known shimmy-type wiggle dance of the same name popular in the post-Beatles era. The 1961 version had a particular content in steps and motions. The dancers would take several steps forward, then a side step. Their arms, held up and bent toward them, would move rhythmically with the shoulders. The Watusi could be danced by couples, in parallel lines, and in a circle. While in a circle, the dancers would pulsate toward the center and then out. It was a very exciting dance to watch. Although largely an r&b phenomenon, the dance was done in some white neighborhoods.

The Watusi, as with many other Chicago dance records, had its origin with black teens. Tony Gideon, a member of the Daylighters, was responsible for discovering and catalyzing interest in the dance while he was working apart from the group. His story shows how a dance record originates and how the little record man invariably gets beaten by the big record man. Related Gideon:

> I was working with Cadillac Baby down at his Bea and Baby Records, and also in his little record shop there. There was a guy named Ted Daniels, another guy named Doc Oliver, and myself. There was a little boy named Herman. I think he was going to either Dunbar or DuSable High School, and he used to come by the record shop every afternoon. He would be doing this little dance to the music, you know. We asked him what the kids called it. He said it was something the kids called "The Watusi."
>
> I then cut a record, which was titled "Wa-Too-Si"; Doc and I wrote the tune. What happened then was, Chuck Barksdale, bass singer of the Dells, he and I were writing together. His father-in-law owned this hotdog stand right next to the record shop. He used to come over there every day. I think what happened was, he knew we were going to do the Watusi thing because he mentioned the fact that we were coming out with it to Ralph Bass and Leonard Chess down at Chess.

They were going to bring the Vibrations in anyway to record them, but they didn't really have a strong tune for them. So they came up with the idea of recording them on a Watusi record. They didn't have a tune. They used—you remember, Hank Ballard and the Midnighters' "Let's Go, Let's Go, Let's Go"—they took the same melody. The only thing they changed was Ralph's using cow bells on the intro and Reggie Boyd's walking bass so it wouldn't sound so similar. But it is still the same tune.

We were ready to release our record and it was on the Miss label, which was a subsidiary label we started at Bea and Baby. We did "The Way You Move Me Baby" and "Wa-Too-Si," but they held us up in the pressing plant; they were having production problems. What happened was we had the tune and we had already cut it, but we didn't have any records to send to the radio stations. So we called Jimmy Gann, who was running Chess's pressing plant over at Forty-eighth and Cottage Grove. He said we could have eleven, that's all he could give us right then! So while we were over at the pressing plant picking up the stuff, waiting for them to get ready for us, Leonard Chess came in with Hoss Allen, of WLAC Nashville. That was on December 19, 1960. Leonard scared Cadillac Baby and told him he would have his Watusi records boxed up and shipped back to him wherever he sent them. With Allen standing right there, the statement seemed to have some weight. He also claimed he owned all the publishing rights to it even though he had a different song.

So what happened was he wanted me to sign with him. I told him I didn't want to sign, so he says he only wants me for a year and not for the Watusi side. He wanted me for the other side, "The Way You Move Me Baby." He told me to come down to the office around three o'clock and "let's talk about it." As a matter of fact, he first offered Cadillac $500 in the pressing plant. Cadillac got scared, because he thought his records would be shipped back to him. So not really knowing and not having distributors across the country, he really didn't know what was going down. So anyway, we went down there the next day and sat down till Cadillac was convinced that leasing the master was best. Also, according to Chess, he was going to make me a star.

Okay, now when I'm released to Chess, Leonard holds the record up until January 12, 1961. By that time the Vibrations' record was several weeks out. Then he released mine, and he went with "The Way You Move Me Baby." The other side, "Wa-Too-Si," he changed the name to "Whatcha Gonna Do" to remove it as competition to the Vibrations song. But Chess did promote the record and it went top forty in Dallas, Los Angeles, Detroit, Birmingham, and sold quite well in Chicago.[15]

Well, there you have it. I do not feel the "Wa-Too-Si" was a strong side, even though it got played in St. Louis and other cities. That Chess would go to the trouble of making sure no one ever heard of Gideon's version despite the obvious strength of the Vibrations' record gives food for thought.

The Continental, or Continental Walk, was another r&b dance of 1961. Dancers formed parallel lines and shuffled in sideways steps first in one direction and then the reverse, clapping their hands. It bore some similarity to the earlier Stroll, from 1957. Helping to popularize the dance were "Continental with Me Baby" by the Vibrations, "Continental Walk" by the Rollers, and "Continental Walk" by Hank Ballard and the Midnighters. This dance was to last well beyond 1961 and into the late 1960s to become virtually a standard form.

In the latter part of 1961 a record called "Foot Stomping" by the Flares became a hit in both the rock 'n' roll and r&b markets. From this record in particular the r&b audience devised a routine called Stomping, or the Stomp, which was not so much a dance but more of a "fun thing." All the dancers did was just stomp on the floor to the beat of the record. Chicago's black youth devised a dance called the Continental Stomp in early 1961, a stomp dance done in parallel lines but with a lighter stomping motion, but no record producer caught on the fad to exploit it. There were several other records important in promoting the Stomp, notably "The Stomp" (1961) by the Olympics, "Bristol Stomp" (1961) by the Dovells, and "Bongo Stomp" (1962) by Little Joey and the Flips.

Probably the most exotic and most quintessential of the black ghetto dances was the Roach, especially popular in Chicago in late 1961 and early 1962. The record "The Roach" by the Los Angeles duo of Gene and Wendell (Eugene Washington and Wendell Jones) can stand on its own as good r&b. It came out on a small obscure Los Angeles label, Ray Star. The Roach was generally a line dance with a somewhat fast tempo, with steps similar to the Watusi. Its most characteristic step was a squishing motion with one's foot on a non-existent cockroach to the song's sharply sung refrain, "kill that roach." For a look at this delightful dance, one should check out *Hairspray*. Often near the end of the record, the dancers would break away from the line (or circle) formation and each would go into his or her individual squashing routine. This in essence was the r&b Stomp. As a consequence Gene and Wendell followed "The Roach" with the identical-sounding "The Roach Stomp," only after it had been discovered that black kids had evolved the stomping routine to the Roach. The follow-up's lyrics specifically point to Chicago as the area of popularity for the Roach.

During the 1961–62 period, the Pony was popular with both blacks and whites. Dancers could Pony with partners, but usually it was done "bunny-hop" fashion in a chain, in which dancers would move around the floor in a high-stepping, gallop-like motion. The appeal in this dance was obvious for whites, who had a long tradition of doing the Bunny Hop. Though it made no reference to the dance, Bobby Lewis's "Tossin' and Turnin'" was considered *the* record for Pony dancing, because rhythmically it most perfectly fit the movements of the dance. Less popular and easily forgettable were actual Pony records—"Pony Time" (1961), in two versions, the original by Don Covey and the Goodtimers, and the cover by Chubby Checker; and "Let's Pony Again" (1961) by the Vibrations. Incidentally, Don Covay discovered the dance in a club in his hometown of Washington, D.C., where the movements of the dance shaped his creation of the song.[16]

Another r&b dance of the period, the Hully Gully, had several records starting with the Olympics' "(Baby) Hully Gully," which came out in 1959. Charles Fizer, who sang second lead with the group, devised a snake-like dance to fit the Hully Gully music. (Fizer, incidentally, was killed in the 1965 Watts riot when he charged a police blockade in his car.) The dance lingered a few years, for in 1962 there was an explosion of Hully Gully records—"Hully Gully Calling Time" by the Jive Five, "The New Hully Gully" (identical to "Continental with Me Baby") by the Vibrations, and "Hully Gully Baby" by the Dovells were the most successful. The lyrics in these songs suggest various pantomimes may have accompanied the sideways steps of the dance.

New Orleans gave birth to the Popeye line dance in 1962. The dance was more popular than the Twist with both blacks and whites in New Orleans, but in the rest of the country it made little impact. Dancers would move in a shuffling motion while making a Popeye arm-flexing gesture (which was the same motion as that of the Hitchhiker dance).[17] The record that launched the fad was "Something You Got" by New Orleans artist Chris Kenner on the Instant label. Owner Joe Banashak told New Orleans researcher Jeff Hannusch, "'Something You Got' was a big record in New Orleans, and I couldn't figure out why because I couldn't even give it away in Baton Rouge. I asked [Ernie] K-Doe and Benny Spellman why the record was selling and they said, 'Don't you know man? The kids are learning the Popeye to "Something You Got." ' I'll tell you how dances affected records. We sold 30,000 singles off the Popeye and that was just in New Orleans."[18]

The New Orleans producers jumped on the Popeye bandwagon in no time and came out with a flurry of Popeye records. The most notable were "Check Mr. Popeye" by Eddie Bo, "Popeye Joe" by Ernie K-Doe, and "Pop-Eye" by Huey Smith and the Clowns, the latter a national hit. Popeye records outside New Orleans that charted nationally were "Pop Pop Pop-Pie" by the Sherrys and "Popeye the Hitchhiker" by Chubby Checker, both records out of Philadelphia. Motown artist Marvin Gaye continued the Popeye dance craze into 1963 with "Hitchhike."

Dee Dee Sharp had her biggest hit in early 1962 with "Mashed Potatoes." The dance it generated was a high-stepping, pigeon-toed dance similar to the Twist, in which the dancers stepped on the balls of their feet and held their arms up like wings. The Philadelphia-produced record was a substantial hit on the popular market, and the dance itself was popular in the white community as well as in the black, maybe even bigger among whites.

Fad Dances, 1963–69

Whereas dancing declined during the 1960s in the white community, within the black community there continued to emerge a great variety of dances, each having form and content to varying degrees. Though some of the dances were rather simple, all had content, so that when blacks went up on the dance floor they invariably had in mind specific moves, motions, and gestures. Generally, the quality of dances was high.

Chicago black teens had their social divisions. As was true of the white kids of the early rock 'n' roll era who tended to place individuals into categories of "nice" and "hoody," usually by their manner of dress, blacks also developed classification schemes from the dim perception of class status. Among males, the respectable middle-class types were generally called "ivy leaguers" after their short haircuts, ivy caps, v-neck sweaters, and peg-leg pants. The largely working-class black versions of young toughs were known as "gousters," who prided themselves on their baggy pants, key chains, long coats, and conical narrow-brimmed hats tilted forward on the head. There was a large middle element, dirt poor, who did not affect a style and who could be found in all seasons and all occasions in their bargain-basement green wash pants and gym shoes. Such dressers sometimes were called "wwigs" (*wear what I gots*).

The girls in the black high schools were not so rigidly characterized. Attractive girls of all classes were generally called "foxes," or "stone foxes," but an attractive girl in a tough crowd might also be known as a "feznecky." Young men were often called "ferns," as in "ferns and fezneckies." Unlike in the white community, the degree of appreciation of dance was not related to one's life-style and peer group associations. Everybody danced in a black high school. Dancing transcended social differences.

Listening to Chicago radio in the mid-1960s one could frequently hear "fox," "gouster," "feznecky," and "fern" bandied about. Disc jockies, particularly Herb Kent, would invariably ask upon taking a call if the caller were a "gouster" or an "ivy-leaguer," or what have you. One can find these social-class terms in a number of Chicago soul records from the period, such as the Five Du-Tones' "The Gouster" (1963), the Joy Rockers' "Gouster Bop" (1962,), the Dukays' "Mellow Feznecky" (ca. 1965), and J. C. Davis's "Feznecky" (1964).

As a universal expression of black kids, dance can also be viewed as a race achievement. Perhaps, consciously or unconsciously, dance was thought to be an expression of blackness and of social solidarity. In the early 1960s, when such feelings were not always so publicly verbalized, there were—as there are today—numerous manifestations of brotherhood such as special handshakes and various styles of talking and joking (jiving). Dance can be seen in the same light. Take the dance the Roach; the kids who did the dance knew it was "their thing," unique to them, and they had a peculiar pride in doing the dance even though it pointed to the reality of the ghetto existence of many of them. The dance really represented a psychological triumph over their physical environment.

Blacks created numerous dances that had to be performed by groups, usually in the form of parallel lines. A young person who could join in on the dance was symbolically demonstrating a solidarity with the group. However, it would be a mistake to read into such dances too much of the idea of black consciousness, for the dancers were usually all young, and there was a focus on communal feelings as well. White youth in earlier years derived a similar sense of solidarity from doing such dances as the Stroll.

Chicago black kids in 1963 went through a slew of new dances—the Dog, Walking the Dog, Bird, Monkey, Crossfire, and Uncle Willie. The Dog and its line form, Walking the Dog, were popularized by the Memphis singer Rufus Thomas with two records, "The Dog" and "Walking the Dog," for Stax records. The song, "The Dog," seems to have been inspired by Willie Mae Thornton's "Hound Dog," to which Thomas had done an answer song in 1953 called "Bearcat." "Walking the Dog," a much superior record, has been frequently covered and still sounds fresh decades later. In the Dog, a dancer with his or her partner would move sensually together in a bent-over position and in such close proximity so as to resemble two dogs copulating. Needless to say, the dog was barred from schools in Chicago and across the nation.

Thomas was part of a dance team of Rufus and Bones in the 1940s, which explains why he specialized in dance records. He discovered the Dog dance while playing at the Danceland Theatre in Millington, Tennessee, where he spotted dancers doing the Dog choreography while he was chanting "Ooh Pah Pah Doo," a song made famous by Jessie Hill.[19]

In its simplest form, the Bird was done by wiggling one's knees back and forth and flapping one's elbows. The best dancers could do it so realistically that they looked as though they were trying to fly away but were held down by some invisible force. There were at least a dozen Bird records in 1963. The big hits were "The Bird" by the Dutones (Richard Parker and Jerry Brown), "Shake a Tail Feather" by the Five Du-Tones, "Bird's the Word" by the Rivingtons, and "Bossa Nova Bird" by the Dells. All but the Rivingtons' record were Chicago products. There was also a record from Philadelphia by the Dial Tones called "Chicago Bird," which was not even a minor hit, but it did point out the city of origin for the dance.

"The Bird" by the Dutones sounded too much like a parody of a dance record, despite its compelling beat. "Shake a Tail Feather" was a real piece of inspiration and was one of the most successful creations of One-derful Records. *Hairspray* does an excellent job in demonstrating the dance to this song. The "Bird's the Word" was a remake of the Rivingtons' earlier hit "Papa-Oom-Mow-Mow," and if one liked the latter, which was as maddenly repetitious as its title, he would surely like the former. Even though these three records, as well as Dee Dee Sharp's "Do the Bird," turned out to be top-forty hits in the pop market, white teens inexplicably never took up the dance. The best of the bird releases, the exciting "Bossa Nova Bird," was not a crossover hit. It came out in late 1962 and probably helped kick off the Bird dance fad. Interestingly, the record also seemed to be trying to capitalize on the Bossa Nova fad popular at the same time.

With the Bird, Chicago began to emerge as *the* dance record center. The recording activity in all r&b records was especially intense in the city during the middle 1960s, and a large number of dance records came out of Record Row during that period. On July 13, 1963, *Billboard* ran an item headlined, "Chi's getting the monkey itch." The story, datelined Chicago, said, "The monkeys have hit the city. Radio stations are playing monkey songs. Kids are buying monkey records. Juke box operators are programming them. There's even a dance called the monkey. Not only the kids, but a limited number of adults are taking part...."[20]

It was not exactly like that. The only stations that were playing Monkey songs were the r&b ones, and virtually the only kids buying the records were blacks. Only one Monkey record in July had any extensive sales and that was Major Lance's "Monkey Time," in my estimation the greatest dance record of all time. "Monkey Time" was not the first Monkey record; there had been in the previous months a number of obscure Monkey records that got no airplay.

Throughout the summer of 1963, "Monkey Time" remained on the r&b charts, and its fantastic success spawned a host of Monkey songs from Chicago. By the fall there were Lance's "Hey Little Girl" (with its Monkey beat and theme) and the Ideals' "Gorilla," both of which were hits, as well as the Five Du-Tones' "Monkey See and Monkey Do" and J. C. Davis's "Monkey," both of which generated few sales and no airplay. The Miracles from Detroit's fledgling Motown organization had a giant hit with "Mickey's Monkey" and Kenny Hamber from Philadelphia hit with "Show Me Your Monkey."

The Monkey is not hard to visualize. It was usually done with vigorous and repetitive overarm motions with a pronounced rhythmic snapping of the neck. In the *T.A.M.I. Show* movie, James Brown demonstrated how this standard version was done. The movie also showed the Miracles doing an exciting and exotic stage version that was not typical of the dance. About a year or so after black teenagers had stopped dancing the Monkey (about 1965), white middle-class kids began picking up on the dance. The kids seemed content to simply wave their arms up and down for a pantomime monkey effect, but with no rhythmic intensity whatsoever. The Monkey had become just another discotheque dance.

Another colorful fad dance of late 1963 was the Crossfire. It was not that popular, but it had a very dramatic movement, a firing gesture made at one's partner. Recording the songs for the dance were Dee Clark with "Crossfire Time" and the Orlons with "Crossfire." Neither was an inspiring number.

Popular in late 1963 and early 1964 was the Uncle Willie, a strange dance that most dancers had difficulty doing. Basically it was a shuffle from side to side in a pigeon-toed movement mostly on the balls of one's feet. The difficulty was that one could continue the sideways shuffle only a short time before one lost momentum and stopped.[21] Bobby Miller was the first Chicago act out of the chute with an Uncle Willie record. His "Uncle Willie Time," recorded for Constellation, was an uninspiring number, but by being the first it got the sales. In December 1963 the *Chicago Defender* reported on the Uncle Willie fad, headlining an item with "new dance to bow into Regal," and then saying, "Chicago's newest dance rage, 'Uncle Willie Time,' is one of the highlights in the Regal Theater's gala holiday stage show opening. Chicago's own Bobby Miller will sing and dance the new dance sensation on the Regal stage. . . ."[22]

Two other Chicago records did well with the Uncle Willie fad in early

1964, Henry Ford and the Gifts' superb teen-lead sound, "It's Uncle Willie," and the Daylighters' pounding stomper "Oh Mom (Teach Me How to Uncle Willie)." The Daylighters' tune fit the difficult Uncle Willie dance just about as well as any of the songs, and Chuck Colbert, Jr., a member of the group and the producer of the record, explained how he got the beat: "We used to take people into the studio all the time and let them dance while we were doing a tune. A lot of people still do that. When they're trying to do dance tunes, they bring in the kids. It's a little trick, you know."[23] Because it was the custom for r&b groups to dance while performing their songs, the Daylighters had to learn how to do the dance for their act, which was undoubtedly a factor in helping to spread the Uncle Willie.

That producers brought kids into their studios helps to explain why so many records of a particular period that were not dance records by name seemed to fit the particular body movements of the day. This was true of the Uncle Willie, which spawned many records that conformed to the rhythm of the dance movements. This happened with Fontella Bass and Bobby McClure's big hit on the Checker from 1965, "Don't Mess Up a Good Thing." The duo was working with Oliver Sain on the song but it was not coming together to anybody's satisfaction. Then Billy Davis came in and made a superb suggestion, according to McClure: "He said, 'Why don't you change the tempo? Do you all do the Uncle Willie?' We said, 'Yeah.' He said, 'Let's put [the Uncle Willie tempo in] there.' And we were doing the Uncle Willie while [the session] was going to make sure the tempo was there, and the feel was there. Then it picked up. I liked it because it was bright, it did something."[24]

Obviously, some dances were created in a producer's head, but most evidently had a spontaneous origin in the experiences of black high-school youth. The relationship between the kids and the producers was often closely intertwined. To determine the origin of a dance, it is sometimes hard to separate the role of a producer from the invention of the young people. A record helped to popularize a particular dance in some respects, but the content of the dance necessarily had to be demonstrated by the youth, which in turn boosted the record. Record companies, of course, did not just depend on kids to do the work of promotion. Major Lance said that when he first started, live monkeys in cages were sent to radio stations and used in personal appearances to promote his "Monkey Time" record.[25]

Chuck Colbert and Billy Davis were producers who made records in an area close to the black neighborhoods, which kept them in touch. In contrast was Carole King, who wrote magnificent songs in a cubbyhole in the Brill Building in New York City. She wrote a dance tune called "Locomotion" and had Little Eva record it in 1962, but a dance never emerged from it. There were numerous records like "Locomotion" released during the 1960s that bore dance titles unconnected to any known dance. Usually such records came about because the writers and producers plied their trade isolated from the real creators of popular dance, black youth.

A mildly popular r&b dance of 1964 was the Sloop, or Sloop Dance. The Vibrations, who had just joined OKeh, recorded "Sloop Dance," and it became a small hit. Its flip, "Watusi Time," unsuccessfully attempted to revive the Watusi. Both sides were produced by Carl Davis and were tremendous dance sides, the best the Vibrations ever did in that idiom. The Sloop itself was a line dance patterned after the Continental Walk. What distinguished the dance was a peculiar swing of the arms pulled upward from the shoulders. (The Vibrations got no more dance hits on OKeh, but did score national hits with ballads, notably "Misty" [1965] and "And I Love Her" [1966].)

The most popular r&b line dance of 1963–64 was the Barracuda, a dance with various prescribed steps in which the dancers made parade-ground turning movements and executed steps forward, backward, and sideways. Both lines of dancers moved precisely in unison, which made this legendary dance one of the most visually exciting dances of all time. Alvin Cash and his Crawlers came out with "The Barracuda" in early 1965, but the dance was popular well before that time.

The Barracuda was one of the few black dance fads that crossed over into the inner-city white dance halls, at least in Chicago. Apparently, white kids from two integrated West Side high schools, Harrison and Farragut, picked up the dance and introduced it into dance halls throughout the city. The kids from these two schools also gained the reputation for being able to perform the Barracuda best and closest to the black original.

Alvin Cash and his Crawlers were not a vocal group but actually a dance team from St. Louis. After gaining a reputation for their dancing, the Crawlers came to Chicago to record a series of dance records for Leaner's Mar-V-lus label. Most of the group's records are hard to listen to as they basically consisted of a series of punctuated dance rhythms interrupted in various places by Cash calling out the dance steps. But they were usually perfect to dance to, filling a social need that was the traditional *raison d'être* of rock 'n' roll and rhythm and blues.

The first and probably best of Cash's records was "Twine Time," which came out in late 1964. "Twine Time" was only a limited crossover hit in the pop market, partly because of its alleged tastelessness. A top-forty station in New York City refused to play it because the deejays thought the "ooh ahhs" in the opening of the song sounded suggestive.[26] Another record that tried to cash in on the Twine was the "Woodbine Twine" by the Five Du-Tones, released in February 1965. The name of the dance came from a particular variation of the Twine that developed at Budland (Sixty-fourth and Cottage Grove), where deejay Herb Kent regularly held sway. He went to George Leaner with the idea for a record, and the upshot was the Five Du-Tones' disc—which, however, was a dud and made no impact in the dancing market outside Budland.

The Twine, like the Barracuda, was one of those dances that emerged from the black high-school kids before it was put on record. Months before the record was released kids around Thirty-fifth to Thirty-ninth streets were doing the dance to the Miracles' "That's What Love Is Made of." Most of the kids in that area attended Dunbar High, and it was at one of the school's dances that one of Leaner's producers, Andre Williams, discovered the dance.[27]

Similarly, the Charge began at least a year and a half before a record of the same name came out in early 1967, Cash's "The Charge." It was a moderate soul hit with sales primarily in Chicago. The dance was seen at private parties in the city in late 1965 and early 1966, where it was usually done to Lowell Fulsom's "Tramp." The Charge was a line dance in which dancers faced their partners and sort of "charged" in a march-step at each other. Also in the dance were steps backward and parade-ground turning movements.

In early 1965 a California group, the Larks (Don Julian, Charles Morrison, and Ted Walters), who came out of the old 1950s doowop group the Meadowlarks, got a national hit with "The Jerk," which promoted a new dance that arose in Los Angeles.[28] Julian told interviewer Steve Propes how he discovered the dance: "I went over to my sister's house, the kids were dancing to Martha and the Vandellas' 'Dancing in the Streets.' I said, 'Hey, what's that you're doing?' She said, 'The Jerk.' I said, 'The Jerk?' She said, 'If you don't know how to do it, come on I'll teach it to you.'"[29]

A local Chicago act, the Dukays, had a weaker and different song also called "The Jerk." In it they claimed the dance started in Chicago, but the record came too late for the claim to be valid. Producer Jerry T. Murray wrote, produced, and released the song on his own label, Jerry-O, and became something of a specialist in dance records. There was a host of Jerk records out of Los Angeles, but the only other records that got national exposure were "Jerk It" by the Gypsies, a girl group from New York; "Can You Jerk Like Me" by the Contours; and "Come on and Do the Jerk" by the Miracles; the latter two were examples of inferior Motown products. This was one of the few r&b dances that became tremendously popular in the white community. It was done by raising one's hands over the head and snapping the neck upon bringing them down. The principle was similar to the original Monkey, but the form of the Jerk was somewhat more restrictive, which did not allow for individual creativity.

The Jerk was not very popular among blacks, at least in Chicago. When they did do the Jerk, they generally combined it with the Twine, which was similar but with more fluid and sweeping motions. The combination permitted the necessary flexibility that the Jerk did not possess. Jackie Ross, in her "Jerk and Twine" (January 1965), suggested that the Jerk did not come from Chicago but pointed out that the Twine did, and suggested combining the two into a single dance. The combined Jerk and Twine probably had already emerged in Chicago before the record came out.

A popular black dance of 1965–66 was the Boston Monkey, which presumably came from Beantown. The dancers would move their arms in a whiplash back-and-forth swing; there was also much swinging back and forth of the torso and knees. The motions were fluid, not jerky. Alvin Cash, after having failed to get a hit with "The Penguin" (June 1965), failed again with the "Boston Monkey" (November 1965). The dance's popularity continued, however, and Billy Butler got some airplay in the summer of 1966 with "Boston Monkey," the B side of his hit "Right Track."

The most successful new dance of 1965–66 was the Boogaloo. The dance had a totally new look compared to previous dances, and its popularity crossed over to whites. In the dance, the entire body moved in a pulsating motion from side to side. The rhythmic impulse seemed to have been centered in the upper torso, shoulders, and head. There were numerous Boogaloo records, the first of which was "Boo-Ga-Loo," a Chicago creation by Tom and Jerrio, who were a dance/comedy/singing act. Tom was Robert Tharp (aka Tommy Dark), who came out of the Ideals, and Jerrio was producer Jerry T. Murray. The duo got the idea to do the dance record from seeing the Boo-Ga-Loo done at a Herb Kent record hop at the Times Square, Forty-eighth and Wabash.[30]

The record, released on ABC, was a huge hit for the pair in April 1965, going as high as position eleven and lasting eleven weeks on *Billboard*'s r&b chart. Said Tharp, "It sold a million, but we didn't get anything out of it. The backing came from Motown. Berry Gordy sued us and said the tune was copyrighted, and we lost all the money we earned from the record."[31] Gordy could not have been claiming the tune for esthetic reasons, because "Boo-Ga-Loo" was an exceedingly unappealing record. Any interest in it came from its funky Boogaloo beat that rode the popularity of the dance. The record was basically an instrumental punctuated by vigorous calls of encouragement, such as "Hit it," or "Come on girl."

Tom and Jerrio worked a lot off the song. Said Tharp, "We played everywhere—Michigan, the West Coast, East Coast, the South. . . . We played a lot of dates with the Temptations. We were a comedy-dance act and warmed up the audiences."[32] Commented former Ideals member Wesley

Spraggins, "Robert became a hell of a choreographer. I didn't know he could dance as well as he could."[33] After two follow-ups—"Great Goo-Ga-Moo-Ga" and "(Papa Chew) Do the Boogaloo"—failed to interest the public, the team broke up. Jerrio went on to record a number of highly successful funky dance numbers, notably the "Karate-Boo-Ga-Loo" in 1967 and "Funky Boo-Ga-Loo" in 1968. He died sometime in the mid-1970s.

Another Chicago Boogaloo record was "Alvin's Boogaloo" (November 1966), which signaled the return to the charts of Alvin Cash and the Crawlers. Chess got a hit out of "Boo-Ga-Loo Baby" by Tommy and Cleve (Tommy Bullock and Cleveland Horne) in 1966, but the record was an independent production by Gene Redd picked up in Detroit by the company.[34] Also, elsewhere in the country the Flamingos came out with "Boogaloo Party" (September 1966) and Don Gardner recorded "My Baby Likes to Boogaloo" (November 1966). All of these records were at least moderate hits in the soul market, but as far as listening pleasure is concerned, none exhibited any lasting qualities. In 1968 the Boogaloo became an enormous fad in the Puerto Rican community, which produced dozens of Latin-styled Boogaloo records.[35]

A variation of the Boogaloo was the Funky Broadway, in which the bending of the knees provided somewhat more leg action than the standard version, and it was generally done as a line dance. The Funky Broadway was largely a black dance; its limited popularity resulted in minimal crossover into the white community. The records promoting the dance were more widely known. Dyke and the Blazers, out of Arizona, launched the fad with "Funky Broadway" in February 1967, but Wilson Pickett had the bigger hit with his cover version later in August of that year. No Chicago company jumped on the fad dance, peculiarly.

The year 1966 also saw the Philly Dog. The dance was not very big in the black community, although there were numerous records promoting it. Perhaps the jerky up-and-down bobbings of the dance hadn't any appeal. Some of the records were the Manhattans' "Teach Me the Philly Dog," the flip to their excellent "Baby I Need You"; the Olympics' "Baby Do the Philly Dog," and Chicagoan Johnny Williams's "Philly Dog," the flip to his "My Baby's Good" on Chess. All were dismal. A fine record, however, was the Mar-Keys' big instrumental, "Philly Dog," from Memphis.

A substantial national r&b hit in the summer of 1966 was Alvin Cash's "Philly Freeze," a variation of the Philly Dog that used the old dance gimmick of suddenly halting the music at the shout of "freeze," upon which all the dancers would hold whatever positions they were in at the moment.

About the same time as the Philly Dog records, Holly Maxwell came out with "Philly Barracuda," which got some local play. It apparently was supposed to combine the Barracuda line dance with the movements of the

Philly Dog. It also had something that other dance records had lacked for some time—instructions on how the dance was to be done. The close relationship between Chicago's record men and the people of the city was evidenced by the special promotion Maxwell's company, Star, used to get the record noticed. In late January 1966, Maxwell appeared with deejay Herb Kent at Crane High in a special lunch-hour show. There she got up on the table to do her song and demonstrate the Philly Barracuda dance.[36] The probable reason for this flamboyant promotion was that the "Philly Barracuda" was one of those records in which the dance had not emerged from the r&b audience or through the audience's interaction with the producer, but primarily from the producer alone, thus, the public needed to be taught the content of the dance.

The last great black line-dance of the 1960s was Function at the Junction, from the winter of 1966–67. It was done to Shorty Long's "Function at the Junction," a Motown hit. The dance's basic movement was a simultaneous swing-dip by all the dancers in two parallel lines. The record had been released in the first months of 1966, was played a few weeks, and then died. By September, however, a dance had developed around the record; Milwaukee seems to have been the point of origin. As a result, "Function at the Junction" developed a second life and became a national hit. It was one of those records that unintentionally gave rise to a dance, and for this reason the dance it spawned is a prime example of a folk creation.

The biggest r&b dance of 1969 was the Popcorn, an exuberantly flashy and vigorous dance. The dancers swung their torsos back and forth, held their arms out, snapping their fingers, and took forceful steps in various directions. The Popcorn was ideal for dance contests, allowing much individual creativity and many showy moves. James Brown developed a mini-industry with the Popcorn, coming out with four Popcorn records—"The Popcorn," "Mother Popcorn," "Low Down Popcorn," and "Let a Man Come in and Do the Popcorn."

Almost as a reaction to the flamboyance of the Popcorn was the Yolk, a tight, highly controlled r&b dance that developed later in the year. It seemed to have started on the East Coast. Dancers would vibrate up and down like birds dropping eggs, while their arms were bent and held close to their sides, hands turned palms down. The hand movement was a lifting, fluttering motion as if the dancers were holding marionettes. Dyke and the Blazers' "We Got More Soul" and "Let a Man Be a Man—Let a Woman Be a Women" were favorite records to which the Yolk was done. Chicago producer Lenny LeCour recorded "The Yolk" by a Milwaukee group, Harvey Scales and the Seven Sounds. The record, released on Chess, was probably the best selling of several Yolk records, but the dance was so pinched and off-putting it could not sell many records.

Standard Black Dances in Chicago

Standard dances, the old reliables, were always around, and were something that dancers fell back upon for a change of pace or mood between the usually upbeat fad dances. Standard dances were broad enough and flexible enough in form so that their popularity was not dependent on a particular record or an especially limiting type of beat or rhythm. They could survive changing tastes in music. The principal standard dances in Chicago during the soul era were the Slow Dance, the Bop, and the Walk.

A standard through the 1970s, the Slow Dance was popular with all groups, black and white. It was done at all levels of proficiency and all styles of footwork and technique. The degree of affection the partners had for each other usually determined how close they would hold each other. The main excuse for the existence of the very close variety was that it gave the kids the opportunity to rub their bodies against one another under the guise of innocent (or not so innocent) entertainment. In the 1940s a close Slow Dance was known as Slow Dragging, especially among blacks, but by the 1960s this name had disappeared and had given way to a name equally unrefined, Belly-Rubbing.

The Bop was generally done among black youth only, at least in Chicago. In the Carolinas white kids did a Bop-like dance called the Shag to rhythm-and-blues music that they called "beach music." The Bop obviously had its origin in the Lindy Hop and the Jitterbug, and more directly the Two Step, as it seemed to be a sort of slowed-down, cool version of the Jitterbug or stylish Two Step. It was not until the mid-fifties that black youth were doing the Bop formally as a distinct dance.

Actually, there was not one Bop but numerous Bops, each with its own footwork and sense of timing to fit the music of a particular record. For example, a popular style in Chicago in the early 1960s was the Gouster Bop, which took its name from the young hoodlum style of dress affected by certain black kids, as mentioned earlier. Riding the popularity of the dance was the Joy Rockers' "Gouster Bop" (1962) on the local Penny label. Of all the black dances, the Bop was the most sophisticated and subtle in its rhythms and tempos. By slight modifications, a dancer theoretically could Bop to just about any record. With a quiet, subliminal awareness of the fact, the Bop was considered a supreme example of black achievement in dance. To do the Bop was literally to demonstrate one's blackness.

For writers on rock 'n' roll and rhythm and blues, the Bop does not seem to exist. Neither do books on social dance include it. That one of the most fundamental popular dances among youth is presumably unnoticed demonstrates the complete neglect of black popular dance.

In the Walk, partners would hold onto each other, side by side, and stroll across the floor in a slow walk tempo. The dance had its origin in the early 1950s. Herb Kent oftened claimed that the Spaniels' "Play It Cool" (1954) was the first Walk record. At record hops he would also play as a Walk record the Diablos' "The Way You Dog Me Around" (1955). California blues singer Jimmy McCracklin did a record called "The Walk" (1958), but it had little relationship to the popularity of the dance. Martin Denny renewed interest in the dance with "Quiet Village" (1959), an instrumental popular with black kids—one of the reasons being that the Walk could be danced to it. Because of Denny's record, in the 1960s the Walk also became known as the Village Walk.

Fad Dances, 1970–78

The early 1970s saw what I call the dark ages of r&b dancing, at least it seemed that way in Chicago. Virtually no dance records were coming out of the city, and most of the non-local creations seem to have been promoted by Rufus Thomas, who had been somewhat quiet for a few years after his Dog records. Within a short time span, Thomas had hits with "Do the Funky Chicken" (January 1970), "(Do the) Push and Pull" (December 1970), "The Breakdown" (August 1971), and "Do the Funky Penguin" (December 1971). Chicago chipped in with a Rufus Thomas imitation, "Funky Chicken" (February 1970), by Willie Henderson, a Brunswick Records producer turned dance master.

Most of the dances were characterized by robot-like movements, and although some could look spectacular at times, as in the Breakdown, each new dance looked like the previous creation, with the same jerky, quirky, stiff-arm and stiff-leg movements.

The year 1974 finally offered relief, ushering in a new era by providing a new look with The Bump, a simple but entertaining dance in which the partners maneuvered around the floor to bump hips. Its success soon spawned a new creativity in r&b dancing, resulting in the Bus Stop, the Hustle, and the Spank. Chicago's last great contribution to black popular dance was the latter dance, which was created in the city's discos by black and Latin teenagers in 1977. There was not much of a record industry in Chicago by the late 1970s, and the big hit record "Le Spank" by Le Pamplemousse had to come out of an alliance between a California label, AVI, and a Chicago disco pool called Dogs of War. The pool, headquartered at 2112 South Michigan, was organized and headed by veteran record man Eddie Thomas after he left Curtom Records. As Thomas conceived it, the "pool" was an organization of club deejays who by acting as a collective would ensure that they would receive promotional product from the record companies and in return would provide a powerful marketing push to their releases.[37]

As to the origin of "Le Spank," the city's deejays noticed the new dance and through their marketing man, Harry Webber, contacted AVI. The company, armed with the reports and observations and music samples from the Dogs' deejays, was able to design a record with music that was "most conducive to spanking."[38] "Le Spank" was recorded in Los Angeles and released first in the discos of Chicago in October 1977. The record in early 1978 went to number six position and lasted twenty-one weeks on *Cash Box*'s black singles chart.

That the Spank emerged as a fad dance was something of a freak occurrence, because in the late seventies, at the height of the disco era, specific dances were generally subsumed within individualistic free-form choreography. The great era of fad dances had actually died with the coming of disco.

NOTES

1. Charlie Gillett, *The Sound of the City*, rev. and enl. (New York: Pantheon, 1983), pp. 209–10.

2. Langdon Winner, "The Strange Death of Rock and Roll," *Rock and Roll Will Stand*, ed. Greil Marcus (Boston: Beacon Press, 1969), p. 40.

3. Nik Cohn, *Awopbopaloobop Alopbamboom* (St. Albans, Eng.: Paladin, 1970), p. 89.

4. Mike Jahn, *Rock* (New York: Quadrangle/The New York Times Book Company, 1973), pp. 101–2.

5. Lynn Ellis McCutcheon, *Rhythm and Blues* (Arlington, Va.: Beatty, 1971), p. 26.

6. Marshall and Jean Stearns, *Jazz Dance* (New York: Macmillan, 1978), p. 4.

7. Ibid., pp. 4–5. In 1988, another authoritative writer on black popular dance, Brenda Dixon-Stovall, apparently got her primary sustenance from the Stearnses in developing her examination of postwar dance trends. See Brenda Dixon-Sovall, "Popular Dance in the Twentieth Century," in *Black Dance from 1619 to Today*, by Lynne Fauley Emery, 2nd ed., rev. (Princeton, N.J.: Princeton Book Company, 1988), p. 354.

8. Carl Belz, *The Story of Rock* (New York: Oxford University Press, 1969), p. 89.

9. John Waters, *Hairspray* (New Line Cinema), 1988.

10. Jay Bruder, "R&B in Washington DC: The TNT Tribble Story," *Blues and Rhythm: The Gospel Truth* 45 (July 1989): 7.

11. Jim Dawson, "The Twist: Around and Around and Up and Down," *Goldmine*, December 16, 1988, p. 96; Robert Pruter, "Hank Ballard and the Twist: The Original Twist," *Goldmine*, August 12, 1988, pp. 30, 79.

12. Hank Ballard interview.

13. [Dan Kochakian and George A. Moonoogian], "Little Joe Cook: The Original Thriller," *Whiskey, Women, and...* 15 (December 1985): 21.

14. John Abbey, "The Vibrations," *Home of the Blues* 1 (May 1966): 8–9; Marvin Goldberg, "The Jay Hawks/Vibrations," *Bim Bam Boom* 5 (April-May, 1972): 12.

15. Tony Gideon interviews, August 6 and 8, 1976.

16. Drew Williamson, "Don Covay, Veteran Vocalist and Successful Songwriter, Cites Dominoes, Little Richard as Early Influences," *Record Collector's Monthly* 44 (July-August 1989): 4.

17. [Jeff Hannusch] Almost Slim, "The Popeye: Strong to the Finish," *Goldmine*, November 4, 1988, pp. 73, 80.

18. Ibid.

19. [John Abbey], "Rufus Thomas: Have No Fear—The Dog Was Here," *Home of the Blues* 4 (August 1966): 9–10.

20. "Chi's Getting the Monkey Itch," *Billboard*, July 13, 1963, p. 48.

21. Robert Pruter, "The Uncle Willie: A Chicago Contribution to Dance Records," *Goldmine*, January 29, 1988, p. 24.

22. "New Dance to Bow into Regal," *Chicago Defender*, December 21, 1963.

23. Chuck Colbert, Jr., interview August 20, 1974.

24. Bill Greensmith, "The Bobby McClure Interview," *Blues Unlimited* 147 (Spring 1986): 25.

25. Major Lance interview.

26. Renata Adler, "Onward and Upward with the Arts: The New Sound," *The New Yorker*, February 20, 1965, p. 100.

27. Liner notes, Alvin Cash and the Registers, *Twine Time*, Mar-V-lus MLP 18270, 1965; Herb Kent interview.

28. Steve Propes, "The Larks and the Jerk: Jerked Around and Still a Hit," *Goldmine*, August 25, 1988, pp. 72, 76.

29. Ibid., p. 72.

30. Herb Kent interview.

31. Robert Tharp interview.

32. Ibid.

33. Wesley Spraggins interview.

34. Dan Nooger, liner notes, The Fiestas, *The Oh So Fine Fiestas*, Ace CH 173, 1986.

35. John Storm Roberts, *The Latin Tinge* (New York: Oxford University Press, 1979), pp. 167–68.

36. Ronnie Jones, "Crane Cool-Gars," *Chicago Defender*, January 22, 1966.

37. "Dogs of War: Disco Jocks Unite," *Soul*, June 6, 1977, p. 18.

38. Alan Penchansky, "Chi Pool Alliance with AVI," *Billboard*, November 5, 1977, p. 67.

9

One-derful Records

The Vee Jay–OKeh–Chess axis of companies so dominated the Chicago music scene in the 1960s with their styles of uptown soft soul, it would be easy to overlook the output of the city's many fine raw and gritty singers of hard soul. Much of it was provided by George Leaner in his label group, One-derful/M-Pac/Mar-V-lus. A veteran of the record business since the 1940s, when blues dominated the r&b charts, Leaner specialized in urban heavily blues-flavored soul, and like its often indistinguishable counterpart, southern soul, this northern variety had that black church element, gospel. George's brother, Ernest, ran the distributing arm of their business, United Record Distributors, at 1827 South Michigan.[1]

George Leaner was born in Mississippi on June 1, 1917. He first came to Chicago in 1923, when his family moved there from Mississippi. The Leaners returned to their home state in 1929, but moved back to Chicago nine years later. George's entry into the record business was a little indirect. His sister, Bernice, was married in 1940 to Bill Chavers, who owned the Groove Record Shop at Forty-seventh and South Parkway. During World War II, Leaner served in the Army and occasionally would drop by the store. In 1945, Bill Chavers was divorced from Bernice and gave her the store, which she operated until 1949. According to Chavers, the Leaner family was close-knit, and Bernice would get other members of the family to help out at the store.[2] Ernie became involved in 1940 and George in 1946.

Also in 1946, George Leaner became an assistant to Lester Melrose, then the top blues-recording man in Chicago. George recalled recording blues artists above Eli's Pawn Shop on the 3400 block of South State. Most of what he recorded was audition records and demos. George told interviewer

Steve Tomashefsky that it was Melrose who "taught me everything I know about the blues."[3]

In late 1947, George and Ernie Leaner joined M.S. Distributors, George working as a sales representative. The brothers stayed with M.S. until 1949, when they joined Monroe Passis, who owned Chord Distributing Company. While at Chord, where they stayed only about six months, the brothers made a small foray into recording, producing in 1950 eight legendary sides of classic Chicago bar-band blues on the Parkway label. Their artists were the Little Walter Trio and the Baby Face Leroy Trio, both of which contained the cream of the city's postwar bluesmen, including Muddy Waters.

Ernie and George formed United Record Distributors in March 1950. George was the junior partner in the operation, which flourished during the fifties and sixties when independent record companies and distributors were competing successfully against the majors.

The success of Chess, Vee Jay, and other Chicago independents during the 1950s probably encouraged George to attempt another venture into the record company business. The catalyst was McKinley Mitchell, who brought a demo of "The Town I Live In" to George, who decided to record the song and release it by forming his own company, One-derful Records, in March 1962.[4] In a short time, as the company prospered, Midas, M-Pac, Mar-V-lus, and Halo (for gospel recordings) were added to the One-derful label.

Leaner intended from the beginning to build his company with hard-soul artists, feeling those artists had been neglected by other Chicago companies thus leaving One-derful a substantial niche in the marketplace to exploit. He gave his aims to *Billboard* in language both vague and arch, mainly because such shorthand terms as "hard soul," "deep soul," or "downhome soul" had yet to be coined, and "soul" was barely in currency. Related the magazine, "the producing would consist of material of a specific type, locally oriented, not being done by other firms. Leaner cited certain types of folk music and some unusual music peculiar to Chicago as examples."[5] To be sure, "folk music" was intended to describe artists such as McKinley Mitchell rather than Peter, Paul, and Mary. Throughout the history of the firm Leaner stayed with the hard-soul approach, not only because he believed in its commercial viability but because he valued it artistically.

Leaner established a crack A&R and production department centered around Monk Higgins (Milton Bland), Andre Williams, and Jimmy Jones, and found excellent writers in Otis Hayes, Eddie Silvers, and Larry Nestor. Typical of many companies of the day, George placed his wife's maiden name, Verlie Rice, on many of the songs. His artists, most notably Otis Clay, McKinley Mitchell, Harold Burrage, Johnny Sayles, Dorothy Prince, and the Five Du-Tones, sounded deeply soulful, raw, and aggressive. It was hard-soul music as vibrant and rowdy as the urban ghetto streets of Chicago from which it sprang.

The company had a workshop type of environment, as Clay related to blues researcher Steve Tomashefsky:

> Things were always open there; we had rehearsal rooms and the writers, musicians, and singers would always be around, exchanging ideas, helping each other out—what George Leaner called a "workshop." I used to think...going to One-derful [was] like a job I had to do every day, and we'd all put in a full day's work, even a night's work too. We were able to do this because there wasn't a big jealousy thing.
>
> We had unique musicians, people like James Green, who played bass on most of the sessions, Cash McCall, Mighty Joe Young, Jimmy Jones on guitar, Ira Gates, a drummer—everybody had ideas about things, and nobody would hesitate to say, "Hey, let's try this. . . . " The sessions were really no problem at all, even though most of them were just two-tracks, because the musicians and the singers and the writers would all be around the offices all the time, and by the time we went to the studio to cut a record, we had so many ideas already done. Even the secretaries got into the act—really. The janitor might come in and sing a background vocal. That was the great thing about One-derful. It wasn't a big thing with superstars and heavy producers. . . . We'd get an idea, and we'd go to George and say, "We want to do this. . . . " and he'd say, "Fine, go ahead."[6]

Leaner, unlike many record people of the era, tried to place himself in the history of Chicago music. He was particularly proud of his hard-soul performers, especially Otis Clay and Johnny Sayles, and thought of them as "artists" for the ages as opposed to transitory entertainers. "George Leaner," recalled Clay, "was a very strong man. He wasn't involved in every aspect of the music, but he had a very sharp ear, and we'd run down an idea to him, he'd know if it was quality material or not. George and I had sort of a father and son relationship. I think he had that with some of the other fellows too."[7]

Leaner's biggest successes were not his hard-soul artists, however, but Alvin Cash, a St. Louis dancer who chanted his way through a succession of funky dance numbers, such as "Twine Time," "The Barracuda," and "The Philly Freeze." Leaner dismissed the records as merely money-making endeavors of little merit.[8] Of significant merit, however, was McKinley Mitchell.

McKinley Mitchell

McKinley Mitchell, who died in 1986, was a distinctive rhythm-and-blues stylist of the first rank. His recording output was not that substantial, but over the years—first in Chicago during the 1960s and later in Jackson, Mississippi—Mitchell came up with a solid and consistent body of downhome blues and rhythm and blues. Mitchell was born in Jackson on December 25, 1934. His earliest experience in music was in church, and in 1950 at the tender age of sixteen he became lead for a Jackson-based gospel group, the Hearts of Harmony.[9]

The manager of the ensemble in a short time moved to Springfield, Massachusetts, and took the group with him. There Mitchell attended Gloucester High and got married, the first of three marriages. While still with the Hearts of Harmony, he tried his hand at secular music, working with the Tiny Button Quintet during the mid-1950s around Springfield. For two to three years Mitchell headed his own gospel group, the Mitchellairs, in Philadelphia.

By 1958, Mitchell was ready to go solo. "I had a lot of relatives living in Chicago. My uncle lived there and he said, 'Hey, man, you ought to come to Chicago because there are a lot of clubs here where you can peform and people can hear you.' So what I did, I just made up my mind to move to Chicago. I went to Forty-third Street, to Pepper's Lounge. Muddy Waters was performing there with his band. I got together with Muddy and began to sing on his show a lot. That's how I got started in Chicago."[10]

Mitchell made his first recording in November 1959, for the Boxer label, which was owned by the El Dorados' manager, Johnny Moore. The sides, made with guitarist Willie Johnson and other members of the Howlin' Wolf band, were blues with a rock 'n' roll beat. Maybe only a few hundred copies of the record were pressed.

In 1961, Mitchell brought a demo of a song he wrote, "The Town I Live In," to George Leaner. Leaner loved it and put him in the studio with producer King Kolax and his band to record the song. "The Town I Live In" was quite remarkable. Mitchell, showing his years of gospel experience, sang it exceedingly raw, but it was a lyrical, enchanting song, urban yet urbane. The arrangement by Kolax added much to the atmosphere with blaring horns, pulsating organ, jangling guitar. Launching One-derful Records, the song became a national hit in early 1962.

The record also launched Mitchell on a national tour in which he played the entire chitlin' circuit, including such famous theaters as the Regal, the Apollo, and the Cow Palace (in Oakland). A first national tour is a particularly heady experience, but the Cow Palace was unusually overwhelming for the young star. Said Mitchell, "I did a show there with the

Miracles, Mary Wells, and others. Well, I came out on stage and started singing 'The Town I Live In.' There was so much excitement that the ladies started grabbing me and taking my clothes off. They stripped me, leaving me up there on stage with just my shorts and necktie. I was almost smothered. The police rescued me and took me to my dressing room. I was excited, I was scared, I didn't know what to do. That was my first taste of success, but I prayed to God that it would never happen to me again."[11]

Released in the summer of 1962 was "I'm So Glad," which got tremendous play in Chicago. It was an instant classic, exhibiting the same raw but lyrical approach. Mitchell sang with such aching feeling that one is left drained of emotion after hearing it. For the first time he used a girl chorus and they enhanced the song well in an emotion-wringing call-and-response routine.

In 1963 the company teamed up Mitchell with producers Otis Hayes and Monk Higgins, and "A Bit of Soul" was the happy result. The theme was like that of King Curtis's "Memphis Soul Stew" or Brook Benton's "Hit Record." Mitchell catalogued the ingredients of a soul record—"words tender and bold," "a piano man," "a great big band," "trumpets blowing out loud," and so on. He gave a good, smooth reading rather than singing in his usual raw voice, and created the best of the "ingredients" records. "A Bit of Soul" failed to chart nationally but it sold well in Chicago and other locales.

Mitchell's last three singles on One-derful, though fine efforts, did not find an audience, and he left the label in 1964. Leaner had just signed Otis Clay and perhaps he thought he did not need another hard-soul singer, since Mitchell's last few records did not exactly burn up the charts. But Mitchell was none too pleased with One-derful either. Said he, "There were a lot of things that weren't right at One-derful. My arranger was King Kolax on 'The Town I Live In,' and we both came into the company together. But then King Kolax wasn't the arranger anymore, so they put me with Monk Higgins, and I didn't think he was qualified then. It just wasn't working out after a while."[12] Also, he suffered an injury causing hospitalization and he never returned to the company.

Mitchell's injury was most peculiar, as he explained: "I had gone to California for a while, but before I had left, I had a tooth pulled in Chicago. When I got to California I discovered that my sinus was broken in half at the top. That was the last part of 1964, the time when Sam Cooke was killed. I flew back to Chicago with his body, and then I went into the hospital to get my sinus taken care of. The doctor said I wouldn't be able to go back on stage for at least a year. I went back on stage in two weeks. I still faked it, because I couldn't do what I wanted to for some time, but I didn't quit singing."[13]

Indeed he did not. For the next three years Mitchell was a mainstay in Chicago clubs, especially at the Bonanza (7641 South Halsted), where he practically lived. Ever since the success of "The Town I Live In," Mitchell was one of Chicago's biggest club performers. Charles Keil in his groundbreaking book *Urban Blues* made this very point in 1966: "Cry singers [his term for emotional, hard-soul singers] may also be considered a part of the blues community. McKinly [*sic*] 'The Soul' Mitchell is Chicago's best known performer in this category and appears frequently at blues clubs, shows and festivals."[14]

It was not until 1968 that Mitchell got on record again, hooking up with blues composer and producer Willie Dixon. For the next seven years there was a series of mediocre-to-lamentable singles on Dixon's and other smalltime labels, none of which did anything to enhance Mitchell's career. Willie Dixon had recorded an album on Mitchell but let it sit in the can, apparently because there was so little interest in the singer. This great soul singer seemed destined to be remembered only for his early 1960s Onederful sides and no more. But then in 1976 came a breakthrough single, "Trouble Blues." It was released on Big Three, a small Chicago label owned by Bill Collins, and became mainly a southern hit.

"I moved to Jackson when I brought 'Trouble Blues' down here," said Mitchell. "I took it first to James Bennett, because he had a distributorship here. After the record started getting big, I didn't think Mr. Bennett would be able to handle the record. That's when I signed up with Malaco."[15] Jackson was a perfect place for Mitchell to settle. In Chicago and other northern communities, interest in hard soul was rapidly declining with the onset of funk and disco. The South was still receptive to the kind of music Mitchell had cut his teeth on, and during the 1970s and 1980s Mitchell was a regular hit-maker for Malaco and later for James Bennett's Retta's label.

Harold Burrage

Harold Burrage is a little known but important figure in the development of soul music in Chicago. A recording artist from 1950 on, he saw Chicago through its transition from a blues and r&b center to a major soul center during the 1960s, helping to shape the hard-soul style. Burrage, however, was perhaps the least known of all the principal artists who recorded for Leaner. Part of the reason was because he died in 1966, well before the advent of record collecting, fanzines, and blues journals of later decades that delineated careers of favorite artists.

Burrage was born on the West Side, March 30, 1931, the son of Leslie Burrage and Pensacola Hudnall Burrage. His family, which included five other brothers and three sisters, originally came from Meridian, Mississippi, but moved up to Chicago in the mid-1920s. His father found a job working in the steel mills, but on the weekends gave himself to the Lord, forming and becoming minister of a Baptist church.[16]

Harold received a very religious upbringing. He and his brothers and sisters would sing each Sunday in their father's church choir, and occasionally he would solo. One of his older brothers, Eugene, was choir director and he said, "Well, him and I would sing together on 'Precious Lord,' which was his favorite gospel hymn. He would sing a verse, I would sing a verse, and so on. He really sang good on it, and as a gospel singer I think Harold would have been great, because he had a pair of lungs on him."[17]

In the late 1940s Harold Burrage was attending Cregier High, but his mind was on music more than his studies, and he was drawn to the many clubs on the West Side. Because he was big for his age, questions as to whether or not he was of age were rarely raised.

In 1950 young Burrage got on record with Decca Records, and the upshot was a successful local hit, an aggressive jump called "Hi-Yo Silver" that was very dependent on the vigorous interaction between Harold's spirited vocals and the echoing chorus. Releases in the urban-blues vein followed on Los Angeles-based Aladdin and on Leonard Allen's United label in Chicago, but nothing came of them. From 1952 to 1954 his career was interrupted by service in the U.S. Army.

Burrage had established himself by the mid-1950s as a regular fixture on the club scene, but not always lucratively. As Rev. Eugene Burrage told it:

> Like, he would go visit a place. They would have a live band on stage, the audience would be clapping for him, and they would always call him up to sing. He would love to sing and go up. I'd tell him, "You ain't getting anything for this. This guy is selling all this alcohol and you're drawing a crowd, and you're not even on the show. You're just a neighborhood boy and they're always calling you up to sing. But if a club owner wants to put you to work, hey, have him pay you." These guys who owned these places, I wouldn't say they used him, but they would say we have Harold Burrage in the house, Harold "West Side" Burrage! He'd come up on stage and do a medley of songs. But there was never any money from day one, until he got hip.[18]

In 1956 Burrage joined the newly formed Cobra label. This legendary West Side company owned by Eli Toscano and Howard Bedno created some of the most fiery and fierce Chicago bar-band blues ever put on wax, mainly with Magic Sam and Otis Rush. But for Burrage, the company with Willie Dixon producing took a lighter approach. That direction was set in 1957 with his second release, "Messed Up," which can best be described as rock 'n' roll with a blues feel. Later in the year he came out with an appealing rock 'n' roll novelty, "Stop for the Red Light." The following year Cobra, heavily influenced by the New Orleans-style rock 'n' roll of Little Richard, Larry Williams, and Lloyd Price, began recording Burrage in that vein. Two releases, "She Knocks Me Out" and "Betty Jean," were truly knockouts in that style and perhaps the best Burrage ever did at the label. Burrage in his tenure at Cobra came out with singles he could be proud of, but he never found an individual style for his talents there.

Burrage went to Vee Jay in 1959, and his first release was "Crying for You Baby," an effective moaning r&b number that took the singer in a stylistic direction that was more soul oriented. On the record he sounded a lot like Jackie Wilson. "Crying for You Baby" was a solid local hit, but it did nothing nationally. After Vee Jay, Burrage teamed up with deejay Richard Stamz's two labels, Paso and Foxy, during 1960–62. He was free to create music to fit his singing style and to develop his producing and writing skills, and even though the songs he recorded were not very good, the Stamz association was a good training period before he went to his next company, One-derful Records.

It was in late 1962 that Burrage joined Leaner's operation. The company, on the strength of its initial hit, "The Town I Live In," was signing up a slew of artists, mostly of the hard-soul variety. Burrage had finally found a company for which he could fully develop his talents. Said Clay, "Harold was somewhat both a staff person and an artist person at One-derful. He was, of course, an artist, but Harold always went down to One-derful every day religiously, as if he was going to a job. Harold was a very good musician, and he did some staff things as far as production was concerned. We really had a creative thing going at the time, working there in the studio putting ideas down."[19]

The first two releases at One-derful on the M-Pac label, however, did little to enhance Burrage's career. The songs, "Master Key" (October 1962) and "Long Ways Together" (early 1963), were produced with too much uptown flair and with intrusive girl choruses. Someone at One-derful had to unleash Harold. "Baby I'm Alright," released in late 1963, did just that. Supported by sympathetic downhome horn riffing, Burrage tore through this mid-tempo number with superb authority. The song was written by Burrage, Higgins, and Hayes, and produced by Higgins and Hayes.

"Got to Find a Way," released in the summer of 1965, became Burrage's main claim to fame, and for good reason. The record was a monster, with its overpowering bass-heavy beat, Burrage's impassioned full-throated vocalizing, and the backup singers' sassy chorusing. The better song, the better band, and the better arranging and producing meant Burrage's delivery dramatically got better. He seemed to sing to the level of his material. The record was not a big national hit on the *Billboard* r&b chart (position thirty-one and eight weeks), but on *Cash Box*'s chart it went top ten (position seven and thirteen weeks). In Chicago the record was a giant hit.

The success Burrage achieved with "Got to Find a Way" was of course a marvelous thing for a man who had worked so hard and so long for recognition. He even toured for the first time in his life, playing in such cities as Memphis and Cleveland. But the success had a detrimental effect on the creative end of his recording career. One-derful, perhaps hoping the magic could be conjured again, saddled Burrage with two successive "Got to Find a Way" sound-alikes, "You Made Me So Happy" (November 1965) and "More Power to You" (January 1966). They were not bad songs, just not original, although many listeners may find them perfectly satisfactory. At the time, however, they did not catch on with the public.

During his One-derful years, Burrage was still a relatively young man— early to mid-thirties in age—but he was looked up to by many younger artists as a veteran of the city's music scene, which of course he was. Otis Clay said, "Harold was kind of a father figure to all of us down there in those days. If he saw a guy trying to make it, he would help him if he could, and he never asked for anything in return. When you come to people like the Five Du-Tones, Johnny Sayles, Tyrone Davis, and myself, there were very few things that Harold didn't inspire."[20]

On November 25, 1966, Burrage died suddenly from a heart attack in Tyrone Davis's backyard. His death made a small paragraph in *Billboard,* but on the West Side it was a momentous, tragic event.[21] Larry Nestor, who worked at One-derful, attended Burrage's funeral on Roosevelt Road and remembered being amazed at the size of the crowds. Said he, "The lines of people were humungous, they went around the block. I knew he sold a few records, but I had no idea he had that kind of following."[22]

The black West Side community had always had something of a complex about being less established, less economically well-off, and lesser in size than the South Side. For that reason West Siders seem to show greater appreciation and loyalty to the entertainers who come out of their community. Such blues singers as Magic Sam and Otis Rush have had a special relationship with the West Side; Tyrone Davis years after moving from the area continued to visit his old haunts; and likewise Harold Burrage was held in special esteem by his West Side fans. They remembered all those years when he was introduced in the clubs as Harold "West Side" Burrage, and they came and showed their respect.

Otis Clay

Otis Clay was a veteran of fifteen years of singing gospel when he joined One-derful, and his approach to a song was more heavily gospelized than some of Leaner's other hard-soul acts. Whereas Harold Burrage had much of the blues club in his singing, Clay had the inner-city church in his. One-derful launched and established Clay on a highly successful career, which was sustained by stays at Atlantic Records, Hi Records, and Malaco Records; he recorded at the great southern studios throughout the 1970s. In the 1980s he built a career as a steady club performer in Chicago and as a major soul star in Japan, with several albums of material.[23]

Clay was born February 11, 1942, at a little junction in rural Mississippi called Waxhaw. He came from a musical family and at the age of twelve began his career in gospel music, first singing in quartets with members of his family and then in various quartets based in the city of Chicago. In 1962, while a member of the Pilgrim Harmonizers, he was able to record four sides on his own for Carl Davis at Columbia Records. The songs sounded closer to uptown singer Chuck Jackson in style than to Clay's later gospelized recordings. Columbia kept all four sides in the can. "I kept the session a secret," confessed Clay, "because you know the thought of what people in gospel might say to know I was singing blues. I kept that under my hat for a long time."[24]

In late 1963 Clay joined the Gospel Songbirds as one of the group's leads. The quartet recorded many records, but Clay showed up on just one single. Not long after the record's release, however, Clay joined one of the most famous gospel groups of all time, the Sensational Nightingales. He was a member of the quartet from May 1964 to the middle of 1965. Before he toured the country with the group, he signed a contract with One-derful. Leaner let him go with his blessings. "We were always on the road," said Clay, "basically the East Coast and the Carolinas. We were working our way out to the West Coast, then most of the dates came up cancelled. The farthest we got was Amarillo, Texas, where we played out our last date."[25]

One can easily see why Clay decided to forgo the gospel life. With Leaner's organization, he had to make perhaps only a small step stylistically. His first hit was mostly a local phenomenon, "Tired of Falling In and Out of Love," in October 1965. It was a splendid ballad but did not best showcase Clay's hard gospel roots. However, the song got him his first engagement, in Miami, of all places. His first big auditorium show was at Chicago's Capitol Theater (7941 South Halsted), where he played on Herb Kent's Christmas Benefit Show, December 18–19, 1965. So between Chicago and Miami, Clay got his start in the secular field. "I'm Satisfied," an intense ballad backed with "I Testify," a secularized hard-gospel raver, was released in early 1966 and proved to be a double-sided hit. "I'm Satisfied" made the *Cash Box* chart.

Following a dead period, hit-wise, Clay once again made the charts with a nationwide hit, "That's How It Is," in August 1967. Clay projected an intense emotionality that made the song compelling without hitting the listener over the head with histrionics. "I worked like mad on that record," said Clay, "all over the country. I remember I was booked in Memphis, in this big auditorium there. They had about thirteen acts on the show." He added, ruefully, "I was starring the show and getting $250."[26]

Most of Clay's songs for One-derful were written by Jimmy Jones and Eddie Silvers. Other writers also contributed, notably Clay's friend from his gospel days, Cash McCall, who wrote "That's How It Is." "One-derful had their own studio and I learned a lot," said Clay. "Making records there was pretty much an open thing. Unlike with other companies, at One-derful I had the feeling of not being restricted." Clay contributed toward writing many of the songs, but at the time he was not attuned to "paperwork as far as songs were concerned" and he missed out on the credit for such compositions as "Tired of Falling In and Out of Love."[27]

One-derful went out of business in mid-1968, and Clay's contract was sold to Atlantic's Cotillion subsidiary for $5,000. During the next two decades Clay's material was produced in the South, but since his One-derful material was not all that stylistically different from southern deep soul, his sound changed imperceptibly from his Chicago recording days. By the mid-1980s Clay had established himself as one of the hottest acts in the extensive Chicago blues-club circuit.

The Five Du-Tones Review

Five Dutones–Johnny Sayles–Duettes

The Five Du-Tones Review was a package of three One-derful acts—the Five Du-Tones, Johnny Sayles, and the Duettes—put together by Louis Tate, a longtime gospel promoter and manager out of Gary, Indiana. The review with its own backup band, the Exciters, traveled around the country playing innumerable small-town clubs as well as the major theaters and venues on the chitlin' circuit. Tate supplied the review with its own bus, a luxury that few acts of the day had. The centerpiece of the review was the Five Du-Tones vocal group which achieved fame with a tremendous crossover hit, "Shake a Tail Feather," in early 1963.

"Shake a Tail Feather" was three minutes of unrelieved frantic madness propelled by demonically screaming voices demanding that one "bend over and shake a tail feather" to the bird-dance beat. The song was one of those periodic reminders during the early 1960s that rock 'n' roll—and its primary source, rhythm and blues—could push to the utmost in energy without losing its swing. The group recorded its material in Chicago, but the performers were originally from St. Louis, where they started as a typical doowop street-corner group out of Patrick Henry High School around 1957. Members at that time were Robert Hopkins, lead and founder, LeRoy Joyce, Willie Guest, Oscar Watson, and James West.[28]

The Five Du-Tones, after some three years of scuffling in clubs in the St. Louis area, knew from a recording standpoint that their opportunities were exceedingly limited in St. Louis and so around 1960 they moved to Chicago. There the group consisted of LeRoy Joyce, Willie Guest, James West, Frank McCurrey, and Andrew Butler. Said Joyce,

> We came to Chicago where the market was and things were more open for us. My mother had moved to Chicago six months before we did. We stayed with her for over a year. We worked odd jobs until we could get enough gigs together to support ourselves.
>
> We went to every record maker in Chicago. We went to King, to Chess, to Vee Jay. During that time, I can't think of the lady's name—I would hate to use her name anyway—she was our manager. She was a white lady out of St. Louis. As a matter of fact she rented the car that we drove up to Chicago in. She was helping us a lot, and meeting people in the business. But most of the guys that worked in the studio were more interested in her than us, if you know what I mean. She got disgusted and discouraged and went back to St. Louis.
>
> We stayed and we in turn ran into some guys that were producing recordings, like Andre Williams and Monk Higgins. We had a lot of gigs now, working in Gary, Indiana, mostly. We were working on Ninety-fifth at the Spark Club in Chicago and at the White Rose in Phoenix [a suburb south of Chicago], and that's how we started meeting people. We met people from One-derful out there in Phoenix. They told us to come in and we met George and Ernie Leaner.[29]

The Five Du-Tones' first record was "The Flea," a dance record that sold a few copies in the summer of 1962. Their third record was "Shake a Tail Feather," in March 1963, and was a smash in all markets. On *Billboard*'s top-hundred pop survey, it reached as high as fifty-first position and lasted some twelve weeks. The song had a lesser life on the magazine's r&b chart, lasting only two weeks in July and getting no higher than position twenty-eight. The chart action, however, was a poor reflection of the popularity of the record, which had been around in various markets selling like hotcakes long before July. *Cash Box* had the more accurate chart during this time and on it the song lasted eighteen weeks and went as high as the nine position. Butler did the exciting lead vocals and Guest maniacally banged the piano that helped give the song its propulsive drive.

The record's flip, "Divorce Court," was a tremendous little playlet in the grand tradition of Andre Williams's "Jailbait" and the Robins' "Framed." Butler played the sonorous judge and narrator, McCurrey with his piercing tenor played the wronged wife, and Guest acted the part of the put-upon, sobbing defendant. It was a great piece of humorous theater, which the group effectively presented in live performance by all dressing in costume to portray the respective parts.

The group toured extensively because of "Shake a Tail Feather" and performed in all the big venues across the country. "They had us at the Regal for seven days," recalled Joyce. "They put us up against groups like the Contours, the Vibrations, and the Dells. We worked the Howard Theater in Washington, D.C., the Royal in Baltimore, and Paramount and Uptown in Philadelphia, and of course the Apollo in New York."[30] The group also made a long swing through the southern states during the summer of 1963.

The touring took its toll on one of the members, James West, who died at the age of twenty-six from heart failure in late 1963. Selected to replace West was David Scott, who had been a vocalist in the Exciters Band. The band—Sydney "Pinchback" Lennear (guitar), Warren Haygood (drums), David Henderson (bass), and Eugene Rogers (rhythm guitar)—were picked up in Washington, D.C., when the Five Du-Tones needed a band behind them for their gig at the Howard. They established roots in Gary and were subsequently used in One-derful recording sessions.

The next few releases by the Five Du-Tones were commercial bombs. The magic ingredients that made for the marvelous success of "Feather" just were not there in the later records. In desperation, the company had them do a close remake of the song, the second-rate "The Cool Bird," in early 1964, which did nothing. The "Woodbine Twine," from early 1965, was likewise a dud.

The Five Du-Tones' last release was "Outside the Record Hop," in 1965. Less frantic and slower than most of the songs the group had been doing, the record represented an attempt to regain popularity by a change in style. It was one of the strongest releases, but alas, it did not return the group to the charts. Having released a half dozen records by the group during a three-year period following "Shake a Tail Feather" and never having scored another hit, One-derful decided to drop the Five Du-Tones in 1966.

The group continued to perform in local clubs for at least a year more. In 1967, however, a combination of pressures from the Selective Service and continued stagnation of their fortunes served to break up the Five Du-Tones. Frank McCurrey and David Scott joined the Exciters Band to form the South Shore Commission, which got some national hits on the r&b charts in the mid-1970s.[31]

In 1980 "Shake a Tail Feather" as sung by Ray Charles was one of the featured musical numbers in the *Blues Brothers* film. This was the fifty-fourth time the song had been recorded (most notably by Ike and Tina Turner, Mitch Ryder, Tommy James, and the Kingsmen), but unfortunately it was the first time Leaner's Vapac Music Publishing Company did not receive credit and royalties. The film makers followed the standard procedure of obtaining the rights to the song through the Harry Fox Agency. The agency gave them the rights for $3,000, but for the wrong song. Leaner successfully sued and received a "substantial cash settlement," plus future royalties and credit for the song. Said the judge, "Ray Charles did that song proud, and if I wrote that song I'd want him to infringe on my copyright. It's a great song. Now I have to see the movie."[32]

The Five Du-Tones will go down in rock 'n' roll history as an obscure one-hit group, but they deserved better. They were hampered throughout their career by poor material, but judging from the unreleased songs unearthed by the Japanese in a 1979 record-reissue project, the singers could have established a greater reputation if they had been guided better and had been given more bluesy material to work with. They had the vocal chops.

One of the finest of Leaner's singers was Johnny Sayles, who during his career never attained the success of such compatriot hard soulsters as Tyrone Davis, Otis Clay, and McKinley Mitchell, but who nonetheless left an indelible mark. Sayles was born February 9, 1937, in a small town in east Texas called Winnsboro. He attended Prairie State A&M, in Prairie View, Texas, and at the school formed his first band to play at fraternity parties and the like.[33]

In 1955 Sayles left school with his new wife and moved to St. Louis. He worked for a drugstore chain for a few years, and for the post office, to support his rapidly growing brood of five kids. He also began dabbling in music again, eventually joining a band called Eugene Neal and the Rocking Kings, which was a spinoff group from Ike Turner and His Kings of Rhythm. Following the Neal association, Sayles joined the Ike Turner band as vocalist about 1958. Sayles also fronted his own band for a while at Chuck Berry's Paradise Club. There during 1959-60 he played on the same bill with such entertainers as the Five Du-Tones, Alvin Cash and the Crawlers, and Bop and the Paper Sack, all acts that eventually made their way to Chicago.

Jan Bradley with her producer, Don Talty, 1964. With her innocent-sounding soprano voice, Bradley established a sound that was emulated by many later Chicago soul artists. Courtesy Janice McVickers.

The Daylighters, 1964. By 1964 the group had undergone several personnel changes, but they were still making some of the most enduring soul music records ever to come out of Chicago. Left to right: Ulysses "Bunky" McDonald; Chuck Colbert, Jr.; Eddie Thomas; and Tony Gideon. Courtesy Tony Gideon.

Phil Upchurch, 1961. Upchurch was nineteen years old when he recorded "You Can't Sit Down" as part of the Philip Upchurch Combo. Courtesy Janice McVickers.

Marvin L. Sims, 1968. Courtesy
Marvin L. Sims.

Making music for Witch/Cortland. At this
August 1963 recording session, the local hit
"Shining Armor" was recorded by the
Versalettes. In front, left to right: producer
Bob Catron, guitarist Kermit Chandler,
and bass player Douglas Anderson. Courtesy
Bob Catron.

Monk Higgins. Higgins (Milton
Bland) was a multitalented
instrumentalist, arranger, producer,
composer, and recording artist who
was essential to the success of
many Chicago recording
companies, especially St.
Lawrence/Satellite.

The Drew-vels, 1964. This family group from Evanston scored with several local hits in early 1964 and launched Patti Drew on a highly successful solo career. Left to right: Patti, Erma, and Lorraine Drew, and Carlton Black. Courtesy Patti Drew.

Shirley Wahls, 1968. Wahls had a fabulous local hit with "Why Am I Crying?" Courtesy Shirley Wahls.

The Esquires, 1967. This Milwaukee-based group kept Bill Sheppard in the record business during the late 1960s. Left to right: Shawn Taylor, Alvis Moorer, Gilbert Moorer, Sam Pace, and Millard Edwards. Courtesy Alvis Moorer.

The Vibrations, early 1960s. This group got its start in Los Angeles in the mid-1950s, but during the early 1960s the Vibrations were making hugely successful dance records in Chicago, first for Chess Records and later for OKeh.

Tom and Jerrio, 1965. This duo launched the Boogaloo dance craze with their hit "Boo-Ga-Loo" for ABC-Paramount. Left: Jerry T. Murray (Jerrio); right: Robert Tharp (Tom). Courtesy Michael Ochs Archives, Venice, California.

McKinley Mitchell, 1968. Hard-soul singer Mitchell was One-derful's first recording star and throughout the 1960s was one of the most popular of Chicago's club performers. Courtesy *Blues and Soul.*

Harold Burrage and Otis Clay woodshedding at the One-derful studio, 1965. Burrage (left) was one of the older performers who acted as mentor for many of the label's younger artists, notably Otis Clay. Courtesy *Blues and Soul.*

Montage for the Five Du-Tones Revue. Upper left: Johnny Sayles; standing by bus: manager Louis Tate; around bus: the Five Du-Tones (A.B. = Andrew Butler; T.J. = guitarist Tommy Jamison; F.M. = Frank McCurrey; W.G. = Willie Guest; J.W. = James West; L.J. = LeRoy Joyce); bottom right: the Duettes (B.L. = Barbara Livsey; M.H. = Mary-Francis Hayes). Courtesy Louis Tate.

Alvin Cash and the Crawlers, 1964. An all-brothers dance act, this group included Alvin Cash, standing, who managed to chant his way to stardom on a group of funky dance numbers.

Sharpees, 1965. The Sharpees came to One-derful via the company's St. Louis pipeline. Several members of the group had earlier been part of the Ike and Tina Turner Review. Top, left to right: Stacy Johnson, Benny Sharp, and Herbert Reeves; bottom: Vernon Guy. Courtesy Bill Greensmith.

Darrow Fletcher, 1965. This South Side singer was fourteen years old when he hit with "The Pain Gets a Little Deeper." Courtesy Johnny Haygood.

Cicero Blake. Courtesy Cicero Blake.

Syl Johnson, mid-1970s.

About 1960, Sayles left St. Louis with his band and headed for Texas. "When we got to El Paso," said Sayles, "we played there for about a year. After playing there, we toured Texas, playing Wichita Falls and all those places. We made pretty good money, playing the Air Force bases, the Army bases, everything. Then my wife and I got a divorce. It kind of shook me up, because we had the kids and everything. So I quit."[34] Sayles went to Houston to attend school around 1961.

During the summer of 1963, a big show came through town, featuring the Five Du-Tones and Moms Mabley. Sayles made his reacquaintance with the group and was asked to join the tour. He was billed on the show as "Little Johnny," and his featured song was "Part Time Love," which as recorded by Little Johnny Taylor was one of the biggest blues hits of all time. Sayles went all through the South with the song. "Everybody thought I was Johnny Taylor," said Sayles, " 'cause he wasn't making no appearances nowhere. Then we later found out why, because he just didn't have it as far as getting on stage was concerned. People laughed at him and everything else. When he did come through, he was a damn near flop, because Johnnie Taylor and I had taken advantage of the whole thing."[35] (This is the Johnnie Taylor who would later become a big hitmaker on Stax, but he launched his solo career as a Little Johnny Taylor imitator.)

Sayles ended up in Chicago with the Five Du-Tones, and there he began his recording career, joining One-derful and kicking off a new label for the company, Mar-V-lus. He did four sides and they proved to be four of the most uncompromising raw soul treatments ever performed on record in the 1960s. The first release, in late 1963, was "Don't Turn Your Back"/ "You Told a Lie." "Back" was an exceedingly aggressive, upbeat number with Sayles's screaming vocals providing an intensity that made the record a southern hit over Nashville's WLAC. The moody "You Told a Lie" was a fine example of blues performed in a soul style. The next release, in May 1964, "You Did Me Wrong"/"Got You on My Mind," was likewise superb on both sides. The riffing of the horn section rivaled the great brass treatments on Bobby Bland's legendary "Your Friends."

With these songs Sayles established himself as an artist in the hard blues–soul vein, and all his subsequent recordings reprised this style. But Sayles felt constricted being typecast this way and wanted to do smooth, sophisticated ballads: "They just never did want me to go in that direction. By me going to college and everything, I wanted to do other stuff. I used to sing Roy Hamilton songs like 'So Let There Be Love,' 'Hurt,' all his songs. They typecast me because of the excitement I would create on stage. I had my act, sometimes I would do this James Brown medley. I used to tear off two or three shirts a night. Rip them off and all kinds of stuff. That's why they would always have me come on just before the Du-Tones."[36]

Sayles was ready to tour the South based on his Mar-V-lus singles, but instead he got a lucrative offer to go to Alaska with Lou Rawls. He left sometime in 1964. Upon his return in 1965, Sayles formed another band and began playing around Chicago. He got a recording contract with producer Monk Higgins, first on Chi-Town, later on St. Lawrence and Chess. "Nothing But Hard Rocks" was Sayles's first post-Alaska release, and although it did nothing in the market, the Otis Clay–composed hard blues ranks among his best. The next release, "Never Let Me Go," was a paradoxical number, insipid lyrically but outstanding in its raw emotional delivery and heavy dramatic blues instrumentation. It appeared on the local charts in December 1965.

Sayles's recordings after "Never Let Me Go" never equalled the commercial and artistic success of his first four releases. His opportunities were severely limited as well, as evidenced by his Dakar association, 1969-71, in which the company released just two singles and an album. "Carl Davis didn't handle me right," asserted Sayles. "'Somebody's Changing (My Sweet Baby's Mind)' was supposed to be a Tyrone Davis tune, right after 'Can I Change My Mind.' They actually wrote it for Tyrone, but he didn't want the tune, and they didn't put nothing behind it."[37]

Despite infrequent appearance on wax and the lack of hits, Sayles continued for many years as a popular nightclub act in the blues and soul clubs. He was numbered among those performers in the city, such as the Scott Brothers and Hi Fi White, who had a larger impact in the club scene than the recording field. People came to see Johnny Sayles as a performer, not simply to hear him do his hits. But his early recordings should not be overlooked, for few artists have equalled Sayles in the sheer gut-wrenching power of delivery.

The story of the Duettes is the story of Barbara Livsey, who had two careers. In the 1960s, when she signed with One-derful, she was a member of the Duettes, a vocal duo. In the 1970s she was the lead of a successful recording trio, Barbara and the Uniques. Unlike many female groups, Livsey's acts did not sing sweet soft music. Hers was a raunchy, aggressive, and often frantic kind of hard soul for teenagers. Livsey was born in Atlanta, Georgia, May 27, 1946. Around 1958 she and her family moved to Chicago, where as a teenager she attended Parker High on the South Side. There she developed an interest in music, attending music class with relish and then forming a duo with her first cousin, Mary-Francis Hayes. They called themselves the Duettes.[38]

Typical of so many r&b acts of the 1960s, the girls' break in the recording business came via winning a talent contest at a local club. Representatives of One-derful Records were attending the show, saw the Duettes' winning performance, and awarded them a contract. The records the girls made at One-derful were all shouters, the best of which was "Please Forgive Me," which did very well in August 1964. That and "Mr. Steel," their first record for the company in 1963, were the girls' only sellers. The Duettes toured extensively during 1963–64 as part of the Five Du-Tones Review, sometimes under the name Tate's Duettes.

By 1966 the Duettes had broken up. Livsey got married and moved to Detroit, but that did not last long and soon she was back in Chicago. She began appearing in local clubs, and this went on for a time before a record company again took notice. From 1969 to 1974, Livsey had several chart successes singing with her sister in a duo called Barbara and Gwen and later in a trio with Gwen and Doris Lindsey called Barbara and the Uniques.

Alvin Cash

One can not write about black music of the 1960s without considering the principal disseminator of dance tunes, Alvin Cash (born Alvin Welch, February 15, 1939). His story is a crucial part of the history of black dance. He was the eldest of what became a large sibling crew of eight other brothers and sisters. Cash and most of his brothers attended Sumner High in St. Louis. When Alvin was about twenty-one he formed with three of his brothers—Robert, Arthur, and George, whose ages ranged from eight to ten—a dance troupe called the Crawlers.[39] They made all the clubs in St. Louis and across the river in East St. Louis and other communities of Illinois. Sayles remembered taking the boys around from club to club until they fell asleep at about three in the morning.[40]

About 1963, after the Crawlers had progressed a little with their act, Alvin took his brothers to Chicago. "I came to Chicago," said Cash, "to try to make my career better and to meet other people and be known. Chicago was a bigger city than St. Louis and my brothers and I could at least get exposed a little more. I intended to come to record."[41]

The Crawlers had some success as a stage act in Chicago, but it took a while before they came out with a record. The break came with the Twine dance fad that emerged in late 1964. "Andre Williams told me to come down to the studio," said Cash. "He had a dance that the kids were doing and it was the Twine. And I came down and cut it with a band that I was traveling with called the Nightlighters. They were from Louisville, Kentucky. For the records we changed their names to the Registers."[42] The records were recorded for the Mar-V-lus label.

"Twine Time" became a national hit in November 1964, selling some nine hundred thousand copies. On the *Cash Box* r&b chart it went to number one position and lasted sixteen weeks. After the record, Leaner regularly teamed up Cash with the Registers to produce a large number of dance records. Although some of the records had "Crawlers" listed on the labels, Alvin's brothers never participated as singers. (Eventually Cash split from his brothers, who continued as the Little Step Brothers.) Cash's follow-up record, "The Barracuda," in January 1965, proved to be another national chart hit, riding the crest of the Barracuda dance craze.

Cash seemingly could do no wrong during this period, because in July 1966 he hit again with the "Philly Freeze," and in November with "Alvin's Boo-Ga-Loo." While "The Twine" was excellent, and "The Barracuda" satisfactory, "Philly Freeze," "Alvin's Boogaloo," and many of Cash's subsequent records were not very interesting. Other Cash records worthy of mention—only because they had their origin in the development of dance fads in Chicago—were the "Boston Monkey" (late 1965) and "The Charge" (July 1967), as discussed earlier.

In 1967 Cash did the first of his Muhammad Ali–tribute records, "Doin' the Ali Shuffle." The dance Alvin was trying to promote (without success, as it turned out) was based on the moves used in Ali's boxing workout shuffle. "Doin' the Ali Shuffle" was the first intriguing evidence of the extent to which the black boxing superstar had taken hold of Cash's imagination. In later years Cash would rerecord "Doin' the Ali Shuffle" for Brunswick and get a local hit in 1976, and he also recorded something called "Ali" in 1979.

Upon One-derful's collapse in 1968, Cash immediately became one of the talents of Ernie and Tony Leaner's newly formed Toddlin' Town label. His stay at the company produced a national hit, "Keep on Dancing" (November 1968), which had the beat and rhythm for dancing the Funky Broadway, popular at the time.

Cash left Toddlin' Town in 1969 and thereafter his releases were intermittent; he usually stayed on a label for no more than one or two releases. The unfortunate fact is that his later records were generally without distinction. But for people who appreciate the visual—whether it is the physical grace of a Muhammad Ali in the ring or of dancers on the floor— Alvin Cash was an important figure in rhythm and blues. In no small way, he helped to provide the music and inspiration by which black America danced in the 1960s. That is some achievement.

The Sharpees

The Sharpees—Herbert Reeves, Vernon Guy, and Stacy Johnson—were yet another talented act obtained by the One-derful company via its pipeline from St. Louis. The group had its origin in a band organized by Benny Sharp, and as true of many black acts during the early 1960s Sharp followed a review format, with various comedians, vocalists, and MC's. The Sharpees coalesced within Sharp's review around 1961. Members then were Stacy Johnson (born in St. Louis, April 13, 1945), Vernon Guy (St. Louis, March 21, 1945), and Horise O'Toole (St. Louis, 1943).[43]

In 1962 Johnson and Guy left Sharp and joined the Ike and Tina Turner Review. The two stayed with Turner until 1964 and each released some singles put out by Turner. The genesis of the One-derful version of the Sharpees goes back to Johnson's and Guy's departure from Sharp. Only O'Toole remained, and Sharp needed a true lead singer, He found him in Herbert Reeves, a St. Louis native born in 1947. In late 1964 Guy joined O'Toole and Reeves to form a new Sharpees group.

The Sharpees would be recording within a year as a result of Sharp's bringing the group to the attention of One-derful's St. Louis connection. In East St. Louis, George Leaner had Mack McKinney working A&R and Eddie Silvers, who would go back and forth between his East St. Louis home and Chicago, writing and arranging for One-derful acts. In the 1950s Silvers had been a horn man in Ike Turner's Kings of Rhythm.

The upshot was that McKinney brought the group to Leaner, who signed them up. The first session was recorded at Oliver Sain's studio in St. Louis, and it produced a hot number called "Do the 45," a takeoff on Junior Walker's "Shotgun." With Sain's jumping sax, Reeves's swinging vocals, and the group's rousing chorusing, the song really cooked. It was on *Cash Box's* r&b chart in July 1965 for three weeks, and succeeded especially well in a number of markets, particularly Chicago.

During the group's first tour, O'Toole came down with a serious illness and had to leave the act. When they got back to St. Louis, the Sharpees inducted Stacy Johnson into the group. The new lineup went to One-derful's Chicago studio for its next session, which yielded the group's biggest hit, "Tired of Being Lonely," written by Larry Nestor and Jimmy Jones, and produced by Jones. Reeves's lead was marvelously forceful and soulful, and perfectly showcased by the rest of the group's chorusing and Nestor's imaginative arrangements. "Tired of Being Lonely," one of the top-notch records from the One-derful organization, first made the charts in several locales in late 1965, and it made the lower reaches of the *Cash Box* r&b chart in January 1966.

"Do the 45" and "Tired of Being Lonely" turned the Sharpees into a nationally known act. The group did the whole chitlin' circuit, playing all the major theaters of the day. Related Guy, "We were doing so much. George really did his best for us. Like when we played the Howard Theater in Washington, D.C., we did TV things as well. We played the Apollo twice, we played the Regal in Chicago twice. We were on a Smokey Robinson and the Miracles show: we were on a Stevie Wonder show."[44] The Sharpees were not exactly unknowns.

The group never charted again. The Sharpees stayed together until November 1972, when Herbert Reeves was shot and killed, putting an end to one of the finest r&b acts ever to come out of St. Louis.

One-derful's Soft-Soul Acts

Leaner's company was not known for its soft-soul vocal groups and young sopranos. Its stable of hard-soul performers essentially defined the character of the company's music. But it would be negligent to ignore some of Leaner's soft-soul acts, because they recorded a body of music that got local notice and that stands up well in the 1980s.

The Accents were a South Side group from Parker High that was organized in 1963. Members were James Short (lead), James Brown, Robert Hill, and Oliver Jackson. After some months of street-corner harmonizing and developing a few original songs, the group managed to obtain a recording contract with Mercury. The Accents recorded two sides that went nowhere.[45]

In 1964 the Accents found a home at One-derful. Leaner turned the group over to songwriter Bernice Williams to help work the Accents' songs into shape for recording. What they came up with was a marvelous up-tempo number written by Hill and Williams about a new girl in the neighborhood, called "New Girl." The song turned out to be a big hit in Chicago during July 1964, when it was a top-five record on WVON, and a crossover success on WLS. The record got the group some work in the Midwest at such theaters as the Fox in Detroit and the Regal in Chicago. After a follow-up failed to score, the small amount of fame they garnered soon dissipated and the Accents broke up.

The Young Folk, featuring a Frankie Lymon sound, had a local hit, "Joey," on the Mar-V-lus label in May 1967. The song was written by Otis Hayes and Jimmy Jones and was produced by Jones, but unlike their other work with hard-soul artists their production on the Young Folk was light and airy with a pop, upbeat sound.

The group, from Harrison High, was brought to the company by Alvin Cash, who discovered the youths singing at an amateur show on the West Side. The group was formed in 1964 while the members were still in grade school, performing Miracles' songs under the name "Baby Miracles." Lead singer was Madeline Strickland, and she was supported by her brother Glenn Strickland, Patrice Scaggs, Jerry Starks, and brothers Johnny and Arthur Mcthune.[46] The group broke up within a year of the release of "Joey." In the late 1980s Patrice Scaggs surfaced in a local play, *Ma Rainey's Black Bottom*, playing the lead role of 1920s blues singer Ma Rainey, and also building a career in the local blues clubs.

Other excellent soft-soul vocal groups recorded by the company included the Inspirations (William Miller, Willie Patterson, and Clarence Campbell), a group from Milwaukee that had a fine record in "I'll Take a Chance on You" (1967); and the Ringleaders (Willie Hawkins, Edgar Donahue, Vandy Lane, and Brent Anderson), a group from Saginaw, Michigan, that had the beautiful "Let's Start Over," a local hit in the fall of 1966.[47]

Beverly Shaffer superbly typified the young-soprano sound of Chicago. She made but two records, and on her one local hit, "Where Will You Be Boy," she evidently possessed the right vocal equipment to build a mini-career in the city's recording field. She was born on the West Side on August 2, 1947, and attended Hess Upper Grade Center and Farragut High. At Hess she was a classmate of Jo Ann Garrett, and they were both in the same choir.[48]

Shaffer entered a talent contest sponsored by the *Chicago Defender*, and she sang at the talent show audition the first verse of Dionne Warwick's "You'll Never Get to Heaven," *a cappella*. She made the audition and went on to win the contest held at the Aragon Ballroom on the North Side. There she made an impression on WVON kingpin Herb Kent. She said, "He told me he knew this guy at One-derful Records, and everything else is history. I went down there and talked to the guys. They said can you write a song? And I said I can write, not knowing that I could. So they said you go home and write a song. I went home and wrote 'Where Will You Be Boy.' "[49] The song was slightly rewritten by Larry Nestor and Jimmy Jones, who produced and arranged the record. The arrangement was restrained and featured a nice lyrical guitar, which set the appropriate mood for Shaffer's lovely vocals.

"Where Will You Be Boy" did not show up on any national charts after its release in October 1965, but that did not mean the record had no impact outside Chicago. Related Shaffer, "I traveled a little bit on it, went to Philadelphia, Washington, D.C., Cleveland, a lot of places. I used to be taken out of school on Thursdays, and be gone Thursday, Friday, and Saturday, and I'd come back Sunday night for return to school Monday. I had one of my English teachers to travel with me on some of the tours."[50] When a weak follow-up, "When I Think About You," did not do anything upon its release in early 1966, Shaffer left the business.

Another fine female singer in the light-soul vein was Josephine Taylor, from the northern suburb of Evanston. She had a super local hit on the Mar-V-lus label with "What Is Love?" (1966), a song composed and produced by Jones and Nestor. Although Taylor made more records for Mar-V-lus and other labels she never made an impact again.

The Final Years

By 1968, the One-derful/M-Pac/Mar-V-lus group was meeting hard times and hits appeared all too elusive. Leaner shut down his operation and went into semiretirement. A few remaining artists in the stable continued with a new company begun by Ernie Leaner and his son Tony, operating as two labels, Midas and Toddlin' Town. The operation was started after a local producer, Bill Cody, who felt the city needed another Leaner label to record local talent, successfully implored Ernie and Tony to begin anew.

During the late 1960s and early 1970s Toddlin' Town/Midas was sustained by a whole raft of hits, most notably Alvin Cash's "Keep on Dancing" (1968), Bull and the Matadors' "The Funky Judge" (1968), and Thomas East and the Fabulous Playboys' "I Get a Groove" (1969). These hits, as with most of the company's releases in this period, were unappealing, unmelodic funk numbers. Bull and the Matadors was a three-man group out of St. Louis—JaMell "Bull" Parks (born June 7, 1945), Milton Hardy, and James Otis Love. Andre Williams discovered them on a talent-scouting trip to St. Louis for Toddlin' Town.[51] Thomas East and his group were brought to the company by WVON deejay Joe Cobb.[52]

Eventually, the company hit a dry spell and collapsed in early 1971. George Leaner continued to handle the publishing end—Vapac Music for the One-derful group and Tony Tunes for the Toddlin' Town group—which had a number of valuable properties, most notably "Shake a Tail Feather." He also did some leasing of the company's masters to reissue firms. During 1979–81 a Japanese firm, P-Vine, released six marvelous albums of material from the One-derful vaults.

By the late 1970s, Ernie Leaner had retired from the record business and moved to Lakeside, Michigan. George Leaner died in 1983 after a short illness, and his brother died in 1990.[53] Bill Chavers commented at the time of George's death: "He was a principled, enterprising man. What he got, he worked hard for; the success he achieved in the music business was deserved."[54]

NOTES

1. One-derful has not elicited much interest from rhythm–and–blues researchers. The company was given some coverage by a record reissue project of a Japanese recording firm in 1979-81. The liner notes were in English: Otis Clay interviewed by Steve Tomashefsky, liner notes, Harold Burrage, *Pioneer of Chicago Soul,* P-Vine Special 9003, 1979. Also see Robert Pruter, "George W. Leaner" (obituary), *Living Blues* 58 (Winter 1983): 46; Bill Chavers interview; Ernest Leaner interview.

2. Chavers interview.

3. Steve Tomashefsky, to the author, 1983.

4. "Leaner Breaks with United Distributing; Forms One-derful Label," *Billboard,* March 31, 1962, p. 40.

5. Ibid.

6. Otis Clay interview with Steve Tomashefsky, *Pioneer of Chicago Soul.*

7. Ibid.

8. George Leaner, to the author, 1980.

9. Robert Pruter, "McKinley Mitchell: Down-home Rhythm 'n' Blues," *Goldmine,* August 30, 1985, pp. 30, 67, 78-79; idem, "The McKinley Mitchell Story," *Juke Blues* 12 (Spring 1988): 7-12; McKinley Mitchell interview.

10. Mitchell interview.

11. Ibid.

12. Ibid.

13. Ibid.

14. Charles Keil, *Urban Blues* (Chicago: University of Chicago Press, 1966), p. 158

15. Mitchell interview.

16. Robert Pruter, "Harold Burrage: Pioneer of Chicago Soul," *Juke Blues* 8 (Spring 1987): 22-25; Rev. Eugene Burrage interview; Otis Clay interview, July 10, 1984; Irene Ferguson interview.

17. Burrage interview.

18. Ibid.

19. Clay interview.

20. Otis Clay interviewed by Steve Tomashefsky, *Pioneer of Chicago Soul.*

21. "From the Music Capitals of the World: Chicago," *Billboard,* December 17, 1966, p. 55.

22. Larry Nestor interview.

23. Thomas J. Cullen III, "Otis Clay: Chicago Soul Man," *Soul Survivor* 5 (Summer 1986): 14-18; Dave Hoekstra, "Otis Clay Is Still Soul's Shining Star," *Chicago Sun-Times* May 27, 1988; Robert Pruter, "Otis Clay: The Arkansas Yardbird," *Juke Blues* 7 (Winter 1986-87): 4-9; Lynn Van Matre, "Gospel Truths: Otis Clay's Days in Blues May be Numbered," *Chicago Tribune,* June 12, 1988; Otis Clay interviews.

24. Clay interview, August 19, 1976.

25. Clay interview, April 20, 1979.

26. Ibid.

27. Ibid.

28 Robert Pruter, "The Five Dutones," *Goldmine,* January, 1982, pp. 172-73; LeRoy Joyce interview; David Scott interview.

29. Joyce interview.

30. Ibid.

31. Scott interview.

32. Lynn Sweet, "Court Hears the Blues—and It Shakes Judge," *Chicago Sun-Times,* August 16, 1980.

33. Robert Pruter, "The Johnny Sayles Story," *Juke Blues* 10 (Autumn 1987): 8-11; Sayles interview.

34. Sayles interview.

35. Ibid.

36. Ibid.

37. Ibid.

38. Robert Pruter, "The Barbara Livsey Story," *Goldmine,* September 1981, p. 183; Barbara Livsey interview.

39. John Abbey, "Alvin Cash and the Crawlers—A Few More Facts," *Home of the Blues* 8 (March 1967): 10; Dave Hoekstra, "Alvin Tries to Cash In on Latest Dance Craze," *Chicago Sun-Times,* April 24, 1988; Robert Pruter, "The Alvin Cash Story," *Goldmine,* August 1980, pp. 168-69; Alvin Cash interview.

40. Sayles interview.

41. Cash interview.

42. Ibid.

43. Pip, Penni, Terry Joe, Brandi and Lee, "The Lowdown," *Chicago Defender,* August 28, 1965; Robert Pruter, "The Sharpees," *Soul Survivor* 6 (Winter 1986/ 87): 23-25; Vernon Guy interviews; Stacy Johnson interviews.

44. Guy interview, December 10, 1985.

45. Clifford Curry interview; One-derful papers, *Living Blues* archives.

46. "Highlighting Teens with Talent," *Chicago Defender,* May 2, 1964; Patrice Scaggs interview.

47. One-derful papers, *Living Blues* archives.

48. Negro Press International, "Up and Coming Tunes, Teens," *Chicago Defender,* January 15, 1966; Beverly Shaffer interview.

49. Shaffer interview.

50. Ibid.

51. Wayne Jancik, "Bull & The Matadors," unpublished manuscript, 1989.

52. Billy Leaner interview.

53. Kenan Heise, "Former Record Distributor Ernest Leaner, Sixty-eight," *Chicago Tribune*, April 24, 1990.

54. Chavers interview.

10

The Small Entrepreneurs of the 1960s: Hard Soul

In the shadow of One-derful Records there were innumerable small record men who tried to make their mark in the soul market with powerful blues-based and gospelized hard-soul singers. Such entrepreneurs as Leo Austell, Willie Barney, Bill Lasley, Bob Lee, and Jack Daniels generally were unable to garner anything more than local hits. On the level at which they were operating, however, local hits could sustain such companies, at least until they hit a dry spell, which invariably had to happen. A few managed to get a national hit or two, as in 1963 when Mel London scored with "Cut You A-Loose" by Ricky Allen, and in 1966 when Bob Lee hit with "I Can't Please You" by Jimmy Robins.

The small record men (and indeed they all were men) worked with hard-soul singers mostly because they were familiar with that kind of music and felt comfortable working with it. The opportunity to make money in the field was undoubtedly more limited than had they worked with soft-soul acts, but they persevered—or better, gambled against the odds—because there was always that chance of success, no matter how slim.

The artists these record men worked with invariably were born in the South and had earlier careers in gospel or blues, and like many singers with that kind of background, they sang in an often uncompromising, raw and intense manner. The consequence was to limit their audience to much the same constituency as that of the city's blues artists—the adult working-class black population not long out of the South. Thus, there were a number of hard-soul singers who never even had a local hit, and at least one discussed here who never recorded a respectable-sounding record.

Regardless of their success or lack of success at recording, the hard-soul singers played week in and week out at numerous inner-city clubs and occasionally worked as opening acts on the big stage shows. Such artists as Roy Hytower, Bobby Jones, Cicero Blake, and Nolan Struck were far from invisible, and without their contributions to the Chicago soul scene the city would have been far poorer.

King Records

Much of the foundation for the activities of the small record men in Chicago was established by King Records. From its offices first at 1255 South Wabash and later at 2131 South Michigan, the company signed a host of Chicago hard-soul singers to record for its King and Federal labels. Syd Nathan had founded the company in 1945 in Cincinnati, and during the postwar years it emerged as one of the most successful independents.[1] The company was one of the few independents to operate a network of branch distributorships; during the sixties King operated its Chicago office as both a distribution branch and an A&R office. The label had a studio in its Chicago building but it was used mainly for woodshedding. When ready, the acts would record in Cincinnati.

During King's last years in the city, Alphonso "Sonny" Thompson was head of A&R. Thompson was born in Centreville, Mississippi, on August 22, 1916, but while a toddler he moved with his parents to Chicago. He was trained as a pianist, and began recording in 1945. In 1948 he hit with "Long Gone" on Lee Egalnick's Miracle label in Chicago, and two years later he joined King Records as both a recording act and a session musician. Gradually, he assumed more and more of a studio role, and when the label's A&R director in Chicago, Ralph Bass, left for Chess Records in 1959, Thompson ably stepped into his shoes.[2]

King's biggest Chicago-based act was bluesman Freddy King, who had a host of hits for the label during 1961. The one Chicago success the company had in the soul idiom was the King Pins' "It Won't Be This Way (Always)," in 1963 (number twelve on *Billboard*'s r&b chart). The King Pins were actually a long-time gospel group, the Kelly Brothers (Andrew, Curtis, and Robert Kelly, Charles Lee, and Offe Reece), and the song was essentially a "gospel number" thinly disguised with secular lyrics.

But for its size, King's efforts in mining Chicago talent proved mostly futile. During his A&R tenure, Thompson got Syl Johnson, Wylie Dixon and the Wheels, James Robbins (Jimmy Robins), Emmett Sutton, and Lloyd Nolan on wax, but never got more than a few radio plays on each. In 1964 King closed its Chicago offices, and many of its failed artists were picked up by small entrepreneurs in the city who turned them into hitmakers. Sonny Thompson remained a fixture in Chicago rhythm and blues for many years afterward, playing in clubs and in sessions until he died in 1989.

Four Brothers

Four Brothers Productions was a recording company operating out of Barney's Records store at 3234 West Roosevelt on the city's West Side. The operation was founded in 1965 by Willie Barney in partnership with one of his employees, Jack Daniels, and a Columbia Records promotion man, Granville White. (White was a secret partner to avoid conflict of interest with his Columbia job.)

The principal operator of the label was Daniels, who handled administration, A&R, production, and promotion.[3] "They asked me to become a partner," said Daniels, "because I was the only one who had the time to do the promotion and, you know, whatever. Basically, when it came to going on the road, I would do that. On several occasions I did make tours throughout the South to promote a record. When it came to booking the artists on local shows and managing, I did all of that. Barney and White weren't really involved in that aspect of it."[4] Barney did have a lot of irons in the fire. Besides his record shop he also operated a one-stop distributorship at 1144 South Kedzie (later on Ogden Avenue), also on the West Side.

Daniels was born in Crossett, Arkansas, December 23, 1936, and moved to Chicago in 1954. His entry into the record business was his work as manager of the Kedzie location. His lack of musical background in part shaped his strategies as an A&R man. Said he, "I felt more comfortable specializing in the blues and more downhome sound. That's perhaps the easiest kind of music to write, and I guess the easiest for Johnny Moore, my songwriting partner, and myself to relate to. At that time I was just getting into the music and I really had no musical background. It was out of necessity that I got into it."[5]

The company did not have a studio of its own and relied on various studios around the city. Naturally, without a home studio the company did not have a house band. Daniels generally relied on head arrangements when recording his acts, but when he used horns he had Monk Higgins come in to do the formal arrangements. Reggie Boyd was also used on some sessions for arranging. The company had a national hit with bluesman G. L. Crockett, and a host of regional hits with Johnny Moore, Junior Wells, Ricky Allen, and Tyrone Davis.

G. L. Crockett was the artist who put Daniels into the recording business and in effect launched Four Brothers and its subsidiary label, Bright Star. Related Daniels:

> Paul Glass, who at the time was the owner of All State Record Distributors, had a studio at Forty-eighth and Cottage Grove run by a friend of mine, Al Perkins. I stopped by to see Al one day and I met this guy in there, G. L. Crockett, who was singing a

song he wrote, "It's a Man Down There." It was kind of catchy. I sort of rewrote the lyrics to it right there. There were some musicians around there and I asked them to try to play some music to the song, and asked Al to run the tape. He ran the tape and got it down.

Barney had just started Four Brothers. He wanted me to be a part of the company, and I also brought that particular song in. I was convinced that "It's a Man Down There" could be possibly a hit record, and I asked Barney if he could release it. I think sort of to appease me, more than having confidence in the record, he had five hundred records pressed and mailed them out to some disc jockeys throughout the South. And one of the jocks who played the song was John R [John Richbourg] on WLAC in Nashville. They got on the record and started playing it, and we started getting calls from all over the country. And the record was the biggest we had.[6]

Indeed it was. "It's a Man Down There" was the only record put out by the company that was a genuine hit on the national charts, lasting thirteen weeks and going to position ten on *Billboard's* r&b survey in the summer of 1965. The record had an appealing Jimmy Reed–type sound, for Crockett had perfectly captured Reed's lazy drawl. (The song was derived from Sonny Boy Williamson's "One Way Out," released on Checker in 1962.)

Daniels followed up with another solid Reed sound-alike, "Every Good-bye Ain't Gone," which briefly made *Cash Box's* r&b chart in the fall of 1965. Perhaps because Crockett made music that was so derivative, blues researchers have not sought any biographical information on him. The basic details of his life are sketchy.[7] He was born George L. Crockett around 1929, in Carrollton, Mississippi, to Esther (father's name) and Mattie Martin Crockett. He moved to the West Side of Chicago in 1949 and by the mid-1950s was well involved in the flourishing music scene there. Crockett's first record was with blues impresario Mel London, who produced the rocking "Look Out Mabel" in 1958.

While at Four Brothers, Crockett had a drinking problem, and recalled Daniels: "He was very fond of alcohol and he had high blood pressure. When he drank and his blood pressure went up, he was very difficult to deal with."[8] Daniels decided he did not need any more headaches and chose not to record Crockett after his third release. On February 14, 1967, after several months of declining health, G. L. Crockett died of a cerebral hemorrhage brought on by hypertension.

Andrew Brown was the company's first artist and came to Barney through Al Perkins, with whom he had recorded one single previously, in

1964 on Glass's USA label. Brown was born in Jackson, Mississippi, February 25, 1937, and in 1946 he moved to Chicago with his mother.[9] While still in early adolescence he began playing guitar in blues bands in the south suburbs.

In 1965 Brown's contract was picked up by Four Brothers, and Brown, working with Perkins and Daniels in Glass's studio, came out with three releases within a year. But the company had absolutely no success with them, and Brown was out of the business for many years. In the early 1980s he revived his career, recording two well-received albums for a Dutch label. Sadly, before he could benefit from his new-won fame he died of lung cancer, on December 11, 1985.

"Johnny Moore was singing locally and was doing some writing when I met him," related Daniels. "After G. L. Crockett's first record other artists were coming to me and I didn't have a source for material. Johnny and I started working together during that time. We started developing new artists, and you know, making the scene every night. In fact we became extremely close and worked extremely well together. It was a great relationship. Johnny was like a brother during that era. And we did quite well."[10]

Moore, who played piano, was more the musician of the two, but each man created both lyrics and music. Said Daniels, "Personally, I think one of Moore's attributes is that he didn't have a formal musical background, because in our later writings a lot of things our arrangers would listen to they would say were incorrect according to theory. But you know it sounded real good. So you know a person with formal musical training would probably not write a lot of stuff we did write for that very reason."[11]

Moore was born on September 1, 1940, in West Point, Mississippi, where he was raised. About 1960 he moved to Chicago and began his musical career singing in various South Side clubs. He cited Fats Domino and Little Richard as his earliest influences, but as the emergent soul sounds took hold in the city, Moore came under its sway as well.[12]

Joining Four Brothers, Moore entered the studio for the first time, and he got a successful local hit with "Your Love's Got Power" in the fall of 1966. Capturing the very essence of subtle hard soul, Moore's edgy vocal approach gave the gently rolling ballad a blues feel. The singer did not immediately sustain his recording career with a follow-up hit, but it did not matter much because he was more interested in composing anyway and working behind the scenes with Daniels.

Junior Wells's squalling harmonica-blowing and gritty, spunky blues singing had always epitomized Chicago bar-band blues, and his path to them, like much of the city's blues fraternity, began in the South. The singer was born Amos Blackmore in Memphis, Tennessee, December 9,

1934, and in 1941 he moved to Chicago with his mother.[13] After a youthful apprenticeship in the Aces and then the Muddy Waters band, he made his first sides for Leonard Allen's States label in June 1953.[14]

In 1957 Wells began a long association with Mel London, who recorded the bluesman first on his own Chief and Profile labels and later on USA, sometimes with dire consequences but more often with magnificent results. Some notable London-produced records were "Come on in This House," "Prison Bars All around Me," and "Messing with the Kid." In March 1966 Wells joined the Bright Star label, and in the fall of the same year he had a giant local hit with "Up in Heah," which spectacularly shot up to number two on WVON's playlist.

Daniels related how "Up in Heah" came about:

> There was some kind of connection with Atlantic. They asked me to cut a record on Junior, and I didn't have a tune. But Johnny Moore and I went up to a place called the Grove Ballroom at Sixty-second and Cottage Grove, and we wrote that song in about a hour. Ed Cook was on WVON at the time, he and Bill "Butterball" Crane. And a lot of the lyrics to the song were some of the things they used to say when they came on the air. Ed Cook would talk about "putting the white rug on the floor, we're gonna cook," and Butterball had this thing about "up in heah." I just kind of incorporated it all in a song, and it turned out to be successful.[15]

Follow-up records with similar soul-style blues sold some, but failed to equal Wells's initial success.

To many purist blues fans of Wells, Daniels's work with the famed musician was considered nothing but soul music. But by the standards of the mid-1960s Wells's Bright Star sides were genuinely downhome, and for Wells to come out with the records featuring harmonica was extraordinary. The Monk Higgins horn arrangements were superb in updating Wells yet keeping to the downhome approach and staying true to the esthetic considerations of the black working-class audience.

Ricky Allen had an extensive career with London prior to his Daniels association. Because he recorded for labels heavy on blues artists and he used blues musicians in his band and on his recordings, he had always gotten a certain amount of attention from blues researchers. But his records were generally in the hard-soul vein and some of his songs because they were "fast blues" could rightly be characterized as rock 'n' roll. Blues researcher Neil Paterson called his style "pop blues."[16]

Allen was born in Nashville, Tennessee, January 6, 1935. He started in church choirs but soon gravitated to blues. In 1958 he moved to Chicago where he immersed himself in the West Side blues scene, playing clubs whenever he could find gigs. In 1961 Allen began recording for London's Age label with the rousing "You Better Be Sure," a great fast blues with a rock 'n' roll feel.

In August 1963 Allen had the biggest record of his career, "Cut You A-Loose." The up-tempo number with a pulsating, throbbing rhythm (courtesy of an organ) propelled Allen's riveting soul/blues vocals to perhaps his best performance. The record went to position twenty on *Billboard*'s r&b chart, establishing Allen as a first-rank performer in Chicago so that in 1964 Paterson would report that Allen was "one of Chicago's most popular singers."[17]

Allen joined Four Brothers in the summer of 1966, and got strong local hits with "Nothing in the World Can Hurt Me" and "It's a Mess I Tell You." The latter song featured a relaxed lope with a blues intensity like most Daniels/Moore compositions. Another fine song written by the pair for Allen was "I Can't Stand No Signifying." The record went halfway up the local charts in the summer of 1967 and was one of the last records put out by the company.

"Tyrone Davis was about the second or third artist we had," recalled Daniels. "Harold Burrage brought him to me. Harold was a guy I was working with very closely and respected quite a bit, and he had a lot of experience. At the time he was working with Ernie and George Leaner at United. And he brought Tyrone to me, 'cause we were all West Siders. He and I made Tyrone's first record, 'You Made Me Suffer.'"[18]

Tyrone Davis was born in Greenville, Mississippi, May 4, 1938. When he was a year old, his parents divorced, with the father taking the infant Tyrone to Saginaw, Michigan, to live. By the late 1950s, Davis was married and had moved to Chicago's West Side. During 1961 he somehow insinuated himself into bluesman Freddy King's entourage. He got a job as King's valet and for more than a year toured with the artist.[19]

In 1962 Davis was back in Chicago and supporting his family working at a steel mill in which Otis Clay worked. Davis, however, aspired to be an entertainer and on weekends worked in West Side clubs. He told *Blues and Soul* editor John Abbey in 1970, "Harold found me singing at a little club, and he seemed to like what I was doing. So one night he came over and said, 'I'm gonna get you a song and produce a record on you.' I thought he was putting me on, so I told him that. And he said he wasn't, and he did come back with a song, 'You Made Me Suffer.'"[20]

Once Davis started recording for Four Brothers he quit the steel-mill job and began working for Barney. Because he was not big enough yet to earn a living as an entertainer, Davis labored for Barney in various capacities, one of which was driving around the city to make all the pickups from the record distributorships for the one-stop operation. In November 1966, Davis's mentor, Harold Burrage, died.

Davis had come out with two releases with Burrage songs, and he made one more for Four Brothers with a Daniels/Moore song, "Please Consider Me." Released in January 1967, it was his most commercially successful release on the label. But it had a derivative sound; Davis made a conscious effort to imitate his idol, Bobby Bland, and it sadly showed. In subsequent years, Davis, recording in his own style, would become one of the biggest soul stylists to come out of Chicago.

By the end of 1967 Four Brothers had in effect closed its doors. The company had suffered a dry spell without hits, so regular production ceased and the artists, except for Junior Wells, left the company. Even before operations ended on the labels Daniels was doing independent productions on Johnny Moore. Their first effort bore fruit when Moore got a local hit in July 1967 with "It's Just My Way of Loving You," which came out on Columbia's Date subsidiary. The song was typical of Moore, featuring a gentle lope with a blues feel.

Barney in subsequent years would on occasion revive both the Four Brothers and Bright Star labels, but one could say that without a regular A&R man the operation was finished at the end of 1967. Meanwhile, in mid-1968, Daniels became A&R director for r&b at Mercury Records.

Tarpon/Gerri/Jacklyn

Tarpon, Gerri, and Jacklyn—three labels active in the mid-1960s—are examples of artist-as-proprietor labels whose sole purpose was to get the owner on wax. The artist usually made the label's releases to serve as demos that could be picked up by a larger company with money and distribution muscle. Of the seven releases on Tarpon, five of them were records by its owner, Billy "The Kid" Emerson; of the four releases on Gerri, all were by its owner, Roscoe Robinson; and of the ten releases on Jacklyn, owned by Johnny Haygood, three were releases by his stepson, Darrow Fletcher (most of Fletcher's releases were leased to other companies).

Billy "The Kid" Emerson was not a kid when he was recording in Chicago in the 1960s: He was in his late thirties and had a long string of recording credits behind him for Sun (1954–55), Vee Jay (1955–57), and Chess (1958–59). He was best known for writing and recording for Sun the rock 'n' roll classic called "Red Hot," which over the years was recorded by such artists as Billy Lee Riley, Bob Luman, Sam the Sham, and Robert Gordon.[21]

Sam the Sham's recording of "Red Hot" provided royalties that gave Emerson a big chunk of seed money to start up the Tarpon label in 1966.

Most of Emerson's releases on himself, in contrast to the prevailing soul sound of the day, tended to have much of the old rock 'n' roll feel of the artist's Sun period. None hit, but Tarpon did have one big local hit in the soul vein, "A Love Reputation" by Denise LaSalle.

Emerson was born in Tarpon Springs, Florida, on December 21, 1925. After service in the U.S. Navy, 1943–46, he returned to Tarpon Springs, learned piano, and joined a band. During the late 1940s and early 1950s, Emerson sang Wynonie Harris songs and other jump blues numbers with various bands in the west Florida coast area. He joined the Air Force in 1952 and while stationed in Greenville, Mississippi, sat in with Ike Turner, Little Milton, and other Mississippi blues artists. With Turner's help he made his first records for the fledging Sun label in Memphis.

In 1955 Emerson moved to Chicago and began recording for Vee Jay. He had little success during his two years with the company, nor any luck with Chess in subsequent years. Likewise, hits eluded him during the early 1960s when he recorded for Mad and other small labels.

Emerson began working in 1964 with Denise Craig, who would record as Denise LaSalle, launching her career in 1966 with "A Love Reputation." (LaSalle would go on to become a big hitmaker in the 1970s on her own.) The first session of his own that Emerson did for Tarpon yielded two Emerson-LaSalle compositions, "Every Woman I Know," a blues-based ballad, and "A Dancin' Whippersnapper," a rock 'n' roll shouter that was stylistically anachronistic. Though recorded in 1964, both sides did not appear on Tarpon until 1966–67. The ten sides Emerson put out on himself on Tarpon combined newly recorded material with earlier recorded songs, but new or old, nobody was interested in them.

After 1967, Emerson did not get on record again in the United States. But as true of most Chicago hard-soul artists, one should not measure his contribution solely in terms of recorded output. He was long a figure in the blues and soul-club scene, he ran a record company, and he produced and wrote for other Chicago artists, most notably for Denise LaSalle on Tarpon and Chess and for Carol Vega on Constellation. During the 1970s and 1980s, Emerson made a living playing piano in cocktail lounges through-out the Midwest.

Gerri Records launched gospel singer Roscoe Robinson on his secular music career in 1966 with "That's Enough." Few artists have brought as much experience to their first rhythm-and-blues recordings as Robinson did. When he entered the soul field he had been singing in the gospel field for some twenty-three years with some of the greatest gospel quartets ever put on wax.[22] The experience was evident in his superbly crafted and sung records.

Robinson was born in Dumont, Alabama, May 22, 1928. His father, who was a minister, and his mother both sang spirituals and imparted their interest to their son. His family moved to Gary, Indiana, in 1938, and around 1942 Robinson started singing lead in a quartet called Joiner's Five Trumpets. Three years later he joined the Royal Quartet, and for five years he jumped from quartet to quartet—the Highway QC's (with Sam Cooke), the Kelly Brothers, the Norfolk Singers, back to the Royals, and then to the famed Southern Sons, who were based in Little Rock, Arkansas. That was in the early 1950s.

The latter part of the decade saw Robinson continuing his nomadic career with various groups—the Fairfield Four out of Nashville, the Gate City and the Gospel Jays in Philadelphia, and the Paramount Singers in Oakland. About 1960 he joined the great Five Blind Boys of Mississippi, who were based in Chicago. Robinson stayed with the Blind Boys for some five years.

Robinson's first secular release was "What Makes a Man Do Wrong," which came out in 1965 on the Chess-distributed, New York-based Tuff label. The song was basically a gospel shouter and unexceptional. In April 1966 Robinson came out with the biggest hit of his career, "That's Enough." The song was produced and arranged by Robinson and employed a girl chorus in an exciting gospel-style call and response. The record was originally released on Gerri but when it looked as though it would be a national hit Robinson leased it to Scepter-Wand for release on the Wand label. He also signed with the company. "That's Enough" went to the number seven position and lasted thirteen weeks on *Billboard*'s r&b chart.

On the strength of "That's Enough," Robinson was able to chart with his follow-up, "How Much Pressure (Do You Think I Can Stand)"/"Do It Right Now," both sides of which lasted about a month on the chart in December 1966.

Robinson signed with John Richbourg's Sound Stage 7 in late 1967 and started recording in Nashville, coming out with ten sides all heavily in the southern soul style. Whereas much of the Wand material was written, arranged, and produced by Robinson, the poorer Sound Stage 7 sides were generally the work of the in-house staff at the company.

Robinson moved to Atlantic Records in 1969 and came out with his last chart record, "Oo Wee Baby I Love You," a remake of the Fred Hughes hit from 1965. Produced by Robinson, he gave it a heavily gospelized treatment that worked well for the song, and it lasted four weeks and went to position forty-two on *Billboard*'s soul chart.

In 1971 Robinson joined Stan Lewis's Paula label in Shreveport, Louisiana. Most of his sides for Paula were produced by Cash McCall and most were written by Robinson, but no hits resulted from the partnership. Robinson left the world of soul in 1973 and resumed his gospel career.

Jacklyn Records was operated out of a record shop at 2200 East Seventy-fifth Street owned by Johnny Haygood. Although he signed several acts, Haygood had one purpose in mind, to get his stepson, Darrow Fletcher, on wax. The company existed for four years in the late 1960s, but Fletcher was only on the label during 1966–67 because Haygood got him signed with MCA in 1968. Essentially Haygood was running a production company and only secondly a label. Two veterans of the 1950s vocal-group scene, producer Ted Daniels and songwriter Maurice Simpkins, were the creative team for the label. Burgess Gardner did some arranging.

Haygood began his recording activities in late 1965 with Fletcher. The young man genuinely deserved the paternal effort because he had a magnificently expressive voice, which was put to good use on a string of hard-hitting, soulfully sung records. Fletcher was born January 23, 1951, in Inskter, Michigan, a community eight miles outside of Detroit. When he was three years of age his family moved to Chicago. Young Darrow began singing at the tender age of six and recording at the age of fourteen while a freshman in high school (he attended first Hirsch and later South Shore).[23]

Fletcher's first record, in December 1965, was "The Pain Gets a Little Deeper." Written by Fletcher and producer Daniels, the funky song with its compelling Latin rhythm was an impressive debut. The record was leased to Groovy, a small New York label owned by Sam and George Goldner and Kal Rudman. They got the record on the national r&b charts for seven weeks in early 1966.

"Pain Gets a Little Deeper" generated such recognition for Fletcher that he could make a tour of the entire chitlin' circuit, playing the Apollo, Howard, Uptown, as well as the Regal. At the Regal, in July 1966, he shared the bill with B. B. King, the Elgins, Stevie Wonder, the Capitols, Lee Dorsey, Jimmy Ruffin, the Swan Silvertones, and from Chicago, the Sharpees and Jo Ann Garrett.

Following three failed follow-ups on Groovy and dissatisfied with the financial aspects of the association, Haygood in 1966 formed Jacklyn, named after one of his daughters. The company immediately scored with a Fletcher great, "Sitting There That Night," which was written by Haygood. The Gardner arrangement, with its marvelous Mayfield-styled guitar intro, brassy horn charts, and loping beat, made the record a genuine Chicago-style classic. Haygood claimed twenty-five thousand sales for the record in the city alone, but because of distribution problems it did nothing elsewhere.[24]

In 1968 Haygood got a production deal with MCA, which released Fletcher on its various labels—Revue, Congress, and Uni. Said Fletcher, "I did some things for [Jacklyn], but it was tough. When you don't have the financial resources and the staff, it's almost impossible for a small label to survive."[25] No hits developed out of the MCA relationship until 1970 with "I Think I'm Gonna Write a Song," in February, and "When Love Calls," in October. Haygood said "When Love Calls" sold at least sixty-five thousand in the Chicago area.[26] The former made the *Billboard* soul chart and the latter made the *Cash Box* r&b chart.

Fletcher moved to the West Coast in 1974 and recorded six sides for Ray Charles, after which his career simply withered away. Meanwhile, Haygood continued with his Jacklyn label for a few years before calling it quits in 1970. In the early 1980s he returned to Detroit, and around 1987 Fletcher returned to Chicago, but not to the music business.

Jerhart

Jerhart was the label and publishing-company operation owned by Bob Lee, who throughout the 1960s was involved with dozens of recording endeavors. His business during most of the decade was conducted from his home at 6253 South Greenwood on the South Side. Most of his recording was done at Sound Unlimited Studio at 93 West One Hundred Fifty-Ninth Street in the south suburb of Harvey. Lee worked not only with hard-soul singers, but also soft-soul solo artists and vocal groups. His acts appeared on Jerhart as well as on the subsidiary labels of Hawk, Big Three, Vick, and Toi.[27]

Lee was born April 12, 1930 in Tuscaloosa, Alabama, and moved to Chicago in 1947. He worked in factory jobs until the late 1950s, attended broadcasting school, and then began deejaying on WOPA. The deejay job did not last long but it drew Lee into the entertainment business. He at first hung around with Leo Austell working with his acts, but by the mid-1960s he was putting out records on his own labels. Unfortunately for Lee, on almost every act he recorded, such as the Vows, the Moments of Truth, Geraldine Taylor, and Verble Domino, the best he achieved was a few plays on local radio. Domino, whose real name was Sherman Nesbary (born May 15, 1940, in Chicago), got on the local charts with "I've Been Fooled Before," in January of 1967. Nesbary's best achievement, however, was writing Jo Ann Garrett's marvelous hit "Stay by My Side" a couple of years earlier.

Lee had better success working as A&R man for Al Benson's Crash/Mica label group. He scored strong local hits with Jimmy Dobbins's "What Is Love?" and Ray and Dave's "Wrong Wrong Wrong," both in 1966.

Lee was hot in 1966 because the one national hit he got also happened that year—"I Can't Please You," released on Jerhart and composed and sung by a remarkable hard-soul singer named Jimmy Robins. Little is known of this singer before Lee recorded him. Robins had earlier made several records under the name James Robbins for Federal, the most notable being "Someone from Somewhere," which got of a lot of play on Chicago radio in the spring of 1964. The song was a secular gospel ballad and one could tell from Robins's deep emoting that he had been thoroughly steeped in a gospel milieu. Said Lee, "He was sort of like a jackleg old preacher."[28]

"I Can't Please You" was Lee's first release on Robins, and it became a surprise national-chart hit in November 1966. On *Cash Box*'s r&b chart it lasted eight weeks and went to the sixteen position. The song had one of the heaviest pounding beats ever put on a hard-soul record, and Robins roared through the song with deep-throated passion equalled by few of his contemporaries. Curiously this Chicago artist recorded the record in California, and it was picked up by Lee in partnership with Purvis Spann.

Lee could not come back with a follow-up hit on Robins, and after 1967 the singer was not heard on wax again. Lee continued to persevere with various small labels and obscure artists, but never again had a national hit.

Brainstorm Records

Brainstorm was founded in 1966 by veteran record man Leo Austell and two young partners, Archie Russell and Hillery Johnson.[29] The label and its subsidiary, Twin Stacks, never achieved more than some regional success during their four years of existence. As a production company, however, the operation had magnificent success with Betty Everett, getting several national hits on her, notably "There'll Come a Time," in 1969. All the Everett recordings were leased to MCA's Uni label. Brainstorm's other acts— the Emotions, John Edwards, Cicero Blake, Roy Hytower, and others—did little to sustain the company.

At its founding the company was located at 1508 East Sixty-eighth Street. Then it moved to a street away from Record Row at 1809 South Indiana, and at its end the company was operating out of 1321 South Michigan.

Austell made his money from a maintenance service business, and first invested in the record business in 1960 when he founded the Renee label, named after his daughter. With Renee he recorded Cicero Blake, Eddie Sullivan, and Betty Everett. Vee Jay picked up Everett from Austell, who in subsequent years became bosom buddies with Calvin Carter, Bunky Sheppard, and other Vee Jay executives. For a time Renee operated out of the Vee Jay building at 1449 South Michigan. The collapse of Vee Jay led to Austell's forming Brainstorm with Russell and Johnson.

Russell, who became vice president, had been singing with his sisters in a vocal group called the Preteens. When nothing seemed to be developing for the group he decided to go into the business end. Johnson, who became the promotion man, was in the insurance field. All three took part on the production and writing. The company's principal arrangers were Tom Washington and George Patterson.

Brainstorm had notable local chart success with a girl group called the Emotions and a rock 'n' roll group called the Sounds of Dawn. The latter recorded a blue-eyed soul number for Twin Stacks, "How Many Times," which went high on the WVON chart in December 1967. The Emotions, while on Brainstorm, consisted of three daughters of Joe Hutchinson—Sheila (born 1953), Wanda (born 1951), and Jeanette (born 1950).[30]

The Hutchinson girls had sung gospel as the Hutchinson Sunbeams almost since they were toddlers. In 1962 they made a brief foray into r&b when they recorded a Christmas record for George Leaner called "Santa Got Stuck in the Chimney." In 1967 Joe Hutchinson decided to have his girls enter the booming soul-music field. While still attending Parker High the girls signed with Brainstorm and began recording as the Emotions. In December 1967 "I Can't Stand No More Heartaches" hit the local charts, and in March 1968 "Somebody New" charted.

Brainstorm put out four singles on the Emotions, but none had that spark needed to launch the girls nationally. Pervis Staples (formerly of the Staple Singers) became the group's manager and in 1969 he got the girls signed with Stax, the same label that was recording the Staple Singers. At Stax, the Emotions went on to become internationally acclaimed recording stars. They were on the national charts regularly through the mid-1980s.

But it was with the hard-soul singers that Brainstorm seemed to excel, creatively if not commercially. The company managed to capture the essence of black working-class esthetics with such artists as Cicero Blake, Roy Hytower, and John Edwards (the latter of whom achieved fame in the eighties as lead for the Spinners).

Cicero Blake's story runs the gamut of black r&b styles, whether 1950s vocal harmony, soul, or blues. His history of entertaining goes back to the twilight of the vocal-group era, in the early 1950s, when he helped form the famous Chicago ensemble the Kool Gents.[31]

Blake was born February 20, 1938, in Jackson, Mississippi, but around the age of fourteen he and his family settled on Chicago's West Side. There he attended Marshall High and became involved in the burgeoning street-corner vocal-group scene. With Johnny Carter, Teddy Long, and other classmates, he formed the Goldentones around 1952; the group eventually became the Kool Gents, led by Dee Clark. Blake also gained valuable experience during 1959–62 as a member of Sonny Thompson's touring r&b review.

Blake got his first recording break in 1961, when he hooked up with Austell, and he got his first notices in 1962, when he recorded "Don't You Do This to Me," an Austell production released on the Iowa-based Success label. In 1964 two more Austell productions on the Renee label, "Soul of Pain" and "Sad Feeling," got considerable play in Chicago and other locales.

Blake had four more Austell-produced releases before the 1960s decade closed, two on Brainstorm ("If I Had My Way" and "Loving You Woman Is Everything"), and two on Capitol's subsidiary label, Tower ("Here Comes the Heartache" and "Don't Wait until Tomorrow"). Although these four are only modest songs, they splendidly typified the Chicago hard-soul sound, which was richly deep and genuinely soulful. None of these sides became a hit, but Brainstorm had some regional success with "Loving You Woman Is Everything."

In 1975 Russell produced a fine record on Blake called "Love Is Like a Boomerang." Released on Capitol, the record proved to be one of Blake's biggest sellers. After leaving Austell in 1978 the singer came out with the finest record of his career, "Dip My Dipper," a salacious downhome blues song. The record did well in several markets and gave Blake's fading career a shot in the arm. During the 1980s he established himself on the North Side as a hard-soul and blues singer, playing the blues clubs regularly.

Roy Hytower had one of the most ominous, menacing-sounding baritone voices ever put on wax. Few hard-soul singers could invest a deep blues feeling into soul as much as Hytower, who had the vocal quality of the great Delta blues singers such as Muddy Waters, Howlin' Wolf, and Robert Johnson. Hytower never had a hit, even on the local level, but some of his records got airplay and he was a regular on the West- and South-Side club scene.[32]

Hytower was born in 1943 in Coffeyville, Alabama. At the age of fifteen he began singing in clubs in nearby Mobile. In 1962 Hytower moved to Chicago and hooked up with the great bluesman Otis Rush, replacing guitarist Mighty Joe Young. Hytower performed around the city and by 1965 made his first record for the local Avin label, "Since I've Been Away," a fairly crude and amateurish effort.

In 1965 Hytower's career was interrupted by the draft, and the young man spent 1966 serving as a machine-gunner in the Vietnamese highlands. Back in Chicago in 1968, Hytower began recording for the Brainstorm label. His first release, "Your Good Man Is Going Bad," was a southern soul-style number much in the manner of Joe Tex. But it was the flip, "Must Be Love," with its chunky beat and Hytower's deep bluesy vocals that best demonstrated the singer's talents. The lyrics were obviously romantic, but

Hytower's vocals suggested something far more raunchy and sweat-drenched. The next Brainstorm release was a solid up-tempo blues, "You Pleases Me," one of the Hytower's best compositions and vocal efforts.

In 1969 Hytower left the collapsing Brainstorm organization and recorded the finest two sides of his career—"I'm in Your Corner"/"Undertaker"—on Mercury's Blue Rock subsidiary. "I'm in Your Corner," which got some play on WVON in November 1969, had a forceful beat. Coupled with Hytower's magnificent vocals it made for a classic Chicago hard-soul record. The flip, "Undertaker," with its rumbling driving beat and Hytower's menacing vocals, was thoroughly evocative of its morbid subject.

Hytower stayed in the music business as best he could during the 1970s and 1980s, but Chicago was drying up as a music center and opportunities were gradually ceasing to exist. Hytower developed a career playing in black musicals, performing such roles as Muddy Waters and Otis Redding to rave notices.[33]

Brainstorm went out of business in 1969, but during the following decade Austell, Russell, and Johnson continued in the record business as a production company, recording sides on Betty Everett as well as on some of their Brainstorm artists. The 1980s saw Johnson moving to Los Angeles and an ailing Austell disengaging himself from the record business. When Austell died in 1988 at the age of seventy-one, Russell was still persevering at making records in Chicago.

Don Clay Productions

Don Clay, like many small record men, began his career as an entertainer. He was born and raised in Evanston, Illinois, and while still a teenager he formed a vocal group, the Foster Brothers. Besides Clay, the group consisted of Les Gayles, Ray Johnson, Lindsay Langston, and George Lattimore. In 1958 the group scored with a sizable local hit on Mercury called "If You Want My Heart." Subsequent releases in the following years failed to ignite much interest, and by the early 1960s Clay was working behind the scenes as a producer and writer.[34]

In 1961 Clay joined R. C. "Bobby" Robinson in the formation of the Boss label. Robinson had been a member of another Evanston group, the Gems (Ray Pettis, David Taylor, Wilson James, Rip Reed, and Robinson), who recorded a number of fine sides for the local Drexel label. The two neophyte record men put out around ten releases on Boss, by such artists as Ray Pettis and Perk Lee (of the El Dorados), but nothing happened except for some local action on "Cotton" by the Duvals (Naturals).

Clay and Robinson had gone their separate ways by 1963, Clay forming Dawn Records and Robinson starting up Dee Dee Records. Robinson got a sizable hit on Dee Dee with an instrumental called "Dawn" by the David Rockingham Trio (Robinson, the producer and writer, on guitar; Dave Rockingham on organ; and Shante Hamilton on drums). The record was leased to New York-based Josie in 1963 and became a national hit.[35] Other releases on Dee Dee, mainly by Ray Pettis, did little.

Clay likewise got only one national hit, a remarkable blues called "Rough Dried Woman" by Big Mack, written and produced by Clay. It was released locally on his Dawn label in late 1966, and the following year became a national sensation after it was leased to Louisiana-based Ronn Records. Meanwhile, in 1965 Clay had taken the job as general manager of St. Lawrence Records, but by the following year was doing independent production work. Besides "Rough Dried Woman," Clay got a fine local hit on his own Flash label in November with "Mr. Shy" by Billy McGregor. The song was a typical Chicago medium-tempo number that got superb arrangements from Eddie Silvers. Although the song was decidedly soft soul in sound, McGregor imparted a depth to the vocals that evoked a hard-soul sensibility.

In 1967 Clay launched his Wise World label in partnership with local rock 'n' roller Phil Orsi. They recorded a bunch of local groups without any noticeable success. Clay joined the Chess staff the same year, but because he was the last man in the pecking order he was given virtually no opportunity to produce.

Clay worked as road manager for cocktail-lounge singer Azie Mortimer from 1968 to 1973. In 1969 Clay formed Number One Records with Mortimer's husband, Mort Kaplan, to record the singer.[36] Although Mortimer in live performance was a singer of jazzy standards, Clay produced her as a hard-soul singer, both on the Number One label and on others such as OKeh. He also produced a Roy Hytower single for Number One, but none of his production efforts in the late 1960s and early 1970s yielded hits.

In 1973 Clay became regional promotion man for New York-based Chelsea Records, ending his career as a Chicago record producer and label owner. He died of cancer sometime in the mid-1980s.

Expo Records

Expo Records was a short-lived label of Bill Lasley's from mid-1968 through early 1970. Lasley established offices for the company at 58 East Roosevelt, a site vacated earlier by Carl Davis when he moved into the old Vee Jay offices at 1449 South Michigan. Lasley never had any real success with Expo (which metamorphosed into Opex before it was finished), other than getting a few plays on his two principal acts, Bobby Jones and Pauline Chivers.

Lasley produced most of the records and normally used Johnny Cameron as arranger. His favorite songwriter was Maurice Simpkins.

Expo was not the first of Lasley's labels. As early as 1957 he was the proprietor of the Amp-3 label out of New York, and in the early sixties he owned the Success label in Des Moines, Iowa. He put out some good records on bluesman Mighty Joe Young during 1966-67 on his Webcor and Celtex labels, but late in the decade Bobby Jones was his principal project.[37] Jones was one of those myriad Chicago singers who never made it from a recording standpoint. For some twenty years he was a regular on the South- and West-Side club circuit, usually sharing the bill with blues singers, and thus made his contribution to the scene largely as a live performer. Jones did record some two dozen sides from 1965 to 1984, but never had even a local hit. It was not that he lacked anything; he had a richly expressive vocal approach with a raw timbre that proved ideal for his blues-based hard-soul material. The unfortunate thing is that his records were not especially interesting.[38]

Jones was born in Farmerville, Louisiana, sometime during the war years of the early 1940s. He had the usual start in gospel, but it was not until he moved to Chicago in the early 1960s that he went into singing seriously. Said he, "I was walking down Forty-third Street and Drexel and heard music coming from a lounge called Freighter's Juke Box. I went in and told the proprietor, Jimmy Mitchell, that I could sing. So he told me to get on up there and sing. My career began from there."[39] Soon Jones was playing such clubs as Peppers (Forty-third and Vincennes), sharing the stage with the likes of Muddy Waters.

Jones's first effort on record for Vee Jay was in 1965, when he came out with "A Certain Feeling," which was a mushy ballad. During the late 1960s Jones was regularly produced by Lasley, who first put out a record on Jones on the USA label before starting Expo. Although without distinction, all the records exhibited the classic Chicago hard-soul sound, especially those written by Maurice Simpkins, such as "Check Me Out" (1967) on USA and "Welcome Back a Foolish Man" (ca. 1970) on Kack. Jones also recorded one single with Pauline Chivers as Pauline and Bobby. (Pauline Chivers, incidentally, had a national hit in 1963 with "Spring," on which she and her husband, Sidney Chivers, were billed as Birdlegs and Pauline.) Jones got his best airplay with the funky "Talkin' 'Bout Jones's" on Expo, which reputedly went as high as number nine on WVON's survey in 1968.

Jones scored with perhaps his biggest-selling record, "I'm So Lonely," which went high on the WVON chart in the summer of 1971. The record was put out on the New York-based Lionel label and was produced by Lasley and Bill Sheppard (old friends from their Gene Chandler days), and written by the Dells. It was a softer soul number than those that Jones had usually done.

Nothing much was heard from Jones during the late 1970s and early 1980s, mostly because of the declining state of Chicago's record industry. He was still appearing regularly in the clubs and developed quite a following for his energetic and top-quality presentation. Blues authority Steve Wisner saw him at a concert around 1985—which featured Denise LaSalle, Z. Z. Hill, and Syl Johnson, among others—and found him to be one of the strongest acts on the bill.[40]

Twinight Records

Twinight Records was founded in 1967 by a former All State Distributors' promotion man, Howard Bedno, and artist management executive Peter Wright. They established headquarters at 166 East Superior on the near North Side, but also maintained a woodshedding studio at 2131 South Michigan. (The South Michigan building was previously the headquarters of USA Records and before that the Chicago offices of King Records.)[41]

The genesis of the label partly stemmed from Bedno's frustration from working at All State and its house label, USA. He explained, "What I was doing, I was a damn fool, because I was getting acts and giving them to Paul Glass, whom I was working for. If I had taken all those acts myself, I could have built a hell of a label. I had the Buckinghams, the New Colony Six, the Rivieras, and then all the blues acts."[42] Before he worked at All State, Bedno owned Cobra Records with Eli Toscano. Sunlight, a subsidiary label to Twinight, briefly surfaced in the early 1970s with releases by the New Colony Six, a rock group managed by Wright. But the operation was essentially an r&b one, because, according to Wright, it was easier to get r&b exposure on radio.[43]

Twinight's A&R man and principal producer was Syl Johnson. Wright's role in the company, however, was very hands-on; he did much of the A&R work and took a production role at each session. The investment in the company was for the most part split between Wright and Bedno, but Johnson had a 5 percent share.[44]

In producing records on himself and on the labels' other artists, Johnson at first worked with arranger/producer Johnny Cameron and writers Carl Smith and Joshie Jo Armstead. Later he worked with writer/producer Jimmy Jones and with two bands, the Deacons (featuring his brother, Jimmy Johnson, on guitar) and the Pieces of Peace (featuring Jerry Wilson on alto sax, Byron Bowie on tenor sax, Michael Davis on trumpet, Bernard Reed on bass, John Bishop on guitar, and Hal Nesbitt on drums). With the bands he made a lot of recordings with head arrangements. The company mainly used the Paragon, RCA, and Eight Track studios. Johnson only got hits on himself and a vocal group called the Notations ("I'm Still Here" in 1970). The records he did on the Guys and Dolls, the Dynamic Tints, Josephine Taylor, Johnny Williams, and others did nothing.

Johnson began as his fellow hard-soul singers did, recording for small, insignificant companies and getting nothing but local hits. But before his career was over he achieved success with some fifteen national hits and eight albums to his credit, impressive numbers by the standards of these artists. The singer, however, never made an impact with members of this nation's critical fraternity, who at most considered him an above-average journeyman entertainer.[45] But if one examines Johnson's career closely, one can find plenty of evidence that he created a body of work that ranked in artistry with most giants of the soul field—Otis Redding, Sam Cooke, Solomon Burke, and Gene Chandler.

Johnson had a strong, sharp, and wailing voice that could dramatically etch a song into one's consciousness. He almost unconsciously projected a deep contradictory bittersweet feeling; he seemed as though he was crying even when he sang a joyful rouser. His lyrics were functional and sometimes awkward, but more often they were exactly right. As with most soul, one should not closely examine attitudes, feelings, and thoughts as expressed in lyrics, but rather concentrate on the nuances and subtleties of the music and vocal delivery, and that was where Johnson was a master.

Johnson was born in Holly Springs, Mississippi, on July 1, 1936,[46] the son of a farmer named Samuel Thompson. His family was steeped in music. The father knew guitar, harmonica, and organ, and Syl's two brothers were noted musicians—Mac Thompson was a long-time sideman in Chicago blues bands and Jimmy Johnson was a fine bluesman who recorded a number of well-received albums during the 1970s and 1980s.

Influenced by his older brother, Jimmy, Syl was learning guitar before his teens, but as he related, "by the time I was in high school, I got serious. Jimmy was working in the steel mills and I was going to Phillips High; therefore, I started playing in the little clubs on weekends. I started out playing all blues. That was my background."[47] Some of the musicians he played behind were the great West Side guitarist Magic Sam, Elmore James, Billy Boy Arnold, and Junior Wells. On the latter three, he also cut some records as a sideman.

Johnson was discovered while backing Jimmy Reed on a Vee Jay session. Calvin Carter asked to see some songs and Johnson subsequently worked one up with Howard Scott called "Teardrops." He recorded a demo in a novelty recording booth and went back to take it to Vee Jay—only he never got there, as Johnson related: "I took a bus to Record Row on Michigan Avenue to take my songs to Vee Jay. I got off the bus at Wabash

Avenue because it did not stop at Michigan. I walked down Wabash and saw King Records. Went in there and said I want to see someone who is in charge of the music. Ralph Bass comes out and says, 'What can I do for you kid?' I said, 'I got a song, would you listen to it?' I gave him the record and he played it. He said, 'You just hold right here, we're going to record you.' He called Syd Nathan in Cincinnati and told him, 'We've got a kid here that you've got to hear man, someone we're going to do something with.'"[48]

Despite this encouraging beginning, King failed to do much with Johnson other than changing his name from Thompson to Johnson. Of the twelve sides released on the company's Federal subsidiary from 1959 to 1962, none did better than getting a few plays on local radio.

Johnson's first substantial hit was "Straight Love, No Chaser" on the Zachron label (owned by John Zachary and Johnny Cameron). It broke big in Chicago in 1966 but did little outside the city. The sound was sassy, aggressive, and harsh, and although not top-notch the song was a strong building-block to Johnson's career. He was coming on fast.

Finally, in April 1967, Johnson had the record that made him a national star, "Come on Sock It to Me," his first on Twinight (originally Twilight). It exploited the "Sock it to me!" expression that was long popular in the black community. (Johnson wrote the music; Joshie Jo Armstead, the lyrics.) From the opening infectious guitar riff, to Johnson's wailing vocals, to the chunk-chunk beat, the record had all the ingredients for a powerful hit. But the record was quintessential hard soul without a whisper of pop to it, and thus had not a chance of crossover success. It sold like crazy in the black community though, lasting twelve weeks and going as high as the twelve position on *Billboard's* r&b chart.

"Different Strokes," written by Zachary and Cameron, was a strong follow-up commercially, lasting ten weeks and going as high as seventeen on the r&b chart, in September 1967. As with many follow-ups, however, "Different Strokes" was something of a sound-alike. But it was done at a slower, funkier tempo and was effective for it.

Three quick releases followed "Different Strokes," but all were poor numbers and failed. Johnson redeemed himself in November 1968 with "Dresses Too Short," a sharply etched, funky up-tempo tune written by Johnson and Carl Smith. It was produced and recorded in Memphis by Willie Mitchell of Hi Records, but it came out on Twinight.

Johnson hit with one of his finest efforts in November 1969, "Is It Because I'm Black," which reached as high as eleven on the r&b chart and stayed on for fourteen weeks. In this superbly arranged and produced song by the Pieces of Peace, Johnson's plaintive vocals evoked the moodiness of this lamentation over the struggle of being black. The song, however, strangely suggested pride rather than defeatism. "'Is It Because I'm Black,'" said Johnson, "was my second biggest to 'Sock It to Me.' People remember it. That was a college record, black college kids. They're political. But these kinds of records tend to hurt you. You've got white people, and then you've got white liberals. There are white people who care nothing about me talking about being black. They just don't care for it. Not that they hate it, but they're not going to pay five, six dollars to buy an album of it."[49]

"Concrete Reservation," written and produced by Jimmy Jones, was a successful follow-up in February 1970, in which Johnson sang a laundry list of ghetto problems. He returned to a lighter vein in May, with a rousing horn-driven number written by Jack Daniels and Johnny Moore called "One Way Ticket to Nowhere." It was the same song that Tyrone Davis hit with a year later, and as good as Johnson's version was, Davis's version had an arrangement that more fully realized the song.

"Get Ready," in April 1971, was Johnson's next chart record. It was a cover of the Temptations' hit, but Johnson made the record his own with one of his grittiest and funkiest vocal performances. That was the singer's last hit on Twinight.

Johnson moved to Willie Mitchell's Hi Records in late 1971. In a 1975 interview with Michael Haralambos, Johnson reported how he got with Hi:

> Willie Mitchell discovered me in a Chicago club called the Burning Spear. I'd usually come out and sing a couple of numbers and open the show with my band. I think at the time I had a thirteen-piece band. One night we had Johnny Nash on the show and I came out and sang a couple of songs, and Willie Mitchell heard it. He said the voice stuck in his head. It was a strange voice, he called it. And later he was on the road and heard "Sock It to Me." He said, "That's the S.O.B. I heard in Chicago. I'm gonna get that cat on this label [Hi]." Willie then did some things on me with Twinight. Before I got away from Twinight he offered me big bucks. And after I waited my contract out with Twinight, automatically I went to Willie Mitchell.[50]

From 1971 to 1976 Johnson had a splendid recording career at Hi, coming out with three superb albums—*Back for a Taste of Your Love* (1973), *Diamond in the Rough* (1974), and *Total Explosion* (1975)—and a passel of great singles, notably "We Did It" (1972), "I Want to Take You Home (To See Mama)" (1974), "Take Me to the River" (1975), "I Only Have Love" (1975), and "Star Bright Star Lite" (1976). His output on the label was of a consistently higher quality than his Twinight work. In most respects, the Hi material possessed better melodies, had more rhythmic punch, and were just better produced. But despite this, the Twinight songs had great qualities that should not be overlooked. The occasional looseness of the production allowed Johnson to sing with more abandon and funkiness. The records were grittier and funkier, and whereas the Hi records evoked the spirit of a well-meshed studio system, the Twinight records seemed to recall more of the spirit of life. They sounded like they came out of the mean urban streets of Chicago. Johnson felt that his best work was on his Twinight records.[51]

Twinight closed its doors in 1972, but Bedno and Wright continued in the music business as independent promotion men, and during the latter part of the decade they published a highly respected tip sheet. Wright continued to do independent productions for years afterward, but in the 1980s he was in the advertising business. Bedno, ever the record man, stayed a full-time promotion man.

Shama Records

Shama was Syl Johnson's personal label that he operated out of his home at 6843 South Aberdeen. But the company was in business while Johnson was working at the 2131 South Michigan building for Twinight, and much Shama woodshedding was done at that location.[52] Johnson worked with artists who didn't interest Twinight, mainly Simtec and Wylie, Lee "Shot" Williams, and Nolan Struck. Johnson produced the acts with the help of Twinight creative people, namely Carl Smith, John Zachary, Johnny Cameron, Jimmy Jones, the Deacons, and the Pieces of Peace.

Shama was started in 1968 with independent distribution and achieved some national success with distribution by Atlantic Records in 1970. The label's only hitmakers were the Deacons, who had an instrumental hit of Johnson's "Sock It to Me" in late 1968, and Simtec and Wylie, who scored with "Do It Like Mama" in 1970.

Simtec and Wylie had their origin in two 1960s groups—Wylie Dixon and the Wheels, a vocal group under the musical direction of Bobby Pointer, and the Tea Boxes band led by guitarist Simtec Simmons.[53] The two aggregations came together in 1967.

Wylie Dixon and the Wheels came out of gospel music. Lead singer Dixon was born March 19, 1936, in Columbus, Mississippi, and moved to Chicago in 1957. Dixon early on was heavily involved in gospel quartet singing and even for a time sang in the famed Highway QC's. He was in a quartet called the Traveling Kings when Pointer met him in the early 1960s. Pointer was born in Hayti, Missouri, in 1945, and moved to Chicago when he was eight years old. He attended Englewood High and by the time he had graduated was in the gospel field. In 1963 Pointer (guitar and alto vocals) then left gospel music to get together with Dixon (baritone lead) and James Carr (high tenor) to form Wylie Dixon and the Wheels.

The group's first recording session was with Federal Records, and the disc the group released was "Uncle Willie's Got a Thing Going On," one of the numerous failed Uncle Willie records put out by local acts to capitalize from the Uncle Willie craze of early 1964. In the next two years the Wheels came out with various releases on small Chicago labels that did nothing. By 1966 the Wheels were evolving into Simtec and Wylie.

Simtec Simmons, whose given name was Walter, was born in Chicago, December 19, 1944, and grew up on the South Side, attending Bowen High. While going to Loop Junior College he formed the Tea Boxes band around 1964. Within two years Simmons and his brother Ronald on bass were working with the Wheels. "We joined up with Dixon in the club," said Simmons, "to become Wylie Dixon and the Tea Boxes Revue. I would open the show and then Wylie would follow. We started traveling with Sonny Thompson. He was our manager and would get the Tea Boxes to back various singers. We grew from five to seven pieces with the addition of horns."[54]

In 1967 Simmons hooked up with Maurice Jackson and began recording for his Maurci label. His first record, the instrumental "Tea Box," became a popular hit throughout the Midwest. Several other records by Simmons on Maurci failed, so by 1969 Simmons and the Tea Boxes were still a nightclub act working largely with Wylie Dixon. The nightclub act, however, served as a catalyst for Simmons and Wylie to record together as a duo, and that began with a recording contract with Toddlin' Town. The records they did for the company, alas, were dismal.

The duo's fortunes turned around when they joined Shama in 1969. In November, they hit with "Do It Like Mama," which entered *Billboard's* national r&b chart early in 1970. With sharp brassy horns, a driving funk beat propelled by Fred White's drumming, and the wailing vocals of Simtec and Wylie, this self-produced record is a perfect example of funk that has a whole lot of soul. "Put an Extra Plus to Your Heart," in 1970, followed the same aggressive formula, but did not earn a whole lot of sales.

"Those records on Shama," said Simmons, "got us our first national recognition. Syl was at Twinight at the time, but he used to work at the old King studio. We used to write and practice with Syl at the studio, and when we came up with material, he just decided to record us. We established our sound with those records. We had a new drumbeat that Fred had come up with—two backbeats. He changed the beat around in it to follow the dancers, and the musicians then expanded on it. Then I sat down to write lyrics to it and then the brothers and I began scientifically writing songs to that particular beat."⁵⁵ In 1970 Simtec and Wylie left Johnson to record for Gene Chandler.

The career of Lee "Shot" Williams was similar to a dozen or so hard-soul singers who plied their trade in Chicago. His gravelly tenor voice was perfect for the type of songs he did, but not distinctive enough to separate him from others recording in the style.⁵⁶ His association with Shama was typical of his records, some of which occasionally got good play in Chicago.

Williams was born in 1938, in Lexington, Mississippi. When he was in his teens he moved to Chicago, and there he became involved in the city's thriving blues scene, working with such artists as harmonica player Little Mack and guitarist Earl Hooker. In 1962 while fronting the Hooker band he made "Hello Baby," his first record for deejay Richard Stamz's Foxy label.

During 1963–64, Williams came out with four sides on the Federal label, a mixture of blues and hard soul produced by Sonny Thompson. A particularly fine side was a cover of Freddy King's "I'm Tore Up," but as with most Federal sides from this period it did not sell. After King left Chicago in 1964, Williams bounced from small label to small label without success.

The year 1969 found him on Syl Johnson's Shama label. He came out with two releases. The first, "I Like Your Style," had a funkier and lighter touch than his earlier projects, and it got a lot of play on Chicago radio. The follow-up, "Get Some Order," was pretty awful and did not go anywhere.

During the late 1970s Williams's recording activities dwindled to nothing, but during the early 1980s they picked up enough for him to have five releases from 1980 to 1984 on various small labels.

Nolan Struck had one of the most fascinating tenors ever put on record. It had an eerie, sensual quality that brought a depth of expression to blues and hard soul. The shame is that he recorded too few records and too few quality records worthy of his talent. One of his less than sterling efforts was recorded for Shama in 1968. But Struck was long active on the city's club circuit, where he was put on many a bill to open for the top blues and soul acts. His immensely entertaining show reflected an old black tradition of having someone first come on to loosen up the audience before the star came on. He was not just put on as filler; he served a definite purpose. Struck was especially suited for this job because he was broadly talented as a singer, dancer, and clown. In the eccentric dance tradition that went back to Earl "Snake Hips" Tucker in the 1930s, Struck entertained with hilarious rubbery movements that were as flexible as his vocal gymnastics.

Struck was a product of the city's blues field. He was born Nolton Antoine, on June 16, 1940, in Duson, Louisiana. His family was filled with entertainers, and he had four brothers—Fulton, Sterling, Wilburt, and Edward (King Edward)—who all played guitar or bass. Antoine began as a professional dancer, and his singing career started after he won a dance contest in Port Arthur, Texas. Bluesman Lonnie "Guitar Junior" Brooks was so impressed by his performance that he added Antoine to his band, teaching him to play bass. Antoine played in Brooks's band for eight years, first in Texas and Louisiana, then in Chicago after the band moved to the city in 1959. Antoine in Chicago played bass for Tyrone Davis, Denise LaSalle, Otis Clay, and appeared on many sessions at One-derful.[57]

Around 1967 Antoine got on record as Little Nolan and the Soul Brothers with "My Baby Confuses Me" on Bill Tyson's Ty-doo label. The following year, recording for the first time as Nolan Struck, he did two sides for Shama—"Too Many Irons in the Fire"/"Anyone But You." The A side, unfortunately, was undistinguished funky hard soul, but the flip was a highly appealing funky ballad.

The next time on record for Struck was in 1973, when he recorded "Welfare Problems" and "She's the One that Hits the Spot" for Tyson's ICT label. Both ranked as the best recordings Struck had ever done. In the late 1970s Struck was in the South recording for a label in Jackson, Mississippi, with little success.

After Johnson moved to Hi in 1971, he closed down his Shama operation for several years. He revived it for a while in the late seventies and early eighties, putting out records on himself and others, notably his fine hit "Ms. Fine Brown Frame" in 1982. By the mid-1980s Johnson was basically semiretired from the music business. He opened a string of fast-food fish restaurants and made occasional gigs at blues clubs. As the city's record industry went into decline during the 1970s, Chicago's other hard-soul singers were forced to adapt as Johnson had by entering other employment fields. Some sustained their names through forays into the blues clubs and by putting out records on their own labels.

NOTES

1. Arnold Shaw, "Record Company in an Icehouse," in *Honkers and Shouters: The Golden Years of Rhythm and Blues* (New York: Macmillan, 1978), pp. 275–89; Steve Tracy, "King of the Blues, Part 1, *Blues Unlimited* 87: 4–8; idem, Part 2, *Blues Unlimited* 88: 7–10; idem, Part 3, *Blues Unlimited* 89: 8–10. These are general histories of the label with few specifics on the Chicago operation.

2. Tony Burke and Dave Penny, "Screaming Boogie," *Blues and Rhythm: The Gospel Truth* 37 (June-July 1988): 9–14; Robert Pruter, "Sonny Thompson, R&B Bandleader and Pianist, Dies, Age 72," *Goldmine,* October 20, 1989, p. 5; Catherine Hayes Thompson interview.

3. Robert Pruter, "Jack Daniels and the Four Brothers/Bright Star Story," *Juke Blues* 14 (Winter 1988/89): 8–13; Jack Daniels interviews.

4. Daniels interview, October 15, 1987.

5. Daniels interview, October 5, 1987.

6. Ibid.

7. Robert Pruter, "G. L. Crockett: It's a Man Down There," *Goldmine,* April 8, 1988, p. 16.

8. Daniels interview, October 15, 1987.

9. Dick Shurman, liner notes, Andrew Brown, *Big Brown's Chicago Blues,* Black Magic 9001, 1982.

10. Daniels interview, October 5, 1987.

11. Ibid.

12. Bill Dahl, "Johnny Moore: Turning Back the Hands of Time," *Goldmine,* October 9, 1987, pp. 24, 88; Johnny Moore interview.

13. The birthdate is subject to some dispute. Wells may have been born in 1932, or even earlier, as some blues researchers have speculated.

14. Bob Koester, "Junior Wells: Eighteen Years at Forty-eighth and Indiana," *Come For to Sing* 2, no. 3 (Summer 1976): 5–9; Neil Slaven, liner notes, Junior Wells, *Messin' with the Kid,* Charly R&B CRB 1133, 1986.

15. Daniels interview, October 5, 1987.

16. Neil Paterson, "Ricky Allen," *Nothing But the Blues,* ed. Mike Leadbitter (London: Hanover Books, 1971), p. 92.

17. Ibid.

18. Daniels interview, October 5, 1987.

19. Robert Pruter, "Tyrone Davis," *Goldmine,* December 1980, pp. 23–25. This is the most extensive treatment of Davis's early years.

20. John Abbey, "Tyrone Davis: They Changed Their Mind About 'Change My Mind,'" *Blues and Soul,* June 19-July 1, 1970, p. 10.

21. Jim O'Neal, "Living Blues Interview: Billy 'The Kid' Emerson," *Living Blues* 45/56 (Spring 1980): 25–48.

22. Robert Pruter, "Roscoe Robinson: One More Time...," *Goldmine,* February 27, 1987, pp. 79, 82. This article and this section are largely based on an unpublished interview with Robinson by gospel researcher Ray Funk.

23. David Nathan, "Darrow Fletcher: Trying Something New," *Blues and Soul,* December 23, 1975, p. 8; Robert Pruter, "Darrow Fletcher," *Goldmine,* August 1981, p. 144; Johnny Haygood interview; Maurice Simpkins interview.

24. Haygood interview.

25. Nathan, "Darrow Fletcher."

26. Haygood interview. His figure sounds improbable, but the point is valid that it sold a lot of copies in Chicago.

27. Private papers of Bob Lee, Chicago; Bob Lee interview; Sherman Nesbary interview.

28. Lee interview.

29. Archie Russell interview.

30. Few of the many feature articles on the Emotions cover much of their Chicago recording career. The following provide the most extensive treatments:

Geoff Brown, "Kalimba Kuties," *Black Music,* March 1978, pp. 22–25; Alan D. Elsey, "Make Up for Lost Time—A Look at the Emotions," *Hot Buttered Soul* 39 (1975): 5–6.

31. Dave Hoekstra, "Cicero Blake Takes Soul to Country," *Chicago Sun-Times,* October 17, 1986; Robert Pruter, "The Cicero Blake Story," *Goldmine,* October 1981, p. 189; Blake interviews.

32. Dave Hoekstra, "Upbeat Performance Fuels 'Muddy Waters,'" *Chicago Sun-Times,* November 15, 1984.

33. Lon Grahnke, "'Mojo' Works for 'Muddy Waters,' " *Chicago Sun-Times,* November 12, 1984; Sid Smith, "Music—And Not This Play's Script—Tells the Real Story of Otis Redding," *Chicago Tribune,* September 24, 1987.

34. Bob Stallworth, "The Gems and the Drexel Label," *Yesterday's Memories* 6 (1976): 9–10; Don Clay interview; R. C. Robinson interview.

35. Robinson interview.

36. Earl Paige, "Azie Mortimer's Wide Range, Phrasing Audience Grabber," *Billboard,* April 26, 1969, p. 12.

37. Galen Gart, *ARLD: The American Record Label Directory and Dating Guide, 1940–1959* (Milford, N.H.: Big Nickel, 1989), p. 8; Bruce Heather, letter to the author, March 1, 1989.

38. Eddie Sullivan, "Bobby Jones—A Chicago Superstar, *After 5,* May/June, 1982, pp. 38–40; "Bobby Jones Singer Extraordinare [*sic*] Coming on Again," *Chicago Metro News,* March 21, 1981.

39. "Singer Extraordinare."

40. Steve Wisner, comment to the author, January 18, 1987.

41. Howard Bedno interview; Syl Johnson interviews; Wright interview.

42. Bedno interview.

43. Wright interview.

44. Johnson interview, April 14, 1983.

45. Indicative of Johnson's lack of impact, there have been few serious articles on his career: Tony Cummings, "Different Strokes," *Black Music,* June 1974, p. 47; Michael Haralambos, "Syl Johnson Interview," *Hot Buttered Soul* 38 (1975): 2–7; Robert Pruter, "The Syl Johnson Story," *Goldmine,* October 1983, pp. 68–76.

46. Haralambos, "Syl Johnson," p. 2. Johnson also has given 1939 and 1944 as the years of his birth. Both dates seem unlikely and were given by Johnson to interviewers in an obvious attempt to appear younger.

47. Johnson interview, April 14, 1983.

48. Ibid.

49. Ibid.

50. Haralambos, "Syl Johnson," p. 6.

51. Johnson interview, April 14, 1983.

52. Johnson interview, February 25, 1988.

53. John Abbey, "Introducing Simtec and Wylie," *Blues and Soul,* Sept. 24–Nov. 7, 1971, p. 6; Robert Pruter, "Simtec and Wylie," *Soul Survivor* 9 (Summer 1988): 24–26; Bobby Pointer interview; Walter "Simtec" Simmons interview.

54. Simmons interview.

55. Ibid.

56. Bill Dahl, "Lee Shot Williams: Chicago's Bluesy Soul Man," *Goldmine,* December 2, 1988, pp. 30, 87; Dick Shurman, "Feel Like a Millionaire, I Haven't Got a Dime," *Blues Unlimited* 114 (July/August 1975): 16–17.

57. Jim O'Neal, "Nolan Struck," in untitled program for the "American Blues Legend 1979 Tour," [1979]; Robert Pruter, "Nolan Struck: My Nerve's Gone Bad," *Goldmine,* August 12, 1988, pp. 69, 79.

11

Brunswick Records

The story of Chicago soul in the 1970s was substantially that of Carl Davis and his productions at Brunswick and its sister label, Dakar. Vee Jay, One-derful, and many other companies were gone by the opening of the decade, and Chess Records began running out of gas rapidly after Leonard Chess died in 1969. Brunswick started as a New York-based subsidiary of Decca Records (now MCA) in 1957. The label revived the Brunswick name, which was a long-time popular logo, especially in the late 1920s and 1930s.

During the late fifties and early sixties, Brunswick survived on an endless stream of hits by the great rhythm-and-blues performer Jackie Wilson. In 1966, however, the label hired Davis as A&R director. The company's vice president, Nat Tarnopol, split Brunswick from Decca in 1970, and the stage was set for making Brunswick one of the most successful independent r&b companies of the 1970s. With such artists as the Chi-lites, Tyrone Davis, Gene Chandler, and Barbara Acklin, the company sustained Chicago as a center of black popular music.[1]

Nat Tarnopol was born January 26, 1931, in Detroit, where he was raised. He entered the music business in 1956, when in partnership with Al Green he opened an artist-management firm. Among its clients were LaVern Baker and Jackie Wilson. Green died in 1957 and Tarnopol inherited the business.[2] As a condition for renewing Jackie Wilson's contract with Brunswick in 1964, Tarnopol received half the label.[3]

The key to Brunswick's success, of course, was Carl Davis. When he was forced out of OKeh near the end of 1965, he had not burned his bridges with the music industry. With Irv Nahan he still owned Jalynne Publishing and he used that as a basis for setting up an independent production operation. Said Davis, "We opened up some offices on Roosevelt Road [58

East Roosevelt, around the corner from Michigan Avenue] and we started working out of there more or less as a production company, a publishing company, and a management company—because I was still managing Gene Chandler, Major Lance, Walter Jackson, and all those different acts."[4]

The operation became a beehive of activity in which the Chicago sound would continue to thrive. "I brought with me Otis Leavill, Gerald Sims, Billy Butler, Sonny Sanders, and a lot of musicians from OKeh," related Davis. "We went out and bought lumber and partitioned off the space and made offices, and turned it into our own little studio. So we used to do what we called woodshedding. Sit down every day and come up with new songs, write new songs, and keep woodshedding until you find something that was good."[5]

Davis's association with Brunswick came when the company was at low ebb and its one star, Jackie Wilson, had not been selling records for some time. Said Davis, "In August of 1966 I went to a disc jockey convention in New York and that's when I met Nat Tarnopol relative to doing a production on Jackie Wilson. That's what we started off with, just a production deal between my company and Brunswick. And then after we did 'Whispers' and the record was a huge success, then that's when Nat offered to bring me on as a staff person."[6] Davis was made A&R director in October. In the February 1967 auction of Vee Jay's assets Davis bought most of the contents of the 1449 Michigan Avenue building, and he moved in four to six weeks later.

At the time Davis came on board, Len Schneider, a veteran of the record business since the 1920s, was president of Brunswick. Tarnopol was vice president. The label was distributed through Decca's Coral subsidiary. Dick Jacobs, who worked as arranger and orchestra director for Coral/Brunswick, said about the situation, "Whatever the title, Nat was running the company."[7] Davis reported to Tarnopol.[8]

Tarnopol bought the remaining half of Brunswick in 1970. Said Jacobs, "There were very big arguments between Nat Tarnopol and Marty Salkin, who was in charge of the whole A&R department of Decca-Coral-Brunswick. Nat made up his mind he wanted to get out. He either wanted to sell his half of Brunswick or he wanted to buy the whole thing. And he went to California and had a meeting with Lew Wasserman, who was the president of MCA, which owned Decca. Basically he gave Nat the whole company. I think he was causing them too much aggravation. He was making too many demands as far as advertising, publicity, and things like that. Wasserman wanted him out; they were getting rid of a headache."[9]

Tarnopol made himself president and Davis executive vice president of the independent Brunswick. Davis had been given 10 percent of Tarnopol's

50 percent when he was hired in 1966, and now his percentage was doubled when it became 10 percent of 100 percent.[10]

Davis within months after assuming his A&R duties at Brunswick signed and recorded a load of new acts to the label, namely the Young-Holt Trio, the Artistics, Billy Butler, Barbara Acklin, and Gene Chandler. The hits began to flow and Brunswick was flourishing again. In 1967 Davis started a new label, Dakar, on which he recorded Major Lance (briefly), Otis Leavill, and Tyrone Davis, among others. Dakar was at first wholly owned by Davis but soon became a subsidiary label of Brunswick. It was independently distributed through a different group of distributors. However, Tyrone Davis's "Can I Change My Mind," an early release on the label, in late 1968, proved to be a monster hit and Carl Davis felt the need to secure a distribution pact with Atlantic Records for Dakar. With distribution by a major label, Tyrone Davis became one of the biggest hitmakers from Chicago. In December 1971 Dakar's promotion and distribution was taken over by Brunswick.[11]

Why did Davis launch Dakar when he had already developed a successful operation at Brunswick? Explained Davis, "I wanted to hire our musicians, put them on staff, give them a weekly salary, and give them a chance to make some extra money. The only way we could do it was to work out a thing where they could do sessions for this new label, and if it could earn enough money then I would put them on weekly salaries. Plus, whenever we did a session they would get scale."[12]

Many of the musicians Davis used at Brunswick/Dakar were those that he regularly employed at OKeh. Phil Upchurch, John Bishop, Danny Leake, and Byron Gregory were the most frequently used on guitar. Bernard Reed was invariably on bass, and Quinton Joseph was on drums. Keyboards were Tennyson Stephens (a recording artist in his own right) and Floyd Morris, and on vibes was Bobby Christian. The brass included John Avant and Morris Ellis on trombone, Maury Watson and Lionel Bordelon on trumpet, and Willie Henderson, Cliff Davis, and Steele Seals on saxes.

By the 1970s, strings were playing an ever larger role in making soul records. Even on records with a somewhat downhome earthy sound, as on Tyrone Davis releases, strings were invariably employed. At the Chicago companies that specialized in soul, strings came from outside and were provided by a string contractor, who more often than not was Sol Bobrov. He played in the symphony orchestra in Kansas City in the late 1930s. In the 1940s he worked for orchestras at NBC and then ABC radio. Late in the decade he began contracting strings for recording sessions and in 1953 he left ABC and went into recording full time. During the 1960s Bobrov regularly contracted strings for Chess, OKeh, Vee Jay, and other Chicago r&b labels. Related Bobrov, "I would be told by the arranger how many strings he wanted and what the ratio as to instruments was—violins, violas, cellos, string basses. Then I would get them and would get the type of men who could cut that kind of stuff."[13] The two mainstays in the string sections on Chicago soul records were violinists Bobrov and Elliot Golub.

Most of the writers at Brunswick came from the group of artists the company recorded. Eugene Record wrote for his own group, the Chi-lites. The Lost Generation and the Artistics both wrote their own songs, and Barbara Acklin wrote a lot herself. Also, the company's producers—Carl Davis, Willie Henderson, Leo Graham, Otis Leavill, and Richard Parker—contributed many songs, especially for Tyrone Davis.

The arrangers Davis hired for Brunswick were the best in the city's r&b industry, namely Sonny Sanders, Tom Washington, Willie Henderson, and James Mack. During Davis's first few years at Brunswick the company also had an orchestra director, a position first held by Gerald Sims and later by Willie Henderson. Sonny Sanders was from Detroit and after arranging some hits for the Ric Tic label there he moved to Chicago and joined Davis during his last months at OKeh. Tom Washington was Brunswick's principal arranger. He grew up in one of the worst sections on the South Side and was raised in the Ida B. Wells projects. He first played drums, then keyboards, and became an arranger after receiving formal music training from James Mack at Crane Junior College.

Like Washington, Henderson studied with James Mack at Crane. In 1968 he joined Brunswick as an arranger, but after he established himself as an ace producer, he left much of the arranging work to Washington. Henderson's very first arranging and producing effort, "Can I Change My Mind" by Tyrone Davis, sold a million and a half copies, and subsequently he was responsible for a good portion of the singer's recordings. He occasionally recorded instrumentals on the studio band under the name Willie Henderson and the Soul Explosions. The ensemble had a minor chart hit in 1970 with "Funky Chicken."

James Mack was brought to Brunswick by his former pupil, Henderson. Mack was classically trained, having earned a master's degree in composition and theory from Roosevelt University. His first teaching job was at Crane. Most of his arranging work at Brunswick was for Tyrone Davis, and when another of his former students, Leo Graham, became the singer's producer almost exclusively sometime after 1973, Mack became the artist's principal arranger.

Jackie Wilson

When Jackie Wilson came to Davis he was the biggest r&b star Davis had ever worked with, having been a major artist during the late fifties and early sixties. Wilson was born in Detroit on June 9, 1934. His early enthusiasm was boxing, and in 1950 he won the Detroit Golden Gloves. During the early fifties he struggled to pursue a solo singing career in the Detroit area. In 1953 he was discovered by Billy Ward, who recruited him to replace the departing Clyde McPhatter as lead of his vocal group, the Dominoes, one of the big r&b acts of the day. Finding a career in a group too restrictive, Wilson used one of the few hits by the Dominoes under his lead, "St. Therese of the Roses" (1956), as a springboard to strike out on his own.[14]

Wilson again was making the circuit of Detroit nightclubs, and in one such club, the Flame Show Lounge, he was discovered by Al Green, who owned the hatcheck concession at the lounge and who managed the careers of LaVern Baker and Johnnie Ray. Green became Wilson's manager and got him signed to Brunswick in 1957. He teamed Wilson up with a hot new songwriting pair from the city, Berry Gordy and Tyran Carlo (aka Billy Davis). The recordings were made in New York with backing by the Dick Jacobs Orchestra. Brunswick used rather pop-like melodramatic arrangements by Jacobs (and sometimes by Milton DeLugg) for Wilson's records, but the result was an almost ceaseless string of top-notch songs that made Wilson one of black music's biggest hitmakers from 1957 through 1963.

Live, Wilson was a great showman, performing splits, spins, and great dancing movements that matched his full-range flamboyant singing. "He was dynamite," Davis related to journalist Dave Hoekstra in 1984. "You almost had to ask the man to come off the stage. He was perpetual motion. He would dance, skip across the stage, hit all the notes and dress well. I felt for him like I feel for Michael Jackson."[15]

Wilson made the Brunswick operation virtually a one-artist label. When Green died, Tarnopol took over management of Wilson's career. But as the artist's hitmaking abilities soured during 1964-65 so did the fortunes of Brunswick. Tarnopol made the wisest move of his career by developing an alliance with Carl Davis. Davis told Hoekstra, "When I began working with Jackie he was disenchanted with his management company because he wasn't getting the kind of material he wanted to do. I found him a beautiful person to work with, and he had a great deal of confidence in me. If he came into Chicago and I wasn't there, he wouldn't work until I got there. He knew what I was trying to do."[16]

With his career revived by "Whispers," Wilson managed to stay high on the charts for the next four years. In 1967 he got a two-million seller with "(Your Love Keeps Lifting Me) Higher and Higher." Recalled Davis, "[Wilson] came to town to sing 'Higher and Higher,' and he started singing it like a soul ballad. I said that's totally wrong. You have to jump and go along with the percussion. I would tell him that if he didn't want to sing it that way, I would put *my* voice on the record and sell millions of records."[17]

Davis got "Higher and Higher" from two young songwriters, Gary Jackson and Carl Smith, who had just come down the street from Chess Records. Shortly after the release of the record, the blind Chess songwriter Raynard Miner heard the song on the radio, and had a fit after discovering the writers' credits on the song. Miner had written the song with Billy Davis, and he asserted that Smith and Jackson took the tune out of his briefcase one day when he was in the studio. They changed the lyrics a bit and took it to Davis as a tune for Wilson to record. Billy Davis and Miner waited until the record hit number ten and then they sued; they won 80 percent of the song, leaving Smith and Jackson with 20 percent.[18]

Wilson had some other outstanding hits, notably "I Don't Want to Lose You" (number eleven on the *Billboard* r&b chart in 1967) and "I Get the Sweetest Feeling" (number twelve on the soul chart in 1968). During the early 1970s, however, Davis failed to come up with consistently strong songs for Wilson, and he faded as a contemporary artist. In his last years on the label he was playing the oldies circuit regularly, sustaining his career on past glories. On September 29, 1975, he suffered a severe heart attack while performing in Cherry Hill, New Jersey, on a Dick Clark oldies review. Wilson was left in a coma and came out of it with severe brain damage that left him unable to walk, speak, feed himself, or perform any essential functions. After spending years in nursing homes he died in 1984.

Gene Chandler

Gene Chander's previous label was Constellation Records, and when the label folded in late 1966 Ewart Abner sold Chandler's contract to Chess Records. Chess began releasing his records on its Checker subsidiary. But a conflict developed because Chandler also signed with Brunswick in early 1967. Tarnopol and Leonard Chess reportedly then agreed to alternate Chandler's releases to avoid fighting each other and cutting into each other's sales. Davis produced the records for both companies. It was a virtually unprecedented arrangement that settled some Byzantine intrigues surrounding the artist's contract situation.[19]

The first release for Chandler was on Checker. "I Fooled You This Time" was a splendid ballad that came out prior to the Brunswick/Chess deal. The record lasted fourteen weeks and went to position three after entering *Billboard*'s r&b chart in November 1966.

In February 1967 Chandler hit with his first Brunswick release, "The Girl Don't Care," a compelling ballad that lasted nine weeks and went to position sixteen. The song was written by Chandler and Keni Lewis, the team that would write much of the singer's Brunswick output. In April, Chandler quickly followed on Checker with "To Be a Lover," a riveting Karl Tarlton ballad that lasted ten weeks and went to number nine on *Billboard*'s r&b chart. Brunswick followed with the up-tempo "There Goes the Lover" in September, which entered the r&b chart for two weeks. As true of many Chandler singles, it had a great flip, the secular remake of James Cleveland's gospel classic "Tell Me What I Can Do." Listening to Chandler use his melismatic and other vocal gifts on the song, one can appreciate that this Chicago singer was one of the best soul stylists of the sixties.

Checker came out with "River of Tears," a ballad composed by Eugene Record, in the summer of 1968 and it did a respectable ten weeks on *Billboard*'s r&b chart. Chandler got his last hit on Brunswick with a rapid-fire cover of James Brown's "There Was a Time," in September 1968, which was a big departure from Chandler's usual fare.

With no hits and with sales lagging in 1969, Chandler decided some changes were needed. He joined Mercury Records in 1970. Said he, "I had felt like Carl and I were not clicking as we had been in the past. So I wanted to produce myself. Nat Tarnopol wouldn't allow me to produce myself. He said Carl and I should stay together. Carl and I had some differences of opinions so I decided to go out and try it on my own. So I asked for my release. They wouldn't give it to me at first, but eventually after six months they gave it to me. Because it wouldn't do any good to take me into the studio because I wouldn't feel all right about the company and I wouldn't have performed my best. So I went into the Mercury deal."[20] Chandler would eventually team up with Davis again in another company in the late 1970s.

Barbara Acklin

Barbara Acklin typified the light pop-soul kind of soprano singer that was immensely popular in the 1960s and early 1970s. She contributed in no small part to developing Chicago's reputation for the soprano sound, with seventeen singles and six albums to her credit. Acklin was born in Chicago, February 28, 1943. Like many r&b singers she got her start in the church, at Big Zion Baptist Church (521 West 66th Place). There at the age of eleven she emerged as a featured vocalist in the choir.[21]

While still a student at Dunbar Vocational High on the South Side, at about seventeen, Acklin began performing secular songs in local clubs. After graduating from school, she got a job as a part-time secretary with St. Lawrence Records where her cousin Monk Higgins was a producer. He recorded her on one single on his Special Agent label under the name of

Barbara Allen, but it achieved nothing. When Higgins moved to Chess in early 1967, he called upon Acklin whenever he needed some background vocals.

In 1966 Acklin joined Carl Davis's independent operation as a secretary-receptionist and songwriter. Her break into the recording end was not long in coming. Said she, "I had kept asking Carl to record, and he kept saying, 'I will, I will, just keep writing.' I wrote a tune with another person called 'Whispers,' and Jackie Wilson heard the tune and really liked it. He recorded it and after it became a big hit for him, he told me, 'If there is anything I can do, you let me know.' I said, 'You tell Carl I want to record!' Jackie asked, 'Can you sing?' He didn't know that. I said, 'A little bit,' and he took me into the back and listened. About three weeks later I was in the studio."[22]

Acklin's first solo records, released in 1967, did nothing, but then she teamed up with Gene Chandler. "It was Gene's idea," said Acklin. "He heard me singing and thought that I had a pretty good voice. The first record, 'Show Me the Way to Go,' did so-so, but the second one, 'From the Teacher to the Preacher,' did really well. So Gene took me on the road with him and gave me five hundred dollars a night to sing one song."[23] "From the Teacher to the Preacher" did exceedingly well, lasting eleven weeks on *Billboard*'s r&b chart and going as high as position sixteen in the fall of 1968.

The big record for Acklin was "Love Makes a Woman," which made it to number three in July 1968 and lasted fifteen weeks on the r&b chart. The song had all the ingredients for a hit: a catchy hook, a forceful drive, a good sax break, and some outstanding vocalizing from Acklin. The song demonstrated Davis's studio system at its finest. The worth of the song was confirmed in the years that followed when it was covered both in the country and the rock markets, most notably by Phoebe Snow.

"Just Ain't Enough Love" was another catchy up-tempo record, and as a follow-up to "Love Makes a Woman" it was perfect. The song lasted eight weeks on the r&b chart and went as high as position twenty-three, ranking as the second-most successful single of Acklin's career.

"Am I the Same Girl," released in early 1969, was something of a sore point with Acklin. Its instrumental backing served to provide Young-Holt Unlimited a hit with "Soulful Strut." Said she, "I had originally recorded the record and they took my voice off and added a piano. Most people do not know that. I was pretty ticked off about that, but you know that's what happens. Of course the earlier release of 'Soulful Strut' completely undercut the success of 'Am I the Same Girl.' They told me mine did better overseas than it did in the United States."[24]

Throughout Acklin's Brunswick association she worked with Eugene Record in many fine collaborations. Mostly Acklin was the lyricist while Record was the tunesmith. "Lots of times I came up with melodies," said she, "but most of the time it was Eugene. Carl used to tell Eugene and I that we tended to write seven years ahead of ourselves. He said we were too deep. He wanted stuff more commerical. I wanted stuff that was more pop and he wanted a more r&b-type thing."[25]

The year 1970 saw the release of the perky "I Did It," which made *Billboard*'s soul chart in October, but with modest numbers, five weeks and position twenty-eight. Acklin entered the soul chart twice more for Brunswick, but with even more undistinguished numbers, "Lady Lady Lady" (position forty-four in 1971) and "I'll Bake Me a Man" (position forty-nine in 1972). She left Brunswick in 1973, and in 1974 got a big hit on Capitol Records, "Raindrops," a Willie Henderson production. In subsequent years, however, she failed to return to the charts.

Otis Leavill

Otis Leavill was best remembered for his up-tempo falsetto hits "I Love You" and "Love Uprising" on Dakar. His role, however, was more far-reaching than indicated by his modest recording career. His contribution was often behind the scenes, in discovering acts, administering, producing, and composing. Where there was Major Lance, the Artistics, Gene Chandler, or Carl Davis, Otis Leavill was sure to be around.[26]

Born Otis Leavill Cobb on February 8, 1941, in Atlanta, Georgia, he was the eldest of seven children of Clarence and Ruby Cobb. When he was about two years of age his family moved to Chicago. Leavill grew up on the rugged West Side and there developed a boyhood friendship with Major Lance. With Lance, he attended McKinley Upper Grade Center and Crane High. When Lance moved to the near North Side in the Cabrini-Green projects, Otis took to hanging out with him at Seward Park. Leavill soon found himself associating with Curtis Mayfield, Jerry Butler, and Billy Butler. A compact, solidly built man, he also boxed along with Lance.

The first singing Leavill did was in church with a family gospel group, the Cobb Quartet. Despite a family prohibition against secular music Leavill eventually found himself drawn to the burgeoning r&b scene in the city. He organized and sang with a group call the Floats, whose other members consisted of Major Lance, Barbara Tyson, and another girl whose name Leavill cannot recall. After a while, he and Lance paired off from the group to form a duo to work dances, shows, and the Jim Lounsbury teen dance show on local television.

Leavill's break into the music business as a recording act was a little slow going. He recounted:

> I think I sat in front of the Vee Jay building for two years trying to get in as an artist. One of the reasons why I finally made it was because I wrote a song called "I'm a Soldier Boy," which Dee Clark recorded. I just sent the tape in. They liked the voice, but they just didn't have time to look at new artists. But at Vee Jay I met Doc Oliver, who was writing for Vee Jay. He was also working for Arthur Grant and he and Grant decided to record me on their Lucky label.
>
> My first record was "I Got a Right to Cry" and "Rise Sally Rise." I think "Rise Sally Rise" was really the A side. I got a lot of pop play on it. I think even WLS played it. I got a lot of work on that record.[27]

Although "I Got a Right to Cry" was a fine early Mayfield composition, the company decided to push "Rise Sally Rise" because it was a dance side with a familiar theme taken from a nursery rhyme, "Little Sally Walker." The song got Leavill good notices upon its release in 1963, but Leavill was not entirely happy, confessing, "really to be very honest, I hated the record. . . . ooh, I hated it. I hate to bring it up, because, listen, it just turns me off. It was something they wanted to go with."[28]

During 1964, Leavill did two more records for Grant and Oliver, and both appeared on Mercury's Limelight label. One of them, "I'm Amazed," did well in the Washington-Baltimore area, but nowhere else. Lance was then riding the success of one million seller after another and Leavill had the opportunity to tour with him on Dick Clark's Caravan of Stars, which also included Gene Pitney, Brian Hyland, the Supremes, Shirley Ellis, and Fabian. They did sixty-five dates in seventy-two days, but Leavill did not perform every show, because his principal role was that of Lance's road manager. Leavill also co-wrote a number of B sides on some of Lance's earlier records, most notably "Sweet Music," the superb flip to "Um Um Um Um Um Um."

In the winter of 1964/65, Leavill established his reputation with the classic "Let Her Love Me," an incredibly beautiful Billy Butler composition. Produced by Lance, the song typified the Chicago brand of subtle soft soul. It became a number-one hit on WVON, but only went as high as thirty-one on *Billboard's* r&b chart. On the strength of the song, which was released on Mercury's Blue Rock subsidiary label, Leavill with Lance played the Regal in March 1965. Later, he would perform in the theaters on the entire chitlin' circuit.

In the spring, Leavill followed up with another Butler-penned tune, "To Be or Not to Be." It never charted nationally, but Leavill said it was the kind of hit that sold a lot of records quietly over a long period of time. During much of the rest of the 1960s Leavill experienced a few lean years hit-wise, although he was recording consistently.

During the time of Lance's early successes on OKeh, Leavill was brought in by Carl Davis to be his right-hand man in administering the business and in managing the artists. When Davis moved to Brunswick, Leavill went with him. On Dakar, Leavill made a few records, mostly Eugene Record compositions. Usually, Leavill sang his songs in a normal tenor, but on his Dakar hits he chose to sing in a falsetto and the result was a voice uncannily similar to Record's lead on Chi-lites' records. "I Love You," which rose to number ten on *Billboard*'s soul chart in late 1969, was the biggest national hit of the singer's career. It was a peppy, up-tempo number that showcased his falsetto to perfection. The following year Leavill came out with the stunning "Love Uprising." It lasted eleven weeks on *Billboard*'s soul survey and went to position nineteen.

Leavill for the most part stopped recording after his last Dakar release in 1972. He continued to have hits though, in England, and throughout the 1970s he toured the Mother Country repeatedly. Most of his English hits were re-releases of old stateside hits. In 1976 Leavill left Brunswick/ Dakar with Carl Davis to set up Chi-Sound Records.

The Artistics

The Artistics—Marvin Smith, Larry Johnson, Aaron Floyd, Jesse Bolian— had much better success on Brunswick than on their earlier label, OKeh. Departing from their imitative Detroit style, the four wrote "I'm Gonna Miss You," a spectacular song thoroughly Chicagoan in its sound. Beginning in November 1966, the song stayed some four months on the national *Billboard* charts and became close to a million seller. The song quickly vaulted the Artistics into their second national tour, in which they hit just about every famous theater on the chitlin' circuit.

While the Artistics were peaking, they were also undergoing a rift. Marvin Smith was trying to establish himself as a single artist and had a pretty good hit going with "Time Stopped." After the initial tour of "I'm Gonna Miss You," he left the group to exploit the "Time Stopped" solo opportunities. Another compelling reason for his departure was suggested by Leavill: "Basically he just couldn't get along with the group. They never fought, but they were always arguing. It's kind of hard for anybody to stay in a group if you don't have the harmony going. There were several guys in the group who were leaders and that was the problem."[29] Added Gerald

Sims, "Marvin Smith always had a personality of his own. He would follow Gene Chandler around, and looking at Gene blew his mind. So he wanted to be lead all the time. His leaving the group destroyed everything we worked on with the group. But he had a great voice."[30]

Without hardly taking a breath, the Artistics found a replacement in Tommy Green, an old school chum from their Marshall days. Also formally added to the group at this time was bassist Bernard Reed, who helped the Artistics in developing their choreography. Although the loss of Smith meant the loss of their best songwriter, the group was able to score again with the second-best song of their career, "Girl I Need You." Like "I'm Gonna Miss You," the record demonstrated that Chicago was coming out with music that could rival that of any other music center in the country. Unfortunately for the Artistics, in subsequent years they could not come up with material good enough to keep them high on the charts.

The Artistics left Brunswick in disgust in 1973. "We asked for a release," said Johnson, "they wouldn't give it to us. So we refused to record anymore. Why should we go into the hole if the records weren't selling and they weren't promoting them. We were just getting deeper in debt to the company. You know you record, the cost goes against your record sales. So we sat it out."[31] The Artistics not only sat it out, they broke up.

Meanwhile, after Marvin Smith left the Artistics he tried to establish a solo career but met with little success. Smith is a virtual unknown in recording history, but his career was far more eventful than his obscurity would suggest. Besides his career in the Artistics, he was lead for the 1950s ensemble, the El Dorados, and was a songwriter of no mean ability.[32]

Smith was born on October 8, 1940, in Palestine, Arkansas, a small hamlet near Forrest City. He moved to the West Side of Chicago with his family in the late 1940s. "My career started a long time ago," related Smith, "right before I went to Crane High. We used to sing on the street corners in the neighborhood. And from there I went to church, and I was very popular in church. I belonged to church choirs and also a quartet. From the church group I went on to my first professional group, the El Dorados. That was around 1957. They were the originals—Jewel Jones, James Maddox, and Louis Bradley. I was their new lead."[33]

In 1966, when the Artistics recorded "I'm Gonna Miss You," Smith recorded "Time Stopped." The Artistics backed him but the record had a solo approach. The record was a fine example of how Chicago soul producers could create a magnificent tapestry of sound in their productions, which in this case marvelously married r&b to a waltz tempo. "Time Stopped," which made it for four weeks on *Cash Box*'s r&b survey, remains today as one of the unheralded songs of the era.

Smith parlayed a number of gigs from "Time Stopped," including the Capitol Theater in Chicago in the fall of 1966 and the "Dick Clark American Bandstand" television show early in 1967. The follow-up hits, however, did not come, and in 1969 Smith obtained a release from Brunswick. Curtis Mayfield signed him up, but only one mediocre record was the result, "You're Really Something Sadie," in 1971. Smith continued to write for other artists and came up with the superb "I Never Thought I'd Be Losing You" for Major Lance in 1978. By the 1980s he was out of the music business.

Young-Holt Trio—Johnny Williams—Lost Generation

Before the Young-Holt Trio was signed with Brunswick in 1966 it formed two-thirds of the famed Ramsey Lewis Trio—bassist Eldee Young and drummer Isaac "Red" Holt.[34] The group's first record, "Wack Wack," was a sizable hit in December 1966. With Ramsey Lewis's "One Two Three," Joe Cuba's "Bang Bang," and Hector Rivera's "At the Party," "Wack Wack" married Cuban rhythms and r&b to generate a "Latin Soul" rage during 1966–67.[35] The record was released as by the Young-Holt Trio, which reflected the membership of veteran jazz keyboardist Hysear Don Walker.

Within two years Walker was dropped and Young and Holt continued as a duo under the name Young-Holt Unlimited. They subsequently scored with a number of hits, the most spectacular being the two-million-selling "Soulful Strut" in 1968. Ironically, neither Holt nor Young was on the record. The instrumental was actually a fine creation of the Brunswick session orchestra. Originally, the number was recorded as the backing track to Barbara Acklin's "Am I the Same Girl," but someone at the company heard an appealing instrumental in the track and then added the superb piano of session man Floyd Morris. The "Young-Holt Unlimited" name on the record was the result of a marketing decision.[36] In 1974, Young and Holt left the company and then broke up to pursue other interests. Morris, who contributed so much to the success of Young-Holt Unlimited, died in 1988 at the age of sixty-two.

Johnny Williams was one of the myriad of Chicago hard-soul singers who sang in a raw forceful style in the manner of gospel singers. During his decade of recording from the mid-1960s to the mid-1970s he put out an average of only one release a year, but he was a mainstay on the city's club circuit and much bigger than his recordings. Two of his releases were recorded for Carl Davis, and one of them, "I Made a Mistake," was the best recording of his career.[37]

Williams was born in Tyler, Alabama, on January 15, 1942. When he was fourteen years of age he moved to Chicago's South Side, and he attended

DuSable High. From his early training-ground in a church choir he graduated into a local gospel quartet, the Royal Jubilees.

The excitement was in the flourishing world of soul music, however, and Williams switched to rhythm and blues. He came under the management of Purvis Spann and E. Rodney Jones. Williams wrote a song, "My Baby's Good," which was recorded and released on Chess Records in 1966. The record got good play on WVON, but the gospelized shouter was not a good record and was what the trade called a turntable hit—one that got good play on radio but few sales in the stores.

In 1969 Williams joined Carl Davis and was assigned to launch a Dakar subsidiary, Bashie. The first release, "I Made a Mistake," was obviously the product of a brainstorming session because it featured four writers— Carl Smith, Simtec Simmons, Johnny Williams, and producer Willie Henderson. It was a great expressive ballad, the type of song Gene Chandler cut his teeth on. It would have been a terrific Chandler vehicle, and perhaps if he had done it the record would have been the hit it deserved to be. Instead, it inexplicably died. In early 1970 a follow-up release, "Your Love Controls My World," a blatant Motown imitation, turned few heads, and Williams and Davis went their separate ways.

As evidence of the declining role of Chicago as a music center during the 1970s, Williams moved to the then flourishing Philadelphia International Records (PIR) label of Kenny Gamble and Leon Huff. The company got Williams his first national chart record with "Slow Motion" in the summer of 1972. Williams left PIR the next year and returned to Chicago. He made a few more singles, with producer Johnny Moore, but within a couple of years he was no longer recording. His death, in December 1986, went virtually unnoticed.

Lowrell Simon was well known in Chicago as a background talent, one who wrote for and produced other Chicago artists. He composed songs for such famous talents as Barry White, Johnny Mathis, Loleatta Holloway, the Dells, and the Impressions. More important, however, he was a successful recording artist in his own right. Followers of 1980s black music may recall Simon as simply Lowrell, the master of mellow-funk with such hits as "Overdose of Love," "Mellow Mellow Right On," and "Love Massage." But Simon, in his relationship to Brunswick, was the lead singer and writer for the vocal group the Lost Generation, who came out with two albums and a number of singles for the label.[38]

Simon was born March 18, 1943, on the South Side. His early years were spent at Stateway Gardens projects at Thirty-fifth and State, one of the poorest areas in Chicago and a rich spawning-ground for groups in the 1950s, though less so in the 1960s. While still in grade school he developed a friendship with Gus Redmond which eventually developed into a business partnership.

By the time Simon was attending high school, he was involved in a vocal group, the LaVondells. Three members of the group attended Phillips High—Lowrell Simon (lead), Glen Murdock (tenor), William "Butch" McCoy (baritone)—and two attended Dunbar, Jesse Dean (tenor) and James Neely (bass). (Murdock, who Simon cited as the group's choreographer, was in the late 1970s lead singer of a black/white rock group called Mother's Finest.)

The Vondells, having dropped the "La" from their name, signed a recording contract with King Kolax's Marvello label. They had a local hit with "Lenore." With its brassy flourishes in the intro, followed first by the group blowing notes together and then by Simon's deeply soulful lead singing, the song was a great blend of 1950s doowop and 1960s soul. Simon said the record sold some twenty-five to thirty thousand copies in Chicago and environs.[39] Unfortunately for the group, lack of distribution limited the record's success to a regional phenomenon.

The Vondells broke up not long after their modest success with "Lenore." Jesse Dean was drafted into the armed services and Glenn Murdock started teaming up with local recording star Joyce Kennedy (the future nucleus of Mother's Finest). As for Simon, he said he became "stagnant."[40]

A few years later, however, the situation changed after Dean got back from the Army. Simon formed the Lost Generation with his brother Fred, Dean, and Larry Brownlee (from the C.O.D.s). Simon's longtime friend Gus Redmond was working in promotion at Brunswick and in 1969 he brought the group to Carl Davis, who had them in the studio in a matter of days. The first release, "The Sly, Slick, and the Wicked," lasted thirteen weeks on *Billboard*'s soul chart in the spring of 1970. The song was written by Simon, Brownlee, and Redmond, and was typical of the group's output, Simon's rather dry lead contrasting vividly with the sweet echoing choruses of the other members.

"Wait a Minute," a Eugene Record composition, was the group's follow-up in late fall of 1970. The song was a little sweeter and featured more echoing, and the record did not do as well, lasting five weeks on the soul chart. "Someday," in February 1971, was a fine Simon-Brownlee-Redmond song well within the prevailing neo-doowop sweet-soul style of the day. It lasted only two weeks on the lower reaches of the soul chart.

For the Lost Generation's next hit, the group returned to the studio and recorded "Talking the Teenage Language." The result was practically a new sound, tough and ominous with a rumbling beat. As usual, it was written by Simon-Brownlee-Redmond. The record lasted for six weeks on the soul chart in the spring of 1971.

Subsequent records failed to chart, and in 1974 the Lost Generation moved to Carl Davis's and E. Rodney Jones's Innovation II label. The group put out "Your Mission (Should You Decide to Accept It)," which managed to go only to the sixty-five position and last seven weeks on the soul chart—not a very big hit. After "Mission" the group disbanded. The departure of the Lost Generation left Carl Davis with few acts by 1974. Brunswick/Dakar sustained itself with basically two Chicago acts, the Chi-lites and Tyrone Davis, and a Detroit-based funkster, Hamilton Bohannon, during its last years.

The Chi-Lites

The Chi-lites were one of the most famous vocal ensembles ever to come out of Chicago and they put the city on the international map. The group exploded on the soul scene in 1969, at the very beginning of the early 1970s vocal/dance-group renaissance. It was an era when such ensembles as the Delfonics, the Stylistics, and the Moments, as well as the Chi-lites, achieved great crossover popularity and significantly shaped the popular music of the era with a soft kind of soul that emphasized high-tenor leads.

Eugene Record was the group's lead and its creative force as songwriter, producer, and all-around instrumentalist. His earliest ballads, especially "Have You Seen Her," "Oh Girl," and "Coldest Days of My Life," featured strong, pretty melodies sung with a high-tenor soulful edge, and Record projected an appealing persona, vulnerable and forlorn. Yet in his up-tempo hits, he presented a vivid contrasting image: In such early songs as "Give More Power to the People" and "We Are Neighbors," it was one of black militancy that fitted the times.

Marshall Thompson was the group's baritone, but his role was that of the Chi-lites leader. He was the go-getter who took care of the group's business. Robert "Squirrel" Lester, as second tenor, and Creadel "Red" Jones, as bass, rounded out this remarkable group.[41]

The Chi-lites went back to the age of doowop, when groups worked their chops on the street corners of the big urban centers of America. The group came out of two such doowop groups, the Desideros and the Chaunteurs. The latter came together about 1958, and consisted of Eugene Record (lead), Burt Bowen (baritone), Eddie Reed (bass), Robert Lester (second tenor), and Clarence Johnson (baritone). Scraping around for the group finally resulted in several records done for Leo Austell, who released them on his own Renee label as well as on Vee Jay and Mercury with no discernible impact.

The Chaunteurs eventually bumped into the Desideros, since they were from the same South Side area: "There was a little movie theater on Forty-third Street," related Record, "and it would have talent shows on weekends. That's when we first met the Desideros, Marshall and Red. We would sing against each other, and the Desideros would win. They won because they would be doing all the dancing and that. It was *their* neighborhood, too. We were just a singing group."[42]

The Desideros came together around 1959 and consisted of Marshall Thompson (baritone), Eddie Sullivan (tenor), Del Brown (tenor), and Creadel Jones (bass). The Desideros came to the attention of Austell, who had the group record "I Pledge My Love" about 1960 on Renee. The record did nothing, but the Desideros under Thompson's leadership became an outstanding choreographed live act.

Soon a friendly rivalry developed between the Chaunteurs and the Desideros, and it was not long before the two groups joined forces. The new group—Record, Lester, Thompson, Jones, and Johnson—called themselves the Hi-lites. They hooked up with Daran Records, a small label owned by Thompson's cousin, James Shelton. After one release on Daran, Johnson left the group, in 1964. The group's next release, "I'm So Jealous," proved to be a moderate local hit upon its release in 1964, and seemed promising enough for Mercury to lease it from Shelton and put it out on its Blue Rock subsidiary. At Blue Rock, the group changed its name to the Chi-lites.

Two more Blue Rock releases followed in 1965 and both went clunk, so the Chi-lites found themselves back with Shelton in 1966. Their release for him, "Pretty Girl," was a lovely ballad and made some noise locally, but the truth of the matter was that the Chi-lites were not going anywhere and they clearly needed something to happen to keep the group together. That something was Carl Davis. "Otis Leavill," related Record, "whom Marshall had known, met Marshall on the bus and told him to come down and see Carl, who had just started a company at Roosevelt and Wabash. So we went to Carl's company. We got in a little office and we showed him some of the songs we had. So he liked what we were doing. He found out then that I was writing good stuff. We signed and we did 'Price of Love.' That song really started our career."[43] The record was released on Dakar in 1967, but the label was still too small to do much with the Chi-lites nationally.

The Chi-lites were signed to Brunswick in late 1968. The result proved immediately beneficial when the group scored with their first national hit, "Give It Away," in January 1969, which made top ten on *Billboard*'s soul chart. It was a delightful up-tempo ballad in which the pretty Chi-lites harmonies really shone. Said Record:

> That was the first hit, that was the first *hit*! We were like in the twilight zone. We didn't know what was happening. We had never

had a hit record before. It's kind of hard to explain the feeling. We weren't really aware of what was going on. All we knew was that the record hit the charts, but we couldn't appreciate at first what it meant. Then we started going to the Apollo Theatre and that was exciting, but at the same time we were scuffling, because there was still no real money. That came later. Then I don't see how we survived off the money we made. At the time you don't look at the money, the money wasn't even important to us. The whole fact was that we finally got a hit record. Nothing else mattered. We got a hit record, and that's what we were trying to do for ten years.[44]

"Let Me Be the Man My Daddy Was" was another terrific ballad for the group that proved its worth by becoming a substantial soul hit in the summer of 1969. Brunswick released the Chi-lites first album, *Give It Away*, which was two hits with a lot of filler. But the basic ingredients were there and they were impressive—Record's wonderful melodies and the singing that brought the deep feeling of the doowop era to soul harmonies of the 1970s.

The group's second album, *I Like Your Lovin'*, was released in 1970. It was a weak effort. The ballad material was not up to par, and the two songs released as singles, "I Like Your Lovin'" (June 1970) and "Are You My Woman" (November 1970), do not stand up two decades later although they became very large hits for the group. The album copied the sound of the Temptations then, when the Motown group was in its "psychedelic soul" period.

The year 1971 was the break-out one for the Chi-lites. They had already established themselves in the soul market but they were still unknown in the popular market. *Give More Power to the People*, the first million-selling album for the group, changed all that and launched the Chi-lites as international entertainers. The first two singles from the album, "Give More Power to the People," in April (number four on the soul chart), and "We Are Neighbors," in July (number seventeen on the soul chart), introduced the theme of black assertiveness and were strong r&b hits. They had limited appeal to the crossover audience.

"Have You Seen Her," a beautiful, haunting ballad released in October, zoomed to the top of both *Billboard* charts and brought the Chi-lites their first crossover hit. Yet Record never guessed that song would be the one to do it. "It was the furthest thing from my mind," he confessed. "I had the song for at least two or three years. But it was so long; five minutes long! You were lucky at that time if you got a record played that was three minutes long. But then, what really made me put it on the album was when

Isaac Hayes came out with that *Hot Buttered Soul* album. He did something that was eighteen minutes and I said ahhh. . . . So we put it on the album, and then, wow, whew. I never seen anything like that record!"[45]

By 1972, the Chi-lites could do no wrong. *A Lonely Man* easily matched *Give More Power to the People* in the number of hits and selling power. Heads above all was "Oh Girl," released in March, which was a multimillion-selling ballad and number one on all the charts. The album contained three other standout ballads: "The Coldest Day of My Life" (top-ten soul), "A Lonely Man" (number twenty-five soul), and "Living in the Footsteps of Another Man" (November 1972). Only "Living" failed to click. Instead, the record's flip, "We Need Order," became the hit side.

The Chi-lites were on a roll and the albums started coming out a bit quicker, with two released in 1973. The first, *A Letter to Myself*, contained "We Need Order" and featured the outstanding title cut, which went to number three on *Billboard*'s soul chart early in the year. Sometime during the year Creadel Jones left the group. He had developed a drug dependency problem and decided to drop out to get his personal life together. He did, however, sing bass on the second 1973 album, called simply *The Chi-lites*. A strong contribution came from lyricist Stan McKenny, a country music deejay from Kentucky. He provided the lyrics for four of the album's songs, most notably the magnificent "Homely Girl," a wistful ballad about a plain-Jane schoolgirl who blossoms beautifully upon reaching adulthood. It went to number three on the soul chart in 1974.

Toby, released in 1974, ranked as one of the Chi-lites' finest albums, producing three superb hits, "There Will Never Be Any Peace" (number eight in the spring of 1974), "You Got to Be the One" (number fifteen in the summer), and "Toby" (number seven in the winter of 1974/75). Another terrific song, "That's How Long," was the flip to "Toby" and was credited alongside the A side on the charts, indicating a double-sided hit. For the *Toby* album, the group tried out a new bass singer, T. C. Anderson, but he was uncredited as they considered him to be a trial candidate.

The Chi-lites next album was *Half of Love*, in 1975. It was perhaps their weakest LP for some time, and only one single came out of it, "It's Time for Love"/"Here I Am," a double-sided hit that reached the twenty-seven position on the soul chart. Still trying out basses, the group had Anderson on some cuts and Willie Kensey, a fellow they discovered in Florida, on others.

The group tried out three basses in all, and finally settled on Doc Roberson, whom they picked out of a local Chicago vocal ensemble, the Five Wagers. The Five Wagers, out of Marshall High, consisted of Larry Maxington, Maurice Dobson, James Price, Harry Price, as well as Roberson, and cut some very good sides in the city without any success. Roberson joined the Chi-lites for two excellent up-tempo songs, "The Devil Is Doing His Work" (number thirty-two in December 1975 on the soul chart) and "You Don't Have to Go" (number fifty in the spring of 1976).

The year 1976 was a difficult one for the Chi-lites. Their company's New York-based officers were tried and convicted of fraud and conspiracy. This brought the feds down on all the company's artists as well, and, added to the difficulties the group was having with Brunswick and with their management (Carl Davis), such a situation only served to bring the group into disarray.

In January 1976, the Chi-lites pleaded guilty to tax evasion charges, and in May they were sentenced to a year's probation and ordered to pay fines.[46] "There was a complete breakdown of just about everything," explained Record. "Our company was in trouble with the government, and when the IRS came into the company they began looking at the artists as well. We felt management was partially responsible for what happened to us. I'm not saying a personal manager should take you to the bathroom and all that, but if you're on the road as we were, you can't do some things. We were on the road so much between 1969, when we started touring, and 1976, that a couple of those years we were away for a least three hundred days each. That's how much we worked."[47]

Added Thompson, "We needed business agents, we needed business accountants, but we didn't have that at the time. Hey, we came off of Forty-third Street! Somebody tells you, 'Here's $100,000, just put it in your pocket and go crazy.' So that's what we did, went crazy, went out and bought Cadillacs, whatever, the money was coming in so fast. So we had to learn. It took us a while. After we had all them tax and other problems, that's when Gene left."[48]

The upshot was that in 1976 Record left the Chi-lites to establish a solo career. Thompson reorganized the group and brought in a new lead. Both Record and Thompson's Chi-lites then signed with major labels, Record with Warner Brothers, the Chi-lites with Mercury. The records both acts made with these labels were not equal to the Chi-lites' Brunswick hits, and chart success was much less. In 1980 Eugene Record reunited with Thompson, Lester, and Jones to form a "reunion" Chi-lites. They signed with Carl Davis's Chi-Sound Records.

Tyrone Davis

Tyrone Davis was one of the brightest stars in the 1970s galaxy of soul artists. After he hit with "Can I Change My Mind" in 1968, Davis had top-twenty hits annually—and often more than that—for a decade, a track record equalled by few in the business. Leavill said his records rarely sold less than three hundred thousand to four hundred thousand for the company.[49] But despite his tremendous recording success, Davis remained fairly obscure to white America, at least compared to leading 1970s crossover stars Al Green, Teddy Pendergrass, and Donna Summer.[50]

Perhaps Davis's music was too alien to the white middle-class youth who constituted the bulk of the popular music audience. He sang in a slightly softer version of an urban blues-soul style pioneered by such early 1960s hard-soulsters as Otis Clay, Johnny Sayles, and Harold Burrage. His vocals ranged from energetic shouting to the most subtle of soft whispering, but mostly he sang in the relaxed, cool, confessional style that characterized so many of Chicago's soul singers. The subject matter of his songs— domestic discord and reconciliation, infidelity, and friends who can't be trusted—reflected his black adult working-class constituency, and like the blues artists of an earlier era, Davis's most loyal following was always that audience.

In 1968, after local success on Four Brothers, Davis made his big break into stardom. It came after years of work and seasoning in which Davis, who had started out imitating other singers, finally found his own style. The record that brought him fame was the two-sided masterpiece "Can I Change My Mind"/"A Woman Needs to Be Loved." The two songs, along with two other sides, were first recorded by Wally Roker for ABC, but Davis wanted to leave that company and asked Roker if he could place the songs with a Chicago company.

Davis took the masters to Carl Davis, and as he told John Abbey: "Carl had been listening to my tapes, and he liked one of the songs, 'A Woman Needs to Be Loved.' He wanted to recut it along with the other three songs, one of which was 'Mind.' So we cut them again. Everybody in the studio cracked over 'Mind,' and when Carl got back we all told him how much we preferred it. But Carl stayed with 'Woman,' and so it was issued as the top side. I think Carl thought of me as a hard-blues singer and that may be the reason he stayed with the blues side."[51]

"A Woman Needs to Be Loved" was released to massive indifference. Some weeks later, a Houston disc jockey known as the Wild Child flipped the record and started the ball rolling to make "Can I Change My Mind" a national hit and number one on *Billboard*'s soul chart.

"Can I Change My Mind," the first Davis release on Dakar, served as the archetypical record that established the Davis confessional style. The persona he projected was that of a vulnerable, easily wounded, contrite lover, eschewing the usual macho stance of so many of his soul contemporaries. The comedian who usually preceded his Chicago nightclub shows, Manuel Arrington, would often teasingly rebuke Davis for his seeming weakness: "Tyrone, why are you always pleading with your women?"

Nonetheless, Davis was rewarded by becoming a genuine love object. "The ladies really like me, you know," he told me in 1979. "I really don't have a clue what it is about me that they like, and it's something I've often wondered about."[52]

If his lyrics made Davis sound unconfident, the Willie Henderson productions and Tom Washington arrangements certainly did not. There was the usual combo of piano, guitars, and drums, but invariably there was also a fat sassy brass section that provided a nice counterpoint to the blues-based lope of the rhythm track. Often used to add even more fullness to the already naturally full sound were chick choruses and strings for sweeteners. More important, Davis's Chicago musicians swung and rocked with a vengeance, creating a sound so powerful and tight, it was exhilarating.

The next four singles for Davis were poor records, futile attempts to recapture the successful formula of "Can I Change My Mind." Surprisingly, one of them, "Is It Something You Got," was a top-five r&b hit. In February 1970 Davis got another huge hit with "Turn Back the Hands of Time," which made it to the number one position on the soul chart. Henderson conservatively followed the same formula, but this time he was able to produce—with the help of a great song by Jack Daniels and Johnny Moore—another timeless record for Davis.

After "Turn Back the Hands of Time" the hits came a lot faster and easier. Davis had top records with "I'll Be Right Here" (July 1970), "Let Me Back In" (October 1970), and "Could I Forget You" (March 1971), the latter introducing the composing talent of Leo Graham, who ultimately would play a much larger role in Davis's career. Davis closed out 1971 with two more hit records, "One-Way Ticket" (a cover of Syl Johnson's hit from a year earlier) and "You Keep Me Holding On."

The year 1972 continued the string of hits with "I Had It all the Time," "Come and Get this Ring," and "If You Had a Change in Mind." The marvelously hokey "I Had It all the Time" was the standout of the lot. The record opened with a refrain from "Is It Something You Got," then went into a highly effective Davis recitation.

Starting in 1973 Davis and his producers began to vary his sound a little more, and the hits did not stop. A double-sided standout opened the year, "Without You in My Life"/"How Can I Forget You." "Life" with its magnificent drive got the most airplay and was a top-five hit on *Billboard*'s soul chart. "How Can I Forget You" was equally good, but perhaps because it followed the old Davis formula so closely its sound was considered stale by the deejays. One of his finest releases, featuring a gloriously rich brassy sound, was "There It Is," a top-ten soul hit in the summer. It was the last Henderson-produced hit, and thereafter Richard Parker and Leo Graham took over the producing chores.

The Parker-Graham team produced the majestically hard-driving "What Goes Up (Must Come Down)," a hit that reached the number eleven position on the soul chart in the summer of 1974. The song superbly exemplified the approach to black music in which artists worked to generate tremendous energy without sacrificing the craftsmanship of the music (something not always true of 1960s and 1970s rock music).

The year 1975 proved to be one of Davis's best, both artistically and commercially. "Homewreckers," number thirty-six on the soul chart in the spring, was produced by Carl Davis and Otis Leavill, and presented Davis in a bluesier, more downhome manner. Then "A Woman Needs to Be Loved" was re-released and proved to be a solid hit in the summer (number thirty-eight on the soul chart). A justification of Davis's faith in the song, this masterful blues-based record was his most powerful effort and became one of the highlights of his concerts.

In November 1975 Davis hit with his third number-one hit on *Billboard*'s soul chart, "Turning Point." The song was written and produced by Leo Graham, who with this record emerged in full command of Davis's artistic direction. "Turning Point," which lasted twenty weeks on the chart, was probably a million seller but it did not get official certification from the Record Industry Association of America (RIAA). Said Davis, "I had records like 'Turning Point,' which easily went a million, but Brunswick never gave me an accurate accounting. I had records like 'I Had It All the Time' and 'Without You in My Life'; all of them went real big. They weren't fair you know, but I don't even care to talk about it much, if you know what I mean."[53]

By the mid-1970s Tyrone Davis was at the peak of his career. From the evidence of the several concerts I attended during 1976–79, I can testify that the Tyrone Davis band during those years was the most magnificent-sounding in any form of popular music, be it rock, blues, or soul. I have seen Al Green, the Rolling Stones, the Band, Bruce Springsteen, and numerous others all at the height of their careers, and only the James Brown aggregation had a band that could equal the live Davis band in rhythmic fury and overall flash and tightness of sound.

Concerning the Davis band, Chess staff member Gene Barge related, "Oh yeah, he had a hot band then. They had that typical down-South r&b arrangements, and the thing you got there was the groove and the beat. The musicians poured so much into it, they're good enough to bring it out. They had that old churchy, foot-tapping feeling. Tyrone had a lot to do with the way they sounded. He stayed on top of them and knew the kind of drive he wanted, and that inspired them. Sometimes it's half-scared, half-inspired. You could call Tyrone crazy. He fussed and raised cain, and his application in the rehearsals [was] what made the band have its drive. He liked that big beat, he liked that drive."[54]

Davis left the crumbling Brunswick/Dakar organization in 1976, and reflecting the trend of the day joined a major, Columbia. He stayed at Columbia for six years and came out with seven albums, all produced by Leo Graham and arranged by James Mack. Davis gradually evolved away from his blues-based, horn-driven music, and although early on at Columbia he had hits equal to the best of his Brunswick material, such as "Give It Up (Turn It Loose)" and "This I Swear," his late 1970s and 1980s material was overly heavy on ballads and disco-influenced numbers. The Dakar hits of Tyrone Davis represented some of the best soul music ever put out and was the best of the Chicago Sound of the 1970s.

The Fall of Brunswick

Brunswick in 1975–76 was doing well. Although not the hit-making entity it had been a few years earlier, it was still scoring hits by its two principal artists, the Chi-lites and Tyrone Davis. But then in March 1976, following the 1975 indictments, Nat Tarnopol and three other Brunswick officers were convicted of various fraud charges and one conspiracy charge. The government found that the defendants sold nearly five hundred thousand singles and albums at discount for $300,000 cash and $50,000 in merchandise. Such transactions according to the government defrauded the company's artists and writers of rightful royalties and the government of tax monies.[55] Carl Davis, as vice president, and Melvin Moore, as national promotion director, were also tried, but were found innocent on the grounds they were not privy to what was going on in the New York office.[56]

Despite the seeming dishonesty of such practices, the defense contended that selling records at discount was a common means of doing business and a necessity for an independent company competing against the majors in the 1970s. Furthermore, Nat Tarnopol and the other defendants were not intentionally trying to defraud anybody.[57] In an elaboration to me, Tarnopol asserted that selling records wholesale at discount was a means to get the volume to put a record on the charts, which in the end helps an act rather than hurts it. He suggested all companies at one time or another did this, and said that compared to others, "Brunswick was a baby."[58]

Tarnopol appealed his conviction, and in December 1977 the convictions were overturned.[59] In June 1978, following a retrial, a judge dismissed the charges and declared a mistrial after the case fell apart.[60] Undoubtedly contributing to the weakness of the government's case was the prosecution's failure to bring any witnesses to the stand to testify that they had been defrauded.[61]

Davis said he was mystified by the events: "Nat was a very good executive and that's one of the reasons why I was confused, that he would do something like that. I really liked him and I considered him a good friend of mine, but then after the trial started, I realized that he wasn't as good a friend as I thought. He destroyed something that I had worked hard for all my life. I had always said that when I got to be around forty-five years old, I would have liked to have been able to, you know, sit back and clip coupons. There I was starting all over again in my forties rather than being able to retire."[62]

During and after the trial Davis and all the key creative persons abandoned the company, and all the important artists left as well. Tarnopol continued the Brunswick operation while attempting to sort out his legal difficulties, but obviously he did not have much of a company to work with. The Chicago office mysteriously was kept open, but the staff's principal function seemed to be to turn the lights on in the morning and turn them off at night. After 1981 Brunswick was moribund as an active label, and existed only to license old masters to other firms for reissue purposes. About 1985 Tarnopol moved to Las Vegas and found employment through friends there. On December 25, 1987, he died of a heart attack.

Joe McEwen, a well-respected writer on black music and an A&R man at CBS Records, said of Brunswick that it had a "dubious reputation."[63] He was being kind. Brunswick had been the subject of a lot of nasty stories over the years, many of which related to presumed links with the mob. Record testified at the Brunswick trial that he was roughed up by an associate of Tarnopol when he demanded an advance for re-signing with the label. I asked Record why a company would treat its artists that way, and he replied, "Hey, it wasn't the company. It was the people who were maybe connected with the company who weren't involved in recording per se. In other words they were outside people that was on the company side."[64] When I pointedly asked if these "outside people" were gangsters, Record silently nodded affirmatively, fully cognizant that the tape recorder was on.[65]

Sonny Woods, for many years a member of the Detroit-based Mid-nighters vocal group, told a tale that at best should be classified as hearsay, but it indicated how artists viewed Brunswick. According to Woods, when in 1964 Jackie Wilson refused to re-sign with Brunswick, Tarnopol and his associates hung the singer by his feet outside the window of a high-rise hotel until he agreed to put his name on the dotted line.[66] Bill Pollak in his revealing portrait of Jackie Wilson in a 1978 *Village Voice* article detailed many nefarious practices of Brunswick that served to keep their great artist in debt despite several million-sellers to his credit. Wilson when he was stricken owed the company some $150,000 in advances on royalties.[67] Yet except for the trials in 1976 and 1978, the reader of trade journals will find little negative reporting on the label.

The positive image of Brunswick stems from the remarkable body of magnificent music that the creative end of the company produced. Those same executives who were brought to trial, Tarnopol and his New York staff, certainly should get the credit along with Carl Davis for building the label into a major force in the soul music industry in the late 1960s and early 1970s.

NOTES

1. Robert Pruter, liner notes, *Chicago Soul: The Legendary Brunswick/Dakar Hits*, Epic 39895, 1985; idem, "Sonny Sanders," *Goldmine*, May 1980, pp. 20–21; Carl Davis interviews; Dick Jacobs interview; Nat Tarnopol interview. *Billboard* and *Cash Box* in occasional articles and news items provided a good history of the company from 1966 to 1978.

2. Tarnopol interview.

3. "Brunswick May Do Indie Thing," *Billboard*, January 17, 1970, p. 1.

4. Davis interview, April 27, 1986.

5. Davis interview, March 9, 1986.

6. Davis interview, April 27, 1986.

7. Jacobs interview.

8. "Executive Turntable," *Billboard*, October 8, 1966, p. 4.

9. Jacobs interview.

10. Davis interview, December 11, 1986.

11. "Brunswick in Atlantic Split; Name Officials," *Billboard*, December 11, 1971, p. 3.

12. Davis interview, March 9, 1986.

13. Sol Bobrov interview.

14. As a rhythm-and-blues superstar Jackie Wilson had been the subject of many fine articles. The most thoughtful and comprehensive are: Dick Jacobs as told to Tim Holmes, "Jackie Wilson," *Musician*, January 1988, p. 21; Kevin Keegan, liner notes, Jackie Wilson, *My Way—Jackie Wilson*, Brunswick Collector Series P18816, 1985; Joe McEwen, "Jackie Wilson," in *The Rolling Stone Illustrated History of Rock and Roll*, ed. Jim Miller, rev. and updated (New York: Random House/Rolling Stone Press, 1980), pp. 117–19; Ralph Newman and Alan Kaltman, "Lonely Teardrops: The Story of a Forgotten Man," *Time Barrier Express* 24 (April-May 1979): 29–32; Bill Pollak, "Jackie Wilson's Lonely Tears," *The Village Voice*, August 14, 1978, pp. 1, 15–18; Clive Richardson, "Hot Gospel: Jackie Wilson's Voice Smashed Musical Barriers," in *The Marshall Cavendish Illustrated History of Popular Music*, Vol. 3, 1959–60 (New York: Marshall Cavendish, 1989), pp. 330–32.

15. Dave Hoekstra, "Producer Gives His Final Tribute to Singer-Dancer Jackie Wilson," *Suburban Sun-Times/West*, February 17, 1984, p. 23.

16. Ibid., p. 21.

17. Ibid.

18. Miner interview.

19. Unsavory elements in the record industry had created a pressure that required Chandler to sign with Brunswick. Leonard Chess understood what was involved and agreed to Chandler's two-company commitment. My source does not want to be identified. Tarnopol disingenuously contended in 1987 that he had no knowledge of Chandler's Checker recordings.

20. Chander interview, February 6, 1979.

21. Robert Pruter, "Barbara Acklin," *Goldmine*, July 1983, pp. 169–70; Acklin interview.

22. Acklin interview.

23. Ibid.

24. Ibid.

25. Ibid.

26. John Abbey, "Otis Leavill," *Blues and Soul* 41 (August 28–September 10, 1970): 41; Melody McDowell, "Whatever Happened to: Otis Leavill?," *Chicago Defender*, July 30, 1977; Robert Pruter, "Otis Leavill," *Soul Survivor* 3 (Autumn 1985): 29–30; "New Rock Singer on the Rise, Hails from Singing Family," *Chicago Defender*, September 21, 1963; Leavill interview, April 19, 1976.

27. Leavill interview.

28. Ibid.

29. Ibid.

30. Gerald Sims interview.

31. Larry Johnson interview.

32. John Abbey, "Time Hasn't Stopped Marvin Smith," *Blues and Soul*, July 6–19, 1973, p. 20; Robert Pruter, "The Marvin Smith Story," *Goldmine*, July 1980, pp. 166–67; Smith interview.

33. Smith interview.

34. Tom Nuccio, "History of Chicago Jazz, Part 16: Ivory Trios," *Illinois Entertainer*, April 1986, p. 69; "Eldee and 'Red' Leave the Ramsey Lewis Trio," *Soul*, July 7, 1966, p. 1.

35. Claude Hall, "Latin Rock in Sales Upswing," *Billboard*, January 21, 1967, p. 1.

36. Leavill interview, July 20, 1984.

37. Robert Pruter, "Johnny Williams: They Loved Him in Chicago," *Goldmine*, April 24, 1987, pp. 16, 22; "Seventy-Two Was Williams' Year For Recognition," *Soul*, February 26, 1973, p. 19.

38. Robert Pruter, "The Lowrell Simon Story," *Goldmine*, April 1982, pp. 182–83; Simon interview.

39. Simon interview.

40. Ibid.

41. Perhaps because it was a vocal group, the Chi-lites elicited little interest in the United States from popular music critics. Therefore almost all of the best profiles on the group come from British writers who were unburdened by biases:

John Abbey, "Eugene Record: Today's Genius," *Blues and Soul*, February 1971, pp. 12–13; idem, "The Chi-lites," *Blues and Soul,* June 4–13, 1974, p. 3; Tony Cummings, "The Chi-lites Story," *Black Music*, July 1974, pp. 8–9; Bob Fisher, "The Eugene Record Interview," *Hot Buttered Soul* 27 (1973): 4–6; Denise Hall, "Eugene Record: Poet of Bittersweet Soul," *Black Music*, October 1975, pp. 24–25; Robert Pruter, "The Chi-lites Story: From Street Corner to Court Room," *Goldmine*, November 8, 1985, pp. 13–18; Chris Savory, "Chi-lites Rappin'," *Hot Buttered Soul* 44 (Feb./Mar. 1976): 16–17; Eugene Record interviews; Marshall Thompson interview.

42. Record interview, November 11, 1980.

43. Ibid.

44. Ibid.

45. Ibid.

46. Ted Watson, "Chi-lites Sentenced," *Chicago Defender*, May 8, 1976; Is Horowitz, "Five Plead Guilty as Federal Probe of Industry Ignites," *Billboard*, January 17, 1976, p. 1.

47. Record interview, November 11, 1980.

48. Thompson interview.

49. Leavill interview.

50. Practically all the published sources about Tyrone Davis lament the artist's undeserved obscurity: John Abbey, "Tyrone Davis: They Changed Their Minds about 'Change My Mind,'" *Blues and Soul*, June 19–July 1, 1970, pp. 10–11; Larry Birnbaum, "The Distinctive Style of Tyrone Davis Still No Household Sound," *Chicago Tribune*, March 22, 1985; Clarence Brown, "Tyrone Davis: A Successful Unknown," *Black Stars*, April 1975, pp. 6–10; Dave Hoekstra, "Oak Brook's Tyrone Davis Hones Singular Soul Style," *Suburban Sun-Times*, January 17, 1983, pp. 17–18; Bret Kennedy, "Tyrone Davis: The Man Upstairs Is My Silent Partner," *Soul*, April 7, 1969, p. 12; Robert Pruter, "Tyrone Davis," *Goldmine*, December 1980, pp. 23–25; Otis Clay interviews, May 22, 1979, and September 9, 1980; Tyrone Davis interview.

51. Abbey, "Tyrone Davis," p. 11.

52. Tyrone Davis interview.

53. Ibid.

54. Gene Barge interview, January 16, 1982.

55. Rudy Garcia, "Trial of Brunswick Execs Nears End: One Acquited [*sic*]," *Billboard*, February 28, 1976, p. 3.

56. Rudy Garcia, "Newark: Four Guilty, Two Are Acquited [*sic*]," *Billboard*, March 6, 1976, p. 12.

57. Rudy Garcia, "Tarnopol Files Appeal: Hearing to Be March 29," *Billboard*, March 27, 1976, p. 95.

58. Tarnopol interview.

59. "Convictions of Tarnopol, Three Others Are Overturned," *Billboard*, December 3, 1977, p. 4.

60. "Judge Dismisses Tarnopol Charges, Declares Mistrial," *Billboard*, June 3, 1978, p. 3.

61. Pollak, "Jackie Wilson's Lonely Tears," p. 18.
62. Carl Davis interview, March 9, 1986.
63. McEwen, "Jackie Wilson," p. 119.
64. Record interview, November 11, 1980.
65. Ibid.
66. Beachley interview, January 27, 1988.
67. Pollak, "Jackie Wilson's Lonely Tears," p. 16.

12

Mercury Records

Mercury Records was formed in Chicago in 1945 by Irving Green and Berle Adams. Green was the owner of pressing plants in Chicago and St. Louis and Adams was a booking agent and also manager of several acts, notably Louis Jordan.[1] At first the company recorded local rhythm-and-blues acts that the majors had ignored, such as Bill Samuels and His Cats 'n' Jammer Three, and the Four Jumps of Jive (who included blues great Willie Dixon). Quickly, however, the company jumped into the pop field and by the end of its first year of business was ranked sixth in national sales.[2] In 1948 Mercury signed Chicago-based singer Dinah Washington, who immediately became their biggest r&b act. The company was originally located in the Loop at 215 South Peoria, then in mid-1946 it moved to 839 South Wabash, south of the Loop. In 1954 the company relocated north of the Loop at 35 East Wacker.[3]

Mercury by the 1950s was fully involved in most fields of music, recording pop, jazz, and classical, as well as being highly active in rhythm and blues. The company, ironically, drew little from Chicago for r&b talent. Brook Benton, the Del Vikings, and the Danleers, for example, were all East Coast–based artists recorded in New York. Mercury's biggest r&b vocal group, the Platters, came from Los Angeles and recorded in that city. In the late 1950s the company hired as A&R man and producer Clyde Otis, the first black to work A&R at a major label.[4] From New York he produced a spate of hits for Brook Benton, Dinah Washington, Clyde McPhatter, and others.

In November 1961 Mercury was acquired by North American Philips, which was part of the huge European firm, Philips Records. Following the acquisition, Mercury decided on a marketing approach by which they would sell records through several labels, called divisions, each with its own A&R and promotion and publicity departments. The Philips division was set up in New York and began operations in February 1962. Smash, which had been formed in the spring of 1961, was likewise turned into a separate division.[5] (In early 1965 the Fontana label was added as a companion label of Smash.)

Irwin H. Steinberg, Mercury's executive vice president in 1964, that year reportedly "likened the Mercury idea to the General Motors concept of separate divisions for each car, each autonomously organized and operated." He claimed the concept worked, citing Mercury's stable of labels together ranked fourth in national sales after Columbia, RCA Victor, and Capitol.[6]

Only a few Chicago acts in the 1960s appeared on Mercury and its confederate labels, namely, the Naturals and Constellations on Smash, Diane Cunningham on Fontana, and Jerry Butler on Mercury. Most of the company's soul acts, however, were directed through two small labels, Limelight, begun in late 1963, and Blue Rock, started in late 1964. Limelight, headed by Eddie Mascari, put out records by such Chicago soul artists as the Classmen, Doris Smith, and Otis Leavill, all without any notable success.[7] When the label was terminated in 1965 it was specializing in jazz, but halfheartedly.

Blue Rock, headed by Carl Proctor, was a slightly more successful effort.[8] The label sustained itself on records leased from independent producers around the country and on in-house production efforts from A&R man Andre Williams in Chicago and from producer Ed Townsend in New York. The label got two national hits in 1965 with Otis Leavill's "Let Her Love Me" (out of the Chicago office) and with Dee Dee Warwick's "We're Doing Fine" (out of the New York office). Most sales came from regional hits, but that was not good enough for a major label, and Mercury suspended Blue Rock in 1966. Only Warwick proved strong enough to stay on, moving to the Mercury label.

Blue Rock had higher visibility in Chicago than in the rest of the nation because of the strength of its local acts, Leavill, the Chi-lites, and Joyce Kennedy. The latter was well known in the mid-1980s as a California-based singer, but she had deep roots in the Chicago music scene dating to her days as a high-schooler singing soprano ditties. Kennedy was born about 1948 in Anguilla, Mississippi, but grew up in Chicago. While attending Lucy Flower High on the West Side she made her first record, at the age of sixteen, called "I Still Love You" (1964).[9] The song came out on the Ran-dee label, a near North Side company owned by Roy Love, Udie Coffman, and Phil Rifkin. The moody-sounding ballad was written by Andre Williams, William McKinley, and Ted Daniels. Williams produced the record, as he would all her subsequent releases. The song got good play on the local stations and Kennedy often cited it as her "local hit."

In 1965 Williams took Kennedy to Blue Rock, and put out two releases on her. The first was a shouter called "I'm a Good Girl," a Karl Tarlton/Andre Williams composition reflecting Williams's aggressive approach to soul. It got good play on WVON, but the second Kennedy release never clicked.

Around this time, while singing at a record hop in suburban Maywood, Kennedy met Glen Murdock, who came out of the Chicago vocal group the Vondells. They found compatibility as a duo and eventually as husband and wife. The duo evolved into a band and for several years crisscrossed the country playing clubs, hotel lounges, and military bases. In 1976 the band emerged as the Atlanta-based Mother's Finest, which was considered the first hard-rock band fronted by blacks.

In 1968 vice president Steinberg revived the Blue Rock label, and in a surprising development put Four Brothers' label producer Jack Daniels in charge of A&R and production.[10] Generally the hard-soul and blues acts Daniels worked with did not generate the sales volumes that could keep a major label interested, but Steinberg probably figured that with limited financing the label could fill a niche in the marketplace and still earn profits. Also, given the growing popularity of blues with the rock audience, Blue Rock could tap that market as well.

Daniels inherited several acts, notably bluesman Junior Parker, but he brought in a few pet acts of his own, primarily Johnny Moore and Junior Wells from Four Brothers and veteran pianist Floyd Morris. Some, such as Morris, were put on Mercury's other labels—Fontana, Philips, as well as Mercury. Daniels during his time at the helm got national chart hits with Wells's "You're Tuff Enough" (July 1968) and Parker's "Ain't Goin' Be No Cutting Loose" (April 1969), and a few local hits.

In retrospect, Blue Rock's successes were small potatoes. Compared to the achievements of Columbia's OKeh subsidiary and Decca's Brunswick subsidiary, Mercury's efforts to record soul, especially Chicago-based soul, were feeble. The company for the most part neglected Chicago and was not strongly committed in the 1960s to mining the rich vein of regional soul-music talent in its own backyard. The company saw itself as national in scope, competing for the same acts as Columbia, Warner Brothers, and Capitol, and as such it maintained offices and recording studios in New York, Los Angeles, and Nashville, as well as Chicago.

In 1969 Steinberg replaced Green as president, and sensing that the company was weak in the vibrant and growing soul market he began a committed policy to strengthen the company in the field by building a stable of soul artists drawn from Chicago.[11] To signal the company's stepped-up efforts he terminated the Blue Rock label and placed all r&b signings on the prestigious Mercury label. He also decided to end in-house production and so Daniels left the company to work as an independent producer.

Steinberg during 1970 signed production deals with Jerry Butler to receive product through his Fountain Productions, and with Gene Chandler to do business through his Mister Chand label. Both artists were noted for their pop-like, soft-soul stylings and both were major artists, a reflection of Mercury's new energized commitment to establish itself in r&b with Chicago talent. Steinberg recognized that Mercury during much of the previous decade had great difficulty in developing soul talent from its in-house staff and thus believed that the best approach would be to use independent production agreements. Butler and Chandler were closer to the street than the Mercury executives and thus better situated to develop talent for the label.[12]

At least, that was the theory. Unfortunately for Mercury it had decided to work with Chicago talent at a time when the city was on the downslide in the soul music arena. The independent production deals with Butler and Chandler were not nearly as successful as all parties had hoped.

Jerry Butler and the Butler Songwriters Workshop

Jerry Butler was Mercury's most successful soul artist, having been with the label since 1966 when he moved from the bankrupt Vee Jay. Butler's move was certainly a boost to his career, but also was disquieting evidence that the Chicago independents were beginning to lose ground to the majors. Because of his association with Mercury, Butler was not much of a regionally based artist any longer. Most of his biggest records on the label were produced in New York and Philadelphia, first with Mercury staff producers Luchi DeJesus and Jerry Ross, and then spectacularly with the Philly-based independent composing/producing team of Kenny Gamble and Leon Huff.

Many rock writers have tended to rate Butler's Mercury years (1966-74) above his Vee Jay years. This opinion is shaped by the common phenomenon among popular-music observers that the degree of familiarity determines the degree of appreciation. Butler's Mercury hits—notably "Mr. Dream Merchant" (1967), "Never Give You Up" (1968), "Hey Western Union Man" (1968), "Only the Strong Survive" (1969), "Moody Woman" (1969), and "What's the Use of Breaking Up" (1969)—were undeniably tremendous hits, commercially and artistically. They were, however, popular at a time when rock critics were writing about popular music. Butler's Vee Jay hits, prior to the advent of publications such as *Rolling Stone*, were not less inferior, just less noticed.

Brunswick/Dakar Records' Chicago headquarters. This building at 1449 South Michigan was previously the headquarters of Vee Jay Records. Photo by Cary Baker.

Jackie Wilson, late 1960s. This legendary singer's career was fading when producer Carl Davis revived it in 1966.

Barbara Acklin, late 1960s. Courtesy Barbara Acklin.

Otis Leavill, late 1960s. Courtesy Otis Leavill.

The Artistics, 1966. After recording for OKeh Records for several years, the group had its biggest success at Brunswick. Standing, left to right: Jesse Bolian, Aaron Floyd, Larry Johnson, and Tommy Green; bottom, guitarist Bernard Reed.

Tyrone Davis, 1968. Courtesy Michael Ochs Archives, Venice, California.

The Chi-lites, 1969. Clockwise from top: Eugene Record, Marshall Thompson, Robert "Squirrel" Lester, and Creadel "Red" Jones.

Jack Daniels signs new acts to Mercury, 1968. Left to right: Johnny Moore, Morris Vaughan, Floyd Morris, and Jack Daniels. Courtesy Jack Daniels.

Billy Butler and Infinity, 1972. Clockwise from top: Errol Batts, Phylis Knox, Larry Wade, and Billy Butler. Courtesy Billy Butler.

Curtis Mayfield, early 1970s.

Leroy Hutson, 1976. A native of Washington, D.C., Hutson helped keep Curtom Records on the charts in the 1970s.

The Impressions, 1979. Left to right: Sam Gooden, Fred Cash, Reggie Torian, and Ralph Johnson.

The Notations, 1975. Left to right: Bobby Thomas, Clifford Curry, and LaSalle Matthews.

Linda Clifford, 1978. Curtom Records depended on Clifford, its only genuine disco star, to produce hits during the disco era of the late 1970s.

The Staple Singers, 1976. This Chicago-based family group was a mainstay first in gospel circles and then in soul music for a quarter of a century before recording under the aegis of Curtis Mayfield in the mid-1970s. Standing, left to right: Cleo, Mavis, and Yvonne Staples; seated: Roebuck "Pop" Staples.

Brighter Side of Darkness, 1972. Top, left to right: Randolph Murph, Larry Washington, and Ralph Eskridge; bottom: Darryl Lamont. Courtesy Clarence Johnson.

Patti and the Lovelites, 1971. These singers were producer Clarence Johnson's first hitmakers. Left to right: Patti Hamilton, Joni Berlmon, and Rhonda Grayson. Courtesy Clarence Johnson.

E. Rodney Jones and Denise LaSalle. WVON deejay E. Rodney Jones presents a gold-record award to Denise LaSalle for her 1971 million-selling hit "Trapped by a Thing Called Love." LaSalle and her husband, Bill Jones, owned a local label, Crajon. Courtesy Denise LaSalle/Showtime Archives (Toronto).

Willie Henderson, 1974. After producing many hits for Tyrone Davis, Henderson left Brunswick Records in 1974 to begin a career as an independent producer and recording artist. Courtesy Willie Henderson.

The Sequins, 1970s. Crajon Productions got its first national hit, "Hey Romeo," with this girl group from Chicago's South Side.

Carl Davis, 1976. Davis is shown in his Chi-Sound offices. Courtesy Carl Davis.

Manchild, 1977.

Margie Alexander, 1977.

Gene Chandler, 1979.
Chandler is shown in
the recording studio.
Photo by D. Shigley.

Magnum Force, 1982.

Butler's string of Gamble-Huff hits ended in 1970. The Philadelphia team left the arrangement when Mercury would not meet their demands for a larger share of the pie. Butler, who was signed to a long-term contract with Mercury, still needed songs. The answer was the formation of the Butler Songwriters Workshop in January 1970 at 1402 South Michigan.[13] In March 1971 the workshop got sustaining support of $55,000 a year from Chappell and Company, the old-line music publishing firm, half of which was then owned by North American Philips.[14]

Butler explained to *Rolling Stone* writer Stuart Werbin in 1973 the reasons behind his concept: "The idea for the workshop came out of self-interest. I had obligations to do thirty sides a year for Mercury...and I didn't know what to do. Tin Pan Alley, where you used to be able to go to get a couple of songs, has died for all intent and purposes. That situation changed when artists started writing their own material....I knew Chicago was not the music center that it once was. But at the same time, I knew there were a number of young cats in Chicago with a lot of songwriting talent, who just didn't have any place to take it to. And even more important, nobody to encourage them."[15]

Also, in January 1970 Butler made a production deal with Mercury through his Fountain Productions, which had been operating as a label at 1402 South Michigan since 1967 without much success. Fountain Productions, with Gerald Sims, Sam Brown, and Billy Butler as producers, produced not only Butler's albums for Mercury, but also Jackie Ross, the Knight Brothers, and Billy Butler and his group, Infinity.[16] Butler and his brother also started up in Memphis a recording studio, a production firm, and a label called Memphis in the fall of 1970.[17]

From 1970 through 1974, the last years of his Mercury association, Butler continued to get moderate hits in the soul market, but his crossover successes were behind him. His two big hits were "If It's Real What I Feel" (a workshop number written by Chuck Jackson), in March 1971, and a duet with Brenda Lee Eager, a four-and-a-half-minute ballad called "Ain't Understanding Mellow" (also a workshop number, by Herscholt Polk and Homer Talbert), in December 1971. The latter was Butler's last million seller and it made that figure on the basis of r&b sales alone. The song was a classic quiet hit that sold and sold and sold; when the total sales finally passed a million copies, Mercury was surprised, and even Butler was surprised. The Butler and Eager team would hit twice more with "Close to You" (1972) and "Can't Understand It" (1973).

Meanwhile, Butler's Fountain Productions and his Memphis operation had yielded but a few hits outside of his own. Records by Jackie Ross, the Knight Brothers, the Unifics, and the Girls all failed. Ollie Nightingale succeeded in getting a moderate hit in 1971 on the Memphis label with

"It's a Sad Thing," but Billy Butler and Infinity had the best success.[18] Besides Butler, Infinity consisted of Errol Batts (from the Enchanters), Phyllis Knox, and Larry Wade. The group got its first recognition in 1969 with "Get on the Case" on the Fountain label. After a few deplorable releases on Mercury, Infinity got another moderate national hit in 1971 with "I Don't Want to Lose You" on the Memphis label. A deal with MGM Records resulted in an uneven album, *Hung Up on You* (1973), produced by Billy Butler and James Blumenberg (a workshop talent).

The workshop was a better success than were Butler's production companies.[19] Among the talent that passed through its doors were Johnny Jones and James Blumenberg, who later recorded as a duo for Stax Records. Another team, Zane Grey and Len Ron Hanks, later recorded as Grey and Hanks for RCA and scored with a number of hits during 1979-80. One singer, Lee Charles Nealy, had prior to his workshop experience already got a national hit as Lee Charles with a Carl Davis production, "Standing on the Outside," in 1968. He would later record for Gene Chandler's Bamboo label with no success, but received some national recognition in 1973 with "I Just Want to Be Loved" on Hot Wax.

The most successful team to come out of the workshop was Chuck Jackson and Marvin Yancy, Jr., who had immense success throughout the 1970s writing and producing hits for the Independents, Natalie Cole, and others. Other fine writers from the workshop included Larry Wade, Terry Collier, Homer Talbert, and Michael Sutton.

That the workshop helped aspiring songwriters to learn the craft and art of composing songs was undeniable. Chappell found the results strong enough to renew the workshop in early 1973 after a two-year trial period. By the mid-seventies, however, the workshop was dead. Butler's hits had dried up and on his last two albums for Mercury he did not use workshop material. His brother's group, Infinity, broke up in 1974 having never gotten off the ground. From the standpoint of hits, the workshop's successes were far too infrequent, especially in the later years. The venture's real success should be measured in terms of the future talent it helped to train, which was considerable.

After Mercury, Jerry Butler moved to Motown in 1975. Instrumental in his joining the organization was Motown president Ewart Abner, Jr., who had been the president of Butler's old company, Vee Jay. Butler's first album for the company was produced and written by a host of Motown talents and it left the artist very dissatisfied. Much of his later work for Motown was recorded in Chicago, where he relied on the songwriting and producing skills of Homer Talbert. Despite Butler's confidence in Talbert, no memorable recordings came out of the association. By the mid-1980s, after brief flings with Gamble and Huff's Philadelphia International Records and with his own revived Fountain label, Butler left the recording business to concentrate on his beverage distributorship and a career in politics.

Gene Chandler

Gene Chandler signed with Mercury in 1970 after a decade of working with producer Carl Davis. He felt constrained at Brunswick Records and wanted the freedom to write and produce his own recordings, control his destiny, and manage his career. Nat Tarnopol would not give him the opportunity, but at Mercury he got it. "I started producing myself," said Chandler, "and I turned out to be successful on my first record, which was 'Groovy Situation.'"[20]

"Groovy Situation" was indeed successful. It became Chandler's first million seller since "Duke of Earl" in 1962, and went high on both the pop and soul charts in the summer of 1970. On the *Cash Box* r&b chart it lasted sixteen weeks and went as high as position four. He also had big hits with "Simply Call It Love," in October 1970, and "You're a Lady," in June 1971, both of which made the national soul charts. A surprising miss was the superb Eugene Record composition "Yes I'm Ready," which failed to reach the charts upon its release in late 1971. Chandler also had mild success in 1971 recording a duet album with Jerry Butler.

When Chandler signed with Mercury, he was already heavily involved in the business end of the music industry, managing and producing acts for the Bamboo label in his offices at 1321 South Michigan. In 1969 he had a big hit with Mel and Tim's "Backfield in Motion," but had no comparable success with the company's other acts—Lee Charles, the Profiles, and the Voice Masters, although some records managed to scrape the bottom of the national charts for a few weeks. In August 1970 he signed a production deal with Mercury, in which the Chandler-produced acts would be released on his own Mister Chand label, distributed by Mercury.[21] Bamboo was phased out shortly afterward. Mister Chand had only four acts, two of which reached the charts in 1971, Simtec and Wylie, a self-contained band led by two singers, as mentioned earlier, and the Krystal Generation, a girl group.

Simtec and Wylie had earlier recorded for Syl Johnson, but were ready to move on in 1970. Simtec Simmons explained how the duo joined Chandler: "He had Mel and Tim at the time and he was accompanying them to the Apollo Theatre in New York. He happened to see us at the show and saw that we were very entertaining. Wylie had a strong spiritual voice that was rather dynamic. And we got a strong response from the audience. Our contract was up at Shama, so when we came back to Chicago we hooked up with Chandler."[22]

By the time Simtec Simmons and Wylie Dixon were recording for Mister Chand in the latter part of 1970, they were working with drummer Wilbur "June" Mhoon. Their old drummer, Fred White, had joined up with Ramsey Lewis, and later he would join his brothers in Earth, Wind and Fire. The sound Simtec and Wylie established at Mister Chand was slightly lighter than that of their Shama sides and to me not as good. At Shama the beat and groove seemed more focused and tighter. Simmons concurred, explaining, "I personally prefer the Shama beat, because it has more funk. We had to change with the trend and had to go more mellow. Gene Chandler wanted us to get the pop appeal."[23]

The group's biggest hit was their third Mister Chand release, "Gotta Get over the Hump," which lasted nine weeks and went to position twenty-nine on *Billboard*'s soul chart. Mercury even released an LP to exploit the single's success. Unfortunately, Simtec and Wylie failed to satisfactorily follow with respectable singles, and by 1974 the duo and their band had broken up. Dixon retired from the business and moved to Bloomington, Illinois.

Simmons continued a few more years with a solo career. In late 1974 he had a huge local hit in Chicago with "Some Other Time," which briefly made *Cash Box*'s national r&b chart in February 1975. The record was a marvelous piece of soft soul, with Simmons's high tenor vocals wonderfully matched with an engagingly catchy arrangement. A few years later Simmons recorded for California-based AVI, but with no success. He quit the business in the late 1970s.

The Krystal Generation was an outgrowth of the Simtec and Wylie organization, as their material was written, instrumentally backed, and produced by the duo's Tea Boxes Band. The group consisted of lead Joyce Smith, Darlene Arnold, Mary Shelley, and Mary Lead.[24] They released seven records, three of them on Mister Chand, but only one charted, a Mister Chand release called "Wanted Dead or Alive," in 1971. It was not a good record, but a release on the Tea Boxes Band's own label, CMC, was a dandy. The song was a cover of Sam Cooke's "Wonderful World," and every soul fan owes a listen to this marvelous rendition with its delightful lope. After Simtec and Wylie broke up, Krystal Generation continued off and on for the next decade trying to make something happen again, but without success.

Chandler, besides attempting to sustain his own recording career, found himself working as an administrator, producer, writer, and publicist for Mister Chand. He closed down the label in 1972. He explained:

> I didn't have any help. When I set up this big plan, I thought I was going to get Eugene Record as a producer, and somebody else.

I didn't get Record from Brunswick because of situations I wouldn't want to discuss. The people that had him would not let him go. So that kind of killed what I had planned.

I had got all the money, made all the deal in one week—I wouldn't make them at separate times because I didn't want someone to say, "No, you got too much to do now." But anyway, it didn't come through. I ended up recording nearly every damn day of the week. I was picking the songs for the artists, working with two different arrangers, Tom Washington and Richard Evans. I kept Universal Studios booked up and just constantly working. But after a while my sound was beginning to repeat itself. If I had the Huff I would have been fine, like Gamble and Huff. I had nobody else.[25]

Chandler left the Mercury organization in 1972.

Mercury Skips Town

In January 1972 Mercury was purchased by the Polygram group head-quartered in Baarn, Holland.[26] Under Steinberg the company continued to draw on Chicago soul talent throughout the 1970s, mainly by picking up acts previously developed by Chicago independents as Steinberg did with Jerry Butler and Gene Chandler. As the independent companies sank, Mercury picked up the flotsam. In 1975 after Chess went out of business, the independent that picked up the remnants of the company, All Platinum, could not afford the Dells contract, and the group went to Mercury. The following year, after the breakdown of Brunswick, the Chi-lites sans Eugene Record signed with Mercury. Other Chicago signings were Heaven and Earth, produced by Clarence Johnson, and Kitty and the Haywoods, produced by Mercury's big self-contained r&b funk band, the Ohio Players.

With both the Dells and the Chi-lites, Mercury felt the talent in Chicago no longer was capable of creating hits, and after both groups had failed albums the company sent them to Philadelphia, the hot city in the 1970s for recording black music. Justifying the label's contention, both groups made their best albums on Mercury with Philadelphia producers. But in the late 1970s, vocal groups were fading as a force in black music, and neither the Dells nor the Chi-lites got substantial hits with their made-in-Philly albums. In late 1980, Mercury, deciding that the music business had gravitated so strongly toward both coasts, moved its headquarters to New York. Chicago thus lost the one major in the best position to discover and record black music talent in the city.

NOTES

1. "Reflections: Mercury," Phonogram Inc., [company history from about 1976]; Peter Grendysa, liner notes, *The Vocal Group Collection*, Mercury 830 283-1 M-2, 1986. The latter source serves as a good survey of Mercury's r&b efforts in the 1940s and 1950s minus any discussion of Dinah Washington and Brook Benton.

2. Grendysa, liner notes.

3. Galen Gart, *ALRD: The American Record Label Directory and Label Guide* (Milford, N.H.: Big Nickel, 1989), p. 142.

4. Colin Escott, *Clyde McPhatter: A Biographical Essay* (Vollersode, West Germany: Bear Family Records, 1987), pp. 40-41; Jim Haskins, *Queen of the Blues* (New York: Morrow, 1987), p. 149.

5. Charlie Gillett, *Sound of the City*, rev. ed. (New York: Pantheon, 1983), p. 51; "The Men Behind the Music: Polygram Records Group," *Soul*, January 16, 1978, p. 16; "Reflections: Mercury."

6. "Mercury Launches Limelight Campaign," *Billboard*, May 30, 1964, p. 3.

7. "Mercury Launches Limelight Records," *Billboard*, November 9, 1963, p. 4.

8. "Blue Rock and Limelight Consolidated by Mercury," *Billboard*, October 23, 1964, p. 3.

9. Charley Crespo, "Joyce Kennedy Play [sic] Her Game," *Rock and Soul*, March 1986, p. 21; Patrick Goldstein, "A Band that Does What It Can't," *Chicago Sun-Times*, October 25, 1976; "Mother's Finest Zooming to Galaxy of Stars after a Decade," *Chicago Defender*, March 24, 1979.

10. Jack Daniels interview, October 15, 1987.

11. "Chicago—To Build a Creative Soul Center," *Billboard*, August 22, 1970, pp. 20, 22; "Merc to Handle Mr. Chand; Helps to Form Workshop," *Billboard*, August 1, 1970, p. 4.

12. Patrick Goldstein, "Making Hits and Big Money at Chicago's Mercury Records," *Panorama—Chicago Daily News*, October 16-17, 1976, pp. 2-4; "Mercury—Chicago's World Ambassador," *Billboard*, April 19, 1975, p. C-8; "The Men Behind the Music."

13. "Merc and Fountain Production Deal, Plan Writers' Workshop," *Billboard*, January 31, 1970, p. 80.

14. "Butler, Chicago Workshop Join Chappell Group," *Billboard*, March 27, 1971, p. 1.

15. Stuart Werbin, "Jerry Butler, Mr. Contemporary," *Rolling Stone*, February 15, 1973, p. 18.

16. "Merc and Fountain," *Billboard*.

17. "Memphis Label Distrib Net," *Billboard*, February 20, 1971, p. 66.

18. Robert Pruter, "The (other) Butler Did It...(too)!!: The Billy Butler Story," *It Will Stand* 19 (1981): 16–18; Billy Butler interview.

19. Workshop sources: Steve Bryant, liner notes, The Independents, *The First Time We Met—The Greatest Hits*, Charly R&B CRB 1146, 1986; Werbin, "Jerry Butler"; "Chicago—To Build a Creative Soul Center."

20. Gene Chandler interview, February 6, 1979.

21. "Merc to Handle Mr. Chand," *Billboard*.
22. Simtec Simmons interview.
23. Ibid.
24. Ibid.
25. Chandler interview.
26. "Polygram Buys Merc, Interest in Chappell," *Billboard*, January 29, 1972, p. 3.

13

Curtom Records

Curtom Records was founded by Curtis Mayfield and Eddie Thomas in March 1968 as an independently distributed label.[1] It is surprising that Mayfield started the label, given that during the previous two years he had started up two labels, Windy C and Mayfield, and was forced to close them down. Mayfield gave a simple reason why he gave it another try: "Because I wasn't a quitter. Sometimes these things are like marriages. You don't give up wanting to be in love and having the best you can expect, just because your marriage fails."[2] The company's motto was "We're a Winner," taken from one of the Impressions' last big hits at ABC. And unlike Mayfield's previous attempts at establishing a company, Curtom *was* a winner, successfully recording acts for more than a decade before succumbing to the major labels.

What made the label a success? The talent of Mayfield for one thing. With his songwriting and producing abilities, he created many hit records for the other acts on the label, not to mention the hits he created that fueled his own enormous success as a solo artist. As the 1970s wore on another important strength was the company's getting distribution through larger labels rather than by direct independent distribution. In June 1968, distribution was assumed by Buddah Records, a powerful New York independent headed by Art Kass and Neil Bogart (a former executive at Cameo-Parkway). In 1975 a major, Warner Brothers, replaced Buddah as the parent company.

Curtom also had wise management. Mayfield was too busy on the creative end to manage the business aspects of the company, and he found a top manager in Marv Stuart, a young man whose only previous experience was as manager of such rock acts as American Breed, New Colony Six, and Baby Huey and the Babysitters (a black act with a large white following). He effectively took over direction of the company from Eddie Thomas in 1970, and formally took the reins in May 1971.[3] Mayfield cites Stuart as a key ingredient in the company's success: "As green as he was, he was very ambitious. I taught him the record business, and how to relate to these people. And of course through his own know-how and his own go-gettingness, he learned. He was able to find weak spots in Curtom and he turned them around."[4]

The name Curtom comes from "Curtis" and "Thomas," obviously taken from the two early owners. The name was actually used first for a publishing company Mayfield and Thomas established in 1960, when Mayfield started writing songs for Jerry Butler at Vee Jay (Butler had a small piece of the company). That Mayfield, under twenty-one and black to boot, started his own publishing company was unprecedented then. Said Mayfield, "I had a big run-in with Ewart Abner and Calvin Carter at Vee Jay, they weren't used to that! I was working with Dick Shelton at the time, who helped me negotiate these things. He made a lot of money in the music business."[5]

In 1965 Mayfield formed Chi-Sound Publishing, which he owned 100 percent, and in 1968 when the Impressions switched to Curtom he formed Camad, sharing ownership with Carl Davis.[6] In 1975 after Curtom moved to Warner Brothers distribution, Mayfield started yet another publishing company, Mayfield Music. Curtom at one time was handling six different publishing companies.[7]

Curtom at its founding was located on the far South Side at 8541 South Stony Island Boulevard. After Stuart came on board the offices were moved to 6212 North Lincoln, in Lincolnwood, a suburb north of Chicago. After 1973 the offices were located at 5915 North Lincoln on the North Side.

Mayfield from the company's inception was the principal producer and A&R man, and veteran Johnny Pate and newcomer Donny Hathaway were arrangers. Pate left in 1972, but as the company grew, Stuart beefed up the in-house staff, especially after Curtom took over the RCA Studio in 1973. Curtom, one of the steadiest customers of the studio, in a sense inherited the operation and its engineer Roger Anfinsen. Also in 1973 Richard Tufo came in as an arranger, producer, and A&R man. Other producers who came later were LeRoy Hutson, Lowrell Simon, Ed Townsend, Gil Askey, and the team of Marvin Yancy and Chuck Jackson. Most of Curtom's artists did not write their own songs, and thus the producers were the company's writers as well. Curtom during the 1970s was rivaled as a creative force for black music in Chicago only by Carl Davis's operations at Brunswick Records and later Chi-Sound Records.

Curtis Mayfield

Curtis Mayfield's debut on Curtom was as lead and the creative force for the Impressions. The three Impressions albums he recorded on Curtom were marginally better than his last ABC albums, but frankly by the end of the 1960s Mayfield's best composing work was behind him. But he was taking greater command of his career by this time in assuming the sole job as producer. The later albums on ABC listed Johnny Pate as producer, but in actuality they were co-produced with Mayfield.

The first Curtom release, *This Is My Country*, from late 1968, was a solid work with several excellent songs, notably "This Is My Country," "Fool for You," "My Woman's Love," "Stay Close to Me," and "Love's Happening." (The latter two cuts were also recorded by the Five Stairsteps on their Curtom releases.) Just two singles were taken from the LP, however, "Fool for You," which went to position three and lasted twelve weeks on *Billboard*'s soul chart, and "This Is My Country," which went to position eight and lasted eleven weeks on the chart. The album had a good-feeling atmosphere helped immensely by Johnny Pate's bright cheerful horn charts. "This Is My Country" was a paean to black pride in America, a sentiment that clashed sharply with the growing militancy that was then engulfing the country.

Young Mods' Forgotten Story, with arrangements by Pate and Donny Hathaway, was a weaker album than its predecessor, but it did well upon its release in the spring of 1969. It produced three hit singles: "My Deceiving Heart" (which went to position twenty-six and lasted six weeks), "Seven Years" (position fifteen and seven weeks), and "Choice of Colors" (position one and thirteen weeks). The last Impressions album with Mayfield was *Check Out Your Mind* (1970), which yielded three pounding hits: "Check Out Your Mind" (three position and twelve weeks in the spring of 1970), "(Baby) Turn on to Me" (six position and ten weeks), and "Ain't Got Time" (twelve position and ten weeks). The album signaled a new direction in Mayfield's music, a move from soft ballads and bright mid-tempo tunes to funkier, more ominous-sounding driving tunes.

The most significant event for Curtom in 1970, however, was Mayfield's leaving the Impressions to establish himself as a solo artist. In the latter part of the year, he released his first solo effort, *Curtis*. Mayfield later claimed, "I had never intended on leaving the Impressions permanently. Then I came out with the *Curtis* album and in doing so I discovered we had *two* acts on Curtom."[8] By the 1970s, the trend in both rock and r&b music was toward self-contained acts that wrote and performed their own material, and Stuart sensed this and felt Mayfield would be better off not subsumed within a vocal group. Marv Stuart told journalist Cary Baker in the Chicago *Reader*, "I told Curtis, 'Everyone makin' it was a singer-songwriter, Curtis. You're an artist, you should go off on your own.' "[9] That Mayfield decided to make his solo foray permanent did not make Stuart unhappy. The solo albums included cuts as long as ten minutes and thus worked to establish Mayfield as an album artist.

Mayfield's solo career was decidedly mixed artistically. His thin high-tenor vocals were faulted for lacking punch, his jarring rhythms for being unfocused, his lyrics for being wordy and pretentious, and his songs for lacking melodic meat. Yet some of the very best black popular music of the 1970s came from Mayfield, who despite the many misses during the decade was one of the creative leaders in establishing a new contemporary style of rhythm and blues, one with a militant, harder edge. Mayfield's style may best be described as rumbling funk, in which he sings his didactic lyrics of social commentary over an instrumental accompaniment of wah-wah guitar, heavy bass lines, swirling strings, and blaring horns.[10]

Mayfield's solo work was harder-sounding than anything he did while with the Impressions. "There was some things that I long had wanted to do," he confessed, "but they were out of the category of what was expected of me and the Impressions. When I got off in the *Curtis* album it allowed me to be more personal for myself."[11]

What was happening was that a new urgent sense of militancy and social concern was coming out of black America during the early 1970s, and many rhythm-and-blues artists of the era were reflecting those feelings in their music. Soul lyrics went beyond the elemental subjects of love, sex, and dance to encompass ghetto anger, such as Marvin Gaye's "What's Going On," the Chi-lites' "(For God Sakes) Give More Power to the People," the Undisputed Truth's "Smiling Faces Sometimes," and the Staple Singers' "Respect Yourself." All these songs came out in 1971 and Mayfield more than any of these artists reflected those times.[12] "It was the era that was 'happening,' " related Mayfield, "when people stopped wearing the tuxedos and such. People were getting down a little more, and of course marijuana was the prime happening. All these things were going on."[13]

Curtis was a bit schizophrenic, with two cuts reflecting Mayfield's bold rumbling funk style and the remainder being softer tunes in the style of the Impressions. It was "(Don't Worry) If There's a Hell Below We're All Going to Go," a rumbling funk number that became a hit single, which went to the three position and lasted thirteen weeks on *Billboard*'s soul chart in late 1970.

The next album, *Curtis Live*, from 1971, was intended to introduce Mayfield's new contemporary style in a nightclub setting. The LP was a terrific showcase for rumbling funk, in which the heavy bass lines magnified by a live recording contributed immensely to the ominous, militant tone of the music. The effectiveness of the live approach was particularly evident on the opening cut, "Mighty Mighty Spade and Whitey." The album easily ranked as one of Mayfield's best solo efforts. Said he, "If I had to pull out a favorite album it would probably be the *Curtis Live*, simply because it did break down my feelings in a context of intermingling and intimacy with a live audience."[14]

Mayfield followed with *Roots* in late 1971, which yielded top singles in "Get Down" (thirteen position and nine weeks on the chart), "We've Got to Have Peace" (thirty-two position and five weeks), and "Beautiful Brother of Mine" (forty-five position and two weeks).

Mayfield's next album, *Superfly*, the soundtrack of the black action film of the same name from 1972, was his most notable solo achievement. Mayfield and his band also appeared in this movie about a drug pusher, playing in a nightclub the pusher frequented. Praise for the album was almost universal, as Mayfield's jagged guitar lines seemed just right for conveying the nervous energy of the black urban ghetto and the pusher's milieu. In the standout numbers, "Freddie's Dead," "Pusherman," and "Superfly," the lack of melody served as a strength, allowing the rhythms to shine and resonate. Mayfield's vocals sympathetically came across more laid-back cool than thin. Said Mayfield, "It was something I was inspired from the reading of this heavy script of *Superfly*. Of course, I could relate with a lot of it, because I lived enough throughout the city to sense what a 'Priest' and what a 'Superfly' was. It allowed me to get past the glitter of the drug scene and go to the depth of it—allowing a little bit of the sparkle and the highlights lyrically, but always with a moral to that."[15]

Superfly was Mayfield's second million-seller and was a number-one record on the top charts. The album produced two top singles, "Freddie's Dead," which went to number two and lasted seventeen weeks in the late summer of 1972, and "Superfly," which went to the five position and lasted fifteen weeks on the chart in late 1972.

The album made Mayfield a crossover artist, with huge sales in the white community, but as a live performer he was still a "ghetto act." Most white rock-fans did not attend shows by black acts in the early 1970s even when they were held in rock venues. Chicago's Jam Productions tried booking Mayfield at its big North Side rock palace, the Aragon. Jam's co-owner, Jerry Mickelson, told rock scribe Bruce Meyer in 1977, "You learn the market. Take Curtis Mayfield. He was hotter than a pistol, and he died in the Aragon. So we learned that you can't do a black act up there."[16]

Mayfield's *Back to the World*, released in 1973, was the follow-up to *Superfly*, and the fall-off from the latter made *Back to the World* a gold record. It was not a strong record, however. The rumbling funk had evolved into something closer to meandering funk. But the album produced three hit singles, "Future Shock" (eleven position and eleven weeks), "If I Were Only a Child Again" (twenty-two position and eleven weeks), and "Can't Say Nothing" (sixteen position and twelve weeks). A tad better was *Sweet Exorcist* from the spring of 1974. "Kung Fu" was a solid, effective funk number and went to the three position on *Billboard*'s soul chart. *Got to Find a Way*, released in late 1974, was Mayfield's last album on Buddah and was simply terrible. A single spun off the LP, "Mother's Son," was bearable funk and managed to go to position fifteen and last eleven weeks on the chart.

On Warner Brothers the following year Mayfield released *There's No Place Like America Today*, which unfortunately sustained the artist's downward creative slide. The saving grace was the outstanding single it produced, "So in Love," which has a brass-style accompaniment reminiscent of 1960s soul. "So in Love" proved to be a big hit, lasting eighteen weeks and going to the nine position on the soul chart.

Mayfield's next album, *Give Get Take and Have*, was likewise uninteresting, yet as with the previous album it yielded a truly exceptional single, "Only You Babe." The ballad possessed a recognizable and appealing melody and managed to showcase Mayfield's difficult-to-record thin vocals especially well. The record deservedly went to the eight position and lasted thirteen weeks on *Billboard*'s soul chart.

Never Say You Can't Survive, from 1977, also produced only one respectable single, "Show Me Love," which didn't do a whole lot on the soul chart, however. Mayfield in his previous three albums certainly demonstrated he was still capable of writing solid, memorable songs, but not the number as in earlier years. The record business required that he keep churning out albums every year whether he had enough songs to fill an album or not. Mayfield obviously did not, yet many of his best songs during this time, ironically, went to other artists on the label, notably on movie soundtracks.

The one other soundtrack on Curtom featuring Mayfield was *Short Eyes*, from 1977. The film for which it was scored was several steps above the usual black action films of the period, having been based on Miguel Pinero's award-winning play from 1974. Curtom was also one of the investors in the film, but unfortunately *Short Eyes* did not do well at the box office, despite critical praise. Said Mayfield, "We got great recognition and real good write-ups. However, the documentary type of stuff with the foul language of the characters, of people just rapping, it was probably too real. You can always look back and tell what happened. When we did it, it was during the times of escapism, of *Star Wars*, things like that."[17]

The soundtrack, however, yielded a sharp-selling single, "Do Do Wop

Is Strong in Here," which went to position twenty-nine and lasted sixteen weeks on *Billboard*'s soul chart in late fall of 1977. The album also contained an excellent remake of "I Can't Work No Longer," which Mayfield wrote back in 1962. The new version, which appeared as the flip to "Do Do Wop," was called "Need Someone to Love."

Other soundtracks from Curtom written and produced but not performed by Mayfield were *Claudine* (1974), performed by Gladys Knight and the Pips; *Let's Do It Again* (1975), performed by the Staple Singers; *Pipedreams* (1976), performed by Gladys Knight and the Pips; *Sparkle* (1976), sung by Aretha Franklin; and *A Piece of the Action* (1977), rendered by Mavis Staples. Only the two Staples albums appeared on Curtom. In the *Sparkle* movie, incidentally, the then unknown actresses Lonnette McKee, Irene Cara, and Dawn Smith sang the score, but the soundtrack had Aretha Franklin singing, apparently for sales purposes. The soundtracks proved immensely successful, and in 1976 Marv Stuart reported that *Superfly*, *Let's Do It Again*, *Claudine*, and *Sparkle* each grossed more than one million in sales.[18]

In 1978 Mayfield reached his creative nadir with the *Do It All Night* album. Disco was at the peak of its popularity, and Mayfield found himself following a trend instead of making one in black music. The album was endless disco, in which even the ballads were given a metronomic beat. Askey, who did some fine disco albums for Curtom's one true disco star, Linda Clifford, replaced longtime arranger Rich Tufo. Of the three singles spun off the LP only "You Are You Are" did anything respectable, lasting twelve weeks and going to position thirty-four on *Billboard*'s soul chart. Confessed Mayfield about his disco foray:

> In all honesty, it wasn't even me. It was just my allowing Marv and allowing the disco thing to influence me. The disco influence was so strong that it made a lot of artists, a lot of creative people try and be and do what they weren't.
>
> Well, what was happening during those times, I was allowing myself to be for the first time wearing too many hats. I had spread myself to thinly through doing all these movie scores, trying to keep my own career going, working on the road, and trying to make decisions in the studio, and trying to watch money, as well as handle my own personal affairs in life. Thus, I began to allow other people with bad decisions to influence me. That was probably no good for me, the company, and for the customer that had so much expectations for me.
>
> The whole name of the game was to make money, too. The investors want to hear one thing—"I want to make money." Probably what people should have done, and I probably should

have done myself, was just laid back and kind of watch things for a while.[19]

Unfortunately Mayfield did not lay back and for the next two years, 1979–80, he perserved with albums that tried to reflect the trends in music. RSO picked up distribution from Warner Brothers in 1979, and Mayfield's first release under the new arrangement, *Heartbeat*, sold well but was an uninteresting album. The second release, *Something to Believe In*, gave the record buyer little to believe in. The third album, *The Right Combination*, a duet album with Linda Clifford, featured an outstanding ballad, "Between You and Me Baby." In 1980, Curtis Mayfield decided to pack it in and disband Curtom.

LeRoy Hutson

LeRoy Hutson came to Curtom through the Donny Hathaway connection. The artists were roommates and music students at Howard University, Washington, D.C. While still there they collaborated on several songs, notably "The Ghetto," which was a hit for Hathaway in early 1970 on Atco Records. Hutson graduated from Howard in the summer of 1970, and was asked to replace Mayfield in the Impressions a short time later. The first Impressions record with Hutson as lead came out in mid-1971.[20]

Hutson was born June 4, 1945, in Newark, New Jersey. While in high school he performed in a vocal group called the Nu-tones. At Howard, Hutson joined Hathaway and some other fellows to form the Mayfield Singers, who recorded a single on Mayfield Records. Later Hutson teamed up with Deborah Rollins to form Sugar and Spice, and they recorded a couple of singles on Kapp Records out of New York without much success. As one can surmise, Hutson not only brought a solid academic musical training with him but an experienced r&b background as well when he joined the Impressions.

Replacing Mayfield in the Impressions was not a satisfactory experience for Hutson, however, as the two post-Mayfield Impressions albums with Hutson as lead sadly gave evidence. The first Hutson-led album, *Times Have Changed*, released in early 1972, was a considerable step down both artistically and commercially from *This Is My Country* or *Check Out Your Mind*. Two singles, "Love Me," from July 1971, and "This Love's for Real," from April 1972, spent a few weeks on the charts and promptly disappeared. Mayfield wrote, produced, and arranged the album, but his work just seemed to lack the Mayfield spark. Hutson did a little arranging on *Times Have Changed*, but with his musical background he probably chafed at his constricted role in the group. His supple tenor voice was put to good use as lead, but Hutson did not enter the music business to perform only as a vocalist.

The next Hutson-led album, *Preacher Man* from 1973, was an even more dismal failure. The record was written, produced, and arranged by one of Curtom's strong new talents, Rich Tufo, but it yielded no records that made the charts.

Hutson left the Impressions after *Preacher Man*. The artist was undoubtedly filled with pent-up frustration at not having been able to use fully his musical talents, as the Curtom publicity release suggested: "The Impressions' tight stylistic focus did not satisfy his total musical personality."[21]

From 1973 through 1980, Hutson established himself at Curtom with a moderately successful recording career, coming out with seven albums and charting some thirteen singles. On nearly all his work, he wrote, produced, arranged, and played multiple instruments, demonstrating that he had superb talent. But Hutson never made a truly top-notch album with a solid body of music. He knew how to create well-crafted r&b tunes, but could not write a memorable melody. His best charted singles were "All Because of You" (thirty-one position and twelve weeks on the *Billboard* soul chart in 1975), "Feel the Spirit (in '76)" (twenty-five position and ten weeks in 1976), and "I Do I Do" (fifty-five position and thirteen weeks in 1976), "Where Did Love Go" (forty-five position and eleven weeks in 1978), and "Right or Wrong" (forty-seven position and ten weeks in 1979). But honestly there is not one song among them that I would unreservedly recommend.

When Curtom went out of business in 1980, Hutson made a couple more albums for other companies and then disappeared from the music world. Hutson's career at Curtom can be easily summarized as one in which he exhibited a tremendous amount of talent, a moderate amount of commercial success that helped sustain Curtom as an ongoing concern, and a small amount of artistic success.

The Impressions

One of the surprising and most impressive achievements of Curtom in the mid-1970s was the resuscitation of the Impressions. During 1974–75, the group placed high on *Billboard*'s soul chart with "Finally Got Myself Together," which went to number one, and "Sooner or Later" and "Same Thing It Took," both of which went to number three. Considering the situation of the group this was a superb achievement. The failure of the Impressions during 1971–73 with LeRoy Hutson as lead was an ominous sign for the group's future. Curtom could no longer depend on Mayfield, who in the mid-1970s seemingly no longer had the ability to spread his talents around in a consistent fashion, or to provide hits for the label's other acts. The other members of the in-house staff also seemed to lack the inspiration to sustain the Impressions. Fred Cash and Sam Gooden correctly perceived that to make themselves into hitmakers again they would have to bring in new talent.[22]

At Cash's behest, Curtom did two things: the company reshaped the group and it brought in a new writer/producer/arranger, the veteran producer Ed Townsend. Cash told *Black Music*'s Denise Hall, "Basically we knew we had to make a change. That's why we moved so fast when LeRoy left, we knew we wanted to get into something else, whilst maintaining our own sound. Over the years Sam and I had often talked about different numbers we would like to have done, but were never in a position to, because we hadn't the right lead vocalist. So we always ended up in the real soft gentle bag, which we loved, don't get me wrong, but we wanted to be able to do the other stuff too."[23]

In late 1973, two new leads were brought in, both tenors: Ralph Johnson, who came out of the gospel field and provided the aggressive strong gospel sound Cash and Gooden were seeking, and Reggie Torian, who could provide the soft ballady sound for the group's material from their Mayfield years. Johnson was from Greenville, South Carolina, and was discovered through an audition tape he sent to Chicago. He was inspired to send the tape by the success of a fellow Greenville resident, Chuck Jackson, who had established a successful songwriting and singing career as a member of the Chicago-based Independents. Torian was born and raised on the South Side; early in 1973 as a member of a vocal group the Enchanters, he had a small local hit, "A Fool Like Me," which came out on Jimmy Vanleer's Golden Ear label.

Ed Townsend had been in the music business since the early 1950s and had a national hit in 1958 with the lovely ballad "For Your Love." During the 1960s he worked as a producer and A&R director first for Scepter and later for Mercury, and in the early 1970s he worked with Motown great Marvin Gaye. Townsend brought an invigorating new element into Curtom, which was evident in the Impressions very next record, *Finally Got Myself Together* (1974).

Half the album was written and produced by Curtom's in-house staff, and the songs were stale rehashes of earlier Curtom material. The first single from the LP, "If It's in You to Do Wrong," was written by Lowrell Simon and produced by Simon and Tufo, and had the typical mellow-funk Mayfield sound with swirling strings and wah-wah guitar. The ballad did not do poorly, lasting thirteen weeks and going to number twenty-six position upon its release in December 1973. It was the Impressions' biggest hit since their last Mayfield-led song, "Ain't Got Time," in early 1971, but it was not a memorable tune.

"Finally Got Myself Together," which became a number one record in the spring of 1974, was another matter. The mid-tempo song written and produced by Townsend featured vigorous up-front singing perfectly showcased with bright, spirited arrangements refreshingly free of the typical Curtom approach. Another excellent song from the LP was "I'll Always Be Here," in which producers Tufo and Simon took a page from Townsend's book and came up with another solid, spirited number. Although much of the rest of the album was marred by too many Simon/Tufo mellow-funk numbers, *Finally Got Myself Together* rejuvenated the Impressions.

The group took a step back in later years with *Three the Hard Way,* a soundtrack album written and produced by Simon and Tufo for the black action film of the same name. The singing was vigorous but it was expended on weak material. The album was the Impressions' last under Buddah distribution.

Townsend was given the job of writing and producing the Impressions' next album, *First Impressions,* which was released in 1975. It was the group's best album in years, the first that could be enjoyed all the way through since their Mayfield-led albums. The album yielded two number-three hits, "Sooner or Later," in April, and "Same Thing It Took," in September. With *First Impressions* the group had fully emerged out of the shadow of Mayfield and had achieved an identity and a body of music distinctly its own.

Unfortunately, the Impressions dissipated their success with subsequent albums. Late in 1975 came the *Loving Power* album, which did not receive the full hands-on treatment from Townsend, who directed the project as "executive producer." Perhaps he had run out of inspiration, because he brought in several new cooks—with Chuck Jackson and Marvin Yancy producing some cuts, Rich Tufo producing others, and Townsend producing some. The resulting stew yielded two tepid singles, "Loving Power," which lasted thirteen weeks and went to position eleven, and "Sunshine," which lasted nine weeks and went to position thirty-six.

Curiously, the Impressions left Curtom at this point. Lead singer Ralph Johnson remained with Curtom and formed a new group around him called Mystique. Cash, Gooden, and Torian added Nate Evans, another lead with a heavy gospel background, and went to Atlantic's Cotillion subsidiary label. But bereft of Curtom's in-house staff, the Impressions floundered badly and were never again a strong factor in the recording business.

In forming Mystique, Johnson brought in an old friend from Greenville, Charles Fowler, and two Chicago vocal-group veterans, Larry Brownlee and Fred Simon, the latter the brother of Lowrell. The Simon brothers and

Brownlee, as mentioned earlier, were previously members of the Lost Generation at Brunswick.[24]

Despite the high hopes Curtom and Warner Brothers had for the group, Mystique never got off the ground. Maybe it was the case of too many cooks, because Bunny Sigler, Jerry Butler, Gene McDaniels, Rich Tufo, and Lowrell Simon—among others—all had a hand in producing the group's one album, *Mystique*, released in 1977. Or maybe the ingredients were poor, because there was not a song on the album that could stick in one's memory.

Curtom's Other Vocal Groups

In 1968 the Five Stairsteps returned to Mayfield and joined Curtom Records after a one-year stay and one album at Buddah. Their stint at Curtom was just as brief, with one album to their credit, *Love's Happening*. Curtom, however, pulled four singles off the album and released one other single on the group, so the Five Stairsteps got four chart singles while on the label. The group at this time was billing itself as the Five Stairsteps and Cubie.

At Curtom, the Burkes seemed to have lost some of their creative juices. The album was produced by Mayfield and he wrote all the album's songs. The five singles that were put out on Curtom were: "Don't Change Your Love" (nine weeks and position fifteen on the r&b chart in the early fall of 1968), "Stay Close to Me" (no chart position in late 1968), "Baby Make Me Feel Good" (nine weeks and position twelve in early 1969), "Madame Mary" (two weeks and position thirty-eight in the summer of 1969), and "We Must Be in Love" (seven weeks and position seventeen in the fall of 1969). The best of the lot was ironically "Stay Close to Me," a rousing, up-tempo number. The painful truth of the matter, however, is that none of these singles was equal to any of the group's Windy C hits.

The Five Stairsteps ended their Chicago years in 1970 and began recording for Buddah Records again under producer Stan Vincent in New York. The group dropped Cubie and became officially the Five Stairsteps again. With Vincent they got their first million seller, the splendid "O-o-h Child," which was also their only real crossover hit. The following year the group moved to New Jersey and Alohe dropped out to attend college. Under the name "Stairsteps" the group had two more hits, "I Love You—Stop" (1972), a weak, imitative Jackson Five type of song, and following a three-year breakup, "From Me to You" (1975), recorded on George Harrison's Dark Horse label. Despite lack of a memorable hook, the song lasted seventeen weeks and went to position ten on *Billboard*'s soul chart.

In 1976 the Stairsteps broke up again, but during 1980–81 they were together as the Invisible Man's Band and made two albums. The first yielded the superb hit "All Night Thing" (1980). Then during the remainder of the

1980s, Keni Burke, who had taken over leadership of the Stairsteps from Clarence Jr. after 1971, established a moderately successful solo career. The Five Stairsteps were one of the more impressive talents to come out of Chicago, and their work with Mayfield was rarely equalled by their subsequent efforts.

The Natural Four were signed by Curtom in 1972 at the height of the vocal-group renaissance. The group originated in the mid-1960s in San Francisco, and in the late 1960s recorded with mild success for ABC Records. Its "Why Should We Stop Now" made *Billboard*'s national soul chart for eight weeks in 1969. The group broke up by the turn of the decade, but one of the members, Chris James, kept the idea of the group alive. In 1971 he joined with Steve Striplin, Darryl Cannady, and Delmos Whitley to form a reborn Natural Four. They recorded an excellent ballad, "Give a Little Love," for Bay-area producer Ron Carson, who leased the record to Chess Records. The company, which was going downhill rapidly, neglected it.[25]

Marv Stuart auditioned the Natural Four at an Oakland concert and signed them. The group was not well served by Curtom's various producers; of three albums and nine singles none could stand up in quality to the few singles they had recorded earlier for ABC and Chess. The Natural Four's third release for Curtom, "Can This Be Real," was perhaps their best, with a nice dry tenor-lead singing delightfully over a mid-tempo lope. The record went to the number ten position and lasted eighteen weeks on *Billboard*'s soul chart in late 1973 and early 1974. The song was one of LeRoy Hutson's best compositions.

The follow-up releases, "Love that Really Counts" (position twenty-three and twelve weeks) and "You Bring Out the Best in Me" (position twenty and twelve weeks), could be considered moderately successful commercially, but artistically they were undistinguished. During 1975 and 1976 the Natural Four came up with four more chart singles, but at most they stayed five to six weeks on the chart and then disappeared. By the end of 1976, the group was no longer with Curtom. Because vocal groups had become passé, the Curtom departure spelled the end for the group, a talented singing outfit whose career was never properly realized.

The Notations were a Chicago-based vocal quartet, and consisted of four veterans of the Chicago vocal-group scene. The group was signed to Curtom's Gemigo subsidiary in late 1974 and recorded for the label during the next two years. While on the label members were Clifford Curry (lead), Robert Thomas, Walter Jones, and LaSalle Matthews.[26]

The origins of the Notations go back to 1965 when Curry contacted Matthews, a buddy from his football days at Parker High, about forming a group. They were soon joined by Thomas out of Harrison High on the West Side and Jimmy Stroud from Dunbar High on the South Side. Their

break into the recording industry was a long time coming, but in 1970 it
arrived when they signed with Twinight Records. Their first record, "I'm
Still Here," was produced by Syl Johnson and became a national hit in
December 1970. The follow-ups, "At the Crossroads" (April 1971) and
"Just You and Me" (August 1971), did well in Chicago but nowhere else.
This lack of success was aggravated when Twinight went out of business,
and the group remained in limbo for a time until the legal wrinkles could
be ironed out.

The group under the management of Emmett Gardner continued to
grow professionally and artistically. The singers acquired their own traveling
band, Nitro, and made a personnel change, replacing the retiring Jimmy
Stroud with Walter Jones. The Notations were soon ready for the big time,
and the "big time" in Chicago meant Curtom Records. Gemigo was formed
in November 1973, and Curtom saw in the Notations an ideal act to fill
the label's stable of artists.

Success came immediately when the Notations' first Gemigo release,
"It Only Hurts for a Little While," a splendid ballad written and produced
by Tufo and Gerald Dickerson, took off in March 1975. Two more fine
hits that year—"Think before You Stop," written and produced by Tufo
and Dickerson, and "It's Alright this Feeling," written and produced by
Jackson and Yancy—kept the group's name before the public.

By 1977 things had cooled off considerably for the Notations. Walter
Jones had dropped out and the rest of the Notations group had left Curtom
in a dispute over royalties. They signed with Mercury but produced only
one single, "Judy Blue Eyes," which got a little airplay and fewer sales.
Not long afterward, the Notations broke up.

The Staple Singers had been together almost a quarter century when
they began recording for Curtom Records in 1975. The group was actually
signed to Warner Brothers, but the soundtrack albums they did with Mayfield
came out on the Curtom label. The Staple Singers were four members of
the Staples family from Chicago. Over the years the group would change
personnel as different members of the family would slide in and out. At
Curtom the four members were father Roebuck "Pop" Staples (lead and
guitar), and daughters Mavis (contralto lead), Cleotha (alto), and Yvonne
(soprano).[27]

The Staple Singers for most of their career were a gospel group, one
of the most distinctive and successful in the business. A strong ingredient
contributing to the uniqueness of the group's sound was Pop Staples's
guitar, which amazingly was played in the style of pre-war Mississippi Delta
blues. Pop was born in Winona, Mississippi, in 1915, and absorbed the
blues of the Delta before moving to Chicago in 1935 with his wife Oceola
and their first two children, Pervis and Cleotha. In 1939 Yvonne was born,

followed by Mavis in 1940. Roebuck, who was a member of various gospel quartets in the 1930s, started training his kids in gospel music in the late forties with the intention of forming a group. By the early 1950s, he and Pervis, Cleotha, and Mavis were singing in local churches. Even at an early age Mavis was a remarkable singer and by her early teens possessed one of the most expressive and exhilarating contraltos in black music. Pop built the vocal sound of the group around his excellent dry tenor and Mavis's contralto.

From 1953 to 1955, the Staple Singers recorded for Leonard Allen's United/States label complex, but the gospel records they recorded for the company did not properly showcase them, submerging Pop's guitar in favor of a piano accompaniment. However, after the group's move to Vee Jay, Pop with his folk-style songwriting and blues guitar made the Staple Singers a giant in gospel circles. From 1955 to 1960 the group recorded some of the most splendid spiritual music ever put on record, and Vee Jay eventually came out with five albums of its tunes.

In 1960 the Staple Singers moved to Riverside Records in New York, but continued to record in Chicago. Riverside, taken with the group's antiquated blues sound, recorded the Staples as a folk-gospel act with hopes of breaking them into the flourishing folk music market. After several fine albums that failed to excite the public, the Staple Singers moved to Columbia Records' Epic division. Again the Staples were recorded as a folk-gospel group, but gradually the lyrics of their songs became more secular. The inspirational messages were still in the songs but with fewer direct religious references. The group made a lot of fine music during the seven years it was at Epic, but the best it could do was to put two singles low on the charts, "Why (Am I Treated So Bad)" and "For What It's Worth," both in 1967.

For many years there was speculation as to when the Staple Singers would cross over into rhythm and blues. That happened in 1968, when the group signed with Stax Records in Memphis. It took a while for Stax to break the group, but once they did, in 1971, the Staples became one of the biggest soul groups of the early 1970s with such great hits as "Respect Yourself" (1971), "I'll Take You There" (1972), and "If You're Ready (Come Go with Me)" (1973).

In 1975 Stax collapsed, and the Staple Singers signed with Warner Brothers. The first album in the new association was a soundtrack for *Let's Do It Again*, a film directed by Sidney Poitier and starring Poitier and Bill Cosby. Mayfield wrote one of his best scores, coming up with two excellent songs for the group, "Let's Do It Again" (number one and eighteen weeks) and "New Orleans" (number four and thirteen weeks). Despite all their top hit records at Stax, *Let's Do It Again* proved to be the Staples' all-time best seller.

Because of Mayfield's success with the Staples, Warner Brothers had Mayfield produce the group's next album, *Pass It On*, which appeared on the Warner label in 1976. It yielded one hit single, the fine "Love Me Love Me Love Me," which went to position eleven and lasted fourteen weeks on *Billboard*'s soul chart. The album, however, did not sell well, and Warners turned to other producers on subsequent Staples albums. One other soundtrack, however, appeared on Curtom, *A Piece of the Action*, which Mayfield recorded with Mavis alone in 1977. The film of the same name was also directed by Poitier and starred Poitier and Cosby, but it was a box office failure. The music was not especially memorable either.

The Staple Singers recorded for several labels in the late 1970s and in the 1980s, but their last big hit appeared on Curtom in 1975. However, one should not measure the remarkable Staple Singers by their commercial appeal, because they have created an amazingly large body of music, both secular and gospel, that ranks with the best music ever recorded by black Americans. They are one of Chicago's greatest gifts to black music.

Major Lance–Gene Chandler–Billy Butler

Major Lance, Gene Chandler, and Billy Butler were three of the biggest beneficiaries of Mayfield's songwriting talents during the 1960s. In the seventies, however, their reputation was up and down (mostly down) and they found themselves at Curtom for a brief time in hopes that the Mayfield touch could get them hits. Unfortunately, Mayfield had neither the time nor enough solid material that could benefit these artists.

Major Lance had the best success. After a brief stay with Carl Davis during 1968–69, he joined Curtom and came out with four sides. "Stay Away from Me," an up-tempo composition by Mayfield, was Lance's biggest hit since 1965, going as high as position thirteen and lasting thirteen weeks on *Billboard*'s soul chart during the summer of 1970. A follow-up, "Must Be Love Coming Down," charted for six weeks in early 1971. Lance left Curtom and Chicago in 1971, recording for Stax in Memphis, for several labels in Great Britain in the early 1970s, and for Playboy Records in the mid-1970s.

Gene Chandler came to Curtom after an up-and-down stint at Mercury. He had a million seller with "Groovy Situation" in 1970, but by 1972 the fire was gone from Chandler's career and he had joined Curtom. The association resulted in some of the most uninspired and poorly done material of Chandler's career. What went wrong? It was "weird, awfully weird," as Chandler tried to characterize the situation:

They signed a contract with me, paid me money for publishing, paid me money to produce, paid me money for several things as an artist. An advance. Curtis and I sat down and talked and talked. The idea was that because Curtis was in as writer on most of my hits, "Man's Temptation," et cetera, "Rainbow," we can get together and bring Gene Chandler all the way back into new songs up-to-date, because we're smarter, we're older, and we're producing ourselves now....Curtis Mayfield—and I love the brother—but Curtis did not show up. Don't ask me what happened, I don't know.

Even to Marv Stuart it was a mystery, "Gene," he said, "I don't know what to tell you. But I'll tell you what, we got to get you started, because we're not making any money. So you just have to go in there and produce it yourself." Well, I didn't want to do that. Curtis and I had sat at home and he played some stuff, and listening to the tape of it I said we're gonna be big. And I was ready to get into those tunes. But Curtis didn't even remember where he put that tape at, so I couldn't even get that from him even though I couldn't get him down there. Anyway, that type of frustration and the fact that I didn't like the way they dealt up there after a while, I left.[28]

Billy Butler had not done anything for several years when he came to Curtom in 1976. His last hit was in 1971 with Infinity, "I Don't Want to Lose You." After the group broke up in 1973, Butler took off from recording for a while to study arranging and recording. He then got some things on tape and took it to Mayfield who signed him to his label. In December 1976 the company put out a single, "Feel the Magic," but it did nothing. An album followed in March 1977, but it was a wretched effort. The chirpy girl chorus was overbearing, the songs boring, and Butler's voice had somehow lost its riveting soulfulness. Butler never made another record, and during the late 1970s and 1980s he played guitar in his brother's band.

Linda Clifford

Linda Clifford was Curtom's attempt to come to terms with the disco era. She had a sassy, slightly high-bred vocal tone that fit well with the slightly snotty airs that seemed to be associated with the disco scene in the clubs. Curtom managed to do quite well with Clifford, and sold a lot of her records. But I was never a big fan of the type of disco that Clifford represented, which is not to say it was not any good. The problem was, as disco developed its own esthetic in the dance clubs, the songs were gradually extended in length, so that good solid three-minute songs were stretched to interminable ten-minute workouts. All of Clifford's albums suffered from an unnatural lengthening of songs to fit disco esthetics.

Linda Clifford had been in the entertainment business a long time before she hit it big in the late 1970s and for that reason she kept her date of birth a secret. She was raised in Brooklyn and by the age of seven was appearing on television shows, such as "Startime" (1950–51) on the Dumont network. At the age of seventeen she won the Miss New York State beauty pageant. In 1966 she was singing as part of a six-member lounge act on the "borscht" circuit in the Catskills, in upstate New York.[29]

For the next eight years, Clifford crisscrossed the country with various lounge aggregations, singing Broadway show tunes, old standards, and a smidgen of rhythm and blues. The year 1974 found her in Chicago, where she was discovered by Stuart working one of the city's lounges. Curtom recorded her on "A Long Long Winter," but leased the record to Paramount. The record lasted six weeks on the national charts in early 1974. Another release followed early in 1975 on the Gemigo label.

In 1977, disco was the rage and Curtom needed a disco artist to compete. Linda Clifford was the perfect candidate, and because the company did not feel it had the in-house staff to record disco properly, it brought in Gil Askey from Motown Records to produce her. In a sense Clifford ceased to represent a regional scene with the coming of Askey. The recording industry in the late seventies had become such that companies tended to draw talent from a national talent pool rather than a regional one. Regional scenes were quickly breaking down.

Askey's first album with Clifford, called *Linda*, got the artist her first notices, as a single from the LP, "From Now On," got good play in a number of areas in late 1977. But it was the second album, *If My Friends Could See Me Now*, that propelled Clifford to international stardom in 1978. A single from the LP, "Runaway Love," went to number three and lasted sixteen weeks on *Billboard*'s black singles chart in the spring of 1978. The album was a top seller also.

The following year, Clifford was on the RSO label, which was having great success at the time as a disco label with the Bee Gees (the Curtom logo also appeared on Clifford releases). RSO obviously poured a lot of money into her first album for the label, a double gate-fold package. Two whole sides were devoted to a ten-minute discofied version of Paul Simon's "Bridge over Troubled Water" and a twelve-minute rendition of "One of Those Songs." The company expected great things with "Bridge over Troubled Water," but it was mainly a hit in disco clubs. Better results came with another of the LP's singles, "Don't Give It Up," which went to fifteen position and lasted twelve weeks on the black singles chart. The album went to position twenty-six and lasted seventeen weeks on the pop chart, so RSO probably got its money back from its investment.

There was something of a backlash against the kind of disco Clifford was associated with in 1979 and 1980, so the music was re-labeled "dance music" and reverted to the disco clubs from which it sprang. Record sales were considerably more modest thereafter for Clifford. Her *Here's My Love* album, from late 1979, produced no hit singles, and *I'm Yours*, from 1980, produced only two moderate-size hits, "Red Light" and "Shoot Your Best Shot." Late in 1980, with the dissolution of Curtom, Clifford went to Capitol Records. During the 1980s she recorded a number of albums for several labels, but without the success of her Curtom years.

The Decline and Fall of Curtom

Curtom seemed to reach the apex of its success in 1976, the second year of its Warner Brothers affiliation. The company had gross sales of between nine and ten million dollars that year, and felt prosperous enough to become an investor in the film *Short Eyes*, which was released the following year.[30] But two developments served to undermine the strength of Curtom in the late 1970s, the rise of disco and the collapse of the black film market.

The company did a fair job of coping with pop disco by bringing in producer/arranger Gil Askey and by promoting and pushing Linda Clifford as a disco diva. But there were no other riches in Curtom's coffers that it could offer the public. Mayfield, the company's creative core, by his own admission was not temperamentally or creatively qualified to record disco. As a result the company's stable of artists gradually was reduced to Clifford and Mayfield, with the latter having a diminishing impact on the charts.

Curtom got a little success with TTF, a disco-funk self-contained group from Homestead, Florida. Members were Willie Brown (keyboards); his brother, Brett Brown (bass); Andrew Most (guitar); Alton Hudson (drummer and lead vocals); Tony Izquierdo (saxophone); Tony Gonzales (trumpet); and Deborah Peevy (lead vocals).[31] TTF had a couple of chart entries with Hudson as lead featuring a disco-funk sound, but the standout hit was "(Baby) I Can't Get Over Losing You" in 1980. The song featuring Peevy as lead was a throwback to the classic Chicago-style girl-group sound made famous by Patti and the Lovelites. The record went to position twenty-one and lasted eighteen weeks on *Billboard's* black singles chart.

The talent depth at Curtom had never been great, and when the producers could not come up with saleable records on the few artists they had, the company was bound to fail. Aside from the work of Mayfield with Rich Tufo, and the Staple Singers, and the Impressions with Ed Townsend, there was little that truly distinguished the company's output. By the latter part of the 1970s the releases were mostly of second-rate disco and its second cousin, disco-funk (disco with an r&b approach rather than a pop one). The black film industry collapsed soon after Curtom's soundtrack, *Short Eyes,* appeared in 1977. In June of that year a journalist for *Soul,* Renee Ward, reported that "black movies are losing their audience." She added that the 1976 gross income from all black movies was down 35 percent from 1974, and that production of such films had dropped from twenty-five in 1974 to fifteen in 1976. Ward pointed out that despite the excellence of Mayfield's music in *Sparkle,* the movie lost money.[32] By the end of the decade there were few black-oriented films released, and after 1977 Curtom never made another soundtrack.

When Curtom switched from Warner Brothers distribution to RSO distribution in 1979, the company was not given its own release series. Instead, its logo was put alongside the RSO logo in the RSO series of releases. Such was the status of independent labels at the time. Curtom, which was little more than a logo, had dropped most of its acts, and by 1980 when the company went out of business there was only Clifford, Mayfield, and TTF. Clifford went to Capitol and Mayfield went to Boardwalk Records, which was founded by Neil Bogart. Marv Stuart bravely tried to make it with his own Gold Coast label, but his principal act, TTF, was not high powered enough to keep the label in business.

Mayfield, who had maintained a home in Atlanta, Georgia, for many years, moved to the city permanently in 1980 and took many of the company's physical assets with him. "What I did," Mayfield later said from his Atlanta home, "I took the Curtom Studio, moved it and all my equipment down here, and put it in my old house. The music scene was kind of drying up in Chicago. Of course, you know Chicago is my home. I love it, but my needs and my desires were quite different. I guess after coming up in the city all your life, you can appreciate a little bit of ground around you. And of course, 'the Hawk,' the weather, probably helped persuade me to move."[33]

NOTES

1. Peter Burns, "The Curtis Mayfield Story: Part 6—Curtom," *Blues and Soul,* April 1969, n.p.; idem, "Curtom Records," *Hot Buttered Soul* 21 (August 1973):2–8; Anne Duston, "Chicago Thriving Area for Indie Labels: Curtom," *Billboard,* April 19, 1975, p. C-6; Ilene Rothman, "Curtom Changing, Challenging, Creating and Comin' Atcha," *Illinois Entertainer,* August 1976, p. 18; Jacqueline Thomas, "He's Seeking Black Music Liberation," *Chicago Sun-Times,* November 14, 1976; Mayfield interview.

2. Mayfield interview.

3. "Curtom Revamps Structure, Format, Mayfield President," *Billboard*, May 8, 1971, p. 74.

4. Mayfield interview.

5. Ibid.

6. Ibid.

7. Burns, "Curtom Records," p. 3.

8. Mayfield interview.

9. Burns, "Curtom Records," p. 4.

10. Most of what has been written on Mayfield has been of the most ephemeral sort, brief interviews designed to promote his latest album. The following are a few of the substantial treatments: Tony Cummings, "The Gentle Genius Writes On," *Black Music*, September 1974, pp. 19–20; Paolo Hewitt, "So Proud: The Moral Standard of Soul," *New Musical Express*, July 9, 1983, pp. 24–26, 43; Earl Ofari, "Curtis Mayfield: A Man for All People," *Soul Illustrated*, Summer 1973, pp. 19–20; Clarence Page, "Does Curtis Mayfield Sincerely Want to Be Rich?," *Chicago Tribune Magazine*, February 10, 1974, pp. 35–41; Sharon Wood, "A Profile of Curtis Mayfield," *Blues and Soul*, September 24–October 7, 1974, pp. 14–15; Mayfield interview.

11. Mayfield interview.

12. For an excellent essay on the turning of early 1970s rhythm and blues toward militancy and social concerns, see Greil Marcus, "Sly Stone: The Myth of Staggerlee," in *Mystery Train: Images of America in Rock 'n' Roll Music*, rev. ed. (New York: Dutton, 1982). However there is something tendentious in Marcus's efforts to make Sly Stone's *There's a Riot Goin' on*, from late 1971, the central impulse behind the trend, which appears to have started at least a year earlier.

13. Mayfield interview.

14. Ibid.

15. Ibid.

16. Bruce Meyer, "Praying for a Packed House: The Saga of Jam Productions," *Triad*, February 1977, p. 11.

17. Mayfield interview.

18. Thomas, "He's Seeking Black Music Liberation."

19. Mayfield interview.

20. Cliff White, "Keep on Pushing, LeRoy Hutson: The Man," *Black Music*, September 1974, p. 21; "The Impressions Make One," *Soul*, February 28, 1972, p. 11; "LeRoy Hutson: Performer, Producer, and Writer," *Soul*, July 5, 1976, p. 11.

21. Published as an article, "He Took Over for Curtis in Three Days," *Soul*, June 23, 1975, p. 11.

22. Denise Hall, "Lasting Impressions," *Black Music*, September 1975, pp. 46–47; David Nathan, "The Impressions: Sooner or Later and Right Now!," *Blues and Soul*, July 22–August 4, 1975, pp. 32–33; Robert Pruter, "The Impressions: Finally Got Themselves Together," *Goldmine*, October 9, 1987, pp. 89, 94; David Schultz, "Ed Townsend," *After 5*, April 1976, p. 40.

23. Hall, "Lasting Impressions," p. 46.

24. "Mystique," undated press release.

25 David Nathan, "The Natural Four: Naturally Together," *Blues and Soul*, July 22–August 4, 1975, pp. 32–33; "Fate Brought the Four Together," *Soul*, July 19, 1976, p. 11.

26. Robert Pruter, "Windy City Soul," *Goldmine*, January 1979, p. 10; "Take Note: Nothing Sounds the Same," *Soul*, July 19, 1976, p. 11; Clifford Curry interview.

27. John Abbey, "The Staple Singers, *Blues and Soul*, January 1971, pp. 12–13; Lacy J. Banks, "The Staple Singers...The Message Is the Music," *Black Stars*, June 1972, pp. 17–22; Viv Broughton, *Black Gospel: An Illustrated History of the Gospel Sound* (Poole, Eng.: Blandford Press, 1985), pp. 103–7; Tony Cummings, "The Staple Singers," *Black Music*, March 1974, pp. 8–9; Dave Hoekstra, "Love Guides Soul Patriarch," *Suburban Sun-Times*, January 20, 1984, pp. 1, 13.

28. Gene Chandler interview, February 6, 1979.

29. Earl Calloway, "Linda Clifford's on the Move and There's No Stopping Now," *Chicago Defender*, July 8, 1978; Nina Gaspich, "My Friends Can See Me Now," *Illinois Entertainer*, August, 1978, pp. 1, 45; David Nathan, "Introducing Linda Clifford, a Runaway Success" *Blues and Soul*, September 1978, pp. 36–37; Robert Pruter, "Linda Clifford: Runaway Love," *Goldmine*, September 11, 1987, pp. 24, 76.

30. Thomas, "He's Seeking Black Music Liberation."

31. "TTF," undated publicity release.

32. Renee Ward, " 'Sparkle': Best of What?," *Soul*, June 20, 1977, p. 34.

33. Mayfield interview.

14

The Small Entrepreneurs
of the 1970s

As they moved through the 1970s Chicago record men found it increasingly evident that their industry was in decline, and they began to look back wistfully to the previous decade as truly the best years of Chicago soul music. The 1960s could boast of several major independents and innumerable mom-and-pop firms putting out records and getting big hits. Yet during the 1970s there were a lot of flourishing small operations besides those of Brunswick/Dakar, Curtom, and Mercury, at least during the first half of the decade. The records that came out of these firms on such artists as Patti and the Lovelites, Denise LaSalle, General Crook, the Southside Movement, and the Independents helped keep Chicago on the map as a soul music center even as the industry was in the process of gravitating to both coasts.

Clarence Johnson Productions

Clarence Johnson by himself, but more often in business partnerships with other record men in Chicago, operated a series of production companies and record labels that put out records on such national hitmakers as Patti and the Lovelites, Brighter Side of Darkness, Heaven and Earth, and Coffee. His companies included Lovelite, G.E.C. Records, and Starvue, and although he was not always the sole owner, he always had a hand in the production end. In the mid-1970s his Lovelite and Starvue companies operated out of the old Chess building at 320 East Twenty-first Avenue.[1]

Johnson was born in Chicago on January 17, 1942. His first taste of the music business was with a vocal group called the Chaunteurs, which he joined around 1958. This is the same group that evolved into the Chi-lites, which Johnson left in 1964 to go into production work. Following early production work on Diane Cunningham's "Someday Baby" (1967) and the Lovelites' "How Can I Tell My Mom and Dad" (1969), Johnson entered the 1970s riding the success of the Lovelites. He cited the group as the best he had ever worked with, their principal talent being Patti Hamilton, whose expressive teenagy lead and songwriting abilities essentially made the group.

The Lovelites came out of the Altgeld Gardens projects, the community farthest south on the city's South Side. The original group consisted of Patti Hamilton; her sister, Rozena Petty; and Barbara Peterman; and it was formed when the girls were sophomores and juniors at Carver High.² They managed to get on record in 1967 for the local Bandera label, owned by Vi Muszynski. The two sides, "You Better Stop It"/"I Found Me a Lover," were spirited but just did not have the ingredients for a hit. After this record, Peterman left and was replaced with Ardell (Dell) McDaniel.

The Lovelites, after playing numerous talent shows, in 1969 joined the Lock label. Hamilton wrote a marvelous song, "How Can I Tell My Mom and Dad," which dealt with the plight of a pregnant teenage girl. Johnson, who produced, and Johnny Cameron, who arranged, gave the record a bright-sounding, mid-tempo lope thoroughly Chicagoan in style. It was evident Lock had its first hit on its hands when in the fall of 1969 the record sold some fifty-five thousand copies in Chicago alone and became a top-five record on station WVON.³

Nationwide the record sold some four hundred thousand copies, and lasted fifteen weeks and went to position fifteen on *Billboard*'s soul chart. The song probably could not have become a national hit had not California-based Uni Records, a division of MCA, leased the record and distributed it. Russ Regan, then president of Uni, picked up the record after it nettted some five thousand sales on the Lock label. It had been his policy for a year to make alliances with Chicago producers to get hits in the r&b market. It paid off with "How Can I Tell My Mom and Dad." The record, however, did not cross over to the pop market, because as Hamilton explained, there was a line in the song, "Oh he made me mother-to-be," that was not considered acceptable on the pop stations.⁴

After "Mom and Dad," Petty dropped out and was replaced with a girl out of Hyde Park High, Joni Berlmon. Uni in the spring and summer of 1970 put out an album and two more singles on the Lovelites, "Oh My Love" (a splendid song) and "This Love Is Real," but they did not click and Uni dropped the group.

Johnson then put together Lovelite Records with partners Ed Douglas (a businessman), Lamar Greer (a singer/friend), and Bill Watkiss (a bass player on all the Lovelites' records). The label's first release on the Lovelites

was another Hamilton-written song, "My Conscience." Johnson and Cameron gave the record the same bright, bouncy beat typical of the Lovelites,
and in the late fall of 1970 the record made a considerable noise in Chicago,
selling more than seventy thousand copies. With the help of Summit
Distributors the record did about four hundred thousand nationally.[5]

"My Conscience" was released with photos of the girls' faces on the
label. This was to show the public what the Lovelites looked like, so that
they would not be fooled by counterfeit groups. According to Hamilton,
there was a counterfeit group touring the Midwest under the name of
Lovelites and reaping the benefits.[6] In 1971 McDaniel was replaced with
Rhonda Grayson.

In 1972 Johnson got a deal with Cotillion, an Atlantic subsidiary label
out of New York, and recorded the Lovelites in Muscle Shoals, Alabama.
None of the Cotillion sides, despite their uniform excellence, made any
impact in the market, however. Around this time Johnny Cameron, Johnson's
collaborator for several years, died. In 1973 Berlmon and Grayson called
it quits. The breakup was inevitable because the group had not had a big
hit for some time and the money was not coming in. After a brief reunion
of the original Lovelites in 1975, Hamilton called it quits as well. Berlmon
and Grayson, working with Theresa Davis, developed a thriving career in
the late 1970s and early 1980s as one of the most in-demand trios of
background singers in Chicago.

The male vocal group the Brighter Side of Darkness was Johnson's
first big success for his General Entertainment Company (G.E.C.), a production company and sometime label he co-owned with Lucky Cordell, a
former station manager at WVON. The ensemble was formed in 1971 at
Calumet High on the South Side. At that time Brighter Side consisted of
Ralph Eskridge (age seventeen), Randolph Murph (eighteen), and Larry
Washington (seventeen).[7] After playing local gigs for a few months, they
came to the attention of local r&b maven Anna Preston. She took them
under her wing and became their manager and music director, and she
added as lead to the group a youngster she had been grooming, twelve-
year-old Darryl Lamont. With his dry, fetching vocals, young Lamont added
a highly appealing pre-teen sound to the group, in the manner of the
Jackson Five. Preston also gave the group its name, Brighter Side of
Darkness.

The Preston-remade group in short order won a local talent contest,
and sufficiently impressed Johnson to have him sign them up immediately.
Johnson was working with a number of other groups at the time. Russ
Regan had just moved from Uni to become head of a newly resuscitated
20th Century label in Los Angeles. He flew to Chicago hoping to find acts
from the local producers that he could sign to the label. Johnson played a

number of songs by various artists for Regan, but it was Brighter Side's "Love Jones" that caught his ear, a song written by two members of the group and Johnson.

"Love Jones" was the second release on the revived 20th Century label in September 1972, and by February 1973 had become a gold record. It went to the number three position and lasted twenty-one weeks on *Billboard*'s soul chart. The song's appeal has faded with time because it was mostly one long cloying recitation by lead singer Lamont with the rest of the group chorusing in the background, "Love Jones, I want a Love Jones." ("Jones" is street slang for "addiction.") The record's sound was marvelously deepened by arranger Tom Washington, who provided gobs of swirling strings as sweetener. His arranging on the record cemented a working relationship with Johnson that lasted several years.

Despite the million seller from Brighter Side, 20th Century dropped the group after just one album, the culmination of a series of events that started when the label demanded Johnson fire two members of the group for reputed misbehavior on a trip to L.A. to appear on the "Soul Train" television show. Johnson in 1974 managed to release a fine record on a reconstructed group, "Because I Love You," on his Starvue label, but the group had been effectively killed two years earlier.

Heaven and Earth came out of the middle-class South Shore community on the South Side, and was formed when the members were in their senior year at South Shore High, in 1974. Members were Dwight Dukes (falsetto lead); his brother, James Dukes (bass); Keith Steward (first tenor); and Michael Brown (baritone). The sound of the group was built around the ethereal high-tenor lead of Dwight Dukes, one of the highest and delicate among vocal groups in the 1970s. The singers were soon discovered by manager Lil Schneider who brought them to the attention of Johnson.[8]

Johnson and Cordell were sufficiently impressed to sign the group to their newly formed G.E.C. label. Johnson obtained the services of two fledging songwriters, Jerline Shelton and Maurice Commander, to come up with some good songs for Heaven and Earth. And as usual Johnson hired Washington to arrange the sessions. The first fruit of this collaboration was the single "I Can't Seem to Forget You," which became a top-ten hit in Chicago in March 1976. Nationally, its success was negligible.

Johnson was not pleased with the way the record was handled nationally. Said he, "The record came out on 'G.E.C., distributed by 20th Century,' which means they were supposed to help us. But we did the promotion in our own area. We sold fifty thousand records in Chicago, where they played it like the national anthem. But it didn't do anything anyplace else. What does that tell you? It means that the company did not have any interest in promoting it anyplace else. Because of that we asked for release from the label."[9] An album on the group was likewise a local phenomenon.

In 1977 Heaven and Earth underwent a reorganization. For a start, Michael Brown was dropped from the lineup. Johnson also reassessed the sound of the group. The great era of high-tenor led vocal groups that began in the early 1970s was evidently coming to a close. Said Johnson, "What happened around this time, you had the resurgence of the baritone lead becoming popular again. The falsetto thing had become a little tired. We knew we got to change with the times. I tell the guys, 'We got to get a new lead singer, a baritone.' So we started auditioning people and we came up with Dean Williams. It was a good and bad decision. It was bad because the three guys did not want a new singer. I made them accept Dean Williams [from another local ensemble, the Soul Majestics]. That was a mistake in the fact that there was never any unity from that point on. That's what destroyed Heaven and Earth."[10]

The good side of the decision was that Johnson got a deal with Mercury in 1978 to record two albums on Heaven and Earth. He had withdrawn from G.E.C. in 1977 and produced the group under his own Starvue production firm. He teamed up with Ric Williams to produce some cuts, and on the others Rodney Massey and Lawrence Hanks at Jerry Butler's Fountain Productions were given the job. The strongest songs came from the pen of Massey and Hanks, two compelling, urbane ballads led by Williams, "Let's Work It Out" and "Guess Who's Back in Town." The two were put out as singles, but only the latter made *Billboard*'s national soul charts, in 1978.

Heaven and Earth's second album for Mercury yielded two chart singles, a hard-funk tune, "I Feel a Groove under My Feet," led by Greg Rose, who had replaced Williams, and (surprisingly) a neo-doowop, "I Only Have Eyes for You," led by Dukes. Although the album lasted ten weeks on *Billboard*'s soul album chart, Mercury was not impressed with the sales figures and dropped the group.

Coffee was organized around 1973 by Elaine Sims who was joined by Betty Caldwell (as lead), Gwen Hester, and Dee Dee Bryant. All the members were from the West Side, Sims and Caldwell having attended Marshall High, and Hester and Bryant having gone to Crane High.[11] In 1977, Coffee was approached by Johnson. He had the group record a splendid spirited song called "Your Love Ain't as Good as Mine," which used the same lively beat as the Lovelites' "My Conscience." With Caldwell's plaintive teenagy vocals evoking Patti Hamilton's voice, the record was thoroughly Chicagoan in sound, and WVON gave it good play upon its release on the Lovelite label. After the record, Caldwell left and was replaced in the lead spot by Gwen Hester.

Coffee's next record, "I Wanna Be with You," was released in 1979 on Johnson and Williams' MIR label just at the end of the disco rage in the pop market. The song had the typical disco flash and fire, but the singing-in-unison vocal arrangements made it a little too characterless to click. Johnson cited bad timing as the problem: "This was a record we recorded to try to get into disco. What happened, by the time we got the record out, disco had faded out. The record didn't happen. So Coffee [basically Elaine Sims] with our permission used the album we did on them as a demo and through them we get a deal with Delite Records."[12]

The year 1980 was most successful for Coffee. New York-based Delite released the album, called *Slippin' and Dippin'*, and radio programmers jumped on "Mom and Dad 1980." As a result the song was released as a single in November 1980. Johnson's genius was to add a long recitation to expand the Lovelites' original "How Can I Tell My Mom and Dad." Although it got a lot of radio play in Chicago and other places, the song, alas, did not chart. Coffee, however, experienced great popularity in Great Britain. The big hit song from the album was a disco remake of Ruby Andrews's "Casanova."

The *Slippin' and Dippin'* album was the last association Coffee had with Johnson. In 1982 Delite had an East Coast producer, Tony Valor, record the group on a second album. It continued the disco sound of the group, but not very successfully, and Delite dropped Coffee, ending their recording career.

Johnson's career in the 1970s was obviously one of ups and downs. On only one group was he able to sustain a recording career for any length of time, and that was the Lovelites. Brighter Side of Darkness, and Heaven and Earth, for example, seemed to contain the seeds of their own destruction. Johnson's most fundamental problem seemed to be that Chicago was declining as a recording center, and equally important, declining as a distribution center, and small producers like him were at the mercy of the major labels based, except for Mercury, outside the city. A number of his potential hits were lost due to the majors' lack of sustained interest in pushing his records. "All the records I made money with," noted Johnson, "I did the promotion on. Those four records—'How Can I Tell My Mom and Dad' (55,000 units sold in Chicago), 'My Conscience' (70,000 plus), 'I Can't Seem to Forget You' (50,000), and 'Love Jones' (120,000)—where did we make our biggest sales? It's 'cause we promoted the records ourselves."[13]

Crajon Productions

Crajon Productions was operated by Bill and Denise Jones, first out of a home office at 4873 South Langley Avenue and later at the Chess Records building at 320 East Twenty-first.[14] Denise wrote the majority of the songs recorded by the company's artists, and both shared in the production work. The recordings were either put on one of the company's labels—Crajon, Parka, or Gold Star—or leased to other companies, usually to Fantasy in San Francisco or Westbound in Detroit. Although the company's earliest recordings were done at Universal Recording with Eddie Silvers as arranger, most of the later work was done in Memphis with Willie Mitchell and Gene "Bow Legs" Miller as arrangers. All of Crajon's labels were independently distributed.

Crajon's most successful artist was Denise Jones, herself, who recorded as Denise LaSalle.[15] She was born Denise Craig in a rural area of LeFlore County, Mississippi, near Greenwood, on July 16, about 1939, and grew up about forty miles away in Belzoni. About 1954 she moved to Chicago. Young Craig had always aspired to be a writer and as a teenager managed to get two soap-opera-like stories published, in *Tan* and *True Confessions*. But as she confessed in 1987 to interviewer David Booth, "After that I had so many stories rejected, I started writing songs. That's how I got off into this [music] business, by writing songs."[16]

Craig's earliest music experiences were in the church, where as a member of a female gospel ensemble, the Sacred Five, she sang throughout Chicago. She got into secular music when around 1965 she made a tape of one of her compositions and took it to Billy "The Kid" Emerson. He signed her up, and in the spring of 1967 produced a top local hit on her called "A Love Reputation." He put it out on his Tarpon label under the name he gave her, Denise LaSalle. The song was a magnificent example of hard soul, marrying a hard-pounding blues drive with soul emoting. Other releases by LaSalle during 1968–70, however, died. In 1969 Craig met businessman Bill Jones. He took command of her career and together they formed Crajon Productions ("Cra" from Craig and "jon" from Jones), and before the year was over they were married.

In late 1969 LaSalle began going down to Memphis to record Crajon acts; the following year she herself recorded. And why did she go to Memphis? She explained to Booth: "Al Perkins, a famous disc jockey that was killed in [Detroit in 1983], was a good friend of mine. He couldn't sing that well, couldn't keep time with the music. Al went down to Willie Mitchell's studio and cut a smash hit. So I said, 'If this man can make Al sound that good that's where I'm going.' Al Perkins told me, 'He's a good guy, call him up.' So we called Willie and he told us to come to Memphis. Everything we cut at Hi just turned out to be great. We had great tunes, great sounds, and the musicians we used were the Hi Rhythm Section."[17]

Armen Boladian of Westbound Records was so impressed with LaSalle's own work in Memphis that he signed her to his label. During her six-year association with Westbound, she came out with twelve singles and three albums, and ten of those singles charted on either the *Billboard* or the *Cash Box* r&b chart, or both. She had a million seller and number one hit in 1971 with "Trapped by a Thing Called Love," and other top-ten hits with "Now Run and Tell That" (1962), "Man Sized Job" (1972), and "Married, But Not to Each Other" (1976). The latter song was covered in the country-and-western field by Barbara Mandrell with tremendous success.

Crajon had national hits with two acts, a hard-soul singer by the name of Bill Coday and a sweet-sounding girl vocal group called the Sequins. Coday had a downhome raspy voice that worked well with LaSalle's more bluesy songs. LaSalle discovered the singer in 1969 at the Black Orchid, a club at Sixty-ninth and Racine. As was true of many hard-soul singers, Coday had roots in the South. He was born in Coldwater, Mississippi, May 10, 1942, and was raised near Blytheville, Arkansas. While in high school he sang in a band that included bluesman Son Seals. In 1963 he moved to Chicago, and began performing in clubs under the name of Chicago Willie.[18]

Coday's first release, "Sixty Minute Teaser," was recorded at the Hi studio in Memphis and put out on the Crajon label. It did well in Chicago, St. Louis, and Detroit, but nowhere else. Coday's third record, the splendid "Get Your Lie Straight," broke the singer into stardom. The record lasted twelve weeks and went to position fourteen on *Billboard*'s soul chart in 1971.

Although the Joneses got most of their sales on the record through independent distribution, they leased the record to Galaxy, a subsidiary of Fantasy. A follow-up on Galaxy, "When You Find a Fool Bump His Head," was another fine bluesy stomper and made the national chart for four weeks in the summer of 1971. In 1987, Eddie King, recording for Chicago blues producer Steve Wisner, came out with an excellent version of this classic. More superb singles followed on Galaxy and other labels, but Coday never got another national hit. However, in early 1973 he scored strongly in Chicago with the fine "I'm Back to Collect," on the Crajon label. By 1972 he had moved to Macon, Georgia. Coday made one more single in Muscle Shoals in 1975 and then left the recording scene.

The Sequins were three teenage girls—Ronnie Gonzales, Linda Jackson, and Dottie Hayes—and they all came out of Harlan High. They got their first notice when they took first place in a talent contest at the Regal Theater, and soon they started making the rounds of the local nightclubs. In one such club they came to the attention of Bill and Denise Jones, who were impressed enough to sign them immediately to their Crajon Productions.[19]

The girls' first session for the Joneses, in Memphis, yielded "Hey Romeo," which became an across-the-nation hit in August 1970 on the Gold Star label. A national tour followed, and the Sequins found themselves on such legendary stages as the Apollo, Howard, and Royal theaters. An excellent follow-up, "The Third Degree," in April 1971, had a smattering of regional success for the girls, but after "It Must Be Love" became only a local hit in June of 1973 the Sequins disappeared as a recording act.

"It Must Be Love" was the last release on Crajon, and by 1974 LaSalle had moved to Memphis and was no longer involved in recording other artists, or involved with Bill Jones, for that matter. In 1977 she married James Wolf and moved to Jackson, Tennessee. During the late 1970s she had more moderate recording success first with ABC and then MCA. In 1983 LaSalle signed with Malaco, in Jackson, Mississippi, and began recording in a highly bluesy vein.

Lamarr Records

Lamarr Records was an outgrowth of Gardner's One Stop operation at 746 East Seventy-fifth Street. The label was founded in 1970 by Walter Gardner, owner of the one-stop, and his brother, Burgess Gardner, a bandleader and longtime r&b arranger in the city. The company released records on three labels—Lamarr, Down to Earth, and More Soul—on only a handful of artists, notably the Esquires, the Startells (aka Chymes), General Crook, and Burgess's band, the Soul Crusaders Orchestra. Burgess did most of the producing and arranging for the company and the Soul Crusaders Orchestra served as the house band.[20]

The biggest hit for the company was its one release on the Esquires, "Girls in the City," which on the Lamarr label was a top-twenty r&b hit in early 1971. The company had a little local success on Lamarr with the Startells (brothers David, James, and Victor Martin), but its most outstanding success was with hard-soul singer General Crook, who had a string of national chart records on the Down to Earth label during 1970–71.

General Crook created a unique sound that managed to convey a downhome blues flavor in a modern hard-driving funk context. Perhaps the style reflected his roots. He was born February 28, 1945, in Mound Bayou, Mississippi, and was raised forty miles away in Greenville. There he was involved in playing in bands, but to further his career he moved in 1963 to Chicago, which had the recording studios and record labels that Mississippi lacked.[21] In 1967 Crook got a position as vocalist for the Soul Crusaders Orchestra. (Burgess Gardner was a fellow Greenville native, and the connection was made from the common roots.) The band played everything from current soul songs to pop tunes to old standards, and toured extensively, playing mainly in hotel ballrooms.

Following an unsuccessful year at Capitol with producer Phil Wright, in 1970 Crook signed with Down to Earth. Of the four records put out by Crook on the label, three made the r&b charts—"Gimme Some" (1970), "Do It for Me" (1970), and "What Time It Is" (1971). The biggest hit was the James Brown imitation, "Gimme Some," but by far the best release was "What Time It Is," a perfect blend of downhome sound with contemporary funk.

In 1973, after a dispute with the Gardners over just about everything, Crook signed with Scepter-Wand and continued with a string of hits through 1974. In the late seventies and eighties he established himself as one of the city's better producers, most notably with Syl Johnson's "Ms. Fine Brown Frame" in 1982 and Willie Clayton's "Tell Me" in 1984.

The Gardners closed down Lamarr in early 1972, and a few years later shut down the one-stop as well. Burgess, who had advanced degrees in music, in the 1980s left Chicago's fading record business to pursue a career as a college teacher.

On Top Records

On Top was a label and production company owned by former Vee Jay A&R man Calvin Carter. The label was located at 1809 South Indiana in the offices formerly occupied by Brainstorm Records. Carter founded the operation around 1970, producing acts for Fantasy/Galaxy in San Francisco. Essentially he was working with Betty Everett and Bobby Rush. In 1972 he added to the production company a house label called On Top, on which he put out records by Rush and a vocal group called Shades of Brown. Assisting him with the acts were outside arrangers Burgess Gardner and Donny Hathaway.[22]

Carter was born May 27, 1925, and entered the record business in 1953 as A&R man for his sister's and brother-in-law's Vee Jay label. After the company folded in 1966, Carter kept busy with independent production work. His productions with Everett yielded two mild r&b hits, "I Got to Tell Somebody" (1970) and "Ain't Nothing Gonna Change Me" (1971), but neither was an appealing song. After Carter failed to produce another hit on Everett, Fantasy got another producer for the singer. But as it turned out, subsequent producers at Fantasy failed to equal the success Carter had achieved with Everett for the label.

Carter's most successful work from an artistic standpoint was with Bobby Rush. The singer was born Emmett Ellis, Jr., on November 10, 1940, in Hommer, Louisiana, a town near Shreveport. Around the age of ten he got the name Bobby Rush, because he was always speedily dancing around. He later moved with his brother to Chicago's West Side, where he lived a decade before moving to the South Side. Rush formed a band when he was a student at Dunbar High and by the time he graduated he was playing a lot of blues.[23]

From 1964 to 1970 Rush recorded on a variety of local labels, but most of the releases were undistinguished blues and hard soul. A record produced by Barry Despenza for ABC in 1968 saw the glimmerings of a unique bluesy soul approach with "Gotta Have Money." When Carter began recording Rush in 1971 the singer had formed a fully developed style of his own.

And what was that style? Rush explained: "I'm what you call folk-funk. I do dialogue and I'm just folkish with it."[24] By "folkish" Rush was probably driving at the idea that his music had appeal to the everyday, earthy working-class black constituency that had always supported hard soul and blues.

Carter got Rush the biggest hit of his career with "Chicken Heads" in 1971, which was leased to the Galaxy label. The record went to position thirty-four and stayed eight weeks on *Billboard*'s soul chart, soon becoming a standard in the city's blues clubs. The disc represented the full flowering of the Rush style—bluesy, funky, and folksy.

In 1972 Carter put out two records on Rush on his own On Top label— "Gotta Be Funky" and "Bowlegged Woman, Knock-kneed Man." Neither record got more than local play and some southern sales, but both were superb records. Jewel, out of Shreveport, was impressed enough with the southern sales to pick up Rush's contract in 1973 and reissue "Bowlegged Woman." The singer put out four more Chicago-produced sides on Jewel during 1973–74, and all were prime Rush. Most notable was "Niki Hoeky," with a supremely riveting lowdown funky groove.

Rush achieved more success in the late seventies recording for Phila-delphia International and in the mid-eighties recording for James Bennett's LaJam label in Jackson, Mississippi. His success in the South encouraged him to move to Jackson around 1983.

Meanwhile, Carter was finding it more difficult to continue in the record business in Chicago. He shut down On Top in 1973 and the following year produced an album on Jerry Butler for Mercury called *Sweet Sixteen*. It met with little interest, and in 1975 Carter moved to California to try to make a go at it in the industry there. His son, Tollie, recalled at the time: "He said the industry was basically in New York and California and that's where he had to go."[25] But Carter never could successfully establish himself in L.A., and during most of the late 1970s and 1980s he was troubled by various physical ailments and disappointments.

Jimmy Vanleer Productions

Jimmy Vanleer was an aggressive, go-getting kind of guy who picked up several acts in the 1970s and put out a load of records on them. His most extensive work was with songstress Jackie Ross, the hard-funk band Southside Movement, the girl group Barbara and the Uniques, and bluesman Little Milton. Vanleer originally made a name for himself in booking shows for the prestigious High Chaparral. In 1971 he opened an office and began signing acts to his production company. He was a prolific songwriter and composed nearly all the songs for his artists. Like most small record-company owners Vanleer would test the waters by releasing an artist's record first on one of his own labels—either Segrick or Golden Ear—and if he got a nibble and garnered some interest he'd lease it with a company who had a national distribution network. He usually dealt with Scepter-Wand and 20th Century Records.

Vanleer's most successful act was the Southside Movement, perhaps because the band fit the trend in black music toward self-contained bands. The ensemble was an outgrowth of Simtec and Wylie's Tea Boxes Band. When Simtec and Wylie fell into disarray in 1972, guitarist Bobby Pointer held the band together. It signed with Vanleer and changed its name to the Southside Movement.[26] The group's first single, "I've Been Watching You," was leased to Wand and in early 1973 the record lasted fourteen weeks and went to position fourteen on *Billboard*'s soul chart. The single featured Pointer on guitar, Ronald Simmons on bass, Willie Hayes on drums, Morris Beeks on keyboards, trumpeter Steve Hawkins as an overdubbed brass section, and Melvin Moore as lead vocalist. The single elicited an album for Wand, *I've Been Watching You*, and in recording it the group was augmented by jazz veteran Bill McFarland on trombone and Milton Johnson on alto saxophone.

In 1974 Vanleer moved the Southside Movement over to 20th Century and produced two more albums on the band, *Movin'* (1974) and *Moving South* (1975), plus several singles. The group, however, could not break into the charts with any of the releases despite their excellence and in 1975 the musicians felt compelled to disband.

Vanleer had one other group with 20th Century during 1974–75, Barbara and the Uniques. The core of the group was lead singer Barbara Blake (aka Barbara Livsey). In the 1960s she was paired with Mary-Francis Hayes in an act called the Duettes who recorded with modest success for Onederful. By 1966 the Duettes had broken up. In 1969 Blake teamed up with her sister, Gwen Livsey, and recorded two singles for New Chicago Sound Records (owned by Leo Westbrook, C. D. Wilson, and Bill Parker). The duo got good play in Chicago with "Right On," in February 1970.

Later in the year the company added Doris Lindsey to Barbara and Gwen to form Barbara and the Uniques.[27] The trio's first single, a rousing song written by Eugene Record, called "There It Goes Again," became a national hit upon its release on the New York-based Arden label. The record lasted eleven weeks on *Billboard*'s soul chart in the winter of 1970–71.

Follow-ups produced by New Chicago Sound failed to garner anything more than local play, and in 1974 Barbara Blake signed with Vanleer. She put out three Vanleer–produced singles and one album on 20th Century billed as "Barbara Blake and the Uniques." The "Uniques," however, were simply ad hoc backup singers hired for the recordings. The records failed to get more than a few plays in Chicago, and in 1975 Blake's recording career was essentially over.

Vanleer's first act as well as one of his last was Jackie Ross. She was a hitmaker as a teen soprano for Chess in the mid-1960s, but when she came to Vanleer in mid-1971 several years of recording failure lay behind her, including an unproductive association with Fountain Productions earlier in the year. The approach Vanleer used was a harder, more adult sound. Gone were the sweet-sounding teenage ditties on which Ross had built her career. Despite an association that lasted until 1982, Vanleer never got more than local airplay on any of his records on Ross, which included nine singles and two albums.[28]

During the early 1980s Vanleer worked with Little Milton, and teamed up the blues singer with Jackie Ross on a few sides, an incompatible union to say the least. Milton never got any hits with Vanleer, and in 1983 he signed with MCA. Deprived of his one remaining name artist, Vanleer essentially closed shop.

Chuck Jackson and Marvin Yancy Productions

Chuck Jackson and Marvin Yancy, Jr., were easily the most successful alumni of the Butler Songwriters Workshop. After their workshop experience the pair formed a production company and as a songwriting and producing team they had scores of million-selling records during the 1970s, most notably with the Independents (a vocal group whose members included Chuck Jackson) and Natalie Cole. The team, however, was hot for only a few years, because by the end of the decade the two had gone cold and had split up.[29]

Marvin Yancy, Jr., was born in Chicago, May 31, 1950, the son of a Baptist minister. He attended Cooley High and later the Moody Bible Institute and the Chicago Bible Institute. Yancy had been playing piano in his father's church since he was thirteen and by the end of the 1960s was playing keyboards for such big-time Chicago gospel singers as Rev. James Cleveland, Jessy Dixon, Inez Andrews, and Albertina Walker.

Chuck Jackson was born March 22, 1945, in Greenville, South Carolina, and is the half-brother of civil rights activist Jesse Jackson. In college he majored in commercial art and minored in music. He left college in 1964 and joined a rhythm-and-blues group, but in 1968 moved to Chicago and got a job as art director for *Playboy* magazine. The lure of music remained strong, however, and in 1970 he quit his *Playboy* job to join the Butler Workshop. Although he penned several songs that subsequently were recorded, notably Butler's "If It's Real What I Feel," Jackson was primarily a lyricist and he needed a tunesmith to work with.

In 1971 Jackson met Yancy at Jesse Jackson's Black Expo, playing piano for Albertina Walker. The two hit it off and Jackson brought Yancy into the workshop as a working partner. The duo soon came up with a fistful of songs, and recorded a number of demos to hawk the songs to interested artists. One such demo was "Just as Long as You Need Me." Veteran record man Eddie Thomas was so impressed with it that he went out and secured a recording contract for the duo with Scepter/Wand.

Jackson and Yancy decided the record would be by a group, and put on the label "Independents," and then recruited a group after "Just as Long as You Need Me" became a hit in the spring of 1972. The record went to position eight and lasted eleven weeks on *Billboard*'s soul chart. An album was released, *The First Time We Met*, featuring besides the voices of Yancy and Jackson two new voices, those of Helen Curry and Maurice Jackson (no relation). The two were Chicago-based singers, both of whom had recorded solo singles earlier without any success. Curry was born in Clarksdale, Mississippi, but later moved to Chicago where she attended Chicago State University as an English major. Maurice Jackson was born in Chicago, June 12, 1944, and throughout the 1960s struggled in the music business.[30]

The First Time We Met yielded a million-selling single, "Leaving Me," which in early 1973 went to the number one position and lasted thirteen weeks on *Billboard*'s soul chart. Also from the album was the group's second-biggest hit, "Baby I've Been Missing You," which in the summer went to position four and lasted thirteen weeks on the chart. The Independents' style was distinctive. Practically all their songs were soft ballads in which the lead vocalists, usually Chuck Jackson and Helen Curry, would trade leads in the gospel tradition. The vocals were heavily melismatic but in a very quiet, soft manner, and were perfectly set off by beautifully harmonized choruses. All the songs were nicely accompanied by instrumental tracks that put Yancy's piano way out front.

For the second album, *Chuck, Helen, Eric, Maurice*, Yancy, who preferred the behind-the-scenes work, was replaced with Eric Thomas. The new member was born in Chicago in 1951 and had majored in sociology at Augustana College. After leaving college he became involved in the Operation Push Choir, where he met Chuck Jackson. The second album was considerably weaker than the first and produced only one single, "It's All Over," which went to twelve on the soul chart after its release in 1973.

Despite getting good hits on the Independents in 1974, Jackson and Yancy lost interest in maintaining the group and disbanded it before the year was out. The duo then began concentrating on their producing and writing. The upshot was a deal with Capitol Records, recording Natalie Cole, a pop-ish singer with a soulful edge who sounded a lot like Aretha Franklin. The daughter of the great pop singer Nat King Cole, she was born February 6, 1950, in Los Angeles, and went to school in the East. When she met Jackson and Yancy she was working the lounge circuit on the East Coast. The songwriting/producing team had immense success with Cole, producing four gold albums—*Inseparable* (1975), *Natalie* (1976), *Natalie...Live!* (1978), and *I Love You So* (1979), plus two platinum albums, *Unpredictable* (1977) and *Thankful* (1977). In the 1980s Jackson and Yancy's well had run dry and Capitol switched Cole to other producers.[31]

Inseparable was recorded at Curtom Studio, and Marv Stuart, seeing that record become a hit, hired Jackson and Yancy to work with Curtom acts during 1975–76. The two came up with some good cuts on the Notations, but their work with the Impressions and the Natural Four was not all that hot.

In late 1977, Jackson and Yancy abandoned Chicago for Los Angeles to work there on Cole's albums. Yancy had a personal reason for the move because he and Cole were married and Cole did not want to live in Chicago. However, Yancy's father died the same year and Yancy took over the reins of his father's church, Fountain of Life Baptist Church on Chicago's South Side. Not surprisingly the couple could not resolve its differences, and Yancy and Cole legally separated in 1979 and Yancy moved back to Chicago. The following year they were divorced.

Jackson, meanwhile, made an attempt to record as a solo artist, and in 1978 came out with his *Passionate Breezes* LP on Capitol, which did not do very well. A second album did not fare well either. Jackson continued to work on the West Coast after Yancy returned to Chicago, working with such acts on Arista as Aretha Franklin, Michael Henderson, and Phyllis Hyman.

Jackson and Yancy were one of the last producing teams in Chicago to create soul music, that is, black music with a gospelized style and depth of feeling. Although their work with Natalie Cole on her later albums too often veered to supper-club pop, their biggest success was on soul tunes recorded by her. In 1985 Marvin Yancy died of a heart attack while he had a gospel album, *Heavy Load*, on the charts.

Willie Henderson Productions

Willie Henderson, who had become a first-rate producer and arranger at Brunswick, left the company in 1974 to establish himself as an independent producer. His subsequent work with Barbara Acklin, Essence, Johnny Sayles, and on his own recordings demonstrated his versatility, which reflected his diverse musical experiences. Henderson was born in Pensacola, Florida, August 9, 1941, and while still a youngster moved with his family to Chicago, on the near South Side a block away from Record Row. By the early 1960s Henderson was playing baritone sax behind such bluesmen as Mighty Joe Young and Otis Rush. After studying with James Mack at Crane Junior College, he graduated to leading bands that backed the city's soul artists, notably Syl Johnson, Harold Burrage, and Alvin Cash. He was well prepared when he joined Brunswick in 1968.[32]

The first artists Henderson had any success with after leaving Brunswick were himself and Barbara Acklin. In 1973 he recorded a hard-driving instrumental called "Dance Master," and put it out on his own Now Sound label, but to no great acclaim. The next year, however, he leased the record to Playboy Records and got a top-twenty r&b hit out of it. A follow-up, "Gangster Boogie Bump," also charted. Henderson signed Acklin to Capitol and got a big hit with "Raindrops" in the summer of 1974. He could not do much with follow-up singles, however.

Essence was a West Side male vocal group whose lack of success recording for Epic was as mystifying to Henderson as it was to me. Said he, "The group was really a talented bunch of singers and we had Jim Peterek writing some fantastic songs, so I don't know why it didn't happen."[33] (Peterek had achieved fame earlier as chief writer and member of the Chicago rock group the Ides of March, who hit with "Vehicle" in 1970. Later he returned to the charts as a member of Survivor, who hit with "Eye of the Tiger" in 1982.)

Essence dated back to 1967, when a group of students at Marshall High formed a vocal ensemble. After several lineup changes and a lot of scuffling the membership of the group jelled in 1973 with Marzette Griffith (lead), Fred Smith (baritone), Bob Tabor (second tenor), Marcus Alexander (bass), and Anthony Redmond (first tenor). The sound of the group was centered around Griffith's beautiful falsetto lead, a voice which was a truly outstanding instrument.[34]

Essence was discovered by former Chess producer Charles Stepney. He made a demo and took it to Brunswick, but Carl Davis passed on it. Henderson, however, was impressed, and upon leaving Brunswick produced a demo and with it got the group signed with Epic. On the Essence records Henderson shared producer credit with Peterek and had James Mack do the arranging. Of the eight sides that came out on the group during 1975–76, two Peterek compositions, "Sweet Fools" and "Relax, It's Just Like Dancin'," were the most outstanding and deserved to become big hits. Only "Sweet Fools" charted, however, but pathetically, staying six weeks and going no higher than eighty on the *Cash Box* r&b survey. All the singles were a bust and Epic shelved the planned album on the group.

Henderson's production work after 1976 was much more sporadic. During the 1980s he put out an occasional single on his Now Sound label, with notable efforts by Johnny Sayles ("Food Stamps" in 1983) and Magnum Force ("Say I Do" in 1984). But his career in production wound down as the Chicago record industry declined.

Playboy Records

Playboy Records was part of Hugh Hefner's Playboy empire, and aspired to be an all-around label, recording rock, country, and rhythm and blues. Although headquartered in Los Angeles, Playboy mined Chicago for much of its r&b talent to build its stable, and managed to sign Major Lance, Willie Henderson, and the Weapons of Peace, among others.[35] During its years of existence from 1972 to 1977, the company put out more than one hundred fifty singles but its only big hits were by the rock act Hamilton, Joe Frank and Reynolds, and by the country singer Mickey Gilley. The r&b acts had only modest success, and only on the r&b charts.

Playboy was not a creative company. It maintained no woodshedding studio and had no production staff. The company preferred to pick up artists from outside producers. The Major Lance singles it put out were earlier productions done in Great Britain. "Um Um Um Um Um Um," from 1974, was an excellent remake of Lance's OKeh hit, and "Sweeter," from 1975, was another fine remake of an earlier Dakar release. Both made the charts and drew attention to Lance again, albeit briefly. The Willie Henderson hit, "Dance Master" (1974), was a record the producer brought to the label.

The one other Chicago act that achieved a modicum of success on Playboy was a self-contained band, Weapons of Peace. The act was brought to Playboy by former Brainstorm executive Hillery Johnson. Weapons of Peace was formed in 1970 by Finis Henderson III, lead vocalist and percussionist for the group. Other members were keyboardist Lonnell Dantzler, guitarist and vocalist Randy Hardy, bassist and vocalist David Johnson, and drummer Ike Davis. Hardy and Johnson usually wrote the arrangements, and they wrote the songs with Henderson and outside composer Charles Franklin.[36] The Weapons of Peace charted with "Just Can't Be that Way" (1976) and "Roots' Mural Theme" (1977) before disappearing as an act. Years later, in 1983, Finis Henderson got a big hit on Motown called "Skip to My Lou."

Golden Tone Productions

Golden Tone was a West Side label owned by Reggie Sykes and Marvin Smith. Sykes was president of the firm and Smith (who should not be confused with the recording artist of the same name) was the label's songwriter and producer. The company was essentially a one-artist firm, having only one big hit in the Midwest with "Remember the Rain." The song was recorded by a Jackson Five–type group called 21st Century.

Sykes and Smith put the record out on their own Golden Tone label in January 1975, and within two weeks it sold twenty thousand copies in Chicago and environs. That interested RCA and they picked up "Remember the Rain" and pushed it nationally. However, the record and its follow-up, "Child," did poorly on the national charts. One wonders why. The song, featuring a pre-teen sound, was a beautifully and excellently sung ballad and was as strong as anything the Jackson Five put out. Chicago loved it though.

The members of 21st Century were from the West Side and consisted of lead singer Pierre Johnson, plus Alonzo Martin, Tyrone Morris, Alphonso Smith, and founder/leader Fred Williams.[37] The group got together in 1973 and made its professional debut in February 1975, singing "Remember the Rain" at the High Chaparral. I saw the group not long after at the McVickers Theater in the Loop and they were simply sensational.

In 1977, the 21st Century went to Motown and recorded under the name 21st Creation with no particular artistic or commercial success. Motown was the last appearance for the group on wax.

Captain Sky Enterprises

Captain Sky Enterprises was a production company owned by Daryl L. Cameron and operated at 9939 South Green. Cameron was born in Chicago on July 10, 1957. While in high school he began working in bands as vocalist and rhythm guitarist. He went out on his own in 1977 to perform under the name of Captain Sky, and not long afterward formed his own production company. He wrote, arranged, and produced all his songs, which were of an exceedingly hard funk variety, and conceived the image of Captain Sky as a type of comic-book superhero, which was reflected in the graphics of the album covers. Cameron put out his records on the California-based AVI label.[38]

Captain Sky got his only substantial hit with a funky number called "Wonder Worm," which lasted eighteen weeks and went to position twenty-seven on *Cash Box*'s contemporary black singles chart in late 1978. During the next three years Sky charted occasionally, but never got as big a hit as "Wonder Worm." In 1980 he moved to Philadelphia and recorded for the TEC label there. The emergence of Captain Sky with his hard-funk oeuvre—highly unappealing to me—reflected black music's move from soul and toward funk, disco, and new international sounds.

NOTES

1. Cary Baker, "Two Chicago R&B Producers & the Death of the Small Label," *Shout* 97 (July 1974): 4–5; Clarence Johnson interview.

2. Robert Pruter, "Patti and the Lovelites," *Goldmine*, June 1981, p. 161; Patti Hamilton interview.

3. Johnson interview.

4. Hamilton interview.

5. Johnson interview.

6. Hamilton interview.

7. John Abbey, "Introducing Brighter Side of Darkness," *Blues and Soul*, January 19–February 1, 1973, p. 22; Robert Pruter, "Brighter Side of Darkness: Addicted to Love," *Goldmine*, June 5, 1987, pp. 32, 36.

8. Robert Pruter, "Heaven and Earth: Heavenly Harmonies and Earthly Delights," *Goldmine*, March 27, 1987, pp. 22, 92.

9. Johnson interview.

10. Ibid.

11. Robert Pruter, "Coffee," *Goldmine*, March 1981, pp. 213–14; Elaine Sims interview.

12. Johnson interview.

13. Ibid.

14. Cary Baker, "Two Chicago R&B Producers," p. 4.

15. G. Fitz Bartley, " 'Trapped'—Releases Denise LaSalle," *Soul*, January 17, 1972, p. 6; David Booth, "Denise LaSalle," *Soul Survivor* 7 (Summer 1987): 4–7; Tony Cummings, "Denise LaSalle; Doin' It Right," *Black Music*, December 1974, p. 35; Wayne Jancik, "Denise LaSalle: Sassy, Suggestive, Sultry...and Determined," *Goldmine*, January 30, 1987, p. 65.

16. Booth, "Denise LaSalle," p. 4.

17. Ibid.

18. Bill Coday interview.

19. Richard Pegue, "Richard Pegue's Chicago," *Soul*, November 20, 1972, p. 7; Robert Pruter, "The Sequins," *Goldmine*, June 1979, p. 16.

20. General Crook interview.

21. Robert Pruter, "General Crook: Fever in the Funkhouse," *Goldmine*, May 20, 1988, pp. 14, 66; Crook interview.

22. Tollie Carter interview.

23. William Cochrane, Bill Ferris, Peter Lee, and Jim O'Neal, "Bobby Rush," *Living Blues* 84 (January/February 1989): 23–33; Jim O'Neal, "A Blues Quartet," *Southern Magazine*, August 1987, pp. 49–51, 71; Robert Pruter, "Bobby Rush: A New Blend of Music," *Living Blues* 84 (January/February 1989): 26–30; Rush interview.

24. Rush interview.

25. Carter interview.

26. Bill McFarland interview; Bobby Pointer interview.

27. Robert Pruter, "The Barbara Livsey Story," *Goldmine*, September 1981, p. 183; Livsey interview.

28. Robert Pruter, "Jackie Ross," *It Will Stand* 20 (1983): 6–8; Ross interview.

29. Steve Bryant, liner notes, The Independents, *The First Time We Met— The Greatest Hits*, Charly R&B CRB 1146, 1986; Adam Finn, "Chuck Jackson and Marvin Yancy: Behind the Scene Heavies," *Black Music*, March 1977, pp. 9–11.

30. John Abbey, "Independently Speaking," *Blues and Soul*, June 4–17, 1976, p. 4; Bryant liner notes; Denise Hall, "Declaration of Independents," *Black Music*, August 1974, p. 20.

31. Bruck Chadwick, "Natalie Cole: Out of Her Father's Illustrious Shadow," *Black Stars*, February 1978, pp. 41–46; Herschel Johnson, "Natalie Cole," *Ebony*, December 1975, pp. 35–42.

32. "His Labor of Love Makes You Take Note," *Soul*, September 30, 1974, p. 11; Willie Henderson interview.

33. Henderson interview.

34. Marzette Griffith interview.

35. "Playboy Records Vows Good Taste," *Rolling Stone*, March 2, 1972, p. 24.

36. Earl Calloway, "Reviewing an Historic Debut," *Chicago Defender*, January 8, 1977; Billy Foster, "Weapons of Peace: From the Green Bunny to Playboy," *Illinois Entertainer*, September 1976, p. 26.

37. Naomi Rubne, "21st Century: Another Jackson 5?," *Soul*, September 1, 1975, pp. 6–7; "The 21st Century: A Group to Watch in '76," *Black Stars*, April 1976, p. 74; "Local Group with Motown: The 21st Creation," *Chicago Metro News*, February 25, 1978.

38. John Abbey, "Wham Bam It's Captain Sky," *Blues and Soul*, November/ December 1980, p. 31; "Captain Sky," Captain Sky Enterprises, Inc., [1979]; "The Artist as Business Man," Captain Sky Enterprises, Inc. [1979].

15

Chi-Sound and the Demise of the Chicago Soul Industry

The decline of independent record companies during the late 1960s and early 1970s was an industry-wide trend.[1] Steve Chapple and Reebee Garofalo in *Rock 'n' Roll Is Here to Pay,* a survey of the record industry from 1977, reported that "by 1970 few independent companies of any significance were left," and that in 1973 the top four record companies "accounted for 52.8 percent of all records and tapes sold."[2] Their statement regarding the indie companies in 1970 was an exaggeration, but they got the nature of the trend correct. By 1987 the percentage figure of the top four would be 86 percent.[3] *Billboard* would report that for the last half of 1975 four of five majors posted "all-time highs."[4]

Much of the growth of the majors was fueled by their move into black music. Lee Underwood and Cynthia Kirk in *Soul* magazine in mid-1975 reported that "between 1971 and 1974 Capitol, RCA, and Columbia entered the black market heavily by signing on new black acts."[5] All three companies increased their percentage in market share at the expense of independents such as Motown.[6] The majors moved into black music partly because it was becoming increasingly lucrative as black acts evolved from singles hitmakers to best-selling album artists.[7] The majors had the deep pockets to provide the big advances necessary for album projects.

Chicago, where independent operations made up the bulk of its recording industry activities, obviously was especially hard hit by the decline of the independents. Particularly noticeable at first was the collapse of Record Row during the late 1960s and early 1970s. One obvious reason for the collapse was that there were too few lines for too many distributors, and not just because there were fewer independent record companies around. The majors, which in the early 1960s had relied on a combination of independent distribution (especially for r&b records) and distribution by company-owned branches, began to give up on the indies. The rationale was that branch operations saved on middleman profits and gave the company better control over distribution.[8] The downside to branch operations was that the overhead had to be paid regardless of profit or loss statements. But in the 1960s with sales growing in volume every year for most of the majors, the expansion of branch operations made sense. Warner Brothers, for example, had to close its branch in Chicago in 1960 because its product line was insufficient to sustain a branch, but later it achieved tremendous growth in sales and reestablished a branch operation by the late 1960s.

During the late 1960s and 1970s, *Billboard* and other trade publications were filled with reports of majors dropping independent distribution. For example, in April 1969 Columbia announced that its Epic label would henceforth use branch operations for distribution.[9] Also in 1969 ABC Records switched to branch operations in several areas of the country, as did United Artists Records.[10] In 1970 MCA discontinued its Revue and Congress labels, which were largely r&b labels distributed by independents. The reason given for their being phased out was that MCA was concentrating on distribution through its branches.[11] Not only were distribution functions taken over by the majors, but also promotion and publicity.[12]

"The business was becoming a big business," said Jack White of Summit Distributors, "and because it was becoming a big business the major labels were interested in taking back their subsidiary labels from the independent people. They no longer wanted M.S., or Garmisa, or All State, or Summit to handle them. Summit lost three or four labels like that. We lost Epic because Epic became such a money-making proposition that CBS wanted to take it back and put it under its own umbrella."[13]

Summit and other independent distributors were useful in the 1960s when the subsidiary labels were smaller and the majors wanted aggressive promotion and push on them, as White related: "They were minor labels, they weren't doing that much business and they wanted to get concentration and exposure. They figured an outfit like us would run around like crazy for them. Which we did for Epic Records. We took Epic when it was a very small, quiet label and we ran with it for five, six, seven years. We ran around and really promoted them."[14]

The independent distributors were also squeezed out by the rise of one-stops and rack-jobber distributors. Rack jobbers provided service to drugstores, variety stores, and department stores. Originally the rack jobbers went to the distributors for product, but as volume grew they bypassed the middlemen and bought direct from manufacturers, or would set up "paper" distribution companies to buy from the manufacturer.

As department stores, drugstores, and other outlets serviced by the rack jobbers increased their share of the retail business, the moms and pops—the traditional customers of independent distributors—went out of business. The independents with their functions and business taken away either closed shop or expanded to become rack jobbers or one-stops. Many one-stops became rack jobbers as well.[15] *Billboard* devoted an article in February 1974 to the acceleration of this trend and saw little or no prospect for its reversal.[16]

Another trend detrimental to the independents, particularly in the 1970s, was the growth of chain record stores. Related Seymour Greenspan of Summit:

> Prior to the growth of multi-store chains, if an outlet was in our area we had access to the sales to that store. We had our own promotion people, calling on the radio stations to create demand for product. What was happening, the chains would come in and they would be distributor-affiliated and buying from their central distribution point. Musicland, for example, was affiliated with a distributor in Minneapolis. We, the Chicago distributors, were supporting the promotion efforts, which wasn't cheap. We were covering 100 percent of the promotion costs and getting 50 to 60 percent of the volume that was being created. Our costs were in excess to what they should have been. That was one of the principal things that happened.[17]

In 1974, Chicago could claim only four indie distributors—Paul Glass's Hitville, M.S., Summit, and United—but within two years three of them would close down.[18] In the summer of 1973, Ernie Leaner turned United into a one-stop, but continued to go through the motions as a full-service distributor for a year or so. Leaner explained he "was joining a trend wherein independent distributors were treating a broader base, necessitated by the inroads of major branch operation."[19] Summit closed its doors before the end of 1974 and by the spring of 1975 Glass was gone. Glass had been distributing Motown product exclusively and in May 1975 Motown switched distribution to M.S., the only game left in town.[20] Glass then left the business. M.S., however, was no longer located on Record Row, but in the northern suburbs, where many branch operations were also headquartered.[21]

In 1980 Chicago writer Cary Baker reported on what was left of Record Row: "It's a little difficult to picture the segment of South Michigan Avenue between Roosevelt Road [Twelfth Street] and Twenty-sixth Street as the one-time recording hub of the city. To be sure, the district that once teemed with recording artists, entrepreneurs, and distributors leaves little evidence of past glories. To drive southward along Michigan from Roosevelt, one passes vacated furniture warehouses, factory-to-you wig outlets, and quiescent corporate headquarters. Only a few landmarks attest to the neigh-borhood's one-time grandeur."[22] What Baker meant by "landmarks" were vacated record-company headquarters, namely those of Brunswick and Chess.

In 1974 there was still enough vigor in the city's soul music industry for *Chicago Daily News* rock critic Jack Hafferkamp to single it out as a lone success: "Right now, where it's at—in fact the only place it's at commercially—in Chicago music is the rhythm-and-blues field." He then cited a 1974 issue of *Billboard* that listed six Chicago artists in the top forty of its soul chart.[23] Despite Hafferkamp's upbeat assessment, the music veterans he interviewed were not impressed. Calvin Carter said the scene was "pretty dismal," and Jerry Butler said, "As the blues and r&b capital long before Motown or Memphis, Chicago had given the world some large doses of music. It was great history, but unfortunately for the last ten years, that's mostly what it has been—history."[24] Instead of deriding the achieve-ments of the previous decade Butler probably would have hailed them had he been prescient enough to know that the city would eventually have virtually no rhythm-and-blues scene by the mid-1980s.

Although most Chicago record companies were no longer located on Record Row in the 1970s, they fared a bit better than the independent distributors—at first. This is because many opted to be distributed by a major, or if not a major, a company with great promotional and financial resources. The Chicago companies thus benefitted not only from solid distribution but from more aggressive and effective promotion and publicity.[25] For example, Carl Davis for several years distributed the Dakar label through Atlantic. Curtis Mayfield distributed Curtom through Buddah and, as the majors gained ascendency, through Warner Brothers. Clarence Johnson at first had his records independently distributed, but by the mid-1970s he had begun placing his productions with larger labels.

By 1976, however, the Chicago recording industry was in dire straits with the collapse of Brunswick. A number of Chicago r&b acts transferred to majors, notably the Chi-lites (from Brunswick to Mercury), Tyrone Davis (from Dakar to Columbia), the Dells (from Chess to Mercury), and Bo Diddley (from Chess to ABC). This reflected a nationwide development that year. *Billboard* commented, "Independent distributed labels are seen devoting more effort to building new artists in the face of an accelerated trend by name acts to abandon their indie homes in favor of labels with branch operations...more than twenty-five acts transfer[red] their allegiance from indie distributed labels in the past year."[26]

Commented Greenspan, "As the majors got bigger they acquired some of the smaller labels, where they would acquire the artists. A lot of these labels would have one or two hot artists, and the majors would either sign the artist or take over the label. For example, Bobby Shad had a label, Mainstream Records, and Janis Joplin was on Mainstream. Janis started to look like she was going to make it, so Bobby Shad sold her contract to Columbia. That was repeated over and over again."[27]

It was in this climate for the record industry that in June 1976, Carl Davis left Brunswick to form his own company, Chi-Sound Records. He relocated from faded Record Row to a building at 10 East Huron on the edge of the glitzy Rush Street nightclub district on the near North Side. There he rented one floor and quickly expanded into a second floor. Almost all of the company's recording was done at Universal, a short walking distance from the company.

Given the realities of the record business at the time, it was obvious to Davis that setting up an independent operation was no longer a viable option, so he established a distribution and financial alliance with United Artists Records in Los Angeles. Chi-Sound became what was called a "custom label" of the company. In this setup Chi-Sound product would be released on United Artist releases, but the Chi-Sound logo would appear on the label as well. All manufacturing, distribution, and promotion (the latter outside Chicago) would be handled by United Artists.

The alliance with United Artists was ended in the spring of 1978, when the label was purchased by Capitol Records, and a corporate reshuffling left Chi-Sound on the outs. Davis established a new "custom label" relationship with a revived 20th Century Fox (renamed from "20th Century") Records. The company was infused with a load of new cash from sales of the *Star Wars* soundtrack and was hiring new executives, signing new talent, and making deals. The key to the Chi-Sound tie was Davis's old friend and associate Bunky Sheppard, who became the new vice president of 20th Century Fox in the summer of 1978. He had been on the coast for several years working under Ewart Abner at Motown. After stints at CTI, Mercury, and other labels he found a home at 20th Century Fox, to which he brought Chi-Sound.[28]

Chi-Sound broke some new artists in its first years, but was unable to follow strongly on their artists' initial successes. One such group was Manchild, a self-contained jazzy-r&b group from Indianapolis. The ensemble was founded in the spring of 1974 and consisted of Reggie Griffin (lead guitar, sax, and vocals), "Flash" Ferrell (lead singer), Chuck Bush (keyboards and vocals), Kenny Edmonds (guitar and vocals), Anthony Johnson (bass), Daryl Simmons (percussion and vocals), and Robert Parson (drums). After developing an original repertoire in Midwest clubs the group was signed by Davis in late 1978.[29]

Manchild during 1977-78 came out with two albums, *Power and Love* and *Feel the Puhff,* but was able to get only one single on the charts—an airy ballad with a jazz feel, "Especially for You." It lasted twelve weeks and went to position sixty-seven on *Cash Box's* black singles chart, essentially a non-hit. The first album, on the other hand, *Power and Love,* went to fourteen on the *Cash Box* r&b album chart. *Feel the Puhff,* released in early 1978, did not create any excitement, and when Chi-Sound moved to 20th Century Fox later in the year the California label did not pick up the group.

One of the first acts signed by Chi-Sound was Margie Alexander, who recorded two singles for the company, one of which was "Gotta Get a Hold on Me." It lasted ten weeks and went to position fifty-eight on the *Cash Box* chart in the summer of 1977. She brought a vigorous gospelized soprano sound to her songs, and the only thing that separated her from stardom was sufficient opportunity.

Alexander was born on October 11, 1948, in a rural town in Georgia, fifty miles from Atlanta. Like many a soul singer she began her singing in the church. Her first professional singing was a member of the Gospel Crusaders out of Los Angeles. In 1968, however, she went into secular music and moved to Atlanta. There she came under the mentorship of hard-soul singer Clarence Carter who produced her first hit, "Keep on Searchin'," in 1974. In 1976 she signed with Chi-Sound. Despite the promise shown by her singles on the label, Davis never did much with Alexander and eventually dropped her.[30]

The principal Chi-Sound artist during its United Artists years was Walter Jackson. He revived his career while on the label and helped immensely in sustaining the company in its first years. Before coming to Chi-Sound, Jackson experienced a real drought in hits; his last was from late 1969, when he got a top-ten r&b record with "Anyway You Want Me," on Cotillion. A brief early-1970s association with Davis at Brunswick did not work out.[31]

Starting fresh at Chi-Sound, however, Davis signed Jackson with the intention of having the singer play a prominent part in launching the label. While some of the other Chi-Sound acts were started off with single releases, Davis started Jackson with an album, *Feeling Good.* It proved to be a new direction for the artist. Whereas his earlier material by and large could be classified as rhythm and blues, albeit a soft variety, the placing of *Feeling Good* in that genre seemed a lot more problematical. The sophisticated pop performer in the man had triumphed over the r&b singer. The album was essentially a collection of pop and pop-soul tunes previously done by other artists, notably Morris Albert's "Feelings," Margie Joseph's "Words," and Elton John's "Someone Saved My Life Tonight." "Welcome Home" was revived, but with a longer and more leisurely arrangement. Basically, *Feeling Good* was soul-styled mood music, but it resuscitated Jackson's career.

"Feelings" lasted twenty-one weeks and went to the eight position on the *Cash Box* black singles chart in late 1976.

Continuing in the same vein as *Feeling Good* were *I Want to Come Back as a Song* (1977) and *Good to See You* (1978), both containing lush covers of popular hits and smooth revivals of Jackson's old OKeh hits. While much of the material failed to make an impact on this listener, both albums featured some standouts that sustained Jackson's reputation. For example, "Baby I Love Your Way," which lasted eighteen weeks and went to position nine on the *Cash Box* chart in early 1977, must certainly rank among the best recordings he had ever made.

After 20th Century Fox picked up Chi-Sound, it released one other very poor album on Jackson, *Send in the Clowns,* and then dropped the artist. Davis managed to get Columbia to pick up another album he did on Jackson, *Tell Me where It Hurts,* which was released in 1981 to no great acclaim. A single of the same name did moderately well, however, lasting sixteen weeks and going to position twenty on the *Cash Box* chart. In June 1983 Jackson died of a stroke, at the age of forty-five. Just three days before his death, Chi-Sound released what would be his last single, "It's Cool." A memorial album, which included "It's Cool," followed within a few months, but the limp evidence on the wax showed how far Carl Davis's operation had fallen as a creative force.

During Chi-Sound's 20th Century Fox years Gene Chandler was the label's most prominent artist. After he was released from Curtom in 1973, he was left with no recording contract. A deal with Columbia did not work out when the album he recorded in England and Jamaica for an independent producer was found by the company to be unacceptable for release. Chandler did not have his record companies either; his life had hit a low point and he was beset with a multitude of personal problems. In December 1976 he was convicted of selling 388 grams of heroin with a street value of $30,000. Gene Chandler by this time was a name that only conjured up the past.[32]

In early 1978, however, Chandler while in the midst of his problems rejoined Carl Davis and began recording again. He had an immediate hit with the splendid mellifluous ballad "Tomorrow I May Not Feel the Same." Despite its excellence, from first listen one could tell it was not going to be the record on which Chandler would stage a comeback. It seemed more like a reprise of his 1960s ballad style than a now sound. Although the record lasted a hefty twelve weeks on *Cash Box's* black contemporary singles chart in March 1968, it never rose higher than position forty-eight.

After serving a four-month sentence for his drug conviction, Chandler came out with "Get Down," released in October 1978 through 20th Century Fox. It was disco, it was hot, a definite comeback sound, and it did not submerge his distinctive vocals as disco sometimes did. The single went to position four and lasted twenty-four weeks on the *Cash Box* chart. He also released a fair album containing a wide range of song styles, not just disco. A good portion of its success rested on the contributions of Chandler's old friend, composer James Thompson (who was a member of the Voice Masters, on Bamboo).

The one hit of "Get Down" was not enough to bring about Chandler's comeback in the concert arena. A fine show in Chicago, in March 1979, filled less than half of the auditorium. He needed more hits. "When You're Number One" had moderate success in June of 1979, but like "Walk on with the Duke" of sixteen years earlier, "Number One" was a mere contrived follow-up. An album of the same name sold enough for 20th Century Fox to get its investment back.

In May 1980 Chandler returned to his hit-making form with "Does She Have a Friend?," a mid-tempo ballad superbly fitted to the singer's way with a song. It went to position seventeen and lasted fifteen weeks on the *Cash Box* chart. With "Friend," Chandler had to break from his usual procedure of picking songs from his own publishing company. Said he, "To be honest there wasn't too many things from my sources that I could hear as a hit. Then I remembered these tunes that had come in to Chi-Sound from this white firm in Los Angeles. I particularly liked this one tune, 'Does She Have a Friend?' I thought it was a great pop record and that it opened my eyes to a lot of things that were coming from other companies, from the white firms."[33] The song was the first single taken from Chandler's third LP on Chi-Sound, *Gene Chandler Eighty.*

In 1981 Chandler took over from Davis the production of his music and came out with the *Here's to Love* album. Although a pleasant-sounding LP, there just were not any particularly memorable cuts on it. Even Chandler admits that the first single taken from it, "I'm Attracted to You," written by folk singer Steve Goodman, could not have been a hit. The second single, "Love Is the Answer," had potential but lacked a forceful enough production to connect with the disco-oriented public.

Under independent distribution, Chi-Sound put out in the spring of 1982 "Make the Living Worthwhile," a moderate-size hit lasting eleven weeks and going to thirty-third position on *Cash Box's* survey. One other single on Chi-Sound, in 1983, was hardly distributed beyond the confines of Chicago.

In 1985 Chandler put out a Chicago-made album on the New York-based Fastfire label. The album, *Your Love Looks Good,* produced two singles that had moderate success on the r&b charts. That we were still hearing from Gene Chandler a quarter century after his first records were released was testimony to the durability and greatness of this artist.

As the 1980s began, it seemed that Chi-Sound was on the verge of actually reviving Chicago as a record town. Chandler was riding high with "Does She Have a Friend?," and the company was having considerable success with the Dells and the Chi-lites. Eugene Record had rejoined the Chi-lites after a three-year absence, and he also entered Chi-Sound as the company's principal writer and producer. Besides working with the Chi-lites, he produced albums on the Impressions and the Dells. Also, Davis purchased a handsome three-story brownstone at 8 East Chestnut, a couple of blocks from his old address. In the new headquarters, which he lavishly remodeled, he scheduled the building of an in-house state-of-the-art twenty-four-track recording studio. But as indicative of the fortunes of the label, the studio was never completed.

The Dells had initial success with the company owing to the talents of Record. He wrote and produced an album, *I Touched a Dream,* from which the title cut, a ballad, lasted seventeen weeks and went to position twenty on *Cash Box's* contemporary black singles chart in the late summer of 1980. Record had less success with the Chi-lites LP, *Heavenly Body.* The title song was only a modest single hit, lasting fourteen weeks and going to position thirty-six on the *Cash Box* chart in late 1980. "Heavenly Body" was a ballad, and Record, sensing that the era of ballady vocal groups was fast ending, concentrated on producing up-tempo hard-driving dance tunes on the Chi-lites next album, *Me and You* (1981). Drawn from the album was a dancer, "Hot on a Thing (Called Love)," which in early 1982 lasted nineteen weeks and went to position twelve on the *Cash Box* chart.

During 1981-82, the Chi-lites proved to be the only bright spot for the company.[34] A second Dells album flopped, as did albums by Gene Chandler and the Impressions. Early in 1982, 20th Century Fox dropped Chi-Sound, leaving the company without a financial backer or solid distribution. Apparently 20th Century Fox felt Davis no longer possessed the touch to make it worthwhile to keep advancing money for albums that were not going to bring returns on the investments.

Davis during 1981 and 1982 was forced to place more and more of his acts on his independently distributed Kelli-Arts label. He got a strong single on a self-contained band, Magnum Force, who hit locally with "Share My Love with You" in early 1982. However, it took Davis a year to follow through with an album. He also placed acts with some majors, Walter Jackson with Columbia in 1981 and Merge with RCA in 1982, but neither did well enough to keep the labels interested. Eugene Record, finding the future prospects at Chi-Sound bleak, left with the Chi-lites. His group continued a few more years, recording with some success for Los Angeles-based Private I Records. The Dells and the Impressions also left in 1982.

During 1983 Chi-Sound was practically moribund. The company was low on financing and the few singles it put out were barely distributed outside the city, besides being pretty wretched. It was obvious that Carl Davis, the major force in the Chicago record industry for more than twenty years, was fast fading from the scene. He was the only one left. Vee Jay went asunder in 1966, Chess was shuttered in 1975, Curtom disintegrated in 1980, and most of the mom-and-pop companies had bit the dust as well. In January 1984 Davis quietly closed the doors of Chi-Sound. The Chicago soul music recording industry was no more.

NOTES

1. There have been two excellent book-length treatments of the record industry as it operated in the 1970s from which the reader will get a good understanding of the industry-wide trends in that decade, particularly the concentration and consolidation of the industry into a few major companies and the decline of independent distribution: Steve Chapple and Reebee Garofalo, *Rock 'n' Roll Is Here to Pay* (Chicago: Nelson-Hall, 1977); R. Serge Denisoff, *Solid Gold: The Popular Record Industry* (New Brunswick, N.J.: Transaction Books, 1975).

2. Chapple and Garofalo, *Rock 'n' Roll,* pp. 87, 93.

3. "N.A.A.C.P., in Report on Hiring Bias, Criticizes the Recording Industry," *New York Times,* April 27, 1987.

4. Stephen Traiman, "Four of Five Majors Post All-Time Highs," *Billboard,* March 27, 1976, p. 6.

5. Lee Underwood and Cynthia Kirk, "Music Industry: Black Money Is Black Power," *Soul,* July 21, 1975, p. 16.

6. Ibid.

7. [Lee Underwood and Cynthia Kirk], "Black Recording Artists: No Longer Second Class," *Soul,* July 7, 1975, p. 14.

8. Chapple and Garofalo, *Rock 'n' Roll,* p. 198.

9. "Col. Branches Will Handle Epic Label," *Billboard,* April 12, 1969, p. 4.

10. "ABC Shifts to Own Outlet in Denver," *Billboard,* April 12, 1969, p. 3; "ABC Distrib Net Gets a Reshuffling," *Billboard,* April 19, 1969, p. 3; "Lib./UA Opens Distribution Outlets in Three Major Areas," *Billboard,* June 28, 1969, p.6.

11. "MCA Phases Out Shambley, Revue," *Billboard,* July 11, 1970, p. 3.

12. Denisoff, *Solid Gold,* p. 196.

13. Jack White interview, June 21, 1988.

14. Ibid.

15. Chapple and Garofalo, *Rock 'n' Roll,* p. 90.

16. John Sippel, "Profit Jam Forcing Indie Distrib Acceleration into One-Stop and Racking," *Billboard,* February 7, 1974, p. 1.

17. Greenspan interview.

18. *Chicago Yellow Pages: C-Commercial/Industrial Directory, 1974* (Chicago: Reuben H. Donnelly Corporation, 1974).

19. "Leaner Opens Memphis One-Stop," *Billboard,* December 15, 1973, p. 47.

20. "Motown Switches Chicago Operation," *Billboard,* May 3, 1975, p. 4.

21. *Chicago Yellow Pages: C-Commercial/Industrial Directory, 1976* (Chicago: Reuben H. Donnelly Corporation, 1976).

22. Cary Baker, "Recording Activity in Chicago: From Four-Track to State-of-the Art," *Illinois Entertainer,* May 1980, p. 4.

23. Jack Hafferkamp, "Rhythm and Blues a Lonesome Soul," *Chicago Daily News,* June 3, 1974.

24. Ibid.

25. Chapple and Garofalo, *Rock 'n' Roll,* p. 90.

26. "Acts Prefer Branch Distrib; Flee Indies," *Billboard,* February 28, 1976, p. 1.

27. Greenspan interview.

28. Earl Calloway, "Dreams Keep Him Spinning," *Chicago Defender,* April 22, 1978; idem, "Carl Davis Uses His Influence to Sustain Chicago Entertainers and the City as a Producing Center," *Chicago Defender,* August 15, 1981; "Mogull, Rubenstein Buy UA; EMI Distributors," *Billboard,* April 15, 1978, p. 1; "20th Century: Film Label Restructuring Sees New Management, Image, Acts," *Billboard,* April 29, 1978, p. 24; "20th Century Fox Aproach [*sic*] to Our Music" and "Chi-Sound Records: It's a Family Affair," *Blues and Soul,* August 1980, p. 16; "20th Century-Fox Records Goes after Black Music Dollar with Addition of 'Bunky' Sheppard," *Soul,* August 28, 1978, p. 2.

29. "Manchild," Chi-Sound/United Artists, [1977].

30. Margie Alexander, "Auto-Biography of Margie Alexander," [1976], unpublished manuscript; copy in author's files.

31. Robert Pruter, "The Uphill Climb of . . . Walter Jackson," *Goldmine,* August 1979, pp. 20-22.

32. John Abbey, "Gene Chandler, the Duke of Earl, Is Back," *Blues and Soul,* August 1978, p. 33; idem, "Duke of Earl Goes over the Rainbow Again," *Blues and Soul,* August 1980, pp. 20-21; David Nathan, "Gene Chandler: Back to Number One . . . ," *Blues and Soul,* January 1980, p. 18; Robert Pruter, "Time Gives Mature Duke of Earl a Brand New Rainbow," *Illinois Entertainer,* August 1980, pp. 72-73, 84; Lee Strobel, "Ex-rock Star Jailed in Heroin Sale," *Chicago Tribune,* December 22, 1976.

33. Chandler interview, February 6, 1979.

34. John Abbey, "The Chi-lites: Back Together Again," *Blues and Soul,* August 1980, p. 18; Robert Pruter, "The Chi-lites, Part 2: 1976-1984," *Goldmine,* November 22, 1985, pp. 16-20.

Appendix: List of Interviews

Except where noted the following were telephone interviews conducted by the author. All transcripts and notes of the interviews are in the author's files.

Acklin, Barbara, Chicago, December 4, 1982
Andrews, Ruby, Chicago, April 12, 1982
(anonymous), Chicago, January 16, 1979
Armstead, Joshie Jo, Chicago, February 5, 1986
Austell, Leo, Chicago, August 3, 1980
Ballard, Hank, New York City, March 15, 1988
Barge, Gene, Chicago, September 8, 1981, and January 16, 1982
Barksdale, Chuck, Harvey, Ill., January 15, 1981, and March 20, 1984
Bass, Ralph, Chicago, April 29, 1988
Beachley, Chris, Charlotte, N.C., June 7, 1986, and January 27, 1988
Bedno, Howard, Chicago, March 2, 1988
Black, Carlton, Evanston, Ill., July 16, 1977
Blake, Cicero, Chicago, June 23, 1981, and February 24, 1988
Bobrov, Sol, Chicago, December 31, 1986
Bradley, Jan, Country Club Hills, Ill., June 9 and June 14, 1987, and February 6, 1988
Brooks, Jerome, Chicago, April 22, 1981
Brown, Devora, Detroit, July 13, 1986
Burrage, Rev. Eugene, Chicago, May 14, 1985
Butler, Billy, personal interview, Chicago, June 5, 1974
Butler, Jerry, personal interview, Chicago, April 21, 1982
Carter, Tollie, Chicago, March 12, 1988
Cash, Alvin, personal interview, Chicago, May 11, 1980
Caston, Leonard, Jr., Los Angeles, August 4, 1980
Catron, Bob, Memphis, Tenn., January 23, 1988

Chandler, Gene, personal interview, Chicago, February 6, 1979

Chandler, Gene, personal interview with Aaron Fuchs, Flossmoor, Ill., 1979

Chavers, Bill, Chicago, October 20, 1983

Clark, Dee, personal interview, Chicago, December 19, 1979

Clay, Don, personal interview with Jim O'Neal, Chicago, February 25, 1982

Clay, Otis, personal interview, Chicago, April 20, 1979

Clay, Otis, Chicago, May 22, 1979, September 9, 1980, and July 10, 1984

Clay, Otis, personal interview with Steve Tomashefsky, Chicago, August 19, 1976

Coday, Bill, Memphis, February 15, 1989

Colbert, Charles, Jr., personal interview, Chicago, August 20, 1974

Colbert, Charles, Jr., Chicago, January 22, 1988

Collier, Mitty, Chicago, April 18, 1981

Collins, Mel, Chicago, January 12, 1986

Cordell, John, Norridge, Ill., March 1, 1987

Crook, General, Chicago, January 13, 1988

Curry, Clifford, Chicago, September 8, 1976

Daniels, Jack, Chicago, October 5 and October 15, 1987

Davis, Billy, New York City, August 28, 1986

Davis, Carl, personal interview, Flossmoor, Ill., March 9, 1986

Davis, Carl, Flossmoor, Ill., April 27, 1986

Davis, Carl, Homewood, Ill., December 11, 1986

Davis, Carl, personal interview with Dave Hoeskstra, Flossmoor, Ill., 1982

Davis, Charles, personal interview, LaGrange, Ill., January 27, 1978

Davis, Tyrone, Oakbrook, Ill., April 7, 1979

Drew, Patti, Evanston, Ill., July 15, 1977, and May 10, 1980

Dunbar, Richard, Washington, D.C., June 11, 1983

Edmund, Jessica, Chicago, July 19, 1979

Edwards, Earl, Chicago, July 18, 1977

Edwards, Millard, Chicago, September 8, 1981, and February 16, 1988

Erman, Bill, Atlanta, July 23, 1988

Everett, Betty, St. Louis, January 13, 1986

Ferguson, Irene, Chicago, May 10, 1985

Garrett, Jo Ann, Chicago, August 14, 1980

Gideon, Tony, Birmingham, Ala., August 8 and 9, 1976, and January 20, 1988

Giardini, Angelo, Wheeling, Ill., July 23, 1988

Green, Garland, Chicago, February 16, 1979

Greenspan, Seymour, Skokie, Ill., June 21, 1988

Griffith, Marzette, Chicago, January 14, 1988

Guy, Vernon, St. Louis, December 10, 1985, and January 27, 1986

Haley, Ray, Chicago, April 22, 1975

Hamilton, Patti, Chicago, January 17, 1981

Haygood, Johnny, Chicago, December 2, 1979

Henderson, Willie, Chicago, July 23, 1984

Isaac, James Dennis, Chicago, February 20, 1978

Jackson, Reggie, personal interview, Bellwood, Ill., July 29, 1978

Jackson, Walter, personal interview, Chicago, August 10, 1976

Jacobs, Dick, New York City, March 23, 1987

Jenkins, Donald, Chicago, February 23, 1977

Johnson, Clarence, Chicago, December 26, 1986

Johnson, Larry, Chicago, December 15, 1979

Johnson, Paul (Guitar Red), Chicago, January 20, 1989

Johnson, Stacy, St. Louis, January 27, 1986, and February 1, 1986

Johnson, Syl, Harvey, Ill., April 14, 1983, and February 25, 1988

Jones, Hilliard, Chicago, December 23, 1988

Joyce, Leroy, Chicago, July 15, 1979

Junior, Marvin, Chicago, December 15, 1979

Kent, Herb, Tinley Park, Ill., April 8, 1977; Chicago, December 23, 1989

Koester, Bob, Chicago, January 1, 1988

Lance, Major, personal interview, Chicago, April 22, 1976

Leaner, Billy, Chicago, July 6, 1988

Leaner, Ernest, Lakeside, Michigan, October 28, 1983

Leavill, Otis, personal interview, Chicago, April 19, 1976

Leavill, Otis, Chicago, July 20, 1984

Lee, Bob, Chicago, January 28, 1989

Lightner, Maxine Edwards, Detroit, May 9, 1986

Livsey, Barbara, Chicago, March 12, 1981

McAlister, Maurice, personal interview, Chicago, April 20, 1981

McFarland, Bill, Chicago, October 15, 1985

McGill, Mickey, Harvey, Ill., February 21, 1981, and April 28, 1986

McGrier, H. Sam, Chicago, May 6, 1980

McVickers, Janice, personal interview, Sandwich, Ill., January 8, 1989

Mason, Melvin, personal interview, Ford Heights, Ill., August 20, 1977

Maxwell, Holly, personal interview, Chicago, February 8, 1987

Mayfield, Curtis, Atlanta, March 26, 1986

Merritt, Carl, personal interview, Chicago, June 10, 1979

Miner, Raynard, Chicago, July 17, 1979

Mitchell, McKinley, Jackson, Miss., April 19, 1984

Moore, Johnny, Chicago, September 23, 1987

Moorer, Alvis, Milwaukee, October 21 and 25, 1981

Moorer, Gilbert, El Paso, Texas, October 19, 1981

Nesbary, Sherman, (Verble Domino), Chicago, January 26, 1989

Nestor, Larry, Chicago, April 13, 1985

Pegue, Richard, Chicago, January 31, 1988

Perkins, O. C., personal interview, Chicago, October 24, 1977

Perkins, O. C., Chicago, November 13, 1977

Pointer, Bobby, Chicago, November 15, 1984

Record, Eugene, personal interview, Chicago, November 11, 1980

Record, Eugene, Chicago, August 26, 1984

Robinson, R. C., Evanston, April 10, 1989

Robinson, Roscoe, telephone interview with Raymond Funk, Birmingham, Ala.,
    May 13, 1983

Ross, Jackie, Chicago, August 15, 1980

Rush, Bobby, Jackson, Miss., September 29, 1985
Russell, Archie, Chicago, February 29, 1988
Sampson, Wallace, Chicago, April 1, 1981
Sayles, Johnny, personal interview, Chicago, June 27, 1979
Scaggs, Patrice, Chicago, April 2, 1988
Scott, David, Gary, Ind., April 2, 1988
Scott, Howard, Chicago, January 15, 1989
Scott, Robert, Chicago, January 15, 1989
Shaffer, Beverly, Chicago, October 19, 1986
Simmons, Simtec, Chicago, October 29, 1984
Simon, Lowrell, personal interview, Chicago, September 16, 1981
Simpkins, Maurice, Chicago, February 17, 1988
Sims, Elaine, Chicago, October 20, 1980
Sims, Gerald, personal interview, Chicago, October 6, 1978
Sims, Marvin L., Iowa City, Ia., September 21, 1985
Singleton, Ace Leon, Chicago, September 26, 1989
Sladek, Bob, Chicago, August 21, 1986
Smith, Marvin, personal interview, Bellwood, Ill., December 9, 1979
Spraggins, Wes, personal interview, Chicago, June 10, 1976
Stallworth, Dr. Robert, Macomb, Ill., March 1, 1987
Stamz, Richard, personal interview, Chicago, April 13, 1978
Sullivan, Eddie, Chicago, August 16, 1980
Tarnopol, Nat, Las Vegas, July 12, 1987
Tharp, Robert, personal interview, Bellwood, Ill., July 29, 1978
Thompson, Catherine Hayes, Chicago, September 6, 1989
Thompson, Marshall, Chicago, November 13, 1980
Upchurch, Philip, North Hollywood, Calif., September 1, 1988
Vance, Cormie, Chicago, May 9, 1977
Wahls, Shirley, Chicago, May 27, 1981
White, Jack, Highland Park, Ill., June 21 and July 6, 1988
Yarbrough, Henry, Sauk Village, Ill., August 17, 1986, and April 29, 1988

Bibliography

Abbey, John. "Alvin Cash and the Crawlers...A Few More Facts." *Home of the Blues* 8 (March 1967): 10.

———. "Behind the Scenes with Carl Davis." *Blues and Soul*, August 3–16, 1973, pp. 22–24.

———. "The Chi-lites." *Blues and Soul*, June 4–13, 1974, p. 3.

———. "The Chi-lites: Back Together Again." *Blues and Soul*, August 1980, p. 18.

———. "Duke of Earl Goes over the Rainbow Again." *Blues and Soul*, August 1980, pp. 20–21.

———. "Eugene Record: Today's Genius." *Blues and Soul*, February 1971, pp. 12–13.

———. "Garland Green: The Story." *Blues and Soul*, June 20–July 3, 1975, p. 8.

———. "Gene Chandler, The Duke of Earl, Is Back." *Blues and Soul*, August 1978, p. 33.

———. "The Ice Man." *Blues and Soul*, April 10–23, 1970, pp. 20–23.

———. "Independently Speaking." *Blues and Soul*, June 4–17, 1976, p. 4.

———. "Introducing Brighter Side of Darkness." *Blues and Soul*, January 19–February 1, 1973, p. 22.

———. "Introducing Simtec and Wylie." *Blues and Soul*, September 24–November 7, 1971, p. 6.

———. "Otis Leavill." *Blues and Soul*, August 28–September 10, 1970, p. 41.

[———]. "Rufus Thomas: Have No Fear—The Dog Was Here." *Home of the Blues* 4 (August 1966): 9–10.

———. "The Staple Singers." *Blues and Soul*, January 1971, pp. 12–13.

———. "Time Hasn't Stopped Marvin Smith." *Blues and Soul*, July 6–19, 1973, p. 20.

———. "Tyrone Davis: They Changed Their Minds about 'Change My Mind.'" *Blues and Soul*, June 19–July 1, 1970, pp. 10–11.

————. "The Vibrations." *Home of the Blues* 1 (May 1966): 8–9.

"ABC Distrib Net Gets a Reshuffling." *Billboard*, April 19, 1969, p. 3.

"ABC Shifts to Own Outlet in Denver." *Billboard*, April 12, 1969, p. 3.

"ABC-Paramount through the Years." *Billboard*, August 18, 1965, p. 32.

"Acts Prefer Branch Distrib; Flee Indies." *Billboard*, February 28, 1976, p. 1.

Adler, Renata. "Onward and Upward with the Arts: The New Sound." *The New Yorker*, February 20, 1965, p. 100.

Albert, George, and Frank Hoffman, comp. *The Cashbox Black Contemporary Singles Charts, 1960–1984*. Metuchen, N.J.: Scarecrow Press, 1986.

Aletti, Vince. "Jerry Butler." In *The Rolling Stone Rock 'n' Roll Reader*, edited by Ben Fong-Torres, pp. 123–32. New York: Bantam Books, 1974.

Alexander, Margie. "Auto-Biography of Margie Alexander." [1976] Unpublished manuscript. Copy in author's files.

Alexander, Michael. "The Impressions." *Rolling Stone*, December 27, 1969, p. 29.

"All Platinum Purchases Three GRT Labels." *Billboard*, August 30, 1975, p. 8.

Anderson, Clive. Liner notes for Billy Butler and the Enchanters, *The Right Track*, Edsel 147. 1985.

"The Artist as Business Man." Captain Sky Enterprises, Inc., [1979].

Baker, Cary. "Chicago Blues News." *Blues World* 43 (Summer 1972): 16.

————. "The Chicago Recording Co." *Triad*, August 1976, pp. 25–28.

————. "Gerald Sims' Homecoming." *Illinois Entertainer,* February 1981, p. 4.

————. "Little Milton Still Singin' Big Blues." *Goldmine*, May 1981, pp. 164–65.

————. "Marshall Chess Comes Full Circle." *Goldmine*, November 1982, pp. 14–16.

————. "Ramsey Lewis: Anatomy of a Reunion." *Goldmine*, November 23, 1984, pp. 46, 48.

————. "Recording Activity in Chicago: From 4 Track to State-of-the-Art." *Illinois Entertainer*, May 1980, pp. 4–5.

————. "Two Chicago R&B Producers and the Death of the Small Label." *Shout* 97 (July 1974): 4–5.

Banks, Lacy J. "Deniece Williams: Niecy's Musical Medicine." *Black Stars*, June 1976, pp. 7–9.

————. "Jerry Butler: The Anti-Perspirant Iceman." *Black Stars*, August 1972, pp. 11–16.

————. "The Staple Singers . . . The Message Is the Music." *Black Stars*, June 1972, pp. 17–22.

Bartley, G. Fitz. "The Stairsteps Take a Step Back." *Soul*, December 6, 1971, p. 12.

————. "Stairsteps Unimpressive at Apollo." *Soul*, December 4, 1972, p. 12.

————. " 'Trapped'—Releases Denise LaSalle." *Soul*, January 17, 1972, p. 6.

Belz, Carl. *The Story of Rock*. New York: Oxford University Press, 1969.

Benjaminson, Peter. *The Story of Motown*. New York: Grove Press, 1979.

Berry, Jason, Jonathan Foose, and Tad Jones. *Up from the Cradle of Jazz: New Orleans Music Since World War II*. Athens, Ga.: University of Georgia Press, 1986.

Betrock, Alan. *Girl Groups: The Story of a Sound.* New York: Delilah Books, 1982.

Birnbaum, Larry. "The Distinctive Style of Tyrone Davis Still No Household Sound." *Chicago Tribune*, March 22, 1985.

Biro, Nick. "Chicago Radio: Kings Remain Assumptive; Heirs Presumptive." *Billboard*, March 28, 1964, p. 12.

———. "Lots of Smoke, No Fire, in Chicago Distrib Picture." *Billboard*, October 26, 1963, pp. 6, 8.

———. "R&B Roundup." *Billboard*, May 11, 1963, p. 22. "Blue Rock and Limelight Consolidated by Mercury." *Billboard*, October 23, 1965, p. 3.

"Bobby Jones Singer Extraordinare [sic] Coming on Again." *Chicago Metro News*, March 21, 1981.

"Bobby Moore Tells How It Happened." *Soul*, July 21, 1966, p. 6.

Booth, David. "Denise LaSalle." *Soul Survivor* 7 (Summer 1987): 4–7.

———. "Etta James." *Soul Survivor* 3 (Autumn 1985): 4–8.

"Bribe Case Turns Touchy and Go." *Billboard*, March 4, 1967, p. 4.

Broughton, Viv. *Black Gospel: An Illustrated History of the Gospel Sound.* Poole, Eng.: Blandford Press, 1985.

Broven, John. *South to Louisiana.* Gretna, La.: Pelican, 1983.

———. *Walking to New Orleans: The Story of New Orleans Rhythm and Blues.* Bexhill-on-Sea, Sussex, Eng.: Blues Unlimited, 1974.

Brown, Clarence. "Tyrone Davis: A Successful Unknown." *Black Stars*, April 1975, pp. 6–10.

Brown, Geoff. "Free!" *Black Music*, June 1977, pp. 24–26.

———. "Just a Matter of Time." *Black Music*, January 1978, pp. 18–20.

———. "Kalimba Kuties." *Black Music*, March 1978, pp. 22–25.

Brown, Marcia L. "Jerry Butler: The Ice Man Keeps on Rolling Along." *Black Stars*, September 1974, pp. 11–16.

Brubaker, Robert L. *Making Music Chicago Style.* Chicago: Chicago Historical Society, 1985.

Bruder, Jay. "R&B in Washington DC: The TNT Tribble Story." *Blues and Rhythm: The Gospel Truth* 45 (July 1989): 4–7.

"Brunswick in Atlantic Split; Name Officials." *Billboard*, December 11, 1971, p. 3.

"Brunswick May Do Indie Thing." *Billboard*, January 17, 1970, p. 1.

Bryant, Steve, Liner notes for the Independents, *The First Time We Met—The Greatest Hits*, Charly R&B 1146. 1986.

———. "Ruby Andrews." *Souled Out* 2 (May 1978): 2–5.

Burke, Tony, and Dave Penny. "Screaming Boogie." *Blues and Rhythm: The Gospel Truth* 37 (June–July 1988): 9–14.

Burns, Peter. "Billy Butler: Nearly a Decade of Writing and Recording." *Blues and Soul*, June 8–21, 1973, pp. 24–25.

———. "The Curtis Mayfield Story: Part 6—Curtom." *Blues and Soul*, April 1969.

———. "Curtom Records." *Hot Buttered Soul* 21 (August 1973): 2–8.

"Butler, Chicago Workshop Join Chappell Group." *Billboard*, March 27, 1971, p. 6.

Bynum, Roland. "I'm Ready If I Don't Get to Go." *Soul*, February 28, 1972, p. 14.

Callahan, Mike. "Both Sides Now, the Story of Stereo Rock and Roll, Vee Jay Records." *Goldmine*, May 1981, pp. 170–72.

———. "The Vee Jay Story, Part 1: Scenes from a Family Owned Company." *Goldmine*, May 1981, pp. 6–18.

———. "The Vee Jay Story, Part 2: Vee Jay Is Alive and Living in Burbank." *Goldmine*, May 1981, pp. 161–63.

Calloway, Earl. "Carl Davis Uses His Influence to Sustain Chicago Entertainers and the City as a Producing Center." *Chicago Defender*, August 15, 1981.

———. "Dreams Keep Him Spinning." *Chicago Defender*, April 22, 1978.

———. "Linda Clifford's on the Move and There's No Stopping Now." *Chicago Defender*, July 8, 1978.

———. "Raynard Miner Gets BMI Award." *Chicago Defender*, July 8, 1978.

———. "Reviewing an Historic Debut." *Chicago Defender*, January 8, 1977.

"Captain Sky." Captain Sky Enterprises, Inc. [1979].

Chadwick, Bruce. "Natalie Cole: Out of Her Father's Illustrious Shadow." *Black Stars*, February 1978, pp. 41–46.

Chapman, Sammy. "The Fascinations." *Soul Survivor* 1 [1985]: 30–31.

Chapple, Steve, and Reebee Garofalo. *Rock 'n' Roll Is Here to Pay*. Chicago: Nelson-Hall, 1977.

"Chess Moves into Its Own Building." *Billboard*, September 3, 1966, p. 4.

"Chicago: Jukebox World Capital." *Billboard*, April 19, 1975, p. C-23.

"Chicago Loses Chess Records." *Illinois Entertainer*, December 1975, p. 25.

"Chicago—To Build a Creative Soul Center." *Billboard*, August 22, 1970, pp. 20, 22.

"Chi's Getting the Monkey Itch." *Billboard*, July 13, 1963, p. 48.

"Chi-Sound Records: It's a Family Affair." *Blues and Soul*, August 1980, p. 16.

Clark, Jack. "Mercury Vapor Lights." Chicago *Reader*, January 21, 1977, pp. 9–10.

Clay, Otis, interviewed by Steve Tomashefsky. Liner notes for Harold Burrage, *Pioneer of Chicago Soul*, P-Vine Special 9003. 1979.

Cochrane, William, Bill Ferris, Peter Lee, and Jim O'Neal. "Bobby Rush." *Living Blues* 84 (January/February 1989): 23–33.

Cocks, Jay. "Sounds Like Old Times." *Time*, January 5, 1981, p. 75.

Cohn, Nik. *Awopbopaloobop Alopbamboom*. St. Albans, Eng.: Paladin, 1970.

"Col. Branches Will Handle Epic Label." *Billboard*, April 12, 1969, p. 4.

"Combine Bids for VJ—with Condition." *Billboard*, May 14, 1966, p. 4.

"Convictions of Tarnopol, Three Others Are Overturned." *Billboard*, December 3, 1977, p. 4.

Crespo, Charley. "Joyce Kennedy Play [*sic*] Her Game." *Rock and Soul*, March 1986, p. 21.

Cullen, Thomas J., III. "Otis Clay: Chicago Soul Man." *Soul Survivor* 5 (Summer 1986): 14–18.

Cummings, Tony. "The Chi-lites Story." *Black Music*, July 1974, pp. 8–9.

———. "Denise LaSalle: Doin' It Right." *Black Music*, December 1974, p. 35.

———. "Different Strokes." *Black Music*, June 1974, p. 47.

———. "The Gentle Genius Writes On." *Black Music*, September 1974, pp. 19–20.

———. *The Sound of Philadelphia*. London: Eyre Menthuen, 1975.

———. "The Staple Singers." *Black Music*, March 1974, pp. 8–9.

"Cunningham and 'Kittens' Headline at Blue Angel." *Chicago Defender*, December 27, 1965.

"Curtom Revamps Structure, Format, Mayfield President," *Billboard*, May 8, 1971, p. 74.

Dachs, David. *Anything Goes: The World of Popular Music*. Indianapolis: Bobbs-Merrill, 1964.

Dahl, Bill. "Johnny Moore: Turning Back the Hands of Time." *Goldmine*, October 9, 1987, pp. 24, 88.

———. "Lee Shot Williams: Chicago's Bluesy Soul Man." *Goldmine*, December 2, 1988, pp. 30, 87.

———. "Oliver Sain: Soul Sax Serenader." *Goldmine*, October 21, 1988, pp. 34, 103.

Dance, Helen Oakley. *Stormy Monday: The T-Bone Walker Story*. Baton Rouge: Louisiana State University Press, 1987.

Davis, Sharon. *Motown: The History*. Enfield, Conn.: Guinness Books, 1988.

Dawson, Jim. "The Twist: Around and Around and Up and Down." *Goldmine*, December 16, 1988, p. 96.

Denisoff, R. Serge. *Solid Gold: The Popular Record Industry*. New Brunswick, N.J.: Transaction Books, 1975.

Dexter, Dave, Jr. "Music Cities, U.S.A." *Billboard*, December 27, 1969, p. 45.

Dixon, Robert M. W., and John Godrich, comp. *Blues and Gospel Records 1902–1943*. 3rd ed., rev. Chigwell, Eng.: Storyville, 1982.

Dixon-Stovall, Brenda. "Popular Dance in the Twentieth Century." In Lynn Fauley Emery, *Black Dance From 1619 to Today*, 2nd ed., rev. Princeton, N.J.: Princeton Book Company, 1988.

"Dogs of War: Disco Jocks Unite." Soul, June 6, 1977, p. 18.

Duis, Perry. *Chicago: Creating New Traditions*. Chicago: Chicago Historical Society, 1976.

Duncan, Dee. "The Steelers (Re-emerge)." *After Five*, July/August 1982, p. 33.

Duston, Anne. "Chicago Thriving Area for Indie Labels: Curtom." *Billboard*, April 19, 1975, p. C-6.

Eckstine, Edward. "Natra: Black Music in the '70's." *Soul and Jazz Records*, August 1974, pp. 6–7.

Eisenstein, Paul. "Motor City's Rebirth in High Gear." *Christian Science Monitor*, July 14, 1987.

"Eldee and 'Red' Leave the Ramsey Lewis Trio." *Soul*, July 7, 1966, p. 1.

Elsey, Alan D. "Make Up for Lost Time—A Look at the Emotions." *Hot Buttered Soul* 39 (1975): 5–6.

Escott, Colin. *Clyde McPhatter: A Biographical Essay*. Vollersode, West Germany: Bear Family Records, 1987.

"Ewart Abner Exits Vee Jay; Big Shake-Up." *Billboard*, August 3, 1963.

"Executive Line-Up." *Billboard*, September 18, 1965, p. 32.

"Executive Turntable." *Billboard*, October 8, 1966, p. 4.

"Fate Brought the Four Together." *Soul*, July 19, 1976, p. 11.

Feather, Leonard. "Johnny Pate." In *The New Edition of the Encyclopedia of Jazz*. New York: Horizon Press, 1960.

Finn, Adam. "Chuck Jackson and Marvin Yancy: Behind the Scene Heavies." *Black Music*, March 1977, pp. 9–11.

Fishel, Jim. "Specialty Labels Abound." *Billboard*, April 19, 1975, p. C-20.

Fisher, Bob. "The Eugene Record Interview." *Hot Buttered Soul* 27 (1973): 4–6.

———. "The Impressions." In *The Marshall Cavendish Illustrated History of Popular Music*, vol. 7, 1967–68, pp. 793–95. New York: Marshall Cavendish, 1989.

"Five Thousand Vee Jay Masters on Auction Block on February 24." *Billboard*, February 11, 1967, p. 10.

Fleming, John. "A Life Recording." Chicago *Reader*, March 7, 1980, pp. 1, 29–32.

Foster, Billy. "Weapons of Peace: From the Green Bunny to Playboy." *Illinois Entertainer*, September 1976, p. 26.

Fox, Ted. *Showtime at the Apollo*. New York: Holt, Rinehart, and Winston, 1983.

"From the Music Capitals of the World: Chicago." *Billboard*, December 17, 1966, p. 55.

Fuchs, Aaron. "The Duke of Earl Gets into Studio 54." *Village Voice*, April 16, 1979, pp. 69–71.

Fukayama, Bob. "Etta James: Twenty Years On." *Soul and Jazz*, April 1976, pp. 46–48.

Galkin, Peter. "Black White and Blues: The Story of Chess Records." Parts 1 and 2. *Living Blues* 88 (September/October 1989): 22–32; 89 (December 1989): 25–29.

Garcia, Rudy. "Newark: Four Guilty, Two Are Acquitted [*sic*]." *Billboard*, March 6, 1976, p. 12.

———. "Tarnopol Files Appeal: Hearing to Be March 29." *Billboard*, March 27, 1976, p. 95.

———. "Trial of Brunswick Execs Nears End; One Acquitted [*sic*] *Billboard*, February 28, 1976, p. 3.

Gart, Galen. *ARLD: The American Record Label Directory and Dating Guide*. Milford, N.H.: Big Nickel, 1989.

Gaspich, Nina, "My Friends Can See Me Now." *Illinois Entertainer*, August 1978, pp. 1, 45.

George, Nelson. *Where Did Our Love Go?: The Rise and Fall of the Motown Sound*. New York: St. Martin's, 1985.

Gilbert, Paul. "Prairie Avenue, Chicago's Ghost Street." *Townsfolk*, June 1947, p. 23.

Gillett, Charlie. *Making Tracks*. New York: E. P. Dutton, 1974.

———. *The Sound of the City*. Rev. and enl. New York: Pantheon, 1983.

Glubok, Norman. "D.J. Al Benson Tells of $855 Monthly Take." *Chicago American*, January 7, 1960.

———. "Howard Miller in Payola Quiz." *Chicago American*, January 4, 1960.

Goldberg, Marvin. "The Jay Hawks/Vibrations." *Bim Bam Boom* 5 (April–May, 1972): 12.

Goldstein, Patrick. "A Band that Does What It Can't." *Chicago Sun-Times*, October 25, 1976.

———. "Making Hits and Big Money at Chicago's Mercury Records." *Panorama-Chicago Daily News*, October 16–17, 1976.

Gray, Michael. "Chess at the Top." *Let It Rock*, September 1973, pp. 30–33.

Greensmith, Bill. "The Bobby McClure Interview." *Blues Unlimited* 147 (Spring 1986): 23–25.

———. "The Fontella Bass Interview." *Blues Unlimited* 147 (Spring 1986): 18–22.

Grendysa, Peter. Liner notes for *The Vocal Group Collection*, Mercury 830 283-1 M-2. 1986.

"GRT Wrap-Up Near Chess Purchase." *Billboard*, January 4, 1969, p. 1.

Guralnick, Peter, *Sweet Soul Music*. New York: Harper and Row, 1986.

Hafferkamp, Jack. "Rhythm and Blues a Lonesome Soul." *Chicago Daily News*, June 3, 1974.

Hall, Claude. "Latin Rock in Sales Upswing." *Billboard*, January 21, 1967, p. 2.

Hall, Denise. "Declaration of Independents." *Black Music*, August 1974, p. 20.

———. "Eugene Record: Poet of Bittersweet Soul." *Black Music*, October 1975, pp. 24–25.

———. "LA Lowdown." *Black Music*, November 1976, p. 10.

———. "Lasting Impressions." *Black Music*, September 1975, pp. 46–47.

"Hambone Kids." *Ebony*, June 1952, pp. 71–76.

Hannusch, Jeff. *I Hear You Knocking: The Sound of New Orleans Rhythm and Blues*. Ville Platte, La.: Swallow, 1985.

[Hannusch, Jeff.] Almost Slim. "The Popeye: Strong to the Finish." *Goldmine*, November 4, 1988, pp. 73, 80.

Haralambos, Michael. *Right On: From Blues to Soul in Black America*. London: Eddison Press, 1974.

———. "Syl Johnson Interview." *Hot Buttered Soul* 38 [1975]: 2–7.

———. "Tony Clarke—A Summary of the Official Biography." *Hot Buttered Soul* 20 (July 1973): 9.

Haskins, Jim. *Queen of the Blues*. New York: Morrow, 1987.

Hawkins, Shirley. "Queen of Soul?...Who Cares?" *Soul*, December 19, 1977, p. 19.

"He Took Over for Curtis in Three Days." *Soul*, June 23, 1975, p. 11.

Heim, Chris. "Radio Roots." *Chicago Tribune Magazine*, February 12, 1989, pp. 10–14, 23–28.

Heise, Kenan. "Former Record Distributor Ernest Leaner, Sixty-eight." *Chicago Tribune*, April 24, 1990.

———. "Musician, Composer, Monk Higgins, Fifty." *Chicago Tribune*, July 16, 1986.

——. "Paul Glass, Sixty, Once Top Record Distributor." *Chicago Tribune*, April 1, 1986.

Hess, Norbert. "Living Blues Interview: Etta James." *Living Blues* 54 (Autumn/ Winter, 1982): 12-20.

Hewitt, Paolo. "So Proud: The Moral Standard of Soul." *New Musical Express*, July 9, 1983, pp. 24-26, 43.

"Highlighting Teens with Talent." *Chicago Defender*, May 2, 1964.

Hirshey, Gerri. *Nowhere to Run: The Story of Soul Music*. New York: Times Books, 1984.

"His Labor of Love Makes You Take Note." *Soul*, September 30, 1974, p. 11.

Hoare, Ian, Clive Anderson, Tony Cummings, and Simon Frith. *The Soul Book*. New York: Delta Books, 1976.

Hoekstra, Dave. "Alvin Tries to Cash in on Latest Dance Craze." *Chicago Sun-Times*, April 24, 1988.

——. "The Chicago Sound." *Suburban Sun-Times*, June 11, 1982, p. 12.

——. "Cicero Blake Take Soul to Country." *Chicago Sun-Times*, October 17, 1986.

——. "Love Guides Soul Patriarch." *Suburban Sun-Times*, January 20, 1984, pp. 1, 13.

——. "Major Lance." *Goldmine*, October 1983, pp. 114-26.

——. "Oak Brook's Tyrone Davis Hones Singular Soul Style." *Suburban Sun-Times*, January 17, 1983, pp. 17-18.

——. "Otis Clay Is Still Soul's Shining Star." *Chicago Sun-Times*, May 27, 1988.

——. "Producer Gives His Final Tribute to Singer-Dancer Jackie Wilson." *Suburban Sun-Times/West*, February 17, 1984, p. 23.

——. "Upbeat Performance Fuels Muddy Waters." *Chicago Sun-Times*. November 15, 1984.

Horowitz, Is. "Five Plead Guilty as Federal Probe of Industry Ignites." *Billboard*, January 17, 1976, p. 1.

Hoskyns, Barney. *Say It One More Time for the Broken Hearted*. Glasgow: Fontana/ Collins, 1987.

Huggins, Cilla. "A Little More on Milton." *Blues Unlimited* 144 (Spring 1983): 30-34.

Hunter, Bob. "WVON New King of Chicago Radio." *Chicago Defender*, September 21, 1963.

"The Impressions Make One." *Soul*, February 28, 1972, p. 11.

Jacobs, Dick, as told to Tim Holmes. "Jackie Wilson." *Musician*, January 1988, p. 21.

Jahn, Mike. *Rock*. New York: Quadrangle/New York Times Book Company, 1973.

Jancik, Wayne. "After Ninety Years: A New Generation of Juke Boxes." *Illinois Entertainer*, May 1979, p. 1, 22-23.

——. "Denise LaSalle: Sassy, Suggestive, Sultry...and Determined." *Goldmine*, January 30, 1987, p. 65.

——. "Bull and the Matadors." [1989]. Unpublished manuscript in author's files.

Johnson, Herschel. "Natalie Cole." *Ebony*, December, 1975, pp. 35-42.

Jones, Ronnie. "Crane Cool-Gars." *Chicago Defender*, January 22, 1966.

"Judge Dismisses Tarnopol Charges, Declares Mistrial." *Billboard*, June 3, 1978, p. 3.

Keegan, Kevin. Liner notes for Jackie Wilson, *My Way—Jackie Wilson*, Brunswick Collector Series P18816. 1985.

Kennedy, Bret. "Tyrone Davis: The Man Upstairs Is My Silent Partner." *Soul*, April 7, 1969, p. 12.

Kinder, Bob. *The Best of the First: The Early Days of Rock and Roll*. Chicago: Adams Press, 1986.

[Kochakian, Dan, and George A. Moonoogian]. "Little Joe Cook: The Original Thriller." *Whiskey, Women, and . . .* 15 (December 1985): 21.

Koester, Bob. "Junior Wells: Eighteen Years at Forty-eighth and Indiana." *Come for to Sing* 2, no. 3 (Summer 1976): 5–9.

Koppel, Martin. "The Chicago Sound of OKeh," *Soul Survivor* 5 (Summer 1986): 24–25.

"Leaner Breaks with United Distributing; Forms One-derful Label." *Billboard*, March 31, 1962, p. 40.

"Leaner Opens Memphis One-Stop." *Billboard*, December 15, 1973, p. 47.

Lenehan, Mike. "Conversations with the Dells: Twenty-Eight Years of Rhythm and Blues, from Doowop to Disco." Chicago *Reader*, November 14, 1980, pp. 1, 20–40.

"Leroy Hutson: Performer, Producer, and Writer." *Soul*, July 5, 1976, p. 11.

"Lib./UA Opens Distributing Outlets in Three Major Areas." *Billboard*, June 28, 1969, p. 6.

Lind, Jeff. "1950's–60's Chicago Scene: Predecessor of Jazz-Rock Style." *Illinois Entertainer*, January 1978, pp. 6–7.

Liner notes for Alvin Cash and the Registers, *Twine Time*, Mar-V-lus MLP 1827. 1965.

Liner notes for Betty Everett/Lillian Offitt, *Betty Everett/Lillian Offitt*, Flyright 589. 1985.

Liner notes for Cash McCall, *No More Doggin'*, L&R Records 42.058. 1983.

Liner notes for Fred Hughes, "Oo Wee Baby, I Love You," DJM Records 10717. Undated.

"Local Group with Motown: The Twenty-first Creation." *Chicago Metro News*, February 25, 1978.

Logan, Sandra J. "Randolph of New Radio Station Makes WYNR a Winner with Teens." *Chicago Defender*, October 20, 1962.

McCutcheon, Lynn Ellis. *Rhythm and Blues*. Arlington, Va.: Beatty, 1971.

McDowell, Melody. "Whatever Happened To: Singer Otis Leavill?" *Chicago Defender*, July 30, 1977.

McEwen, Joe. "Jackie Wilson." In *The Rolling Stone Illustrated History of Rock and Roll*, edited by Jim Miller, pp. 117–19. Rev. ed. New York: A Random House/Rolling Stone Press Book, 1980.

———. Liner notes for *The Vintage Years: Featuring Jerry Butler and Curtis Mayfield*, Sire 3717-2. 1976.

———. Liner notes for *OKeh Soul*, Epic 37321. 1982.

"McLendon's Hardest Sound in Town Makes Rating Noise." *Billboard*, March 16, 1963, p. 70.

"Manchild." Chi-Sound/United Artists. [1977].

Mandel, Howard. "Phil Upchurch Greases the Groove with His Intellectual Guitar Creativity." *Illinois Entertainer*, May 1981, pp. 34–35.

Marcus, Greil. "Sly Stone: The Myth of Staggerlee." In *Mystery Train: Images of America in Rock 'n' Roll Music*. Rev. ed. New York: Dutton, 1982.

"MCA Phases Out Shambley, Revue." *Billboard*, July 11, 1970, p. 3.

"Memphis Label Distrib Net." *Billboard*, February 20, 1971, p. 66.

"The Men Behind the Music: Polygram Records Group." *Soul*, January 16, 1978, p. 16.

"Merc and Fountain Production Deal, Plan Writers' Workshop." *Billboard*, January 31, 1970, p. 80.

"Merc to Handle Mr. Chand; Helps to Form Workshop." *Billboard*, August 1, 1970, p. 4.

"Mercury—Chicago's World Ambassador." *Billboard*, April 19, 1975, p. C-8.

"Mercury Launches Limelight Campaign." *Billboard*, May 30, 1964, p. 3.

"Mercury Launches Limelight Records." *Billboard*, November 9, 1963, p. 4.

Miller, Jim, ed. *The Rolling Stone Illustrated History of Rock and Roll*. Revised New York: A Random House/Rolling Stone Press Book, 1980.

"Mother's Finest Zooming to Galaxy of Stars after a Decade." *Chicago Defender*, March 24, 1979.

"Motown Switches Chicago Operation," *Billboard*, May 3, 1975, p. 4.

Murphy, Frederick Douglas. "Ruby Andrews Explores Her Bittersweet Career." *Black Stars*, February 1978, pp. 26–29.

"N.A.A.C.P., in Report on Hiring Bias, Criticizes the Recording Industry." *New York Times*, April 27, 1987.

Nathan, David. "Darrow Fletcher: Trying Something New." *Blues and Soul*, December 23, 1975, p. 8.

———. "Gene Chandler: Back to Number One" *Blues and Soul*, January 1980, p. 18.

———. "The Impressions: Sooner or Later and Right Now!" *Blues and Soul*, July 22–August 4, 1975, pp. 32–33.

———. "Introducing Linda Clifford, A Runaway Success," *Blues and Soul*, September 1978, pp. 36–37.

———. "The Natural Four: Naturally Together." *Blues and Soul*, July 22–August 4, 1975, pp. 32–33.

———. Liner notes for Sugar Pie DeSanto, *Down in the Basement*, MCA-Chess 4275. 1988.

Nathan, David, and John Abbey. "Marlena Shaw: Sweet Beginnings." *Blues and Soul*, August 2–15, 1977, pp. 5–6.

Negro Press International. "Teen Musical Notes." *Chicago Defender*, January 15, 1966.

———. "Up and Coming Tunes, Teens." *Chicago Defender*, January 15, 1966.

"New Chess R.&B. 'Baby' Shows Face in Chicago." *Billboard*, April 13, 1963, p. 24.

"New Dance to Bow into Regal." *Chicago Defender*, December 21, 1963.

"New Rock Singer on the Rise, Hails from Singing Family." *Chicago Defender*, September 21, 1963.

Newman, Mark. *Entrepreneurs of Profit and Pride: From Black-Appeal to Radio Soul*. New York: Praeger, 1988.

Newman, Ralph, and Alan Kaltman. "Lonely Teardrops: The Story of a Forgotten Man." *Time Barrier Express* 24 (April–May 1979): 29–32.

Nooger, Dan. Liner notes for the Fiestas, *The Oh So Fine Fiestas*, Ace 173. 1986.

Nuccio, Tom. "History of Chicago Jazz, Part 16: Ivory Trios." *Illinois Entertainer*, April 1986, pp. 62–69.

Oates, Max. Liner notes for the Four Jewels, *Loaded with Goodies*, DJM 001. 1985.

Ofari, Earl. "Curtis Mayfield: A Man for All People." *Soul Illustrated*, Summer 1973, pp. 19–20.

O'Neal, Jim. "A Blues Quartet." *Southern Magazine*, August 1987, pp. 49–51, 71.

———. "Living Blues Interview: Billy 'The Kid' Emerson." *Living Blues* 45/46 (Spring 1980): 25–48.

———. "Nolan Struck." Untitled program for the "American Blues Legend 1979 Tour." [1979].

O'Neal, Jim, and Dick Shurman. "Living Blues Interview: Ted Taylor." *Living Blues* 25 (January–February 1976): 10–18.

Page, Clarence. "Does Curtis Mayfield Sincerely Want to Be Rich?" *Chicago Tribune Magazine*, February 10, 1974, pp. 35–41.

Paige, Earl. "Azie Mortimer's Wide Range, Phrasing Audience Grabber." *Billboard*, April 26, 1969, p. 12.

Paterson, Neil. "Ricky Allen." In *Nothing But the Blues*, edited by Mike Leadbitter, p. 92. London: Hanover Books, 1971.

Pegue, Richard. "Richard Pegue's Chicago." *Soul*, November 20, 1972, p. 7.

Penchansky, Alan. "Chi Pool Alliance with AVI." *Billboard*, November 5, 1977, p. 67.

Penni, Terry, Joe, Pip, Brandi and Tee. "The Low Down." *Chicago Defender*, September 4, 1965.

Pip, Penni, Terry, Joe, Brandi and Lee. "The Lowdown." *Chicago Defender*, August 28, 1965.

"Playboy Records Vows Good Taste." *Rolling Stone*, March 8, 1972, p. 24.

Pollak, Bill. "Jackie Wilson's Lonely Tears." *The Village Voice*, August 14, 1978, pp. 1, 15–18.

"Polygram Buys Merc, Interest in Chappell." *Billboard*, January 29, 1972, p. 3.

Propes, Steve. "The Larks and the Jerk: Jerked Around and Still a Hit." *Goldmine*, August 25, 1988, pp. 72 and 76.

Pruter, Robert. "The Alvin Cash Story." *Goldmine*, August 1980, pp. 168–69.

———. "Barbara Acklin." *Goldmine*, July 1983, pp. 169–70.

———. "The Barbara Livsey Story." *Goldmine*, September 1981, p. 183.

———. "Beach Music from the Windy City: The Story of the Artistics." *It Will Stand* 12/13 [1980]: 14–16.

———. "Betty Everett: Thirty Years of Bitter-Sweet Recordings." *Goldmine*, April 10, 1987, pp. 97–99.

———. "Billy Stewart." *Soul Survivor* 9 (Summer 1988): 18–20.

———. "Billy Stewart: The Fat Boy Lives On." *It Will Stand* 17/18 [1981]: 18–20.

———. "Bobby Rush: A New Blend of Music." *Living Blues* 84 (January/February 1989): 26–30.

———. "Brighter Side of Darkness: Addicted to Love." *Goldmine*, June 5, 1987, pp. 32, 36.

———. "Cash McCall: When You Wake Up." *Goldmine*, August 14, 1987, p. 107.

———. "The Cheers." *Goldmine*, March 1979, p. 29.

———. "The Chicago Soul of Major Lance." *Time Barrier Express* 24 (July–August 1979): 31–34.

———. *Chicago Soul: The Legendary Brunswick/Dakar Hits*, Liner notes, Epic 39895. 1985.

———. "Chicago Starlets Created 'Junkman' Sound that Launched Blue-Belles' Career." *Record Collector's Monthly* 36 (December–January 1986/87): 1, 10–11.

———. "The Chi-lites Part 2: 1976–1984." *Goldmine*, November 22, 1985, pp. 16–20.

———. "The Chi-lites Story: From Street Corner to Court Room." *Goldmine*, November 8, 1985, pp. 13–18.

———. "The Cicero Blake Story." *Goldmine*, October 1981, p. 189.

———. "The C.O.D.s." *Goldmine*, December 1977, p. 12.

———. "Coffee." *Goldmine*, March 1981, pp. 213–14.

———. "Collectible Bel Aires Disc Precursor of R&B/Soul Hits by Chicago's Sheppards." *Record Collector's Monthly* 37 (February–March 1986): 4.

———. "Darrow Fletcher." *Goldmine*, August 1981, p. 144.

———. "The Daylighters." *Goldmine*, February 1981, pp. 12–14.

———. "The Dee Clark Story." *Goldmine*, May 1981, pp. 19–21.

———. "Don Talty and Formal Records." *Juke Blues* 19 (Spring 1990): 6–11.

———. "Donald Jenkins' Story." *Record Exchanger* 28 [1979]: 14–15.

———. "The Dukays." *Record Exchanger* 27 [1978]: 4–7.

———. "The Emergence of the Black Music Recording Industry, 1920–1923." *Classic Wax* 3 (May 1981): 4–6.

———. "Evanston Soul: Patti Drew and the Drew-vels." *Record Exchanger* 26 [1978]: 22–24.

———. "Fascinations: Girls Are Out to Get You." *Goldmine*, March 27, 1987, pp. 20, 94.

———. "The Five Chances and Their World of Chicago R&B." *Goldmine*, April 6, 1990, pp. 19–20, 33.

———. "The Five Dutones." *Goldmine*, January 1982, pp. 172–73.

———. "G. L. Crockett: It's a Man Down There." *Goldmine*, April 18, 1988, p. 16.

———. "Garland Green." *Soul Survivor* 7 (Summer 1987): 12–14.

———. "The Gems." *Goldmine*, December 1979, pp. 25–26.

———. "Gene Chandler." *Goldmine*, January 1980, pp. 13–17.

———. "The Gene Chandler Story." *It Will Stand* 35 [1987]: 6–11.

———. "General Crook: Fever in the Funkhouse." *Goldmine*, May 20, 1988, pp. 14, 66.

———. "George W. Leaner." *Living Blues* 58 (Winter 1983): 46.

———. "Gerald Sims." *Goldmine*, December 1978, p. 26.

———. "Get on Up...And Get Away: The Esquires." *It Will Stand* 26 [1982]: 6–9.

———. "The Hambone Kids." *Goldmine*, September 1980, pp. 180–81.

———. "Hank Ballard and the Twist: The Original Twist." *Goldmine*, August 12, 1988, pp. 30, 79.

———. "Harold Burrage: Pioneer of Chicago Soul." *Juke Blues* 8 (Spring 1987): 22–25.

———. "Heaven and Earth: Heavenly Harmonies and Earthly Delights." *Goldmine*, March 27, 1987, pp. 22, 92.

———. "Henry Ford and Gifts Keep Kid-Lead Vocal-Group Sound Alive in Chicago." *Record Collector's Monthly* 37 (May–June 1987): 1, 5.

———. "Holly Maxwell: From Opera to Soul." *Goldmine*, January 1, 1988, pp. 100, 106–7.

———. "How Herb Kent, the Kool Gent, Got Burned." Chicago *Reader*, April 15, 1977, pp. 11, 17.

———. "The Impressions: Finally Got Themselves Together." *Goldmine*, October 9, 1987, pp. 89, 94.

———. "Island of Soul: The Sheppards." *Time Barrier Express* 27 (April–May 1980): 69–73.

———. "Jack Daniels and the Four Brothers/Bright Star Story." *Juke Blues* 14 (Winter 1988/89): 8–13.

———. "Jackie Ross." *It Will Stand* 20 [1983]: 6–8.

———. "Jan Bradley." *Soul Survivor* 8 (Winter 1987/77): 18–20.

———. "The Jerry Butler Story." *It Will Stand* 27/28 [1982]: 6–10.

———. "The Jewels: The Most Angelic Voices Ever Waxed." *Goldmine*, January 2, 1987, pp. 14, 20.

———. "JoAnn Garrett." *Goldmine*, January 1981, p. 173.

———. "The Johnny Sayles Story." *Juke Blues* 10 (Autumn 1987): 8–11.

———. "Johnny Williams; They Loved Him in Chicago." *Goldmine*, April 24, 1987, pp. 16, 22.

———. "Knight Brothers." *Goldmine*, December 1983, pp. 137–39.

———. "Linda Clifford: Runaway Love." *Goldmine*, September 11, 1987, pp. 24, 76.

———. "The Lowrell Simon Story." *Goldmine*, April 1982, pp. 182–83.

———. "McKinley Mitchell: Down-home Rhythm 'n' Blues." *Goldmine*, August 30, 1985, pp. 30, 67, 78–79.

———. "The McKinley Mitchell Story." *Juke Blues* 12 (Spring 1988): 7–12.

———. "The Major Lance Story." *It Will Stand* 34 [1986]: 6–10.

———. "The Marvelows." *The Time Barrier Express* 24 (April–May 1979): 19–22.

———. "The Marvin L. Sims Story." *Soul Survivor* 4 (Winter 1985/86): 14–15.

———. "The Marvin Smith Story." *Goldmine*, July 1980, pp. 166–67.

———. "Minnie Riperton 1947–1979." *Goldmine*, October 1979, pp. 10–11.

———. "The Mitty Collier Story." *Goldmine*, November 1981, pp. 25–26.

———. "Monk Higgins 1936–1986." *Living Blues* 72 (1986): 41.

———. "The Multifaceted Career of Joshie Jo Armstead." *Soul Survivor* 5 (Summer 1986): 20–23.

———. "Nolan Chance." *Goldmine*, July–August, 1978, p. 23.

———. "Nolan Struck: My Nerve's Gone Bad." *Goldmine*, August 12, 1988, pp. 69, 79.

———. "The (Other) Butler Did It...(too)!!: The Billy Butler Story." *It Will Stand* 19 [1981]: 16–18.

———. "Otis Clay: The Arkansas Yardbird." *Juke Blues* 7 (Winter 1986/87): 4–9.

———. "Otis Leavill." *Soul Survivor* 3 (Autumn 1985): 29–30.

———. "Patti and the Lovelites." *Goldmine*, June 1981, p. 161.

———. "The Patti Drew Story." *It Will Stand* 20 [1981]: 14–15.

———. "The Philip Upchurch Combo." *Goldmine*, December 30, 1988, pp. 24–25.

———. "The Prairie Avenue Section of Chicago." Master's thesis, Roosevelt University, 1976.

———. "The Radiants." *Soul Survivor* 1 [1985]: 9–13.

———. "The Radiants Story." *It Will Stand* 22/23 [1981]: 4–7.

———. "Roscoe Robinson: One More Time." *Goldmine*, February 27, 1987, pp. 79, 82.

———. "Ruby Andrews." *Goldmine*, July 1982, pp. 26–27.

———. "The Sequins." *Goldmine*. June 1979, p. 16.

———. "The Sharpees." *Soul Survivor* 6 (Winter 1986/87): 23–25.

———. "The Shirley Wahls Story." *Goldmine*, December 1981, p. 172.

———. "Simtec and Wylie." *Soul Survivor* 9 (Summer 1988): 24–26.

———. "Sonny Sanders." *Goldmine*, May 1980, pp. 20–21.

———. "Sonny Thompson, R&B Bandleader and Pianist, Dies, Age Seventy-two." *Goldmine*, October 20, 1989, p. 5.

———. "Sugar Pie DeSanto: Go Go Power." *Goldmine*, July 31, 1987, pp. 20, 26.

———. "The Syl Johnson Story." *Goldmine*, October 1983, pp. 68–76.

———. "A Talk with Daddy G." *Goldmine*, March 1982, pp. 24–25.

———. "Time Gives Mature Duke of Earl a Brand New Rainbow." *Illinois Entertainer*, August, 1980, pp. 72–73, 80.

———. "Tony Clarke: The Entertainer." *Goldmine*, January 30, 1987, p. 22.

———. "Tyrone Davis." *Goldmine*, December 1980, pp. 23–25.

———. "The Uncle Willie: A Chicago Contribution to Dance Records." *Goldmine*, January 29, 1988, p. 24.

———. "The Uphill Climb of...Walter Jackson." *Goldmine*, August 1979, pp. 20–22.

———. "The Vontastics." *Goldmine*, January 1978, p. 20.

———. "Windy City Soul." *Goldmine*, November 1978, p. 25.

———. "Windy City Soul." *Goldmine*, January 1979, p. 10.

———. "Windy City Soul." *Goldmine*, February 1979, p. 11–13.

Pruter, Robert, and Wayne Jones. "The Dells Part 2: The Soul Years in Chicago, 1960–1972." *Goldmine*, July 20, 1984, pp. 15–26.

"Randall Wood Exits." *Billboard*, June 19, 1965, p. 10.

Redd, Lawrence N. *Rock Is Rhythm and Blues: The Impact of Mass Media*. Grand Rapids, Mich.: Michigan State University Press, 1974.

"Reflections: Mercury." Phonogram, Inc., Chicago [ca. 1976].

Regal advertisement. *Chicago Defender*, April 23, 1966.

"Richard Parker to OKeh A&R Post." *Cash Box*, February 22, 1969, p. 30.

Richardson, Clive, "Cash McCall—A Biography." *Soul Music* 2 (January 1968).

———. "The Dells." *Shout* 61, December 1970.

———. "Hot Gospel: Jackie Wilson's Voice Smashed Musical Barriers." In *The Marshall Cavendish Illustrated History of Popular Music*, vol. 3, 1959–60, pp. 330–32. New York: Marshall Cavendish, 1989.

———. "Ted Taylor" (obituary). *Juke Blues* 11 (Winter 1987/88): 18–19.

Roberts, John Storm. *The Latin Tinge*. New York: Oxford University Press, 1979.

Rothman, Ilene. "Curtom Changing, Challenging, Creating and Comin' Atcha." *Illinois Entertainer*, August, 1976, p. 18.

Rowe, Mike. *Chicago Breakdown*. London: Eddison Press, 1973.

Rozenweig, Arnold. "Blind Collegian-to-be Likes It that Way, Making It as R&R Composer." *Chicago Defender*, February 29, 1964.

Rubne, Naomi. "21st Century: Another Jackson Five?" *Soul*, September 1, 1975, pp. 6–7.

Rudis, Al. "...and a Singer with Sounds that Are Beyond Belief." *Chicago Sun-Times*, July 14, 1974.

Savory, Chris. "Chi-lites Rappin'." *Hot Buttered Soul* 44 (February-March 1976): 16–17.

Sbarbori, Jack. "The Dells...Twenty-three Years Later." *Record Exchanger* 22 [1976]: 4–11.

Schiffman, Jack. *Harlem Heyday*. Buffalo: Prometheus Books, 1984.

———. *Uptown: The Story of Harlem's Apollo Theatre*. New York: Cowles, 1971.

"Schlachter Will Head GRT Records Group." *Billboard*, March 13, 1971, p. 3.

Schultz, David. "Ed Townsend." *After Five*, April 1976, p. 40.

Seroff, Doug. "Polk Miller and the Old South Quartette." *Seventy-eight Quarterly* 1, no. 3 (1988): 27–41.

———. "Pre-History of Black Vocal Harmony Groups" (parts 1 and 2). *Goldmine*, March-April 1977, p. 17; and October 1977, p. 10.

"Seventy-two Was Williams' Year for Recognition." *Soul*, July 19, 1976, p. 11.

Shaw, Arnold. *Honkers and Shouters: The Golden Years of Rhythm and Blues*. New York: Macmillan, 1978.

Shurman, Dick. Liner notes for Andrew Brown, *Big Brown's Chicago Blues*, Black Magic 9001. 1982.

———. "Feel Like a Millionaire, I Haven't Got a Dime." *Blues Unlimited* 114 (July/August 1975): 16–17.

Sippel, John. "Profit Jam Forcing Indie Distrib Acceleration into One-Stop and Racking." *Billboard*, February 7, 1974, p. 1.

Slaven, Neil. Liner notes for Junior Wells, *Messin' with the Kid*, Charly R&B CRB 1133. 1986.

Smallwood, David. "Radio's Great Black Sound." *Chicago Sun-Times Midwest*, January 9, 1977, pp. 6–9.

Southern, Eileen. "James Bracken." In *Biographical Dictionary of Afro-American and African Musicians*, p. 43. Westport, Conn.: Greenwood Press, 1982.

Spiegelman, Judy. "Five Little Stairsteps and How They Grew." *Soul*, August 24, 1970, pp. 1–6.

———. "Why Are the Stairsteps Hiding?" *Soul*, August 30, 1971, p. 1.

Stallworth, Bob. "The Gems and the Drexel Label." *Yesterday's Memories* 6 (1976): 9–10.

Stearns, Marshall and Jean. *Jazz Dance*. New York: Macmillan, 1978.

Strobel, Lee. "Ex-rock Star Jailed in Heroin Sale." *Chicago Tribune*, December 22, 1976.

Sullivan, Eddie. "Bobby Jones—A Chicago Superstar." *After Five*, May/June 1982, pp. 38–40.

Summers, Lynn S., and Bob Scheir. "Living Blues Interview: Little Milton." *Living Blues* 18 (August 1974): 17–24.

Sweet, Lynn, "Court Hears the Blues—and It Shakes Judge." *Chicago Sun-Times*, August 16, 1980.

"Take Note: Nothing Sounds the Same." *Soul*, July 19, 1976, p.11.

Taraborrelli, J. Randy. *Motown*. Garden City, N.Y.: Doubleday, 1986.

Tesser, Neil. "The Men in the Glass Booth." Chicago *Reader*, December 5, 1975, pp. 1, 32–35.

Thomas, Jacqueline. "He's Seeking Black Music Liberation." *Chicago Sun-Times*, November 14, 1976.

Tiegel, Eliot. "New Home, Face, Philosophy—ABC/Dunhill on Fifteenth Anniversary." *Billboard*, September 12, 1970, pp. ABC-4 and ABC-8.

Tomashefsky, Steve. "Farewell to the Regal." *Living Blues* 15 (Winter 1973/74): 20–21.

"Top Level Changes at VJ." *Billboard*, February 27, 1965, p. 3.

Tortorici, Joan. "The Chicago Recording Scene—Past, Present and Future through the Eyes of a Man Who's Seen It All." *Illinois Entertainer*, July 1976, pp. 1, 21.

———. "Phil Upchurch a Natural Resource as a Studio Guitarist." *Illinois Entertainer*, December 1976, p. 16.

Tracy, Steve. "King of the Blues." (Parts 1–3.) *Blues Unlimited* 87: 4–8; 88: 7–10; 89: 8–1.

Traiman, Steve. "Four of Five Majors Post All-Time Highs." *Billboard*, March 27, 1976, p. 6.

Travis, Dempsey J. *The Autobiography of Black Jazz*. Chicago: Urban Research Institute, 1983.

"20th Century Fox Aproach [*sic*] to Our Music." *Blues and Soul* August 1980, p. 16.

"The 21st Century: A Group to Watch in '76." *Black Stars*, April 1976, p. 74.

"The 21st Creation." *Chicago Metro News*, February 25, 1978.

[Underwood, Lee, and Cynthia Kirk]. "Black Recording Artists No Longer Second Class." *Soul*, July 7, 1975, p. 14.

Underwood, Lee, and Cynthia Kirk. "Music Industry: Black Money Is Black Power." *Soul*, July 21, 1975, p. 16.

"Upchurch and Fennyson [*sic*], Explosive New Duo." *Soul*, July 5, 1976, p. 10.

Van Matre, Lynn. "Gospel Truths: Otis Clay's Days in Blues May Be Numbered." *Chicago Tribune*, June 12, 1988.

Vee Jay advertisement. *Billboard*, March 7, 1964, p. 37.

"Vivian Bracken, Sixty-nine; Brought Records of the Beatles to U.S." *Chicago Sun-Times*, June 15, 1989.

Waller, Don. *The Motown Story*. New York: Charles Scribner's Sons, 1985.

Walls, Malcolm, and Robert Pruter. "Mamie Davis." *Living Blues* 57 (Autumn 1983): 31.

Ward, Renee. "'Sparkle': Best of What?" *Soul*, June 20, 1977, p. 34.

Waters, John (director). *Hairspray*. New Line Cinema, 1988.

Watson, Beatrice. "From Bea...to You." *Chicago Defender*, June 19, 1965.

Watson, Ted. "Chi-Lites Sentenced." *Chicago Defender*, May 8, 1976.

"WBMX Sold, Kernie Anderson to Remain." *Chicago Defender*, January 26, 1987.

Werbin, Stuart. "Jerry Butler, Mr. Contemporary." *Rolling Stone*, February 15, 1973, p. 18.

Whitburn, Joel, comp. *Joel Whitburn's Top Rhythm and Blues Records 1949-1971*. Menomonee Falls, Wis.: Records Research, 1973.

White, Adam. Liner notes for Billy Stewart, *One More Time—The Chess Years*, MCA-Chess 6027. 1988.

White, Cliff. "Dee Clark: In from the Cold." *Black Music*, December 1975, pp. 23, 61.

———. "History of an Ice Man." *Black Music*, February 1977, pp. 44-53.

———. "James the First." *Black Music and Jazz Review*, October 1978, pp. 22-23.

———. "Jerry Butler, Curtis Mayfield and the Impressions." *Time Barrier Express* 23 (July-August 1977): 28-32.

———. "Keep on Pushing." *Black Music*, September 1974, pp. 16-19.

———. "Sugar Pie DeSanto: Use What You Got." *Black Music*, July 1974, p. 10.

"Will It Be Any Day for Young Diane?" *Soul*, December 11, 1967, p. 15.

Williams, Bill. "Chicago Gains as a Studio Center." *Billboard*, April 19, 1975, pp. C—3, C-20.

Williamson, Drew. "Don Covay, Veteran Vocalist and Successful Songwriter, Cites Dominoes, Little Richard as Early Influences." *Record Collector's Monthly* 44 (July-August 1989): 4.

Winner, Langdon. "The Strange Death of Rock and Roll." In *Rock and Roll Will Stand*, edited by Greil Marcus. Boston: Beacon Press, 1969.

Wood, Sharon. "A Profile of Curtis Mayfield." *Blues and Soul*, September 24-October 7, 1974, pp. 14–15.

Wright, Doug, and Richard Pack. "Laura Lee." *Soul Survivor* 5 (Summer 1986): 4–7.

"WYNR Case Goes to D.C. as Probe Here Closes." *Chicago Defender*, April 20, 1963.

Index

407

A Note on the Author

Robert Pruter is a senior editor in the Social Science Department of New Standard Encyclopedia in Chicago. He has a master's degree in history from Roosevelt University. Mr. Pruter also is the R&B editor for *Goldmine* magazine. He is the author of scores of articles that have appeared in many journals and magazines, including *Goldmine, Living Blues, Juke Blues, Record Collector's Monthly,* and *Soul Survivor.*

A Note on the Author

Robert Pruter is a senior editor in the Social Science Department of New Standard Encyclopedia in Chicago. He has a master's degree in history from Roosevelt University. Mr. Pruter also is the R&B editor for *Goldmine* magazine. He is the author of scores of articles that have appeared in many journals and magazines, including *Goldmine, Living Blues, Juke Blues, Record Collector's Monthly,* and *Soul Survivor.*

Books in the Series Music in American Life